The Cars of Oldsmobile

Dennis Casteele

Motorbooks International
Publishers & Wholesalers ®

This edition first published in 1992 in the Crestline Series by Motorbooks International Publishers & Wholesalers, PO Box 2, 729 Prospect Avenue, Osceola, WI 54020 USA

Originally published by Crestline Publishing Co., 1981 Editor/Designer: George H. Dammann

The information in this book is true and complete to the best of our knowledge. All recommendations are made without any guarantee on the part of the author or Publisher, who also disclaim any liability incurred in connection with the use of this data or specific details

We recognize that some words, model names and designations, for example, mentioned herein are the property of the trademark holder. We use them for identification purposes only. This is not an official publication

Motorbooks International books are also available at discounts in bulk quantity for industrial or sales-promotional use. For details write to Special Sales Manager at the Publisher's address

Library of Congress Cataloging-in-Publication Data
Casteele, Dennis.
    The cars of Oldsmobile / by Dennis Casteele.
        p.   cm.—(Motorbooks International Crestline series)
    Originally published: Sarasota, Fla.: Crestline Pub. Co., 1981.
    ISBN 0-87938-677-0
    1. Oldsmobile automobile—History.   I. Title.   II. Series.
TL215.04C37   1992
629.222′2—dc20   92-25318

Printed and bound in the United States of America

Many Thanks

A variety of people have helped make this book a reality.

Initially I would like to thank Crestline Publishing and George Dammann for their faith in me and George's long standing patience throughout the research term on this book. I'd also like to thank fellow automotive historian, literature collector and Crestline author Don Butler of Detroit, for getting Crestline and me together.

My family has always been interested in cars. My Grandfather Knoop and father Frank Casteele started me out on this trail. My mother Rosemary Casteele and wife Diane Casteele have suffered through too many loads of greasy coveralls, early morning swap meet trips, junkyard scroungings, parts hoarding and late night arrivals home from far flung car racing sessions. My son Scott, at age 8, appears to have the Casteele automotive curse already.

The Lansing Board of Water and Light has given me steady employment and income while I was writing this volume.

A variety of people at Oldsmobile have helped out. They include: my old boss - the "coach" — Fritz Bennetts; Dave Jarrard, Jerry Holmes, Jerry Robbins - who brought me into Oldsmobile in 1972, Dave Violetta and a special thanks to the first lady of Oldsmobile public relations, Helen Early, to whom hundreds of vintage Olds owners owe a special debt.

There were certain people who helped on special research areas: Dick Neller and Jack Gardner of Lansing (early Oldsmobiles); Gary Halford of Strongsville, Ohio (1916 Oldsmobiles); Dale Smith and Rod McLean (racing and high performance Oldsmobiles) and Woodie Hyde (1949's).

From the Oldsmobile Club came help from Karl Foss, Hank Pinckney, Don and Sarah Spieldenner (who have restored some of the most beautiful cars in this book), Max Hineman, and OCA president Newell Stuhlfaut.

Thanks also to Willie Hentges of Warren, Michigan, for his timely work on the book cover.

I'd like to thank my garage and racing partner Marvin Townsend for his help and support and the many nights he worked alone in our garage so I could work on the book. The late Jim Bradley made me feel welcome at the Detroit Public Library and I thank Crestline for my introduction to Jim.

Others who have helped along the way include: Dale Van Houten, Andy Such, Joyce Church and Bill Hersey.

Again, thanks to one and all.

Preface

There are many fascinating aspects of Oldsmobile. It certainly has one of the longest historical trails ever blazed in the auto industry, dating back directly to 1897 and traceable into the 1880s.

Over the years Oldsmobile has ridden a rollercoaster in the industry sales race. In the days of the Curved Dash, Oldsmobile was the nation's leading seller of automobiles and a pioneer in the assembly line production of vehicles. By 1908 and into some years through the early 1920s, Oldsmobile was at best a secondary producer of a limited number of cars. This is not to say a good product was not built, it is just that volume was limited. There were several years when Olds did not appear in the top 15 in sales standings. If there had not been an affiliation with General Motors there are some very real doubts as to whether or not the Oldsmobile nameplate would have survived. During the Depression years the ill-fated Olds companion car, the Viking, was launched and promptly sunk. Just a couple of years later serious consideration was given to some type of merger between Buick, Oldsmobile and Pontiac. From the mid-1930s through the 1960s Oldsmobile earned a solid, if unspectacular, reputation in the car business. The tag of innovator was hung on Oldsmobile and deservedly so for advances such as the HydraMatic transmission (1940 model year), Rocket V-8 engine (1949 model year) and the re-introduction of the full sized front wheel drive car (Toronado: 1966). By the 1970s and into the 1980s Oldsmobile had come full circle in the marketplace and had a firm grasp on the third position in car sales behind Chevrolet and Ford.

Another very interesting aspect of Oldsmobile history was the involvement, and in a good many years the lack of involvement, of Ransom Eli Olds — the fellow's name that was on the buildings and the cars. Like fellow General Motors pioneers, David Buick and Louis Chevrolet, Olds left the company bearing his name in the very early going. But unlike the other GM namesakes, Ransom Olds got back into the auto business and made it in a big way for awhile. Olds left Oldsmobile in 1904 and by late 1905 he was well on his way to establishing the Lansing based Reo Motor Car Company as one of the most complete vehicle building complexes anywhere to be found. It must have brought immense satisfaction to Ransom Olds that in just a few years, and just a few blocks down the street from Oldsmobile, he was handily outbuilding, outengineering, and outselling his former firm and doing so using ideas that essentially were turned down at Oldsmobile. By the late 1930s the tables were turned for Olds as Reo fell into gradual decline amidst corporate bickering not unlike that Olds had seen years earlier at Oldsmobile. The direct descendants of Reo did not totally collapse until the mid-1970s. It is interesting to note that in the late years of R.E. Olds life (he died in 1950) Olds was again recognized as the man whose name was on the building and on the cars, and he was again welcome at Oldsmobile.

Several books covering partial aspects of Oldsmobile have been written. After writing this book it is easy to understand why this is the first comprehensive effort on the Oldsmobiles of every year since 1897. From 1907 through 1917 was one of the hardest bits of research I have ever encountered. From 1923 through 1927 Olds built an absolutely bewildering trail of models.

In this book we at times encountered too little or no data and at other times ran across significant differences on information. We were fortunate to have had a great deal of research help on various Oldsmobile years and were able to talk to a number of Oldsmobile factory sources who were on the scene at the time. Where duplicate data existed we tried to use the source that had the best documentation. A variety of Oldsmobiles have been built in Canada since the early years. These Oldsmobiles have been mechanical similar to U.S. models and there simply wasn't enough time and room to cover Canadian cars separately.

After a period of seven years, this book is finally a reality in paper and ink. I hope this can give enthusiasts the standard Oldsmobile reference they need in the easy to read and use Crestline format that has become a valuable tool in the old car hobby. Hopefully this book is a good start in obtaining everything a collector or researcher wants to know about his or her Oldsmobile. Might I suggest a membership in the Oldsmobile Club of America as another step? The club was founded in 1970, is approaching 4,000 members and can be contacted at: Oldsmobile Club of America; P.O. Box 16216; Lansing, Michigan; 48901.

Thank you very much for your interest in Oldsmobile and this book.

Dennis Casteele

Some automotive historians are convinced that Ransom Eli Olds is one of the more under rated and lesser known automotive pioneers. Others believe Olds has been accorded his just position in the annals of auto history.

One thing for certain there would have been no Oldsmobile automotive nameplate without R. E. Olds, and yet he ended his association with the firm carrying his name only a few years after its founding. In fact Olds went a few blocks from his original Lansing, Michigan manufacturing site to found a rival motor vehicle building concern. The REO name was derived by using Ransom Eli Olds initials and for a time that firm out engineered, out built and outsold his namesake Oldsmobile.

Early literature put out by Oldsmobile made two rather consistent claims for the company. One claim was that Olds was the first organization to produce passenger cars commercially. That claim will draw arguments from auto historians everywhere. The second claim was Olds started the first assembly line for quantity production in building its Curved Dash models. This claim probably has more validity than the first and Olds was a pioneer in assembly line techniques.

The man behind the Oldsmobile — at least in its early stages — was Ransom Eli Olds, born in 1864 in Geneva, Ohio. At the time of his birth, Olds father operated a combination locksmith shop and machine shop. In 1870 the Olds family moved to Cleveland and for awhile was involved in farming for a living. By 1880 the family moved again, this time to Lansing, Michigan.

In the fall of 1880 Pliny Olds (R. E.'s father) and brother Wallace opened a shop on River Street in Lansing. Advertisements for that business — P. F. Olds and Son — billed the firm as practical machinists: manufacturers of steam yachts, vertical steam engines and iron and brass castings.

By 1883 Ransom Olds had become a member of the family business as a machinist and bookkeeper. Later R. E. purchased brother Wallace's part of the business and became his father's partner. Ransom Olds quickly became the company's driving force and the fledgling firm rode through some tough times to the early 1890's when it became nationally known as builders of all types of engines. In 1889 Olds married Metta Ursula Woodward. By 1890 the business had been incorporated and by 1894 Pliny had withdrawn from active management of the firm.

All the while Olds was building his machine shop and stationary engine business, he was also tinkering with what people of the era called "horseless carriages." By 1887 he had built and driven a crude — but none the less workable — three wheeled steam propelled carriage. Olds then quickly advanced to the construction of four wheeled steamers — one of which was exported in 1893 for sale to the Francis Time Company of Bombay, India. Olds early years were also filled with experimentation with electric powered cars. Although this facet of his work is largely undocumented, several finished versions of the silent running electrics were perfected by the auto pioneer.

But the most promise came with the internal combustion gasoline engine and by the mid-1890 Olds was headed on this path almost exclusively. In both 1895 and 1896 Olds applied for and obtained some motor vehicle patents.

By the end of 1896 Olds felt ready to go into commercial manufacturing of motor cars. Not having the resources to handle such a venture himself and not really wanting to risk the still profitable business at P. F. Olds and Son, R. E. tried another route. He would seek financial backers and form another company.

One of R. E. Olds earliest attempts at a horseless carriage was this three-wheeled steam powered machine. Although this probably wasn't the first commercially built automobile, it was among the first. The tiller bar steering arrangement, of course, carried past the turn of the Century and found itself used on the popular Curved Dash models which saw volume production in 1901.

Olds progressed rather quickly on to four-wheeled steam powered vehicles such as the one shown here. This machine is equipped with a flash boiler and an engine horsepower output estimated at four. Top speed was said to be about 15 mph. Olds exported this car — or one similar to it — to India. There was a rumor years later in the auto industry that the ship carrying this exported auto sank and the transaction was never completed.

Early in his life R. E. Olds grew a mustache and that stayed with him for a great part of his adult life. Pictured without that mustache here is a sixteen year old Olds. This is the point in Olds life that his family moved from Ohio — where they had several early homesteads — to Lansing, Michigan.

Moving into the 1890's, when this photo was taken, Ransom Olds was already an experienced hand at assembling horseless carriages. Several of his early creations were steam powered and later cars were also built using electric power. Olds finally concluded, as did other automobile pioneers, that the gasoline fueled internal combustion engine held the most future promise.

R. E. Olds is shown here in later life. Olds enjoyed a unique position in automotive history as for a good share of his life two car building companies carried his name: Oldsmobile, which exists today as a division of General Motors and R.E.O, which was formed in 1904 by using Ransom Eli Olds' initials. All traces of the Reo nameplate faded in 1975 with the bankruptcy of Diamond-Reo and subsequent demolition of what once was the Reo complex in Lansing.

Pre-1897

Old's formation of that new company will be covered in the next chapter along with the vehicles that firm built in its early going. It was a dispute with one of his early financial backers that led Olds to resignation from Oldsmobile in 1904.

From 1904 until well into the 1930's Olds was active in his management and board of directors duties at R.E.O. It must have been an interesting position for Ransom Eli Olds to watch the firm that he'd founded and nurtured and that carried his name grow into a strong part of the General Motors family and be a survivor in the modern auto industry.

That watch ended on August 25, 1950 when R. E. Olds — automotive pioneer — died.

A great number of men destined for leadership roles in the growing auto industry at one time or another worked with or for R. E. Olds. He carried the affectionate nickname "School-master of the auto industry." Olds had some early training in bookkeeping and this, along with his abilities as a master machinist, served him well in the early phases of Oldsmobile and Reo.

In 1897 Olds moved firmly into the automobile business and subsequent Oldsmobile publications and sales literature have traced the beginning of the firm to this year.

The actual organizational session for the Olds Motor Vehicle Company was conducted on August 21, 1897. The firm was capitalized at $50,000 and the list of investors read like a Who's Who of Lansing, including: Edward W. Sparrow, Arthur C. Stebbins, Alfred Beamer, Fred W. Seibly, Frank G. Clark and Eugene F. Cooley.

Olds' instructions from his business associates are famous in company history but also proved to be rather elusive for the entire automobile industry even after nearly eight and one-half decades. R.E.'s marching orders were to, among other things, "build one carriage in as nearly perfect manner as possible."

There is an indication that Olds was well on his way to completion of this carriage by the end of 1896, prior to establishing the new firm. It is believed that a total of five machines of the same general design were built in 1896 and 1897 and one of those units, an 1897 model, is today in the collection of the Smithsonian Institution. In later years a controversy developed about whether or not R. E. Olds had the right to donate this vehicle to the institute. Olds' old nemisis F. L. Smith raised the point in a series of letters to the Institution and General Motors.

A general description of the 1896-7 Oldsmobile, which carried four persons — on two seats — both facing forward, came from "The Horseless Age" of the era:

"Underneath the box, and in every way independent of it, is a 5 h.p. gasoline motor, which in operation makes scarcely any vibration. The vehicle is steered with the left hand. The lever at the right of the buggy when thrown forward throws in the back gear; when turned in the opposite direction, a fourth of a turn, it throws in a four-mile speed which is used for rough roads and hill climbing. If higher speed is desired another quarter turn gives eight miles an hour, still another is twelve miles an hour, and if still greater speed is desired the speed is increased at the governor of the motor and as high as eighteen miles can be obtained. The machinery is said to be very simple, not even a countershaft being used in its construction; it is practically noiseless and impossible to explode, as the fuel supply is below the engine."

Soon after the fledgling auto building firm began, a successful effort was made by one of the chief financial backers of the concern — F. L. Smith — to move the operation to his home town of Detroit. Lansing had a population of about 2,000 and didn't appear capable of supporting a massive manufacturing effort. Detroit had skilled workers and others already involved in machine shop work and engine production. Anxious to establish his two sons, Frederic L. and Angus S. Smith in business, the elder Smith backed his relocation pitch with cash.

The Olds Motor Works was incorporated for $500,000 on May 8, 1899. The new company acquired all the assets of the Olds Gasoline Engine Works (the old P. F. Olds and Son) and the Olds Motor Vehicle Company.

Despite its move to Detroit, Olds never completely broke with Lansing. Some manufacturing efforts continued to be based there and factory literature of the era lists both Detroit and Lansing prominently.

Following the incorporation of the Olds Motor Works and into the new century no fewer than eleven prototype autos were built, tested and perhaps several even sold. Journals of the era indicated the newly formed concern might be about ready to vend a car "with the latest improvements including pneumatic clutch and cushion tires and selling for $1,250."

The main engineering and manufacturing site for Oldsmobile was its Detroit Jefferson Avenue complex which was located near historic Belle Isle. The auto business — even into 1900 — continued to be a loser, to the tune of $80,000. Manufacturing of various types of stationary and marine engines were the firm's staple product.

Olds continued to rack up automotive patents in 1898 through 1900. He even did some early work a type of "self starter" which Charles "Boss" Kettering was to perfect in years later. Through 1900 R. E. Olds and his business associates continued to look for "the car that would put America on wheels."

In 1901 they would take a giant step down that path.

R. E. Olds did not have the financial resources to launch a car building firm on his own in 1897. Stock was sold and the Olds Motor Vehicle Company was formed. Here is a photo of the original stock certificate of Alfred Beamer who had 187 shares of the infant motor car concern valued at $10 per share. The certificate is dated September 7, 1897. The Olds Motor Vehicle Company was phased out soon after its formation and it was replaced by the Olds Motor Works.

1897-1900

One of the least known phases of the early work of R. E. Olds was the electric cars built shortly before and shortly after the turn of the Century. Olds built steamers and internal combustion engined cars — but the electrics remain a mystery even today. These rather fashionable ladies were out for a spin in an Olds electric around 1899 or 1900.

Pictured here is one of the 1897 Oldsmobiles, produced after the formation of the Olds Motor Vehicle Company. Note the front end differences from the 1896 car. Estimates disagree on the exact number of cars like this built, ranging from 4 to 6 units not considering the 1896 model. This is probably what could be called the first Oldsmobile model built. The entire engine and all mechanical components were located beneath the body.

In 1972 the author had the privilege of photographing the Smithsonian Institution's 1897 Olds. This car is preserved in remarkably original condition and has changed little since it was received by the museum in 1915. There was a squabble over the donation procedure used and former Oldsmobile executive F. L. Smith made claims that R. E. Olds donated the car to the museum without proper authority to do so. The drive on this car was by double belts and pulleys directly connected to the rear axles.

This is an electric with slightly different coachwork than the other car shown on this page and without the top assembly. The lines on this car somewhat follow later Curved Dash models. To the author's knowledge none of these early electric cars built by Olds survive and that's a shame because so little is known about these interesting vehicles.

This is one of a handful of gasoline fueled, internal combustion engined cars that Olds built prior to the turn of the Century. This car is probably Old's first such effort and it was probably chugging around the streets of Lansing by late 1896. It is pictured here so it can be directly compared to photos of other pre-Curved Dash models. At the tiller is R. E. Olds with coach builder/stockholder Frank Clark as the front seat passenger. In the rear compartment are Mrs. Clark, left, and Mrs. Olds.

1901

The year 1901 was a truly historic year for Oldsmobile - the year that the delightful Curved Dash runabout came of age. Oldsmobile's 425 sales for the year paced the infant auto industry.

In R.E. Olds experimental work he built a car, or cars, similar to the production Curved Dash of 1901. Easily the most popular car of its era, the Curved Dash was powered by a horizontally mounted, four-cycle engine of single cylinder design. The transmission was a spur gear affair with two forward speeds and a reverse. The unit was steered by a tiller like earlier Olds vehicles. Based on a 60-inch wheelbase, the Curved Dash weighed 700 pounds and carried a price tag of $650.

The Curved Dash, and its successor the straight dash model, was built commercially from 1901 through 1906. The changes in design for this little car were almost on going and over its life span these changes were significant. Some of the changes were subtle, others rather major in nature. In fact if an early 1901 car is placed side by side with a 1905 or 1906 model there are immense differences. Some of these changes — unfortunately most — did not follow the lines of model year changes. In photo selection for this book we've tried to do the best we could with this ever changing little auto in order to stay within Crestline's year by year format. In the process we are offering some never before published photos of Curved Dashes.

The early Curved Dash models could range in speed from 3 to 25 mph. On the average road, a well tuned model could achieve up to 25 miles per gallon of gasoline. The gas tank held about four gallons of fuel and there was a water capacity of roughly the same amount. Wire wheels of twenty-eight inches were standard equipment and the car was based on a normal wagon tread of 4 feet and seven inches. The front axle was slightly crowned, reinforced steel tube. A foot operated brake was applied by a clutch band to a flange attached to the driving sprocket. There was also an emergency brake acting directly on the rear axle.

Most sources rated the engine at four horsepower. Starting was via a non-detachable crank at the right hand of the driver. Motor speed was controlled by a foot lever. Two sets of batteries were used and the factory suggested battery life at three to four months.

Two stories abound on exactly how the Curved Dash was finally selected for production among the fleet of Olds prototypes in existence in early 1901. By the end of March, 1901, most of the other Olds experimentals would lie as piles of ashes and heat tortured metal. Both accounts agree that a Curved Dash prototype was pushed from a flaming building within the Olds Detroit complex when that facility was nearly completely destroyed by fire in the spring of 1901. Legend has it that employee James Brady pushed the Curved Dash model from the flames. Thus, that was

the model Olds would hang its future on simply because it was the one that survived. More careful research, in particular by George S. May, indicates that much groundwork had already been laid to produce the Curved Dash and that detailed plans and patterns survived the fire and enabled Olds to resume production relatively soon after the disaster. Brady's rescue, thus, was very important but not as fatalistic as once thought.

In October of 1901, Olds employee Roy Chapin, who would later rise to automotive fame with other firms, primarily Hudson, drove a Curved Dash from Detroit to New York for the opening of the second annual auto show at Madison Square Garden. It took Chapin more than seven days to complete his trek and he arrived so disheveled that a doorman at the Waldorf-Astoria wouldn't admit him through the front door.

The people running the Olds Motor Works were very promotion conscious in the early going and the little cars racked up several other attention getting schemes in 1901. The Oldsmobile was the first car used by the U.S. Postal Services. Several dirt track racing trophies were garnered and first place was won in a 100-mile non-stop endurance race.

In 1901 Olds was still operating both its Detroit and Lansing plants at full tilt and rebuilding efforts were undertaken in Detroit after the fire. Employment combined for both factories totalled 386.

The little Curved Dash was a capable performer and that is one reason it went on to become the most popular car in the country. Ease of repairs was another reason for the Curved Dash's popularity. Where there were no franchised dealers a local blacksmith's shop often successfully made Oldsmobile repairs. Here the car is climbing a test hill near the factory.

The early Curved Dash even proved to be a good mudder. In 1901 the standard Olds equipment included a lamp, tools and an odometer. Most early Curved Dashes were outfitted as shown with wire wheels. An option that would have helped the driver pictured here were the factory mud guards or fenders. These didn't appear on many early cars and were priced at $10. How many of today's cars could get through this mess?

New cars today are sold and then dealers attempt to load them with factory options which increase their profits and make the price of the car higher. This is hardly a new practice as in 1901 a two-passenger Curved Dash could haul a couple of more folks when equipped with the accessory Dos-a-Dos seat shown here. This unit listed for $25 and proved to be a handy option. Olds pushed several factory options — tops, fenders, extra lights — in its early catalogues.

In the automobile still appeared to be more of a gadget than anything else. Here a giant teeter-totter supports three Curved Dash models. The factory called this setup a "balance board." It was set up before a crowd of 8,000 on October 10, 1901 at an auto race. The purpose of the demonstration was to "show the control of the Oldsmobile."

Roy Chapin, who went on to an illustrious automotive career on his own, waits pensively before a big trip behind the tiller bar of a factory owned Curved Dash. Chapin, accompanied only by some tools and a box of spare parts, made an historic trip from Detroit to the second annual auto show in New York's Madison Square Garden. Chapin's trip took more than seven days, but he made it.

1901

By 1901 even the U. S. Government had heard about the virtues of the Curved Dash Oldsmobile and several were placed in mail service. Neither rain, nor sleet or even the snow pictured here kept the little car from its appointed rounds. The driver even looks comfortable in this rig with a woolie lap robe and a jaunty cap.

This early advertisement stressed the positive aspects of the Olds calling it noiseless, odorless speedy and safe. An early Oldsmobile slogan was also included: "Nothing to watch but the road." The Curved Dash pictured in this ad is equipped with a top which in leather cost $50 and in rubber was $25. Both tops featured dash mounted carrying cases.

This heretofore unpublished photo gives testimony that many early Curved Dash collectors thought their cars were really earlier than they actually were. Fred Caven of Cascade, Idaho believed his 1901 model to be an 1897 Olds. Fred offered to sell this car to Oldsmobile in 1920. He had owned the car for 14 years and had driven it from Ohio to Idaho at one point. Note the very "non-stock" mufffler and side-pipe.

Although Locomobile outsold Oldsmobile in 1901, the company still considered the horse as its primary competitor. This advertisement was an attempt to pursuade the horse owner to consider the cost advantages of owning an Olds. Horse board was computed at $180 annually and this was compared to $35 gasoline cost for 10,000 miles. The Olds in this ad is shown with the optional top.

The little Curved Dash runabout continued to be the bread and butter product for the Olds Motor Works in 1902. With its peppy performance and favorable weight distribution the little Olds made for good winter transportation even in its frozen home state of Michigan. By 1902 runabouts without wire wheels were more common than in the previous year.

This is what a well factory optioned Curved Dash Oldsmobile looked like in 1902. This car is equipped with the optional wheel package ($25), a Dos-A-Dos Seat ($25) and the optional top ($25 in rubber and $50 in leather). Visable in this car is the top carrying case which is mounted inside the dash. This was part of the factory top package, which also included the roll-up rear curtain.

By 1902 Oldsmobile had gained a world wide reputation as an automobile building concern. International customers included Sir Thomas Lipton and the Queen of Italy. Despite its international good will and national popularity, some early records show Oldsmobile stood number two in the auto business behind Locomobile. Olds sales rose to 2,500 for 1902 with the price remaining at $650 and most of the other details on the little car staying the same as well.

Oldsmobile had renewed its Detroit factory and office operations and despite intense pressure from a group of interested Lansing citizens to do otherwise, Olds at least in part rebuilt its Detroit operation following its earlier fire. For this model year, 415 workers were employed at the Detroit and Lansing complexes. Using this large number of workers, and two different manufacturing locations, gave Olds Motor Works strong claim to its statements about being a leader in mass production and automotive assembly line work.

Even with two manufacturing sites and 415 employees, Olds contracted a great deal of work out to Detroit based suppliers. Several of these suppliers went on their own to eventually make it in the auto industry including; the Dodge brothers, Briscoe brothers and Henry Leland.

R. E. Olds and the people running Oldsmobile in the early going were good product promoters. They came up with many ways to get their little car in the public limelight. Olds and Winton battled it out in Ormond Beach, Florida in 1902 and a 57 mph tie was claimed by both car builders. Olds' factory racer was the "Pirate" which is pictured in the 1903 chapter of this book. In the early going, just displaying an automobile would sometimes draw a crowd. Olds encouraged his dealers — and there were at least 58 selling agents by mid-1902 — to display Oldsmobile whenever and wherever possible.

The Curved Dash model offered in 1902 differed little from those offered the previous year. There really was no such thing as a model changeover, as improvements were on going within the model year. Sometime in 1902 Olds hung the Model R tag on the Curved Dash. Cars built in 1901 carried an identification number between 6000 and 6500. Those numbers ran between 6500 and 8990 on 1902 Curved Dashes. This number usually can be found between the seat and body stamped on a main spring and it was also found on the original water tank.

Appearance-wise and mechanically the 1901 and 1902 models were close to the same. In 1902, some cars came equipped with the stager-spoked "Midgely" wheels as factory equipment. But for the most part wheels continued to be of the spoked "bicycle" variety. The Curved Dash color scheme was black with wine trim.

R. E. Olds actually got into the auto exporting business years before when he shipped an early steam car to a customer in India. By 1902 the Olds Motor Works had developed a rather extensive exporting network. One early customer in England is pictured here. It is Sir Thomas Lipton of tea fame, who is shown behind the tillar bar of his 1902 Curved Dash.

One key to the popularity and survival of so many Curved Dashes was the flexible chassis under the car. Early roads left a lot to be desired and some cases roads didn't exist where an Olds driver wanted to travel. Yet most of the Curved Dashes managed to take on whatever terrain their drivers would venture onto. If a Curved Dash was broken it was a simple machine to repair.

Curved Dashes served so faithfully as pieces of transportation that they were on the roads for many years after Olds halted their production. This 1902 model was still in good operating order in 1921 as indicated by its New York license plate of that year. Note the bicycle type bell which is mounted on the tiller bar near the driver's hand. Despite its performance, this really was not the car to use on a cold, wet, slushy New York winter day, as can be evidenced by the two occupants who are bundled up to their necks in heavy woolen overcoats.

This is another Curved Dash that probably saw daily service until well into the 1920's. Motor power for the little runabout was transmitted directly from the motor shaft to the rear axle by chain. This chain was a 4,000 pound test unit and was said, by the manufacturer, to be the heart of a reliable power transmission setup. This car is wearing 1921 Illinois dealer plates, and the photo was posed in front of some hotel — probably as a local publicity stunt since the car's occupants are wearing costumes more akin to the turn of the century than to the styles of the early 1920s.

Curved Dashes have long been the fancy of antique car collectors — particularly in the early stages of that hobby. This particular Oldsmobile is from Harrah's collection. It sports several options including a top assembly and carrying case, Dos-A-Dos Seat and all white tires. The Curved Dash was such a popular model car that it boasts its own car club.

1902

The Oldsmobile

Nothing to watch but the road

An unbroken record of success attests the high state of perfection attained by the Oldsmobile.

Two blue ribbons in the Chicago Endurance Run; first honors against the crack French and American racers in the two five-mile events at St. Louis; the only automobile in its class to finish in the New York-Boston Reliability Run without a penalized stop; and three cups for first places in the Chicago Automobile Club Meet, prove the Oldsmobile is built to run *and does it.*

For a Christmas Present

The Oldsmobile with its leather or rubber top and storm apron, essentially "the all year round" motor car, can be delivered Christmas if ordered now.

Price $650.00 f. o. b. Detroit.

Call on any of our 58 selling agents or write direct for illustrated book to Dept. G.

Olds Motor Works, Detroit, Mich.

The Oldsmobile made a neat little all-weather package when several factory options were ordered. This early advertisement stressed the Olds was an all weather car. The car pictured here is outfitted with a full top and also a factory "storm apron." Lighting was adequate on the Curved Dash with some extra factory and aftermarket lighting packages also offered.

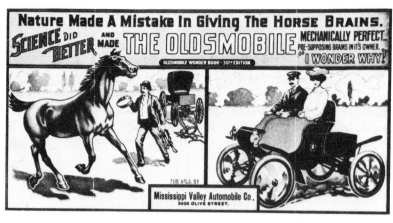

Although a number of other car building firms had sprung up across the country by 1902, a chief Oldsmobile rival remained the horse. Olds advertising of the day took every opportunity to point out the potential problems of horse drawn transportation. Olds listed its range of speeds as from three to 20 miles per hour in 1902.

Another area Oldsmobile sought to concentrate on in 1902 was sales to businesses. This advertisement, which lists only Detroit as an Olds location, talks about the Curved Dash for "practical business use." This is a very early 1902 advertisement, as only 11 dealers — or selling agents — are listed by the factory. This was the first Olds ad to appear in the Saturday Evening Post. Brownell and Humphrey of Detroit was the ad agency.

The price of the Oldsmobile Curved Dash remained at $650 throughout 1902. This was due largely to volume purchasing and assembly line production work achieved in both the Detroit and Lansing shops. Olds estimated the cost of running one of its Curved Dash runabouts — in 1902 — at about ⅜th of one cent per mile, which was far cheaper than keeping anyone of the three horsey types shown here. On the other hand, if Mama keeps driving while looking backward, the horses might just find themselves back in business towing the car home.

1903

Oldsmobile had a number of firsts in the infant automobile industry. Noteworthy was the fact that they were certainly among the first car builders to actively pursue the overseas market. Olds dealers quickly sprang up in Great Britain, European countries and South America. As this picture indicates "Oldsmobiling" was also a very popular activity in Australia. Note the reflection of the rear wheel in the high gloss finish of the body.

Oldsmobile continued to lead the automotive sales race in 1903 as 4,000 buyers opted for the Model R. Curved Dash Runabout. This is the only car production records show Olds building this model year, but there are indications that some railway inspection cars and other models might have been included in the sales total. Meanwhile within the Olds Motor Works there was strong disagreement on what type of automobiles Oldsmobile would build in the future. In 1904 this disagreement would lead to R. E. Olds leaving the firm.

From a product point of view the 1903 Curved Dash models were among the best cars built by the company in its early years. The design of the little runabout was tried and true and several years of manufacturing experience had been gained with this model. The later one-cylinder Curved Dash and Straight Dash models were a heavier and somewhat more complicated car. Some collectors view the 1903 Model R as the ultimate Curved Dash. It was quicker than the heavier, later models and more reliable than those built the previous two years.

Model numbers for the 1903 Curved Dash ran from 13050 through 19999. This year the cars had an exclusive finned section on the engine casting. Also, a distinctive radiator was placed on the 1903's. A 28 x 3 inch clincher tire rim was used. Wire wheels were still available along with stagered wooden spoked wheels and straight wood spoked wheels. A few cars were even built with a special type of cast steel wheels. One 1903 exclusive was the stacking, or piggybacking, of the gasoline and water tanks. This arrangement for a variety of reasons proved unsatisfactory and most 1903 models were later modified.

Olds continued to operate both its Lansing and Detroit plants and employment stood at 450 for the combined operation. The firm continued to promote its products at special events of all types. A Curved Dash won the Tour de France, a difficult reliability and endurance road race. In 1903 Olds returned to Ormond Beach, Florida with his factory racer "Flyer." In 1902 this car was known as the "Pirate." Modified little from the previous year, the single cylinder Olds in 1903 established a world's speed record for lightweight cars at 54 mph for a single mile run.

In 1903 a Curved Dash was shipped to San Francisco. A cross country trek was then attempted by L. L. Whitman and Eugene Hammond. Sixty days from San Francisco they were greeted at the Oldsmobile factory and thirteen days later the pair of cross country motorists arrived in New York.

In 1903 the automobile was still unique enough to be a real attention grabber. Oldsmobile was good at getting its cars out where they could attract attention. Here a 1903 Oldsmobile Curved Dash and its two drivers pause in route on a San Francisco to New York run that helped prove the reliability of the little Michigan built car. The drive took two and one-half months to complete.

The Curved Dash Oldsmobile has long been popular with people who collect and restore vintage automobiles. This sharp looking Maryland-based car was on display at Oldsmobile's 75th anniversary meet in 1972 in Lansing, Michigan. Rather than a bicycle bell this restored auto has a bulb horn mounted on the tiller bar.

The Curved Dash quickly became a reminder of a bygone era. This restored Curved Dash — which at one time is believed to have belonged to Californian Ray Nelson — was used to create some street scenes which could have taken place just after the turn of the century. This car is equipped with accessory wheels and at one time (if it is the Nelson car) was painted green with black trim.

This fascinating photo was taken in late 1929. Russell C. Frey, pictured, had offered his Curved Dash for sale to the Oldsmobile firm. Frey claimed his car was a 1900 model, but more likely it was a 1903. Notice the very interesting items which are displayed in front of Frey's runabout and the mid-1920's Oldsmobile in the background. It was first thought these items were toys, but a closer inspection indicates that they were patent models, which were required to be submitted with a patent application in that era. Apparently Mr. Frey was an inventor of sorts, and seemed to be involved with an eight-wheel bus and what appears to be some sort of a steam engine. At this point, nothing further could be learned about this picture, Mr. Frey, or his interesting ideas.

It Costs ⅜ of a Cent a Mile to travel in the **Oldsmobile**

The Best Thing on Wheels.

The Oldsmobile is the cheapest *reliable* automobile in the world, as well as the most economical in operation. Its premier position has been won by inventive genius and is maintained by progressive methods of manufacture. **Price $650.00**

Write for illustrated book to Dept. 10.

Olds Motor Works, Detroit, Mich. FACTORIES, DETROIT AND LANSING

Oldsmobile doubtlessly built a few cars other than the Curved Dash model in 1903. Production records don't exist however for interesting things like this Oldsmobile Railway Inspection Car. Olds built a number of these cars for obvious use along the nation's rail systems. The author has never seen one of these cars and wonders if any remain.

One of the sources of problems between R. E. Olds and other members of the Olds Motor Works management in 1903 was the type of vehicles the firm should build. Olds wanted to continue to offer cars that were inexpensive to buy and inexpensive to run. This advertisement emphasized these qualities.

This was the first of several factory backed racing Oldsmobiles. In 1902 this machine was called the Pirate and with very little modification the car became the Flyer in 1903. It set a world's light weight record over a sandy Ormond Beach, Florida mile course in 1903. The record speed was 54 mph. This car was powered by a single cylinder engine. The rocket like units on its flanks are fuel tanks.

Oldsmobile retained a firm grasp on its first place slot in the sales race of 1904. Total sales for the firm were 5,508 — but there is a great deal of question as to exactly what model was responsible for what number of sales. This was an all-time high mark for Oldsmobile sales and for 1904 employment totals combined for both plants rose to 500. One person leaving the employment of the Olds Motor Works in 1904 for good was the firm's founder R. E. Olds.

For the first time since its founding in 1897 Olds offered a rather extensive model lineup for the year. The firm did not count just on the Curved Dash model as it had since 1901. For the 1904 model year the Curved Dash faced its first major model change since its inception in 1900. For 1904 the Curved Dash was known as model 6-C. Also offered in the 1904 Olds catalog were a Curved Dash delivery or express model, a railway inspection car, an all new light tonneau car and a similar car called the touring runabout. All models were powered by varying horsepowered versions of the tried and true Olds one lunger engine. Prices ranged from $450 to $950.

The big product news for Olds in 1904 was one of the first new products offered by the firm in three years, the light tonneau and touring runabout models. These cars shared a similar design but were in fact almost totally different machines. For the first time ever an Oldsmobile production model was equipped with a steering wheel rather than a tiller bar arrangement. Both new models were steering wheel equipped.

The light tonneau was the most expensive car in the Oldsmobile lineup for 1904 carrying a price tag of $950. This car was basically a four passenger model, but had a detachable rear seating compartment which was designed to be easily and quickly removed. The entire body could be quickly taken off, for that matter, as only four bolts held the entire body assembly in place. The engine was not located under the hood, but instead the hood area housed batteries, gasoline and water tanks. This new model was based on an 82-inch wheelbase, 55-inch tread and rolled on 30-inch artillery wheels with 3½-inch detachable tires. The transmission had two forward speeds and a reverse. The brakes were activated on the rear hubs and transmission. Fuel and water capacities were seven gallons each and standard equipment included a complete set of tools and a large pair of brass lamps. Color selection was dark green or dark red.

The 1904 touring runabout looked very similar in overall appearance to the tonneau with its rear seating deck removed. The runabout was actually a different and smaller car, however. Wheelbase was 76 inches, wheels were 28 inches and the motor was rated at 7 horsepower, as opposed to 10 horsepower on the bigger car. Colors were again dark red and dark green and the price tag of $750 probably brought it into competition range with the Curved Dash.

From 1904 and through its final offering in 1907 the Curved Dash was a larger, heavier, more powerful and different car than those offered in earlier years. Designated the 6-C, serial numbers ranged from 20000 through 24999. The Holley Carburetor was introduced on the Olds in 1904 and it must be remembered that Holley produced a car that for a time was competition for the Curved Dash. The cylinder bore was increased to five inches. The wheelbase was upped to 66 inches. Colors were black with red trim and the price remained at the introduction level of $650. In addition to heavier running gear and a more powerful 7 horsepower engine other changes included: a larger capacity cooling system, improved main bearing design and adjustment procedures and the addition of rear drum type brakes.

Olds built a very sharp little Curved Dash model called the light delivery car or express. Mechanically it was similar to other Curved Dash models. Price on this unit was $850. The railway inspection car continued to be offered in the Olds catalog for $450. This model could be ordered for standard gauge track or any gauge down to 36 inches. It was equipped with 20-inch steel wheels and carried ample water and gasoline for an 100-mile run.

From a corporate point of view 1904 was an interesting year because it marked the departure of the Olds Motor Works' namesake, Ransom Eli Olds. Olds wanted the firm to continue to build lightweight, inexpensive cars, while others in company management wanted to build heavier and more expensive cars. Olds quickly set up shop across town with his Reo firm and by 1905 he was selling a competitive line of cars.

The Olds experimental shops were not content with a line of cars that were powered by single cylinder engines. They were hard at work on a twin cylinder Olds which would be known as the "double-action" Oldsmobile.

Ransom E. Olds said goodbye to his namesake firm, the Olds Motor Works, in 1904. Olds quickly rallied some new financial backers around him and by the end of the year he had formed a new company — Reo — just a few blocks from Oldsmobile's Lansing factory. In the matter of a few short years Reo would consistently outpace Olds in the sales race.

The Curved Dash remained the seller for Oldsmobile in 1904, but production records are unclear on how many of this popular model were produced. For this model year the Curved Dash was known as the 6-C. For 1904 the Curved Dash was powered by a slightly larger and more powerful one cylinder engine. It was a 5 x 6 inch unit with turned out 7 horsepower.

1904

The curved Dash could be a useful little car, even in the foulest of weather. Pictured here is a 1904 6-C Curved Dash in bad weather gear. Tops had been an accessory since the introduction of the little car in 1901. The storm front on this car did little to help visability, but it could be counted on to keep the driver and a passenger reasonably dry, at least from the neck down.

The 1904 6-C Curved Dash was actually a substantially different car than the machine Olds offered the previous three model years. One of the new items added to the popular Oldsmobile runabout for the new model year was rear brake drums, which are very evident on this 6-C. This car is also outfitted with the optional Dos-A-Dos seat.

A prospective antique car collector could have gotten into a bargain basement deal with this car in 1930. Despite signage proclaiming it a 1902, the car was actually a later Curved Dash. In 1930 its Colorado owner was anxious to part with the car, which he listed in good running order. The price was a mere $25.

Many people tend to think that one Curved Dash model was the same as the next. This simply wasn't true and a major change took place in 1904. Curved Dash models built after that date were bigger, heavier and more powerful than the cars produced from 1901 to 1903. A number of small changes were made during each model year. Curved Dash models were offered by Olds from 1901 through 1907.

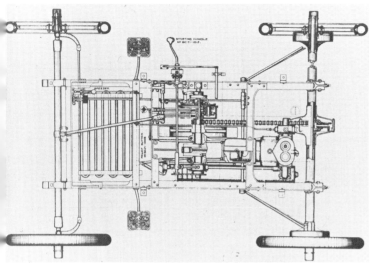

This bird's eye view of a working Curved Dash chassis gives an idea of how rugged the construction of the little car really is. Ignition came from a jump spark system. Despite major changes in 1904, the Curved Dash stayed with its traditional tiller bar steering arrangement. The differential was of the bevel-gear type.

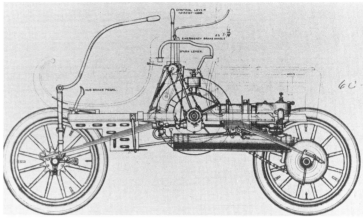

Despite the substantial changes and improvements that were made in the Curved Dash model in 1904, the little car remained simple to operate and simple to work on. The radiator was of the copper disk type and water capacity was five gallons. Gasoline capacity was five gallons as well. Price on the Curved Dash remained unchanged from its introduction in 1901 at $650.

A strong and flexible chassis remained the key to the Curved Dash runabout's success. For 1904, the Curved Dash model's wheelbase was expanded to 66 inches. The frame was constructed of angle steel. The standard wheels were 28-inch wood artillery units with 3-inch standard tires. The factory paint package was black with red trim.

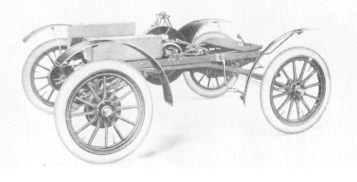

A couple of years down the road Oldsmobile would offer some huge trucks. This Curved Dash offshoot actually got Oldsmobile firmly in the truck business, which they would be in, off and on, through the 1920's. This unit was known as the Oldsmobile Light Delivery Car of Express model. Price was $850. Olds claimed this model "does the work of three men, three horses and three wagons and the maintenance cost is nominal.

Little is known about the Oldsmobile Railroad Inspection Cars, but apparently a fairly large number of these were built. Most of the distribution was handled by Railway Appliances Company with offices in Chicago and New York. The unit pictured was called Model No. 2 — the Oldsmobile Tonneau Railroad Inspection Car. It was larger than previously built Olds units and both the top and rear passenger compartment were designed for easy removal.

1904

Long a favorite of old car collectors, it is logical that automotive modelers would try to recreate a curved Dash. Here a scale model of the 6-C Curved Dash has been built nearly to perfection. In 1972 — for its 75th anniversary — Oldsmobile commissioned the construction of a small number of glass whiskey decanters that look very similar to this model.

Even though the Curved Dash model continued to be the big seller for Olds in 1904, the Olds Light Tonneau attracted a lot of attention at auto shows and the like. This was the highest priced 1904 Olds, listing for $950. The rear seating compartment on this model could be easily removed and an all-weather rear deck cover was furnished to each buyer.

The light tonneau certainly gave Oldsmobile a different appearance from the front. Those looking for a motor under the all-new hood compartment were disappointed as the only things this area contained were gas and water tanks and batteries. The engine location in this model placed the cylinder head forward beneath the hinged floorboards. This Olds was powered by the firm's most powerful engine to date — a 10 horsepower unit.

An Oldsmobile with a steering wheel? The two new 1904 models were the first to give up the traditional tiller bar steering arrangement that had been with Olds since 1897. The light tonneau chassis was the largest Olds this year, as it was built on an 82-inch wheelbase. Wheels were of the 30-inch wood artillery type, mounted with 3½ inch detachable tires. Colors were dark green or dark red.

This Olds wound up chugging around the city streets for a good number of years. Standard equipment on an Oldsmobile Light Tonneau included a complete set of tools and a pair of large oil brass side lamps. Each car could hold seven gallons of water and seven gallons of gasoline. The radiators on these cars were of the honeycomb design.

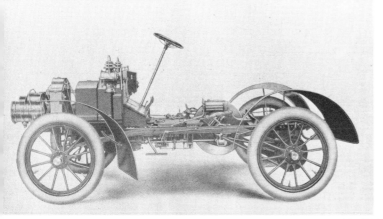

For just $100 over the price of the Curved Dash 6-C model — a total of $750 — a buyer could move up into the all new Olds Touring Runabout in 1904. This model had a ten inch longer wheelbase than the Curved Dash. The new model's wheelbase was 76 inches. There was a hint of family resemblence between the touring runabout and the redesigned Curved Dash.

These photos were taken by H. E. Armstrong in late 1927 of an Olds Touring Runabout. The location is Donnelly, Idaho, just down the street from Kendale's Pool Hall. This rear shot shows the back of the bucket seats and the sloping rear deck of this model Olds. The differential on this model was of the bevel gear type. Brakes operated off the rear hub and the transmission.

The new model Oldsmobiles carried an Olds logo similar to the one carried for years on the Curved Dash. In an effort to keep things simple the coachwork on the Light Tonneau and the Touring Runabout was simple to remove, with only four bolts holding it in place. Colors on this model were either dark green or dark red.

The new design of the Olds Touring Runabout gave Oldsmobile a more conventional look for 1904. The touring runabout had 28-inch wooden artillery wheels with three-inch detachable tires. Power for this model came from the same 5 x 6 inch, 7 horsepower, one-lunger which powered the 6-C Curved Dash. The transmission was of the all-spur type with two speeds forward and reverse.

Although a quick look might indicate otherwise, the Touring Runabout and the Light Tonneau were completely different cars. The tonneau was a larger car and there were substantial differences between the two all-new Olds models. The two cars did, however, share some parts and there was some interchange between the new 1904 offerings. This is another of the interesting photos made in Donnelly, Idaho, by H. E. Armstrong in 1927.

This would mark the final year that Oldsmobile would top the sales race in the automobile industry. Olds secured the top sales spot with a total production of 6,500 vehicles and once again an exact production breakdown by model was not available.

By this time Olds was rapidly phasing out its Detroit operation. The employment totals for both plants combine were 612. During this period Oldsmobile reached its early peak production output of 36 cars per day. The next few years Olds didn't approach the sales volume it reached in 1905, and this production capacity was largely uneeded.

This would be the last meaningful year of production for the now famous Curved Dash runabout. Oldsmobile continued to offer this car in its catalog for 1906 and 1907 but it is doubtful that many Curved Dash models were built past 1905. Still when the factory needed an entry in a New York to Portland jaunt

under the sponsorship of the National Good Roads Association, two Curved Dash models were picked. These cars, dubbed "Old Scout" and "Old Steady" took a tremendous pounding throughout the 3,890-mile trek yet both cars made it. It interesting to note that Oldsmobile retains "Old Scout" in its antique car fleet today. In 1905 the Curved Dash still meant Oldsmobile to some buyers and the price tag remained $650.

The new car in the Olds lineup for 1905 was the two cylinder Oldsmobile Touring. This was by far the most expensive Oldsmobile offered with a price tag of $1,400. The car bore a strong family resemblance to the light tonneau and touring runabouts of 1904 and 1905. The new touring model could be easily distinguished by its larger radiator and the fact that the rear passenger area was side entrance rather than rear entrance. Big news of this model was the 20 horsepower, two cylinder engine that powered the 90-inch wheelbased machine. It weighed 2,350 pounds, had 30-inch wheels and 3½ inch tires in front and 4 inch tires in back. Olds claimed a top speed of 40 mph

By 1905 Ransom E. Olds had left Oldsmobile to lead another automotive concern, this one bearing his initials — R.E.O. His new company got into production in 1905 and this was the type of car that Reo built in the early going. With Reo and Oldsmobile operating in Lansing by 1905, that city's automotive output was significant. The two auto concerns' main plants operated within several blocks of each other for nearly seven decades.

Oldsmobile has at least two Curved Dash models in its divisional antique car collection. One of those is the fabled "Old Scout" one of the factory team cars involved in a historic cross country jaunt in 1905. Olds drivers Percy Megargel and Dwight Huss traveled light on the trip with less than 200 pounds of luggage, tools and parts.

By 1905 Oldsmobile dealers saw the popularity of the Curved Dash models begin to fade. For the year a total of 6,500 cars were sold — but no accurate breakdown has been found on exactly what model represented what sales total. When Olds needed an entrant for a difficult cross country race, however, it went to the nimble little Curved Dash model. This model stayed at the 1901 introduction price level of $650.

in high gear. Gasoline capacity was 15 gallons with 8 gallons of water carried under hood. This was a striking looking Oldsmobile, as most were finished with deep blue bodies, white striping, yellow running gear and wheels and black leather upholstery.

There were two carryover models in the 1905 lineup with the light tonneau and touring runabout essentially unchanged from the previous year. Both were one-cylinder powered with the light tonneau listing for $950 and the touring runabout going for $750. In an advertisement of the period Olds called its touring runabout "an ideal machine for pastor, busy doctor or any professional man — it never gets tired — is as willing at the end of the trip as the start".

Olds also eased into the truck business in 1905 with several large trucks and a continuation of the Curved Dash Express model. The big truck, called the Olds Commercial Wagon, was built on an 83-inch wheelbase. It was powered by a 15 horsepower, two cylinder engine. The unit ran on 30-inch wheels and 4½ inch solid tires. It had a payload of 87 cubic feet or 1,500 to 2,000 pounds. The Detroit Post Office used this model in its 1905 Christmas mail rush. The truck could be ordered in either green or maroon finish.

Oldsmobile also continued to market a limited number of its railway inspection cars in 1905.

In addition to its cross country jaunt with Olds Scout and Old Steady, a Curved Dash outfitted with Michelin Tires and no other modifications completed a 3,000-mile midwinter European trip in 16 days. Olds officials invited its active Moscow dealers, M. Andrew Zenliczka and M. Nicholas Sommerfield, to the Madison Square Garden Auto Show. The Russians said out of 150 cars registered in Moscow in 1905, 80 were Oldsmobiles. During the year F. L. Smith of the Olds Motor Works created his "Six Shooter," a 34-foot long, white oak keel, mahogany decked motor launch. The engine in this craft was a 60-horsepower Olds built six cylinder.

Oldsmobile gained a good bit of free publicity in 1905 when Gus Edwards wrote the big selling song "In My Merry Oldsmobile".

Oldsmobile received a number of letters from car owners wanting to sell their Curved Dash models back to the factory. This case was unusual because the letter was written by nine-year-old Raymond Jarvio of South Braintree, Mass. He is apparently the passenger in this photo. Young Jarvio said in his June, 1928, letter that his father's Curved Dash "looks good and runs like the town clock".

The year 1905 marked the last time Oldsmobile ever topped the automotive sales race. Olds had a good mix of cars for this year and most continued to be powered by one-cylinder engines. The touring runabout was basically a carryover from 1904. Selling for $750, just $100 more than a Curved Dash, this proved to be a lot of Oldsmobile for the money. This was also one of the first Olds built cars to be steered by a steering wheel rather than a tiller bar.

Several of the 1904 and 1905 touring runabouts have survived and today are in various car collections across the country. One such survivor is the one-cylinder powered machine belonging to former Oldsmobile Club of America president Russ Yoder of Louisville, Ohio. Yoder's car is in remarkably good condition and it was one of the earliest cars to be displayed at several national meets.

1905

Carried over into the 1905 model year with a small number of changes was the light tonneau car introduced the previous year. This car appeared like many other cars of the era, complete with a hood or bonnet. Under this hood was no motor, but instead fuel and water tanks and batteries. The entrance for the tonneau was at the rear, in the center of the detachable seating section.

Russ Yoder seems to enjoy driving his 1905 single cylinder Olds as much as any in his antique car collection. Yoder, who for years operated an Oldsmobile dealership in Louisville, Ohio, always found willing passengers for a vintage car ride. Yoder's runabout — as were all the 1904 and 1905 models — is powered by a one-cylinder engine very similar to the Curved Dash powerplant.

Early motoring was an adventure — even in one of the more reliable one-cylinder Oldsmobiles. Here a 1905 light tonneau gets ready to take to the road with a woman behind the steering wheel, and another in the front seat, while the men rode behind — a novelty in this era. The rear portion of this car was easily detached and a deck lid could be installed. Notice the really nifty wicker picnic basket mounted on the side of this early Olds.

The only really new Oldsmobile car for this model year was the two cylinder touring. With R. E. Olds gone from the Olds Motor Works management team, Olds moved more and more toward larger, more sophisticated and more expensive cars. The touring model was a first step in that direction. Powerplant on this machine was a 20 horsepower engine with 5¼ by 6 inch horizontal opposed cylinders. The price of the touring was $1,400, by far the most expensive 1905 Olds.

1905

By far the heaviest Olds car built to date was the 1905 touring. It weighed 2,350 pounds and was on a 90-inch wheelbase with a 55-inch tread. This was the second year for an Oldsmobile to carry an upfront honeycomb radiator and this was by far the largest radiator ever used on an Oldsmobile. The factory claimed a top speed of 40 mph for this model's 2-cylinder, 20 horsepower opposed engine.

For several years Olds built its Curved Dash express model trucks, but in 1905 the firm got into some heavy duty trucking. These machines were powered by a two cylinder vertical engine of 5x5 inch bore and stroke developing 15 horsepower. The engine was located under the seat. An 83-inch wheelbase provided an ample cargo area adequate to carry up to 2,000 pounds. This particular truck configuration was known as the delivery wagon.

Oldsmobile built some unique truck type vehicles in 1905 including this single cylinder model based on the light tonneau chassis. The rear portion of this model was similar in design to the Curved Dash express model. The standard color was black and the rear compartment could be ordered with wood paneling or latticed wire sides. It had a carrying capacity of 41 cubic feet of light cargo, and was built on the 82-inch wheelbase chassis. As before, it could be ordered with 55-inch standard tread or 60-inch southern tread, which was better suited to the ruts made by the cotton and tobacco wagons.

For 1905 Oldsmobile was becoming even more involved in the production of trucks. It continued to offer this Curved Dash - based express model. Olds also began selling a larger line of trucks which was expanded in 1906. The express, or Delivery Car, was the first step into the world of the horseless carriage for many merchants and businesses.

Oldsmobile continued to offer several versions of its railway inspection car of 1905. The powerplant remained a slightly smaller version of the same engine that drove the Curved Dash. This particular car was used to provide passenger service on the Sierra Railway Company Line between Oakdale and Jamestown, Cal. Three passengers and a driver were the total capacity of this unit. The engine had a 4½ x 6 inch bore and stroke, and developed 4½ horsepower. The locomotive-type headlight looks a bit whimsical on this little car.

Oldsmobile fell back dramatically to 6th place in the sales race for 1906 and would never again hold first place. Fewer of the popular little Curved Dashes and Straight Dashes were seen in the model mix for 1906 and maybe the buying public was looking for more sophistication than a one cylinder runabout could offer. Sales totalled 1,600 with only 100 of those sales the single cylinder models. The bulk of the sales, 1,400, were of the all new four cylinder machine. The other 100 sales were of a warmed over two cylinder model known as the Model L.

For the first time, the cross-town rival Reo outsold Oldsmobile as R. E. Olds moved his company into fourth spot in the sales race.

Lansing officially became Oldsmobile's only home in 1906 thanks to the efforts of local citizens who had worked for several years to permanently lure the car builder back from Detroit. A 1906 Oldsmobile publication said, "You will notice the various buildings composing the 'works' extend for several blocks, covering a large portion of the area which was formerly used for the State Fair grounds. Previous to 1906 two separate factories were operated, one in Lansing and one in Detroit. During the summer of 1905 its was deemed advisable to concentrate at the former place, and therefore the entire office and works were moved. Additions have constantly been made until the present plant occupies a space of 56 acres."

Big product news for the new year was the four cylinder Model S, which was offered in two versions: the Palace Touring Car and the Gentleman's Roadster. These new fours had a 28 horsepower engine with mechanical valves, forged steel connecting rods and a two section aluminum crankcase. The carburetor was a new unit of Olds design and it was gravity fed from a 15 gallon gas tank. Ignition was of the jump spark type with four unit dash coils. Cooling water was circulated with a gear driven pump and cooling was aided by a belt driven fan. The transmission was controlled by a single lever which actuated sets of sliding gears. The clutch could be activated by a foot pedal or the emergency brake lever. The transmission had three speeds forward and one reverse. Wood artillery wheels were supplied with 10 spokes in front, 12 in the rear. Tires were 32 inch by 3½ up front and 32 inch by 4 inch in the rear. The top of the line Olds model came equipped with two acetylene lamps, two oil lamps, one tail lamp and a horn. Also included was a full set of tools secured in a portion of the battery box which was located on the right running board. The Palace Touring weighed 2,300 pounds,

A new look for a tried and true model came in 1906 as Olds introduced a straight dash version of the famed Curved Dash Olds. Power for this car continued to come from a single cylinder, 7-horsepower engine. Standard equipment on this little runabout included lights and tools. A top, including storm curtains with celluloid windows was also provided. All this still was priced at $650.

New on the scene for 1906 was the Model L, Double Action Olds. This was the second year of production for a twin cylinder Oldsmobile. Offered either with or without (as pictured) the rear tonneau seating compartment, the horsepower rating on this model was 24. There were a number of parts that interchanged between the Model L and Model S including the frame, transmission, controls and some of the running gear. Price on this model was $1,250.

The Curved Dash runabout — complete with its traditional front styling treatment — continued to be offered. Mechanically this car was identical to the straight dash model. Both models were equipped with a planetary transmission outfitted with two speeds forward and a reverse. All gears were constructed of either bronze or machine steel.

rode on a wheelbase of 106 inches and sold for $2,250. The Gentleman's Roadster was of the same general construction with the only major changes being body design and larger wheels and tires.

The powerplant on the Model L "double-action" Olds had been around for awhile and it wasn't a very popular 1906 car. The motor was based on a 5-inch bore and a 5-inch stroke and the unit developed 24 horsepower from its twin cylinders. This car was similar in many ways to the Model S machines, using many of the same components. The Model L had wooden artillery wheels front and rear. The wheelbase was 102 inches, weight was 2,000 pounds and base price was $1,250.

Continued to be found in the Olds catalog for 1906 was the standard runabout, for this year known as the Model B. The Curved Dash could also be ordered with a straight dash front panel. The powerplant remained the reliable single cylinder, 7-horsepower unit. In an effort to make this a more comfortable car, the Model B in either straight or curved dash form, came standard with a top and side curtains with celluloid windows.

Olds also built a very limited number of fascinating trucks, which it called commercial cars. Coachwork on these units included a closed delivery van, an 18-passenger wagonette and a unit with roll up side curtains known as a winged express.

With the noticeable reduction in car sales, employment in the Olds factory dropped to 600 in 1906. The Olds experimental department was already dabbling with several six cylinder models. Erstwhile Olds employee and cross country driver Roy Chapin and several others left Oldsmobile to form the E. R. Thomas Company of Detroit which eventually and round-aboutly led to the Hudson Motor Car Company. Olds had a 1906 Vanderbilt Cup Race entry driven by Ernest Keeler with Harry Miller — of later Indianapolis fame — as riding mechanic.

The base weight on the Model L Olds was 2,000 pounds. The wheelbase was 102 inches. As pictured here the model L is equipped with the rear seating section. Standard equipment on this model included two acetylene lamps, two oil lamps, one tail lamp, horn and a full set of tools. The tools shared a running board mounted box with the batteries.

Oldsmobile continued to offer larger and more powerful cars. In 1906 the top of the line was the four cylinder Model S. Offered in both a touring car and a roadster, the wheelbase for this series was 106 inches. The touring car weighed 2,300 pounds. Running boards and fenders were designed for ease of removal.

Carrying a price tag of $2,250 the Palace Touring, Model S, was the most expensive Olds car in 1906. This model came equipped with wooden spoked wheels front and rear. Brakes were on the rear wheels and also on the transmission shaft. Standard Model S equipment included two acetylene lamps, two oil lamps, a horn and a full set of tools.

This roadster was one of the sportiest cars ever offered by Oldsmobile. It was one of the two Model S, 4-cylinder cars available in 1906. The roadster could be ordered with additional rear deck seating. List price on this model was a sizeable $2,250. Although exact production numbers are not available, it was a rare car. Its engine, located under the hood, turned out a maximum of 28 horsepower.

Olds used this demonstration of pulling against a team of 20 horses to point out the power of its new four cylinder model. The Olds four put out 28 horsepower from a 4¼ inch by 4¾ inch powerplant. Pistons were cast iron, connecting rods were drop forged steel and the two section crankcase was aluminum. The ignition was a jump spark type with a storage battery or set of dry cells.

Olds expanded its production of its heavy duty line of trucks in 1906. This particular model was known as the delivery wagon. The factory rated its range as up to 100 miles per day. This particular truck was designed to carry a payload up to 2,000 pounds. Not very many of these early trucks survive and the author has never seen one at an old car meet.

OLDSMOBILE

A rather interesting entry into the mass transit market by Olds came in 1906 with this 18-passenger wagonette. Running on a wheelbase of 108 inches, this truck, or bus, could achieve speeds up to 20 mph. Tires were solid rubber Firestones and the powerplant was a vertical twin cylinder 20-horsepower job of 5x5 inch bore and stroke. Price on this people moving unit was $2,600.

Despite the fact that by 1906 Oldsmobile had moved most of its operation from Detroit to Lansing, the Detroit Post Office remained a customer for Olds built trucks. In fact the Detroit mail carriers had used Oldsmobile in their delivery efforts since the early days of the Curved Dash. This is a specially built mail delivery version of the Oldsmobile truck. Solid rubber Firestone tires on all four wheels must have provided a delightful ride over Detroit's cobblestone and brick surfaced streets.

Oldsmobile built several special types of heavy duty trucks in 1906, including this one-off delivery wagon for Emery, Bird, Thayer, a Kansas City dry goods firm. Like most large vehicle building companies of the era, the Olds Motor Works had a special test track on its grounds. By this time most car and truck building tasks had been moved to Lansing and were located with a 56-acre complex.

For 1907 sales continued to dwindle for Oldsmobile as increased emphasis was placed on bigger and more powerful cars. A total of only 1,200 sales were made this model year, causing Oldsmobile to drop to ninth in the sales race, while crosstown rival Reo rose to third place. Employment at the Olds complex in Lansing dropped dramatically to only 215, its lowest level since 1901.

One of the biggest pieces of news during this model year was the introduction of nickel plating. Olds brought out four basic auto models — and a smattering of specially built trucks — to the market place in 1907. They included the four-cylinder powered A Model tourings and limousines and the H Model Flying Roadster. Also listed in the 1907 catalog, "A Busy Man's Textbook on Automobiles," were the one-cylinder curved and straight dash offerings. It is believed very few of these old standbyes were produced in 1907.

The mainstream of the Olds lineup was powered by a 40-horsepower engine. Cylinders were gray iron and cast in pairs. Bore was 4½ inches, stroke was 4¾ inches. Cast iron pistons were supported by drop forged steel connecting rods. A copper gasoline tank was located under the front seat.

The Model A — either open or closed — rode on a 106 inch wheelbase. Weight was 2,600 pounds. Color choices included: gray, brewster green or red. Wheels were of the wooden artillery type. Standard equipment included a full set of tools, two acetylene head lights, two oil lamps, large horn and luggage carrier. The limousine was the first closed car offered by Olds and indications are that very few were produced. Features of the Model A closed car included: beveled glass, leather or satin interior, a speaking tube to the chauffeur's compartment and a full toilet set consisting of clock, perfume bottles, card case and ash tray. There are indications that if a buyer selected it, he could purchase a Model A chassis with both the open and closed bodies in the one purchase. Supposedly, it would then be up to the chauffeur to switch bodies back and forth at the whims of the owner.

An era ended in 1907 when the legandary Curved Dash Olds was last listed in the company catalog. Oldsmobile had been building Curved Dash models since the turn of the century and this was the first auto that many people had either owned, driven or seen. For 1907 the single cylinder runabout could be ordered either as a straight dash, as pictured, or with the traditional Curved Dash front, with its price remaining at $650 completely equipped with lights, tools, removable folding top, and storm curtains.

However, this was not as great a chore as might be expected, as the bodies were basically bolt-on units which, in a well equipped shop, could be interchanged rather readily.

The Model H Flying Roadster rolled on a 106½ inch wheelbase and was powered by the same four cylinder engine as the Model A. Color choice was either red or french gray. Olds called this body design "a racing type with aluminum running boards and footboards."

An era ended in 1907, as that was the final appearance of the faithful Curved Dash models in the company catalog. Both the straight and curved dash front end were offered. Power continued to come from a single cylinder, 7 horsepower engine. A final, and very fitting slogan for the Curved Dash Model B was, "You see them wherever you go; they go wherever you see them."

There was a great deal of trouble on the horizon for the Olds dealers across the country, and even a link with General Motors didn't solve the problem. From 1901 through 1905 the standard Olds car, the Curved Dash, cost $650. By 1907 the standard Oldsmobile was the four cylinder Model A Palace Touring Car priced at $2,750. So Oldsmobile was suddenly faced with attracting an entirely new type of car buyer.

The bread and butter car in the 1907 model lineup was the Model A Palace Touring car. With a base price tag of $2,750 Olds was trying to appeal to a new class of customers. By 1907 all factory and office operations had been moved to Lansing within a bustling 56-acre complex. Olds had a special half-mile test track within that complex.

Oldsmobile factory literature of the day said of the Model A "it is a model which will stand the test of time, or, in other words, will represent a standard machine — not in style one year and out the next — but one which can be purchased with the feeling that one is getting a practical, serviceable car of long life and enduring design."

1907

The Model A Palace Touring pictured was caught by a photographer in front of the Michigan State Capitol Building in Lansing. Olds had some exotic metals within its 40-horsepower engine. The crankcase was cast aluminium and weighed only 43 pounds. The crankshaft bearings were made of white bronze. A glass bull's eye in the front wall of the crankcase showed the oil level.

Olds patterned its four cylinder models after the 1906 models — with some styling changes and some design improvements. There were substantial suspension changes in the new models as well as some under the hood refinements. Speed control or gearshifting was maintained by a single lever. Spark and throttle levers were placed on the steering post just below the steering wheel.

The Olds shipping department was not as busy in 1907 as it had been in previous years. Here several Model A Palace Touring models await rail shipping with a sprinkling of Curved Dash models also on the dock. A dealer had his choice of receiving new cars by rail or coming to the factory and picking them up.

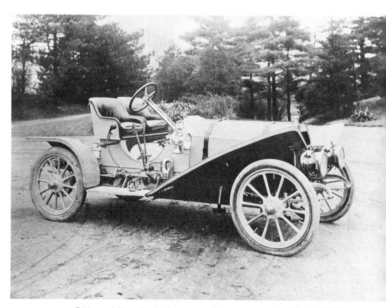

Oldsmobile selected a romantic name — the Model H Flying Roadster — for its sportiest offering in 1907. This machine rode on a wheelbase a half inch longer than the Model A touring. Olds called this rakish body a "racing type." Factory colors were red or French gray. The transmission on this roadster was of the sliding gear type with three speeds forward and reverse.

This Model H Flying Roadster offered extra seating capacity in the rear. Four small people could ride in this sporty Olds. Drive on all four cylinder models came through a 1 ⅛ inch machined propeller shaft to the bevel gear on the rear axle. Universal joints were protected by a steel sleeve and a heavy leather boot.

1907

Long distance motoring was becoming a more popular thing by 1907 and this motorized adventurer selected a Model H Flying Roadster to do his traveling in. He is seen here partway through his trip from Los Angeles to Boston. Note the extra tires on the side, items like a block and tackle in the rear and the searchlight driving light mounted in front of the steering wheel. The frame on each Olds four cylinder was made of $\frac{5}{32}$-inch pressed steel, made up in channel sections and riveted together.

This is a rear view of an H Model Flying Roadster complete with a single seat and the optional top. On all four cylinder models the clutch was of the internal reverse cone type made of aluminum covered with leather. To aid in smoother starts a spring device was provided which allowed the load to be taken up slowly. Note the large auxiliary fuel tank mounted between the rear spring shackels.

The first closed car that Oldsmobile offered to the buying public was the Model A Limousine. This machine was offered on the same four cylinder chassis as the Palace Touring model. A buyer could order both the open and closed bodies with one Model A chassis if he had the inclination and the money. Passenger compartment upholstery options included leather or silk, while the front seats were always done in leather.

Oldsmobile advertising for this model year attempted to capitalize on those already familiar with Olds products. Olds offered copies of its weekly newsletter the "Oldsmobile News Letter," to any Olds owner submitting his name to the factory. Olds pointed out in this ad that it would be displaying cars in the upcoming shows at Madison Square Garden and the Chicago Colliseum.

Olds built a few special trucks in 1907 including this nifty stake side unit. The company dabbled in truck production for several years, but their most serious effort at mass truck marketing came in 1919 through 1921 with the Olds Economy Truck. Note the solid wheels on this truck and the drive chain arrangement extending to the rear wheels. Power was by a 2-cylinder vertical plant.

For Oldsmobile, 1908 became a historic year - not so much for the cars produced - but for the fact that the Olds Motor Works was taken over by General Motors in this year. Sales continued to dwindle in 1908 as only 1,055 Oldsmobiles were sold during the year. Still, this was good for 12th spot in industry sales standings for the year.

Big news on the product side of things was the long awaited introduction of the all new six cylinder Model Z. Olds began experimenting with a six cylinder

With a carryover to 1907 styling, this was the 1908 Model X touring car. Unique to these touring cars for this model year was the "bat wing" design front fenders. The Model X was the smallest car in the 1908 lineup with a wheelbase of 106 inches. The car was offered only as a five-passenger touring. The Model X carried a slightly smaller cylinder bore than the four cylinder engine which powered the M models.

This very nice example of the rare 1908 Model X Oldsmobile belongs to E.R. Ruby of Pontiac, Illinois. Ruby and Dick Neller are part of a handful of collectors who have taken an interest in the scarce 1906 to 1914 Oldsmobiles. Ruby's car was photographed at a national meet of the Oldsmobile Club of America. The Model X had a rear axle of the Timken type with the driveshaft carried on Timken roller bearings contained in the outer end of the axle tube.

powerplant back as far as 1905. The powerplant had a 4¾ inch stroke, 4½ inch bore, and developed 48 horsepower. Valves were of cast iron design. The camshaft was a one-inch diameter piece of steel tubing with a flange pinned and brazed on the forward end for the camshaft gear. Hess-Bright bearings were used throughout the engine. Other mechanical features of the Model Z included a three speed transmission, nickle steel I-beam front axle, Timken full floating rear end, 20 gallon copper gas tank with a three gallon reserve, Bosch high tension magneto and an aluminum crankcase. Standard model Z equipment included two acetylene headlights, two oil side lights, an oil tail lamp, a large bullfrog horn and a complete tool set. The Model Z rode on a 130-inch wheelbase and was available only as a seven-passenger touring car.

The Model M continued to use the Palace Touring designation of previous years. This car was an update of the previous year's Model A. The Model M was offered as a touring or limousine with several other specialty closed models available. Power for this series continued to come from a 40-horsepower four-cylinder motor. Wheels were second growth hickory 34-inch units. Limousines were finished in leather or cloth or satin and cloth. Beveled glass windows were standard. Interior conveniences included an electric light, speaking tube and a full toilet set. All mountings were brass while curtains were silk. The usual color combination was dark green and black. Standard M series equipment included two Rushmore acetylene headlights, two Atwood oil side lights, tail lamp, a large bullfrog horn, jack, and a complete tool set.

Offered within the M-series was the model MR, which again this year carried the designation of the flying roadster.

Olds offered a third basic series in 1909 with its four cylinder X model cars. The X and MR series shared a wheelbase of 106 inches, as opposed to the larger 112-inch M series cars. The only model available in the X series was a five passenger touring. It was a slightly smaller engine that powered the X cars when compared to the M models.

In 1908 Olds employment stood at an even 500. The factory chose the annual New York Madison Square Garden automobile show to introduce its new six cylinder Z model. During the year an Olds four cylinder won its class with a perfect score in the Glidden Reliability tour.

A breakdown in sales shows that 1,000 of the Olds Motor Works sales were the four cylinder M, MR and X models, while only 55 of the lately introduced six cylinder Model Z's were sold.

William C. Durant, who had been very successful with his take over of Buick, was looking to expand his automotive empire. General Motors was incorporated in New Jersey on September 16, 1908. Negotiations were carried out with Oldsmobile officials in October and November. Before the end of 1908 Oldsmobile became a cornerstone of General Motors. The Olds takeover involved more than $3 million in GM stock and $17,000 in cash. As a result of the new ownership, in late 1908 W.J. Mead took over the general manager's post from F.L. Smith.

The top seller in the 1908 model lineup was the M touring car. This particular car was outfitted with a special promotional Gabriel horn, probably used as an advertising gimmick for a Gabriel salesman. Base price was $2,750. The Model M was a mild update of the 1907 Model A. Powerplant on all M cars was a 4¾ inch bore and stroke engine that developed 40 horsepower. Cylinders were of grey iron construction and were cast in pairs.

This M-series toy tonneau demonstrates the flat top front fender design exclusive to 1908 models. All cars in this series were driven through a 13/16 nickel steel propeller shaft into bevel gears on the rear axle. Universal joints were of the block and trunion design. These units were hardened ground and protected by a heavy leather sleeve. Running boards were of aluminum construction.

The Model M touring is shown here as an early auto show is being set up. Olds involved itself in a variety of motoring contests to prove the overall favorable performance of its cars. These included a New York City to Poughkeepsie, N.Y., high gear run; the Glidden tour; a New York to Florida test run; a trip up Twin Peakes at San Francisco, and winning of the $6,000 Los Angeles to San Francisco race.

Several limousines were built by Oldsmobile on the 1908 M series chassis. This unit, featuring special cained body work, was a handsome car. The large 1908 Olds catalog said, "For winter use or special functions, limousines are rapidly gaining favor among the exclusive set and no expense has been spared to make them acceptable to the most fastidious." An unusual feature of this car is the fact that roll-up side curtains were used for weather protection for the tonneau. These curtains, when down, only extended as far as the forward edge of the chauffeur's seat, and did not completely enclose the front compartment.

The body work on this 1908 Model is fascinating. Although it would be 1912 before Olds offered a regular coupe model, this might well be the first closed smaller car offered by Oldsmobile on a custom basis. Each Olds Model M contained a tool kit which included a monkey wrench, a bicycle wrench, three engineers wrenches, a Stilson wrench, a Timken bearing spanner, pliers, chisel, hammer, oil can, oil gun, two extra spark plugs, two extra valve springs, cotter pins, jack, tire pump and tire repair kit. Note the extra third seat perched behind the main body.

The MR was another in the Oldsmobile flying roadster series. It was based on a 106-inch wheelbase with the same 36 horsepower engine as the other M series cars. As with all 1908 Oldsmobiles, the transmission had three speeds forward and reverse. The clutch was the same as the rest of the M series, of cone design with leather and cork insert lining. An interesting addition to this model are the Oldsmobile pennants flying from the front fenders.

This was an MR flying roadster with some special rear seating capacity and an optional, covered spare tire. The catalog for 1908 carried a huge full color ad on its back page for the flying roadster. It concluded: "If you enjoy the pleasures of the open road, you should examine the simple Oldsmobile. Duplicates of its most famous cars are on sale at all agencies. There is but one quality and one performance in the Oldsmobile."

Probably based on the MR roadster, this was an interesting one-off model. The seating was the unique part of this particular custom built car. The rear seating or tonneau section was totally upholstered in padded natural leather. Oddly, this tonneau could only be entered by swinging the left front seat forward - as shown here - and then climbing up the step plates provided atop the tool box and under the swing-away seat. In the M series the clutch was of the internal reversed cone type. It was made of aluminum and outfitted with cork inserts. The unit was covered with leather. The MR cooling system was based on a vertical tub radiator. Water capacity was almost four gallons.

This is the Model Z with its top up. The top remained an option for Olds buyers, and was not included in the Z model's base price of $4,500. This model Olds rode on 36 inch wheels with 4½ inch tires up front and 5 inch tires on the rear. Two complete ignitions systems were furnished. One was a set of six Connecticut coils with a storage battery. The other was a Bosch high tension magneto. The motor was wired so either system could be used at the flip of a switch.

New to Oldsmobile in 1908 was the Model Z, the company's first production six cylinder. Olds waited until late in the model year - the Madison Square Garden show -to introduce the Z. For the model year this was an extremely low production car and it was changed very little for 1909. All model Z's rode on wheelbases of 130 inches with a tread of 56 inches.

1909

The 1909 model year is one that poses several problems for the serious student of automobile history. The confusion centers on exactly how many Oldsmobiles were built in 1909. Specifically the problem involves the mysterious Model 20.

Two of the most reliable sources of production figures vary greatly for this model year. Automobile Quarterly's *Oldsmobile the First Seventy-Five Years*, and also available Olds factory records, list Olds total production as 6,575. James Bradley and Richard Langworth's 1896 to 1970 production figure lists Olds 1909 totals as 1,690. The higher figure would give Olds seventh spot in the 1909 sales race, while the lower figure drops Oldsmobile to eleventh. All these production figures basically agree on four cylinder Model D, DR and X model totals at 1,100 and six cylinder production for the Z at a scant 150. That would leave the Model 20 production at between 440 and 5,325.

It is fitting that the Model 20 is the source of the confusion. First that model is not listed in any of the factory catalogs or advertising that the author has researched. Legend has it that this Oldsmobile was born when W.C. Durant became alarmed that Olds had not changed or added to its model lineup between 1908 and 1909. Durant sent a Buick model of the era to the Olds experimental shops. The Buick was cut apart, a few extra inches were added and the "new" model was outfitted with an Olds grille and hood. Probably the most appealing feature of this new car was its price which made it the cheapest 1909 Olds, selling for $1,250. The Model 20 had a far smaller four cylinder engine than any other 1909 Olds. Bore and stroke was a square 3¾ inches. Only 22 horsepower

were developed from 165 cubic inches.

What was the real production of the Model 20? Chances are the actual total didn't approach 5,000 and it may have been nearer the 500 mark. Reasons? An expert in the field of pre-1916 Oldsmobiles, Dick Neller of Lansing, Mich., who has kept intensive files on early Olds owners, indicates he knows of only one surviving 1909 Model 20. Chances are that if thousands of examples of this car were built, there would be more than one known survivor. Production for 1908 totalled 1,055 and 1910 production was 1,850. Even though Olds employment rose to 1,052 for 1909 it is doubtful that Olds could have built more than 5,000 cars in 1909. Finally Durant was quite showy and he or one of his managerial assistants might not have been above padding production figures, particularly since the Model 20 reflected Durant's and General Motors' first year control of Oldsmobile. Finally all factory production records of Olds since the early Curved Dashes were substantiated by serial number records. This documentation included other six and four cylinder Oldsmobiles built in 1909, but no such records exist for the Model 20.

Basic to 1909 Olds production was the D, DR and X four cylinder Oldsmobiles. All, except the X, were powered by a 4¾ inch bore and stroke four. The X special had a slightly smaller bore. Horsepower on most of these cars stood at 40. The D and DR rode on a wheelbase of 112 inches. The X rolled on a 106 inch wheelbase. Standard equipment for these Olds fours included 8-inch headlights, generator, oil side lamps, horn, tail lamp and a full set of tools. Prices on these cars ranged from $2,000 to $4,000. Colors included maroon or brewster green on the D Palace Touring, red on the D toy tonneau, maroon on the DR

Pictured here is the mysterious Model 20 Olds/Buick. This car was offered only in 1909 and it was the smallest Olds built during the year. It was also the least expensive 1909, carrying a price tag of only $1,250. The Model 20 was powered by an engine far smaller than the standard Olds four used in the D models. This model came out at the insistence of GM chief W.C. Durant and was little more than a customized Buick. Educated guesses on Model 20 production ranged from 500 to over 5,000.

1909 Oldsmobile

Smallest and one of the best performing Olds in the 1909 model lineup was the Model X Special. Priced at $2,000, the standard color was English vermillion. The X rolled on a wheelbase of 106 inches. A slightly smaller bored Olds four cylinder turned out 35 horsepower. The X model carried 20 gallons of fuel in the copper fuel tank mounted behind the front seat. Equipment included headlights, oil side lamps, tail lamp, generator and a full tool set.

detachable toy tonneau and the flying roadster and English vermillion on the X special.

Olds continued to produce the six cylinder Model Z in 1909 with modest changes from the previous introduction year. Most Z models were touring cars, but there were several closed cars built in the top of the line series. Model Z prices began at $4,200 for the seven passenger touring. This model rolled on a 130 inch wheelbase. The 4¾ bore and stroke powerplant produced 60 horsepower. Standard equipment for the series included 9 inch headlamps, Prest-O-Lite tank, oil side lamps, tail lamp, tire irons, muffler cut-out and a full tool set.

Olds literature of the era listed the Oldsmobile Company of Canada doing business at 80 King Street in Toronto, Ontario.

The base car in the 1909 big four cylinder lineup was the Model D Palace Touring car. Priced at $2,750 this was a reliable Oldsmobile. Standard color on this model was maroon or brewster green, but it is believed optional colors could have been ordered. Wheel and tire size on the front of this model was 34 x 3½ inches, while the rears were 34 x 4 inches.

Oldsmobile has one of the finest collections of old cars of any manufacturer still in business. This 1909 Model D is often represented by Olds as a 1908 model. The front fenders are a dead giveaway as to the correct year. This nicely restored car has been in the Olds collection since the late 1960's, but actually it is the property of the legandary Detroit hobbyiest Barney Pollard. Pollard is the man who fought off World War II scrap metal hounds to perserve his warehouses full of precious early cars. Some of the cars were stacked end on end or three or four atop each other, but Pollard managed to save hundreds of rare early motorcars.

This interesting photo was taken in front of an Oldsmobile dealership of the era. The lead car in the picture is a 1909 Model D Palace Touring. Behind it is a 1908 Model X touring car. Olds dealers had things rough with the decline of sales since the hay day of the Curved Dash. The dealership pictured-like many Olds dealers of the period-picked up some extra profits selling accessories from the "Automobile Owners Supply Depot."

Most expensive among the D series cars was the limousine which was priced at $3,800. These closed cars were exceedingly rare with no more than a dozen or two built. All D series cars were square bored and stroked at 4¾ inches. Each of these cars was designed to carry four gallons of water and eighteen gallons of fuel with an extra four gallon reserve tank.

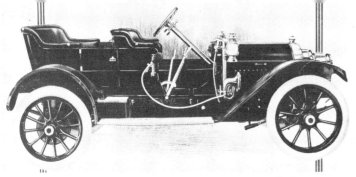

An interesting and rare 1909 model was the four cylinder Model D toy tonneau. This rakish car was priced at $2,750. The standard factory color was red. This was strictly a four passenger car. It rode on the standard series wheelbase of 112 inches. Equipment on this car included 8-inch headlamps, generator, oil side lamps, tail lamp, a full set of tools, horn, trunk rack, coat rail and foot rest.

Another relatively rare and exceedingly sharp 1909 Olds was the Model DR detachable toy tonneau. This machine carried a $2,750 price tag and rolled on a 112 inch wheelbase. Standard color on this four seater was maroon. The radiator was of cellular construction and water capacity was four gallons. Fuel capacity on this model was 15 gallons with an additional four gallon reserve.

A very unusual machine was this closed Model DR Oldsmobile. Needless to say very few of this car ever rolled off the Olds Motor Works assembly line. The price on this car was $3,500 and it was so rare it wasn't even listed in many Olds pieces of literature. An electric source for the Olds was a storage battery and dry cells. The cars were magneto equipped. Olds was several years away from the air starter system and even further away from the Delco electric system.

The well equipped Model DR Flying Roadster came outfitted with this optional top. Oldsmobile took great pride in the fact they built their own tops within the Lansing complex. It is interesting to note that both Oldsmobile and Reo had among the largest and most complete auto building complexes in the industry. The roadster rolled on front semi-elliptic springs and rear full elliptic springs.

This is the Model DR flying roadster. It was the sportiest of the Olds offerings, carrying on a tradition of several years. Price tag on this open job was $2,750, the standard color was maroon, and the seating capacity was two to four depending on which rear seating option was selected. The clutch on this four cylinder model was a leather faced cone unit.

In the early days of the auto business, Oldsmobile accomplished a lot of exposure by being involved at various major auto shows. In 1909 the company continued to participate in these events. Here a Model DR flying roadster and a Model D Palace touring are identifiable. The previous year Olds brought big news to the Madison Square Garden Auto Show with the introduction of the Model Z six cylinder line.

The Model Z was never a big seller for Olds, either in its introduction year of 1908 or in 1909. The car, however, was very well received in the automotive community. The next step was to the three-year model run of the mighty Limited series which was to be introduced in the next production year. Olds began experimenting with six cylinder engines several years before the introduction of the Z.

Standard of the Model Z series was the impressive touring car. Base price on this model was a sizable $4,200 and the standard colors were maroon or brewster green. The Model Z rode very well on an 130 inch wheelbase. Tread was 56½ inches. Front tires were 36 x 4½ inches, while rear tires were 36 x 5 inches. The Olds six cylinder powerplant had a 4¾ inch bore and stroke. Horsepower rating was 60.

A very, very few closed Model Z's were actually built in 1909. This limousine is obviously very plushly outfitted on the inside. This Z limo rode on smaller wheels and carried a price tag of more than $5,000. All cars in this series carried five gallons of water and eighteen gallons of fuel. All Z models were equipped with a three-speed transmission.

The pride of Lansing's early Oldsmobile collector Dick Neller's collection is this magnificent 1909 Model Z touring car. Neller's car is often driven to car shows and recently was driven more than 200 miles in a single day. It has racked up major awards from several clubs. Standard Model Z equipment included 9 inch headlamps, Prest-O-Lite tank, oil side lamps, tail lamp, full set of tools and tool box, trunk rack, coat rail, foot rest, tire iron and muffler cutout.

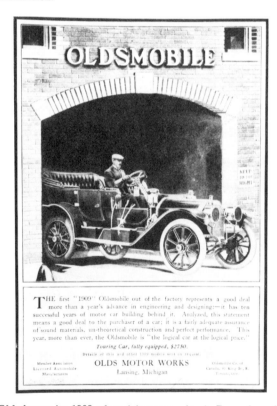

Olds began its 1909 advertising campaign in December of 1908. This advertisement was found in the automobiles, parts and accessories section of Scribner's Magazine. Since the early days of the Curved Dash, Olds placed a great deal of print media advertising. Oldsmobile was also noted for its vast network of road signs. In 1909 Olds remained a member of the Licensed Automobile Manufacturers Association.

1910

Oldsmobile sales and employment totals dropped dramatically in 1910, yet Olds introduced one of its legandary vehicles during this model year. The mighty Limited, one of the largest and most powerful Oldsmobiles ever created, was introduced in 1910. With sales totalling only 1,850 - 325 Limiteds and 1,525 Specials - Oldsmobile failed to make the top 15 in automotive sales for the first time ever in 1910.

Despite the fact that factory employment dipped from its 1909 level of 1,052 down to 850 for this model year and despite the fact that production was down by two-thirds over the previous year, a new assembly plant was completed in 1910. During the year the new Limited model was forever captured in the famous William Harnden Foster painting "Setting the Pace."

The Limited model saw limited production in its first year, but it was a car that commanded attention wherever it was displayed or driven. This model Olds offered the combination of a six cylinder powerplant, a newly refined suspension system and huge 42 inch wheels. Four styles were available on the Limited -seven passenger touring, roadster, close-coupled touring and the limousine - and with a total production of only 325 some of these cars were exceedingly rare.

Three of the Limited models, the open cars, carried price tags of $4,600 with the limousine listing for a whopping $5,800. All models rode on a wheelbase of 130 inches. Bore and stroke on the six cylinder engine stood at a square 4¾ inches. Each Limited carried five gallons of water and fuel capacity ranged from 22 gallons on the touring car to an incredible 40 gallons on the roadster. Each model had a transmission with four speeds forward and reverse. The clutch was of the leather faced cone design and the rear axle was of the full floating type. Standard equipment on the Limited models included a Bosch magneto, 9-inch Solarclipse headlights, combination oil and electric side lamps and tail lamp, Prest-O-Lite gas tank, horn and complete tool set. Colors were Brewster green, dark blue and red. Limousines were upholstered in goat skin with satin trim. Options included tops, glass fronts, speedometer, clock and extra tires.

Olds increased the wheelbase on its four cylinder models, for 1910 known as the Special series, to 118 inches. Few underhood changes were made to the four, but a new transmission with four speeds forward and reverse was added. Specials were available in the same models as the Limited - touring car, roadster, close coupled touring and limousine. Price on the first three models was $3,000 with the rare limousine tagged at $4,200. Special standard equipment included the Bosch magneto, 8 inch headlights, combination oil and electric side and tail lamps, Prest-O-Lite gas tank, horn and complete tool set.

Oldsmobile did offer some specially built commercial vehicles in 1910. Olds continued for the year to be a member of the American Licensed Automobile Manufacturers, licensed under the Selden Patent.

In the early years Oldsmobile did a lot of good promotional work. In 1910 this painting proved to be a great promotional tool. The painter was William Harnden Foster. There were many authorized copies produced of the original work and they were widely distributed to Olds dealers of the era. This painting seemed to vividly portray the power of the mighty Limited, racing or beating one of the many express trains of the era.

Olds lengthened the wheelbase on its four cylinder models and changed the name of the series to Special in 1910. This particular version was the most popular car of the model year, a seven-passenger touring car. It had folding jump seats located ahead of the regular rear seats. Olds also made some improvements on this series. They added a transmission with four speeds forward and reverse.

Smallest and sportiest of the Special series was the roadster. All 1910 Oldsmobile roadsters carried an incredible 40-gallon fuel supply in the round fuel tank located behind the seat. Located at the rear of the tank was a provision for a small trunk or hand luggage. This model Oldsmobile, the Special Roadster, was priced at $3,000.

This is what the well optioned Special series touring car looked like. Base price on this car was $3,000. Tops cost $100 to $125 depending upon the fabric used. Note the leather straps supporting the top. Olds built the touring top assemblies within its own plant rather than ordering from an outside supplier. Other popular accessories included a speedometer and windshield, although the windshield is missing from this model.

A very rare car in either series was the 1910 close coupled touring. Pictured here was the Special series machine priced at $3,000. All Special series cars were powered by forty horsepower, four cylinder engines. All cars from this grouping had a tread of 56 inches and a width of 66 inches. Each 1910 model was constructed on a pressed steel frame.

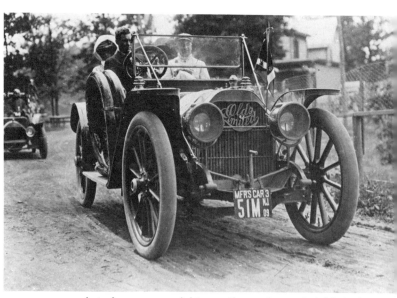

Very few limousines in either series were built in 1910. Olds said the following about its Special limousine which is pictured, "It is essential that the car should easily ride over granite pavements and crossings and the motor should have ample power, run silently and 'pick up' quickly in congested traffic." Base price on this model was $4,200.

A truly awesome sight was the newly created Limited model in any type of view from the front. This was a very early car as identified by the New Jersey manufacturer's license plate from 1909. Part of the hugeness of this car can be attributed to the 42-inch wheels which were on all 1910 models in this top of the line series.

1910

Oldsmobile for a long time has mistakenly identified its own Limited model as a 1910 rather than the 1911 model which it actually is. This car has been in the possession of its manufacturer for a long time. In this rather early shot of the car note the non-stock headlights and the rather questionable location of the spare tire.

The most common model in the low production Limited series was the touring car. It sold for $4,600 without a top. The car pictured here — with the late Bing Crosby at the wheel and in the inset — was a California collector car that was used in the 1939 movie "The Star Maker." The number of kids seated in the rear compartment of the Limited gives an idea of the hugeness of this model.

One of the big differences between the Olds Limited and most other cars on the road in 1910, including the Olds Special, was wheel size. Two roadsters — parked nose to nose — show off the difference between the two series. The smaller wheeled Special is on the left, while the Limited is on the right. The Special had 36-inch wheels, the Limited is outfitted with 42-inch wheels.

A top was considered an option on a car even as expensive as the Limited roadster. For electricity on the 1910 models Olds used a Bosch magneto. Steering on all cars in the series was of the worm and nut type. The roadster was the shortest car in the series with an overall length of 14 feet. Wheelbase on all Limited models was 130 inches. The large wheels and short length give the roadster an ungainly look somewhat akin to a highweeler model.

A true sportster looking for a car in the Limited lineup would have been drawn to the Limited roadster. Carrying a price tag of $4,600 few of these powerful cars ever were built. Each Limited roadster came with 9-inch Solarclipse headlights, a six-volt eighty-hour lighting battery and a complete set of Oldsmobile script tools.

Probably the rarest 1910 car that Oldsmobile built was the Limited limousine. A very nice home could be financed in that era for the $5,800 asking price of this model. Olds introduced its six cylinder powerplant in 1908 and by this model year that engine had been fairly well perfected. Note that the limousine version of the Limited did not use the 42-inch wheels, but appears to be fitted with the 36-inch wheels of the Special Series.

1910

Based on a 1910 Limited chassis, this might have been General Motors first venture into the camper business. Looking like a motorized covered wagon this is an unusual custom bodied Oldsmobile. By this model year Olds production had dropped by two thirds over the previous year. Under those conditions the Olds Motor Works was willing to manufacture special units where orders existed, apparently doing most of the custom body work right in its own shops.

Olds made a small number of trucks and commercial vehicles from 1907 through 1912. This particular police patrol unit was four cylinder powered and based on the Special chassis. This truck is pictured in the 1910 factory catalog. Olds said, "A car for use in connection with mail, fire or police work must be necessarily ready at all times. These cars are all in active service and have proven their worth in many emergencies."

With its Curved Dash models Oldsmobile pioneered assembly line production. By 1910 Olds production had backed off considerably and both the Special and the Limited were large cars not well suited to the assembly line. Olds employment for the year had dropped to 850 from the 1909 employment level of 1,052. In this model year Oldsmobile moved into a new assembly plant.

Oldsmobile continued to be a big advertiser in 1910, even though this was the first year since 1901 that Olds hadn't been in the top fifteen in the auto sales race. With its past history and its recent connection with General Motors, Olds retained a surprisingly strong dealer network. Part of what kept its dealers going were parts sales and repair work on the popular Curved Dash models.

For the third consecutive year Oldsmobile sales slumped and again in 1911 Olds was not to be found in the top fifteen automotive sales spots. A total of 1,250 cars were built for the year, 1,000 of the four cylinder cars — most of which were the Model 28 Autocrats which were new for the year — and Limited production became even more limited as only 250 of the Model 27 six cylinders were produced.

The Olds work force — despite slumping sales over the previous year — rose to 915 for this model year. As a product note for 1911, Oldsmobile had its first self starter, an air type system, installed on an optional basis this year.

The Special series was shown in the 1911 catalog, but indications are this was simply a carryover model and once the supply of already built Specials were gone that was it. The 1911 Special was essentially the same as the 1910 and it did not share the more powerful four cylinder motor used in the new Autocrat. Four Special models were listed at prices ranging from $3,000 to $4,200.

The Autocrat, an interesting choice of names for the new Olds, rode on its own 124 inch wheelbase. Bore and stroke on both the Autocrat four and Limited six was increased to 5 x 6 inches in 1911. The Autocrat was built as both a five and seven passenger touring car, a roadster, four-passenger tourabout and a limousine. All open models carried a price tag of $3,500 with a whopping $5,000 list price for the limousine. Horsepower rating on the new four cylinder was 40. Bodies on this series were wood trimmed in leather. Autocrats held three gallons of oil, seven gallons of water and twenty-two to twenty-eight gallons of gas. Standard colors were brewster green, royal blue or cardinal red. Standard equipment on the series included: eight-inch headlamps, side and tail lamps, Trauffault-Hartford shock absorbers, Oldsmobile dragon horn and a complete tool set. The top assembly and windshield were options.

The Olds Limited, noted for its hugeness and awesome power, got bigger and more powerful in 1911. The engine was rated at 60 horsepower for this model year and the wheelbase went up to 138 inches. Shipping weight on the series touring car was 5,160 pounds. The catalog listed the Limited as being available as a touring, roadster, tourabout and limousine. Given the series extremely limited production record, there is some real doubt that Limiteds in all these body styles were actually produced. Certainly the touring was the most popular model. Open cars listed for $5,000, while the limousine sold for $7,000. Olds again rolled its top of the line model on 42 inch wheels of second growth hickory. Standard equipment included 9 inch Solarclipse headlights, mohair top with dust cover, windshield, Warner 100 mph speedometer, an Oldsmobile dragon horn and a complete tool kit.

The cylinders of the Autocrat and Limited motors were of the vertical T-head design and cast in pairs. Outside the engine block was enammeled black. Pistons came from selected grey iron castings. Connecting rods were forged from high grade steel alloy that had been heat treated. Lubrication was of the positive feed and splash type. Olds stayed with the Bosch magneto system for 1911. The carburetors were of the automatic float feed type with a single jet. Frames on the two top series cars were made of pressed nickel steel alloy. Both the Autocrat and Limited models were upholstered in hand buffed leather.

The Olds Motor Works had remained away from most auto racing ventures since the days of the Olds Pirate. However, a prototype 1911 Autocrat was an entry and did reasonably well in Long Island's Vanderbilt Cup Race.

Essentially a carryover model from 1910, the Special series continued to be listed in the 1911 catalog. There are indications that once the Special models left over from the last model run were sold, that was it. The Specials continued to be powered by a 36-horsepower engine, a less powerful unit than the one in the Autocrat series. Price on the open models continued to be $3,000 — the least expensive 1911 Olds.

A few Special roadsters were sold in 1911. The Special four cylinder engine had both a 4¾ inch bore and stroke. The Specials all rode on 118 inch wheelbases. The 1911 Oldsmobile catalog said, "The Special has an established reputation having been placed on the market during the past year. The design is but little changed for the 1911 season as the degree of satisfaction given by each car is consistent with our manufacturing policy."

When Olds pepped up its four cylinder engine in 1911, it decided to use it to power a new series. The name selected was rather unusual — the Autocrat. Price on this model, the seven-passenger touring, was $3,500. The new four cylinder was — at forty horsepower — the most powerful motor of its type ever built by the Olds Motor Works. This engine had cylinders cast in pairs with a 5 inch bore and 6 inch stroke.

One rather unusual, yet somewhat attractive, 1911 offering was the Autocrat tourabout. This car was priced at $3,500 and few were built. Standard colors for the series were brewster green, royal blue or cardinal red. Colors other than standard were available for an extra $50. Notice the unique cowl design on this car, and the large oval gas tank behind the roadster — like rear seats.

Another rare and appealing Autocrat was the five-passenger touring. Costing $3,500, as with all cars in the series, it rode on a wheelbase of 124 inches. The braking system on the series was an expanding and contracting unit on the rear wheels. Brake activation could be via a foot pedal or the emergency hand lever. Frames were pressed nickle steel, six inches deep, four inches wide and ⅛th inch thick.

The lone closed car in the Autocrat lineup was the limousine. It was also the highest priced car in the series at $5,000. Few of this model ever rolled out of the Lansing plant. The transmission for the series was a unit with four speeds forward and reverse. Gears were of chrome vanadium steel with roller bearings. The limousine rode on larger tires than the rest of the series, using 39 x 5 inch units.

Since 1909 Oldsmobile had been a regular on the Glidden Tour. This was the 1911 entrant for that event, an Autocrat five-passenger touring car. The Autocrat had an 18½ inch cone clutch. Oil capacity was three gallons, water capacity was seven gallons and twenty two to twenty eight gallons (depending upon model) of fuel could be carried.

Sportiest among the Autocrat offerings in 1911 was the roadster. Priced at $3,500, Olds added optional single or double rear seating to its roadster for this year. Standard Autocrat equipment included eight-inch headlights, side and tail lamps, Prest-O-Lite gas tank, tire irons, Oldsmobile dragon horn and a complete set of tools.

The mighty Limited got bigger and even more powerful in 1911. The price of this model was $5,000. The wheelbase was expanded to 138 inches and the huge six cylinder engine put out an underated 60 horsepower. The top of the line Olds continued to ride on massive 42 inch wheels and 4½ inch tires front and rear. The Limited's driveshaft was enclosed in a torsion tube.

One of the premier collections of early Oldsmobiles belongs to Dick Neller of Lansing, Michigan. Here is Neller's very rare 1911 Autocrat roadster which was photographed at a national meet of the Oldsmobile Club of America. There were no standard colors offered for Autocrat roadsters this year, the color choice was left up to the ordering dealer or customer.

OLDSMOBILE

This is the Oldsmobile Division's 1911 Limited. The car company usually identifies it as a 1910 model, but it actually appears to be a 1911 model. Whatever the year, it is one of less than 1,000 of this model built over a three-year span and only a handful of these brutish cars are left today. The Limited's cooling system used a honeycomb radiator with a capacity of seven gallons of water.

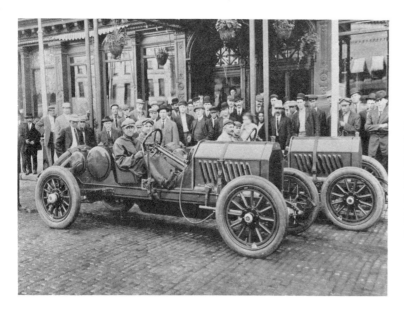

Oldsmobile has had its Limited for quite a long time. Pictorial records show the car in the division's hands as early as 1939 when this promotional scene was set up. Limited standard equipment for 1911 included side and tail lights, mohair top with cover, Warner 100 mph speedometer, Oldsmobile dragon horn, baggage rack, windshield, tire irons and a complete tool kit.

The Olds factory Limited has suffered some indignations over its career and one of the worst was the period that it was nearly covered with white paint. During World War II, when the car scraping zealots were in action, the Olds antique car collection was safely hidden on one of the factory roofs. Olds Limited wheels were made of second growth hickory.

Over the years Oldsmobile was involved in car racing on an on again, off again basis. Olds built these twin racers on its newly pepped up Autocrat chassis and 40 horsepower engine. The Autocrat crankshaft was produced from a steel forging of massive proportions. The unit was mounted on three bronze main bearings. Olds continued to use a crankcase cast in two parts of number 12 aluminum. These racers are similar to the Autocrat roadster shown in Oldsmobile's 1911 catalog, and could be purchased from the factory on a special order basis.

This 1911 Autocrat prototype racer was entered in the Long Island Vanderbilt Cup Race. Driver of the Oldsmobile racer was H.M. Stillman. The Olds averaged 60 mph over the 265 mile event and although it didn't win, it made a creditable showing. As much responsible for the Olds racing success as anything was the chassis which had a great deal of good handling characteristics built in.

With production capacities in excess of car orders that were coming in, the Olds Motor Works continued to build some special vehicles in 1911. Apparently several unique fire trucks were built for the Lansing Fire Department during this era. This unit was based on the huge Limited chassis. Note the chains on the rear wheels, and the unusual whitewall tires on the front. A huge acetylene spotlight and air-powered horn share cowl space with the standard cowl lamps.

Oldsmobile continued its slide in 1912 as three models — the Limited, Autocrat and the new Defender — accounted for only 1,075 total sales. Olds sales toppled from a high of 6,575 in 1909 to their 1912 level. Olds did not appear in the top 15 sales spots. Fortunately for the Lansing-based car maker, this marked the low point in the sales slump. Employment in the Olds Motor Works was also down drastically. It slipped from the previous year's 915 to 563. Despite all this doom and gloom, Olds added to its assembly plant in 1912. During the year W.J. Mead stepped down as Olds general manager and he was replaced by O.C. Hutchinson.

The mighty Limited, one of the most awesome cars ever to cruise the American streets, was in its third and final season as an Oldsmobile. This year the Limited grew a bit more to a wheelbase of 140 inches. Power continued to come from a 60 horsepower monster six cylinder engine. Again year Olds listed six possible ways to order a Limited: Touring, tourabout, roadster, limousine, limousine with extra touring body and chassis only. With only 250 Limiteds built — largely because prices ranged from $5,000 to $6,600 — there are serious doubts that all models listed in the catalog were actually built. Only the touring, tourabout and roadster were pictured in the catalog.

A styling addition on the 1912 Limited was four louvers, similar to the hood louvers, in the front door. All Limiteds were done with full nickle trimmings. Standard Limited equipment included two 10½-inch gas headlights, side lamps and tail lamp, automatic head lamp lighter, Pantasote top with mohair optional, lighted Jones speedometer, dragon horn, and tool kit.

Newest among the Oldsmobile models was the Defender. Powered by a smaller version of the tried and true Olds four cylinder, output was 35 horsepower. The Defender — Model 40 — was responsible for 325 sales. This was the smallest Olds offered during the year as all Defenders rolled on 116 inch wheelbases. Models offered included a touring,

Newest among the Oldsmobile lineup was the Defender series. Running on a wheelbase of 116 inches, tires on most models in this series were 36 inches by 4 inches, of plain tread design. The length of the Defender model was 12 feet, 5 inches, road clearance was 11 inches, and width was 66½ inches. Frames on this series were made from pressed nickel steel. Channel sections were 4½ inches deep and were ⁵⁄₃₂ of an inch thick. Tire rims were Baker bolted-on demountable.

tourabout, roadster, coupe and plain chassis. Prices ranged from $2,750 to $3,900. Defender series cars carried 2½ gallons of oil, 5 gallons of water and 22 gallons of fuel. A four speed transmission was provided along with a cone clutch. Front axle design was of the I-beam type with a full floating rear end with a pressed steel housing. A combination of black enamel and white nickle trim was used on all cars in the series. Standard equipment included two 9½ inch gas headlamps, side lamps and tail lamp, top with cover, windshield, dragon horn, Jones speedometer and one spare rim.

The Autocrat continued to be offered as a 1912 model. The wheelbase on this second year Olds series was 126 inches. Horsepower had been upped to 45 from a five-inch bore, six-inch stroke four cylinder powerplant. Autocrat series cars were available in several different forms for this model year including a touring car, tourabout, roadster, speedster, limousine, limousine with extra touring body and as a plain chassis. Prices ranged from $3,200 for just the chassis to $5,000 for the limousine-touring car combination. Black enamel and white nickel trim was used on all models. Standard equipment for the series included 9½ inch gas headlamps, combination oil and electric side lamps and tail lamp, top, windshield, Jones speedometer, dragon horn and complete tool kit.

Olds summed up the outfitting of all its 1912 models in its factory catalog: "To obtain a finish in keeping with the high standard set for Oldsmobile construction, two things are essential: high grade materials and their proper application. As for the paints and varnishes used on the various models, none but the best obtainable are brought into the shops. To secure the best finish, time is an important factor. The number of operations required in finishing a body is from 25 to 30. All models are upholstered in hand buffed leather, selected from the best hides, having a uniform thickness throughout. The cushions are unusually deep and comfortable and the spiral springs are enameled so they cannot rust. In the tufting, extra long curled hair is used. The top is made of the best grade of Pantasote or mohair with a dust cover of the same material. Each car is individually fitted in the Oldsmobile top department. The sockets are leather covered and bows are arched to provide a perfect watershed. When the top is thrown back, it rests in adjustable top supports which hold it at any desired angle with the bows separated."

Base model in the Defender series was the touring car. The price on this model $3,000. The engine on the Defender series was a smaller version of the motor that powered the Autocrat. The Defender powerplant was a four cylinder with cylinders cast in pairs. There was a 4 inch bore and a 5⁵⁄₁₆ inch stroke. Ignition was a high tension magneto and batteries.

Priced at $3,000 was the four passenger tourabout. All of the Defender models were steered by a worm and wheel unit. This was of the ball bearing thrust design. The steering wheel was 18½ inches in diameter. Brakes were of the internal expanding and external contracting on the rear wheels. External activation could be carried out via a foot pedal or the emergency lever would activate the internal expanding units.

1912

An Oldsmobile highlight was the offering of a coupe in the 1912 lineup. The lowest priced Olds series — the Defender — offered this jaunty looking closed model called the coupe. Base price was $3,600. For $3,900 a buyer could purchase this coupe along with an extra touring body. The Defender coupe rolled on the smallest wheels in the 1912 lineup, 34 inches by 4½ inches. It had the most unique cowl lights in the entire Olds lineup.

Despite being the lowest priced Oldsmobiles offered, the Defender series had its own sporty model — the roadster. Price tag on this model was $3,000. Front axles on all Defenders were of I-beam construction of alloy steel. The rear end was of the full floating type with a pressed steel housing. Wheels in this series were wooden, constructed of second growth hickory.

The heart of the Autocrat lineup was the touring car, shown here with its top raised, It carried a price tag of $3,500. All the cars in this series rode on 39x5 wheels and tires with plain tread. The Autocrats had nearly a foot of road clearance, were almost 15 feet long and 68 inches wide. Oil capacity was 3 gallons. Seven gallons of water was carried and this model carried 22 gallons of fuel.

The middle of the Olds lineup was again covered by the second-year Autocrat series, of which this was the touring car. Horsepower on this model was upped to 45 for 1912. Bore and stroke on this four cylinder was the same as the Limited six cylinder. All Autocrats used a selective, sliding-gear, four speed transmission. Gears were of chrome vanadium steel with bearings used throughout. The rear end was of the full floating type with a pressed steel housing.

The Tourabout in the Autocrat series sold for $3,500. Standard equipment on this second year 4-passenger Olds offering included two 9½ inch gas headlamps, two side lamps and tail lamp, automatic head lamp lighter, Prest-O-Lite tank, Pantasote or mohair top, clear vision windshield, Jones speedometer with light, dragon horn, tire iron, extra demountable rim, shock absorbers, tool kit and carpeting.

1912

The award for one of the strangest looking cars of the year had to go to the Autocrat touring roadster. Notice the unique integral cowl lights used on this series, as well as several other 1912 offerings. All motor lubrication was by means of an automatic, positive feed system. The oil was carried in a reservoir formed by the lower half of the aluminum crankcase. An oil pump was located on the left side of the motor and operated by a gear on the exhaust camshaft.

The Autocrat series was the lone Oldsmobile model which offered a pair of two passenger models. Pictured here is the extremely rare Autocrat Speedster, obviously designed to compete against Stutz and Marmon models. This car, finished in a striking red, is owned by Bud Ley of Cleveland, Ohio. The speedster rolled on 38 inch by 4½ wheels and tires. Front wheels had 12 spokes and the rear wheels had 14 spokes. Spokes were oval in design and made of second growth hickory.

One of the few closed cars offered by Oldsmobile in 1912 was the Autocrat limousine. So few of these cars were produced that they were virtually custom built autos. Base price on this car was $4,700 and an Autocrat chassis with both limousine and touring bodies could be had for $5,000. This was the most expensive offering in the Olds Autocrat lineup. Olds called this body a semi-Berline type. Note that the coach lamps are similar but not identical to those used on the coupe.

Oldsmobile continued its advertising efforts in 1912 despite lagging sales and production. A lot of this advertising was centered on the middle series Oldsmobile — the Autocrat. This particular ad sells the virtues of the tourabout and the unique touring roadster. Olds called its interesting looking built-in cowl lights "bull's eye side lights" and indicated they were wired directly to the battery.

In its final year of a three-year production run was the mighty Limited series. By far less than 1,000 of these awesome cars were produced during the three-year period and 1912's output was just 250. Olds provided a compression release mechanism for its Autocrat and Limited motors. This unit was actuated by pulling a rod located near the front of the car.

1912

There were two ways to obtain a Limited touring car in 1912. The first was to order the touring model which cost $5,000. The second was to order the limousine with the extra touring body. Price tag for this combination was $6,600. Tires on the touring and limousine models were 43 by 5 inch, with anti-skid tread design by any standard manufacturer. Wheels were made of second growth hickory.

Another of the 1912 Limited series was the Tourabout. Price on this four-passenger offering was $5,000. For this year horsepower rating on the massive Limited six cylinder was 60. Ignition was via a dual high tension, multi-point magneto and storage battery. The length of this model was 16 feet 8 inches, while road clearance was over a foot and width was 68 inches. This model Olds carried 22 gallons of fuel with an additional small auxilliary tank.

Sportiest of the top of the line Olds series was the Limited roadster. The price on this model was $5,000. Cylinders on the Limited were cast in pairs with a five-inch bore, six-inch stroke. Valves were of the taper seat interchangable design. Bearings were done in what was called Oldsmobile bronze. The carburetor on this model was of Olds design with a constant float level.

This is a photograph that was taken at Lansing's Central Fire Station in 1912. Oldsmobile enjoyed a good working relationship with the local fire fighters. A great number of Lansing's early fire trucks were custom built Oldsmobiles. Vehicles shown here range from 1907 through 1911 in date. This gave Olds some fleet testing of ideas and a local showcase for its products.

1913

The year of 1913 was a pivotal one in the history of Oldsmobile. Sales picked up during the model year with 1,175 Olds sales registered. This left the Olds Motor Works far off the pace set by industry leaders like Ford with 202,667 sales and Willys-Overland with 37,422 sales. Crosstown rival Reo held eighth position with 7,647 sales. Olds again failed to make the top 15 in sales. The disastrous slide in employment continued as less than half the previous years employees worked at Olds. Only 276 workers punched time cards in 1913.

A big change came in Olds vehicle philosophy during this year. Prices on the top of the line Model 53 six cylinder series were down substantially over the price levels of the Limited models of 1910-1912. The Model 40 Defender four cylinder series prices were dropped in this carryover year. During the year corporate executive C.W. Nash, who later had a car company of his own, was named General Manager at Olds. Under Nash's direction Olds immediately began experimenting with quality light cars.

The biggest news in the Olds lineup during the year was the all new six cylinder Model 53. Sales literature of that era pointed up the fact that previously an Olds six cylinder had never sold for less than $4,200. The lowest priced Model 53 carried a $3,200 price tag. The new model rode lower than previous Olds big cars and used 60 inch springs. Olds went back to a three-speed transmission on its new model. The ignition coil was a Delso, spark plugs were Champions of the 7/8 variety. The clutch was a leather surface cone type. Wheelbase was 135 inches. The series 53 powerplant was a six cylinder L-head. Bore was $4\frac{1}{8}$ inch and stroke was $4\frac{3}{4}$ inches. A new innovation in this model year was the use of silent Coventry chains for driving the magneto, water pump and camshaft.

A direct advantage of being in the General Motors family was realized by Olds in 1913 and enabled them to include the Delco starting, lighting and ignition system on the Model 53. The 1913 Olds catalog said of the system, "This is conceded the most positive self-starting device today and possesses a range of efficiency that places it far in advance of any other system. The operator simply retards the spark lever and pushes forward on the clutch pedal; this automatically engages a gear on the electric motor with teeth on the flywheel of the engine which causes the latter to turn over, thereby producing the same effect as by the old method of cranking." The electric starting motor also acted as a dynamo or generator. Energy produced was stored in an 80 ampere hour storage battery. Another new six cylinder feature was a power driven air pump which was attached to the motor by a bracket and was operated by a sliding gear which engaged with a permanent gear on the shaft between the generator and starting motor. The system included 15 feet of tubing, an air pressure gauge and the proper connection for tire pumping.

One puzzling model in the Olds lineup has always been the 1913 Defender. It is believed that these models—designated Model 40—were actually two slightly different models. The first were carryovers from the 1912 model year with identical specifications to those cars. The second series of 1913 Defenders were believed to have carried slightly different styling. Serial numbers ranged from 80325 to 80999 and only a touring car was offered. Wheelbases were 120 inches. The powerplant had a 4 inch bore and $5\frac{5}{16}$ inch stroke, 267 cubic inch four cylinder engines. The author has seen several Olds catalogs featuring the six cylinder Model 53, but has never seen a catalog or ad mentioning or picturing the four cylinder 1913 models.

In 1913 the Olds Motor Vehicle Company listed 12 distributors for its products. These were on a more or less regional basis and included cities like Boston, Chicago, Detroit, Los Angeles, St. Louis, San Francisco, New York, and Cleveland.

Carrying over into the 1913 model year were the Defender models which were produced in 1912. Indications are that most Defenders sold in 1913 were touring cars. One change in the Defender series was that the price on the touring car was lowered from $3,000 in 1912 to $2,500 in 1913. The Defenders used a 35 horsepower, four cylinder T-head engine. Axles were of the I-beam type in front with a full floating rear end.

There were some special Defender models built in 1913, but exactly how many of these cars were built remains a mystery. Notice the cowl treatment and the rear end styling on this model. Oldsmobile factory employment reached a low point in 1913 and there apparently was a gap after most Defender models had been produced and start-up for the Model 53 was slow coming. Only 276 people were employed by Olds in 1913.

1913

Top of the line for 1913 was the Model 53 Seven Passenger Touring Car. Priced at $3,350, the shipping weight on this six cylinder offering was 4,700 pounds. All cars in this series rode on a wheelbase of 135 inches, down slightly from the largest of the Limiteds. Each model 53 carried 23 gallons in its regular fuel tank with a reserve tank carrying an additional two gallons. Frames were of pressed sheet channel steel.

All new for 1913 was the six cylinder powered Model 53, a basic car that would be an Olds mainstay for several years with modest changes. Obviously less of a luxury car than the previous years Limited, it was reflected in the lower price tag which ranged from $3,200 to $3,350 depending on which model was selected. The Olds catalog for 1913 said, "Without sacrificing any of the rugged strength and dependability for which the Oldsmobile is famous, the entire chassis of the new car has been refined, standardized and lightened in weight."

The second basic model in the 53 Series was the five-passenger touring car. Priced at $3,200, the shipping weight on this unit was 4,625 pounds. Standard equipment on all cars in the series included the Delco self-starting, ignition and lighting system, 10¼ inch electric headlamps, two side lamps and tail lamp, power tire pump, top with boot, clear-vision windshield, Truffault-Hartford shock absorbers all around, Klaxon combination horn, Warner speedometer, Waltham eight day clock, jack, complete tool outfit and spare rim.

Rounding out the three-model 54 Series lineup was the four-passenger tourabout. This car was priced at $3,200 and weighed 4,515 pounds. As with most G.M. products of the era, Model 53 Oldsmobiles carried a lot of Delco equipment. This included Delco magneto, storage battery, coil and starter. Factory spark plugs were Champion and brakes were lined with Raybestos.

Down some in size since the days of the mighty Limited, the Olds six cylinder engine was still a fine unit in 1913. The engine was of L-head design with a 4⅛ inch bore and 4¾ stroke. Cylinders were cast in pairs with integral water jackets. Valves were on the left side. The connecting rods were H-section forgings, solid at the top and bushed with bronze for the piston pin bearings. The crankshaft came from a solid forging and was supported by four main bearings. Chains were used drive the magneto, water pump and camshaft. Horsepower was 50.

Things continued on a gradual upswing for Oldsmobile in 1914. A mildly restyled six cylinder lineup was joined late in the model year by the interesting Baby Olds, the four cylinder Model 42. Despite an increase to 1,400 total sales, this left Oldsmobile well out of the top 15 in sales for 1914.

An interesting summation of Oldsmobile's position in the industry — despite an absence in the top 15 — was made by Collier's Weekly auto writer Julian Street, "The first gasoline motor car to achieve what they call 'output' was the little, one-cylinder Oldsmobile which steered with a tiller and had a curved dash like a sleigh. It is to the Olds Motor Works which built that car that a large majority of the automobile manufacturers in Detroit trace their origin. Indeed, there are today no less than a dozen organizations, the heads of which were at one time connected with the original Olds Company — the 16-year-old forefather of the automobile business."

For 1914 Olds Motor Works employment rose to 600, up substantially over the previous year.

Mainstay of the 1914 Olds lineup was the revised Model 54, six cylinder Olds. No major changes were made in this large luxury class auto. Despite some minor improvements, Olds lowered its six cylinder prices for the model year. Three basic 1914 six cylinder models were offered. Two tourings and a limousine were available. One major change over 1913 was that the Model 54 used two different wheelbases. The seven-passenger touring had its own exclusive 139 inch wheelbase. The five-passenger touring and the limousine shared a 132 inch wheelbase. Tire sizes were standardized at 36 x 5 inches, both front and rear with Fisk or Goodyear outfitted. Wire wheels were also a rare option. Standard equipment continued to include the Delco starting, ignition and lighting system, in its second year as Oldsmobile equipment. Horsepower rating remained at 50, but the bore was increased to 4¼ inches and the stroke to 5¼ inches.

The 54 models were cars of good construction and fine appointments. Side curtains were of the Jiffy brand. The radiator was a honeycomb Mayo with a German silver casting. Carpeting was imported horsehair. Headlights were electric, nickel plated on brass with pure white French plate glass. The Model 54 steering wheel was Circassian walnut with a black enameled spider. Interiors were hand buffed leather. Toe boards, heel plates and running boards were of cast aluminum. The Model 54 dash was also of Circassian walnut with nickel trim. The dashboard was lit by an electric light.

Olds added a limousine to its six cylinder lineup in 1914. Mechanical details were the same as the open 54's. The limo was built to accomodate seven-passengers: Three on the rear seat, two on the auxiliary seats and two up front. Bodies were trimmed in French novelty cloth. Metal parts were sterling silver finish. Other refinements included a speaking tube, flower vase, toilet articles, umbrella rack electric lights and French plate glass. Weight was 4,900 pounds.

Prices on the Model 54's ranged from $2,975 to $4,300. Total production for the 1914 six cylinders was an even 1,000.

In April of 1914 Olds added a four cylinder to its lineup. Known both as the Baby Olds and the Model 42, this model was introduced as a five-passenger touring on a wheelbase of 110 inches. Price on this model was $1,450. The 42 was powered by a four cylinder with a 3½ inch bore and a 5 inch stroke. Cubic inches were 192 and horsepower was 30.

Only 400 of the Baby Oldsmobiles were built, due largely to the late introduction of the cars. Shipping weight was only 2,700 pounds — the lightest Olds built in years. William Harnden Foster, who did the famed Limited racing the train painting had actually done several subsequent paintings of Olds built cars. In one of his final efforts, Foster painted a Baby Olds racing a train.

William Harnden Foster painted a series of paintings for Oldsmobile and the subject was always the same, a current model Olds racing a speeding train. Most famous of these works showed the 1910 Limited in action. This particular painting — probably the final one in the series — showed a 1914 Baby Olds at speed. These paintings were widely reproduced, but the 1914 edition is far more rare than the 1910 picture.

The Model 42 was also known as the Baby Olds. Only 400 of this model were built in 1914, but the car was carried over to 1915 with little change. The Baby Olds produced 30 horsepower from only 192 cubic inches. This car was offered in 1914 only as a touring car, but in 1915 a roadster was added. Wheelbase on this model was 110 inches. The car weighed only 2,700 pounds.

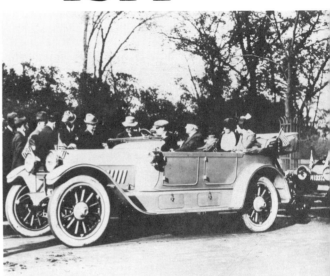

The bulk of the cars sold by Oldsmobile in 1914 were model 54 six cylinders. Standard equipment on this series was impressive. It consisted of combination electric and oil side lamps and tail lamp, electric headlamps, adjustable windshield, top, boot, side curtains, 60 mph speedometer, Waltham clock, extra rim, motor driven air pump, Delco starting, lighting and ignition system, tools, jack, and Klaxon horn. Standard colors were green, lake and gray. The dual spare tires on this model were an accessory, however.

This Oldsmobile saw duty hauling dignitaries around Washington, D.C. The lubrication system was of the splash type and the clutch was of the cone type. The front axle was of the I-beam design. Rear axle was of the floating type. Timken roller bearings were used up front. A Model 54 could hold 23 gallons of fuel with three gallons in a reserve tank. The gas tank had two partitions to prevent fuel from splashing when the tank was half full.

A very rare Olds factory option in 1914 was wire wheels. There were several other options available from the Olds Motor Works during this year. Seat covers were an extra cost option. Tires other than the standard size were available. The standard tires were Goodyear or Fisk. Colors other than standard were available for $50 extra. Olds also offered special touring trunks. The price was $45 for one and $80 for a pair.

Riding on a 132 inch wheelbase was the five-passenger touring car. This was the lowest priced Model 54 carrying a price tag of $2,975. A honeycomb radiator of the Mayo brand name was used. The shell was of German silver. The gasoline tank was lead coated. Base of that tank was high grade steel. The windshield was of plate glass of silvering quality. This car is seen entering Belle Isle, a fashionable Detroit city park in that era.

The seven-passenger Model 54 touring car sold for $3,150; a price reduction over 1913 levels for essentially the same car. This was the largest car offered by Olds during the model year as it rode on 139 inch wheelbase. This year the size of the Olds six cylinder was increased to a 4¼ inch bore and 5¼ inch stroke. Horsepower remained at 50. The engine was suspended on a three-point system.

1914

The Olds Model 54 was the result of several years developmental work. The steering wheel was of Circassian walnut which was imported from Asia. The spider was black enameled to avoid reflection in the driver's eyes. Aluminum was used in toe boards, heel plates and running boards. The Olds six cylinder was an L-head. Valves were enclosed to insure silence, freedom from dirt and to retain oil in its proper place.

Despite the passing of the awesome Limited series in 1912, the Model 54's had plenty of class. Delco supplied a number of components to Olds during this year including the magneto, six-volt storage battery, spark coil, spark control and electric starter. Olds used Baker demountable rims. The frame for the Olds 54 series was constructed of heat treated pressed steel channel.

The Olds limousine was a finely turned out piece of automotive equipment. Carrying a selling price of $4,300, very few of this model rolled out of Lansing. Wheelbase on the limo was 132 inches. The Model 54 closed car was built to carry seven passengers. Bodies were trimmed in French novelty cloth. Metal parts were done in sterling silver finish. Interior nice touches included flower vases and electric lights. The chauffeur of this vehicle could have buttoned up the front compartment with side curtains.

This Model 54 Oldsmobile was at one time owned by California racing champion and old car restorer Phil Hill. This nice Oldsmobile has since been exported overseas. Front springs on the Model 54 were of the semi-elliptic design, while the rear springs were elliptic underslung. Road clearance was 11 inches. The carburetor was of a special design of the float feed type.

1915

Things got a great deal better for Oldsmobile in 1915 as sales soared to 7,696, based largely on the popularity of Olds four cylinder offerings. Olds finally made it back in to the top 15 in sales standings as they captured 15th spot behind Chalmers. Crosstown rival Reo grabbed ninth spot by virtue of 14,693 sales. Olds factory employment swelled to 2,000 for the year.

Style leader among the Oldsmobiles was the Model 55 Olds. This car was priced at $2,975 and was offered only as a seven-passenger touring car. Only 114 of this model were built. This was a logical update of the 1913 Model 53 and the 1914 Model 54. Olds began offering six cylinders in 1908. Timing gears on this motor were operated by silent Smith Coventry imported drive chains. The Delco starting system continued to be offered as standard equipment on 1915 Oldsmobiles.

The Model 55 was a large Oldsmobile running on a wheelbase of 139 inches. Shipping weight on this model was 4,186 pounds. Wheels were of second growth hickory with 5-inch straight side tires. Non-skid units were normally on the rear, even though they were not on this example. A rear mounted tire rack would carry up to two tires. Rims were Baker straight sided of the bolted on type. The radiator was of the honeycomb type with a German silver finish.

Three basic models racked up the Olds sales total in 1915. The Model 42 — with slight modifications, lower prices and the addition of a roadster — accounted for 1,319 sales. A revised four cylinder, introduced later in the model year, the Model 43 accounted for a whopping 5,921 sales. The Model 55 — in its updated six cylinder form from the previous year — accounted for only 114 sales. This model year was credited with 342 Model 44 sales, but this was early production of a genuine 1916 model.

The Olds four cylinder Model 42 was slightly upgraded for 1915. Wheelbase was stretched two inches to 112 inches. Prices were cut noticeably also and a roadster was added. Both sold for $1,285. The 1915 Olds catalog said the "Light Four Oldsmobile probably has as low a center of gravity as any other America made car. This is accomplished by the use of long springs which are underslung from the axle in the rear and are 48 inches in length, and by specially designed axles, spindles and frames."

The cowl dash was made of Circassian walnut as was the 17 inch steering wheel. Upholstery was long grain leather and standard body colors were brewster green or Orriford Lake. The top was standard equipment as were Jiffy side curtains. The engine remained a 30 horsepower job. The front axle was an I-beam while the rear axle was ¾-floating. Brakes used 12 inch drums. Wheels were 33 inch, of natural finished selected hickory. This lower priced car was Delco starter equipped. Weight was 2,615 pounds. A tool kit was standard equipment as was a tire pump and jack.

Although limited in its production, the Model 55 six cylinder was the class of the 1915 lineup. This machine was an update of the 1913 Model 53 and the 1914 Model 54. Prices were reduced on this series, and the seven-passenger touring sold for $2,975. A major change on this model was the switchover to left hand steering. The engine remained an L-head, 446 cubic inch, 50 horsepower job. Standard colors were brewster green or Orriford Lake. Standard equipment included a Warner speedometer, eight-day clock and a dashboard light. There was a 22 gallon fuel tank and gasoline was moved via a Stewart-Warner vacuum system. The Delco starting, lighting and ignition system was in its third year with the Olds six. A three-speed transmission was used and the top was a one-man unit of long grain material to match the upholstery. A tool kit was standard, as was a tire pump and jack.

Also offered in 1915 was an updated and lately introduced four cylinder known as the Model 43. This car was carried over virtually unchanged to 1916. Running gear was very nearly the same as the Model 42, with a 30 horsepower, valve-in-head engine underhood. Wheelbase for this new series was upped to 120 inches. The Delco ignition, starting and lighting system was again standard equipment. Leather upholstery was provided. Other name brand equipment included Baker rims; Collins side curtains; Delco starter, spark coil and generator; Exide 6-volt battery, and bearings by Timken, Hyatt and New Departure. A $1,095 base price was on this series. Production for the year was 5,921.

1915

The sporty tennis set could feel at home with this $1,285 priced 1915 Model 42 touring car. There was a concealed compartment that opened just above the running board. This compartment was locking. In it was a factory tool kit as standard equipment, which included a tire pump and jack. Shipping weight on this model was 2,495 pounds. There was a 15-gallon gas tank suspended on the rear frame side members.

The Model 42 was a nimble, sharp little Oldsmobile. Introduced as the "Baby Olds" the previous year, this was the second year for the Model 42 with minor changes. The potent little four cylinder — an engine type Oldsmobile had offered for a decade — developed 30 horsepower. Olds literature of the day pointed out the fact that valves were enclosed and silenced. Olds also touted its newly designed splash lubrication system. Note that in this view, the valve cover has been removed, showing the placement of valves and rocker arms.

For 1915 the Oldsmobile "one-man" top was standard equipment. This top was of long grain material to match the upholstery. Also supplied were patented Jiffy side curtains. These were made to be carried in a specially designed pocket in the front part of the top. The Model 42 dash was done in naturally finished Circassian walnut. Instruments were flush mounted. They included a Stewart-Warner speedometer and an eight-day clock. Instruments were illuminated by an electric dash light.

New to the Model 42 lineup for 1915 was this jaunty looking roadster. Price on this model was $1,285 FOB in Lansing. Standard colors on the Model 42 were either brewster green or Orriford Lake (maroon). Brakes were controlled via a foot pedal with an additional lever controlling the emergency brake. Brake drums were 12 inches in diameter. The clutch was of the cone design. Clutch diameter was 12½ inches with a 2½ inch face. The frame was of pressed channel steel of four inch sections.

At the time of this photograph, this 1915 Model 42 touring was owned by Dick Neller of Lansing, Michigan. It was displayed at a national meet of the Oldsmobile Club of America. Olds running boards for this model were made of aluminum. Road clearance was 10½-inches. Tires — front and rear — were straight sided and 33 x 4 inches. Nonskids were used on the rear. Rims were Baker brand, demountable of the bolted-on type. There was a tire rack at the rear, as shown on Neller's Model 42.

Later additions to the 1915 line were the four cylinder Model 43 cars. This is the roadster. These machines were carried over essentially unchanged to the 1916 year. Production for the 43's was 5,921 — making this by far the most popular 1915 Olds series. The engine size on this model increased slightly over the Model 42's, although both were four cylinders. Price for both open cars in 1915 was $1,095. This was one of the earliest uses of a true rumbleseat on a roadster.

Probably the most popular 1915 Oldsmobile was the Model 43 touring car. Carrying a $1,095 price tag, this model was part of Oldsmobile's effort to downsize its cars since the monsters of 1910-12. The 43 series used a four cylinder valve-in-head motor outfitted with a Delco electric system for starting, lighting and ignition. Wheelbase was 120 inches.

No, this is not a 1915 Olds. However, this year the livery firm of P.G. Katz & Son of Verona, Penn., totally reworked a used Oldsmobile chassis of undisclosed vintage and then mounted upon it an ambulance body produced by the nearby Pittsburgh firm of G.A. Schnable & Sons. The result was this rather interesting "C" cab vehicle, which probably saw several years of service as a private ambulance in the Allegheny Valley area northeast of Pittsburgh. Schnable was one of a multitude of small firms of the era that would produce commercial bodies of all types for just about any chassis, though professional bodies such as found on ambulances and hearses were considered the apex of the commercial coachbuilder's art.

In 1938 Joe Taffee of Kalamazoo, Michigan wrote Oldsmobile to tell of the 1915 Model 43 that was owned by his grandfather, Joe Cooper, pictured left. Taffee is sitting on the hood of the Model 43 Olds. This photo was taken in front of Cooper's Roofing Company. Oldsmobile received hundreds of letters each year testifying to the good cars built by Olds. Some owners wanted to sell their cars back to the company, others — like Taffee — just wanted to offer praise.

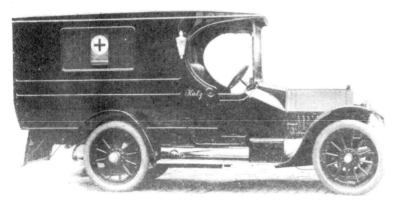

Oldsmobile sales totals were up in 1916. A total of 10,142 sales were good enough to boost the Lansing, Michigan based car builder into sixteenth spot in the sales race. Reo was well up in the standings and others outselling Olds this year were Saxon, Chalmers, Chandler and Paige.

Olds brought a pair of cars to the market place in 1916: the four cylinder Model 43 carried over from 1915 and the division's first V-8 model known as the Model 44. Factory employment for this year rose to 3,600, nearly double the previous year's workforce.

Big news of this year, of course, was the eight cylinder Olds. Since the days of the one-lunger Curved Dash, Oldsmobile had been experimenting with different multiples of cylinders. This was one of the reasons R.E. Olds left his namesake firm in 1904. The two cylinders came in 1904, four cylinders in 1906 and this six cylinders in 1907. According to Strongsville, Ohio, 1916 Olds expert Gary Halford — who helped research this difficult year — Olds actually began selling Model 44 V-8 cars in August of 1915. Halford shared his collection of 1916 Oldsmobilia with the author including records and photographs of surviving cars. His collection is so vast it includes a tracing from the serial number plate from a Model 44 found buried in the mud along a New England river bank.

Olds called its Model 44 "a light eight." This was the lone year of production for this series. Model 44's rolled on a wheelbase of 120 inches. Tread was standard and weight was less than 2,800 pounds. The all-new motor was an L-head eight cylinder putting out more than forty horsepower. The crankshaft was built of heat treated, high carbon steel. Lubrication was force fed and the clutch was of leather faced cone design. The electric system was Oldsmobile Delco and consisted of a starter, generator and distributor. The six volt battery was stored in a steel box under the front seat. Other V-8 series equipment included: natural finished hickory wheels, Circassion walnut steering wheel, French leather upholstered seats, German silver radiator, and a Stewart vacuum system.

The Model 44 came in four body styles: roadster, touring and very rare sedan and cabriolet, which the author has never seen a remaining example of or even a photo or mention of in any printed factory literature of the era. A total of 7,838 open Model 44's — mostly tourings — were built. Only 162 of the elusive closed cars were made. Open car prices began at $1,195.

Running as a companion car to the new V-8 was the tried and true Model 43 four cylinder. This was the second, and final year, for this series. The next four cylinder Olds would be the Economy truck which was introduced in 1919. The Model 43 appeared largely unchanged in 1916, except the roadster was rumble-seat equipped. Power continued to come from a valve-in-head 30 horsepower four. Displacement was 192 cubic inches and lubrication came from a splash system. Other Model 43 features included: leather faced clutch, Delco ignition system, Stewart vacuum system, Delco starter and coil, Exide six-volt battery, Timken front axle bearings, seasoned hickory wheels and aluminum running boards. Standard body colors

for this series were Orriford Lake or Brewster Green. Models offered were the five passenger touring and the roadster. Weight was approximately 2,700 pounds. Prices began at $1,095. A total of 2,142 Model 43's, all open cars, were made in 1916.

Factory backed cross country motoring was not new to Oldsmobile, in fact it dated back to the Curved Dash era. In 1916, however, a new twist was added as a woman took the controls of an Olds for a marathon trek. Miss Amanda Preuss of Sacramento drove a Model 44 roadster from San Francisco to New York via the Lincoln Highway in 11 days, five hours and 45 minutes to establish a transcontinental record for women. The only person — up to that point — to record a better cross country time was the experienced Erwin "Cannonball" Baker in a Cadillac. A previous cross country run by Baker in a Stutz was bettered by Miss Preuss. Later Baker would use an Olds in one of his cross country stunts.

Miss Preuss told why she undertook such an adventure in a specially printed Olds brochure on her trip: "I had read where Miss Anita King, a moving picture star, had made a trip accross the continent the summer in 43 days which was considered a remarkable performance. 'Gracious,' I said, 'I can beat that and never half try.'" Miss Preuss trip included lots of strenuous driving, but according to her account the Model 44 held up well. A small brake part had to be dealer replaced along the way and the radiator started leaking after the lady mowed down a horse in Nebraska. Her Goodyear all weather tread tires held up well as her lone blowout came in Wyoming when she hit a sharp rock "with terrific force." The lady record setter was distraught with having to purchase a pint of radiator water for a nickel in the midst of the desert and she was more upset with 60-cent per gallon gasoline at another out of the way stop.

A bit of mystery exists on exactly who built the Oldsmobile engines of this era. Most reference books indicate or imply Oldsmobile engines were Olds built, but other sources of this time period indicate Olds using a "Northway" engine. Remember, as far back as the Curved Dash era, it was not unusual for Oldsmobile to use an outside engine supplier such as the Dodge brothers and Cadillac designer Henry Leland.

Moved up essentially unchanged from the previous model year were the two open Model 43's. This is the five-passenger touring which carried a price tag of $1,095. Production for the entire series was 2,142 and most of this group were touring cars. Weight was about 2,700 pounds. All these cars had black fenders and under body parts. Standard body colors were Orriford Lake (a shade of purple) or Brewster Green. Road clearance for the series was slightly more than 10 inches.

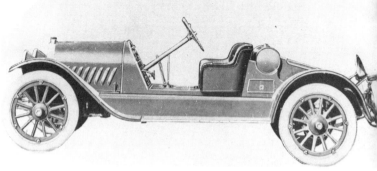

A snappy offering in the Model 43 group was the roadster. The Olds four cylinder was a peppy performer bringing 30 horsepower from 192 cubic inches. Water was circulated by a centrifugal pump through a honeycomb radiator. Tires were 33 x 4 inch, straight sided with non-skid tread at the rear. Rims were Baker brand, bolted on and straight sided. The factory tool kit included: A tire pump, five assorted wrenches, cotter pin extractor, hammer, pliers, chisel and punch.

So rare it isn't even listed in any of the standard factory literature of the day was this 1916 Model 44 V-8 speedster. Olds 1916 expert Gary Halford is attempting to restore a car of this design. Evidently this speedster was a product of the Cuttling Larson Company of New York. It was built for the 1916 New York Auto Show. The engines on all Model 44's were outfitted with a three blade aluminum fan and detachable transmission cover.

This 1916 Olds Model 44 touring was photographed in about 1950. At that time the machine was owned by Harry Olney of Springfield, Vermont. Another 1916 Olds resides in the vast collection at Harrah's in Reno. The windshield on this series was constructed of heavy plate glass in two sections. Extra strength side braces served as a rigid front support for the one-man top. The top had five bows. This car is believed to be outfitted with the original top as pictured. Note the unique rear window design.

The Model 43 and Model 44 offerings shared the same wheelbase dimensions of 120 inches. Front springs on this V-8 chassis were semi-elliptic, two inches wide and 36 inches long. Rear springs were underslung, two inches wide and 48 inches long. The radiator was of honeycomb design with a solid German silver jacket. Olds literature of the day said it was of "European design conforming to the lines of the car." A removable toe board gave access to the clutch.

This sharp Model 44 roadster belonged to Bill Hinrich of Martinsville, New Jersey. As with all 1916 V-8's it had 23-inch width doors. The horn was electrically powered and motor driven. It was concealed under the hood and actuated from the top of the steering column. The standard color for this model Olds was royal green. Upholstery was black, long grain leather.

This is another shot of the New Jersey based Hinrich Model 44. Contrast the radiator shell design here against that of the Spanish catalog cars pictured elsewhere in the chapter. All 1916 Oldsmobiles in this series featured left-hand steering. The steering wheel was of 17-inch diameter and constructed of Circassian walnut. The steering wheel spider was painted with black enamel. Headlamps were of two bulb design. Paint and varnish were hand applied and hand rubbed during this era.

A rear view of the Hinrich car shows it sported the two passenger rumble seat. The Model 44's rode on a floating rear end. Heavy nickel drive gears were outfitted. The differential was mounted on ball bearings. Wheels were mounted on a double row of ball bearings. Wheels were mounted on the axle, not on the driving shaft. Wheels were of seasoned hickory naturally finished.

Apparently a touring car from the 44 series was also available in some Spanish speaking nations, as this catalog illustration comes from a Spanish brochure. The fueling system for all Model 44's worked through a float feed carburetor. Gas was fed from a rear suspended fuel tank via a Stewart vacuum system. The gas gauge was located atop the tank rather than on the dash. Touring cars were outfitted with Collins, quick adjusting curtains, carried in the front, middle and back sections of the top.

Beginning with the earliest days of Oldsmobile production, the export business was important. Although export sales records are sketchy, this Spanish language catalog photo gives evidence Olds was concerned with export sales in 1916. Shown here is a Model 44 roadster. Note the radiator design here differs from most other cars pictured in this chapter. Indications are this radiator style was also used on some U.S. cars during the model year.

Oldsmobile still carried out an active advertisement program in 1916 despite the fact they were in sixteenth spot in the sales race. This advertisement told of the virtues of the light-eight Model 44. All cars in this series were powered by a 246 cubic inch motor which put out 40 horsepower at 2,000 rpm. Olds called its powerplant vibration free. After a long series of one, two, four and six cylinders, this was the company's first try at an eight cylinder.

Miss Amanda Preuss made an amazing new women's transcontinental record in this 1916 Model 44 roadster. She is pictured here at journey's end in front of a combination Olds/Stutz dealership in New York City. Her trip was an 11 day, 5 hour and 45-minute trek between San Francisco and New York via the Lincoln Highway. In 1916 the only person ever to make the trip faster was Erwin "Cannonball" Baker in a Cadillac.

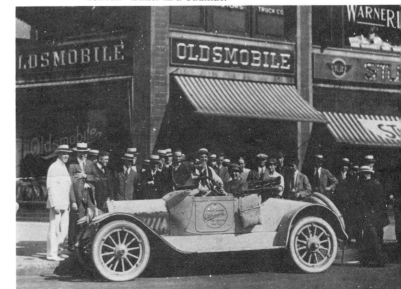

This was the Model 45, V-8 two-passenger roadster. Production between the two V-8 roadsters totalled 3,199. The price on this Olds model was $1,295. The standard color scheme on the 45 roadster was a carmine body and hood with black enameled fenders. The 33 inch wheels were natural wood finish. The electric system on this model was Oldsmobile-Delco. There were three units, a starter, generator and distributor. Each unit was independent. A high grade storage battery was provided also.

This Oldsmobile Model 45 was in the City of Lansing fleet in 1917. Note the Olds made, simplified one-man top. The factory also provided adjustable side curtains with snap fasteners. The curtains opened with the doors. This model carried what Olds called a "auxillary seat in the deck" otherwise known as a rumbleseat. Electric lights provided by Olds on this model included double bulb headlights, tail light and dash light.

An attractive model was this four-passenger Model 45 roadster which sold for $1,295 and was included in the overall V-8 roadster production of 3,199. Standard paint scheme on this model was a blue body and hood with black enameled fenders. Rear axle assembly on Model 45's was a spiral, bevel type, full floating with its pinion and differential in a demountable carrier. A pressed steel housing was reinforced by a truss rod. Drive gears were constructed of extra heavy nickel steel which was heat treated. The differential was mounted on Timken roller bearings.

1917

For 1917 Oldsmobile's fortunes improved dramatically. Sales more than doubled over the previous year and stood at 22,613. This was good enough to move Oldsmobile into the top 10 in sales standings, finishing tenth. Factory employment was on the rise as well to 4,000 for the year.

The larger Olds work force had things beyond the realm of car building beginning in 1917. During the year the Olds Motor Works began a war production effort that over two years saw the construction of more than 2,000 kitchen trailers. Olds also did some production work for the Liberty aircraft engine.

The two basic cornerstone models of the 1917 Olds effort were both new. A six cylinder rejoined the lineup in this year with the Model 37. Production totalled 8,045. In the V-8 catagory Olds sold 31 Model 44's which were left over 1916's. They also built 1,097 of the Model 45-A which was essentially a 1918 model. The real 1917 Olds V-8 was the Model 45 which enjoyed a production run of 13,440.

Over its history Olds had built one, two, four and six cylinder powerplants. In 1916 it offered its first production V-8, the Model 44. In 1917, with the new Model 45, Olds reached a high production with its V-8 design. The new car weighed only 3,000 pounds spread across a 120 inch wheelbase. Models included both two and four passenger roadsters, five-passenger tourings and seven-passenger tourings. Wheels were of the artillery type with natural wood finish. The powerplant was of the V-type, L-head design turning out 50 horsepower. Cylinders were cast enbloc with detachable heads. Features included balanced connecting rods, alloy aluminum pistons and extra large bronze backed, babbit lined bearings. Cooling came from a honeycomb radiator with a nickel plated shell. Transmission was a three-speed unit. A hotchkiss drive system was used. Delco provided an improved starter, generator and distributor. Upholstery was quality leather, brightly finished with box pleated cushions. The instrument panel was walnut. Instruments included oil pressure gauge, speedometer, eight-day clock and ammeter. Instruments were illuminated and nickel plated. Standard series equipment included electric horn, extra rim, license plate hanger, tool set, jack and tire repair kit. Standard colors were black, carmine, blue and royal green.

Model 37's rolled on a wheelbase of 112 inches with a weight of about 2,400 pounds for open cars. Under the hood was a six-cylinder, valve in head 40 horsepower motor. Transmission was a three speed. Wheels were 32 inch made of selected hickory. Upholstery was done in black leather with box pleats. The dash was walnut with a sight-feed oil gauge, speedometer, eight day clock and ammeter. All were illuminated by a standard dash light. The windshield was a heavy plate glass unit in two pieces. A one-man top was furnished. Prices in this series started at $1,185. This was the series that made the most extensive use to date of regularly built closed models. Two closed models were available in the 1917 Model 37 lineup.

1917

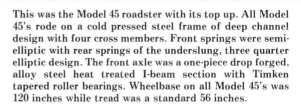

This was the Model 45 roadster with its top up. All Model 45's rode on a cold pressed steel frame of deep channel design with four cross members. Front springs were semi-elliptic with rear springs of the underslung, three quarter elliptic design. The front axle was a one-piece drop forged, alloy steel heat treated I-beam section with Timken tapered roller bearings. Wheelbase on all Model 45's was 120 inches while tread was a standard 56 inches.

Rarest of the 1917 Model 45 V-8's was the five-passenger touring. Only 1,500 of this model were built. Standard color scheme on this model was royal green bodywork and hood with black enameled fenders. Price was $1,295. The Olds V-8 cooling system was based on a honeycomb radiator. Water was circulated by a gear driven centrifugal pump. The system was topped off with a special watertight cap. A four-blade, pressed steel fan was driven by a V-belt of leather. Gasoline was fed by a vacuum system with the gas tank suspended in the rear.

In its second year of offering a light eight, the Olds Model 45 was a rugged car. The powerplant was a high speed, L-head turning out 50 horsepower. Cylinders were cast en bloc with detachable heads. Balanced connecting rods were used along with alloy aluminum pistons. Extra large, bronze backed bearings were used. A jump spark ignition system was employed with current supplied by the Delco unit. There was a combination hand and automatic spark advances. The carb was of the automatic compensating type. Brakes operated on the rear wheels only, with the service brakes being of the external contracting type and the parking or emergency brake of the internal expanding variety.

Most popular of the V-8 Oldsmobiles in 1917 was the seven-passenger touring car. Production on this model was a sizable 9,701. This was the most expensive car in the series, priced at $1,367. The color scheme here was Royal green with black enameled fenders. Driving controls for the V-8 included friction retained spark and throttle levers on top of the steering wheel. Pedals were provided for brakes and clutch. There was a floor mounted gear shift lever and an emergency brake lever located in the center of the floor.

This is an interesting shot of a new Model 45 touring car displayed with a Curved Dash mislabled as an 1897 Olds. The Model 45 is a rare unit due mainly to its wire wheels, which were believed to be a factory option during the year. The Olds touring top was made of a material known as Drednaut. It was a cotton drill base coated with five layers of rubber compound. The new Olds top material could be washed easier than traditional mohair. Side curtains were of the Collins type with curtains in three sections so any door could be opened without unfastening more than one section. The scene, shot in Indianapolis, apparently was set up by a local dealer in that city. The owner of the curved dash was identified as Carl Fisher, but no one else in the photo is named. Note the 21-cents a gallon gas price.

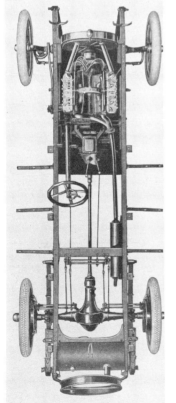

The Model 37 roadster sold for $1,185 making this the least expensive Olds for 1917. All Model 37's rode on a wheelbase of 112 inches. Weight was 2,400 pounds. This marked a return of the six cylinder to the Oldsmobile lineup after a year's absence. Transmission on this series was a three-speed with a leather faced cone clutch. Standard color on the Model 37 roadster was carmine.

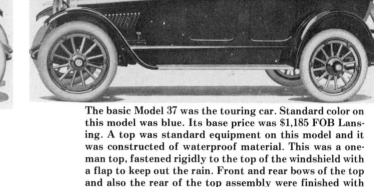

The basic Model 37 was the touring car. Standard color on this model was blue. Its base price was $1,185 FOB Lansing. A top was standard equipment on this model and it was constructed of waterproof material. This was a one-man top, fastened rigidly to the top of the windshield with a flap to keep out the rain. Front and rear bows of the top and also the rear of the top assembly were finished with bright coach mouldings. There was a single tire rack at the rear with the spare tire held by a single bolt.

Olds moved into volume production of closed cars in 1917 with a couple of Model 37's. This coupe cost $1,595. The closed design was carried on for several model years to come. All Model 37's were built on frames of cold pressed steel with channel sections with a maximum of 7 inches in depth. The front axle was of the I-beam design. The service brakes were of the external contracting type actuated by a foot pedal. The emergency brake was operated by a floor mounted lever.

Another in the growing number of closed Oldsmobiles was the Model 37 sedan. This car sold for $1,695. All cars in this series carried their six volt battery under the front seat. The Model 37 used a left hand steering system of the split nut and worm type, fully adjustable. The steering wheel was a 17 inch unit of corrugated walnut. There was a one-piece nickel plated steering column jacket. A specially designed horn button was located in the center of the steering wheel.

The six cylinder Model 37 powerplant developed 40 horsepower. It was of the valve-in-head design with a detachable head. This engine was designed to burn a lower grade fuel than usual. Connecting rods were light weight and drop forged with large bearings. The cooling fan was a three-blade unit of polished aluminum. Lubrication was of the splash type brought about by rod dippers sweeping through the crankcase. Oil level was maintained by a pump inside the crankcase driven off the camshaft.

1918

Things continued to go well for Oldsmobile in 1918, although sales numbers went down slightly from the previous year. Despite the lower number of 19,169 Olds moved up to eighth spot in industry sales standings. There was really little product change for the new year as the Model 37 was carried over and a slightly revised Model 45-A was brought forth for V-8 buyers. A total of 11,037 of the six cylinders were built with 8,132 V-8's coming out of Lansing.

Specifications stayed nearly the same for the 45-A as compared to the Model 45 of 1917. Power continued to come from an L-head V-8. Horsepower rating was increased to 58 for this year and the engine continued to be mounted at three different points. Cooling still came from a honeycomb radiator with a nickel plated shell. A vacuum fuel system was used and a leather faced cone clutch was employed. Twelve spoked artillery wheels were used. The windshield was of heavy plate glass and a slanting two-piece bottom was employed with rubber weather strips. Tires were 33 x 4½ with non-skid treads on the rear. A new model sportster touring — a large four passenger car was added during the model year. Prices on the 45-A's were at $1,700.

Things were changed only slightly on the Model 37 six cylinder series. The wheelbase remained at 112 inches. Prices remained very near the 1917 levels and customers continued to respond well to the two closed models — for 1918 dubbed All Season cars — despite several hundred dollar higher price tags over open models. The six cylinder had some internal modifications and horsepower went up to 44. Delco components continued to be used throughout the car. Tires were 32 by 4 inches with non-skid tread at the rear. These were mounted on demountable straight sided rims and wheels were of selected hickory and naturally finished. A rear tire rack was provided with an area for a tire lock. A rare an interesting addition to the Model 37 lineup was a nifty little pickup truck known as the service wagon. The bed was almost five feet long, 39 inches wide and 14 inches deep.

Because of the war effort some auto building materials were in short supply during parts of this model year. Olds continued to build some of its kitchen trailers for the war effort and also turned out selected Liberty aircraft engine parts. Rail transportation ran into some difficulties in 1918 and Olds continued to emphasize factory driveaways as a way to guarantee fast delivery of a customer or dealer's car. A small fleet of Olds Model 45-A's — finished in battleship grey — were selected to serve as the official cars at several Navy bases.

By August of 1918 Oldsmobile had leaked the word they were planning to build trucks in the near future. Olds dealers began to plan and look forward to this additional segment of business.

Olds put the finishing touches on a new motor plant in 1918.

After a period of dwindling sales, smaller employment and little interest in its cars, Oldsmobile was doing better in 1918. Sales of 19,169 hoisted Olds to eighth position for the year. The division continued to use this logo for the year. It is very similar to the one that decorated the popular Curved Dash models in the early going.

Olds stayed with the Northway V-8 in 1918 to power its slightly revised Model 45-A lineup. The touring car sold for $1,700 and weighed 3,065 pounds. This series was powered by a V-type engine of L-head design. Horsepower was upgraded to 58. The engine was balanced by a three point suspension system. The touring was available in either 5 or 7 passenger form.

The standard roadster continued to be a part of the Olds lineup this model year. Priced at $1,700 this model tipped the scales at 2,905 pounds. All Model 45 A's rolled on a wheelbase of 120 inches. The engine was cooled by water circulated by a centrifugal pump. The radiator was of the honeycomb design fitted in a nickel plated shell. A four blade fan circulated the air. This is the 2-passenger version with its large rear deck area.

Olds tagged its Model 45's and Model 45-A's with a variety of special names. Shown here is the 45-A Pacemaker. Olds said this model utilized a "fuselage" body, which was slightly different than the regular touring body. The transmission on this model was a three speed unit with gears and shafts of special steel drop forged, heat treated and hardened. The clutch was a leather faced cone type.

The V-8 Club Roadster was again produced in 1918. The price was $1,700 and its weight was 3,085 pounds. Lubrication on the Olds V-8 was force feed on an automatic pressure system. Oil pressure was indicated by an oil gauge. Olds used a vacuum system to move the fuel with the gas tank suspended in the rear. The frame was of cold pressed steel of deep channel construction with four cross members.

The sportster was another special model offered in the 45-A series in 1918. This model was special enough to rate a brochure of its own. It was a very large 4-passenger touring model. Special oval rear bevel edged windows were provided. These windows were set in nickel plated frames. Upholstery was of high grade, genuine French leather. Marshall cushion comfort springs were used in both cushions and seat backs.

The Model 37 Olds was the lightest car in the 1918 lineup at 2,350 pounds. Price on this little roadster was $1,195. Olds retained its six cylinder powerplant this year and upped the horsepower count to 44. Lubrication was via a pump circulating splash system. Individual troughs were maintained for connecting rods. A gauge on the dash indicated whether the oiling system was working.

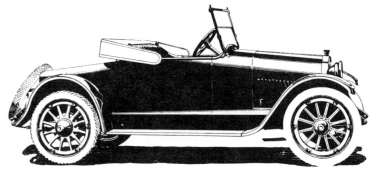

Mainstay of the Model 37 lineup was the touring car. The price on this model was $1,195 and the weight was 2,390 pounds. Gasoline was fed by a vacuum system with a gasoline tank suspended in the rear. The rear axle on Model 37's was of the full floating type. Special bevel gears were constructed of nickel steel. Wheels were mounted on large double ball bearings. The differential was mounted on tapered roller bearings.

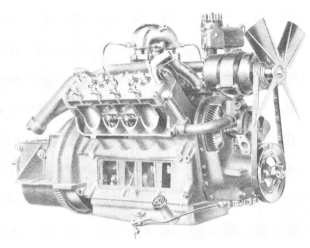

Oldsmobile was in its third year of offering V-8 engines to its customers. The Olds engine this year used aluminum alloy pistons and a steel hardened ground wrist pin. Three compression rings were fitted to the upper part of the piston, while at the lower end was a scraper ring. Tungsten steel valves were used. These valves were opened by valve fitted at their lower ends with hardened and ground steel rollers.

This amazing shot shows the exceptional carrying capacity of a Model 45-A touring. The vanderville troop called Singer's Midgets got their Olds ride in Seattle, Wash. Model 45-A equipment for this year included ventilating windshield, spare rim, Stewart-Warner speedometer, tire carrier, robe rail, foot rail, double bulb headlights, dash light, full tool kit, eight-day clock, ammeter, electric horn, tire pump and jack.

Oldsmobile called its Model 37 cars of this year All Season models. This Sedan, note the placement of the single side door on each side, weighed 2,632 pounds. Price was a top of the line $1,695. Production between the two Olds closed Model 37's was 1,000. On both closed cars the side windows dropped into cushioned pockets in the body. This gave the car a very open look, almost like the hardtops of the 1950's.

This little coupe was an interesting Model 37 Olds. It weighed 2,527 pounds and sold for $1,595. The main seat in this model was to the rear of the driver's seat. An extra seat then could be unfolded from under the cowl. This provided a seat for a fourth person. The instrument board on Model 37's was of genuine walnut with a satin finish. Instruments and clock were nickel finished and set flush.

This was a very unique and very rare offering that Olds made apparently in 1918 only. Based on the six cylinder Model 37 this is an interestingly little pickup factory built by Oldsmobile. The bed on this model was almost 5-feet long, 39 inches wide and 14 inches deep. It is believed that a few of these car/trucks found used at the factory in Lansing and also at the various Olds factory sales branches across the country. It was priced at $1,195 F.O.B. Lansing, fully equipped with roadster top and nickeled box rails.

Sales nearly doubled for the high riding Olds Motor Works in 1919. A total of 39,042 — the highest production ever for Olds — units were sold this year, good for ninth in the sales race tucked between Hudson-Essex and Studebaker.

This new all time Olds sales mark was achieved with mildly updated six cylinder and V-8 cars. Big product news came, however, as Lansing released a line of four cylinder powered trucks. These were not the first trucks to come from Olds, but this was the first volume effort at truck building by the company. Truck production would continue up to the mid-1920's.

The Oldsmobile Economy Truck was responsible for a healthy 5,617 sales the first year with a firm that several years back didn't build that many units in an entire year. This was a light truck that achieved good acceptance in the market place by farmers, merchants

Rounding out the 37-A series in 1919 was the sedan. Price was $1,895 and weight was 2,915 pounds. Service brakes were of the external contracting type on the rear wheels only. They were adjustable by a thumb nut. Front springs were semi-elliptic, 2 inches wide and 36 inches long. Rear springs were semi-elliptic, underslung and 54 inches long. The steering column was nickel plated. The steering wheel was walnut and 17 inches in diameter.

This was a 1919 Model 37-A sedan. Note this car has only one door per side, but the door on the left was for the driver, while the right one opened into the passenger area. The 37-A dashboard was made of walnut with instruments mounted flush. Gauges included oil pressure, speedometer and an eight day clock. Lighting and ignition switches were mounted on a hinged door in the dash.

and municipalities. The Olds Economy Truck rode on a wheelbase of 128 inches. With standard body work the truck was a bit over 177 inches. When a factory installed express body was in place weight was 3,100 pounds. The rated load capacity was an amazing 2,000 pounds. It is rather unusual that Olds selected not to go with either its standard V-8 or six cylinder motor but instead used the first four cylinder in its lineup since 1916. The motor was a valve-in-head unit displacing 224 cubic inches and developing around 40 horsepower. The crankshaft was of high carbon drop forged, heat treated steel. Connecting rods were of the same material. Wheels were 35-inch artillery sytle made of second growth hickory. Tires were all weather Goodyear cords. The carb was a double jet Zenith. Water capacity was 19 quarts, gasoline capacity was 12½ gallons while a single gallon of oil was carried. Standard equipment included dash lights, ammeter, electric horn, side curtains, extra rim and complete tool set. Prices ranged from $1,350 equipped with the express body, $1,295 with just the cab and chassis and $1,250 as a chassis including cowl, fenders, and windshield but no seat.

Three types of V-8 cars were sold over the 1919 model year including a few Model 45's and a nearly equal number of Model 45-A's and Model 45-B's. Total V-8 production was 11,457. Models ranged from roadsters, several touring models and a 45-B Sedan introduced very late in the model year. Prices ranged from $1,700 to $3,450 for a special and rare limousine model. The 45-A's were essentially as described in the previous chapter. The 45-B's rode on an increased wheelbase of 122 inches. Power continued to come from a V-8 with a 2⅞ inch bore and 4¾ inch stroke. Horsepower output remained at 58. Lubrication was via an automatic pressure-gear pump system. Gasoline was fed through a vacuum system from a 20-gallon tank. Transmission remained a three-speed with a large, leather faced cone type clutch. Wheels were 34 inch natural finished artillery type. The instrument panel was of genuine walnut with a shrouded light. Weight was 3,150 pounds.

Most popular of the Oldsmobile series in 1919 was the six cylinder models which were tagged 37-A's. Olds continued to offer two popular priced closed cars in this lineup. Production for the series totalled a sizeable 20,037. Wheelbase on this series was 112 inches. Weight was 2,400 pounds. Power continued to come from a six-cylinder, valve-in-head motor with a balanced crankshaft. This motor featured a detachable cylinder head and the horsepower rating remained 44. A six volt battery was located under the front seat. Steering was done with a 17-inch walnut wheel with a column finished in nickel and bolted to the dash. Upholstery was of the box pleated type of leather. Tires were straight sided, 32 x 4, with non-skid treads on the rear. Prices ranged from $1,295 to $1,895.

Olds Motor Works employment continued at about 4,000. An expansion program was started to handle the increased volume of Oldsmobile production. The new manufacturing areas included final assembly, axles, sheet metal and enameling.

In the All-Season lineup for 1919 was the 37-A six cylinder coupe. Price was $1,895 and weight was 2,830 pounds. The factory catalog listed this model as being either a three or four passenger car. Transmission on all cars in this series was a three-speed. Clutch was a leather faced cone type. An I-beam front axle was provided with taper roller bearings.

Most popular of the Oldsmobile six cylinder was the 37-A touring car. Price tag on this car was $1,295 and weight was 2,510 pounds. Total production on this series was 20,037 for all models. Powerplant for the 37's was a valve-in-head six cylinder. This motor had a detachable head and turned out 44 horsepower. The crankshaft was made of heat treated high grade steel. Connecting rods were light weight and drop forged.

Lowest priced car in the Olds lineup was the Model 37-A roadster. Price on this car was $1,295 and weight was 2,400 pounds. This series continued to roll on a wheelbase of 112 inches. Cooling came via a honeycomb radiator with a nickeled shell. A six volt battery was located under the front seat. The frame on this series was of cold pressed steel with seven inch channel sections.

Very rarely seen was a closed model of any type in the 45-A group. Pictured here is the Deluxe Seven-Passenger Limousine. Price on this model was $3,450 making this the most expensive 1919 Olds. Front axles on the V-8's were a one-piece drop forged heat treated and hardened I-beam section. This axle used tappered roller bearings. The rear axle was of the spiral bevel type, full floating with the pinion and differential in a demountable carrier. Also available from Oldsmobile, on a custom order basis only, were Landaulet, Bristol-Limousine, Salamanca (whatever that was), Landau-Brougham, and Brougham styles. Even though some Oldsmobile literature of the day refers to these models, virtually nothing is known about them and no illustrations can be found of these styles. Prices on these cars ranged from $2,950 to $3,450, and it appears that the cars were custom built in Oldsmobile's own shops only upon special order. It is conceivable that no orders ever materialized for some of these styles.

The Model 45-A touring was a strong and handsome car. Note the rubberized top and the twin rear oval windows. Also notice the top irons at the rear of the car. The big nickel plated radiator was a distinctive Olds appearance item. Springs were semi-elliptic up front and three-quarter elliptic in the rear. The touring car used longer springs than the roadster. Note the body interior and top edge of the doors were leather covered. Power on the Model 45-A came from a V-8 with an L-head design. There were balanced connecting rods and alloy pistons. Extra large bronze backed, babbitt lined bearings were in place. Lubrication was force fed with a bypass governing pressure. There was an oil gauge on the dash. An automatic compensating carburetor was utilized. There was a vacuum fuel system with a gas tank suspended in the rear.

In the early part of the Model year most of the V-8's sold were the 45-A model four-passenger Pacemaker. It was priced at $1,700 and weighed 3,000 pounds. The 45-A cars rolled on a wheelbase of 120 inches. Total production on the entire 45-A series for 1919 was 5,631. A leather faced cone clutch was used as was a three-speed transmission.

The seven-passenger touring in the 45-A series was also tagged the Thorobred. It was priced at $1,700 and weighed 3,150 pounds. Tires on this model were 34 inches by 4 inch, with Non-skid treads being used at the rear. Upholstery was of high grade leather with a box pleated design. The frame was of cold pressed steel with four cross members.

This was the Model 45-B touring car which at some times was also designated the Pacemaker. Priced at $1,895, this was the least expensive car in the series. Weight on this model was 3,150 pounds. For this model year the V-8 wheelbase was upped to 122 inches. The eight cylinder engine remained a V-type with detachable heads. Bore was $2\frac{7}{8}$ inches with a $4\frac{3}{4}$ inch stroke. Horsepower output stayed at 58.

Olds hung the nametag of the Thorobred on this 45-B seven-passenger touring car. Price was $1,895 and weight was 3,210 pounds. Total Model 45-B production — across all model lines — was 5,826. The electrical system consisted of three independent units; starter, generator and distributor. There was automatic current regulation. This was a six-volt system and a three-cell storage battery was used.

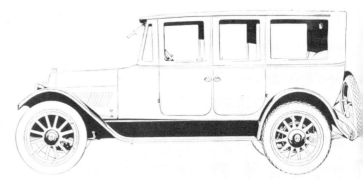

Very late in the 1919 model year Oldsmobile introduced a sedan in its V-8 series. The seven-passenger 45-B Sedan was the most expensive car in the 45-B lineup at $2,950. Weight was 3,420 pounds. Very few of this car were built in 1919, but it became a lot more common in 1920. The 45-B cars used a three-speed transmission with drop forged, heat treated chrome nickel steel gears and shafts.

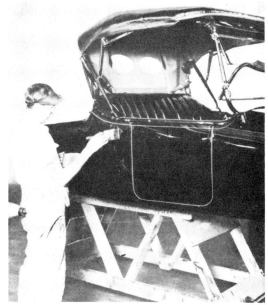

Oldsmobile still used a great deal of hand work in its 1919 painting process. Factory colors included seal brown, periscope green, royal blue and carmine. Notice the twin oval treatment on this roadster. Tops on the Oldsmobiles for 1919 were of the one-man type with Johnson nickel framed plate glass windows in the rear. The windshield was of heavy plate glass construction.

This was the standard Oldsmobile configuration for the Olds Economy Truck. The truck was a new offering from the Olds Motor Works. Oldsmobile for several years had offered V-8's and six cylinders, yet strangely they chose to power their new truck with a four cylinder. That engine displaced 224 cubic inches and developed about 40 horsepower. Three main bearings supported a crankshaft of high carbon, drop forged, heat treated steel.

This was an unusual use for an Olds Truck. Obviously the load made the most of the potent four cylinder engine. The carb was a double jet Zenith. An air intake was provided with a hot air tube and shutter. There was a choke mounted on the dash. The cooling system was a forced water circulation type with a centrifugal pump mounted on the front of the motor. Water capacity was 19 quarts. Oil capacity was 1 gallon.

The Economy Truck gained good acceptance across the country, even in California. This fleet was operated by the California Laundry in Hollywood. With a standard body the Olds truck was just over 177 inches long. Wheelbase on this model was 128 inches. Road weight was 3,100 pounds. Carrying capacity was a goodly 2,000 pounds.

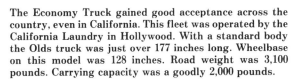

A number of companies were using the Olds Economy Truck in service as small buses. This particular unit operated in Cleveland, Ohio. The Olds truck used 35 inch artillery wheels of second growth hickory. Tires were Goodyear cords. All weather treads were used on the rear with rib type up front. Springs were semi-elliptic all around and made of high grade steel. The gas tank was under the driver's seat with a capacity of 12½ gallons.

1920

Sales declined slightly for the Olds Motor Works in 1920 and the division stood pat with just revisions of 1919 models. A total of 34,504 Oldsmobiles were sold during the 1920 model year. This gave Olds twelfth place in the sales standings between Maxwell and Dort.

The six cylinder continued to pace Olds sales. In 1920 the open six cylinders were known as 37-A's and 14,073 were built. This year the closed sixes were called 37-B's and 3,871 were produced. The 45-B was the mainstay of the V-8 line with 7,215 made. A new 46 V-8 was offered later in the model year with only 497 built. The 43-A, essentially an all-new four cylinder for 1921 (see next chapter), saw early production of 635 in 1920. Truck production reached an all-time peak of 8,213.

This was the last year of significant production for the Model 37's although a few six cylinders were carried over to 1921. For this year Olds tagged the open cars, such as this roadster, 37-A's. The B designation was placed on all closed cars. The roadster was the least expensive and lightest 1920 model. Price was $1,450 and weight was 2,380 pounds. The 37's continued to be powered by a six cylinder, valve-in head 40 horsepower engine.

A popular 37-A model continued to be the touring car. A two piece windshield was used. Construction was of a heavy plate glass. Wheels were of selected hickory with a natural wood finish. Rims were demountable and bolted on. Tires were straight sided 32 by 4's with traction tread on the rear. Price on this model was $1,450 and weight was 2,390 pounds.

In 1920 Oldsmobile completed an expansion program which included new areas for final assembly, axles, sheet metal and enameling. Factory employment dropped slightly for the year to 3,890.

The only real new model in the 1920 lineup was the Model 46. This series was offered for three years. Production was relatively low in 1920 and 1921, but picked up substantially in 1922 — its last year. The Model 46 was essentially an update of the 45-B. Both cars came on a 122 inch wheelbase. Power continued to come from a 246 cubic inch V-8. Detachable heads were used and horsepower remained at 58. The transmission was a three-speed, while the clutch was of the leather faced cone type. One distinctive feature between the Model 45 and Model 46 was the latter's use of small cowl lights.

Most popular among the Olds offerings continued to be the six cylinder 37-A and 37-B models. The A designation was used on the open cars and the B nameplate was on the popular closed cars. Wheelbase on these models was 112 inches. The tried and true powerplant remained a 177 cubic inch, valve-in-head six cylinder. Horsepower remained at 44. Lubrication was of the automatic force feed type. Artillery wheels were used. Leather upholstery was found on the open cars with velour used on the closed cars. The 37-B Sedan became a true four door in 1920. The rather cumbersome seating design was changed on the coupe. Three passengers could now ride in comfort, with an auxiliary seat which faced forward for a fourth passenger.

The Oldsmobile Economy Truck continued to climb in popularity, in fact 1920 was the peak year for production of this vehicle. From this point on production of the truck was limited. For this model year the factory did a great deal of promoting of its truck. Several nice pieces of sales literature were produced, national advertising was placed and factory publications were full of truck news. By this year several other bodies were offered on the truck. The Lansing Body Company built several attractive truck bodies which were pictured in the Olds catalog. The Hayes - Diefenderfer Company of New York made several closed truck designs for Olds. A convertible 8-in-1 farm body was offered through Olds by the American Wagon Company of Dixon, Illinois. The truck wheelbase was 128 inches. The Olds Economy Truck was automatically governed to run 22 mph, unless the orderer directed otherwise. The motor remained a valve-in-head four cylinder which produced 40 horsepower. The starting and lighting system was an Auto-Lite, breaking a Delco stronghold at Olds. It was a six-volt unit using a Bendix drive and an 80 ampere hour U.S. L. battery.

On Nov. 30, W.C. Durant, who brought Oldsmobile into the infant General Motors in 1908, was once again forced from that giant automotive concern. Durant went on to build yet another automotive corporation and in the later years of the 1920's a major Durant plant in Lansing was kept busy building Durant and Star cars. Pierre du Pont and organizational man Alfred P. Sloan were left to pick up the corporate pieces at General Motors and the Olds Motor Works.

1920

The closed cars continued to be a good seller for Oldsmobile in the 37 series. The coupe was priced at $1,995 and weight was 2,755 pounds. Wheelbase on these six cylinders continued to be 112 inches. The electrical system included separate units for starting, lighting and ignition. There was a popular brand six volt battery located under the front seat. The frame on this series car was pressed steel with seven inch channel sections.

Olds by now had a traditional four door sedan in its six cylinder 37-B series. This was the top of the line six cylinder. Price was $1,995 and weight was 2,927 pounds. Cooling for all cars in this series was by a centrifugal water pump. The radiator had a honeycomb design. The transmission was a three-speed unit Olds had offered for several years. The clutch was a leather faced unit of cone design. This photo was taken in front of the fashionable Mayfield Country Club in Cleveland, Ohio.

Oldsmobile Division of General Motors today has this very nice 1920 Model 37-B in its factory collection. This is a highly original car and finished in an attractive green color. Ths is the oldest closed car in the Olds collection. It is often displayed and usually proves to be a crowd favorite. All 37-B's were lubricated by an automatic force feed system.

This is a rear view of the Oldsmobile owned 1920 37-B sedan. Upholstery on all closed models was done in distinctive velours which harmonize with the exterior paint. The instrument panel was walnut finished with instruments mounted flush. Included were an oil pressure gauge, speedometer and an eight-day clock. Lighting and ignition switches were locking.

The flagship in the Olds lineup for 1920 and also the most expensive car in regular production was the Model 45-B Sedan. This car cost a sizable $2,950 and weighed 3,695 pounds. Front and rear springs on this car were semi-elliptic. Shackles were oversized and springs were fitted with phosphorus bronze bushings. The steering wheel was an eighteen-inch corrugated walnut unit. Tires were 34 inches by 4½ inch.

This is an interesting rear view of the Model 45-B touring car. This particular car has optional twin spare tires at the rear. Note the single taillight. Spark controls were mounted inside the walnut steering wheel. The Model 45-B was a large comfortable machine. The interior was of high grade box pleated leather. Seat backs were detachable. The body interior and top of the doors were leather covered.

This cowboy obviously was proud of his Model 45 touring car. A very rare set of wire wheels are seen on this Olds, giving it a lighter and sportier appearance. This model had two independent braking systems. The foot brake controlled an external contracting system. A hand operated brake system was internal contracting. Both operated on the rear wheels only. The top was a simplified one-man with Johnson nickel framed plate glass windows in the rear.

This nicely restored 1920 Model 45-B touring is owned by A. Ray Kyle of Hubbard, Ohio. Mr. Kyle owns several types of old cars and he considers the Olds among his favorites. This particular car was photographed at the rain soaked 1979 Oldsmobile Club of America national meet in Lansing, Michigan. This car was displayed inside a parking ramp.

It was the final year for the Model 45 V-8 series. This model brought a lot of customers to Oldsmobile and for an early V-8 design it proved to be fairly reliable. Price on this touring was $2,045 and weight was 3,195 pounds. This car continued to use a wheelbase of 122 inches. The driveshaft was a tubular unit. There were two universal joints in this set up. An unusual thing about this photo is the ancient riveted lighthouse in the background - where was the photo taken?

This is the Model 45-B Olds V-8 and its was very similar to the Model 46 V-8. Olds dubbed this a "high speed, high efficiency 90 degree engine." Heads were detachable. Bore was 2 and ⅞ inches and stroke was 4 and ¾ inches. Horsepower remained at 58. There was a counterbalanced crankshaft, Lynite pistons and bronze backed, babbit lined bearings. The carburetor was a two stage type. Fuel was fed by vacuum.

A new V-8 came on the Olds scene in 1920. This car carried the designation of Model 46. The Model 46 was offered for three years, the first two seeing very limited production. The Model 46 touring was priced at $1,875 in its introduction year and tipped the scales at 3,195 pounds. Specifications were very similar to the Model 45's which had been offered for several years and were in their final year of production in 1920.

Oldsmobile continued to carry out an aggressive print advertising effort in 1920. This ad was first seen in Literary Digest. It pushed the Olds Model 37 and Model 45-B closed cars. Olds felt the woman had a great deal to say about the family auto purchase and women seemed attracted to the closed Oldsmobiles. The factory emphasized the "power, speed and dependability and remarkable fuel economy" of its cars.

This Model 46 was quite attractive with its wire wheel option. Standard wheels on this model were the wooden artillery type of selected hickory. Also available were these Truarc wires. One difference between the 45 and 46 models were the attractive cowl lights on this model. The windshield was of heavy plate glass. There was a rubber seal between the lower section of the windshield and the cowl.

An early camper was this unit based on the Olds Economy Truck Chassis. Dubbed with the colorful name The Road Lizard, this unit was way ahead of its time. It was equipped with a stove and ice box and had running water. The Olds truck rolled on artillery wheels made of second growth hickory. Demountable rims, such as the one stowed on the roof, were used with 35x5 inch Goodyear cord tires. Timken bearings were used both front and rear. The front axle was a drop forged I-beam section.

A fairly common Oldsmobile Economy truck application was as an ambulance. There is some interesting coachwork in this truck and it looks like a one-off job. This model year was by far the biggest one for the Olds truck. Sales for this year totalled 8,213 and trailed off seriously in the next couple of years. Cooling system for the Olds truck was based on forced water circulation by a centrifugal pump mounted on the front of the motor. Water capacity was 19 quarts.

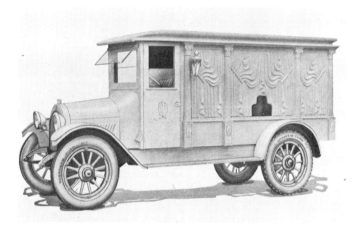

This was one of the standard models offered by Oldsmobile in their truck catalog. This hearse had a loading space of 90 inches and a width of 44 inches. The interior was done in something called vehisote, which the catalog said was "stained and polished to imitate mahogany." This unique carved body was constructed by the hometown Lansing Body Company.

There was a lot of municipal uses for Olds trucks and one of the more popular applications was as a fire truck. To get the engine to the fire quickly, power came from a 224 cubic inch, 4 cylinder motor. Rated at 40 horsepower, the crankshaft was drop forged of chrome vanadium steel. There were three main bearings. The road weight for the standard Olds truck was 3,100 pounds, this fire truck was probably heavier.

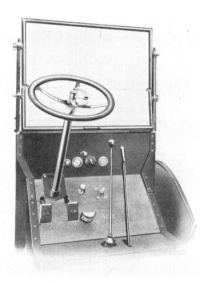

This was the dashboard and control area for the Oldsmobile Economy Truck. The windshield was a two-piece adjustable unit. Regular equipment included dash lights, ammeter, electric horn, complete set of side curtains, seat cushion, extra rim, complete set of tools, jack and tire pump. There was an 18 inch steering wheel. The gasoline tank carried 12½ gallons and was located under the front seat.

1921

After several years of offering mild restyles of the previous year's models, 1921 marked a year of innovation for Olds. Big news came as the all new 43-A four cylinders were introduced. A second new model, the Model 47 V-8, was also in its first year in 1921. This lineup was added to the existing Model 46 V-8's and the truck line which saw a drastic cutback in sales this year.

Despite Oldsmobile's new look, sales numbers dropped more than a third between 1920 and 1921. A total of 19,157 sales was good enough, however, to move Olds up to ninth place in the sales standings between Nash and Maxwell.

For 1921, as the result of the 1920 change in General Motors management, there was a new Olds Motor Works general manager. Taking over was industry veteran A.B.C. Hardy. His work force fell rather dramatically in this model year from 3,890 in 1920 to 2,500 in 1921.

In 1921 there were 948 Model 37's built, but those were essentially leftover 1920 models (see photos last chapter). Olds went without a six cylinder model for 1921 and 1922. The new four cylinder Model 43-A was the big seller at 13,867. Production for the V-8 broke down this way: Nine carryover Model 45 B's, 745 Model 46's, and 3,085 of the new Model 47 V-8's. Finally Oldsmobile sold only 503 of its economy trucks, low point in sales for the truck's five-year history.

The biggest product news in several years at Oldsmobile was the all-new Model 43. Introduction of the new four cylinder came in November of 1920. At that introduction there were two open cars and two closed. The introduction advertising campaign came in magazines like the Saturday Evening Post and Country Gentleman. The 43-A's rolled on a wheelbase of 115 inches. A four cylinder engine had a displacement of 224 cubic inches and horsepower rating of 43. Pistons were of aluminum alloy. Fuel from a 14 gallon tank was moved by a Stewart vacuum system. The electrical system used Auto Lite starting and lighting with a Remy distributor. A six volt Willard battery was located under the front seat. The clutch was of the dry plate type, while a three speed transmission was again used. The rear axle was a semi-floating type. Tires were straight sided fabric type with non-skids on the rear. Closed cars had three inches more leg room over the 37 series cars of a year ago. Closed car interiors were done in high grade fabrics, while open cars were upholstered in leather. Weights ranged from 2,742 pounds to 3,027 pounds. Prices were between $1,445 and $2,145.

The other new offering in the 1921 Olds lineup was the Model 47. This was a slightly smaller and slightly less powerful V-8, as compared to the carryover Model 46. Wheelbase on the 47 was 115 inches. A total of 53 horsepower came from 234 cubic inches. A Delco starting motor was used along with a Willard battery. The clutch was a dry disc plate unit by Borg and Beck. This new V-8 came as a touring, sedan and coupe. The interior work on the open car was done in fine grained black leather. Upholstery work on the closed car was a combination of velour and broadcloth. The instrument panel was of genuine walnut. Tires were 32 by 4 inches. Weight ranged from 2,970 pounds to 3,262 pounds. Prices ranged from $1,695 to $2,395. The top was made of the best weatherproofed material. Five top bows were provided and nickel plated mouldings were used at the front and rear. The top backdrop was fitted with a long rectangular Johnson window.

In 1921 Olds continued to offer the Model 46, though in extremely limited numbers. That model was continued on a 122-inch wheelbase. A 247 cubic inch V-8 produced 58 horsepower.

Another year of Oldsmobile Economy Trucks was offered this model year, with no substantial changes. Wheelbase continued to be 128 inches. Power came from a 40 horsepower four cylinder engine.

In November of 1920 Oldsmobile introduced its first four cylinder car in nearly five years. This 43-A model, heading uphill, was featured on the cover of the "Oldsmobile Weekly Wallop," December 11, 1920 issue. The Wallop was published for several years for Olds dealers and distributors. The magazine, published by Oldsmobile, said of the new fours: "Extreme cars has been given the development of this new model and a great deal of special new machinery of the most modern type has been installed for its manufacture."

$1445

The most popular Olds in 1921 was the all new 43-A touring car. Priced at $1,445 it shared low price honors with the roadster in the same series. Weight on this unit was 2,767 pounds. A total of 11,481 open model 43-A cars were built in 1921. This series rode on a wheelbase of 115 inches, slightly larger than the sixes of the previous years. Frame construction resembled the Model 37's of the past years.

1921

Oldsmobile's new 43-A series all had nice lines. Tires on this touring and all other four cylinders were straight sided 32 x 4's with non-skid tread pattern on the rear and straight tread on the front. Rims were of the demountable, bolted-on type. Most model 43-A offerings rode on wooden wheels built from selected hickory. Finish on these wheels was natural. Each car in the four cylinder series had approximately ten inches of road clearance.

Selling cars was a competitive business in the early 1920's and dealers took every opportunity to showcase their car's performance. Evidently the 43-A's were quite good hill climbers. A Boston dealer took on the notorious Corey Hill in high gear and won. Note the tire chains installed on the rear wheels. A Knoxville, Tenn. dealer had such faith in the 43-A's climbing capacity that he posted a $2,000 challenge to other area dealers. Note that this car advertised a $1,595 delivery price in Boston — which was $100 higher than the factory F.O.B. price at Lansing.

$1445

A basic model in the 43-A lineup was the roadster. Priced at $1,445, the weight on this model was the lightest Olds for 1921 at 2,742 pounds. Electrical equipment for the new fours included an Auto-Lite starting and lighting set with a Remy distributor. Current came from an 80-amp hour, 15-plate, six volt Willard storage battery. The generator was equipped with a new type of third brush regulator.

Closed Oldsmobiles had been popular in past years and the four cylinder line allowed the division to offer its least expensive closed cars ever. This 43-A coupe listed for $2,145 and tipped the scales at 2,917 pounds. Closed cars were trimmed in high grade fabrics. Marshall seat springs were used with graded, curled interlaced hair inside each cushion. Two corner lights and a dome light were found inside each closed 43-A, and roller shades were standard on the back windows.

$2145

$2145

The sedan continued to be a popular offering and the 43-A sedan led the way in 1921 closed car production. A total of 2,386 closed 43-A's were built in the model year. Price of this car was $2,145. This was the heaviest car in the series at 3,027 pounds. Olds still used brush painting and each paint job was hand rubbed. Most cars in the series were standard left hand steering, but some right hand drive cars were built for export. Interior appearance was enhanced through the use of a nickeled steering column.

A late addition to the 1921 Model 43-A series was this closed 5-passenger Brougham. It featured more passenger room than the standard coupe. As with all cars in the series, the walnut finished instrument board featured a flush mounted oil pressure gauge, speedometer and choke control. Instruments were flood lit. A combination ignition switch and ammeter were mounted on an access door on the instrument panel. Note the highly reflective finish on the body — the result of many hours of hand painting and hand rubbing.

By far the rarest Olds series in 1921 was the Model 46. Only 633 of these Model 46 tourings — in both five and seven seat capacity — were built. This seven-passenger job cost $1,875 and weighed 3,195 pounds. The Model 46 cars were very close in chassis and engine design to the previous years of Model 45s, 45-As and 45-Bs. Sometimes the name of Thorobred was hung on the 7-passenger touring cars like this one. Note the extremely rare wire wheels which were believed to be a factory option in late 1921.

Olds used the Pacemaker nameplate on its Model 46 five-passenger vehicle. Price on this Olds was $1,815 and weight was 3,160 pounds. The Model 46 was introduced in the 1920 Model year and its production was continued through 1922. Because of its ninth place sales standings in 1921 Oldsmobile probably could not justify production of two V-8's. A six cylinder offering probably would have worked out better.

Oldsmobile pictured this V-8 model in an issue of its dealer-customer publication "The Pacemaker." Its driver was evangelist Aimee Semple McPherson. The article said, "She is a very expert driver and has not the slightest hesitancy over undertaking even the longest tours." Note the interesting disc wheels — not believed to be factory equipment — and the spotlight. The California style top was not seen on many 1921 Oldsmobiles but the factory proved numerous such installations in 1922. It appears that the wheels were not true disc-type, as no mounting bolts are visible. Rather, they appear to be large wheel covers mounted over the optional wire spoke wheels. Miss McPherson won acclaim from Oldsmobile after driving her car from Philadelphia to San Francisco and back — certainly quite a trip in 1921.

While open cars in the 46 series were rare, closed models were even more scarce. Apparently only a sedan was produced in the 1921 Model 46 lineup. This rather boxy model carried a price tag of $2,575 making it the most expensive 1921 Olds. It was also the heaviest car at 3,695 pounds. Production for closed Model 46 cars this year was a scant 112. All Model 46's were powered by a 247 cubic inch V-8 turning out 58 horsepower.

Early April of 1921 brought another new Olds, the so-called "Light Eight" Model 47. Again Olds announced its new offering to dealers via the "Weekly Wallop." It proclaimed: "The new Model 47 eight cylinder has been designed to satisfy the most exacting automobile experts who demand performance with economy, excellence of materials and workmanship and the necessary style and finish which ranks a job as a high class automobile."

The most popular offering in the Model 47 series was the touring car. It carried a price tag of $1,695 and weighed 2,970 pounds. Only, 2,055 of the open model 47's were made. All cars in the series rode on wheelbases of 115 inches. Upholstery on this model was box pleated black leather. Tires were 32 x 4 on all body styles. Non-skid tread was found on the rears and on the spare. Rims were straight sided and of the bolted on type.

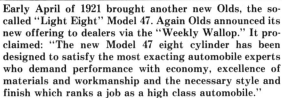

Olds offered a pair of closed cars in the Model 47 series. Shown here is the coupe which was priced at $2,395. Weight on this model was 3,082 pounds. Closed car interiors were done in either velour or broadcloth. The floorboards and running boards were bound with aluminum mouldings. Olds used a spiral bevel, floating rear end with Hyatt roller bearings on wheels.

A Lansing, Michigan country club provided an attractive site to photograph this Model 47 5-passenger Brougham. Total series production for closed cars was 1,030. A spare tire was optional equipment in 1921. Note the covered rear tire carrier on this car. All cars in the series were outfitted with three-speed standard transmissions. Nickel steel gears and shafts were used within. The clutch was a Borg and Beck 10-inch unit.

Model 47

Top of the line in the Light Eight series was the Model 47 sedan. It cost $2,395 and tipped the scales at 3,262 pounds. Powering cars in this series was a new Olds V-8 weighing only 714 pounds fully outfitted. It developed 53 horsepower from 234 cubic inches. Cord tires were standard on all closed cars in this series.

1921

The Model 47 Olds rode on a sturdy chassis based on a frame of sectioned carbon steel with four cross members. The front axle was a drop forged I-beam. Oil cups were used on king bolts with Alemite grease cups on the tie rod bolts. Service brakes were of external contracting design operated by a foot pedal. The emergency brake was of internal expanding design operated by a center control hand lever. These brakes operated on the rear wheels only. A fourteen gallon gas tank was located at the rear of the frame.

A great deal of development work had gone into the all new four cylinder powerplant. This unit developed more than 40 horsepower from 224 cubic inches. A high carbon, drop forged crankshaft rode on three main bearings. Connecting rods were light weight drop forged steel. Special aluminum alloy pistons were used and they carried three rings. Lubrication came from a force feed system with a pressure gauge on the dash. A centrifugal type water pump was built into the block, directly behind the fan, with which it shared a common shaft.

The popularity of the Olds Economy Truck dropped off in 1921, but the truck line continued to be offered for the next couple of years. Only 503 trucks were produced in 1921. Michigan Bridge and Pipe Company of Lansing operated this unit. An Olds truck outfitted with this exact body configuration could be ordered through the Olds factory. Subcontractor for this dump body was the Lansing-based Yule Company. This was a chain activated unit, hand operated by the crank located just behind the cab.

Several police agencies used the Olds truck for patrol and paddy wagon duty. This particular Olds was operated by the Knoxsville, Tenn. police department. For a truck powered by a four cylinder engine, the Olds offered good mileage. Operators reported that fully loaded the Olds could get up to 16 miles per gallon. Oldsmobile was not the only Lansing, Michigan firm to build trucks in 1921 as both Reo and Duplex offered extensive truck lines.

Although truck sales dwindled in 1921 and truck sales disappeared completely by the mid-1920's, owners continued to find a variety of uses for Oldsmobile trucks. Here an Olds is being used as a power source for an ice company plant. Factory literature of the day listed over 220 different uses for the Olds Economy Truck: newspapers, piano movers, painters, road carnival companies, lumber yards, farmers, coal haulers, bakers, bottlers and utility companies.

1922

For the first time in a number of years Oldsmobile stood pat with a model lineup for two consecutive years. For the year 1922 the Lansing based General Motors division continued to offer the popular four cylinder 43-A's, the Model 46 and 47 V-8's and the Olds Economy Truck. For the second consecutive year Oldsmobile ignored the production of six cylinder autos.

Oldsmobile built 21,499 vehicles in 1922 — up substantially from the previous year. Despite increased production, Olds slipped several notches to 13th spot in the industry sales race. Fellow GM car builders surrounded Olds in these standings with Cadillac ranked twelfth and Oakland in fourteenth. Crosstown rival Reo held fifteenth position. The company's work force remained at the 2,500 level for the second straight year.

The four cylinder models were again the bread

The most popular offering in the 1922 model lineup was the 43-A five passenger touring. Oldsmobile prices took a dip this year and this car sold for $1,095. Weight on this four cylinder was 2,767 pounds. Production for open Model 43 A's totalled 12,161. The wheelbase on this series was 115 inches with a standard tread and ten inches of road clearance. The standard wheels were made of selected hickory.

New to the Model 43-A line this year was the four passenger Semi-Sport. A quick tipoff on this model was the Tuarc disc wheels which were finished in the same cordova red as the body work. Ivory painted wire wheels were available as an option. The interior was done in box pleated fine grain black leather. Price on this unique model was $1,225, weight was 2,804 pounds.

winners for Olds, this year knocking down a sales total of 14,839. Mechanically this series remained intact from the previous year which saw its introduction. Wheelbase continued at 115 inches and power still came from a 43 horsepower powerplant. Other 43-A features included: Auto-Lite starting and lighting, nickel finished radiator, Willard six volt storage battery, leather upholstery on open cars and walnut instrument boards. Big news in the 43-A group came from a pair of new offerings: a five-passenger touring with a factory installed California top and a sporty four passenger touring called the Semi-Sport. Special appointments on the Semi-Sport included: black leather side rails, a special cordova red paint job and either Tuarc disc wheels or five ivory painted wire wheels. The California topped 43-A's were really the first hardtopped Oldsmobiles. Prices were reduced on all models in 1922 and several open 43-A's were priced very near the $1,000 mark.

Oldsmobile's so-called Light-Eight, the Model 47, carried modest sales totals of 2,723 for 1922. Big news in this model grouping was a sporty new touring known as the Super Sport. Special equipment here included: Tuarc steel disc wheels, bobbed fenders, short cast aluminum steps, a Boyce deluxe motormeter, beveled plate glass windshield wings and nickel plated triple bar spring steel bumpers front and rear. This must have been a striking auto as the standard color scheme was black fenders, jersey brown body and maroon colored leather upholstery. The Model 47's shared the 115 inch wheelbase with the four cylinder series. Power continued to come from a 234 cubic inch motor. Series features included: Willard six volt storage battery, Johnson carburetor, Delco starter and generator and grey iron pistons.

Rounding out the Oldsmobile automotive lineup in 1922 was the Model 46 V-8 series. Introduced in 1920, this model remained largely unchanged in its last year of production. A total of 2,733 of this model were built making this by far the most successful year for the Model 46. This was 1922's largest Oldsmobile riding on a wheelbase of 122 inches. Power came from a 247 cubic inch, 58 horsepower motor. Features included: a 20-gallon gas tank, walnut dashboard, Willard battery and cord tires on all models. Two Pacemaker tourings — one with wire or disc wheels as standard — were offered. A seven-passenger touring Thorobred was also available along with the most expensive 1922 Olds, the $2,635 sedan.

Truck sales made a slight rebound in 1922 with a total of 1,204 built — more than doubling 1921 truck output. Olds was finding a variety of uses for its truck chassis. The bare chassis continued to sell for $1,095, a steel cab and chassis went for $1,175 and a complete truck with the factory express body sold for $1,245.

Olds dealers continued to demonstrate the performance capability of their cars. The 43-A's still did well as hill climbers. A specially modified light-eight — built by the California Olds distributor J. W. Leavitt & Company — ran 1,000 miles in 899 minutes. This demonstration took place at the Cotati Speedway. During the grueling run the only attention paid to the Olds was to fuel it and add a bit of oil and water.

1922

Oldsmobile introduced its first hardtop model with the 98 series holiday in 1949, but this 1922 Model 43-A came close to the hardtop concept. This was the first year the so-called California top could be factory installed in Lansing. Base price on this rare model was $1,395 and weight was 2,915 pounds. The instrument board on all cars in this series was made of genuine walnut with instruments flush mounted.

This is the 43-A touring with the padded California top's side panels removed. In this configuration the car had particularly nice lines. The 43-A series cars were powered by a 43 horsepower valve-in-head engine. The crankshaft was made of high carbon, drop forged, heat treated steel. Three large main bearings were used. Water cooling for the engine came via a centrifugal pump and a fan driven from the crankshaft.

A basic machine in the 43-A stable was the roadster. Note the nifty rumbleseat, or "convertible auxiliary seat" on this car. The roadster shared low price honors with the touring car at $1,095. This was the lightest Olds of the year, weighing just 2,712 pounds. The radiator was of honeycomb design and was covered by a nickeled shell. The clutch was a single plate dry disc type.

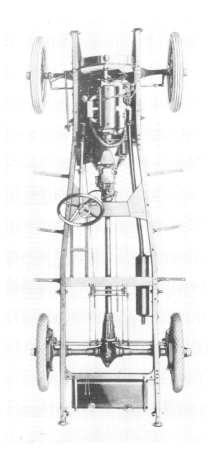

The 43-A was based on a rugged chassis, which was largely unchanged from its introduction in 1921. The frame was of cold, pressed steel. Four cross members were built in. Gasoline from a 14-gallon rear mounted tank was measured by a level gauge installed on that tank. A vacuum system was used to move fuel. The front axle was drop forged, heat treated I-beam with integral spring perches.

1922

Driving controls for the 43-A series were fairly simple. The steering wheel was an 18-inch walnut unit. The windshield was an inclined, two-piece affair with rubber weather stripping. On the touring, the top was of a weather proofed material. It was a one-man type with five bows. The back curtain was fitted with a long rectangular plate glass window. Lighting on the instruments was indirect.

One of three closed cars offered by Oldsmobile in the four cylinder series was this four passenger coupe. Carrying a price of $1,595 this car weighed 3,015 pounds. Production for all three closed cars in the series amounted to 2,678. Olds literature of this era suggested this model would be a good choice for the business or professional man. Seating included a rear seat for two, a driver's seat and an auxiliary front passenger seat which folded under the dash when not in use.

Introduced in late 1921, the 43-A Brougham was a classy looking closed car. It was the least expensive closed 1922 selling for $1,425. Weight was 3,005 pounds. All cars in the four cylinder series used an Auto-Lite starting and lighting system. A Remy brand distributor and coil were outfitted. Brakes were of the service design of the external contracting type. The emergency brake was of the internal expanding type.

Flagship for the 43-A line was the big sedan. Carrying the highest price tag in the series — $1,745 — this car weighed 3,095 pounds. Three of the sedan's doors were fitted with thumb door locks, while the right front door had a key lock. Decorative interior lights were set in silvered fittings. The steering gear on all 43's was of the split nut type with positive adjustment.

The smallest series as far as model offerings went was the Model 46. Olds tagged its seven-passenger touring the Thorobred. It was priced at $1,735 and weighed 3,192 pounds. Open car production in this series totalled 2,600. Cars from the 46 group were the physically largest Oldsmobiles of 1922 based on a wheelbase of 122 inches. A vacuum system fed fuel from a 20-gallon gas tank at the rear.

Two different Pacemaker tourings were available in the 46 series. Shown here is the special Pacemaker outfitted with jump seats and wire wheels. Price on this model was $1,850 and weight was 3,165 pounds. Tuarc disc wheels could also be ordered on this model. The standard Pacemaker had wood wheels and no jump seats. Price was $1,735 and weight was 3,150 pounds. Tops on both models were of the simplified one-man design. A Johnson nickel-framed plate glass window was used at the rear.

This bird's eye view gives a good idea of just how massive the Model 46 Oldsmobile was. The windshield was made of heavy plate glass. Rubber seals were used between the lower section of the windshield and cowl. Upholstery was done in high grade brightly finished box pleated black leather. The body interior and top edges of the doors were leather covered. Equipment on this series included an eight-day clock.

Probably the rarest 1922 Olds was the Model 46 sedan. It was the sole closed car in the series and only 133 were built. It was the most expensive Olds offered this year at $2,435. Weight was 3,365 pounds. This car was a true seven passenger auto. A rear compartment exhaust heater was standard equipment on this massive sedan. Wooden wheels were of artillery design made of selected hickory. A twelve spoke pattern was used along with extra large hub flanges.

The Model 46 powerplant was one that Olds had used for several years. Displacement was 247 cubic inches. Lubrication came from a gear driven pressure pump. The carburetor was a two-stage type with a primary designed for economy, while the secondary was used for maximum power. The clutch was a leather faced cone type. The transmission was a three speed with drop forged, heat treated vanadium steel gears and shafts.

The price leader in the Model 47 series was the roadster. It sold for $1,495 and weighed just 2,922 pounds. Production for all the open cars in this light eight cylinder series totalled 1,988. Model 47's shared a wheelbase of 115 inches with the Model 43-A's of this year. Tires on all models were 32 x 4 of cord construction. Rims were straight sided demountable bolt-ons.

1922

The most popular Olds Model 47 in 1922 was the touring car. This auto shared the series low price tag of $1,495 with the roadster. Weight was 2,970 pounds. The Olds light eight displaced 234 cubic inches. The crankshaft was made of high carbon, heat treated drop forged steel. Extra large, bronze backed, babbitt lined bearings were outfitted. Light grey iron pistons were carried on high carbon drop forged I-beam design connecting rods. The camshaft was of heat treated forged steel supported by three bearings.

Since the days of the Curved Dash models, Oldsmobile was active in various endurance runs for its products. This is a Model 47 Olds specially outfitted by J. W. Leavitt, the California Olds distributor. The car ran 1,000 miles in 899 minutes to average over 66 miles per hour. The run was made around the 1¼ mile Cotati Speedway and was driven mostly by W. L. Cooper. This car carried the stock touring body with obvious modifications like: cutdown windshield, dual spotlights, tonneau cover, special wheel knockoffs and unique outside exhausts.

This very nicely preserved Model 47 is the property of Charles Nagler of Southfield, Michigan. This car came from early in the model year as it carried serial number 235 and motor number 4678. The Oldsmobile Club of America is approaching 3,000 members and is nearing its tenth anniversary. Because of relatively low production figures on V-8 models in the 1920's, there are few such cars in the club. Nagler's machine is among the nicest of those early 1920's cars.

The newcomer to the Model 47 lineup this year was the attractive Super Sport. Carrying a price of $1,725, weight on this jaunty model was 3,007 pounds. A special Olds brochure on this model said, "The Oldsmobile Super Sport is complete in every detail from Tuarc Steel Wheels, nickeled triple-bar bumpers fore and aft to aluminum steps and windshield wings. Nothing needs to bought later." It was finished in Jersey brown.

One of the genuine heroes of this era — particularly in Olds production country — was the Detroit Tiger's Ty Cobb. Here the baseball legend stands proudly with this 1922 Olds Model 47 Super Sport. This front view points up the massive nickeled front bumpers, Boyce deluxe monogrammed motor meter and left front apron mounted spotlight. Other special appointments to this model were: sedan type foot rest, robe straps and beveled glass rearview mirror. The standard body color was Jersey brown with eye catching maroon leather interior.

The most expensive and heaviest Model 47 was the sedan. Priced at $2,145 this Olds weighed 3,262 pounds. A factory catalog on 1922 closed cars said of this model, "These compact eights are so high powered that the weight of the body imposes no strain or retarding effect. The brilliant performance of Oldsmobile enclosed cars is little short of startling."

Oldsmobile claimed the Model 47 four-passenger coupe was a particular favorite with the ladies. It was priced at $1,995 and weighed 3,192 pounds. Production for both closed cars in the series amounted to only 735. Olds closed cars of this vintage featured an attractive curved metal external sun visor. The 43-A and 47 coupes were of similar interior layout.

Auto manufacturers in the 1920's were out for any type of publicity they could get. Olds sent lettered up versions of its products on various jaunts. Here a Model 47 Super Sport was sent on an around Lake Michigan trek. This outing was sponsored by the Michigan good roads people. In addition to using the V-8 for demonstrations, the Olds four cylinder models seemed to make good hill climbers.

As Olds continued to lower its closed car prices, these models became more common. The Model 47 coupe offered very stylish lines. Closed models in this series were upholstered in either velour, broadcloth or mohair. Open cars were done in fine grain black leather. The windshield was of two piece design with heavy plate glass outlines by heavy rubber gaskets. Standard wheels were of the artillery type of selected hickory.

A functional interior layout was offered on the Model 47's. A walnut 18-inch steering wheel was provided. A highly finished walnut dashboard carried instruments flush mounted and illuminated by an independent light. The transmission was a floor shifted three speed. A floor mounted emergency brake lever controlled an internal expanding brake system. Olds continued to finish its cars by brush painting and hand rubbing.

A couple of unique features were on this Model 47 sedan. Most of the sedans carried wooden wheels — but this car is equipped with discs. Also note the interesting winter front installed on the radiator. Along with a 1922 Michigan license plate, a Lansing AAA plate is carried up front. All Model 47's had a spiral bevel floating rear end. The differential housing and wheels were mounted on Hyatt roller bearings. The rear end ratio was a stump pulling 5 and $\frac{1}{10}$ to one.

Oldsmobile continued to offer its line of Economy Trucks in 1922. In today's market this truck would be a collector's item as would be the cargo of milk cans it is carrying. Shown is the standard express body which could be ordered from Lansing as pictured here. The price, complete with coachwork, was $1,245. Olds continued to rate its four cylinder powered truck as a one-tonner.

The Olds truck chassis was suited for lots of things and one near ideal application was that of a small bus. The standard truck wheel was the artillery type with demountable rims. Standard tires were 35 x 5 Goodyear cords. The truck carb was a double jet Zenith. Gasoline was fed from a 12½ gallon tank. Rear end was an Olds-Torbensen internal gear unit. Front axle was a dropped I-beam section.

This boxy delivery model carried work from the Lansing Body Company of Lansing, Michigan — a firm that did a great deal of business with Olds in the 1920's. Standard wheelbase on the truck was 128 inches with a tread of 56 inches. Truck weight was about 3,100 pounds depending upon what bodywork was installed. For 1922 truck production was 1,204 which more than doubled 1921 truck output.

1923

This was a unique year in the annals of Oldsmobile history as it was rather distinctly divided into two model years within a single calendar year. The first months of 1923 were devoted to the production of Model 43-A's and Model 47's. By mid-1923, however, Oldsmobile was slowly starting to work on the all new Model 30 six cylinders. It would be 1929 before Olds would come back with another V-8 model, and that would be the short lived Viking companion car. It took Olds much longer to return to four cylinder production as that came in 1976 with the Starfire model.

This model year brough substantially more sales for Oldsmobile than 1922, but the division held thirteenth spot with 34,758 sales, edging out crosstown rival Reo, which dropped tremendously. Oldsmobile was outsold in 1923 by such makes as Durant (which also had major production facilities in Lansing), Maxwell-Chalmers and Hupmobile.

An all new six cylinder came to Olds in 1923. Production began slowly in July with the building of just four cars and only 16 more were produced in August. Slightly less than 200 cars were made in September and it was October before the new Model 30's were publically introduced. By some standards the Model 30 series should be considered 1924 models, but Olds factory record keeping and most other auto research lists them as 1923's or 1923½ models. From introduction time on the new sixes sold well and by the end of 1923 a total of 11,919 Model 30's had rolled off Lansing assembly lines.

Some confusion exists on exact model year dating on 1923-1927 six cylinder cars, but Oldsmobile did have a system for labeling output by year. Sixes built during calendar year 1923 became Model 30-A's. Production of Models 30-B through 30-E continued through 1927 and will be outlined in subsequent chapters.

From July of 1923 through 1928, for the first time since the Curved Dash era, Oldsmobile would offer cars powered by just a single type of engine. General Motors apparently had a great deal to say where Olds would now fit into the market place and that was as a builder of low priced six cylinder cars. The price leader for the new 30 series were a pair of open cars which sold for $750. Keep in mind this is more than $200 less than comparable four cylinder 43-A's built earlier in 1923! The Model 30-A lineup included: a five-passenger touring, sport touring, roadster, closed cabriolet, coupe and sedan. Prices initially ranged from $750 to $1,095.

For the first time bodies were Fisher-built and several auto magazines of the era commented on the quality of Fisher appointments. The new Oldsmobiles rode on a wheelbase of 110 inches, ran on 31 x 4 tires and had ten inches of road clearance. Weight was reduced several hundred pounds over previous

offerings. The new engine was only 170 cubic inches and developed 42 horsepower. The crankshaft was of high carbon drop forged steel riding on three large babbitt bearings. Lubrication was automatic force feed. Oil capacity was five quarts. A three speed transmission was in unit construction with the engine. Transmission bearings were phosphor bronze. The factory claimed a 20 to 25 mile per gallon range for the new model. Standard equipment included: a Harrison radiator, Delco two-unit electrical system, Willard battery, Zenith carburetor, Thermoid-Hardy universal joints, Brown-Lipe-Chapin differential, New Departure bearings, Alemite lube system, Klaxton horn and Flat-Lite reflectors.

This was the final model year for the 43-A, a successful Oldsmobile offering for several years. In its final year the 43-A was offered in three different touring models, a roadster, and four separate closed versions. Prices came down under $1,000 for the first time. Most four cylinder production came to a halt early in the model year and the sixes took over. Power continued to come from the faithful 224 cubic inch, 43 horsepower four cylinder. Wheelbase was 115 inches. A Delco starting and lighting set was used. The Model 43 was Oldsmobile's top seller in 1923 with 19,114 produced.

Also in its final year as an Olds model was the light eight Model 47. Never a big seller, only 2,258 of this series were produced in 1923. Prices were lowered on this series too, and they ranged from $1,375 for the touring to $2,080 for the big sedan. The 115 inch wheelbase was again used. Power came from the 234 cubic inch V-8 turning out 56 horsepower. Artillery wooden wheels were standard, but disc wheels were an option. Jaxon demountable bolted on rims were outfitted with 32 x 4 cord tires.

An era ended for Oldsmobile this year as the division went out of the truck business and as of this writing they've never re-entered that field. The Olds Economy Truck was introduced in 1919 and volumes steadily declined from the more than 8,000 (almost one-fourth of the total Olds output) in 1920. For this model year 1,382 trucks were sold. A deciding factor for Olds leaving the truck business stemmed from the fact it had discontinued its four cylinder motor production early in 1923.

A complete re-arrangement was found at the Olds Lansing plant. For the first time since the Curved Dash era, Olds was just building one type of motor. The plant was modernized and largely retooled. One entire manufacturing building was cleared of equipment and outfitted as a new Fisher Body plant. Construction was also begun during 1923 for an elaborate oven and conveyor system to facilitate enameling.

In its final year of production the four cylinder Model 43 A's remained popular, and this touring was the most popular Olds for 1923. Production totalled 11,309 with 197 additional cars built with the factory California top option. Price for the standard touring dipped below the $1,000 mark at $975, while the California topped car sold for $1,350. Weight on this model was 2,883 pounds. Most four cylinders were built early in the year as later production was shifted exclusively to the new six cylinder cars.

Price leader in the 43-A series was the roadster. Priced at $955, this machine weighed 2,738 pounds making it the lightest car in the series. Only 1,357 of this square backed model were built. Wheelbase for the four cylinder Oldsmobiles was 115 inches. The engine was a tried and true four holer producing more than 40 horsepower from 224 cubic inches. Engine lubrication was from a force fed and splash system outfitted with a pressure gauge on the instrument board. This model featured a parcel compartment behind the seat, as well as a large luggage area under the rear deck.

Introduced the previous year, Oldsmobile continued to offer the four-passenger 43-A Semi Sport. Tuarc disc wheels set this job off from other cars in the series. A cowl ventilator and cowl lights were standard on this car as was black leather upholstery. The price tag here was $1,075 and weight was 2,931 pounds. Production was 1,446. All 43-A's were built from a cold pressed steel frame with channel sections up to seven inches deep. Four very heavy cross members were installed.

Oldsmobile continued the 4-passenger coupe in its four-model closed car lineup this year. The coupe cost $1,475 and weighed 3,132 pounds. Only 926 were built. The standard wheels were artillery type made of selected hickory. Tuarc steel wheels were an option on this series. Rims were Jaxon demountables of the bolted on type. The radiator was a Harrison honeycomb with a nickeled jacket.

Charles Nagler owns this 1923 Model 43-A Brougham. Early 1920's examples of Olds closed cars are relatively rare and this is a nice one. Nagler's car carries chassis number 1235 and engine number C4225. Indications are that some Oldsmobile closed bodies in 1923 may have been built by Melbourn Body Works in Toledo, Ohio. By late in this model year, however, closed bodies were Fisher built in Lansing. All cars in this series rode on 32 x 4 inch cord tires. Ribbed tread was used up front and all weather tread in the rear. All closed bodies were constructed of steel panels over a frame of seasoned hardwood. Heater and dome light were standard equipment on all closed body styles this year.

Continued in the four cylinder series for this year was the five-passenger Brougham. Carrying a price tag of $1,375 this car tipped the scales at 3,115 pounds. A total of 1,562 Broughams were sold in 1923. All 43-A's had a floating type rear axle utilizing spiral bevel gears. The differential housing and wheels rolled on Hyatt bearings. The gear ratio was 4.7 to 1.

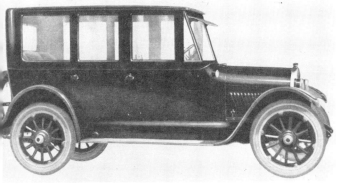

Most popular of all Model 43-A closed offerings was the sedan. This car weighed 3,207 pounds and sold for $1,595. Production totals were 1,605. The carburetor on all four cylinders was air heated. The mixture on leaving the carb passed over a "hot spot" in the manifold to offer a better mixture. Fuel was vacuum fed from a 14-gallon tank suspended at the rear of the frame. The gas gauge was atop that tank.

The least expensive closed Model 43-A was the newest: the Cab. Priced at just $1,195 and weighing only 3,097 pounds, only 712 of this model were built. Olds pitched this model to business men and salesmen. It contained ideal behind the seat storage for luggage and sample cases. The Cab, probably short for cabriolet, had 12 cubic feet of storage area. Interior on this model was done in hand buffed grey Spanish leather. Other interior appointments included: a walnut instrument board, dash lamp and dome light.

New to the series was the Model 47 sport roadster. Only 94 of this jaunty car were built. The price tag was $1,625 and weight was 3,110 pounds. An Olds catalog of the era pointed up the fact this model would appeal to the golfer. It was described as a three passenger car with a spacious luggage compartment. Open cars of this series were upholstered in brown hand buffed leather. The golf bag rack and step plate forward of the rear fender was standard equipment.

This woman appears quite happy behind the wheel of her Model 47 Sport Roadster. Actually Olds made a real sales pitch to the ladies in 1923 with advertisements in leading women's magazines and a special small catalog — complete with a pink ribbon — titled "Oldsmobile from a Woman's Point of View." All other cars in this series were outfitted for a single spare tire, but Sport Roadsters carried two, in addition to standard bumpers, which were considered accessories on all other non-sport Olds.

Offered in extremely limited numbers for 1923 were the Model 47 V-8 Oldsmobiles. Like the four cylinders, the 1923 V-8's were built early in the year, then facilities were converted to exclusive six cylinder production. Most popular among the 47's was the touring car. Priced at $1,385, this machine weighed 3,020 pounds. Production was only 1,111.

The most expensive 1923 Olds was this largish Model 47 sedan. Priced at $2,080 there were only 549 buyers for this auto. Weight was 3,220 pounds making this the heaviest car built this year by Oldsmobile. A rearview mirror and windshield wipers were standard equipment this year on Model 47's. The windshields were inclined, of two-piece design heavy plate glass. Closed cars sported an opaque external sun visor. Upholstery was in plush mohair and interior fittings were of satin silver finish.

1923

Exceedingly rare in the Model 47 lineup was the coupe. One of two closed cars offered with V-8 power, only 187 were built. The coupe sold for $1,875 and weighed 3,110 pounds. All cars in this series were powered by a 63 horsepower, 234 cubic inch V-8. Light grey iron pistons rode on high carbon, drop forged connecting rods. The fourth seat on the coupe continued to be of the auxiliary type, folding under the dash when not in use.

In its second and final year was the Model 47 Super Sport. The most expensive open Oldsmobile for 1923, this sportster sold for $1,680. Weight was 3,140 pounds. Only 504 of this specially outfitted V-8 were made. Special equipment consisted of Tuarc disc wheels, aluminum step plates instead of running boards and special glass wind wings. This was one of the few 1923 Oldsmobiles to offer bumpers front and rear and dual spares as standard equipment.

By the summer of 1923 Oldsmobile shut down all its production facilities for a changeover to build the new six cylinder line. It took until October for full production to return to Lansing. By far the most popular 1923 Model 30-A model was the touring car. In its short production span, 6,015 of this model were built. The $750 price tag would make this the least expensive Olds in many years. Weight on the touring was 2,275 pounds. General Motors seemed to have a lot to say about Olds building this new type six cylinder line.

A 4-passenger coupe was offered in the new 30-A series. It was priced at $1,035 and weighed 2,405 pounds. Production on this automobile was 1,575. Closed car appointments included: heater, dome light, outside sun visor, cowl ventilator, door locks and window curtains. The instrument panel was enameled steel. Nickel faced instruments were flush mounted and illuminated. A single tail lamp was standard on this series.

Closed cars continued to grow in popularity during this model year. The Model 30-A was the most expensive car in the series at $1,095. This was the least costly sedan ever offered by Olds. Weight was 2,462 pounds and production was 2,693. Each of the new sixes rode on a wheelbase of 110 inches. A Klaxton horn was mounted under hood. It was operated by a push button atop the steering column.

Rarest car in the 30-A series was the roadster which saw a production run of only 420. Price on this little open model was $750. This car was the lightest 1923 Oldsmobile at 2,275 pounds. Braking on the series was provided by service brakes on rear wheels. An emergency brake was outfitted on the transmission. The clutch on this series was a Borg and Beck single dry disc of nine-inch diameter.

1923

This sharp little closed car was tagged the Cab. It was the rarest closed car in the 30-A series as only 782 were made. It was also the least expensive closed car selling for just $955. Weight on this model was 2,398. All 30 series cars used a semi-floating rear end with a one-piece housing. New Departure annular ball bearings were used throughout. A Brown-Lipe-Chapin differential was also utilized on the 30 cars.

Olds added a sporty type model to its new 30-A series with this Sport Touring. Only 434 of this model were built with a weight of 2,298. Base price was $885. Standard color on this machine was olive green. Standard equipment included: nickeled bumpers front and rear, monogrammed Olds step plates, brown Spanish leather upholstery, Boyce Motor-Meter, Tuarc disc wheels, black enameled trunk and spotlight. Sorry, but the stamping across this photo was done at the Olds factory when the picture was first made.

Oldsmobile made several across country runs in past years and in 1923 it took to the open road with a 30-A touring car. Doing the driving was Erwin "Cannonball" Baker a veteran traveler. It took Baker just 12½ days to make the New York to Los Angeles trip. He had made faster cross country jaunts, but this one was slowed a bit because the six cylinder Olds was locked in high gear for the entire run. Special modifications to the car were minimal and included extra fuel capacity and special spotlights. Baker's run drew good crowds at some of the stops. Note his aviator-like helmet and goggles. He is shown here in front of the New York City Olds dealership at Broadway and 59th Street.

This is the first non-wood dash panel used by Oldsmobile. Central in the layout was a speedometer by AC of Flint, Mich., which included an odometer and a resettable trip odometer. The oil pressure gauge was a unit by National Gauge of LaCrosse, Wis. A Sterling Manufacturing Co., Cleveland, amp gauge was also mounted. The Delco ignition switch also served as the light switch. Note the indirect lighting unit. Spark and throttle controls were on the steering column. A standard feature this year was a transmission lock, which Oldsmobile claimed would reduce insurance rates by 20% for the owner.

Early in Cannonball's jaunt his Olds retained a factory luster, later that faded somewhat after the ravages of mud, stones and the like. Note the single Olds script tailight and the single tire carried at the rear. Tires offered as Standard 30 series equipment were 31 x 4 inch cords. A spare was an extra cost option in 1923. Cannonball rode on Goodyears and had little tire trouble on his trip. Wheels were of artillery design and rims were Jaxon demountables.

1923

Cannonball ran into problems along the way including this midwestern mud bog. As with all 30-A's the powerplant on this cross country car was the all new six cylinder of 170 cubic inches. This was an L-head design. Crankshaft construction was of high carbon steel riding on large babbitt-lined, bronze backed Chadwick bearings. Lubrication was automatic force feed. The electric system was a Delco 2-unit with a Bendix starter drive. A Willard storage battery was of six volt, 80-ampere design.

An Oldsmobile tradition ended in 1923 as the division stopped production of its Economy Truck models. Built since 1919 this Olds offering was once very popular. In its final year 1,467 trucks were built. Specifications and prices carried over from the previous year. Olds began to offer trucks in the Curved Dash era and offered some specially built units throughout the early years. As this is being written, Olds has still not returned to truck building, since its last unit rolled off the line in 1923.

A unique outfit was this truck and trailer rig based on the Olds Economy Truck. This unit was created as a lumber hauler. Standard truck equipment included: Auto-Lite electric lighting and starting system, headlights, tail and dash lights, electric horn, complete side curtains, extra rim, complete set of tools, jack and tire pump.

Oldsmobile continued to be proud of the large variety of uses — well over 200 — found for its trucks. Here a pair of screen sided Olds trucks found duty as mail carries in Spokane, Washington. These trucks averaged 18 miles per gallon in tough service. Truck models used Zenith Model 0 double jetted carburetors. The air intake had a hot air tube with a shutter. A dash mounted choke was used as were throttle controls on the steering post and a foot accelerator.

Things became much more simple at Oldsmobile over the next few years. In 1923 Olds offered 20 separate automotive models spread across three series. They also built trucks. By 1924 truck production was gone and just six models were available from a single series.

Despite the substantial thinning of the number of cars offered from Lansing in 1924, the Oldsmobile sales position improved dramatically. Total sales of 44,542 moved the division up two notches to eleventh place in the industry sales race. Those outselling Oldsmobile this year included Durant, Willys-Overland, Chrysler-Maxwell and Nash.

A late 1923 introduction of the all new Model-A six cylinder engine set the stage for a little changed Model 30-B as the six cylinder offering for 1924. The monthly six cylinder production peak for the year came in March when 8,144 Model 30-B's rolled off Lansing assembly lines. The significance of this production effort is underlined when it is realized this output exceeds any Olds model year production from 1900 through 1915. Olds reached an all-time high in employment totals for this year with 4,200 workers on the payroll.

Prices rose ever so slightly for the six cylinder Oldsmobiles in 1924. Changes in the 30 series cars were minimal between 1923 and 1924. A wheelbase of 110 inches was used with a standard tread. The Olds six cylinder was well received by the motoring public. It continued to be a 170 cubic inch, 42 horsepower six with a detachable L-head. Lubrication was automatic force feed and cooling was done by a centrifugal pump built into the front of the block. Oil capacity was five quarts and water capacity was 13 quarts. Brand names used included: Delco electrical parts, Willard battery, Zenith carburetor and Borg and Beck clutch. Standard wheels were wooden artillery except on the sport touring. Tuarc discs were standard on the sport touring and optional on some other models.

With the production of the six cylinder models in late 1923 Olds began to use Fisher Bodies to some extent. Fisher Bodies were found on closed models first in 1924 and later this General Motors division would supply open car bodies as well. Olds cleared a portion of its manufacturing plant area to give Lansing-Fisher a home. Several years later things just got too crowded on the Olds grounds and Fisher moved away from the Olds main plant and established its own manufacturing complex in what originally was the Lansing Durant plant.

Increased volumes of car production and new developments within the industry brought Oldsmobile to an era of change and experimentation on how cars were finished. For years Olds had finished fenders and allied parts in black enamel. Varnish was used on bodies and hoods. A main problem with the hand applied varnish was slow drying conditions within the steam heat process used by Olds. Depending upon the year and series of the car, it took from 12 to 23 days to finish an Olds. Bodies had to stand in a darkened room for up to two days to allow proper drying. Matching color to repair a damaged body was difficult and very large areas had to be refinished to make an acceptable color match. The paint process came in the following steps as late as 1922: (1) clean body; (2) apply initial primer coat; (3) putty glaze; (4) apply two coats of sand surfacer; (5) add one coat of color; (6) brush two additional color coats; (7) finish lower panels; (8) add

Most popular in the 1924 lineup was, as usual, the touring car. Priced at $795 the 30-B touring weighed 2,305 pounds. Production for this open car was 10,586 with 514 more cars built for export. The six cylinder engine, in its second year of production, proved to be a winner for Oldsmobile. Advertising of the era claimed gas mileage figures between 20 to 25 miles per gallon and figured oil consumption of a gallon per 1,000 miles.

Cars from the mid-1920's era are relatively rare in the ranks of the Oldsmobile Club of America. This trophy winner is a 1924 Model 30 six cylinder belonging to George Long of Pennsylvania. It was photographed by the author at the 1980 Oldsmobile national meet on the campus of Bowling Green State University in Ohio. Cars of this series had service brakes on the rear wheels and an emergency brake on the transmission.

1924

two finish coats of black; (9) rub out the varnish; (10) add two color coats of varnish; (11) add a heavy final coat of English coach varnish, and (12) final hand rub. All these operations required substantial air drying and some hand finishing in between steps.

By early 1923 Olds had begun to use enamel on some open bodied cars and hoods. Open bodies were sprayed and hoods were enamel dipped. Fenders, running board housings and other lower car parts were dip processed. By 1924 production demands became so heavy that varnishing was discontinued on the remaining open bodies as well as closed cars.

Enameling was short lived and by the end of this model year Olds went to lacquer finishing. The first lacquers used were DuPont. Later Rinshed-Mason, Ditzler and Nubian brands were used. There were early problems, particularly with finding a workable primer, but lacquer's big advantage was that Olds could durably finish a body in a few hours. Lacquer also came in a wider variety of colors and at this point a far larger selection of standard colors were offered by Oldsmobile.

The least expensive car offered this model year was the roadster priced at $785. Prices went up very slightly this year on 30 Series cars, but Oldsmobile still managed to keep several models well under the $1,000 mark. A total of 1,800 Model 30-B roadsters were made with 25 more going for export. Weight on this model was 2,290 pounds. In this series a storage space was offered under the rear deck.

The OLDSMOBILE SIX CAB

Surprisingly high production totals were realized by the 30-B Sport Touring. A total of 8,847 of this model were made with 489 additional cars slotted for export. This was the most expensive open Olds of 1924 with a $915 price tag. Weight was 2,323. In keeping with Olds sporty offerings of the past couple of years, this six cylinder came standard with Tuarc disc wheels. Tops were outfitted with four bows. Side curtains were designed to open with the doors.

Least expensive of the 30-B closed cars was the short coupled Cab model. A purchaser of this model could get change back from his $1,000 bill as list price was $985. Production totals on the Cab were 2,169 with a single additional car built for export. Weight was 2,423 pounds. All six cylinders of this year were outfitted with a drop forged heat treated I-beam front axle.

Two sedans were offered in the 30-B series. Shown here is the standard version. Total sedan production was 3,225 with 16 additional cars exported. Price on this model was $1,135 and weight was 2,487 pounds. By 1924 closed Oldsmobiles were outfitted mostly by Fisher Bodies. Standard sedan equipment included: heater, satin silvered interior fittings, door locks, cowl mounted ventilator and a unique transmission locking device.

Added later in the model year was this deluxe sedan model. The deluxe sedan and the Sport Touring shared several items of special equipment like: spot light, disc wheels, step plates and enameled trunk. Both these special versions also carried nickeled radiator shells, giving a preview of the 1925 upfront styling. The deluxe sedan sold for $1,250 and was the most expensive 1924 Oldsmobile offered.

1924

An Olds publicity photo of the era cited 1924 as a 25th anniversary for Oldsmobile. Actually that milestone came several years earlier. The 1899 model shown here probably was either an 1897 or at the latest 1898 model. Pictured here was a lady of the day with a standard Model 30-B sedan. Again note the relatively rare whitewall tires.

An extremely popular car within the 30-B series was the two-door or coupe. With a base price of $1,075, a total of 8,839 were produced. Sixteen additional cars were exported. Standard two-tone color scheme on this car was Orriford Lake on the body and black top, hood and radiator. As with other closed 30-B's this car had an attractive curved outside sun visor. The coupe was classed as a 4-passenger car. Upholstery was in striped velour.

Oldsmobile, like most manufacturers of this day, liked to show its cars with celebrities of the era. Here the Eddie Foy family is packed into a standard 30-B sedan. This car has some rather unique options, but it is not known whether all of it is factory equipment. Note: bumpers front and rear, a unique winter front radiator cover, dog bone radiator cap and motor meter, through the windshield Clymer spotlight and whitewall tires.

Oldsmobile probably had as much experience as any domestic car builder with different configuration engines. Olds had built single, two, four, six and eight cylinder motors by 1916. The all new six cylinder was several years on the drawing board, followed by extensive testing. Introduced in late 1923, the new six became a proven performer. Oldsmobile's first six cylinder came in 1908. The six was the exclusive Olds powerplant from this model year through the introduction of the Viking V-8 in 1929.

MODEL 3 CHASSIS

Olds started from the ground up when it designed its new six cylinder chassis in late 1923. The 30-A and 30 chassis were virtually the same. A wheelbase of 110 inches was used with standard tread and road clearance of more than 10 inches. The Oldsmobile frame was solidly constructed of channel carbon steel. Four cross members were used. Tires were 31 x 4 inch cords with non-skid tread pattern on the rear.

A pioneer in auto advertising, Oldsmobile continued to agressively sell its products through the pages of magazines like the Saturday Evening Post. By 1924 Olds was offering cars financed by "the GMAC extended payment plan." Olds sold its 30 series cars with a tool kit which included a few wrenches, pliers and tire tools. A starting crank was also included in this packet.

In its third year of offering the 30 series six cylinder cars, Olds expanded its model selection in 1925 and offered some styling changes over 1923 and 1924 models. Sales slipped just a bit this year with totals of 42,701 good for thirteenth place in industry standings. Cars outselling Olds in 1925 included: Hudson-Essex, Studebaker, Durant and Nash-Ajax.

For 1925 Olds actually offered two 30-series cars, the 30-C's and 30-D's. The "C" cars were introduced in the fall of 1924 and the "D" car introduction began in June of 1925. A 1925 Olds could be either a "C" or "D" model and changes between the two were very limited.

The 1925 Oldsmobiles had several major differences from the 1924's. First of all several new models were added. A new business coupe replaced the cab model of the previous couple of years. The business coupe came standard with a blue paint job with ivory striping. Upholstery was done in either velour or a gray Spanish style "Fabrikoid." A sport roadster was added. This car carried a beige paint job as standard. Special equipment included: disc wheels, spotlight and windshield wings. Most popular of the new additions was the closed two door coach which would be a good seller the next few years. The deluxe sedan, introduced the previous model year, and the sport touring, dating back several years, were among the other unique 1925's built.

Several appearance changes were evident in the 1925 Oldsmobiles. A new hood and radiator configuration were most evident. Olds introduced chrome plating late in the model year and radiator shells were either chrome or nickel plated — depending on when the car was produced. Attractive cowl lights were now standard equipment. A new central instrument grouping was the biggest interior change. Power continued to come from a workhorse 40-horsepower L-head six outfitted with Delco ignition and starting components. Closed cars were virtually all outfitted with hardwood framed Fisher Bodies built in Lansing. The wheelbase remained at 110 inches. Options included a balloon tire and smaller disc wheel package that sold for an additional $50. Overall 1925 prices were up slightly over 1924 offerings.

Oldsmobile continued to be concerned about the performance image of its cars. In 1923 the division hired "Cannonball" Baker to make his "locked-in high-gear" cross country run and in 1925 Olds turned to another veteran automotive record setter. Floyd Clymer was well known in automotive circles, being acknowledged as the nation's youngest auto dealer (in the early 1900's) and later a pioneer in the auto publishing and auto accessory field. In the late summer and fall of 1925 Clymer drove a 30-D touring to stock car records for climbing Lookout Mountain in Chattanooga and Pike's Peak. Clymer's efforts were well advertised, particularly in the west, and Olds put out a brochure entitled "Pike's Peak and Lookout Records Both Smashed by Oldsmobile Six: Performance Plus." Clymer's Olds was a stock model with less than 2,000 miles on the odometer. The lone modification was the removal of the top to decrease wind resistance.

By 1925 Oldsmobile was using a finishing process called Duco. This was a DuPont product and widely used in the industry during this period. Duco did not have the brittleness problems of other finishing techniques of the era. Other advantages of Duco included: permanency, resistance to oxidation, ease of finishing and refinishing and better survival in difficult climates. An Olds brochure of the day said, "Clean water alone is all that's necessary to clean a Duco-finished Oldsmobile. In fact you'll find that new lustre is actually brought about by polishing a dusty or muddy Duco-finished car with a dry cloth. Just a few minutes rubbing at any time will make a Duco finished Oldsmobile look as smart as the day it was built."

In 1925 Olds employment rose to a record 4,250 level. In February of 1925 veteran A.B.C. Hardy retired as Oldsmobile general manager. Forty-year old Irving J. Reuter took over the top Olds managerial spot. Reuter had prior auto company experience with Willys-Overland and came to Oldsmobile from automotive industry supplier Remy Electric Company in Indiana.

Least expensive Oldsmobile for 1925 was this roadster priced at $875. Production totalled 2,090 with 13 additional cars exported. Weight was 2,390 pounds. Olds continued to use a wheelbase of 110 inches. There was a convenient locking compartment of 13 cubic feet in the roadster rear deck. An additional five cubic feet of storage space was located just back of the seat. Cowl lights were a new and attractive feature on the 1925 cars.

A second two-passenger Olds for this year was the sport roadster. Price here was $985. Production totalled 1,765 with a single additional unit made for export. Weight was 2,415 pounds. The sport roadster carried the same extra storage capacity as the roadster. Special sport roadster appointments included: disc wheels, step plates on the running boards and a front mounted road spotlight.

1925

A Sunday family drive could be fun in an Olds Model 30 touring car. This family appeared to be enjoying itself. Standard tires were 31 x 4 inch cords. The spare tire was not included as standard equipment. Balloon tires and disc wheels were a $50 option. Standard wooden wheels were of artillery design. Rims were of the Jaxon demountable type.

Very popular among the Model 30's of this year were the touring cars. Price on this model was $875. A total of 7,328 of this car were made with 260 more built for export. This model tipped the scales at 2,405 pounds. Standard equipment included clear vision side curtains. Olds brakes for this year were large service split drum units on the rear wheels. The emergency brake operated off the rear of the transmission.

Oldsmobile continued to offer a line of sporty models in 1925, led by this Model 30 sport touring. This was the most expensive open Olds tagged at $1,015. Production was surprisingly strong on this car at 4,569. Weight was 2,423 pounds. Standard equipment on this model was: Tuarc disc wheels, nickled double-bar bumpers front and rear, windshield wings, road spot light, aluminum step plates and enameled trunk on a special rear platform.

This Olds sport touring had among the nicest lines in the 1925 run. All six cylinder Oldsmobiles were powered by an engine in its third year of production. The Olds six was an L-head of small bore and long stroke. Other engine features included: grey iron pistons, Chadwick bronze backed bearings, Delco ignition components and a Harrison radiator. Olds moved into another body finishing process in 1925. They called this procedure Duco satin finishing and it was widely used in the industry.

For several years Olds offered a model called the cab. In 1925 the cab was dropped and a similar model called the business coupe was introduced. Base price on this two-passenger closed Olds was 1,045 making it the least expensive 1925 closed car. Production was 1,620 making this the rarest Olds of this year. Weight was 2,416 pounds. The cylinder head for 1925 was a single iron casting removable from the top of the cylinder block, being held in place by 16 cap screws.

This nifty business coupe obviously was touted to salesmen, doctors and the like. Upholstery was done in either quality velour or a new type of fabric Olds called "Spanish-style Fabrikoid." The factory listed this as three-passenger model — but it might have been a tight squeeze for any more than two people. Clutches on Model 30's of this year were 9-inch diameter Borg and Becks.

Among the nicer designed 1925 Oldsmobiles was this coupe. Base price was $1,175. Weight was 2,407 pounds. Production totalled 2,338. Oldsmobile mentioned in several of its catalogs: "It is ideally designed for women who drive and desire the companionship of their friends." Notice the large amount of plate glass in this model. It would be several years before Olds would outfit their cars with safety glass.

This front view of the Model 30 coupe showed off the new radiator shell for 1925. At some point during this model year Olds began using chrome plating to replace nickel finishing of some parts. Olds carried this attractive radiator design through 1927 models. Delco continued to supply a large number of Olds six parts including starter motor, generator, distributor, ignition coil and lighting and ignition switch.

Newest of the Olds offerings for this year was the coach. Priced at $1,045 this was the third closed two-door offered in 1925. Shipping weight was 2,523 pounds. The production was sizeable 9,896 with 53 additional cars exported. Each Olds came from the factory with a Willard Type XW-13 battery manufactured by the Willard Storage Battery Company of Cleveland, Ohio.

A late introduction was made of the 1925 series coach. A special folder was issued on the latest Olds closed model. This piece of literature was titled: "An Oldsmobile Six Coach With a Fisher-Built Body." Balloon tires were standard equipment on this car. The Fisher Body featured steel panels mounted atop selected hardwood framing. Other standard coach features included 33-inch doors, automatic windshield wiper, and ventilating windshield of one-piece design.

1925

A cornerstone of Olds closed car production for some time had been the sedan and in 1925 two sedans were again offered. This was the standard sedan. A total of 5,820 were made with 22 additional cars exported. Weight was 2,587 pounds and list price was $1,250. Each Olds of this year was outfitted with an underhood Klaxton Type 8 horn manufactured by the Remy Electric Company of Anderson, Indiana.

Even a spare tire — such as seen on this coach model — was extra cost equipment in 1925. To enter the rear compartment of this Olds the passenger side front seat folded up. Tires on this model were 31 x 4.95 balloons. Hardwood body joints were mortise-wedged, glued screwed together and bolted. Joints that were in high stress areas were given greater strength by the addition of metal corner braces.

With the new styling treatment of 1925 even the largish sedan appeared to be a graceful car. The radiator was of Harrison design. Olds urged the cooling system be kept clean and the system be flushed every 3,000 miles. At zero degrees in the winter the Model 30 owners' manual urged a 50-50 mix of water and glycerine. The Olds cooling system held 13 quarts when full to the top of the radiator.

In its second year as a full fledged model was the popular deluxe sedan. This was the most expensive 1925 Olds tagged at $1,350. Production was 7,075 with five additional cars exported. Weight was 2,607 pounds. As with all special Olds models the deluxe sedan rode on disc wheels. Note the Olds factory mounted road spotlight underneath the driver's side headlight on this model.

Poised between two elegant houses of the day was this 1925 30 series sedan. Fuel for the six cylinder powerplant came through a Zenith carburetor via a vacuum system. The carb was outfitted with a dash mounted choke. Vacuum tanks were of either G.G. or Stewart brand. Olds used a 12½ gallon fuel tank mounted at the rear of the chassis. The tank was built of heavy gauged lead coated steel.

This rear shot of a Model 30 deluxe sedan gives an idea of more additional equipment found on this car. Special step plates were found on the running boards. A rear mounted trunk platform housed a factory outfitted black enameled trunk. Note the special bright strips on the back of this sedan body to protect the paint from vibration of the trunk. The Model 30 rear end was a semi-floating type equipped with New Departure ball bearings throughout.

Floyd-Clymer — pictured here with a special Model 30 touring car — was known for a great many of things in the world of wheels. He was a prolific publisher of auto books and at one time owned the production rights to the Indian motorcycle. This shot was taken in front of Olds dealership of the day and shows the machine in which Clymer broke stock car records for climbing Pike's Peak and Lookout Mountain. Note the two through the windshield spot lights which were marketed by Clymer. Other speed records broken by Clymer in this car were the Bear Creek Canyon run near Denver, and a run between El Paso, Texas and Albuquerque, New Mexico.

Olds stayed with an aggressive advertising campaign for this model year. The Olds Model 30-C's were introduced in late 1924 and this ad actually appeared in late August of that year. It appeared in the Saturday Evening Post and pointed out the fact that more than 40,000 owners had already bought Model 30's. The ad said, "One of your neighbors is driving an Oldsmobile Six! Talk with him — then come in and admire the beautiful lines of this long lived car."

This lady of the 1920's was enjoying the interior of her 1925 Olds. The steering wheel was a 17-inch diameter wooden unit. Closed cars were outfitted with a vacuum operated windshield wiper. The instrument panel was Duco finished with nickel faced instruments flush mounted and illuminated. The horn was operated from a button atop the steering column. The knob the lady is turning raised or lowered the windshield in its tracks, opening just above the dash.

A banner year would be an apt description of Oldsmobile's efforts in 1926. Domestic sales of 51,988 were an all-time high production mark for Oldsmobile and employment of 4,458 also was a record for the division. Olds moved up a notch to twelfth in industry sales standings finishing behind such makes as Nash, Durant, Willys-Overland-Whippet and Hudson-Essex. For the first time ever closed Oldsmobiles became immensely more popular than the open models.

Once again Olds offered just the six cylinder Model 30's. Some confusion on model years existed in 1926 as both the carried-over-from 1925 Model 30-D's were offered as well as the 30-E's which saw production begin in June of 1926. Prices remained very close to 1925 levels.

During this year Oldsmobile dropped the somewhat inappropriate sports designation on some of its models. This tag had been carried for several years on specially equipped models. In 1926 the term deluxe was substituted on those specially equipped models. Standard and deluxe versions were available in touring, coupe, coach and sedan models. Also offered was a deluxe roadster and a late appearing 30-E series landau four door sedan model. Gone were the standard roadster and business coupe designations of 1925.

A slight variation in body lines was apparent on 1926 Oldsmobiles. A lower appearance was achieved by modifying spring shackles and wheel dimensions. Roof height was reduced an inch. Two-tone Duco color combinations, with contrasting striping, were now available. Upholstery was a heavy plush cord on closed cars and genuine Spanish leather on the open cars. Under-hood changes were subtle and included the adoption of a Morse chain drive between the crankshaft and camshaft. Valve diameters were increased slightly and cast iron bearings replaced bronze bearings all around the cam. A lighter weight cast iron piston was employed. A reduction of clutch pressure was utilized in 1926. The deluxe package for this year consisted of disc wheels, trunk rack, black enameled trunk, bumpers, motormeter and rear vision mirror. Naturally finished wood wheels were an option this year. Gradually adopted this year as standard

equipment, after being a popular option in 1925, was a K-S Telegage on the dash to show the amount of fuel left in the tank. Late in the model year an optional wire wheel package was offered, but research indicates few cars were so equipped in 1926.

For this year all Olds bodies, open and closed, were built within the Lansing Fisher Body operation. These units were constructed on staunch hardwood frames topped by metal panels. All closed models this year had the so called Fisher VV windshield of one panel plate glass design. Direct ventilation came via a crank

By 1926 the popularity of open Olds models, including this disc wheeled deluxe roadster, was on the downswing. All bodies this year were Fisher built. Olds continued to carry its unique locking transmission device outfitted to discourage theft. Windshield wings, pioneered several years ago on Olds sports models, were on this car. Bumpers were also standard equipment here. Some early cars sported nickel plated bumpers, others were chrome.

Since the days of the Curved Dash, Oldsmobile had dabbled in the export market — but for the first time ever more of an Olds model was built for export than for the domestic market. A total of 1,124 standard touring cars were built for U.S. sales, with an additional 2,616 made for export. The touring was the lowest priced 1926 Olds tagged at just $875. Weight on this model was 2,200 pounds. All standard cars came without bumpers, although this was a popular option on the standards.

After offering a pair of roadsters for several years, Olds went back to a single two-seat open model in 1926. Offered only as a deluxe model, the selling price on this car was $975. Weight was 2,317 pounds and production was 1,249 with a single additional car built for export. Roadsters of this year came outfitted with either disc wheels, or as shown with naturally finished wooden artillery wheels. The rumble seat added a nice touch and gave extra fair weather seating capacity.

1926

centered in front of the driver above the windshield Olds and Fisher continued the use of DuPont Duco body finishing. In its painting process a body was first cleaned and treated with a rust preventative coating Primer was followed by a surfacer. Then four coats of DuPont Duco were put on. A final polish job was then performed.

For years it seemed Olds operated almost independently of its parent concern General Motors By 1926, however, this was far from the case. GM had carefully placed Oldsmobile and its six cylinder cars in its marketing strategy and it was paying off well in terms of sales. Just about every piece of Olds sales literature and printed advertising played up the fact that Oldsmobile was a part of General Motors. As a result of this new found corporate kinship, Olds continued to push the financial services of General Motors Acceptance Corporation (GMAC). However Olds might have been stretching it a bit in one of its 1926 brochures when it said, "This (financial) service is unique in that GMAC was not primarily organized to earn a profit from financing operations. It is operated instead, to further the sale of cars."

Olds did not get into any major performance record setting in 1926, as in some previous years, but Floyd Clymer did make an interesting Olds powered jaunt in 1926. On March 14, Clymer made a 301-mile run from Chicago to Detroit in slightly less than 6 hours. Olds proudly claimed this was less time than it took the Wolverine Flyer, an express passenger train of the day, to make the same trip.

By the end of 1926, Oldsmobile had announced an ambitious future plan to expand its Lansing production facilities by one-third. Expansion was to come largely in the areas of heat treating, chassis assembly, body building (Fisher), axle, motor and sheet metal production.

Revised body lines on the 1926 Model 30's like this standard touring lended themselves to more two toning. Olds stayed with the Dupont Duco painting process this year and contrasting striping really set off some of these paint jobs. A popular color scheme on 1926 open Oldsmobiles was a moleskin gray above the molding line and a Russian brown on the main body areas. Red striping was found just under the belt line, on hood louvers and on the wooden wheels.

The deluxe touring model could also be outfitted with disc wheels in 1926. For several years Olds called its fancier versions sports models. This really was an inappropriate term and in 1926 it was replaced by deluxe. Olds said of its deluxe cars, "By purchasing a deluxe car, the motorist thus obtains additional features at decidedly smaller cost than he must incur to buy and install them separately, in addition to the fact that they are of a design in pleasing balance with the lines of the car and are properly installed during the process of manufacture."

Rarest among the 1926 offerings was the deluxe touring model. Pictured here with wooden wheels, this model was priced at $980. Production totalled only 744 and weight was an even 2,400 pounds. Cars in the deluxe trim were equipped with a dogbone radiator cap and motormeter. Running board step plates were in their last year on this package. The regular open body upholstery was grey genuine Spanish leather. Cushions and seat backs were done around sets of coiled springs.

Parked uphill at a rakish angle, this Model 30 provided a good view of rear appointments. Photographed on the factory grounds, this deluxe car is missing top, windshield and spare tire. Apparently some cars were shipped this way and the dealer added these items later. Note the split bumper design and the factory trunk.

Disappearing from the Olds lineup this year was the business coupe and replacing it were standard and deluxe coupe models. This standard coupe shared landau irons with the landau model sedan offered later in 1926. A $925 price tag was placed on this 2,347 pound car. Production was just 1,528. Hardwood framing was the basis for 1926 Fisher Bodies. Olds used a vinyl-like covering on rear roof quarters of most of its coupes.

Model 30 coupes continued to be favorites for those people who were on the road a lot and had to carry a good bit of material with them. Olds pitched cars like this standard coupe to people like salesmen and doctors. Note the small access door between the passenger side door and the rear fender. Closed Olds tops were of slot and padding construction with supporting members running from both side to side and from front to rear. The landau irons were strictly decorative.

A bit more popular than the standard version was this deluxe Model 30 coupe. Either wooden artillery or disc wheels coud be ordered. Price was just under the $1,000 mark at $990. Production was 3,296. Weight was 2,470 pounds. Closed cars of this year were outfitted with the Fisher V V windshield. Made of a single plate glass panel, it could be cranked open for ventilation. Closed cars were also windshield wiper equipped. Olds called the device "an automatic windshield cleaner."

Introduced in 1925, the Model 30 coach was a very popular Olds in 1926. In standard form 6,388 coaches were made with 827 more readied for export. This offering shared low price closed car honors with the standard coupe at $925. Weight was 2,450 pounds. Olds rated seating capacity inside the coach at five. Each closed Olds had an inside dome light with a switch that could be easily reached while standing outside the car.

A sharp turn is being made here by a 1926 standard coach outfitted with the optional disc wheels. Lines on this model were set off nicely by the distinctive radiator shell and attractive cowl lights. This model did carry disc wheels and the special radiator cap and motormeter from the deluxe series. It was a standard, however, as no front spotlight or running board step plates were found. Standard models could be equipped "ala carte" with items from the list of 1926 Olds accessories. The radiator shell was very similar in design to that used by Buick during this era.

Folks in the Olds advertising and publicity departments continued to have a facination for displaying cars near powerful trains. Remember the series of paintings from 1910 through 1915 showing various Oldsmobiles racing trains. Pictured here is a 1926 deluxe coach with a giant electric locomotive. Engineer of the train and owner of the Olds was a gent named Henry Steimman shown climbing aboard the train at its terminal near St. Paul, Minn.

A peek inside a closed 1926 Model 30 was afforded as the passenger door on this standard coach was left open. Closed model upholstery came standard in heavy cord of a neutral shade. A lower overall appearance was achieved on 1926 models by modifying the spring shackles and wheel size. Roof height was also chopped an inch. Note the handy pockets built into this coach's door covering material.

Very rare indeed was this wire wheel equipped Model 30 deluxe coach. Wires had been offered several diferent years by Olds, as early as 1914. Of the dozens of photos reviewed by the author in researching this chapter, this was the only one to show a wire wheel equipped car. Base price on the deluxe coach was $1,040. This was the second most popular 1926 Olds achieving a production run of 13,906. Weight on this Olds was 2,620 pounds. This photo was one of a series taken in a special display room of the General Motors Building in Detroit.

Oldsmobile continued to like to show its cars off with celebrities of the day. Here one of Charlie Chaplin's leading ladies — Merna Kennedy — stands with her arm draped over the cowl light of a 1926 Model 30 deluxe coach. Oldsmobiles were becoming more colorful during this period. The color scheme on this coach might have been Buckingham gray on the mid body with black Duco on the upper body and fenders. A fine green pin striping was found on the belt line, hood and wheels.

1926

Offered in standard trim was this 1926 Model 30 sedan. Base price here was $1,025 and weight was 2,690 pounds. A total of 3,404 standard sedans were made with 392 more exported. Olds was generous with its praise of the Duco finishing process. "Oldsmobile bodies are finished in two-tone genuine DuPont Duco, the most practical body finish ever developed for motor cars. It is hard, smooth, lustrious, rich and it is permanent."

Disc wheels gave a nice touch to the 1926 standard sedan. Besides carrying the optional discs, this car also was out-fitted with bumpers and the trunk package. A common color scheme for Model 30 sedans this year was Aquamarine blue main body with black upper structure and fenders. White striping was used. A mild chassis change this year saw the wide flat pressed channel member forward of the engine replaced by a stronger tubular cross member.

Later in the year, when the first 30-E cars were made, the landau sedan appeared. It was the most expensive 1926 Olds with a price tag of $1,190. This model became Oldsmobile's biggest seller in 1927, but in 1926 just 1,205 were made. It was also the heaviest Olds of the year, tipping the scales at 2,705 pounds. As with all closed cars this model had an attractive external sun visor. This car featured special upholstery, interior hardware in satin finish nickel, and two-tone Duco paint, with black fenders and superstructure. The trunk was standard, as were the rub rails on the rear panel to keep the trunk from vibrating against the car's finish.

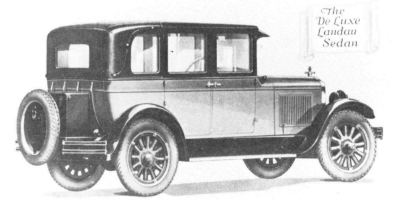

The De Luxe Landau Sedan

Most popular among all the 1926 Oldsmobiles was the deluxe sedan. A whopping total of 15,302 of this stately looking car came off the Olds Motor Works assembly line. Price was $1,115 and weight was 2,690 pounds. This was another photo taken in Detroit's General Motors Building. Just a few years before that same building was known as the Durant Building. Even today, stylized "D" initials remain as part of the building's cornice trim — standing for Durant, of course.

This quiet street setting saw two 1926 Oldsmobiles parked in tandem. Olds head lamps of this year contained bulbs of twenty-one candle power. The tail lamp, instrument board and cowl lights were rated at two candle power. Each lamp was of the 6 to 8 volt type. This was the last year Olds was to stick with the two-wheeled braking system which operated off rear wheel drums. The parking brake was off the rear of the transmission.

In earlier days Olds touted its cars as good hill climbers and the Model 30 could hold its own in this department too. Here a standard sedan heads up a fairly steep hill. Power for hill climbing came from a 40-horsepower L-head six. Olds urged proper tire inflation on all models. A tire pump was part of the factory tool kit that came in each 1926. Front tires were to have 28 pounds of air. Rear tire inflation recommendations ranged from 32-36 pounds depending on the model involved. This hill climbing scene took place at the General Motors Proving Grounds near Milford, Mich.

"You're next," was the greeting of an Oldsmobile service manager as he met a customer wheeling a Model 30 sedan. Olds stressed the cars should be brought back to factory authorized service stations periodically. The Olds guarantee was a rather limited one in 1926 as it covered only 90 days. Not guaranteed by Olds were tires, rims, ignition components, horn, starting devices, batteries or speedometer.

Double decker buses were a common sight on the streets of Detroit when the Model 30 Oldsmobiles were in their prime. Here a pair of sixes chug by these examples of mass transit in 1926. In mid year, with the introduction of the E series cars, Olds jumped the six cylinder displacement slightly to 185 cubic inches. The central instrument cluster for 1926 included an ignition switch and lock, ammeter, choke control, oil pressure gauge, fuel gauge and combination odometer and speedometer.

A good view of the rear of a 1926 sedan was provided as this Olds backed into a parking space. Note the special fabric tire cover this car is carrying. It was lettered with Oldsmobile Six. Ahead of the spare tire is a special factory black enameled trunk resting on a platform. Each Olds carried a fuel tank of 12 gallons. Cooling system capacity was 14 quarts.

Active in the export market since the days of the Curved Dash, this is the Model 30 Olds offered in England for 1926. A main difference is the fender mounted lights which was shown on all cars in the English catalog this year. The English also called this coachwork a saloon. Olds carried its business to Great Britain via General Motors Limited located on Edgware Road in London.

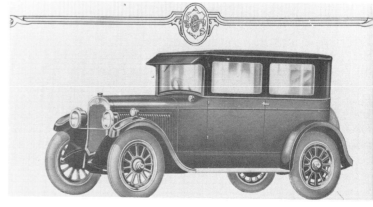

Once again in 1927 Oldsmobile racked up an all-time sales high as Lansing continued to turn out Model 30 six cylinders. A combination of foreign and domestic sales totalled 79,282, good for twelfth position in industry sales standings. This placed them a scant few hundred units behind crosstown Durant which occupied eleventh place. The other major Lansing car builder — Reo — had less than half the Olds output but did manage a sixteenth place showing. Olds employment fell only slightly short of 1926 levels at 4,350.

Thankfully this was the final year for the confusing way Olds used to identify its cars. In very late 1923 Olds brought out the 30-A six cylinder and in 1927 it ended up building 30-E's — but in between series offerings did not exactly follow model years. For example series 30-E production began in mid-1926, But a major change came in January of 1927 when Olds began to build the 30-E's with four wheel brakes. Olds would stay with the six cylinder car as its staple model for the next two decades — but in the next model year the 30 designation was dropped and the all new F-28 was introduced.

As mentioned the biggest change in the 30-model lineup was the introduction of four wheel brakes at the very beginning of 1927. The new Olds braking system, offered with no price increase, was accompanied by a change to 30x5.25 balloon tires. In the new four wheel braking system the rear wheels were stopped by two shoe bands. For parking these brakes were applied independently by the hand lever. The new front wheel stoppers were of the internal expanding type operated by a rotating cam. Olds said its flanged drum and oil cover excluded dirt, water and oil. There were lubrication connectors on all working parts.

The model lineup was essentially the same as 1926, except 1927 found three coupes offered. The standard and deluxe coupes had a conventional hinged trunk opening at the rear. A late introduction was a rumble seated coupe known as the sports coupe. The landau model — introduced in late 1926 — became the most popular Olds model in history with sales totalling 16,792. It's interesting to note this model's sales total in 1927 was nearly as much as the entire Olds auto output just a decade ago. The touring car continued to fade fast this year and for the second straight year export sales for the touring greatly outnumbered domestic sales. Olds changed its deluxe package slightly this year. It now included bumpers front and rear, locking motometer and dogbone radiator cap, and the option of steel disc wheels — finished in main body color — or wooden spoke wheels.

As Olds became more familiar with Duco finishing techniques, it was able to offer a rainbow of two-tone factory combinations in 1927. They included: 1) Russian brown/Moleskin Gray with Red striping; 2) Sea Fog Gray/Ocean Blue with Burnt Orange striping; 3) Buckingham Gray/Black with Pistachio Green striping; 4) Dageston Blue Black with Ivory striping; 5) Bloomfield Gray/Black with Ivory striping; 6) Dawn Mist/Dust Proof Gray with Pistachio Green striping. Open Oldsmobiles of this year were fitted with black pebble grain finished leather. Closed cars were upholstered in genuine mohair in either taupe shade or neutral gray.

Braking changes excepted, most of the mechanical changes in the 30-E's came with their introduction in mid-1926. These mechanical changes included a slightly larger engine displacement of 185 cubic inches, the slight boosting of wheelbase to 111 inches, a redesigned harmonic balancer, an improved air cleaner, a new method for crankcase ventilation, an oil filter and a new walnut finished instrument cluster with a standard fuel gauge. A few wire wheeled cars were made in 1927, but it remained a very rare option.

During this year Olds advance design people were hard at work on the F-28 Oldsmobile, the first all new model since the Model 30 series was added in 1923. A plant expansion on the drawing boards in 1926 became bricks, mortar and structural steel in 1927. This ambitious project included an additional 90,000 square feet of motor plant, a new two-story shipping and loading dock, a new engineering lab and new heat treating facilities.

For some time Oldsmobiles were sold in Canada with few changes from those marketed in the U.S. The Olds Motor Works of Canada, Limited was headquartered in Oshawa, Ontario. In 1927 they offered what was called a "Jubilee Series of Oldsmobiles." These were essentially the same as 1927 Model 30-E's offered in this country. The Canadian cars used Fisher Bodies, offered the same color schemes and interior appointments and introduced four wheel brakes this year.

Deluxe trim was the only way a 1927 Model 30 roadster could be ordered. Price on this model was $975. A total of 2,342 were built with 132 more exported. Weight on this model was 2,317 pounds. Tops were done in khaki colored fabric. Bumpers were outfitted front and rear. The rear deck compartment had side upholstery and a rug. Black pebble grain leather upholstery was found on both open cars.

Probably the best passenger's seat — at least in fair weather — was the rumble seat. Olds lines were still perfect for very nice two toning, and a common deluxe roadster paint combination was Sea Fog Gray and Ocean Blue. These colors were accented by burnt orange striping. This year's twin beam headlights were controlled by a lever centered in the steering wheel opposite the hand throttle.

1927

Olds went rather wild in the offering of coupe models this year as a total of three different Model 30 versions were found in 1927. Pictured is the standard coupe — the least popular of the three with only 3,258 made and 19 more exported. This was the least expensive Olds tagged at $925. Weight was 2,450 pounds. A Klaxton horn was located underhood and again operated from a button atop the steering column. The golf bag door on the right quarter panel was standard on all coupes, but not on the roadster.

Venturing out in winter weather took a hearty individual in an open Olds. This disc wheeled 1927 deluxe roadster shows the side curtains used on this type car. Disc wheels were usually finished in the same color as the main body. Top bows on open cars were naturally finished. Side curtains were designed to open with the doors. Note the little curtain flap to allow a driver to make a turn signal.

A deluxe coupe was offered this year. One option on the deluxe package was a choice of either disc or wooden wheels. Both the deluxe and standard coupes were outfitted with rear opening trunks. Price on this model was $990. Weight was 2,540 pounds. It was the most popular of the coupes with a production run of 5,359. Olds used Duco finishes exclusively this year. Two and three toning were available with contrasting stripes.

Rarest of the domestic Model 30's offered was the standard touring. The least expensive 1927 model, this open car was priced at $875. Just 99 of these cars were sold in this country, while 2,928 were made for export. Weight was 2,335 pounds. The wheelbase had been upped slightly on E series cars to 111 inches. A standard tread was used and road clearance was just shy of 10 inches.

New to the lineup was the rumble seated sports coupe. This was the most expensive of the coupes priced at $1,010. Production was 3,996 and weight was 2,560 pounds. Model 30 coupes continued to carry landau irons over a fabrikoid covering. The front axle was a drop forged, heat treated I-beam. It was similar to units used in the past, but was slightly modified for the addition of front wheel brakes.

Deluxe tourings did not prove to be much more popular than standard versions. A scant 204 were made with 8 additional cars exported. Price on this model was $980 and weight was 2,490 pounds. Equipment on this rare model included a rug in the rear compartment and rubber mat up front. There was a rear compartment foot rest and a robe rail. Upholstery was done in genuine black leather. The trunk was an extra cost option on standard models, but was part of the DeLuxe package.

Late in the model year Olds offered some variations in paint schemes as on this touring car. Note the wide striping on just the doors. Oldsmobiles were outfitted with a floor shifted three-speed transmission. This unit had drop forged, heat treated alloy steel gears and shafts. New Departure ball bearings were used. The speedometer gear was housed in the transmission case. Note that this is a styling studio shot, and the car has been fitted with disc wheels on the right and spokes on the left side.

Bread and butter for Olds sales continued to come from the coach model. This was the last year Olds was to use that name as next year's cars in this configuration became the two-door sedan. The standard coach sold for $950 and weighed 2,570 pounds. Production was an impressive 12,422 with 344 more exported. Upholstery on this model was in a taupe shade of genuine mohair. Both front seats folded forward for entrance to the rear passenger area.

Coach production was split almost evenly between the deluxe and standard versions. Shown is the $1,050 deluxe coach. A total of 11,308 were made. Weight was 2,720 pounds. Deluxe equipment on this model meant: brightly finished bumpers front and rear, disc wheels, trunk rack and trunk, motor meter and dogbone radiator cap, rear window curtain and rear view mirror. A tubular driveshaft was used on all Model 30's with a flexible fabric universal joint at each end.

Two versions of the 30-E sedan were built. This is the deluxe version which had a production run of 11,398. Price was $1,125 and weight was 2,780 pounds. Standard sedan pricing was at $1,025 and weight was 2,625 pounds. Production was 6,945 with 882 cars made for export. All Oldsmobiles rode on a channel-section carbon steel frame. A total of four cross members — including a tubular unit up front — were outfitted.

This restored 30-E sedan appeared at Oldsmobile's 75th anniversary program in the summer of 1972 in Lansing. Biggest news for this model year was the addition of four wheel brakes. External contracting, two-piece bands were used on the rear wheels, while self-energizing, three shoe internal expanding units were used up front. The parking brake was actuated by a hand lever and worked from the rear wheels.

1927

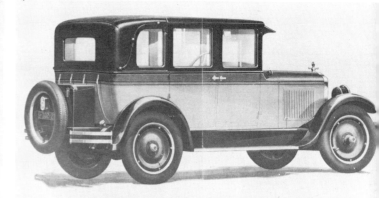

Oldsmobile stylists did a good job with the Model 30-E landau. Introduced in late 1926, this model became the most popular 1927 Olds. The interior on the landau was upholstered in neutral gray mohair. The rear quarter roof was fabric covered and graced by decorative landau irons. The trunk package for this year included a black enamel trunk, rear platform and bright protective rub strips at the rear of the body. Split bumpers were also provided on this model.

It's unusual when buyers make the most expensive car in a series the big seller, but that's exactly what they did with the 1927 landau. An amazing total of 16,792 — the highest Olds tally ever for a single model — were built this year. Export production was an additional 89 cars. Price on this four door was $1,190 and weight was 2,785 pounds. All Oldsmobiles rode on 30x5.25 inch balloon cord tires.

Driving a 1927 Olds Model 30-E would produce this view. The driver held on to a 17-inch walnut rimmed steering wheel. Instruments were grouped in a center cluster, walnut finished panel. The dash was Duco finished. Instruments were glass covered and nickel faced. Instrumentation included a fuel gauge, oil pressure indicator, speedometer/odometer, ammeter and choke control. Illumination was from the rear.

Official duty was found for this Model 30 car as it carried Henry Damm, US Consul at Nogales, Mexico. Pictured here are Mr. and Mrs. Damm following a 6,000-mile U.S. tour in their Olds. South of the border cooling was important and in the six cylinder Olds this was accomplished by a centrifugal pump. A four-blade fan moved air about underhood. Water capacity was 14 quarts. A Harrison honeycomb radiator was again factory standard. Barely visible on each door window are small roll-up awnings. These little after-market accessories could be rolled down and braced in a manner similar to the awnings on today's campers. However, unlike camper awnings which are designed for use only when parked, these car awnings were for keeping the sun from beating in the windows when the car was in motion. Try that today, even with the 55 M.P.H. limit!

This rugged chassis had served Olds well with few basic changes since its introduction in late 1923. In 1928 the chassis and motor would undergo major changes. For 1927 semi-elliptic springs were upfront with underslung springs at the rear. A 12-gallon fuel tank was located at the extreme rear of the chassis. A vacuum fed system was still used. For at least part of this year a one-inch Johnson Model H carburetor was used.

Oldsmobile jumped a spot—to tenth—in the sales ace for 1928. The totally redesigned F-28 odels—with a midyear shot in the arm with the inoduction of sidemounted, wire wheeled deluxe odels—brought sales up to 84,797.

The all new lineup for Oldsmobile was shown for the rst time on January 12, 1928. Olds advertising and roduct literature of the day said the new models were vo years ahead of their time in both styling and ngineering.

Perhaps the biggest news was under the hood as a ew six cylinder powerplant was unveiled. This was ne simple and reliable engine that was to power ldsmobile — with modest changes — well into the ecade of the 1930's. This new engine was an L-head ype which developed 55 horsepower from slightly ore than 197 cubic inches. The crankcase held four ain bearings and the four bearing camshaft was ain driven. Pistons were of cast iron and had the ng skirt design. The oil pump was located in the imp of the oil reservoir and was verically driven off ne camshaft. An impeller water pump was located on ne fan shaft. A new, motor driven fuel pump replaced ne vacuum tank system. This pump was mounted on ne right side of the crankcase and was driven by the amshaft.

F-28 models all rode on 113½ wheelbases with verage overall lengths of 171 inches. Weight was up pproximately 120 pounds over comparable 1927 ldsmobiles. There were numerous new chassis eatures on the F-28's. A three-speed standard ransmission was used. The rear axle was a semioating banjo type with a ratio of 4.41 to 1. Four heel mechanical brakes were used. Rear wheels were xternal contracting on 14-inch diameter drums. ront brakes were internal and self energizing. Total raking area was 244 square inches. Each 1928 Olds as based on a pressed steel frame with a depth of 5½ ches. Front and rear springs were two inches wide nd semi-elliptic. Four Lovejoy shock absorbers were andard equipment. Tyron shackles with oil reseroirs were used on the rear end of the springs.

Seven body styles were offered upon the January inroduction of the F-28 models. These included: the wo Door Sedan, Four Door Sedan, Landau, Sport oadster, Coupe, Sport Coupe and Sport Phaeton. heet metal of the Fisher bodied cars was completely estyled. One distinctive new styling feature was a 1olding and paint scheme which started at the bot-

tom of the cowl, curved upward to the bottom of the windshield and then curved forward over the hood, joining its companion section at the radiator cap.

The Fisher bodies were again of a composit steel and wood construction. F-28 doors were wider than previous years and set flush with the body. Interior width of the new models was increased by a minimum of three inches. Heavy mohair upholstery was used in the closed cars with a neutral taupe shade selected. Landau and Sport Coupe models used a two-tone figured mohair for the seat cushions. Leather upholstery was found on the open cars.

Standard equipment on the F-28's included: a rear view mirror, automatic windshield wiper, combination stop and tail light with a license plate holder and front and rear bumpers. Cowl lights were eliminated from the 1928 models. An offset separate bulb in the headlamp provided parking lights. A new type of artillery wood wheels were standard on all early 1928 models. These wheels had a diameter of 18 inches and were thickly spoked. Full balloon 28 x 5.25 tires were used. Truarc disc or natural wooden wheels were optional on the Landau, Sport Coupe and the open cars

In the summer of 1928, to boost already good sales of the F-28 models, five new deluxe models were added. This new deluxe line consisted of the Deluxe Landau, Deluxe Roadster, Deluxe Sport Coupe, Deluxe Four Door Sedan and Deluxe Phaeton. The deluxe package consisted of sidemounted wire wheel equipment, trunk platform, chrome plated headlamps, leather boots on the springs and some special paint trim work.

Some of the colors offered on 1928 Oldsmobiles included: Trauville blue, London smoke, Launda green, Orinoco green, Locust cream, Crockett brown, Birmingham green, dust proof gray and black.

During 1928 General Motors in Lansing reached a new high employment peak with the combined payrolls of Oldsmobile and Fisher Body reaching 6,234. Olds officials reported that in addition to employing record numbers of people, more than a third of those on the job were working two to three hours of daily overtime. Olds was in the midst of increasing its design and production facilities dramatically. During 1928 work was also underway to create a new companion car for Oldsmobile which would hopefully give General Motors another spot in the automotive market.

One of the rarer models built in 1928 was the Convertible Roadster. With the standard wood wheels and rear mounted spare tire 2,791 were made. Base price was $995 and weight was 2,695 pounds. In addition to a complete restyle job the F-28's had a totally new six cylinder engine which Olds was to hold onto without major changes until well into the 1930's. This powerplant developed 55 horsepower from just over 197 cubic inches.

The F-28 deluxe equipment package was added in the midsummer of 1928 and for this reason the total number of deluxe cars was down when compared to later years. In addition to twin wire sidemounted wheels deluxe equipment included: chrome headlight shells, trunk platform, leather spring covers and special paint trimming. In deluxe form there were only 200 Convertible Roadsters made. Price was $1,115 and weight was 2,845 pounds.

The F-28 Sport Phaeton was the rarest of all standard models offered. As with its sister car the Convertible Roadster, the Sport Phaeton had a leather interior. Production on the standard Sport Phaeton totalled 804 and there are indications that a good number of these were exported. This model carried a base price $995 and 2,915 pounds was the weight.

All Oldsmobiles in standard form carried split rear bumpers to accommodate the rear mounted spare tire. Unlike later years of Oldsmobile, bumpers — front and rear — were part of the standard equipment package in 1928. The factory offered the tire cover that is pictured. It was inscribed "The New Oldsmobile." Dealer price on this unit was 90 cents each and they were offered in January of 1928 with the introduction of the F-28's.

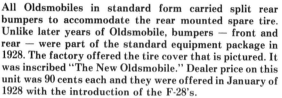

Side curtains were still very much with the Oldsmobile open car owner in 1928. Both the Sport Phaeton and Convertible Roadster came so equipped. Curtains were of the clear vision type and were mounted in rigid supporting frames. Olds literature of the day called them "practically draft proof." When not in use they were stored vertically in a special locker behind the seat back cushion.

The F-28 Sport Phaeton was a rare car anyway, but equipped in anything but the standard five wood wheel configuration it was exceedingly rare. The open four door, as pictured here, was one of several Olds models which could come from the factory with disc wheels on special order. A deluxe Sport Phaeton — with wire sidemounted wheels — was also produced. Eighteen were built in wire wheeled form with a base price of $1,115 and weight of 3,065 pounds.

The standard Coupe was one model that was not offered in deluxe trim in 1928. A total of 9,164 of this model were built. Price on this model was the lowest of any F-28s, $925. Weight was 2,705 pounds. Olds touted this car as being appealing to the business man and it did offer a great deal of room behind its full width front seat. F-28 bumpers were designed with two broad metal pieces and were mounted on special rubber cushions.

The Sport Coupe was a popular Oldsmobile offering for several years. The standard F-28 Sport Coupe saw a production run of 5,079. Base price was $995 and weight was 2,760 pounds. Setting the Sport Coupe off from the Coupe was a cushioned deck seat (rumble seat) for two. Rumble seats were upholstered in leather, while up front the upholstery was done in a good quality mohair.

An F-28 Deluxe Sport Coupe was a nice looking automobile. Only 1,038 of this model were produced. It carried a base price of $1,115 and weighed 2,910 pounds. The all new F-28's were powered by a six cylinder powerplant that in addition to being reliable was also a good performer. It went from 5 mph to 25 mph in 8½ seconds with a great deal of smoothness.

Both 1928 coupe models were nimble little cars. As with all F-28's they rode on an all-new 113½ inch wheelbase which Oldsmobile would use for several years to come. All 1928 Oldsmobiles used the Delco-Remy Lovejoy hydraulic shock absorbers of the strap type as standard equipment. Each car was outfitted with a concealed wiring combination tail light, stop light and license plate holder.

Bread and butter car in the F-28 series was the standard Four Door Sedan. Production on this model totalled a whopping 27,849. Base price was $1,025 and weight was 2,890 pounds. Fenders on each F-28 were extra wide and of the full crown type. Running boards were covered with heavy material and bound with aluminum moldings. The front axle was drop-forged and heat treated and of the I-beam style.

The F-28 Two Door Sedan was another model which was offered only in the standard equipment package. This was the second highest production model of the year as a total of 23,572 rolled off the assembly line. Base price was $925 and weight was 2,790 pounds. Each 1928 Oldsmobile was outfitted with distributor, starter and generator built by Delco-Remy. The battery was an 80 ampere-hour, six-volt, 13-plate Willard.

Most popular among the deluxe equipped cars was the Four Door Sedan. A total of 2,221 of this handsome, side-mounted machine were built. Price was $1,140 and weight was 3,040 pounds. Each Olds for this year was equipped with what the factory called a centrifugal air cleaner. Centrifugal force within a whirling air current thrust dust particles outward against the walls of the cleaner before they reached the carburetor intake.

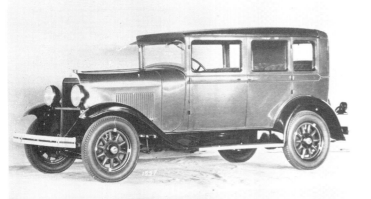

Another relatively popular F-28 Olds was the Landau. This was a four door sedan which offered a blocked rear quarter area with stylish Landau irons hung in that area. Production on this model was a surprising 10,485. Price was $1,085 and this car weighed 2,805 pounds. The Landau was a distinctive looking car both inside and outside. On the inside upholstery was done in a special two toned figured mohair.

Particularly graceful for a larger car was the deluxe version of the Landau. This special model four door was the highest priced F-28 Oldsmobile at $1,205. It weighed 3,050 pounds. The production run was only 1,576. 1928 was the year Oldsmobile decided to discontinue cowl lights. It installed a special parking light bulb in the headlight assembly, a practice that would continue for several years.

The F-28 Landau was one of the few Olds standard models that could be ordered with disc wheels. Here is an auto show model so equipped. Olds kept no records on how many disc wheeled cars it built, but it is believed to be relatively few. In the F-28 series four doors it took nine board feet of lumber and fifteen square feet of sheet steel to make a door.

The F-28's were a new model from stem to stern. Cooling came from a Harrison hexagon honeycomb type radiator with a chrome plated shell. It held 13 quarts of engine coolant. Forced circulation was by a centrifugal pump located in the front end of the engine block. A four blade fan was driven by a V-type belt. Each F-28 had a turning circle of 36 feet and road clearance of more than 8 inches.

Olds had a number of dealers in locations all over the country and Alaska was no exception. Here a group of F-28's wait aboard the S.S. Seattle for northern shipment to a Fairbanks dealer. This shipment included a variety of closed models. Needless to say the Convertible Roadsters and Phaetons were not all that popular up north. This high angle photo shows a good view of the unique F-28 striping layout.

Production continued to climb for Oldsmobile in 1929. The company stayed with a mild update of the previous year's all-new cars, and the motoring public received them well. Production in 1929, less the newly introduced Viking (covered in a separate chapter), was 94,598—good for a move up to ninth place in sales standings. This all-time-high production mark for Olds had several interesting aspects including the fact that in just four years Olds output more than doubled. The Depression hit Olds hard, as it did all auto builders, and it would be 1935 before Olds would surpass sales totals of this year.

Only minor changes were accorded the 1929 Olds models, the majority of the division's innovative work going into the all-new companion car — the Viking. The F-29's brought some changes including a more powerful engine, new style counter weighted crankshaft, adjustable front seat, metal crown panels in the roof and a rubber silenced chassis and body. The 1928 and 1929 Oldsmobiles were very similar with the F-29's adopting a new oval Olds emblem on the headlight tie bar.

The F-29 lineup had the following basic models: two-door sedan, four-door sedan, landau sedan, coupe, roadster and phaeton. Prices on these standard-equipped cars ranged from $875 to $1,035. In addition to standard equipment Olds offered two other packages this year. Special equipment was made up of two sidemounted spare tires, trunk rack and bumpers front and rear. Prices on the special equipped cars ranged from $950 to $1,020. Deluxe model equipment included: sidemounted wire wheels, trunk rack, bumpers front and rear and chrome plated headlight shells. Prices on the deluxe models ranged from $1,005 to $1,165. Interiors on all cars were done in either button tufted mohair or shark grained genuine leather.

Oldsmobiles for 1929 were powered by a 197 cubic inch motor very similar to the all new powerplant introduced just a year ago. Output this year was upped slightly to 62 horsepower. Four large babbitt main bearings supported a drop forged, heat treated high carbon crankshaft. Drop forged I-beam connecting rods carried gray iron pistons. A pressure fed fuel system was used. Fuel came from a 15-gallon rear mounted tank. Delco-Remy supplied the distributor, generator, starter and horn. Standard wheels were 10-spoke artilleries with 18-inch rims. Tires were 28x5.25 inch non-skid balloons. Wire wheels and sidemounts were optional. Each 1929 Olds was fitted with four Lovejoy shock absorbers.

Oldsmobile and Fisher Body, both divisions of General Motors, were familiar production partners by 1929. There was still a great deal of wood in the closed F-29's including nine board feet of lumber in a single door. The Fisher closed body was still based on hardwood framing with steel corner bracing. Roof construction was largely wood with seven lateral cross members and thirteen longitudinal members. The covering consisted of varying layers of padding, cotton cloth and weatherproof fabric. The instrument panel on the F-29 stressed symmetry with a center ignition lock flanked by radiator shutter control and choke lever. Instruments included an ammeter, oil pressure gauge, water temperature device and fuel gauge. A speedometer/odometer combination also featured a trip odometer. Door latches, locks and window controls were supplied by Ternstedt. The steering column could be dealer adjusted and closed cars had adjustable front seats.

By 1929 Oldsmobile employment jumped nearly 2,000 to 7,213 — the largest number ever working for the Lansing car builder. This employment mark would not be equalled again until 1934. Olds continued a massive construction program in 1929. Total holdings were brought to 85 acres with the purchase of three city blocks. Despite the fact that just a year ago new shipping and loading facilities were completed, in 1929 an additional 25% of shipping, loading and warehousing space was added to the Olds complex. Work was also started on a new administration building in this year.

Open cars continued to be rare in 1929. The standard roadster sold for $945, and weighed 2,716 pounds. Only 947 were built. In special form the price was $1,020, weight was 2,730 pounds and production was only 335. The F-29 roadster had natural wood bows and the front windshield could be folded flat. Wooden artillery wheels were naturally finished and used ten spokes. Eighteen inch rims were outfitted. Side curtains could be raised even with the top down.

Convertible roadsters were rumble seated and outfitted with a weather-tight top with a full top boot and crank-up windows in the doors. The trunk rack on the special and deluxe models was foldable. All F-29's rode on a wheelbase of 113½ inches and had road clearance of slightly more than 8 inches. The six cylinder's fuel system was fed from a 15-gallon tank mounted at the rear. A fuel gauge was dash mounted and the system was fitted with a gasoline strainer.

Exceedingly attractive was the F-29 deluxe roadster. It was priced at $1,075 and weighed 2,725 pounds. A total of 1,013 were made and this was a rare case where a deluxe model production was more than either the standard or special versions. The F-29 deluxe package consisted of six wire wheels, sidemounted fenders and fittings, folding trunk rack, bumpers front and rear and chrome plated headlight shells.

Oldsmobile employee Rick Miller of Perry, Michigan has always been interested in vintage cars. This restored 1929 roadster is the star of Miller's collection. Miller and his family did most of the restoration work on this beauty themselves. Olds lighting this year included twin beam headlamps controlled from the steering wheel. The stoplight and rear tail lamp were combined in a single unit with enclosed wiring.

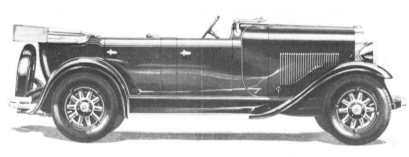

With a total domestic production run of less than 100 the Olds phaeton was a rare car in 1929. In standard form the price was $945, weight was 2,734 pounds and production was only 18. In special fittings the price was $1,020, weight was 2,744 pounds and only 9 were made. As a deluxe the price was $1,075, weight was 2,739 pounds and 51 were made. Besides this, a total of 428 of these cars were produced for export. Upholstery on these cars continued to be in genuine leather.

The Coupe
$875

A pair of slightly different coupes were found among the F-29 offerings. This is the coupe which in standard form was the least expensive car offered this year at $875. Production was 8,135 and weight was 2,830 pounds. In special form the coupe sold for $950, weighed 2,846 pounds and 2,011 were made. As a deluxe, the selling price went to $1,005, weight was 2,840 pounds and only 646 were built. A total of 6 coupes were exported. This version was built in trunk-back style only. The special model offered a single right-hand sidemount and trunk rack.

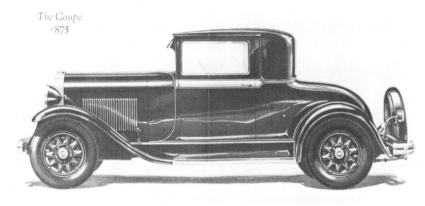

The Sport Coupe
$945

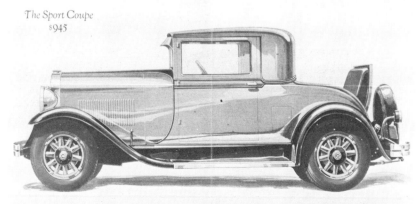

A rumble seat was the distinguishing feature of the sport coupe. As a standard model the price was $945 with a weight of 2,850 pounds. A total of 4,633 were made. As a special the price was $1,020 and weight was 2,866 pounds. Production was 1,281. As a deluxe the price on the sport coupe was $1,075 and weight was 2,860 pounds. A total of 2,871 were built. The export total was 44. All Olds coupes this year had a luggage or golf bag access door on the left rear panel.

The Two-door Sedan
$875
See price notes in back of book

A good sized batch of two-door sedans rolled out of Lansing in 1929. In standard form price was $875, weight was 3,075 and output was a healthy 21,266. As a special the price jumped to $950, weight was 3,085 pounds and 4,284 were built. In deluxe equipment the production was 1,544 with a price of $1,005 and weight was 3,080 pounds. Export total for the F-29 two-door sedan was 144. All Olds were fitted with a hydraulic Lovejoy shock absorber for each wheel.

Few changes were made between the F-28 and F-29 models. One quick way to distinguish between these two years was the 1929's sported a new oval Olds emblem centered in the headlight bar. The horsepower rating was upped to 62 for the F-29. The six cylinder engine continued to displace 197 cubic inches. Four large main bearings were fitted and supported a 51-pound carbon steel crankshaft. Intake valves were made of alloy steel. The two-door sedan, like all closed Oldsmobiles, used the Fisher "VV" windshield — "VV" stood for ventilation and vision.

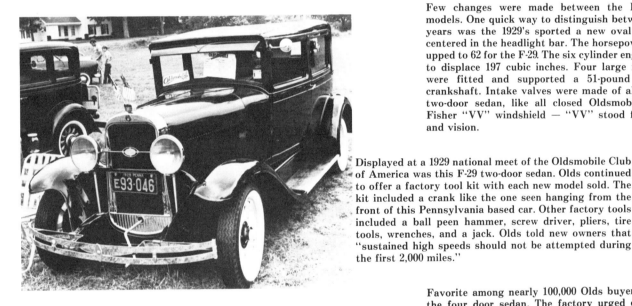

Displayed at a 1929 national meet of the Oldsmobile Club of America was this F-29 two-door sedan. Olds continued to offer a factory tool kit with each new model sold. The kit included a crank like the one seen hanging from the front of this Pennsylvania based car. Other factory tools included a ball peen hammer, screw driver, pliers, tire tools, wrenches, and a jack. Olds told new owners that "sustained high speeds should not be attempted during the first 2,000 miles."

By far the most popular car offered by Oldsmobile in 1929 was the four door sedan. In standard forms as seen here, the price was $975 and weight was 3,128 pounds. Production totaled a whopping 25,443. In special trim the price became $1,050 and weight was 3,138 pounds. A total of 6,620 were built. Export totals for the entire four-door line was 473. A pre-delivery dealer inspection list included 91 items ranging from a visual body inspection to advising the owner regarding service locations.

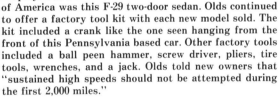

Favorite among nearly 100,000 Olds buyers in 1929 was the four door sedan. The factory urged each owner to bring his new car back to a dealer for a 1,500-mile checkup. This included a dealer road test, adjusting valve tappets, cleaning spark plugs, filling the battery, tightening bumper bolts, checking wheel alignment, lubricating the chassis and a rather complete interior cleanup job. All the services were performed at no cost to the owner.

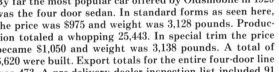

The Four-door Sedan
$975

Profiles of the 1929 four-door sedan were quite attractive. Olds was concerned about why a customer decided to purchase an Oldsmobile. Each new car owner was given a survey that asked how a customer became interested in Oldsmobile, what other car makes were considered, what features of the Oldsmobile appealed the most, what magazines were read by the owner's family and what the owner's occupation was. A large space was left open "for any suggestions or criticisms of Oldsmobile or Olds advertising you may care to make."

Cutting an attractive and stately figure was the F-29 deluxe four-door sedan. This model sold for $1,105 and tipped the scales at 3,133 pounds. Production on the deluxe four-door was 7,197. As with all closed Oldsmobiles, the car was upholstered in button tufted genuine mohair. The rear quarter and side roof panels were covered with sheet metal lacquered in the main body color.

Shown on a dealership floor or in an auto show display was this two toned deluxe four-door. This car was outfitted with several unique items. Note the fabric covering for the sidemounted wire wheel. Also note the attractive trunk on this car. In some earlier years a trunk was included in the deluxe package — but deluxe trim on an F-29 included only a folding trunk platform.

Captured in front of one of the factory buildings was this 1929 landau. A General Motors Division that did a lot of business with Oldsmobile was Delco-Remy. They supplied a cutout relay and thermostatic controlled generator, distributor, positive mechanical engaging starting motor and a six-volt vibrator type horn. Olds continued to use a silent chain to drive the camshaft and generator.

In the span of just a couple of years the landau dropped from one of the most popular cars offered to one of the most rare. As a standard model the landau was priced at $1,035 and weighed 3,140 pounds. A total of 2,459 were built. As a special the price rose to $1,110 with a weight of 3,155 pounds. Only 601 were made. Export totals for the landau were 166. Lovejoy hydraulic shock absorbers were standard on all F-29's. Walnut moldings were used around doors and on the instrument panel.

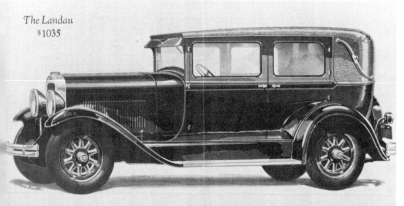

The Landau $1035

The highest priced 1929 Oldsmobile was the deluxe landau. Price was $1,165 with a weight of 3,150 pounds. Production here was 1,774. Front axle construction was based on a drop forged, heat treated I-beam. A ball thrust spindle mounting was used. Semi-elliptic springs were found both front and rear with the rear springs being longer. Both spring sets were two inches wide.

From up front the F-29 was a traditionally styled machine. Olds continued to use an external sunvisor. The visor had a pattern that was carried over to the unique overthehood body line. Bumpers were not part of the standard package this year, but few cars left Lansing without bumpers. Olds had used Harrison radiators for years and this year was no exception. A Harrison hexagon honeycomb was found up front surrounded with a chrome plated shell.

This is what a deluxe equipped Olds sedan looked like from the rear. The folding trunk rack and bumpers were part of the special and deluxe equipment packages. Note the fuel tank location behind the luggage rack. All Oldsmobiles were fitted with a single dry disc clutch. This unit was spring cushioned to prevent chatter. The clutch release bearing was made of baked carbon graphite and was both self lubricating and self aligning.

Four door models in 1929 offered spacious interiors done in mohair. For this year the front seat was adjustable — note the seat adjusting control in the lower center of the seat. A black enameled foot rest was found in the rear compartment. Note the dome light centered in the rear compartment and also the rolled up shades at the rear and rear quarter windows. The steering column was braced to the instrument board. Steering ratio was 16 to 1.

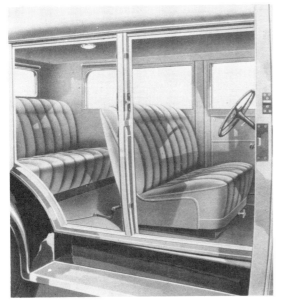

It had been several years since any major motoring stunt had been pulled by Oldsmobile, but this year an Olds made a punishing trip across the Kalahari Desert in South Africa. Shifting sands made it a most difficult trip. The Olds was the first car to complete a cross country mail run. On this trip the Olds really needed its 14-quart cooling system capacity. Circulation was via a centrifugal pump located in the front of the block.

PART 2—PAGE 16.   Chicago Sunday Tribune: FEBRUARY 10, 1929

The 1929 *Oldsmobile is*
FINER THAN EVER
LOWER IN PRICE

—and now it is winning greater and greater public favor in every section of the country. . . .

With all its desirable improvements . . . with all its additional smartness, luxury, comfort and performance . . . the 1929 Oldsmobile is lower than ever in price . . . now only $875.

The 1929 Oldsmobile is more beautiful than ever in appearance—the result of new style refinements and new color combinations now presented in its composite bodies by Fisher.

The 1929 Oldsmobile is more luxurious, more comfortable and offers new conveniences for driver and passengers. Roominess is a feature. Seat cushions are deeper and softer. Upholsteries are richer. And the new Fisher adjustable front seat, combined with Oldsmobile's adjust-

able steering wheel, makes the driving position a matter of individual choice.

The 1929 Oldsmobile provides even more gratifying and dependable performance. Its big high-compression engine now develops 62 horsepower. Typical of its fine car design, oil is forced directly to the piston pins through rifle-drilled connecting rods—a feature

heretofore characteristic of high-priced cars.

Oldsmobile was a remarkable value before. Now that it is finer than ever—and lower in price—it is the outstanding value of its class. Come and see this finer Oldsmobile. Drive it yourself. Compare it with other cars. Know why it is winning greater and greater public favor in every section of the country.

Other important features include double-ribbed crankcase . . . balanced crankshaft . . . rubber engine mountings . . . full pressure-lubrication . . . crankcase ventilation . . . oil filter . . . air-cleaner . . . controlled cooling . . . full-length vertical radiator shutters . . . motor-driven fuel pump . . . silenced chassis . . . silenced interior . . . double-cushioned universal joint system . . . spring-cushioned

NEW LOWER PRICE
TWO DOOR SEDAN
$875
f. o. b. Factory, Lansing, Michigan
Spare Tire and Bumpers Extra

clutch core . . . self-adjusting spring shackles . . . extra-heavy, "low-dropped" tapered frame . . . quick, positive four-wheel brakes . . . 18 to 1 steering gear ratio . . . high-pressure chassis lubricating system . . . four Lovejoy hydraulic shock absorbers . . . Fisher bodies . . . "VV" windshield . . . gasoline gauge and engine temperature gauge on dash . . . and many others.

OLDSMOBILE
PRODUCT OF GENERAL MOTORS

OLDS MOTOR WORKS
CHICAGO BRANCH, 2401 SOUTH MICHIGAN AVENUE. PHONE VICTORY 6800

Viking

Oldsmobile for two years (1929 & 1930) built one of its rarest and most interesting cars: the Viking. The Viking was far more than simply another Oldsmobile model. It had very little interchange with the six cylinder F-series models that were the Olds bread and butter during 1928-31. The division had set up separate production facilities within the Lansing complex for Viking production and the building of major components for the V-8 companion car.

Obviously Oldsmobile and General Motors had set some lofty sales targets for its new car line and just as obviously the Depression wiped out any hope of success for a new car line out of Lansing. Olds spent a bundle designing, tooling up for, placing into production and marketing the Viking. Obviously less than 8,000 sales spread over two years made the Viking a financial loser from the time the first one rolled off the assembly line.

Introduced to the public in mid-April of 1929, the Viking spanned the model years of 1929 and 1930. In 1929 a total of 5,259 Viking sales were made and in 1930 Viking sales dropped to 2,738. By mid 1930 it was obvious - even to the car conscious public - that the Viking was a goner. By 1931 Olds had attempted to completely disengage itself from the orphaned Viking, although a few dealers were stuck with leftover 1930 models which were titled as 1931's. The Viking venture did strain relations for awhile between Olds and some of its dealers and in fact the Viking drove some out of business. It is rather surprising that Oldsmobile itself weathered the whole situation as well as it did.

There were few differences between the 1929 and 1930 Vikings, but there were also a few on going changes made on Vikings from the startup until the finish of the production run. For the purposes of this book we will treat the entire Viking production run as a single output, rather than breaking it into two years.

The Viking was a unique car in the annals of Oldsmobile history - and perhaps its most unique feature was its V-8 engine. Cylinders were bored 3-3/8 inches with a stroke of 3-5/8 inches. Displacement was 260 cubic inches and the horsepower rating was 80. The V-8 engine block was a "monoblock" casting. The crankshaft was less than 21 inches long between end bearings and it was supported by only three oversize bearings. Pistons were made of annealed gray iron and connecting rods were drilled lengthwise for lubrication. Rocker arms actuated the valves directly from the camshaft. Olds made a great deal of the design of the intake manifold which was of the downdraft design. The Viking's Johnson carburetor was mounted in a very high position and Olds claimed this helped in cold starting. Other interesting Viking engine features included: an aluminum oil pan, engine supports of live rubber, alloy steel intake valves, silchrome exhaust valves, a six-volt 15-plate battery and Delco-Remy supplied distributor, starter and horn.

There were other interesting mechanical features on the Olds companion car. It was equipped with a standard selective sliding gear three speed transmission. The clutch was a single-plate, dry disc of 9-7/8 inches

The Viking was a massive car, larger than anything Oldsmobile had built for many years. This was particularly evident in a straight on front view of the machine. Viking headlamps were of the depressed beam type and controlled from the steering column. Parking light bulbs were installed in the headlight assembly. Lights were powered by a six-volt, 15-plate storage battery. It was a 100 ampere hour capacity.

Rarest among the three Viking models was the Convertible Coupe. A total of only 17 were made in standard (non-sidemounted wire-wheels) equipment. An additional 467 deluxe (six wire-wheeled) models were produced. The standard wire-wheeled convertible cost $1,770 and weighed 3,945 pounds. The sidemounted wire-wheeled convertible cost $1,885 and weighed 4,005 pounds. Standard model Vikings came without spare tires and without bumpers - but few cars left Lansing without this optional equipment.

diameter. The rear axle was of the $^3/_4$ floating type with a gear ratio of 4.63 to 1. Brakes were of the mechanical, two-shoe type. Total brake area was 243 square inches. Springs were of the semi-elliptic type of carbon steel in front and silico-manganese steel in the rear. Wheels were 18-inch either wire or wood with 30x6.00, non-skid balloon cord tires. Four Lovejoy hydraulic shock absorbers came standard on all Viking models.

The Viking rode on a stately 125 inch wheelbase. Each Viking had a Fisher Body and came equipped with safety-plate glass in the windshield. As in all Olds-Fisher bodies of the era the Viking was framed entirely in selected hardwood. Joints were mortised, tenoned, glued and screwed together. Included in the construction of a Viking sedan body was: 265 board feet of lumber, 237 square feet of metal and 21.7 square feet of plate glass. Bodies were finished in lacquer. Closed model interiors were upholstered in button tufted mohair with leather available on convertibles. Some interior moldings were finished in mahogany.

Just three basic models were included in the Viking lineup with three types of equipment packages. Closed cars were the Four Door Sedan and the Close Coupled Sedan with the lone open model the Convertible Coupe. The standard equipment package on all body types included Lovejoy shocks and four naturally finished wood wheels. Bumpers and a single spare tire were technically options - but few if any Vikings left the factory without them. The special equipment package included two spare tires and wooden wheels, two welled fenders, hold down irons and locks, front and rear bumpers and a folding trunk platform. The deluxe package included: six wire wheels, tire hold down irons and locks, two welled fenders, bumpers and a folding trunk rack.

Oldsmobile came up with some rather bizarre way for promoting its new product line. Preliminary ads i cluded a four-color, two-page Saturday Evening Po ad in the April 13, 1929 issue. By far the wildest effo was called "the Uniformed Viking Campaign." F several weeks prior to announcement Olds suggeste that its dealers hire actors. The factory suggeste "men of imposing stature, being about six feet height and weighing 180 to 200 pounds" be hired. Fa tory supplied Viking costumes were available fro Olds for $25 each. Olds suggested, "The flashing shields, helmets and spears makes an imposing spe tacle that will cause a great deal of attention in th name of Viking." The factory follow-up sheet showe the program involved: 16 men in Columbus, Ohio; 2 men in Indianapolis; 16 men in Milwaukee, 36 men St. Louis and 72 men in Chicago.

Another interesting promotion involving the Vikin came from April 28 to July 7, 1930 with the running the Elks Prosperity Tour. This involved four separat teams of men from the Elks Lodge carrying a speci prosperity message from President Hoover. The ca used by these teams were four specially painted Vi ings — white with purple trim. All cars were Delc radio equipped. Tie-ins were made with Olds-Vikin dealerships and Oldsmobile officials across th country.

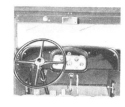

With its top down the Viking Convertible Coupe was an impressive automobile. The top was of a heavy waterproof fabric. Each convertible had folding chrome landau bars. The rear window was rectangular plate glass. The luggage compartment came equipped with a locking door. There was a rubber treated mat in both the front and rear compartments. The windshield was of the swinging type with a chrome plated frame.

Convertible Coupes were built with wood wheels in the Viking series. The least expensive open car was the standard (non-sidemounted) equipped wooden wheeled model which sold for $1,695. It weighed 3,970 pounds and 387 were produced. With special (sidemounted) equipment only 56 were made. Weight was 3,945 pounds and the price tag was $1,770. Viking convertibles came with rumble seats which the factory literature called "rear deck seats.

Viking

Viking

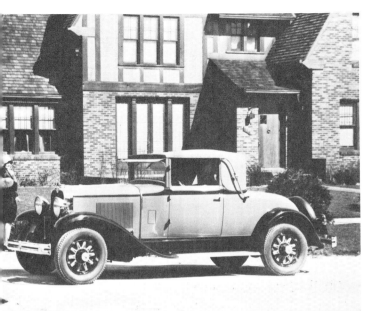

Viking called the smaller of its four doors a Close Coupled Sedan and later this model was also called a Brougham. In standard (non-sidemounted) form with wire wheels the price on the Close Coupled Sedan was $1,770 and the weight was 4,080 pounds. The production run for this car was only 29. With a wheelbase of 125 inches the Viking models had eight inches of road clearance and a turning circle of 44½ feet.

Olds claimed its Viking to be a middle price bracket car — but it worked out to be of the upper middle variety. All Vikings were lacquer finished. They were equipped with adjustable front seat and steering column, cowl ventilators, chrome headlamps, rubber clutch and brake pedal pads, running boards covered with heavy corrugated rubber and bound with a chrome molding. Convertible interiors were done in black genuine leather.

The Viking cars with sidemounts offered a particularly striking form when compared to other Oldsmobile-built cars of the era. The deluxe equppped (six wire wheels) Close Coupled Sedan was priced at $1,855. It weighed 4,145 pounds and 807 were made. Each Viking featured a carburetor adjustment control located at the left of the instrument panel. The Viking also used a "theft-proof" ignition lock assembly.

Vikings, as did all other 1929-30 Oldsmobiles, carried Fisher Bodies. Window sills were of artistically inlaid wood panels with a V-motif of decorative design. Notice the cowl mounted ventilators which were designed to be operated by a foot lever. Viking headlamps were chrome plated and mounted on plated posts. They were fitted with tilt ray bulbs and offset bulbs in these lamps served as parking lights.

Entry to the back seat on the Close-Coupled Sedans was more difficult than on the other Viking four-door model. In standard (non-sidemounted) form with wood wheels 621 Close-Coupled Sedans were made. Base price was $1,695 and weight was 4,105 pounds. With sidemounted wood wheels (special equipment) only 71 were produced. Base price was $1,795 and weight was 4,160 pounds.

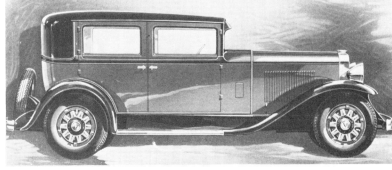

Viking

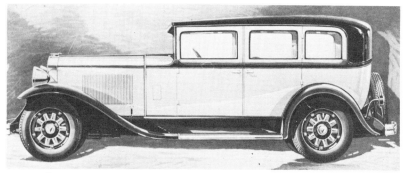

By overwhelming choice the most popular Vikings were the wood wheeled Four-Door Sedans. A total of 2,913 of the standard (non-sidemounted) wooden wheeled Four-Door Sedans were made. Base price was $1,695 and weight was 4,150 pounds. In special equipment (wood-wheeled sidemounts) only 187 Four-Door Sedans were built. Price was $1,795 and weight was 4,205 pounds. Viking tires were 30 x 6 inches, non-skid, balloon cord.

The Viking proved to be a fashionable car for fashionable people in its short-lived new car span. Most popular among the three basic models was the Four-Door Sedan. A Viking in standard equipment came with four wire or four natural wood wheels. Special equipment meant a car had the wooden artillery wheels but carried two spare tires on rims in front fender wells. Deluxe cars had six wire wheels with tires with two spares in the fender wells.

Wire wheeled offerings in the Viking Four-Door Sedans were also popular in a relatively limited model run. As pictured with deluxe equipment (sidemounted wire wheels) 2,353 Four-Door Sedans were produced. Base price was $1,855 and weight was 4,180 pounds. By contrast the standard (non-sidemounted) equipped wire wheeled Four-Door Sedan saw a model run of only 89. Base price was $1,770 and weight was 4,125 pounds. Each Viking came equipped with a Delco-Remy, 6-volt vibrator horn.

The Viking was priced a bit too high to be considered a fleet car. But that didn't stop one California firm from buying ten of the Oldsmobile companion cars. Pictured are the ten wood wheeled four door sedans purchased by the Sutherland Transportation Company of San Diego. It is not known exactly what these cars were used for but they would have been ideal for hauling passengers because of their 125 inch wheelbases. It is assumed that they all went into the taxi or livery business.

Viking never became a household name in automotive circles, but one California woman liked the new Olds model so much she bought two. Mrs. Ruth M. Irwin of Los Angeles bought a close coupled sedan in standard equipment. Just a month later she bought a convertible coupe with deluxe equipment. If more people showed Mrs. Irwin's enthusiasm for the Viking it might have been a sales success.

Viking

Cooling was rather crucial to the newly designed and complicated V-8 engine. The Harrison hexagon honeycomb radiator was up to the job. It was housed beneath a chromium shell. Radiator capacity was 8 gallons of coolant. Controlled type circulation was forced by a centrifugal pump in the front end of the engine block. There was a four-blade adjustable fan driven by a V-belt.

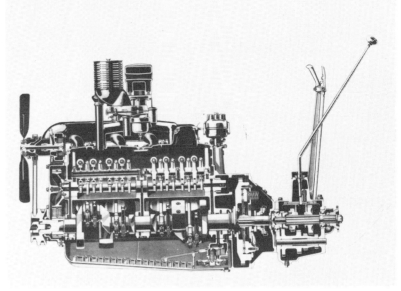

By far the most complicated Olds powerplant in many years was the Viking V-8. The new engine was a 90-degree V-type eight cylinder unit. It displaced 260 cubic inches and in dynamometer tests it was rated at 81 horsepower at 3,000 rpm. The crankshaft was drop forged and heat treated high carbon steel. It rode on three bronze-backed, babbitt main bearings.

General Motors always carried a conservative label and Oldsmobile was among its more conservative divisions. Yet there were some rather wild schemes hatched to promote the short lived Viking. Around the country Olds suggested demonstrations be staged with hired Vikings to familarize people with the new car line. The factory sold Viking costumes to its dealers for $25 and places like Chicago, Milwaukee and Columbus, Ohio saw such demonstrations.

Interior layout on the Viking was decidely different than Oldsmobiles of the era. The Viking dash panel — with an engine turned finish — was particularly attractive. The instrument panel was both directly and indirectly lit. As with most General Motors products of 1929-30 the Viking was outfitted with the VV Fisher Body windshield. Spark and choke controls were located in the instrument panel.

1930

Although the number of cars sold dropped dramatically between 1929 and 1930, Oldsmobile retained its tenth place sales standing in the auto industry. Total sales were 49,395 excluding the Viking which made its final appearance in 1930.

The 1930 models were good solid Oldsmobile rolling stock and mildly revamped editions of the successful 1929 models. Most of the innovations of that Olds era went into the ill-fated Viking, but the F-series Oldsmobiles remained the division's bread and butter cars.

Underhood lurked the familiar 197 cubic inch L-head six cylinder which for 1930 carried a horsepower rating of 62. Olds touted the simpleness and the reliability of this engine. Its features included: full pressure lubrication, automatic spark control, four bearing support for both the camshaft and the counterbalanced crankshaft and mushroom-type valve lifters that were of hollow construction and were faced with chilled cast iron.

For 1930 Oldsmobile's crankcase ventilation system drew about one-third of the carburetor air supply from the crankcase. This air entered at the oil filter port and was swept through the case to a special duct for the carburetor air cleaner. Here any water or fuel vapors were drained off. The air cleaner was of an improved design and employed an oil saturated copper mesh unit which assured an adequate air supply at all times.

Olds used an oil filter on its engines. It was connected into the pressure oiling system on the bypass plan so it didn't restrict lubrication if the filter became clogged. The lead was run through the second camshaft bearing and was drilled so it functioned as a rotary valve. At 25 miles per hour the total oil supply passed through the filter system within approximately ten minutes. The filter itself was placed in a horizontal position on the crankcase so it required very few inches of piping to connect it to the case.

The Olds wheelbase remained at 113½ inches. All closed Oldsmobile bodies were built by Fisher Body. There was a great deal of wood in the Olds-Fisher body of 1930. For example there was nine-board feet of lumber in the typical Oldsmobile door and fifteen square feet of sheet steel. The Fisher one-piece vision ventilating windshield was standard equipment on all closed models. The Olds radiator shell was chromium plated. Shutters were manually operated. Headlamps had double filament bulbs and offset parking light bulbs.

Clutches were single plate and dry disc construction. Brakes were of the mechanical type with a braking area of 244 square inches. Wheels were either wire or of the ten-spoke artillery type. Tires were 5.25 inches by 28 inches and the construction was of the full balloon type. The rear axle was of the semi-floating type with a ratio of 4.41 to 1. Delco-Remy supplied the distributor, generator, starting motor and horn on all F-30 Oldsmobiles. A fifteen gallon fuel tank was rear mounted on the frame. A new instrument panel offered the central grouping of instruments. A chrome plated beading was formed around the control panel. Lighting was indirect from behind each instrument.

In the coupes, the two door sedans and four door sedans the standard upholstery was rubber impregnated genuine mohair. The Patrician, a special deluxe trimmed version of the four door sedan, was finished in broadcloth. The convertible and phaeton, in its last year of production, were upholstered in genuine leather. The sport coupe was rumble seat equipped and the rear window lowered for ease of communication between occupants of the front and rear seats.

There were several ways an Oldsmobile could be outfitted in addition to the individual options which could be added from the factory list. Standard prices did not include bumpers or a spare tire and wheel assembly. The special equipment package was two spare tires and rims mounted in front fender wells, tire hold down irons and locks, both bumpers and a folding trunk rack. The deluxe equipment package included six wire wheels and tires mounted in welled fenders, tire hold down irons and locks, chrome plated headlights, bumpers and a folding trunk rack.

Oldsmobile base prices for the F-30 models ranged from $895 to $1,190 and weights ranged from 2,755 pounds to 3,110 pounds.

Even with the top up, the F-30 Convertible Roadster remained a handsome car. In this model Olds offered pigskin grain upholstery of genuine leather. The standard top fabric was waterproof and tan in color. The windshield could be folded down over the cowl. Landau bars were chrome plated. Other standard convertible features included: cowl ventilator, rear view mirror and automatic windshield wiper.

Wire wheeled convertibles were the more popular in that model line for 1930. With the five wire wheeled package, only 364 Convertible Roadsters were built. Base price was $1,050 and weight was 2,832 pounds. In the deluxe side-mounted wire wheeled version 1,560 were produced. Base price was $1,125 and weight was 2,895 pounds. All F-30 models rode on identical 113½ inch wheelbases as did the F-29 Oldsmobiles. Road clearance amounted to eight inches.

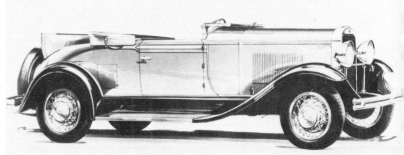

1930

Nice lines belonged to the open F-30 models, particularly the Convertible Roadsters. In standard wood wheel equipment 822 rolled off the assembly line for sale in this country and 27 more were exported. Base price was $995 and weight was 2,745. In sidemounted (special) wood wheeled equipment production equalled only 233. Base price was $1,030 and weight was 2,790 pounds. Steering ratio on all F-30 models was 16 to 1.

Olds kept much of its basic styling from the 1929 to 1930 models. The easiest way to distinguish between the two models is the rather plain hood paint scheme on the 1930 pictured as opposed to the 1929 models which had an intricate pattern on the hoods. There also was a difference in the bumper bolt patterns on the two years. Mechanically the F-29 and F-30 models were nearly identical.

Despite its rare nature, the Phaeton appears in Olds product literature of the day and it wasn't a special order unit. Upholstery was of genuine leather with a shark skin grain finish. All Phaetons had adjustable and folding windshields with chrome plated frames. The tops were of a heavy waterproof fabric with natural wooden bows. Other equipment included a cowl ventilator, automatic windshield wiper and rear view mirror.

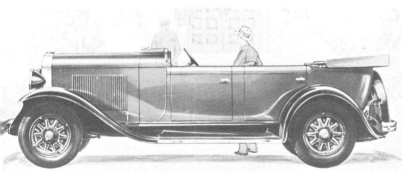

Rarest among all the F-30 Oldsmobiles was the Phaeton. It was probably for this reason that Olds would wait a decade to offer another such a factory built four-door open car. With standard wood wheel equipment 17 of this model were built with an additional 9 exported. Base price was $965, weight was 2,965 pounds. With the special package (wood sidemounts) only 5 Phaetons came off the line. Base price was $1,040 and weight was 3,045 pounds.

Although no Oldsmobile has ever officially been designated a true classic automobile, the F-30 Phaeton — by virtue of its regal lines and low production output — should be considered for classic status. As pictured with the deluxe equipment, 76 F-30 Phaetons were built. Base price was $1,095 and weight was 3,115 pounds. Technically a more rare car was the five whire wheeled Phaeton as only 5 were built. Base price was $1,020 and weight was 3,045 pounds.

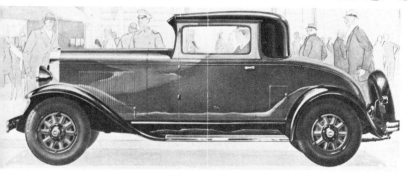

Most basic of the F-30 Oldsmobiles was the Coupe. In its non-sidemounted wood wheeled form 3,726 were produced with an additional five made for export. Base price was $895 and weight was 2,755 pounds. In wire wheel equipment without sidemounts only 343 were made with a base price of $950 and weight of 2,835 pounds. Each F-30 model came standard with four Lovejoy hydraulic shock absorbers.

Even without sidemounts the F-30 Sport Coupe had good lines and was a handsome car. In non-sidemounted wooden wheeled form production totalled 2,214 with a base price of $965 and a weight of 2,810 pounds. With five wire wheels production totalled only 584. Base price was $1,020 and weight was 2,890 pounds. All closed Oldsmobiles — except the Patrician — came equipped with genuine Mohair upholstery. All bodies were Fisher built.

The Sport Coupe offered a step up to Olds small car buyers, and had the attraction of a rumble seat and roll down rear window. In sidemounted wire wheeled (deluxe) equipment production totalled 1,594, price was $1,095 and weight was 2,960 pounds. With sidemounted wood wheels the price was $1,040, weight was 2,890 pounds and there were 478 produced.

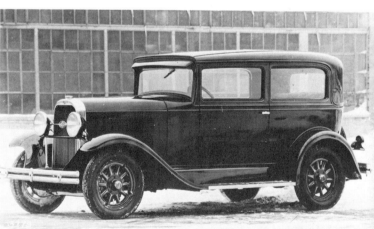

Sidemounted cars in the Coupe series were relatively rare. With six wood wheels, or the special equipment package, production totalled only 633. Base price was $950 and weight was 2,835 pounds. With six wire wheels, or the deluxe package, production of the Coupe was even less at 306. Price was $1,025 and weight was 2,905 pounds. For universal joints, the F-30's used a flexible fabric joint at the front and a sliding metal trunnion joint at the rear.

The wooden wheeled Oldsmobiles were slightly more popular in 1930 than wire wheeled units. Any base priced car — including this Two-Door Sedan — came standard with only four wood wheels and tires. Few cars left the factory, however, without a spare tire and also without bumpers which also were not standard equipment. Production on this version of the F-30 Two-Door Sedan was a whopping 9,295 with 47 extra cars built for export. Base price was $895 (excluding bumpers and a spare tire) and weight was 2,840 pounds.

As with all 1930 models, two wire wheel versions of the F-30 Two-Door Sedans were available. One model came standard with five wire wheels as pictured. It was priced at $950, weighed 2,920 pounds and 1,357 were produced. The sidemounted wire wheeled cars were called deluxe models. Only 615 of the Two-Door Sedans were built with deluxe equipment. Price was $1,025 and weight was 2,990 pounds.

Most popular among all the F-30 Oldsmobiles in all the equipment versions was the wooden wheeled, non-sidemounted Four-Door Sedan. A total of 11,841 of this popular Olds was built with 95 additional cars made for export. Price was $995, weight was 2,940 pounds. With sidemounted wood wheels this car sold for $1,070 and weighed 3,020 pounds. A total of 3,031 were made. Four-Doors came with Fisher V-V windshield, smoking set, dome light, rear view mirror, foot rail and automatic windshield wiper.

A truly handsome F-30 Olds was the wire wheeled, side-mounted (deluxe) Four-Door Sedan. In this equipment 2,973 four-doors were made. Base price was $1,125 and weight was 3,090 pounds. Note the chromed headlamps which were part of the deluxe package. With five wire wheels, four-door production was 1,242. Price was $1,050 and weight was 3,020 pounds. Each Olds was started with a 6-volt, 13-plate battery and a Delco-Remy starter.

Wooden wheeled F-30's equipped with sidemounts were known as special equipment cars. A total of 1,598 of these Two-Door Sedans were produced. Base price was $970 and weight was 2,920 pounds. All F-30 Two-Door Sedans came equipped with chair type front seats which tilted forward. Other equipment included: dome light, rear view mirror, automatic windshield wiper and rear foot rail. The driver's seat was also adjustable on this model.

This was the first year for what was to become a popular Olds model, the Patrician Sedan. This model replaced the fancy Landau sedan offered in 1928 and 1929. Not surprisingly the most popularly equipped Patrician was the side-mounted wire wheeled (deluxe) version. A total of 2,525 of this particular offering were made. Base price was $1,190 and weight was an even 3,100 pounds. With the five wire wheeled package production was only 303. Price was $1,115 and weight was 3,030 pounds.

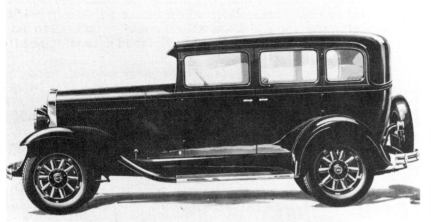

The differences in the Patrician package were mostly confined to the interior of the auto. Despite higher prices, a number of Olds buyers opted for this model. It offered special interior hardware, broadcloth upholstery, Pullman-type quarter lamps, arm rests and mahogany finished garnish moldings. With the standard wood wheel package, 1,015 were sold with 31 more exported. Base price was $1,060 and weight was 2,950 pounds. With side-mounted wood wheels production was 426, price was $1,135 and weight was 3,030 pounds.

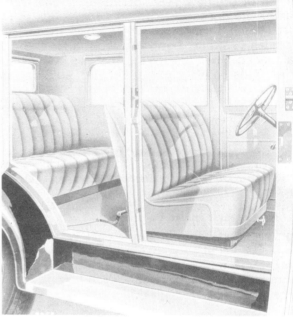

By 1930 most closed cars built by General Motors were equipped with Fisher bodies. Oldsmobile held with that trend. This photo points out some of the rather extensive use that Fisher made of wood during the era. This is the interior of a Four-Door Sedan. Interior fabric was a quality mohair. Notice the seat adjusting device which is located near the middle bottom area of the front seat. Other obvious F-30 features are the dome light and the rear foot rail.

Introduced in 1928 and virtually unchanged from 1929 to 1930 was the simple, reliable L-head six cylinder powerplant. Developing 62 horsepower from slightly more than 197 cubic inches, this was a solid motor. Features included: drop forged valves, special steel camshaft, and a gear type oil pump. Ignition came from a Delco-Remy distributor mounted atop the cylinder head.

The instrument panel of an F-30 Oldsmobile offered a central grouping of instruments. This central cluster housed an amp gauge, oil pressure indicator, coolant temperature gauge and fuel level indicator. The cluster was surrounded by a chromed beading. Lighting came indirectly from behind each instrument. Olds touted its Fisher Vision-Ventilation windshield construction which permitted the control of direct or indirect air circulation.

Every Olds closed car in 1930 had a roof which was constructed a a separate assembly of sturdy roof rails, bows and slats. This unit was then securely fastened to the overall body framework. At points of contact where metal was used, a newly developed anti-squeak material was used to separate wood and metal. Reinforcements were made within the Fisher Body wooden framework with braces of malleable iron or forged steel.

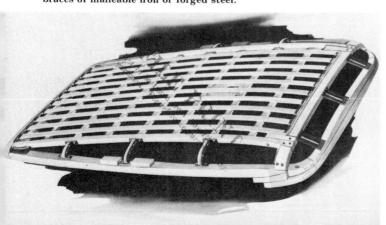

1931

Oldsmobile introduced its 1931 models on January the 5th of the new year. Strangely, 1931 was the one year in the decade of the 30's that Olds didn't start out the model year without at least two series of cars. Its sales ranking, however, was among the best for that decade for Olds. With just its six cylinder F-31 series, Oldsmobile grabbed the industry's eighth sales position on the basis of 47,279 sales.

The last of the Vikings were shuttled out of the factory by mid-1930 and the lone Olds engine offering for 1931 was the tried and true six cylinder. That powerplant carried a 3-3/16 inch bore and a 4-1/8 inch stroke which developed 65 horsepower from 197 cubic inches at 3,350 rpm. Olds improved its intake valve porting for the new year and claimed improved performance due to that change. Other Olds engine features for 1931 included: Stromberg downdraft carb, manifold heat control, block cast from close grained chrome nickel alloy iron, drop forged connecting rods, cast gray iron pistons and a cooling system fed from a Harrison cellular radiator.

For the first time Olds offered a synchromesh transmission in the new models. The term synchromesh referred to the fact that the relative speed of the gears in the transmission was controlled and synchronized so gear shifting could be performed without gear grinding and clashing. This transmission also offered helical cut second speed gears which made for more quiet overall operation.

The braking system was a duo-servo system carried over from 1930. Worm and three-tooth sector steering was also carried over from previous models. The Olds frame was strengthened by increasing the depth of the side rails. Semi-elliptic springs with anti-rattle, self adjusting shackles continued to be used.

Wheel equipment on 1931 models came down to a choice between 12-spoke demountable, painted wood wheels or wire wheels. The Deluxe model package offered by Olds in 1931 included choice of twin side-mounted wire or wood wheels, front and rear bumpers and a rear trunk platform. Standard cars came in five-wheel form and bumpers and a spare tire cost $37.50 above base price. Wire wheels came painted in black, cream or red and wood wheels could be painted to harmonize with body color or be finished naturally for $10 extra.

Fisher Bodies continued to carry a lot of wood including almost exclusive wood framing. Hardwood was found in sills, beams and pillars. Standard 1931 body color included: Venetian blue, Tokio ivory, Beau Brummel tan, black, Crockett brown, Fenway gray, Bennington blue, Bingham green and Viceroy maroon. Olds offered just one open car in 1931; the Convertible Roadster. Other models included: two coupes, Business Coupe and Sport Coupe; a Two Door Sedan and two four-doors, the Patrician Sedan and Four-Door Sedan. On closed cars choice of mohair or whipcord upholstery was offered while leather or whipcord interior fabric was offered on convertibles. The Patrician package consisted of special interior lights, silk robe cord, silk assist cords, arm rests, two ash receivers, extra quality whipcord or mohair upholstery and a special radiator cap.

In 1931 Olds sponsored a transcontinental good roads tour which commemorated the run made by the Curved Dash "Old Scout" in 1905. "Old Scout" reran its original tour from New York to Portland in 1931 accompanied by an escort of new Oldsmobile sedans. The original Olds driver Dwight B. Huss again led the Olds caravan and the company reaped a great deal of publicity out of this program as it got its zone people involved from coast to coast.

By 1931, Olds had 26 factory buildings within its Lansing complex of 87 acres. Olds Motor Works was capable of building and shipping 800 autos each working day. This meant a new car could come off the end of the assembly line every 41 seconds. Fisher Body operated its plant on the Olds grounds in 1931.

The Convertible Roadster with five wood wheels was a very rare F-31 Oldsmobile as only 124 were built. Cost of this model was $935 and weight was 2,965 pounds. Accessory group number three for standard models included the following: front and rear bumpers, spare tire, wheel, tube and lock, special radiator cap, spring covers, fender lights, metal tire cover, spot light and Waltham clock. List installed price for this group was $103.

The most basic Olds offering in 1931 was the Business Coupe. In the production run of wire wheeled cars a total of 802 sidemounted business coupes were made with a base price of $910 and weight of 3,040 pounds. With five wire wheels, production was 1,364, price was $845 and weight was 2,990 pounds. Shatterproof glass was an option on 1931 Oldsmobiles and this option added $30 to the price of either coupe model.

1931

Country clubbers went wild about the sidemounted Convertible Roadster. Price on this car was $1,000, weight was 3,010 pounds. Production totalled 1,179. Note the fold down windshield which was used exclusively on this model. This car is equipped with accessory number 398733, the metal spare tire cover. It could be purchased finished either in black or matching body colors and sold for $11 each installed.

The sportiest F-31 Oldsmobile was again the Convertible Roadster and it was a suprisingly popular car this model year. In five-wheel form it cost $935, weighed 2,965 pounds and 233 were made. But with wire sidemounted wheels, production jumped to 1,964 with an even $1,000 price tag. Weight was 3,010 pounds. Most convertibles came like this one with black top, but a light tan top was available with certain body colors.

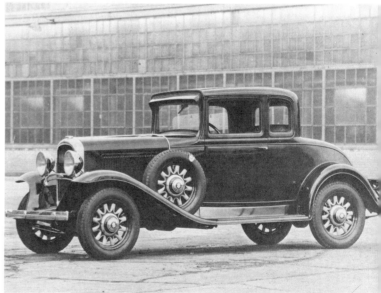

In base form, Oldsmobiles came without bumpers. To add them cost $20 over the list price on each Olds model. Bumpers were also included in certain option groups of the day. The Sport Coupe with five wire or wood wheels cost $895 and it weighed 3,065 pounds. In five wheeled form production was 858 and as shown with wood wheels it was only 687. Factory seat covers were offered. List price for covers for the Sport Coupe was $10 per set or $11 installed.

Wood wheels gave the 1931 Oldsmobile Business Coupe a more massive appearance. Production of the sidemounted (deluxe) Business Coupe with wood wheels was only 475. Base price was $910 and shipping weight was 3,040 pounds. The five-wood-wheeled model sold for $845, weighed 2,990 pounds and 1,059 were built. Standard 1931 equipment included: rear view mirror, automatic windshield wiper, chrome plated head lamps and hydraulic shock absorbers.

1931

If golf was your game then two F-31 models had just the right place to stash your clubs. The Convertible Roadster and Sport Coupe had a handy behind-the-door hatch that was just right to load a couple of bags of golf clubs. This car is outfitted with a couple of interesting accessories. The full chromium finished spot light sold for $16.50 installed. The novel fender lights were not really lights at all—but rather chrome plated reflectors styled to match the headlights. They sold for $6 a pair installed.

Wire wheels looked good on the rumble seated F-31 Sport Coupe. With the Deluxe (sidemounted) package this model cost $960 and weighed 3,115 pounds. Production was 2,067 on wire wheeled models and 1,288 on the wooden wheeled cars. Olds called its F-31 engine "a high compression, six cylinder engine of simple, quiet L-head construction." That powerplant dated back to 1928 and developed 65 horsepower from 197 cubic inches.

A solidly popular car in the F-31 lineup was the Two-Door Sedan. As with all 1931 Oldsmobiles, it was offered in two wooden wheeled versions. With five wheels, it sold for $845, weighed 3,105 pounds and 2,519 were produced. With sidemounted wood wheels it cost $910, weight was 3,155 pounds and 1,756 were made. The two door models had front seats that tilted forward for easy entrance to the rear seat area.

This five wire wheeled F-31 Two Door Sedan sold for $845 and weighed 3,105 pounds. A total of 2,804 of this version of the two door sedan were made. With sidemounted wire wheels the price rose to $910, weight was 3,155 pounds and production was 2,077. Special interior appointments within the two door sedans included a dome light and a rear seat foot rail.

1931

Four Doors continued to be a popular car line for the Olds Motor Works in 1931. A sidemounted wire wheeled Four Door Sedan had a base price of $990, weighed 3,260 pounds and saw a production run of 5,177. With five wire wheels the price was $925, weight was 3,210 pounds and a total of 4,116 were built. Special four door appointments included: two ash receivers, arm rests, dome light and rear foot rail.

Five wooden wheels kept this F-31 Four Door Sedan rolling. Base price on this version was $925, weight was 3,210 pounds and there was a production total of 3,620. This car was equipped with a fabric spare tire cover. Although not listed in the official Olds accessory book, many dealers stocked and sold accessories like this. Some Olds fabric tire covers carried the Oldsmobile name, emblem, dealership name or even list price of the various models.

The luxury cruiser of the F-31 fleet was again the Patrician Sedan. With wooden sidemounted wheels this model -the most expensive 1931 Olds - cost $1,025. Weight was 3,270 pounds. With five wooden wheels the base priced Patrician cost $960, weighed 3,220 pounds and had production of only 510. The Patrician package consisted of special upholstery, Pullman type quarter lamps and assist cords for rear passengers.

The most popular F-31 built was the wooden sidemounted Four-Door Sedan. Production for this model so equipped was 5,309. It carried a base price of $990 and weighed 3,260 pounds. This car also carried the $16.50 (installed price) spot light and a pair of cowl lights. An interior control located above the VV Fisher Body windshield permitted the windshield to be raised or lowered for ventilation.

Surprisingly popular - despite its relatively hefty price tag - was the F-31 Patrician Sedan. Pictured here in side-mounted wire wheels the base price was $1,025 and weight was 3,270 pounds. Production of this version was 3,457. With only five wire wheels the base price was $960, weight was 3,220 pounds and only 448 were made. The Patrician featured a special bird-like ornamental radiator cap that could be ordered on any other model for $5. No, Crestline did not make a mistake by letting a photo stamped "File Print" sneak into the book. This simply was the only original photo that could be found of this particular car.

Front styling of the standard Oldsmobile lineup was redone for 1931. The Olds radiator was of Harrison hexagon honeycomb design. Its capacity was 13 quarts and it was covered by a chromium plated shell and grille. Water temperature was told by a dash mounted indicator. Temperature could be controlled by hand operated radiator shutters.

The major component in the deluxe package was dual sidemounted tires. Again in 1931 Oldsmobile offered no single sidemounted cars. Tires for all models were of the 28 x 5.25 inch variety of non-skid ballon cord construction. Bumpers were available in several option packages in 1931, but as an option by themselves front and rear bumpers cost $20 installed and few cars left the factory without them.

Olds had used the same basic powerplant since 1928, upgrading the six cylinder unit in performance slightly each year. For 1931 all Oldsmobiles were six cylinder powered. This was the only year of the decade that some form of eight cylinder engine wasn't built by Oldsmobile. Sales literature of the time called the powerplant "ample horsepowered and exceptionally efficient." A decal on the engine block advised the use of SAE 20 oil in the winter and SAE 30 in the summer.

Oldsmobile recreated is famous 1905 coast to coast (New York to Portland) run in 1931. In addition to the original driver - Dwight Huss - making the rerun were a fleet of F-31 sedans called "Trail Blazers." Olds got its sales zones from across the country involved in this promotion and it got a fair amount of publicity.

Most of the fleet of "Trail Blazers" for the 1931 Olds coast to coast run were five-wood-wheeled Four-Door Sedans. One reason for the 1931 rerun was to show how far roads had improved over a 25-year period. These particular Oldsmobiles were finished in non-stock colors and featured bold lettering schemes which told of the special purpose cars.

1931

One distinct advantage of owning a sidemounted Olds was that it was easier to carry a trunk. Each sidemounted car came with this trunk platform. Three different trunks were offered - one for the coupes and roadsters, one for two-door sedans and one for four door sedans. The trunks were painted with factory colors and sold for $30 installed.

Again in 1931 production was just about evenly divided between wire and wood wheeled cars and sidemounted and non-sidemounted autos. The deluxe package - which was available on any of the six Olds body styles - included: six wire or wood wheels, six tires and tubes, bumpers-front and rear, folding trunk platform, welled fenders and tire locking devices.

The dash layout on the F-31 Olds was very simple. The far left gauge told water temperature. Next was an AC produced speedometer/odometer which also housed a trip odometer. The next gauge was a dual amp and oil pressure gauge. On the far right was a fuel level indicator. A center cluster housed the ignition key along with controls for lights, radiator shutters and choke.

Overall interior level on the F-31 Oldsmobiles remained at or near the Spartan mark. A floor mounted lever operated the parking brake which worked on both front and rear wheels. A floor mounted pedal directly actuated a Delco-Remy starting motor. A single windshield wiper was standard equipment on 1931 models. The windshield could be raised slightly to allow air flow to passengers.

As with most General Motors products of the era, Oldsmobiles came outfitted with Fisher Bodies. One area in which Fisher claimed to have done a lot of research was in seat design. This cutaway photo shows the spring construction within an F-31 seat. These seats were adjustable. Olds upholstery options included whipcord, mohair and sometimes leather.

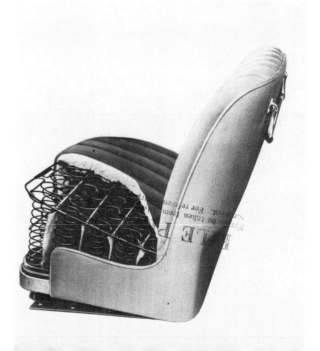

1932

In the sales race Oldsmobile dropped to twelfth position with total 1932 model sales of 19,169. The big news of the new model year was the return to a two model format which departed Oldsmobile in 1930 with the death of the short-lived Viking lineup. For 1932 there were six cylinder models and eight cylinder models designed as F-Series (6) and L-Series (8) cars.

It was very difficult to distinguish between the two series of 1932 Oldsmobiles without a glance in the engine compartment. Bodies, wheelbase and external trim were identical on six and eight cylinder cars. The only readily noticeable difference was that the eights had double windshield wipers and the sixes were equipped with a single wiper arm.

The Depression was firmly entrenched by 1932 and Olds was particularly vulnerable as indicated by its declining sales figures and traditional position in the middle of the GM automotive ladder. General Motors gave some serious thought to dropping or combining some of its vehicle building divisions. Although this did not take place, a corporate arm called B.O.P. (Buick-Oldsmobile-Pontiac) was formed to handle various marketing and manufacturing aspects of these three formerly independent divisions. Dealers resisted the idea and folks in Lansing didn't take too kindly to being lumped with their frequent rivals from the eastern part of the state. B.O.P. was never fully implemented and by the middle of the 1933 model year it went the way of other not too well layed out corporate schemes.

A great deal of the Oldsmobile news for 1932 came in the form of engines: a pepped up six cylinder which could be easily traced back to 1928 and a new straight eight powerplant which Olds dealers welcomed as far less complicted than the last Oldsmobile try at an 8, the ill-fated Viking V-8.

A bore of 3-5/16 and a 4⅛ inch stroke gave the tried and true six a displacement of slightly more than 213 cubic inches. Its horsepower rating was bumped up to 74 at 3,200 rpm. The six cylinder crankshaft rode on four bronze backed main bearings. Carburetion came from a single throat Stromberg downdraft unit.

The new straight eight had a displacement of 240 cubic inches. Horsepower was rated at 87. The engine used five large main bearings for crankshaft support.

Features common to both engines included: one-piece block casting of close grained chrome nickel alloy iron, cast iron pistons, a new automatic choke system, automatic heat control for incoming fuel, a

Model year 1932 brought some up-front styling changes to the Oldsmobile line as well as both six and eight cylinder models for the first time in many years. Both cars shared a 116½ inch wheelbase and there were few distinguishing appointments between the six and eight models without lifting the hood to see what lurked there. Six cylinder cars came in standard trim with only one windshield wiper, as seen here, while the eights came with a dual wiper setup.

A truly dashing Oldsmobile was the Six Cylinder Olds Convertible Roadster with five wire wheels. Price on this open model was $955 and curb weight was 3,025 pounds. Only 88 of this model were built. With wood wheels production totalled 53 in five-wheeled form and 249 with side-mounted wood wheels. The base six cylinder Olds engine dated back to 1928 with the 1932 version getting 74 horsepower from 213 cubic inches.

This flawlessly restored 1932 Olds Convertible Roadster with sidemounts — and powered by a six cylinder engine — was a national prize winner restored by Don Spieldenner of Fremont, Ohio and later sold to Asher Brunes of Indianapolis. List price on the six wire wheeled convertible was $1,000 and production totalled only 333. Weight was 3,045 pounds. Blocks on all 1932 Oldsmobiles were of a special nickel alloy cast iron.

1932

"Remo-Injector" decarbonizer, an oil temperatu[re] regulator, rifle drilled connecting rods, a larger 1[?] quart cooling system with improved water pump an[d] a redesigned cooling fan.

Olds carried over its synchromesh three spee[d] transmission from 1931 and this was the only unit o[f] fered. A new, curious and short-lived free wheelin[g] unit was found on all 1932 Oldsmobiles. The rear ax[le] shafts were made substantially stronger on the ne[w] models. Olds offered a standard rear end ratio of 4.5[?] to 1 and a "mountain" gear set of 4.77 to 1.

Double action Delco-Lovejoy hydraulic shock a[b] sorbers were now standard equipment. A rid[e] regulating system was built into the shocks of eac[h] car and it was remotely controlled by a lever mounte[d] on the instrument panel. Chassis lubrication was vi[a] Alemite-Zerk push type high pressure fittings.

Wheel equipment on 1932 models was optional be[?] tween five and six demountable painted wood wheel[s] or wire wheels. The size of the wheels was reduced on[e] size over 1931 models while tires were increased on[e] size hence a 17 x 6.00 wheel-tire combination.

On the Fisher Body itself the external sun visor wa[s] eliminated, body design was slightly updated, ne[w] and larger fenders were added, hood doors (whic[h] could be ordered in chrome) replace fixed slots or hoo[d] louvers. Either mohair or whipcord was the standar[d] upholstery material used with extra wide panels an[d] special narrow piping on Patrician and Sport Coup[e] models. The wheelbase was up to 116½, a three inch in[?] crease over 1931 models. Olds also employed a grea[t] deal more usage of special insulating and soun[d] deadening materials in the new cars.

In 1932 the Olds plants covered 87 acres in Lansing[.] Oldsmobile was in competition with 40 other makes o[f] automobile built by 25 different U.S. manufacturers[.]

Wooden wheels and sidemounts nicely set off the rumble seated Six Cylinder Sport Coupe. Sidemounted versions of this car sold for $970, weight was 3,190 pounds. Sidemounted production totalled 420 in the wooden wheeled cars and 389 in the wire wheeled machines. Of the five-wheeled models 209 of the wood jobs were built, with 157 wire wheeled cars coming off the line. Each six cylinder car had Delco-Remy distributor, generator and starting motor.

More popular among the Six Cylinder Two Door Sedan buyers were the wood wheeled cars. The sidemounted job shown here was priced at $920, weighed 3,210 pounds and had a production of 539. In five-wheeled form it sold for $875, weighed 3,165 pounds and saw 1,045 produced. Whitewall tires were a popular 1932 option and they cost $7.50 on five wheeled cars and $9 on six wheeled models.

The most basic of all six cylinder Oldsmobiles was the Business Coupe. Shown here is the five-wire-wheeled model which sold for $875 and weighed 3,040 pounds. Only 323 of this car were made in this combination. With sidemounts a Six Cylinder Business Coupe went for $920. Production totalled 159 for the sidemounted wood wheeled car and 164 for the sidemounted wire wheeled car. In five-wooden-wheeled form, 437 of this model were made. Each Olds carried a sixteen gallon fuel tank.

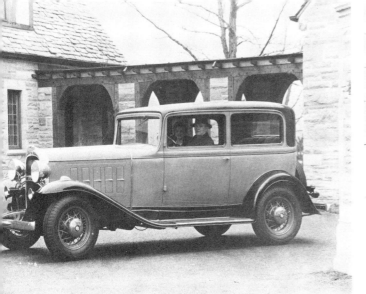

This Six Cylinder Two-Door Sedan with five wire wheels was priced at only $875 and weighed 3,165 pounds. Production of this version totalled 784. A sidemounted sedan with wire wheels cost $920, weight was 3,205 pounds and production was 436. Accessory group number one — for non-sidemounted cars — was a strongly suggested option that included front and rear bumper, electric clock, spare wheel lock and radiator cap lock. Price was $33.

The Six Cylinder Four Door Sedan with five wire wheels had a production run of 1,055. Base price on this model was $955 and weight was 3,240 pounds. All 1932 Oldsmobiles came standard with 6.00 x 17 non skid balloon cord tires. Four Lovejoy double action hydraulic shock absorbers were also standard. Olds continued to use mechanical brakes on all its 1932 models.

1932

In sidemounted form the Six Cylinder Four Door Sedan was a handsome car. Its base price was an even $1,000 and it weighed 3,285 pounds. Production totalled 1,295. All 1932 Oldsmobiles used a three speed manual transmission. Both models of the 1932 Olds also used a free-wheeling feature which was of the roller type design.

Wood wheels made a nice looking package on the Six Cylinder Four Door Sedan. Production of this five wheeled model totalled 1,548. Base price was $955 and weight was 3,250 pounds. Safety glass was standard on all 1932 Oldsmobile windshields. The manufacturer was Libbey Owens Ford. An optional feature was safety glass in all other windows.

Most popular among all the 1932 Oldsmobiles was the Six Cylinder wooden wheeled sidemounted Four Door Sedan. Production of this model was 2,002. It weighed 3,295 pounds and was priced at $1,000. Although this car is not so equipped, any 1932 model could be ordered with chromium plated hood doors. These units were made of sheet brass and chromed. Price was $12.50 installed.

Rounding out the six cylinder lineup in fine fashion was the other Oldsmobile four door sedan, the Patrician. This model differed from the standard four door chiefly due to its fancier interior trimmings. With five wood wheels, the Patrician cost $990, and weighed 3,260 pounds — 146 were made. With sidemounted wood wheels the price was $1,035, weight was 3,305 pounds and production was 1,040. With five wire wheels price was $990, weight was 3,250 and production totalled 90. In sidemounted wire wheels, price was $1,035, weight was 3,295 and 838 were made.

1932

Rarest among the 1932 Oldsmobiles was the Business Coupe equipped with an eight cylinder engine. Five wheeled versions of this model sold for $975 with the sidemounted cars selling for $1,020. Production totalled 37 for five-wood wheeled models, 61 for sidemounted wood-wheeled coupes, 52 for five-wire wheeled cars and 66 for sidemounted wire-wheeled machines. Shipping weight on this model was 3,365 pounds. The eight cylinder Olds engine displaced 240 cubic inches and developed 87 horsepower.

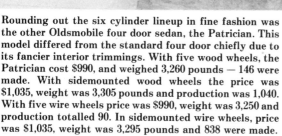

The sidemounted Eight Cylinder Oldsmobile Sport Coupe was just the car for a fair weather trip to the weekend estate. With wood wheels this sidemounted model sold for $1,070 and weighed 3,495 pounds. Production totaled 163. In five-wheeled wooden form price was $1,025, weight was 3,440 pounds and only 44 were produced. Each 1932 Olds came with a semi-floating, pressed steel, one-piece housing rear end. The standard ratios were either 4.56 or 4.77 to one.

The rumble seated Sport Coupe was another relatively low production eight cylinder Oldsmobile. Riding on five wire wheels this model was priced at $1,025 and weighed 3,460 pounds. Only 40 of this model were produced. With wire wheels and sidemounts the base price was $1,070, weight was 3,505 pounds and production totalled 229. Each 1932 Olds was equipped with dual Delco Remy vibrator horns.

Another very low production 1932 Oldsmobile was the Eight Cylinder Two-Door Sedan. Production totals were as follows: 52 five-wood wheeled, 75 sidemounted wood wheeled, 70 five-wire wheeled and 74 sidemounted wire wheeled. The five wheeled cars had a base price of $975 and the sidemounted cars sold for $1,020. Shipping weight was 3,480 pounds. Carburetion on the eight cylinders came from a Duplex downdraft carb with an automatic choke.

1932

Big seller in the Eight Cylinder Olds series was the Patrician. In sidemounted form its $1,135 base price tag made this the most expensive Olds for 1932. In five wire wheeled trim weight was 3,565 pounds and production was only 86. In sidemounted wire wheels weight was 3,610 pounds and production was 1,071. With five wood wheels, as shown here, weight was 3,575 pounds and production totalled only 95. In sidemounted wood wheels weight was 3,615 pounds and production was 1,010. The base price on five-wheeled models was $1,090.

Lines of the sidemounted 1932 Olds were elegant and probably the closest thing the division ever built to a true classic car. Production on the Eight Cylinder Four Door Sedan totalled 507 with wire sidemounted wheels. Base price was $1,100 and weight was 3,600 pounds. With six sidemounted wood wheels the price was again $1,100, weight was 3,610 pounds and output was 698. Eight cylinder Olds pistons were cast of a special gray iron and electro plated.

In the four-door models the lines of the Fisher built bodies were particularly graceful. In the five-wheeled models the wire wheeled job sold for $1,055, weighed 3,555 pounds and production totalled 246. With five wood wheels the base price remained the same, weight was 3,565 pounds and production was up to 279. Eight cylinder Oldsmobiles used a single dry disc clutch which was $9\frac{7}{8}$ inches in diameter.

The lone open car in the 1932 Eight Cylinder lineup was the Convertible Roadster. With five wood wheels it sold for $1,055, weighed 3,340 pounds and only 12 were built. In sidemounted wood wheels the base price was $1,100, weight was 3,385 pounds and 128 were made. Five wire wheeled models cost $1,055, weighed 3,330 pounds and 35 were produced. With wire sidemounted wheels base price was $1,100, weight was 3,360 and production totalled 219. Convertible tops came in black or light tan depending on car body color.

Each Oldsmobile rode on a chassis of 116½ inches. Olds touted the even distribution of weight on the chassis and also talked about its low enter of gravity. Shock absorbers could be controlled via a dashboard mounted lever known as the ride regulator. Olds used double action Lovejoy shocks. This feature didn't wear too well and its rare to see a 1932 Olds with a functioning ride regulator.

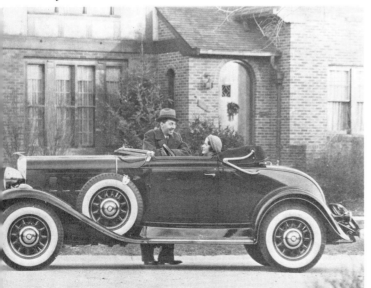

The resting place for the spare tire on a 1932 Olds was behind the rear body on sedans. Although the wood wheeled car in this photograph is not so equipped, there were several tire covers available from the factory. These were metal covers with one or two chrome strips around them. The cover cost $12 in black or $13 finished in a factory color. Note the passenger side taillight carried the Olds logo and the driver's side was a license plate holder.

In 1932 Oldsmobile's Fisher Body still contained a great deal of wood particularly in the top area. The roof assembly was a sub-assembly process in the Fisher factory and required people skilled in working with wood. Roof rails, bows and slats had to be securely mortised, glued, screwed and then bolted to the entire body framework. Anti squeak material was used to separate the wood and metal construction.

The rear end of sidemounted Oldsmobiles looked like this, with the luggage platform being part of the sidemount package. Three separate factory trunks were offered in 1932 with models for the two door sedan, four door sedans and one for coupes and convertibles. Construction was wood with a covering of heavy gauge steel and chrome trim. Price for the trunk in black was $30 installed, with two dollars extra charged if it was painted a color. Specially fitted luggage was also offered for the Olds trunk.

The interior of the 1932 models was nicely laid out. A far right gauge indicated fuel level while a far left gauge told of the battery charging system. On the near left was a large dial type speedometer and odometer and the large right hand cluster housed a water temperature indicator and oil pressure gauge. From left to right the knobs across the bottom of the dash were for free wheeling control, lights, radiator shutters and cigar lighter.

Olds offered only dual sidemounted cars in 1932, while other manufacturers would sell a car with only one sidemounted fender. The factory sidemounted package included: six wheels, tires, tubes; two welled fenders, holdown clamps, tire locks and a luggage trunk platform on the rear. A choice of wire wheels or demountable painted wood wheels was offered. Blackwall tires came standard and optional tire covers were available for the fender mounted tires.

1933

The year 1933 brought a newly restyled Oldsmobile lineup. The previous year the Six and the newly introduced Eight models shared the same chassis and wheelbase, but in 1933 the Eight became a larger car from the ground up. The Six was based on a 115-inch wheelbase, while the Eight grew to a 119-inch wheelbase.

The new styling apparently made a bit of an impression as Oldsmobile moved into ninth place with 36,648 model year sales and calendar year sales of 36,072.

Colors offered included black, two greens, three blues, maroon, gray and brown. Three types of upholstery were used: mohair, whipcord, and leather as an option on the convertibles. Dash panels on the 1933's were among the most striking ever offered by Olds. A grain walnut dash finish was featured and it housed a speedometer similar to 1932 and a second cluster holding an ammeter, oil pressure gauge, gas gauge and temperature indicator.

On the mechanical side, the bore on the Six was increased to 3-3/8-inch with the stroke remaining at 4-1/8 inch. Displacement was up from 213 to 221 cubic inches on the Six. The Eight maintained a displacement of 240 cubic inches. Six cylinder engines were rated at 80 hp while the Eights produced 90 hp. Both models had 16-gallon fuel tanks. Standard tires on the Six were 5:50x17 non-skid balloons, while the Eight utilized 6.00x17 of the same construction. Free wheeling was dropped in 1933, but an automatic clutch was offered as a rarely ordered factory option.

The two series of Oldsmobiles were easily told apart and Eights offered particularly striking styling with an unusual grille treatment. Sidemounts remained an option on both series. Four-doors remained the most popular model and the Sixes continued to sell far better than the Eights.

Several unique marketing approaches were used in 1933. Advertising proclaimed Oldsmobiles as the "style leaders." And in a tie-in with the world of style and fashion, a national program was adopted where new Olds models were displayed at leading department stores across the country. A 1933 Eight was an official car at the Indianapolis 500, but did not handle race pacing duties.

One particularly confusing bit of Olds model terminology began in 1933 and was carried on for several years. Two models of both the 5-passenger coupe and the sedan were offered. The offerings which carried the larger, built-in trunks were called touring coupes and touring sedans. Some confusion existed between these names and the earlier touring car designations hung on open cars.

In November of 1933, C. L. McCuen, who was to bring many innovations to the Oldsmobile product line in years to come, was named president and general manager of the division.

The L-series eight cylinders and the F series six cylinder cars were similar looking in 1933. The cars were completely restyled, however, when compared to 1932 Oldsmobiles. Grilles for the two series were distinctly different and the F series used a 115 inch wheelbase while the L series rode on a 119 inch wheelbase. The free wheeling feature used on previous Oldsmobiles was dropped.

The most basic of the 1933 Oldsmobiles, and also the least expensive, was the F-33 Business Coupe, model number 33407 which weighed 3,045 pounds. A total of 1,361 five-steel wheeled models were made with an additional 100 sidemounted cars sold. Seventy-nine five-wire-wheeled F-33 Business Coupes were produced, with seven more sidemounted wire wheel cars made. In 1933 Olds used full mechanical, servo-type brakes with steel brake cables.

Extra luggage capacity was a special feature of the F-33 Five Passenger Touring Coupe, model number 33431. List price on this model was $775 and weight was 3,185 pounds. A total of 4,940 of the five-steel wheeled model were built with 484 additional cars sidemounted with steel wheels. A total of 35 more cars were made with five wire wheels and five more came with sidemounted wire wheels. The 1933 F-series battery was a 6-volt model with 13 plates and an 86 ampere hour capacity.

1933

Oldsmobile's F-33 Sport Coupe carried model number 33428. This model was priced at $780 and weighed 3,105 pounds. The production total for cars factory equipped with five steel wheels was 1,431 with an additional 286 steel wheeled cars sidemounted. Only 18 cars came with five wire wheels from the factory and three more F-33 Sport Coupes came with wire wheels and sidemounts. Olds offered a synchromesh transmission on both F and L series cars for 1933 and advertising of the era touted the "silent second gear."

By far the rarest 1933 F series Olds was the Convertible, model number 33418. Priced at $825, this model weighed 3,155 pounds. Production broke down this way: 196 five-steel wheeled models, 119 sidemounted steel-wheeled models, and one each of the five-wire-wheeled and side-mounted wire wheeled models. All F series cars came equipped with an 80 horsepower, six cylinder powerplant. Top speed for the Six was advertised at 75 to 80 mph.

The F-33 Five Passenger Coupe was model number 33401. List price on this model was $745 and weight was 3,195 pounds. A total of 3,880 of the standard equipped (5-steel wheels) cars were built with 88 steel wheeled sidemounted cars made. A total of 110 of the five-wire wheeled models were produced but no cars with sidemounts and wire wheels were made. Oil capacity on the six cylinder models was 6 quarts, while the Harrison vee-type radiator held 17 quarts. Standard tire size was 5.50 x 17.

The most popular car among all the 1933 Oldsmobiles was the F-33 Four-Door Sedan. Model number 33409 cost $825 and it weighed 3,215 pounds. A total of 6,360 of the five-steel-wheeled version were made with 474 steel-wheeled cars sold with sidemounts. Wire wheeled production saw 353 five-wheeled models made, while 7 more sidemounted cars were built. F series cars came with down-draft car-buretion, automatic choke and a "Remo Injector" decar-bonizer.

A handsome 1933 L-series offering was the Sport Coupe, model number 33428. Base price on this model was $880 and it weighed 3,350 pounds. A total of 559 five-steel-wheeled cars were made with an additional 251 steel-wheeled sidemounted L series Sport Coupes built. In the wire wheel area only nine five-wire-wheeled models were made with eight sidemounted wire wheeled cars made. Carburetion on the L-series came from a Duplex down draft with an automatic choke, combination air cleaner and intake silencer and a "Remo Injector" decarbonizer.

The most luggage capacity of all F-33 models belonged to the Four-Door Touring Sedan, model number 33419. This was also the heaviest and most expensive six cylinder Olds, costing $855 and weighing 3,255 pounds. The production breakdown went as follows: 3,960 of the five-steel wheeled models, 1,683 of the sidemounted steel wheeled cars, 39 of the five-wire-wheeled F-33's and 38 sidemounted wire wheeled cars. The steering gear of all F-33's was semi-irriversible and of the three worm and sector type. Steering ratio was 16 to 1.

Winter protection was adequate even on the open 1933 Oldsmobiles. The L-33 Convertible, model number 33418, was priced at $925 and weighed 3,305 pounds. An extremely rare car, the production breakdown on the L-33 Convertible went: 146 five-steel-wheeled, 115 sidemounted steel wheeled, 4 five-wire-wheeled and two sidemounted wire wheeled. Cooling on the eight cylinder cars came via a Harrison vee-type radiator, 19 quarts of coolant and a belt driven four-blade fan.

There were a pair of Five Passenger Coupes offered in 1933. The L-33 Five Passenger Coupe, model 33401 was not even listed in most Olds product literature of the era. It was priced at $845 and weighed 3,320 pounds. The production breakdown was: 183 five-steel-wheeled, 17 steel-wheeled sidemounted, two five-wire-wheeled and one wire-wheeled sidemounted. The larger trunked L-33 Five Passenger Touring Coupe, model number 33431, was displayed here in a department store setting. This model sold for $875 and weighed 3,360 pounds. Production for the L-33 Five Passenger Touring Coupe was: 1,493 five-steel-wheeled, 372 steel-wheeled sidemounted, 26 five-wire-wheeled and 10 wire-wheeled sidemounted.

1933

Most expensive among the 1933 Oldsmobiles was the L-33 Touring Sedan, model number 33419. Priced at $955 this oddly enough was the largest production eight cylinder Olds of 1933. It weighed 3,445 pounds. The production breakdown was: 2,516 of the five-steel-wheeled car, 1,773 of the steel-wheeled sidemounted Olds, 26 of the five-wire-wheeled car and 42 of the sidemounted wire-wheeled Olds. The L-series battery was a 6-volt, 13-plate 98 ampre hour capacity unit.

Those looking for basic transportation in the eight cylinder Oldsmobile looked to the L-33 Business Coupe, model number 33407. Base price for this model was $845 and weight was 3,295 pounds. The production breakdown was: 314 five-steel-wheeled cars, 62 sidemounted steel-wheeled cars, 17 five-wire-wheeled cars and three side-mounted wire wheeled cars. The L-series engine was a 90 horsepower, 240 cubic inch job. The engine was mounted in rubber on three-point controlled cushioned mountings.

In 1933 a L-33 Convertible served as an Official Car at the Indianapolis Motor Speedway. It is unclear if the car had any on-track duties. However it was used on official business by Speedway president Captain Eddie Ricken-backer and other speedway officials. All 1933 Oldsmobiles started with the double drop X frame. Another 1933 Olds feature was Fisher No-Draft Ventilation.

One of the more popular eight cylinders was the L-33 Four-Door Sedan, model number 33409. Priced at $925 this machine weighed 3,440 pounds. A total of 2,137 five-steel-wheeled cars were built with an additional 419 steel-wheeled sidemounted cars made. Wire wheeled production included 61 of the five-wheeled type and 22 of the side-mounted version. All L-series cars rode on a 119 inch wheelbase. The standard tire was 6.00 x 17 non skid balloon cords.

There were a few bare chassis produced by Oldsmobile in 1933 including this nice looking L-series car complete with custom coachwork believed to have been done in Germany. Olds made a great deal out of the improved smoothness of its new models from a ride standpoint. Threaded spring shackles were used in 1933 to improve ride and Lovejoy double-action shock absorbers also were standard equipment in 1933.

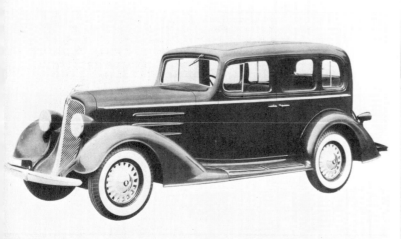

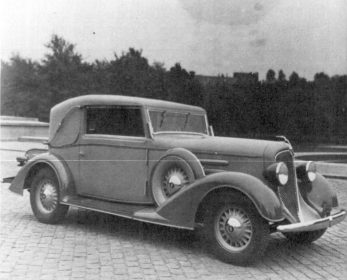

1934

Changes for 1934 came largely on the mechanical side. They included: 4-wheel hydraulic brakes, knee action suspension, a ride stabilizer system, central control steering and Fisher No-Draft ventilation.

This new mechanical package met with widespread customer approval and a model year total of 79,814 was good enough for a climb into sixth place. Calendar year production totaled 82,150.

Two distinctive series, the Six and Eight, continued to be offered with the Six remaining by far the bigger seller. The Eight continued on a 119-inch wheelbase, while the wheelbase of the Six was dropped one inch to 114 inches.

Horsepower on the Six was upped to 84 by virtue of raising the compression ratio slightly. Olds sales literature of the day claimed 17 miles per gallon for the Six at a steady 50 mph. A top speed of 78 mph was also claimed. Specifications for the Eight remained unchanged from 1933.

Colors included: black, maroon, green, two blues, beige and green. Interiors were offered in mohair, whipcord, Bedford cloth, and leather. A growing list of factory accessories were highlighted by Air Mate and Air Chief radios, hot water heater, bumper guards and specially fitted luggage.

Despite progress by other manufacturers to all-metal construction, Oldsmobile Fisher bodies for 1934 used considerable wood framing. Standard tire size on the Six remained 5:50 x 17, while the Eight models came standard with 7:00 x 16. Six models could also be ordered with 6:50 x 16 tires as an option.

Late in 1934, Oldsmobile began an expansion of its production facilities. A total of $2½ million was spent on new machinery, enlargement of assembly lines and the rearrangement of other factory equipment. New equipment included: larger fender presses, new heat treat furnaces, additional crankshaft machining equipment and an enlarged docking area for car shipment.

The price leader among the 1934 Oldsmobiles was the F-Series Business Coupe, model number 34457. This car carried the low price tag of $675 and weighed 2,980 pounds. Production stood at 3,724 with four additional cars made for export. All F series cars were powered by a 213 cubic inch six cylinder engine developing 84 horsepower. Top speed of between 75 mph to 80 mph was claimed by Olds literature of the day.

The Oldsmobile Six

Sidemounts were particularly attractive on model 34457, the sidemounted F Series Business Coupe. Production on this car totalled only 206 with no exports. It was priced at $750 and weighed 3,075 pounds. Each 1934 F Series Olds came with a 15-plate, 100-ampere-hour battery. The manufacturer claimed this unit could handle cars equipped with options like a radio or spotlight.

There were several major differences between the F-Series and L-Series cars. Shown here is a sidemounted F-Series model. All six cylinders were built on a 114-inch wheelbase, had distinctively different radiator mascots and grilles. The crank hole cover also indicated the number of cylinders the car had. Unlike some manufacturers, Olds built only twin sidemounted cars in 1934. All five-wheeled cars had rear mounted spare tires.

1934

For those desiring a bit more room in their six cylinder piece of transportation there was the F-Series Five Passenger Coupe, model number 34451. The non-sidemounted version of this car was priced at $705 and weighed 3,055 pounds. Production totalled 4,628 with four more cars exported. The sidemounted six cylinder Five Passenger Coupe cost $780 and weighed 3,150 pounds. Only 47 of these cars were made. Olds touted the fact that its engine bearings were of the thin wall construction type in 1934.

The main distinguishing feature on 1934 Olds Sport Coupes was the rumble seat equipment. Costing $715, the F-Series Sport Coupe weighed 3,040 pounds. Production on this version of model number 34478 was 2,131 with three additional cars built for export. Olds used a special crankcase ventilation system on all F Series models. Removable valve guides and tappets were touted as being helpful in making low cost service possible.

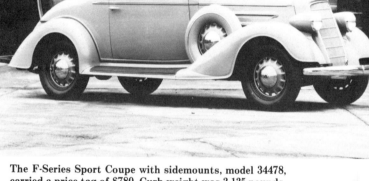

The sidemounted F-Series Five Passenger Touring Coupe, model number 34472, was priced at $805. It weighed 3,230 pounds. Production was 551 with 19 more cars made for export. The 1934 Olds sidemount package included: two welled fenders, two tire carriers, two spare tires and wheels, two ring type metal tire covers, two spare wheel locks, rear spring covers and front and rear bumpers.

The F-Series Sport Coupe with sidemounts, model 34478, carried a price tag of $780. Curb weight was 3,135 pounds. Production on this six cylinder model was 226 with 10 more exported. Olds called its F-Series lubrication system "full pressure lubrication". Each bearing was lubed abundantly and the faster the car was driven, the more oil was pumped to the bearings.

For those looking for a bit more trunk capacity in an F-Series coupe, the Five-Passenger Touring Coupe, model number 34472 filled the bill. It was priced at $730 and weighed 3,135 pounds. Production was at 11,717 with 17 additional cars built for export. All 1934 Oldsmobiles stopped with hydraulic, self energizing brakes. This particular car is equpped with the factory Sportlight which listed for $14.95 and could be installed when the car was built or at the dealership.

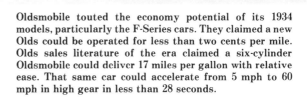

Oldsmobile touted the economy potential of its 1934 models, particularly the F-Series cars. They claimed a new Olds could be operated for less than two cents per mile. Olds sales literature of the era claimed a six-cylinder Oldsmobile could deliver 17 miles per gallon with relative ease. That same car could accelerate from 5 mph to 60 mph in high gear in less than 28 seconds.

The F-Series Four-Door Sedan was model number 34459. In standard five-wheel trim it sold for $765 and weighed 3,130 pounds. Production totalled 6,463 with 29 more cars exported. The sidemounted F-Series Four-Door Sedan cost $840 and weighed 3,225 pounds. Only 452 were built with 70 more exported. This car, displayed at a national Oldsmobile meet in Lansing, Michigan, belongs to Leonard West of Eaton Rapids, Michigan.

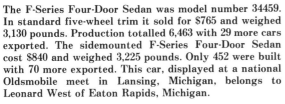

The most expensive and also most popular car in the 1934 Oldsmobile lineup was the F-Series Four-Door Touring Sedan, model number 34469. The standard model cost $795, weighed 3,210 pounds and saw a production run of 19,088 with 11 additional cars exported. The sidemounted F-Series Four-Door Touring Sedan cost $870, weighed 3,305 pounds and had a model run of 1,577 with 105 more cars exported. All F-Series cars had electro-plated cast iron pistons.

Olds built only one open car in 1934 and it was model number 34418, the L-Series Convertible. With five wheels this car cost $990 and weighed 3,350 pounds. With five wheels production totalled 536 with an additional car for export built. The L-Series sidemounted Convertible cost $1,080 and weighed 3,445. This model had a production run of 367 with 11 more cars exported. All L-Series cars were powered by a 240 cubic inch straight eight engine developing 90 horsepower.

The L-Series cars were impressive from the front and showed differences from the F-Series models. Wheelbase on the L-Series was 119 inches. Olds offered a standard tire of 7.00 x 16 inches on eight cylinders. At recommended pressures — 22 pounds cold, 25 pounds hot — Olds claimed a new tread design eliminated tire squeal. The Olds steering gear was of the worm and double roller tooth type with a 21 to 1 ratio.

1934

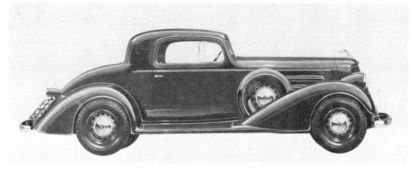

Short on passenger space but long on luggage room was the L-series Business Coupe, model number 34407. As a five-wheel offering 770 were produced. Price was $910 with a weight of 3,330 pounds. The sidemounted version sold for $1,000 and weighed 3,425 pounds. Only 128 of this model were produced with two more built for export. Olds claimed its L-Series cars could accelerate from 5 mph to 60 mph - in high gear - in less than 28 seconds.

Model number 34428, the L-Series Sport Coupe was the lone rumble seated closed car among the eight cylinders. A base price of $945 was established for the five-wheeled models, while the curb weight was 3,395 pounds. Production totalled 1,024 with one more car exported. With sidemounts the base price rose to $1,035 and weight went to 3,490 pounds. Production totalled 248 with five more cars exported. L-Series carburetion was from a duplex downdraft unit.

Model number 34401 was the L-Series Five Passenger Coupe. In five-wheel trim the price was $910 and weight was 3,405 pounds. Production totalled only 620 with one additional car built for export. The side mounted L-Series Five Passenger Coupe cost $1,000 and weighed 3,501 pounds. Twenty-seven of this model were made with one more for export. Each eight cylinder Oldmobile was equipped with an automatic choke and counterweighted crankshaft with vibration damper.

The Five Passenger Touring Coupe, model number 34422, was one of the most popular cars in the L-Series. With five wheels this car was priced at $940 and weighed 3,485 pounds. A total of 3,811 were built with five more exported. The sidemounted L-Series Five Passenger Touring Coupe sold for $1,030 and weighed 3,580 pounds. Production totalled 472 with three more export cars made. All L-Series cars were equipped with a single plated dry disc clutch with a self lubricating release.

The L-Series Four-Door Sedan, model number 34409, sold for $990 and weighed 3,490 pounds. A total of 3,589 of this car were built with four more made for export. The L-Series engine was fitted with electroplated cast iron pistons. Olds touted that these units were made of the same material as the engine block and therefore rates of expansion and contraction were the same.

1934

By laying down $1,020 a 1934 Olds buyer could have owned an L-Series Four-Door Touring Sedan, model 34419. Weight on this model was 3,570 pounds, while a production run of 8,856 — with one additional export car — was tops in the eight cylinder Olds series. A special accessory Group Y was offered for $21.85 on any L-Series car. It included: cigarette lighter, gear shift ball, bumper guards, license plate frames and a mirror watch.

A relatively rare L-Series offering was the sidemounted For-Door Sedan, model number 34409. Carrying a price tag of $1,080 weight on this model was 3,585 pounds. Production was only 547 with 47 more cars produced for export. Electrical energy for L-Series Oldsmobiles came from a 17-plate, 114-ampere hour battery. Each engine was mounted on four, rubber cushioned flexible engine mountings.

The flagship of the 1934 Olds lineup — and the most expensive car offered by Olds in 1934 — was the L-Series Four-Door Touring Sedan with sidemounts, model number 34419. It was priced at $1,110 and weighed 3,675 pounds. Production totalled 3,369 with 76 more cars exported. Accessory Group B was installed at the factory on all L-Series cars for $12.50. It included: double windshield wiper and booster pump, dual trumpet horns and right hand inside sun visor.

One of the Henney Progress models offered in 1934 was based on the L-Series Oldsmobile chassis. Oldsmobile was never as popular as Cadillac in the ambulance and funeral car field, but a few manufacturers did use the Olds chassis in almost every model year for some commercial application. Some of the standard L-Series features for 1934 included: Delco-Remy generator which supplied maximum amperage at 34 mph, a button activated Delco-Remy starter and double action hydraulic shock absorbers front and rear.

A few special Olds chassis were produced in 1934 and wound up in commercial applications like this Cunningham #347-A Limousine-Hearse. This unit was stretched to an 148-inch wheelbase, but still utilized the stock 90-horsepower straight 8 Olds engine. The L-Series powerplant had a pressure feed oil system via a gear driven pump from the camshaft. There was a seven quart oil capacity.

1934

Olds interiors could be ordered in a variety of trims for 1934. Tan mohair or whipcord was available on all coupes and sedans. Gray whipcord was offered in certain L-Series coupes and sedans. Convertible interior options included coffee colored leather, tan Bedford cloth, gray leather or gray Bedford cloth.

Olds shared the Knee-Action suspension system with later years of Oldsmobiles and other General Motors products. The factory claimed this suspension system offered a vast improvement over straight front axle designs. Claims included: easier driving, greater comfort for backseat passengers and a sturdier and safer front wheel assembly. Each Oldsmobile had an emergency brake setup on the rear wheels.

Olds offered a rugged chassis in both 1934 Series. Each frame had an X center member which helped prevent frame twist. Note the in-frame installation of the six volt battery and the far-rear mounting of the fuel tank. Olds used an undisclosed process called "Parkerizing" for the protection of steel under carriage parts from rust.

Interior layout on the 1934 Oldsmobile was uncluttered, efficient and rather attractive. The left side instrument cluster housed a speedometer and odometer combination. The right side cluster was complete with a fuel gauge, amp meter, water temperature gauge and oil pressure gauge. For 1934 Olds used a steel cored, molded steering wheel. Door moldings were done in the same trim as the dashboard.

Obviously the touring coupes and touring sedans of 1934 had a far greater luggage carrying capacity over conventional models. This angle shows the rear mounting of the spare tire which was the standard practice on non-sidemounted cars. In the rear 1934 Oldsmobiles used semielliptic springs. These were attached to the frame with threaded bolts in the front and silent U threaded shackles in the rear.

1935

A complete exterior change was again carried out in 1935 and on the mechanical side it was refinement rather than innovation. Three years previously Oldsmobile was tucked away in 12th sales position, but the post-Depression era that saw a lot of car builders fail, was good to the Lansing-based G.M. division. Healthy sales increases were enjoyed in both 1933 and 1934, and in 1935 the all-time 1929 divisional sales mark was smashed. In 1935 Olds had a firm hold on fifth place with a 126,768 model year total and calendar year sales reaching 183,152.

Knee action and hydraulic brakes were the innovations of the previous year and both these items were improved in 1935. Front suspension systems were improved by redesigning the steering arm and strengthening the steering gear. Brake shoes were wider and drum size was increased. Sixteen-inch tires became standard equipment on all models. Rubber valve stems also were used on 1935 tires replacing metal stems of the previous years. Other subtle mechanical improvements included: a new type generator, a foot pedal starter control, a beefed up frame and a new type muffler fitted on both models.

1935 colors included: black, maroon, grey, blue, two greens, and red. Interiors came in mohair, tree-bark wool, boucle cloth and leather. Accessories included: two types of radios, two types of hot water heaters, defroster, electric clock, and for the first time, factory fender skirts (rear wheel shields).

Redesigned cylinder heads and other internal engine improvements boosted the Six horsepower to 90 and eight output to 100 hp. Sixes outsold the Eights by a three to one margin. One inch was added to the Six wheelbase bringing it to 115 inches, while the Eights grew two inches to 121 inches. Distinctive grilles continued to be the big difference in the two offerings. Double chrome tail and stop lamps were standard on the Eights. The Six came standard with only a painted left stop and tail lamp assembly. A second unit could be ordered as an option on the Six.

Continuing to expand, General Motors paid $6 million for the Lansing facilities of the Durant Motors Corp. This property immediately became the new home of the Lansing division of Fisher Body Corp., a move which allowed Oldsmobile to take over floor space within the Olds complex formerly used by Fisher.

For buyers wishing a bit more flair with their coupe, the F-36 sport coupe was available. Model number was 353657; price was $725, and shipping weight was 3,150 pounds. A total of 2,837 regular sport coupes were produced, with 46 additional sidemounted cars made, and 22 right-hand drive models exported. The main distinguishing feature of this car was the rumble seat. Olds claimed 18 MPG with all of its six-cylinder powered cars including the F-35 sport coupe.

The lowest priced 1935 model was the F-35 business coupe which sold for $675. Model number for this car was 353607 and it was the lightest Olds at 3,110 pounds. This car proved to be fairly popular as 8,390 in standard form with an additional 65 sidemounted models made. Export production was 13. Salesmen were impressed as this coupe boasted a cargo area from the trunklid to the back of the front seat.

A sub-series of the F-35 business coupe was the club coupe. This model was listed in none of the 1935 factory literature. Externally, it was identical to the business coupe, with the lone difference being two jumpseats located in the cargo area. This offering carried the same model number as the business coupe. It had a price of $690 and weight of 3,115 pounds. Only 200 were built with four of that total carrying sidemounts.

Any sidemounted 1935 Olds was a rarity, and only 31 F-35 five-passenger coupes were built. Regular production for this model was 14,751 with three more built for export. Shipping weight was 3,225 pounds and the model number was 353601. The price on the standard model was $725. Sidemounts boosted the price of any six-cylinder $47.50. Safety glass was standard in the windshields and side vent windows, and safety glass could be factory installed in all windows for an extra $10.

1935

Olds models for 1935 and 1936 are look alikes. The quickest ID factor is the 1935's rear hinged suicide doors. Like all F-35s, horsepower on this five-passenger touring coupe was 90. The touring coupe gained its name by virtue of a large trunk area. Model number was 353611, price was $755 and shipping weight was 3,225 pounds. A total regular production of 19,615 made the F-35 five-passenger touring coupe Olds' most popular two-door. An additional 191 sidemounted models were built and export production was 15.

Sportiest of the F-35, or six-cylinder, 1935 Oldsmobiles was the convertible coupe. This model carried designation number 353867 and weighed 3,155 pounds. A total of 1,475 standard 6-cylinder convertibles were made with 80 additional sidemounted cars built. Right-hand drive, export production for this model totalled 43. Base price for the F-35 convertible was $800 making it the second most expensive six-cylinder Olds and the rarest of the six-cylinder models.

The F-35 four-door sedan was a rather unique car from the rear. Note the twin trunk handles and the single taillight. A second painted taillight could be ordered as a $4 option on any F-35 and an attractive trunk lid Olds emblem was available for $1. Model number for this car was 353609; price was $790, and shipping weight was 3,285 pounds. Regular production totalled 12,807. An additional 135 sidemounted cars were built, and 67 more cars were built for export. As with all F-35 models, the wheelbase was 115 inches.

Olds' most popular 1935 offering was also its most expensive six-cylinder. The F-35 touring sedan carried a price tag of $820. Regular production totalled a whopping 33,368 with an additional 1,089 sidemounted cars produced. Export production was 190. Model number for the touring sedan was 353619 and the shipping weight was 3,285 pounds. Unusual accessories offered by the factory in 1935 included: a home battery charger for $7.95, fender markers at $1.25 each, insect screens for $1.50, and two-piece fitted luggage at $22.25.

Factory records and literature do not show a station wagon model, yet this photo proves there was at least one built. This three-seater was a particularly attractive car with its sidemounted fenders. This F-35 had three seats and a stylish fabric roof. A few six-cylinder chassis were sold in 1935 and this car could have had coachwork added at another plant — in fact the body is very similar to those turned out by U.S.F.&B. Corp. Later wood bodied General Motors wagons were produced in Ionia, Michigan, which is 50 miles northwest of Lansing.

Unlisted in any 1935 Olds sales literature was the L-35 club coupe which was actually a subseries of the business coupe. This model featured jump seats located in the cargo area behind the front seat. It carried the same model number as the L-35 business coupe, was priced at $875, and weighed 3,340 pounds. Production was limited to 74 cars. As with all L-35s, the club coupe was powered by a 240 cubic inch, 100 horsepower straight Eight.

Based on a 121-inch wheelbase, as with all eight cylinders, the L-35 business coupe was the least expensive 8 offered, with a price of $860. It was also the lightest L-35 at 3,335 pounds. The L-35 business coupe carried model number 353807. Regular production totalled 1,183 with an additional 43 sidemounted cars built. The sidemounts on any eight-cylinder model cost an extra $50.

Flashiest of the L-35 two-doors was the rumble seated sport coupe. Carrying model number 353857, the sport coupe weighed 3,380 pounds and sold for $895. Production totalled only 891, with an additional 56 sidemounted cars built and 12 right-hand drive models exported. Interior fabrics on the L-35 closed cars were tan mohair or tan or blue grey boucle cloth.

The most expensive two-door car offered by Oldsmobile was the L-35 convertible which was base priced at $950. Carrying model number 353867, the convertible tipped the scales at 3,390 pounds. As with most of the L-35s, the convertible was rare, with only 791 built. An additional 111 with sidemounts were made ane eight more were exported. Convertibles, in both the L and F Series, could be ordered with leather interiors.

Two-door buyers without much luggage were candidates for the L-35 five-passenger coupe. Priced at $870 this small-trunked model weighed 3,480 pounds and carried model number 353801. This was another extremely scarce Olds for 1935, as only 852 were built, with an additional 18 being made with sidemounts. Fisher Body called its 1935 all-steel bodies "Turret Tops" and advertising of the era stressed their safety, strength and rigidity.

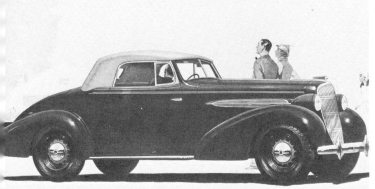

1935

Carrying a base price of $940 was the L-35 four-door sedan, model number 353809. This car weighed 530 pounds and saw regular production of 2,870. Sidemounted production was an additional 92 and 14 right-hand drive models were exported. Most cars coming from the factory in 1935 carried accessory group "A" which included: bumpers, bumper guards, spare tire and rear spring covers. The price on this group was $37.50 on the F Series and $45 on the L Series.

By far the most popular and also the most expensive L-35 Olds was the four-door touring sedan. Priced at $970, this L-35 was model number 353819. It weighed 3,530 pounds. A total of 16,500 were built with an additional 1,491 being sidemounted. Export total was 67. Factory accessory "B" group for the L-35s was popular. It consisted of dual trumpet horns, double windshield wiper and booster pump and a right-hand sun visor. Price for the group was $12.50.

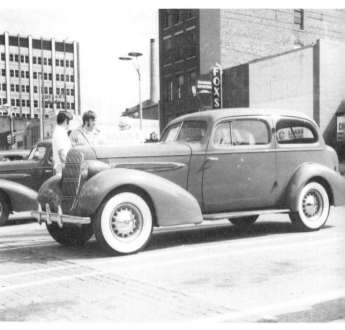

By far the most popular of the L-35 two-doors was the five-passenger touring coupe. This finely restored example belongs to Russ Yoder of Louisville, Ohio, and holds a special place in the Yoder collection because 1935 was his first year as an Olds dealer. Pictured with Yoder, far right, are Fred Gramcko, left, of Olds service department and the author. The L-35 five-passenger touring coupe was priced at $900, weighed 3,485 pounds and carried model number 353811. A total of 4,749 regular models were built with 113 sidemounted cars made and six exported.

Power and torque was increased on the six-cylinder for 1935 via slight head design improvements. Olds made a great deal out of smoother engine operation which was largely due to a new three-point engine mounting setup and additional counterweights on the crankshaft. Other areas of improvement on the popular six-cylinder included: a redesigned crankshaft, materially strengthened connection rods, increased oil pump capacity and improved fuel system.

The hard working Olds L-35 chassis found some use beyond passenger car duty. This graceful Sayers-Abington ambulance shows such an application. This was among the lower priced models offered in 1935 by Sayers & Scoville of Cincinnati. The improved Olds eight-cylinder head offered a 6.2 to 1 compression ratio and allowed the L-35 to better haul around heavier commercial coachwork like this S & S ambulance.

A vast amount of luggage space was available to those who picked a touring coupe or sedan with sidemounted spare tires. This L-35 model is shown with an optional three-piece luggage set offered by Oldsmobile for $32.50. There was another three-piece set of luggage available from the factory with two suitcases and a hatbox and also a two-piece set was offered. In touring models without side-mounts a horizontal spare tire compartment was provided, at the expense of trunk space.

The 115-inch wheelbase for the F-35 was the more popular of the two 1935 chassis. The frame was strengthened for the new models and other stronger components included: steering arm, rear bumper, rear axle and differential. Brakes were improved with more shoe width and additional lining area. Wheels were also restyled for 1935 and 6.25 x 16-inch tires were standard equipment on the F-35s.

This is an interior on one of the six-cylinder four-door models. Olds stayed with both the floor mounted gearshift lever and emergency brake during this model year. Six-cylinder models had plain glovebox doors, while the L-35s came standard with an emblem in the center of the glovebox. This area could also be used to house the accessory clock, and the same setup could be ordered as an F-Series option. A second type of accessory clock was also available, built into the rearview mirror.

Despite its two-door configuration, backseat passengers rode in comfort in both models of the five-passenger coupe. Luxurious armrests were provided. Upholstery on closed models of the F-35 came in tan mohair or tan tree-bark wool. Passengers in L-35 closed models rode either on tan mohair and either tan or blue grey boucle cloth.

A simple but functional instrument cluster appeared on all 1935 models. Gauges included: gasoline, ammeter, oil pressure and water temperature. To the right of the dash, (not pictured) was a panel which housed radio controls, ignition switch and a cigarette lighter. Six-cylinder models had a manual choke knob located in this area also.

Externally the 1936's were difficult to distinguish from the previous year's offering. The biggest difference was the move away from the front opening suicide doors of 1935. The public continued its confidence in Olds and production records again were established with a 1936 model year total of 200,546 and a calendar year mark of 187,638. These totals were good enough to keep fifth spot in the sales race.

Colors offered for 1936 included: black, maroon, brown, gray, two blues and green. Six cylinder upholsteries were taupe mohair or tan tree bark cloth. On the Eights, taupe mohair or boucle cloth were available. Leather was offered as an option on all convertibles.

On the mechanical side, the big news was the adoption of electro-hardened aluminum pistons in both engines. A new vacuum spark advance aided both engines in the fuel economy department, as did the adoption of a new type carburetor and air cleaner system. Other improvements under the hood included a redesigned generator voltage control, improved cooling system, different exhaust valve seat angles and an improved water jacketing system around cylinders.

Chassis size remained the same as 1935. Improvements in the knee action suspension included increased road clearance and simplified adjustments involving the front suspension. The X-type frame construction was strengthened and improved shock absorber arms were also added in 1936.

The most distinguishing feature between the Sixes and Eights from the front continued to be the differing grilles. Headlamps were mounted higher on the hood sides and placed closer together in 1936. The Eights also sported attractive fender mounted parking lights. Sixes continued to come equipped with only one tail lamp, with a second available as an option.

Accessories included deluxe or standard radios, side mounts, heaters, flexible steering wheel, cigar lighter, bumper guards, mirror clock and radiator grille insect screens.

In 1936 Oldsmobile moved ahead with a $6 million expansion which included more and improved manufacturing area and a new engineering center. Assembly of Oldsmobile models was added during the year at Linden, N. J., and South Gate, Calif.

Salesmen and others who valued a cavernous trunk space continued to make the businessman's coupe popular in 1936. Model number for the F-36 version of this car was 363607. It weighed 3,019 pounds and was the lightest and also the least expensive 1936 Olds. Base price was $665. Regular production totalled 20,284, with an additional 62 sidemounted cars built. A total of 90 horsepower came from the 213 cubic inch F-36 powerplant.

Rarest among the F-36s was the stylish convertible, model number 363667. It carried a price tag of $805 and weighed 3,109 pounds. Only 2,026 were made with an additional 47 being exported. Convertible interiors on both the F-36 and L-36 models were done in either tan boucle cloth or tan leather. Oldsmobile changed car slogans often since its 1897 inception. For 1936, the slogan was "The car that has everything."

Olds sales literature of the era touted the F-36 sport coupe rumble seat as extra fair-weather seating capacity. It didn't mention what happened when the weather wasn't so fair. Carrying model number 363657, the sport coupe weighed 3,054 pounds and was priced at $730. A total of 2,803 sport coupes were made, with an additional 28 sidemounted models built and seven right hand drives exported. Although horsepower and displacement didn't change in the faithful six-cylinder engine in 1936, internal improvements included aluminum pistons and rifle-drilled connecting rods.

1936 was a good year for the six-cylinder, five-passenger touring coupe. The spacious trunk and large back seat helped attract 46,101 buyers to model number 363611. An additional 272 sidemounted F-36 toruing coupes were made and 18 more right hand drives were exported. Price on this model was $755 and the shipping weight of Olds' most popular two-door was 3,144 pounds. Most F-36s were ordered with factory-installed Group A accessories which included: bumpers, bumper guards, spare tire and rear spring covers. The price was $37.50 for this package.

Olds continued to call its two-door sedan a five-passenger coupe. Carrying model number 363601, this F-36 was priced at $730 and weighed 3,144 pounds. A total of 13,124 were built with 19 more sidemounted cars made. All F-36 models rode on a 115-inch wheelbase. Big sales points on the F-36 were: knee action suspension, Turret-Top construction, steel floor structure and a ride stabilizer.

Dwindling in popularity in contrast to other F-36 models was the four-door sedan. Carrying model number 363609, it was priced at $795 and weighed 3,179 pounds. Only 4,065 buyers chose this model with 17 more selecting the sidemounted F-36 four-door sedan. A total of 10 of this model was exported. F-36 interiors were finished in either taupe mohair or tan tree-bark cloth.

The big seller in the 1936 Olds lineup was the four-door touring sedan. This was the most expensive F-36 at $820 and also the heaviest at 3,194 pounds. Model number 363619 sold a whopping 69,078 units. Export production was 365. Notice the major external differences between 1935 and 1936 were door hinge location and hood trim. F-36 and L-36 models had differing grille designs as well for 1936.

Only 63 sidemounted F-36 convertibles were produced. This rare beauty is from the collection of Don Spieldenner of Fremont, Ohio. He has produced national prize-winning 1932, 1938 and 1939 Oldsmobiles and prefers the rare sidemounted models. Sidemounted equipment added $47.50 to the $805 base price of the car, but it greatly enhanced the looks. As with all sidemounted cars, underhood access is less than ideal.

A few commercial vehicle builders latched onto the F-36 chassis. This 1936 Olds hearse was built by Brantford Coach and Body Company located in Ontario, Canada. Most ambulance and hearse chassis made by Olds were side-mounted as the coachwork left little spare tire space. An improved X-type frame offered 25% more rigidity in all F-36s and allowed more widespread sales of commercial chassis.

In the early days of the curved dash, Olds rarely lost a chance for showmanship and promotion. Even with General Motors conservatives firmly at the controls in 1936, this flashy model turned some heads in the southwestern U.S. It was produced for the Texas Centennial, and the rooftop speaker got the message across loud and clear. None of the nine Olds standard factory colors were anywhere close to the white of this specially built F-36.

For a trailer no larger than this teardrop job, the F-36 touring sedan made an ideal tow car. In 1936, Olds smashed sales records dating back to 1929 and did so with cars only mildly restyled. F-36 models, such as this trailer hauler, were almost 189 inches long and more than 72 inches wide. They held 18 gallons of gasoline, 6 quarts of oil, 13 quarts of water and two pounds of transmission oil. This commercial unit hailed from Champaign, Ill.

A total of 1,371 sidemounted F-36 touring sedans were produced. This car shared the same model number with the regular four-door touring sedan, and was priced $47.50 higher. F-36 models had a front tread of 58 inches, rear wheel tread of 59 inches and low pressure 6.50 x 16-inch tires. Olds claimed its knee action suspension reduced unsprung weight, increased road clearance, simplified design and greatly improved riding comfort.

The business coupe in the L-36 series was for the traveler who wanted a bit more underhood power. As with all L-36s, model number 363807 was powered by the 100 horsepower, 240 cubic inch straight Eight. Price on this model was $810 and shipping weight was 3,231 pounds. A total of 2,126 were made with an additional 55 sidemounted cars produced.

The lone open car in the L-series was the sporty convertible, model number 363857. This was the most expensive 1936 Olds at $935 and it weighed 3,321 pounds. Only 873 of this model were produced, with 41 sidemounted cars made and 17 more exported. The L-36 convertible interiors were done in either tan boucle cloth or tan leather. Popular L-36 options were: a flexible steering wheel for $12.50, an exhaust extension and deflector for $1, and a rearview mirror-clock for $4.

The L-36 sport coupe was a relatively rare model which continued to appeal to the "wind in the face crowd" because of its handy rumble seat. The fender mounted parking lights on this car were an L-series exclusive. Base price on the sport coupe was $845 and weight was 3,261 pounds. Model number was 363857. Only 909 L-36 sport coupes were built with 41 more sidemounted and 9 more exported. Closed L-series cars were upholstered in taupe mohair or tan or blue gray boucle cloth.

The least popular 1936 Olds was the eight-cylinder five-passenger coupe. Only 224 were made with eight more sidemounted and five exported. Model number 363801 was priced at $845 and weighed 3,376 pounds. The L-series wheelbase was 121 inches, tires were 7.00 x 16 inches with a 25-pound pressure minimum and the frame was of the X-type construction.

Most popular of the Olds eight-cylinder two-doors was the five-passenger touring coupe. A total of 6,466 regular models were made with 155 sidemounted and five export cars. Base price was $870 and shipping weight was 3,376 pounds. Model number was 363811. Compression ratio on the L-36 was 6.1 to 1 and cylinder head construction was cast iron.

The Michigan State Police had several L-36 five-passenger touring coupes in their fleet. The roof mounted device is believed to be a radio antenna. Gasoline capacity on the L-36s was 18 gallons. Other vital capacities included: 7 quarts of engine oil, 16 quarts of engine water, and two pounds of transmission grease. Rear end ratio on all L-36s was 4.55 to 1.

1936

Another of the relatively rare L-36s was the four-door sedan. Only 390 of model number 363809 were made. Eleven additional cars were sidemounted and five more were exported. Base price on this machine was $910 and weight was 3,401. Eight-cylinder models carried an improved air cleaner which drew incoming air across an oil bath and through oil soaked mesh.

The most popular L-series car was the touring sedan. A total of 27,379 of model number 363819 were produced with 78 more exported. Base price was $935 and weight was 3,421. All 1936 Olds models had cowl mounted ventilators in their Fisher Bodies. One windshield wiper was standard equipment on both series with a second wiper package available.

This mighty L-36 touring sedan belongs to Detroiter John Kiritsis and is a familiar feature of most Oldsmobile Club meets. A total of 1,916 of this model were produced with sidemounts. The base price with sidemounted equipment was $985. All Oldsmobiles used coil front springs in the knee-action system. Rear springs were semi-elliptic, permanently lubricated and enclosed by spring covers.

Olds never was extremely active in racing or speed contests. There were, of course, the Pirate racer, Old Scout and Cannonball Baker's cross country jaunt in high gear, but all these came before the mid-1920s. Here an L-36 touring sedan, sidemounted, was used to promote the long forgotten racing movie "Speeding Up." Promoting the movie was one of America's genuine auto racing heroes, Pete DePaolo.

Olds was big on testing back in 1936. This L-36 sedan was undergoing a cold test. Oldsmobiles of this era proved to be fairly good winter transportation. Both L and F-series models featured six-volt Delco-Remy batteries. The six-cylinder battery had 15 plates and carried a 20-hour cranking capacity of 94 amp hours. The eight-cylinder unit had 17 plates and a capacity of 110 amp hours. Winter accessories included: a deluxe heater for $16.75, standard heater for $11.95, a defrosting and ventilating fan for $5.25 and a garage battery charger for $7.95.

The L-chassis found its way into some commercial applications, as this Henney Progress Model 764 ambulance points up. Henney, a popular manufacturer of the era, was located in Freeport, Ill. The fuel system on the L-series Olds was fed from a diaphragm pump to a duplex downdraft carburetor. Both the heat control and the choke were automatic. The fuel gauge was an electric unit.

The sidemount package offered in 1936 differed only slightly from that in 1935. It featured an attractive emblem and full tire coverage. Tire pressure could be checked via the exposed tire valve. Sidemounted cars offered the advantage of increased luggage space and more graceful overall appearance. These cars — built in limited numbers by Olds — are, of course, highly valued by today's collectors. The six-wheel package, as Olds called it, consisted of bumpers, bumper guards, 2 spare tires, two welled fenders, two spare tire covers, an extra wheel, two metal tire covers, wheel locks and rear spring covers. Price was $47.50 on the F-Series and $50 on the L-Series. 1936 was also the last year sidemounts could be obtained on a six-cylinder.

Olds called its 1936 central dash cluster an "aviation type speedometer." Flanking it on either side were a fuel gauge, ammeter, oil pressure indicator and water temperature gauge. The novel looking round glovebox door was lock equipped. All 1936 Oldsmobiles had three-speed floor mounted manual transmission, floor mounted starter buttons and under the dash cowl vent controls. The emergency brake control was a piston grip affair located to the driver's left.

This road ranging GMC tractor-trailer rig brought many loads of 1936 Oldsmobiles right to the dealer showroom. Other 1936 Olds shipping methods included rail and an extremely active factory driveaway program whereby a new car owner came to Lansing to claim his new car. Notice the trunk decoration on the rear facing Olds and also the huge license plate holder. This was one of the many 1936 Oldsmobiles shipped minus a rear bumper.

A new hubcap design was selected in 1936. All models came with 16-inch steel wheels. Olds touted these wheels as being "easy to wash, clean and maintain." F-36 models came standard with 6.50 x 16 balloon tires, while 7.00 x 16 tires were standard on L models. Chrome wheel moldings cost an additional $8.50 on five-wheel models and $10.25 on side-mounted cars.

1937

The straight front view of the 1937 six cylinder model shows the major front end styling change from 1936. The 1937 base price included rather substantial looking bumper guards. The entire F-37 grille was of die cast construction. Olds boosted the horsepower of its L-head six cylinder to 95 and this powerplant displaced 229 bucic inches.

When an F-37 Olds pulled up to a gasoline pump it could take up to 18 gallons to complete a fillup. Olds literature of the era claimed up to 17 miles per gallon. Base price on this business coupe was $765 and shipping weight was 3,220 pounds. A total of 13,853 of model number 373627B were produced, with an additional 105 made for export. For 1937, safety glass was standard equipment in each Oldsmobile window.

The F-37 club coupe had two twenty-inch wide back seats which could be folded up for additional cargo area. Model number 373627 was externally the same as the business coupe. Price was $825 and weight was 3,221 pounds. U.S. sales for the club coupe was 7,224 with an additional 202 exported. All F-37s were on a wheelbase of 117 inches and the standard tire size was 6.50 x 16.

Completely restyled models were readied for 1937 wi significant mechanical changes coming as well. Oldsmob dropped two slots in the production standings, finishi seventh for 1937 with a model year total of 200,886, a calendar year production of 212,767. Both figures we all time highs for Oldsmobile.

Colors offered were: black, maroon, green, two blu gray, tan, brown, red and cream. Six interiors were do in either taupe mohair or tan tween cloth. Eights car with the taupe mohair or gray boucle cloth. Leather w offered on either model convertible.

An all-steel Fisher Body was introduced by Oldsmob in 1937. This body was approximately three inches low than the 1937 models. Under the hood things we pepped up a bit with the Six now displacing 230 cul inches and rated at 95 horsepower. The Eights were upp to 257 cubic inches and gained 10 horsepower, up 110 hp.

Factory accessories for 1937 included a twin speak radio, electric clock, sidemounts, hood louver initia chrome fog lamps, dash controlled radiator shutters a bumper guards.

There was an increasing emphasis placed on making t two models more distinctive. Both cars offered the unusu high level stop and taillight combinations. Standard equi ment on the Six now included two rear lights, but th was a difference in both head and tail lights between t two models. The front ends of both cars were even mc distinctive than previous years. Both models continued grow longer, with the Six on a 116-inch wheelbase, a the Eight on 124 inches.

1937 brought the introduction of the Safety Automa Transmission. This was a first step in shiftless driving th would carry Oldsmobile to its exclusive HydraMa introduction with 1940 models. The safety transmissior so named because the driver could keep both hands the steering wheel more of the time—was offered as option on the 1937 Eights in June. The unit was built Buick in Flint, but was not offered by that GM Divisi until 1938. The option was factory installed, cost $8 and was rarely ordered. It was the first column sh offered by Olds and it did greatly increase usable fro seating capacity.

In 1937 a new customer drive away facility w completed to allow buyers to come to Lansing to dri away their new Oldsmobiles. The division's expansic programs began to pay big dividends as 1937 was the fir year that Oldsmobile assembled more than 1,000 ca during each working day.

With its tan or gray top snugly in place, the F-37 convertible was an attractive and weathertight car. Model 373667 shared honors with the touring sedan as being the highest priced F-37 at $920. Shipping weight was 3,295 pounds. Only 1,402 of this open car were made, leaving it the rarest of the sixes. An additional 217 convertibles were made for export. F-37 convertible upholstery was in leather of tan, black, green, gray, blue or red.

1937

For $825 an Olds buyer could purchase an F-37 two-door sedan. Model number 373601 was shipped at 3,275 pounds. Production totalled 9,597 with an additional 67 built for export. Closed models of the F-37 were upholstered in taupe mohair or tan tweed cloth. Factory accessory group B was very popular in 1937 and it included dual trumpet horns, double windshield wiper and booster pump and an oil bath air cleaner.

By a wide margin the most popular F-37 two-door was the two-door touring sedan, model number 373611. Base price was $850 and shipping weight was 3,275 pounds. Production totalled 37,722 with 321 additional cars made for export. This model had 12 cubic feet of trunk room. An interesting accessory was the hood initials set just behind the hood louvers. These were chromed and were dealer installed. Price was $3.50.

The X-frame is a rather obvious feature of the F-37 chassis. Located under the seat was a Delco-Remy 6 volt, 15-plate, 94 amp hour battery. The oiled copper wool or optional oil bath cleaner perched high atop the single downdraft carburetor. Tires were 6.50 x 16 inches and hubcaps were of a new design in the 1937 model year.

The F-37 four-door sedan carried model number 373609. This car continued to run well behind the other four-door model – the touring sedan – in production. A total of 3,819 F-37 four-door sedans were sold with 201 additional exported. The four-door sedan was the heaviest six cylinder at 3,310 pounds and its base price was $875. F-37 models carried 18 gallons of fuel, 6 quarts of engine oil, 16 quarts of engine cooling water and 2 pounds of transmission grease. The rear end ratio was 4.375 to 1 with an optional package of 4.625 to 1.

Once again the most popular Olds was the six cylinder four-door touring sedan. A whopping 59,794 of this F-37 model were built. An additional 3,139 were produced for export. Olds most popular model carried model number 373619. This car was the second highest priced six cylinder at $920. It weighed 3,295 pounds. Accessory group Z for the sixes included: cigar lighter, gear shift ball, wheel trim mouldings, electric panel clock and license plate frames.

The business coupe continued to be the lightest and least expensive eight cylinder in the Olds lineup. Base price on model number 373827B was $880 and it weighed 3,395 pounds. A total of 2,108 regular L-37 business coupes were made with an additional 28 sidemounted and 14 more exported. The high level tail lamps were ahead of their time and offered a marginal safety feature.

The other coupe in the L-series was the club coupe which could accommodate two smallish passengers in the rear. Model number was 373827 and it weighed 3,405 pounds. The base price on this model was $940. A total of 2,086 L-series club coupes were produced, with 71 more sidemounted and 145 exported. Upholstery on L-series closed cars was done in mohair or boucle cloth.

The most expensive car in the 1937 Olds lineup was the L-37 convertible, model number 373867. For the first time in many years, several Olds base prices crept over the $1,000 mark. This model was listed at $1,035. Shipping weight was 3,450 pounds. Regular production was a rather limited 599 with an additional 34 exported. Convertible interiors for the L-series were done in either tan, black, green, gray, blue or red leather. Tops could be ordered in tan or gray.

The most distinctive eight cylinder grille yet was housed in the front of the L-37. In addition to the grille differences between the 6's and 8's, the L models carried an 8 designation on the front and rear bumper. Hood side louvers were also different. All eights were on a wheelbase of 124 inches Tire size was 7.00 x 16 inches with a front tread of 59 inches.

Sidemounted models were produced only in the L-series for 1937. This convertible was one of only 95 produced. The sidemount package consisted of an extra spare tire and tube, two fender wells, two spare tire carriers, two metal tire covers, two spare wheel locks and an extra wheel. Price on this package was $50. Another eight cylinder only optional package was Group Y, which consisted of: a cigar lighter, gear shift ball, wheel trim mouldings, electric panel clock and license plate frames. Price was $26.45.

The L-37 two-door touring sedan was the most popular 8 cylinder two-door model made. This car was priced at $965, weighed 3,480 pounds and carried model number 373811. A total of 5,712 were made with 97 more side-mounted and nine exported. Olds continued its use of the opening cowl ventilator. Opening vent windows added to the fresh air availability in all models.

Rarest of the 1937 Oldsmobiles was model number 373801, The L-37 two-door sedan. This car carried a base price of $940 and a shipping weight of 3,480 pounds. Only 396 were built, with two more sidemounted models made. Olds used double-action hydraulic shock absorbers on all wheels of all 1937 models. Rear springs were semi-elliptic, permanently lubricated and sealed with metal covers.

Another rare L-37 was the four-door sedan, model number 373809. Base price was $990 and shipping weight was 3,510 pounds. A total of 477 of the L-37 four-door sedan were made with nine more sidemounted and 10 exported. Rear seat width in this model was slightly more than 46 inches, cushion depth was 20 inches, and shoulder room was 55 inches.

Most popular of the eight cylinders was once again the four-door touring sedan. Price on this luxury liner of the roadway was $1,015, model number 373819, and shipping weight was 3,495 pounds. A total of 28,203 of this car were produced, with 1,811 more built with sidemounts and 351 additional built for export. Each 1937 Olds came with two sets of matched tumbler locks. One key operated the door and ignition switch, the other operated the glovebox and trunk.

Dash layout was once again revised in 1937. Instruments were grouped in two dials directly in front of the driver. Located in the glovebox were two additional round structures, one an ashtray and the second an accessory clock ($12.25). Other accessories on this particular car are: radio (standard - $53, deluxe - $66.50), flexible steering wheel ($12.50), and the Safety Automatic transmission.

For 1937, the differences were even more obvious between the six and eight cylinder Oldsmobiles. The F-series fought it out with Pontiac for its share of the General Motors market. A tougher G.M. foe for the L-series was the mighty Buick produced in Flint. By 1937, Olds buyers were aware of and appreciated the Fisher solid steel turret top. This steel roof was reinforced with several steel crossbows which ran across the top of the body and were secured to the steel inner body frame.

The biggest changes for 1938 were up front. This F-38 model displays the distinctive six cylinder grille. Both F and L series cars featured highlights blended in with the fenders. Olds played up the fact that individual grille louvers could be replaced in the event of accident. All six cylinder cars were based on a 117-inch wheelbase. Front tread was 58 inches and rear tread was 59 inches.

Since 1932, Oldsmobile had been offering the buying public two different series of automobiles, but 1938 would be the last year for that lineup. Sales were drastically off industry wide and Olds was hit hard by the slump. Output was less than half the previous year, with 99,951 for the model year and 93,706 for the calendar year. Oldsmobile held onto seventh place, however.

There was little new in 1938, the biggest external change being new grille treatments for both models. Headlights were fender mounted. In the October 9 new car announcement a great deal was made of a so-called safety dash which was free of projecting knobs and even featured radio at the end of the instrument cluster. Like Ford's safety campaign of 1956, there is little evidence that safety helped sell many Oldsmobiles in 1938.

The Safety Automatic Transmission continued to head the factory option list with availability expanded to all Six and Eight models. The price was upped to $100. Other accessories included radio, wheel discs, fender markers, chrome fog lights, winter grille covers and locking gas cap.

Colors for 1938 were black, red, cream, two blues, brown, two grays, green and maroon. Taupe mohair was available on all closed models with a mixture cloth offered on the Six and tan pattern cloth available on the Eight. Tan Bedford cloth was standard on the open car with various colored leathers optional on both Six and Eight models.

Wheelbases and most mechanical specifications remained the same as in 1937. The Six was offered on a 117-inch wheelbase, while the Eight measured 124 inches. Sixes developed 95 horsepower and the Eights were rated 110 horsepower.

The biggest underhood change was the air cooled battery. The battery was moved underhood where it was easier to service and required shorter connections to the starter and generator. The battery was cooled by means of a duct which directed cool air to the battery compartment.

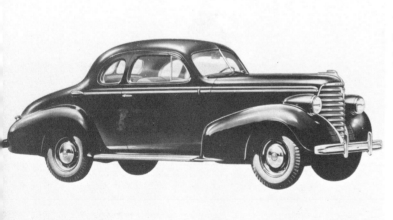

Two coupes were offered in the F-38 series with the main difference being the rear compartment design. Model number of the business coupe was 383627B while the club coupe was 383627. The business coupe was the cheapest 1938 Olds at $870 while the club coupe, which had two 20-inch wide rear jump seats, cost $926. Both cars weighed 3,205 pounds. A total of 8,506 business coupes were produced with 32 more exported. Club coupe production was 5,353 with 279 exported.

Rarest among the F-series cars was the convertible. Only 1,001 were built in regular production with an additional 183 for export. Model number 383667 was priced at $1,043, Oldsmobile's most expensive six cylinder. It weighed 3,360 pounds. Convertible tops came in tan or gray. Convertible upholstery in either series was in tan Bedford cloth or tan, black, gray, green, blue or red leather.

1938

The added luggage capacity continued to make the F-38 two-door touring sedan Oldsmobile's most popular two-door. Its model number was 383611, base price was $941, and shipping weight was 3,265 pounds. Regular production was 22,144 with 246 additional F-38 two-door touring sedans exported. Luggage was housed in a trunk which was 16 inches tall, 49 inches wide and 30 inches deep.

This was the final year in which Olds offered two versions of the two-door sedan. The regular two-door sedan was the less popular of these two offerings and only 3,955 were built with 20 more built for export. Base price was $916 and· shipping weight was 3,275 pounds. As with all F-38 models, 95 horsepower was produced from a 230 cubic inch L-head six cylinder engine.

The bread and butter Olds again in 1938 was the six cylinder, four-door touring sedan. It carried model number 383619, was priced at $992 and weighed 3,290 pounds. Production totalled a whopping 32,257 with an additional 3,657 for export. Rather than vertical hood louvers, the 1938 Oldsmobile stylists hid their louver under a continuous horizontal body moulding. A single handle located at the center of the panel unlatched the hood.

This was also the final year for two F-series four-doors. Continuing to be the less popular of the two was the F-38 four-door sedan, model number 383609. Base price on this model was $967 with a shipping weight of 3,285 pounds. Regular production totalled 1,458 with 19 more exported. Accessory Group X could be ordered on either series. It consisted of: Cigar lighter, dash compartment lights, license plate frames, gearshift ball, exhaust deflector, and header clock. Total price was $11.75.

The L-series grille was similar in shape to the F-series, but construction was of more numerous chrome plated horizontal bars. Both F and L series Oldsmobiles came with wide, single bar bumpers fitted with two sturdy bumper guards. There was also a gravel deflector panel located between the body and the bumper. All L-series cars were on a 124-inch wheelbase. Front tread was 58 inches, rear tread was 59 inches and overall length was nearly 198 inches.

Neither of the L-series 1938 coupes were very popular, with each selling only slightly more than 1,000. Externally the two coupe models were very similar. The club coupe — model number 383827 — had two rear jump seats. Model number of the business coupe was 383827-B. This car provided no rear seating, but had a 50-inch deep and 46-inch wide cargo area. Base price for the business coupe was $986 and the club·coupe sold for $1,032. Both weighed 3,400 pounds. A total of 1,078 business coupes were built with 19 more sidemounted and one exported. Club coupe production was 1,085 with 37 sidemounted and 14 exported.

This L-38 convertible was a standout on the beach. Base price for this sporty model was $1,160, making it Olds' most expensive 1938 model. Model number was 383867 and shipping weight was 3,530 pounds. The L-series convertible had domestic production of 377 with 30 more for export. Notice the special eight cylinder insignia on the car's front bumper.

Probably the most immaculately restored Olds in the country is this sidemounted L-38 convertible owned by Don Spieldenner of Fremont, Ohio. Only 68 of this sidemounted model were produced in 1938. Sidemounts again this year were available only on L-series cars. This marked the final year for sidemounts. The sidemount package cost $65 and consisted of an extra spare tire and tube, two fender wells, two side tire carriers, two metal tire covers, two spare wheel locks and an extra wheel.

The most popular L-series two-door was the two-door touring sedan, model number 383811. Base price was $941 with a shipping weight of 3,265 pounds. Total production of this model was 1,907 plain, with 37 more sidemounted and 4 exported. L-series closed models could be ordered with either taupe mohair, tan pattern cloth or tan leather. Dealer installed accessory group M, available on either L or F models, consisted of: a luggage compartment mat, trunk light, visor vanity mirror and a front grille guard. Price was $6.

The rarest 1938 Olds was the L-38 two-door sedan, model number 383801. Only 137 of these cars were built, with six more exported. Base price was $916 and shipping weight was 3,275 pounds. All Olds eight cylinders were powered by a 257 cubic inch, 110 horsepower, L-head engine. L models held 18 gallons of gas, 7 quarts of oil, 21 quarts of water and 2 pounds of transmission grease.

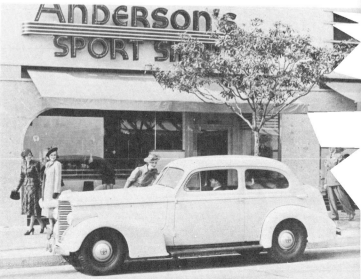

Another relatively rare L-series offering was the four-door sedan, model number 383809. Base price for this Olds was $967 and it was shipped at 3,285 pounds. Only 189 L-series four-door sedans were made with 10 more sidemounted and one exported. Rear seating width was just over 46 inches with a seat depth of 20 inches. L-series models had rear ash trays located in both armrests.

Most popular of the L-series models was the four-door touring sedan, model number 383819. Base price was $1,104 and shipping weight was 3,290 pounds. A total of 13,590 of this model were produced with 461 additional L-38 four-door touring sedans exported. The high level taillights were common to both F and L series models. Safety glass was standard in all windows of all models.

Sidemounts made this four-door touring sedan a more graceful car. Sidemounted production for the L-38 four-door touring sedan totalled 936. Olds used a chemical process called bonderizing on all its 1938 models. This was a combination of rust proofing and primer paint. Oldsmobile claimed this process prolonged finish life, eliminated paint cracking and reduced rust.

Olds interior designers were again busy in 1938 as the dash layout was revised. This layout was dubbed the safety instrument unit. Corners and projections were eliminated by building in curved surfaces and placing controls flush. This car was equipped with the $100 optional Safety Automatic Transmission, in its second year of Olds usage.

A majority of the 1938 models were shipped via truck. The new models had lower body height and less road clearance due to a change in the propeller shaft which allowed the body to sit lower on the frame rails. Notice the extra pair of ramps used to unload the lower 1938s. The center light was a license plate light and bracket. A trunk lock and handle was built into the unit.

For 1939, Oldsmobile buyers had three lines to choose from in the showroom and a bid was made, with the 60 series, to attract buyers who were shooting just a notch above the Ford and Chevy price range. Basic styling was established which would carry the division through to the Futuramics of the late 1940s. Production increased greatly over the previous year, and Olds retained its hold on 7th position. Model year production was 137,249 and the calendar year totalled 158,560.

The new Olds lineup started with the 60 series which was on a 115-inch wheelbase. The 70 and 80 series shared a 120-inch wheelbase, with a difference coming in trim and, of course, in the powerplant. The 60 models were powered by a 6-cylinder engine rated at 90 horsepower, while the 70 series was powered by a 6-cylinder engine similar in construction but turning out an additional 5 horsepower due to an extra ¼-inch bore. The 8-cylinder engine, offered exclusively in the 80 series, remained largely unchanged from 1938. For the first time, a steering column mounted standard shift was incorporated into the Olds lineup on all 1939 cars.

Completely new body styling was introduced in 1939, and the rumbleseat coupes were no longer offered. Visually, the three models were fairly difficult to distinguish. The 70s and 80s sported chrome moldings on the headlights and running boards. Eights carried that Roman numeral on the grille. The designation of touring sedan and touring coupe was eliminated and all cars had full trunks as standard equipment.

The first hint of the disappearing running board came with the announcement that the 70 and 80 Series models could be ordered without running boards. In their place were so called sport side panels—chrome side panels coupled with rear fender rubber scuff pads. This was a no charge option. For 1939, an ad campaign was launched heralding Oldsmobile's "rhythmic ride." Components of this system were coil springs at all wheels, knee-action front suspension, front and rear stabilizer bars, and double action shock absorbers.

For the final time the Safety Automatic Transmission appeared on the option list, this time with the price lowered to $75. Other factory options included push-button radio, rear seat heater, glove box clock, winter grille cover, automatic windshield washer and fender skirts.

Despite a shorter wheelbase, 60 series models were difficult to distinguish from the larger Oldsmobiles. Two identifying factors on the F models were the lack of chrome running board mouldings and an exposed upper front door hinge. This 4-door sedan model was the most expensive in the 60 series with a price tag of $889. It weighed an even 3,000 pounds and carried model number 393519. Regular production was 14,554 with 1,404 exported. Sixty interiors were upholstered in either tan pattern cloth or tan mohair.

Colors included black, maroon, red, ivory, two blue brown, two grays and green. Tan mohair upholstery w available on all closed models. Tan pattern cloth w offered on the 60 Series, with tan Bedford cloth availab on all convertibles and 70 and 80 closed cars. Leather, six colors, was an option on the convertibles.

Prices dropped in 1939 with the addition of the 60, or F, series. Least expensive of the Oldsmobiles, and the division's price leader, was the business coupe at $777. It was also the lightest Olds, as it was shipped at 2,870 pounds. A total of 5,539 of this model was produced and 36 more were exported. They carried model number 393527B. The 60 series had its own distinctive powerplant of 216 cubic inches and 90 horsepower. Tire size was 6.00 x 16 inches.

The main difference between the 60 club coupe, shown here, and the business coupe was the club coupe's two folding auxiliary rear seats. Model number on this offering was 393527, price was $883 and shipping weight was 2,915 pounds. A total of 2,059 of this model was produced with 214 exported. Compression ratio on the smaller six cylinder engine was 6.2 to 1. This model could hold 17 gallons of gas, 5 quarts of oil, 17 quarts of water and two pounds of transmission grease.

For 1939 there was just one F series two-door sedan and it carried model number 393511. Base price on this car was $838 and its shipping weight was 2,965 pounds. This was the most popular 60 series offering with 16,747 made in regular production and 163 exported. All 1939 Oldsmobiles rode on coil springs front and rear. Sixty and 70 series models were started by a 6 volt, 15-plate, 94 amp hour Delco battery.

Least expensive of the 70 series Oldsmobiles was the business coupe. It carried model number 393627B. Base price was $840 and shipping weight was 3,040 pounds. Regular production totalled 5,188 with an additional 23 exported. Interiors on the closed 70 and 80 models could be upholstered in either tan bedford cord or tan mohair. Leather was an extra-cost option.

Since there were no 60 series open cars, the least expensive Olds convertible was the 70, or G, series offering. This car carried model number 393667. Base price was $1,045, making it the most expensive 6 cylinder model. It weighed 3,230 pounds. The convertible was the rarest of the six cylinders with 1,509 produced and 205 made for export. As with all G series cars, power came from a 230 cubic inch, 95 horsepower engine.

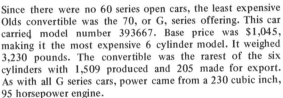

Externally similar to the business coupe was the 70 series club coupe, model number 393627. Base price was $891 and shipping weight was 3,080 pounds. Production totalled 4,653 with 142 more exported. The Safety Automatic Transmission was offered as a $75 option in 1939, but there were few takers. Olds and General Motors were well into the final testing of the fully automatic HydraMatic transmission.

All four-door sedans — including this 70 series model — now had the touring sedan style of trunk. This model carried number 393619. It sold for $952 and weighed 3,180 pounds. The 70 series four-door sedan was the most popular 1939 Olds. A total of 35,972 were made in regular production with an additional 2,173 exported and 79 built with sunroofs. Dealer installed accessory group X consisted of: a cigar lighter, glovebox light, license plate frames, exhaust deflector, electric clock and trunk light. Installed price was $12.

The lone two-door sedan in the 70 series was model number 393611. Base price was $901 and shipping weight was 3,140 pounds. Regular production was a sizable 19,365 with 62 more exported. An additional 17 of this model were equipped with a sunroof. This option was known as the sunshine turret top. It was available only on 70 and 80 series two-door and four-door sedans. It listed for the incredibly low price of $37.50.

The 70 four-door model provided loads of passenger room. One reason for a more spacious front seat was the adoption of an on-the-column shifter in standard shift models. Olds called this arrangement Handi-Shift. Front seats on all models were adjustable. Olds also used a new, three-spoke steering wheel mounted at a different angle.

Two jump seats in the rear compartment distinguished this club coupe from its sister 80 series machine, the business coupe. As with all L-series offerings, it carried Roman numeral VIII in its grille. Base price on this car was $971 and shipping weight was 3,230 pounds. A total of 1,136 of model number 393827 were produced with 13 more exported. No-charge factory option N would eliminate running boards, but few cars came so equipped.

The most expensive of all 1939 Oldsmobiles was the 80 series convertible, priced at $1,119. It carried model number 393887 and weighed 3,390 pounds. This car was also the rarest regular production Olds with 456 made and an additional 16 were exported. This particular car had some interesting accessories including the deluxe radio ($55) and the chrome fender lights ($6 installed).

This beauty belongs to Don Spieldenner of Fremont, Ohio, and it has an interesting background. At one time this particular L-series convertible belonged to Oldsmobile Club of America founder Gary Pinckney. At the time the Olds restorer obtained it, the car gave him a consecutive run of 1936-39 Oldsmobile convertibles. Note the unusual options including the grille guard and fender lights. This car also came without running boards, a rare factory manufacturing option.

A relatively rare offering in the 80 (L) series was the business coupe with only 736 built and an additional two exported. Model number on this car was 393827B. Price was $920 with a shipping weight of 3,190 pounds. The 70 and 80 models shared a wheelbase of 120 inches. L series power came from a 257 cubic inch, 110 horsepower engine.

1939

Top seller in the 80 series was the four-door sedan, model number 393819. Base price was $1,043 and shipping weight was 3,340 pounds. Production totals were 12,242 with an additional 84 sun roof equipped cars made and 100 more exported. Eighty series cars came equipped with a six-volt, 17 plate, 110 amp hour battery produced by Delco.

Model number 393811 was the 80 series two-door sedan. Priced at $992, this model was shipped at 3,290 pounds. Regular production was 1,562 with two more exported and two additional with sunroofs. Wheelbase on the 80 series was 120 inches. Front tread was 58 inches and rear tread was 59 inches. Standard tire size was 6.50 x 16 inches.

For serious winter motoring the optional winter front could be ordered. It could be partially opened to admit varying amounts of air. The winter front was a real bargain at the installed price of $1. The chrome strips atop the headlights were standard on 70 and 80 models and could be ordered on 60 series cars. The center bumper ornament came on all 80 series Oldsmobiles.

Olds went to the touring sedan trunk style on all its 1939 models. Small combination stop and taillights were like most other GM offerings of the year — very difficult to see from a distance. Bumper guards were standard both front and rear. All 1939 Oldsmobiles were equipped with self-energizing hydraulic brakes. Sixty and Seventy models had 11-inch drums, and Eighty series cars were stopped with 12-inch drums.

Oldsmobile and Buick shared this sunroof package in 1939, Few cars so equipped survive, and in numerous trips to old car meets across the country the author has never seen an Olds with the Sunshine Turret Top option. In addition to this hole in the roof concept Fisher Body prided itself on the no-draft ventilation system which utilized vent windows and a functional cowl vent.

1939

This auto show special was as close as Olds got to a four-door convertible in 1939, although such a model was built the next two model years. This was a 70 series sedan painted in a very non-stock white. Ordinarily, the Olds roof was reinforced with steel crossbows. Fisher claimed its body and roof insulation aided in quietness and protection from winter cold. All Olds steel tops had a soft pad cemented to the underside.

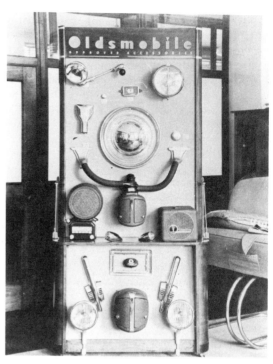

For the Olds owner who appreciates accessories, this board represents a dream come true. This was a 1939 dealership display board. Most items pictured could be dealer installed or ordered from the factory and in some cases a dealer could make more on the sale of accessories than on the sale of a car. Among the items shown were: a spotlight ($14.50). wheel covers and trim rings ($12.00), center radiator-grille guard ($2.00), chrome fog lamps ($5.35), header clock ($3.25), and standard hot water heater ($13.95).

The big difference in the two 1939 Oldsmobile six cylinder engines was the stroke. Bore on both motors was 3-7/16 inches. Stroke on the 60 series 216 cubic inch engine was 3 and 7/8th inches, while the 230 cubic inch, 70 series motor had a stroke of 4 and 1/8th inches. Externally, the two engines were similar. The 70 series had a slightly lower compression ratio, but higher horsepower. Block and cylinder head construction was of cast iron.

Olds called this road-illuminating monster the Super-Ray Driving Lamp. It had a nine-inch lens which diffused a wide flat beam of light directly in front of the car and also directed beams further down the road. Oldsmobile recommended this light for driving in fog, rain or snow. The option could be factory ordered or dealer installed. Price was $10.95. including installation. Note the chromed parking lamps on this car – a $6 option.

This was the basic interior on all model club coupes, and the main distinguishing feature from the business coupe. The tiny jump seats folded away leaving a fair amount of cargo capacity. The biggest space advantage of the business coupe was its through-the-trunk access. In the club coupe the back and sides of the interior were heavily cushioned, permitting passengers to ride either sideways or forward.

1940

In 1940 the three series format was continued, but the top of the line models became the 90 Series rather than the previously designated 80. Sales continued on the upswing and Olds jumped a notch to sixth place in the sales race. Model year production was 192,692 and a new all time high calendar year figure of 215,028 was realized.

The introduction of the HydraMatic fully automatic transmission with the 1940 models was one of the most significant innovations ever to originate from Lansing. Both Oldsmobile and GM engineering staffs had invested great amounts of money and effort in developing the new shiftless transmission. HydraMatic was an efficient, well-designed unit which eventually led to the unit that most of today's automatic transmissions are based upon. Cost of the HydraMatic on 1940 models was $57, cheaper than the less complicated Safety Automatic Transmission it replaced.

For the first time, three separate wheelbases were under the three series Oldsmobiles. An inch was added to the model 60, while the 70 remained at 120 inches. The 90 series had a wheelbase of 124 inches. In overall length the 60 grew almost 9 inches, the 70 was just two inches longer and the 90 was more than a foot longer than the 80 series of the previous year.

On the mechanical side of things, the major change was that the engine on the 60 models grew to the same specifications as the powerplant of the 70 Series. Sealed beam headlights were introduced on all models. The model lineup for the smallest Oldsmobile was expanded to included a convertible for the first time in 1940.

A big effort was made to increase the luxury on the top Olds line, the 90 Series. To achieve a lower profile, the 90 models rode on 15-inch tires. Both the 60s and 70s retained 16-inch rubber. The 90s offered extra wide and extra deep lounge type seats built with foam rubber padding. The 90 models were the only 1940s which came without running boards. This was the first year that the top of the line Olds also carried the designation of Custom Cruiser.

Colors were black, maroon, red, ivory, two blues, tan, two grays and green. Pattern cloth and Canada cloth interiors were offered on all closed 60s and 70s. The 90 series interiors were done in mauvetone broadcloth. Convertible interiors were done in Bedford cloth with six colors of leather optional on all open or closed cars.

Factory accessories included a defroster, electric touch radio, back up lights, visor vanity mirror, fog lamps and fender skirts.

In August of 1940, S. E. Skinner was appointed general manager of Oldsmobile replacing C. L. McCuen who had held that post since 1933.

The convertible was added to the bottom of the line series 60 in 1940. Base price on the convertible was $950, making it the most expensive model in the F series. Shipping weight was 3,150 pounds. Tops were done in either tan or black. Model number on this Olds was 403567. Production was 1,347. For 1940, the 60 and 70 series shared the same six cylinder engine. It displaced 230 cubic inches and turned out 95 horsepower.

Least expensive car in the 1940 Olds lineup was this 60 model business coupe priced at just $765. Model number 403527B was shipped at 2,950 pounds. Production totalled 2,752. Interiors in the 60 series business coupe were done in either tan pattern cloth or Canada cloth, with leather optionally available. Accessory group X was extremely popular and consisted of: cigar lighter, thirty-hour panel clock, glovebox light and chrome exhaust extension. Price for the group was $9.40 installed.

Olds went back to the touring designation on its 1940 sedan models, even though there was just one of each sedan per series. Model number 403511 was the 60 series two-door touring sedan. Base price was $810 and shipping weight was 3,045 pounds. This was the most popular 60 series car with production of 29,220. Starting power on the 60 and 70 models came from a Delco 6-volt, 15-plate battery.

1940

Model number 403567 was the F series club coupe. Base price was $805 and shipping weight was 2,995 pounds. Production totalled 2,752. Sixty F series club coupes, two-door sedans and four-door sedans were upholstered in either duotone pattern cloth or Canada cloth with leather as a special order option. Wheelbase on all 60 series models was 116 inches. Gas capacity was 17 gallons and a 60 series car could hold 5 quarts of oil, 18 quarts of water and two pounds of transmission grease.

Plenty of passenger room at a low selling price was a big point for the F-60 four-door touring sedan. Model number 403519 had a base price of $855. Shipping weight was 3,060 pounds. Production totalled 24,422. Trunk area on the 60 series was carpeted and the spare tire was vertically mounted in the trunk. An underseat heater could be ordered on any 1940 model for $19.75.

A newcomer to the 1940 Olds lineup was this Hercules-bodied 60 series station wagon. This attractively styled model carried a price tag of $1,275. Each wagon came with three seats and two of them were easily removable. White ash was used for the framing with birch finish panels with a high varnish rub. Each wagon had a special tool kit mounted under the front seat. Production for this model totalled 633.

This really nifty continental kit graced all 60 series station wagons. By mounting the spare tire in back it gave the car a lot more luggage capacity. The gate was hinged to provide easy access to the load area. Bumpers were special for this car. The wagon offered special heavy duty coil springs in the rear to accommodate heavy loads. Available colors on the wagon included tan, ivory, blue, gray and green. Note how the lower panel was cut out to allow room for the spare when the tailgate was lowered.

Seats were unique in the station wagon. Each seat was built on a tubular steel frame with deluxe cushion springs used in seat construction. All seats were upholstered in brown imitation leather. Rubber floor mats were standard in both the rear and driver's compartment. The 60 series station wagon was not listed in the full 1940 Olds color catalog, but a special color station wagon folder was circulated.

The least expensive 70 series Olds was the business coupe priced at $820. This was model number 403627B, and it was shipped at 3,090 pounds. A total of 4,337 Seventy series business coupes were produced. Interiors in either of the business coupes could be done in tan bedford cord or Canada cloth. Leather was again offered as a special order item.

An attractive model was number 403667, the 70 series convertible. This was, of course, the most expensive six cylinder, carrying a price tag of $995. Shipping weight was 3,290 pounds. Production totalled 1,070, making this the rarest of the 70 series models. All cars in the G series rode on a 120-inch wheelbase with an overall length of just under 200 inches.

White sidewall tires were offered in 1940, but few cars were so equipped from the factory. The whitewalls on this 70 series two-door touring sedan added $11 to its base price of $865. This car carried model number 403611 and was shipped at 3,190 pounds. Production totalled 22,486. The Sunshine Turret Top was listed as a $37.50 option in 1940, but there are indications that few, if any, 1940 models came so equipped.

Extra rear seating capacity made the 70 series club coupe a bigger seller than the similar business coupe. Base price on this offering was $855 and shipping weight was 3,130 pounds. It carried model number 403627. Production totalled 8,505. Standard equipment on all 1940 models were two windshield wipers with a booster pump to insure more positive operation.

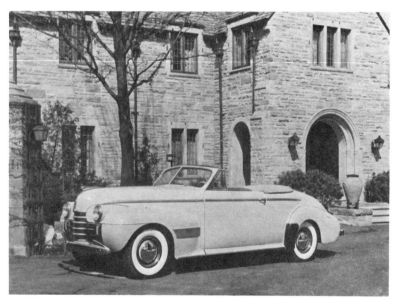

Top seller in the entire 1940 Olds lineup was the 70 series four-door touring sedan. It carried model number 403619 and was base priced at $915. Shipping weight was 3,230 pounds. For 1940, a new type of sealed beam headlight system was adopted by Olds. The new lighting system was much more powerful and reliable than lighting used on previous models. Factory option A was the HydraMatic Drive and it carried the reasonable price tag of $75. A total of 42,467 of the 70 series four-door touring sedans were built.

This is the interior on the 70 series four-door touring sedan. Interior fabrics were vogue weave bedford cloth or Canada cloth with leather available as a special order item. This model had ash trays in both rear side armrests. Fisher Body called its 1940 offerings "Observation Bodies." Each Olds front seat had a front-rear adjustment of 4½ inches.

This 90 series convertible coupe was so rare it was not listed in any factory literature. This car carried model number 403967. Shipping weight was 3,440 pounds. As with all L series cars, it was on a 124-inch wheelbase. For 1940, Olds changed its top series designation from 80 to 90. An exclusive for the 90 series was the front fender chrome trim. Total production for the 90 convertible coupe was 290.

Only one coupe model was produced in the 90 series, and it was in the club coupe configuration. This car carried model number 403927C and a price tag of $1,015. Shipping weight was 3,280 pounds. All 90 series cars were powered by a 257 cubic inch, 110 horsepower L-head engine. Gas capacity on 90 series cars was 17 gallons, oil capacity was 6 quarts and water capacity was 21 quarts.

Top seller in the 90 series was the four-door touring sedan. Model number 403919 was priced at $1,075. Shipping weight was 3,390 pounds. Total production on the L series touring sedan was a surprising 33,075. An innovation for 1940 was two-tone factory paint jobs. This was available only on the 90 series and cost an extra $12.50. This particular car is from the Oldsmobile factory collection and is finished in two-tone combination 45, vagabond blue and mercury blue. This car also has the optional factory fender skirts which were known in the accessory book as streamlined rear fender panels.

1940

Olds production had been on the gradual upswing since the depression. It took the division almost seven years to build a million cars and World War II would make it even longer before the next million milestone was reached. The historic car was a 90 series touring sedan with accessories that included a front center grille guard and whitewall tires.

Rounding out the 90 series was the rarest 1940 Oldsmobile of all, the convertible phaeton. It was the first four-door open car built by Olds in almost a decade. Model number on this car was 403929. Production totalled only 50, and several of these survive today. Olds also started using the Custom Cruiser tag on its top of the line series. Overall length of the 90 series models was 210 inches.

Olds was getting more involved in the chassis business by 1940. This machine was an L-series Miller-Oldsmobile hearse. It is currently owned by Crestline Publishing author Walt McCall of Windsor, Ontario, Canada. This is an attractive styling package with its ornate side coachwork and single window. A rather unusual Olds accessory on this car is the single vertical grille guard which was factory installed for $1.50. Chassis price for a 90 series was $775.

Biggest Olds news in 1940 was the HydraMatic Drive, a bargain at its $75 option price. Demand for this device far outstripped production in this first year. Olds put out a great deal of advertising on HydraMatic and it quickly caught the eye of the motoring public. The transmission selector was actually an attractive unit. This car is also equipped with a deluxe steering wheel, standard on the 90 series and a $12.50 option on the 60 or 70 series.

All 1940 instrument panels were finished in walnut grain. Instruments were placed, according to Olds advertising, for maximum ease of control, visibility and driving safety. A new offering on the 90 series was the use of foam seat padding over the seat springs. The foam was optional on 60 or 70 models. Each Olds was equipped with two sets of matching tumbler locks. One operated the door locks and ignition switch and the other unlocked the glovebox and trunk.

1941

The least expensive car in the 1941 Olds lineup was the 66 business coupe. Model number was 413527B and base price was $805. Shipping weight totalled 3,145 pounds, making this the lightest 1941 Olds. A total of 6,433 66 business coupes were made. All Special series cars rode on a 119-inch wheelbase with an overall length of 204 inches. All 66's came standard with 6.00 x 16-inch tires.

The four-door 66 model slipped a bit in popularity in 1941. It carried model number 413519 and was priced at $895. Shipping weight was 3,230 pounds. A total of 37,820 of this model were produced. Dealer installed accessory Group Y was a popular choice. It included: cigar lighter, electric clock, license plate frames, visor mirror, trunk light, hood light and exhaust extension. The installed price was $21.75 and the same items could be factory installed.

The 66 two-door sedan was high up on the Olds popularity list for 1941. It carried model number 413511 and its base price was $850. Shipping weight was 3,190 pounds and total production was 32,475. In 1941 HydraMatic production began to catch up with demand from Olds buyers. This automatic transmission was listed as factory accessory group A and was priced at $90.

With its new model announcement on September 2 1940, Oldsmobile added versatility to its lineup by offeri for the first time a choice of a 6 or 8-cylinder engine each of its three series.

Olds held onto its sixth place sales standing with an time high of 270,040 model year sales and 230,7 calendar year sales. HydraMatic continued as a big sal builder for the division as almost half the 1941 Oldsm biles sold were equipped with the automatic transmissic In 1940 GM's capacity for building HydraMatics w woefully low, but in 1941 production capacity began meet demand.

New names were tagged on the lowest and middle li models. The 60 Series became known as the Spec Series, while the former 70 models became the Dynam Cruiser Series. Top of the line Oldsmobiles, formerly t 80s and 90s, continued to be called the Custom Cruise as in 1940. The wheelbase on the Special Series w extended to 119 inches, and the Dynamic and Custo Cruisers shared a whopping 125-inch wheelbase.

On the mechanical side of the 1941s, the 6-cylind engine was pepped up a bit by adding 1/8-inch to t bore which brought horsepower output to an even 10 A minor change was made in the 1941 HydraMat adding an interlock which automatically moved the sh lever to neutral when the starter was depressed.

From a styling standpoint, the 1941s received a heavi chrome treatment up front. On all Special and Dynam Cruiser models running boards were hidden behind t doors for the first time. Dash design on the Special Seri was based on American Walnut finish, while other mode were patterned after Bayou wood.

Colors for 1941 included red, two blues, sand, two gray green, brown and black. A variety of two-tone comb nations were available also. Accessories offered includ two types of radios, the Condition-Air heater and defrost system, 30-hour panel clock, directional signals, gas tan door lock and a kit to convert the car to an overnig sleeper (ala Nash).

The 2-millionth Olds was built in 1941. In addition building cars, the division gave a realistic preview of thin to come by devoting increasing amounts of manufacturi space to war production. Government contracts with t Lansing-based GM Division called for building a varie of munitions.

A particularly graceful car was the 66 series convertible, model number 413567. This was the second highest priced Special series Olds at $995. Shipping weight was 3,355 pounds. Total production on this car was 2,822. A deluxe equipment package was offered on any Special or 60 series car. It consisted of: plastic hood ornament, deluxe instrument cluster, deluxe clock and glovebox door, glovebox light and deluxe steering wheel. Price on this factory package was $20 and the items could also be ordered individually.

Model number 413527 was the 66 series club coupe. It carried a base price of $845 and was shipped weighing 3,185 pounds. Production on this model was a surprisingly high 23,796. Six cylinder engines for the first time could be ordered in any Olds series. The 1941 six cylinder displaced 238 cubic inches and turned out 100 horsepower.

The bulk of the 68 series coupes were produced as club coupes, but there were a few business coupes made. Base price on the 68 club coupe was $885, while the 68 business coupe was tagged at $845. Shipping weight on the club coupe was 3,300 pounds and the business coupe weighed 3,260 pounds. The two coupes shared model number 413527 with the 66 series coupes with the business coupe wearing the suffix B. Only 188 Sixty-Eight business coupes were built with 2,684 Sixty-Eight club coupes made.

Most popular of the 68 models was the four-door sedan. It shared model number 413519 with its sister 66 four-door sedan. Shipping weight was 3,390 pounds. Price of this model was $935. A total of 6,009 of this model were built. Standard tires on the 68 four-door were 6.50 x 16 inches. Rear seat width on this model was 57½ inches. Standard rear end ratio was 4.1 to 1 with optional rear ends rated at 4.3 to 1 and 3.9 to 1.

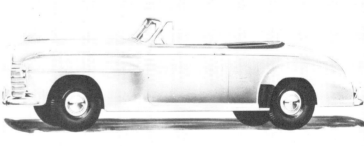

The Special series cars could be ordered with either a six or eight cylinder engine. Quite logically those cars powered by eights were known as 68 models. This is the only year Olds offered so much flexibility with engine selection. This car was model number 413527, a designation the 68 convertible shared with the 66 convertible. Base price was $1,035 and shipping weight was 3,455 pounds. Production on the 68 convertible totalled only 776.

1941

There is some question as to whether a 1941 70 series business or club coupe was built. Most factory literature does not list such a car, but reliable production records indicate 353 were made in the 76 series and 51 were built as 78's. Model number for this car was 413627 in both series. Olds offered to paint any model in a special color if five or more units were involved. In addition, a special fire engine red was available for fire departments on special order.

Fastback styling was the highpoint of the 70, or Dynamic Cruiser, series. Inside Deluxe equipment for the series consisted of a deluxe instrument cluster, deluxe clock and glovebox door, automatic glovebox light and deluxe steering wheel. This equipment was also available on an individual basis. Standard 76 club sedans carried model number 413627 and 41,938 were made. Deluxe 76 club sedans carried number 413627-D and 6,947 were produced. Shipping weight on this car was 3,320 pounds and price was $900.

The 78 club sedan carried model number 413627 or 413627-D in deluxe trim. Visible deluxe equipment on this car included chrome strips on the front and rear fenders, larger hubcaps and wheel trim rings and 7.00 x 15 tires. A total of 8,260 of this model was made in standard trim and 5,338 were built in deluxe trim. Rare optional factory fender skirts carried an emblem and sold for $14 installed. Shipping weight on the 78 club sedan was 3,420 pounds and prices began at $935.

The 78 four-door sedan was model number 413609 in standard trim and 413609-D in deluxe. Standard production of this model was 8,046, while 7,534 deluxes were made. Shipping weight was 3,500 pounds. This particular car was equipped with HydraMatic transmission as evidenced by the chrome letters on the cowl.

Fastback styling was carried over to the four-door Dynamic Cruiser lineup. The 76 four-door sedan carried model number 413609 in standard trim with production totalling 31,074. Model number on the deluxe 76 four-door sedan was 413609-D and 9,645 were made. Shipping weight on the 76 four-door was 3,390 pounds and price was $995. The wheelbase on the Dynamic Cruiser was 125 inches. Standard tire was 6.50 x 16 inches and whitewalls were $8.50 extra.

The only Custom Cruiser model to dip below the $1,000 price barrier was the 96 club coupe. As with all Custom Cruisers, it was built on a 125-inch wheelbase and like all 96 series cars, power came from a 100 horsepower six. This car carried model number 413927 and weighed 3,320 pounds. Production of the 96 club coupe was 2,176.

The Custom Cruiser nametag was used on all 90 series models. Convertibles were model number 413967 and came as a 98 or 96 model. The 96 convertible sold for $1,130 and a 98 convertible went for $1,165. Shipping weight on the 96 was 3,525 pounds and the 98 weighed 3,600 pounds. Interior fabrics offered on Custom Cruiser convertibles included tan bedford cloth, a combination of red leather and tan bedford cloth and leathers in black, blue, green, grey, red and tan. Production totalled 325 in the 96 series and 1,263 in the 98 series.

The top selling model in the Custom Cruiser series was the four-door sedan. A total of 4,176 Ninety-Six four-doors were made, with 22,081 Ninety-Eight four-doors built. Both models of the four-door carried number 413919. The 96 weighed 3,410 pounds and was priced at $1,040 while the 98 tipped the scales at 3,500 pounds and cost $1,075. Another standard feature on the Custom Cruiser, which was optional on other models, was foam rubber seat cushions.

Obviously the ultimate 1941 Olds was the Custom Cruiser convertible phaeton, model number 413967. It was by far the most expensive and rarest of the 1941 Olds lineup and only a handful of these cars survive today. Price on the phaeton — in its last year of Olds production — was a whopping $1,505. It weighed 3,790 pounds and all models were 98's. This HydraMatic equipped beauty belongs to C. Douglas Houston, Jr., of Detroit, and is one of two such phaetons in excellent condition and registered with the Oldsmobile Club of America. Original production of this model was 119, according to one reliable source, but it might actually have been even less.

The other coupe in the Custom Cruiser lineup was the 98 club coupe, model number 413967. This car weighed 3,430 pounds and was priced at $1,020. Production for the 98 club coupe was 1,263. Custom Cruiser interiors for 1941 were done in Royal cloth. Extra-cost upholstery work could be ordered in leather or a two-tone leather and broadcloth combination. An oil filter was a factory option that could be ordered on any model for $5.

1941

The rarest and most expensive of the 66 Series vehicles was the station wagon. This year the models carried wood and steel bodies made by either Hercules or Ionia. The prices were down on this model, dropping to $1,050. Interiors of all wagons were done in simulated brown leatherette. Each station wagon came with three seats, with the rear two seats being designed for easy removal. An underhood light could be ordered on any 1941 Olds for $1.25.

The photo of the 1941 Olds wagon gives a good view of the Ionia supplied body, which differed in a few respects from the Hercules model. Note that on the Ionia body, the stainless steel beltline trim strip, which began just aft of the headlights, was carried along the body and ended at the rearmost D-pillar. On the Hercules bodies, this strip ended at the cowl. In addition, the Ionia bodies had no horizontal rib on the rear quarter panel, while Hercules bodies carried this trim piece.

This artist's rendering of the 1941 Olds station wagon shows the vehicle equipped with a Hercules body. It is not known how many of these bodies were supplied by Hercules and how many came from the Ionia plant. Ionia bodies were supplied by the Yipsilanti Furniture Co. of Yipsilanti, Mich.

Olds continued to supply chassis for the hearse and ambulance manufacturers in 1941. This Miller-Olds service car was manufactured on the 90 Series chassis and was powered by the venerable straight eight engine. The Olds dealer data book listed plain chassis as being available in all series. Prices were: 66 - $600; 68 - $640; 76 - $690; 78 - $725; 96 - $735 and the 98 - $770. Tire makers supplying Olds in 1941 included U.S. Royal, Firestone and Goodrich.

Although Olds did offer its chassis to the professional car trade, overall the cars were not too popular in this side of the industry. The A. J. Miller Co. of Bellefontainne, Ohio, was one of the primary manufacturers that used Olds chassis along with Cadillac. This is the Miller Art Carved model hearse, which featured heavy drapery detail on the rear body sides. These "drapes" were actually cast bronze plaques painted black and attached to the body.

The front end of any 1941 Olds was heavy with chrome. The parking lights were of an attractive design. All grilles were die cast and formed in one basic unit. Each car came with bumper guards as standard equipment and an additional horizontal grille guard could be ordered on the front only of 60 series cars and front and rear on all other models. This particular car was equipped with the rare factory fog and driving lights which sold for the installed price of $10.90.

Oldsmobile seemingly took a page from the Nash book with this "sleeper" option. Those using their Olds for a bed utilized the backseat as sleeping quarters. Room was gained by making it open through to the trunklid. Olds was quite serious about this option and even offered bug screens for the windows. The author has never seen a 1941 model so equipped and this is the only year Olds listed such an accessory package.

Once again the division's bread and butter engine was the L-head six cylinder. It was rated at 100 horsepower from 238 cubic inches and the same powerplant could be ordered in any series car. Compression ratio was 6.1 to 1. At a steady 50 mph Olds advertised economy of 18½ miles per gallon in a six cylinder powered Special series sedan. That same car had a top speed of 86 mph.

A redesigned dash was one of the nice things that greeted owners of all 1941 Oldsmobiles. Panels in the Special series were done in simulated American walnut, while the Dynamic and Custom Cruisers came with simulated Bayou wood finish. Full gauges were housed in an instrument cluster that Olds used until after World War II. Radio installation was in the lower center dash. The glovebox door could be ordered with either an electric clock, a 30-hour clock, or plain.

Most spacious of the interiors on 1941 closed Oldsmobiles was, of course, the Custom Cruiser. Standard upholstery on the Special was heather bedford cloth or Canada cloth. Standard interior on the Dynamic Cruiser series was modern weave cloth or Canada cloth. Custom Cruisers offered Royal cloth as the standard interior fabric. Two-tone upholstery combinations were available at extra charge on the upper two series and leather was also an option. The factory also offered Santoy or satin-rayon seat covers.

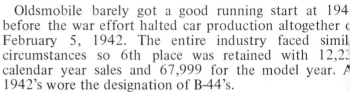

1942

Both convertibles offered in 1942 were extremely rare. Only 848 of the Special (60) series open car were made. A Special series car could be ordered with either a six or eight cylinder engine. Model number for this car was 423567. Price for the 66 convertible was $1,185, while the 68 sold for $1,225. Shipping weight on the 66 was 3,400 pounds, while the 68 weighed 3,515 pounds. The standard convertible top color was light tan, with blue and black available on special order. Two electric motors operated the top.

Oldsmobile barely got a good running start at 194 before the war effort halted car production altogether February 5, 1942. The entire industry faced simil circumstances so 6th place was retained with 12,2 calendar year sales and 67,999 for the model year. 1942's wore the designation of B-44's.

Olds kept its basic styling from previous years with heavier touch up front, due largely to new, massive fro bumpers. Dubbed "double duty" bumpers, the new un consisted of two separate horizontal bars connected vertical bumper guards. Both horizontal bars were join to the car frame by sturdy steel bars.

The Special and Dynamic Cruiser models remained wheelbases identical to 1941. The Custom Cruisers mov up to two inches to a 127-inch wheelbase. Facto literature for the year used the Special, Dynamic Cruis and Custom Cruiser designations interchangeably with t 60, 70 and 90 nomenclature used before 1941. The model was dropped from the lineup in 1942.

Mechanical improvements for 1942 included an a ditional front cross member in the frame and sligh larger braking surfaces. Under the hood, compressi ratios of both powerplants were bumped slightly by redesign of the combustion chambers. The crankshaft w beefed up and connecting rods were made stiffer in t 110-horsepower 8-cylinder engine.

The most striking feature of the 1942 interior was t dark walnut type dash finish. Upholstery in the Spec models was either ripple bedford cloth or mohair. Off ings in the Dynamic Cruisers were modern weave broa cloth or mohair. Top of the line Custom Cruisers we done in tan or gray broadcloth. Full leather upholster or a leather and bedford cord combination, could ordered on a convertible of any series.

Colors for 1942 included: red, tan, ivory, two gray two blues, two greens and black. Nine two-tone com nations were also offered. Accessories were: a dual fl dash heater, three types of radios, electric clock, fend skirts and the in-car bed package. The Dynamic Cruis was also offered in a deluxe package which included spec hood ornament, instrument cluster, clock, steering whe wheel trim rings, larger tires, full size hubcaps, front a rear fender moldings and rear center arm rest.

A Special series business coupe – minus a backseat – continued to be the least expensive Olds built. Model number 423527B's base price was $915 in the 66 model and $955 in the 68. Shipping weight for the 66 was 3,230 pounds and the 68 weighed 3,365 pounds. Sixty series business coupe production totalled 1,166. Standard upholstery of Special series cars was either ripple weave bedford cloth or mohair. Leather was an option.

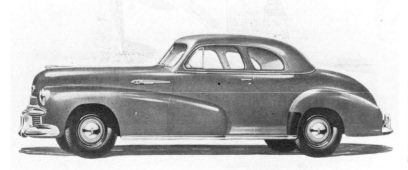

The backseat was a tight squeeze, but by 1942 Olds featured a full width backseat in its club coupe. Model number for the Special series club coupe was 423527. Production totalled 4,173. Base price on the 66 club coupe was $955 and it weighed 3,265 pounds. The 68 club coupe sold for $995 and it was shipped at 3,405 pounds. Two-tone paint schemes, available on all closed Oldsmobiles, cost $10 extra.

An addition to the 1942 Olds lineup was the Special series club sedan. This model carried number 423507. It was the big seller in the 60 series as 10,766 were produced. The 66 club sedan sold for $970 and weighed 3,270 pounds. The 68 club sedan was priced at $1,010 and weighed 3,405 pounds. The same six and eight cylinder powerplants were used across the model lineup, except the 90 series was available only as an eight. The six cylinder developed 100 horsepower and the eight cylinder turned out 110 horsepower.

Model number 423511 was the Special series two-door sedan. Production for this car totalled 3,688. A 66 two-door was priced at $960 and weighed 3,270 pounds. A 68 two-door sedan sold for $1,000 and weighed 3,410 pounds. All 1942 Oldsmobiles carried as standard equipment: safety glass, bumpers, spare wheel and tire, dual horns, dual windshield wipers, vacuum booster pump, two sun visors and a cigar lighter.

Oldsmobile expanded the Special series to include two four-doors in 1941. Model number 423569 was the four-door town sedan. As a 66 this car was priced at $1,005 and it weighed 3,315 pounds. The 68 four-door town sedan sold for $1,045 and weighed 3,455 pounds. Production on the Special series four-door town sedans totalled 3,888. All Special series cars were on a wheelbase of 119 inches.

The bigger seller of the two Special series four-doors was the four-door sedan, model number 423519. Production on this model – which included one extra side window – totalled 8,053. A 66 four-door sedan sold for $1,005 and weighed 3,320 pounds. A 68 four-door sedan went for $1,045 and weighed 3,435 pounds. In 1942, Oldsmobile's tire suppliers were Goodrich, U.S. Royal and Firestone. Sixty-six models came standard with 6.00 x 16 tires and 68's rode on 6.50 x 15 tires. Oversize tires were offered on both models.

The rarest car in the Special series was the Hercules bodied woodie station wagon. It was also the most expensive car in the series, priced at $1,280 as a 66, and $1,320 as a 68. The station wagon carried a shipping weight of 3,515 pounds as a 66 and 3,630 as a 68. Once again the wagon came with brown simulated leather upholstery as standard equipment. Body construction was of white ash and birch with a high varnish finish.

Just two models, in both standard and deluxe trim, were offered in the Dynamic Cruiser (70) series. The Dynamic Cruiser club sedan carried model number 423607 in standard trim and 423607D in deluxe. The deluxe package included: deluxe instrument cluster and glovebox door, electric clock, glovebox and map light, deluxe steering wheel, broadcloth upholstery, foam rubber seat cushions, rear center armrest, wheel trim rings, 7.00 x 15 tires, large hubcaps, plastic radiator ornament and front and rear fender mouldings. Production on the standard model totalled 11,536, while deluxe production was 3,165. The 76 was priced at $1,010, while the 78 went for $1,050. Deluxe models sold for $85 more. Shipping weight was 3,485 pounds on the 76 and 3,620 on the 78.

The fastback styling on the 1941 Dynamic Cruiser lineup carried over to the 1942 models. The 70 series four-door sedan carried model number 423609 in standard trim and 423609D in deluxe form. Price on the 76 four-door sedan was $1,065, while the 78 sold for $1,105. Deluxe models went for $85 more. Shipping weight on the 76 was 3,510 pounds, and the 78 weighed 3,640 pounds. A total of 9,166 of the 70 four-door sedan were produced in standard form, while an additional 3,400 in deluxe trim were made. All Dynamic Cruisers were on a 125-inch wheelbase.

As the winter of 1942 moved on, World War II was about to halt Olds car production completely for several years. For months, the Lansing assembly lines had produced a variety of items for the war effort as well as B-44 Oldsmobiles. This was the rarest of the 1942 models, the Custom Cruiser (90) convertible. It carried model number 423967 and only 216 were made. This was also the most expensive 1942 Olds at $1,450. All Custom Cruisers came on a 127-inch wheelbase and were powered by eight cylinder engines. Ninety-Eight convertibles came with either tan bedford cord, leather or a leather and fabric combination interior.

The lone closed two-door offered in the 98 series was the club sedan. It carried model number 423907 and production totalled 1,771. Price on this model was $1,220. Shipping weight was 3,740 pounds. Standard tire size was 7.00 x 15, and oversize tires were not available. Upholstery on 98 closed models was broadcloth. Fender skirts were standard on 98 models and optionally available on other models for $14.

Rounding out the Custom Cruiser series was the four-door sedan, model number 423969. Price was $1,275 and shipping weight was 3,780 pounds. This was the most popular 98 with a production run of 4,672. The price on the optional HydraMatic was raised to $100. Directional signals were available in 1942 for $11.40. Interior appointments on this model included a folding center armrest. The trunk was carpeted and the spare tire was held in a vertical position on the side.

This Miller Oldsmobile carried a uniquely styled rear panel. This particular Miller unit was available only on the Olds 98 and Cadillac chassis. Drape panels on this car were copper with a dull satin finish. This commercial chassis was a 90 series, and its price was $900 without the Miller body. Other available chassis and prices for 1942 were: 66 – $680, 68 – $720, 76 – $770 and 78 – $810. Chassis assemblies furnished by Olds included: radiator, grille, hood, lamps, fenders and dash instruments.

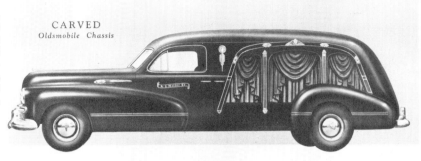

CARVED
Oldsmobile Chassis

Olds sales literature for 1942 stressed the refinement of the chassis. This was a six cylinder machine, but the eight cylinder engine was housed in basically the same chassis. Overall length on the Special series was 204 inches, 212 inches on the Dynamic Cruiser, and 216 inches on the Custom Cruiser. Coil springs were made of silicon manganese steel and were more than 126 inches long before being coiled. The front suspension system remained the knee action unit introduced eight years before.

Oldsmobiles of the 1942 vintage are rare in any car show. This Custom Cruiser was displayed at the 1976 Olds national meet in Geneva, Ohio. This car features some unusual accessories of the era. They include: fog/driving lights – $11.50; whitewall tires – $8.50; spotlight – $14.50; and radio (master electric tune – $68.50; standard pushbutton – $58; and universal – $29.50).

In February, Oldsmobile auto production ground to a halt for four years. A small group of Olds employees and factory officials were on hand to send this 1942 club sedan off into the automotive world. The final cars off the line had painted headlight rims and dully finished items such as grille parts and hubcaps. Despite its otherwise austere appearance this final 1942 Olds sported a two-tone paint job.

Most car makers were hung up with some type of military theme on their 1942 models. Oldsmobile proved no exception with its B-44 designation. Olds called its front end treatment the double duty bumper, and claimed it would help in front end accidents. Fenders were dubbed fuselage fenders. Headlamps on the 1942's were spaced fifteen inches wider than the previous year.

1943 - 1945

For a manufacturer of vehicles during peacetime, Oldsmobile's World War II output was most unusual. The Lansing-based G. M. Division produced no motor vehicles for the war effort.

Olds war production began in the fall of 1940 when a proposal was submitted to the government to build 75 mm and 105 mm high explosive shells. In November of 1940, Olds was awarded its initial shell contract and in April of 1941 that contract was expanded.

By early February of 1942, car production ground to a halt. The Olds slogan became "Keep 'Em Firing" and the division was engaged in the fulltime production of military items.

Oldsmobile controlled the military output from G. M. plants in Janesville, Wis. and Kansas City, Mo. In addition, a vast network of subcontractors—covering 58 cities i 10 states—was needed to meet military demand.

Military cannon built by Olds were used on land and i the air. Tank and tank destroyer cannon built by Old mobile were of the 75 mm M3 and the 76 mm M1A variety. The division also built the gun tube for the M-1 tank destroyer.

Olds built 20 mm and 37 mm cannon and these wei used on both the P-38 Lightning and the P-39 Aircobi airplanes. A variety of production techniques – qui different from those used in the automotive arena were used in wartime machining, milling, grinding an finishing. Olds was successful in its wartime effort i evidenced by receipt of Army-Navy "E" with three star

A number of other war related materials flowed fron Oldsmobile's assembly lines including crankshafts fo English-built Vaxhaul engines used in Army field wagon tank track end connections, B-26 bomber landing gei cylinders and spiders for the Hamilton three-blad propeller.

During the period from before Pearl Harbor until V-Day, Olds produced 48 million rounds of artillery ammi nition, 140,000 aircraft, tank and other types of cannor nearly 350,000 precision parts for aircraft engines and ove 175 million pounds of forgings for heavy duty truck tanks, aircraft and cannon.

In addition to its military production, Oldsmobile wi also used as the location for a series of training classes fe Army personnel working with aircraft and tank weapon

On the human side of the war, a total of 2,255 men le the Lansing GM plants to enter the armed forces and 5 of those men died in the service.

Like other auto producers, Olds did its best in scra drives, prompting an interesting battle between faction who wanted to scrap the division's historical auto colle tion and those who wouldn't hear of such an effort. Th savers won out over the scrappers and because of tha fact Oldsmobile today has the best historical collection c cars within GM. Some secretive methods were used lik hiding the car collection – which dated back to 1901 in several obscure outposts, including at least one plar roof.

A colorful series of full color war posters were used t motivate the work force. Issues of an eight-page newspape the Olds Cannoneer, were mailed to all employees. An sales literature, entitled "Olds Keeps 'Em Firing," an shop manuals for cannon were turned out by those who produced similar literature during peacetime ca production.

During the war years Oldsmobile built a large forg plant. This plant was constructed with an eye to peac time production. Soon after war production was halte the new plant complex began turning out items lik crankshafts and camshafts.

Oldsmobile built a variety of items during World War II, but it did not produce any complete military vehicles. The division numbered more than 200 different items which it built for the war effort. The range was from automatic aircraft cannon to airplane engine parts. This special display showed Oldsmobile war workers their part in the winning battle.

Oldsmobile produced a large number of rockets which were used in a variety of applications during the war. Here a Republic P-47 Thunderbolt was outfitted with triple rocket launchers under each wing. The Olds-built projectiles could be launched by bazookas and this type of weapon was very successfully used in Southwest Pacific fighting.

Olds produced many airplane engine internal parts from 1942 until 1946. One plane that used such parts was the Martin B-26 Medium Bomber pictured. This plane was powered by two, 18-cylinder, 2,000 horsepower Pratt & Whitney engines which Olds supplied parts for. The division also built parts for the Rolls-Royce Merlin aircraft engine.

Before the war effort Oldsmobile's Building 32 was used as a preparation and shipping point for finished cars. By 1944 this area had been converted to the production of 155mm shells. Launched by a powerful gun nicknamed the "Long Tom" these shells could be hurled up to 14 miles. This photo shows a conveyor system carrying the shells from a washing bin to a drying area.

Although Olds did not build any complete vehicles for the fighting front they did produce a number of componet parts for military vehicles. Some main components came from the Olds forge plant, including 78 different parts which were forged for four and six ton truck axles. Here the "Red Ball' express convoy speeds across France carrying 500,000 tons of supplies. Many of these units rode on Olds forged axles.

Oldsmobile built guns were used on a variety of awesome looking tanks. This M-4 tank was outfitted with 75 mm Olds gun. This gun unit weighed 893 pounds and shot a 14.7 pound, high explosive shell. Oldsmobile built several other tank guns in volume production.

The North American Mustang was one airplane equipped with aircraft cannon supplied by Oldsmobile. This particular plane had two 20mm M2 cannon mounted in each wing. Olds built 37 mm aircraft cannon as well and these were mounted on airplanes like the P-38 Lightning and the P-38 Aircobra. The Olds automatic aircraft cannon were a version of the Hispano-Suiza used by the British.

Olds expanded its forge plant operation during the war years, but during this expansion effort it kept the war effort parts coming. Oldsmobile made several forged parts for airplanes like the North American B-25 Mitchell. These parts included several vital landing gear components and other integral parts for propellar assemblies.

1946

Oldsmobile got a good jump on building its postwar cars, as in early 1945 conversion back to building auto parts began in Lansing. Hand-built models of the 1946 Oldsmobile — the first such postwar cars built by any GM division — were displayed in Lansing and major cities across the country as early as July of 1945.

Oldsmobile was among the first car producers to resume auto building following the war. A completely new front end treatment, centering on a new grille design, was created for the 1946 models. Mechanically, most of the car was a carry-over from 1941-2 models. This styling package served the division through the 1948 model year with few changes.

For 1946, the 60 series models were available only with a six cylinder powerplant. This six cylinder, common to both 66 and 76 models, displaced 238 cubic inches and was rated at 100 horsepower. Model number 463519 was the 66 (Special) series four-door sedan. It weighed 3,365 pounds and was priced at $1,169. Domestic production totalled 11,053. Despite wartime startup problems and the crippling UAW strike, an additional 1,694 model 66 four-doors were exported to Australia with right-hand drive setups.

On October 15, 1945 the assembly lines began to turn out 1946 models, but a crippling UAW strike hit GM on November 21, 1945 just as production was hitting its stride. Car production did not resume until April 1, 1946 and for the entire model year it was indeed a seller market. Model year totals were 119,388 with 114,674 Oldsmobiles produced in calendar year 1946, good for seventh sales spot. In addition, a special run of model 66 4-door sedans were built for Australia. A total of 1,694 of this right-hand-drive model were built.

The 1946's were warmed over 1942 models, and this was the styling that Olds would use for the bulk of its cars for the next two years. Gone was the heavy, double-bar bumper styling of the 1942 front end. Front Lucite parking light lenses were inset into the bumper guards. The grille assembly was made of four separate die cast pieces, not including the base. Two colors — amber and red — were offered in the hood ornament which was also made of Lucite. Wrap around bumpers were found on the Dynamic Cruisers and Custom Cruisers, but they were not used on Special Series models. The Specials were available in 1946 only with the 6-cylinder engine.

On the mechanical side of things, the 1946's were nearly identical to pre-war Oldsmobiles. A few refinements were offered under the hood, but horsepower ratings remained the same as 1942. A new, heavier duty connecting rod and improved rod bearings were introduced. A higher rating thermostat was also found on the new models, along with a new type oil resistent synthetic rubber engine mounting block. Brake lining width was increased both front and rear, while steel clutch plates — faced with cork — replaced previously used brass plates. In the tire area 6:50 x 16 were made standard on both sixes and eights in the Dynamic Cruiser series. Specials were equipped with 6:00 x 16's and Custom Cruisers came with 7:00 x 15's. The 15-inch wheels and tires were an option on any Dynamic Cruiser.

Interior changes included a one-piece cast instrument panel grille. Special series interiors were done in tan mixture pattern cloth. Standard models of the Dynamic Cruiser came with modern weave Bedford cloth. Deluxe Dynamic Cruisers and all Custom Cruiser closed cars came with either tan or gray custom broadcloth. Convertibles came with leather and cloth combinations in a variety of colors, or all tan Bedford cloth. Black convertible tops were standard with tan top material an option.

1946 colors included black, ivory, two blues, three greens, red, beige and two grays. Six two-tone combinations were also available on an optional basis.

Popular factory accessories were a seven-tube deluxe push button radio, Condition-Air heater and defroster, electric clock, visor vanity mirror, direction signal system and driving and fog lights.

Oldsmobile worked out and heavily publicized a series of "Valiant" controls designed to aid disabled war veterans and other handicapped people operate cars. The Hydra-Matic transmission helped make such controls possible. There were a variety of special steering wheel devices coupled with a wide brake pedal, hand brake and throttle controls, hand dimmer switch, left-foot throttle and many other special controls.

Oldsmobile called model number 463527, the 66 club coupe, a personal sized car. Rear seating capacity in this model was optimistically rated at three. All Special series models were on a 119-inch wheelbase and the standard tire size was 6.00 x 16 inches. Price on this two-door model was $1,108, making this the least expensive 1946 Olds. Shipping weight was 3,315 pounds. Production on the Special club coupe totalled 4,537.

Fastback styling was expanded to the bottom line series in 1946. It is most difficult to distinguish 1946 models from 1947's. The easiest way to distinguish the two models is by the distinctive front fender chrome moldings. Model number for the 66 two-door club sedan was 463507. Price was $1,134 and shipping weight was 3,330 pounds. Production totalled 11,721 and the Special series club sedan was the most popular 66 offering.

The budget-minded Olds open car buyer was limited to model 463567, the 66 convertible. Only a limited number of buyers were interested, as 1,409 of this model were sold. Price on this offering was $1,327 and shipping weight was 3,480 pounds. Convertible interiors could be ordered in either leather trimmed bedford cord or a variety of colors of leather. This particular car had the specially ordered tan top. Most convertibles had black top material.

The Oldsmobile standard station wagon. The wood bodies were supplied by Ionia and Hercules. The quarter windows were sliders, which was common practice. The rear door is more narrow than the front. Concealed hinges were used for the front doors, exposed hinges for the rear. Oldsmobile, like the other GM divisions, attempted to integrate more sheet metal in the wagons, as evidenced by the front fenders. The rear end was more slanted to give it a more streamlined appearance. The overall wagon design blended well with the rest of the car line.

1946

Rarest of the 1946 Oldsmobiles was the station wagon, model number 463581. Production was only 140. As usual, the wagon came only as a 66 model. Price was a whopping $1,795 which could account for the low sales figure. Weight was 3,680 pounds. The wagon came as a standard model with simulated leather upholstery or as a deluxe model with genuine leather upholstery. Only black top roof coverings were available on the wagon.

From the rear it is obvious that the station wagon was the tallest of the 1946 models. Wagons were available only in black, ambassador red, pawnee beige and forest green. The wagon featured a cargo area in excess of 85 inches long. Both rear seats were designed to be quickly removed. The factory rated the station wagon's load capacity at 1,000 lbs.

The model lineup in the 70 (Dynamic) series continued to be quite limited in 1946. There were just two basic body styles with two different powerplants. Deluxe and standard models were offered as well. Model number 463607 was the 76 (or 78) club sedan and a D after the designation indicated deluxe trim. Price on the 76 club sedan was $1,184 with an extra $100 for the deluxe package. Weight was 3,444 pounds. Production was 30,929 with an additional 1,923 built in deluxe trim. This was the most popular 1946 Olds.

Fastback styling was most obvious from the rear. This 78 club sedan could be distinguished by the numeral 8 located on the trunk lid. Price was $1,264 on the standard with the deluxe package adding $100. Production was 8,723 standards and 2,188 deluxes. Deluxe equipment in the 70 series consisted of a special steering wheel, instrument cluster and glovebox door, rear seat center armrest, 7.00 x 15 tires, chrome wheel trim rings, foam rubber seat cushions and a deluxe electric clock.

Four-doors in the 70 series all carried model number 463609 with deluxe models carrying the suffix D. A total of 18,425 Seventy-six four-door sedans were built in standard trim with 2,179 more deluxes built. In the 78 series, 7,103 were made with 2,939 additional deluxes built. Base prices were $1,234 on the 76 four-door and $1,313 on the 78 four-door. Deluxe equipment added $100 to either model. Shipping weight was 3,515 pounds on the 76 and 3,660 on the 78.

1946

Rarest of the Custom Cruisers was the convertible, model number 463967. Only 874 of these open cars were built. This was the most expensive Olds at $1,840 and shipping weight was 3,750 pounds. HydraMatic was a popular offering, particularly in 90 series cars. The Olds automatic transmission realized various design improvements following extensive World War II tank duty. The Custom Cruiser convertible, like all cars in the 90 series, rode on a 127-inch wheelbase.

Top of the line for Olds again after the war was the plush 90 (Custom Cruiser) series, based on a 127-inch wheelbase. Fender skirts were a 90 series exclusive. All 98's were powered by a 257 cubic inch straight-eight turning out 110 horsepower. Model number 463969 was the four-door sedan which cost $1,490 and weighed 3,725 pounds. It was by far the most popular 98 as 11,031 were sold. Upholstery on all closed 98's was in either tan or gray broadcloth.

The fastback styling wore particularly well on the longer 98 series club sedan. Model number 463907 was priced at $1,442 and weighed 3,690 pounds. Production totalled 2,459. Because of after the war production problems, some accessories were in extremely short supply in 1946. Two hard to obtain optional items were radios and heaters. Supply plants found it difficult to keep up with the postwar auto boom.

Olds basically sold all the cars it could build in 1946, so there was little need to advertise or promote the product in auto shows. The division, however, used this Lansing display to show its new models and also publicize its Valiant control system which aided handicapped people, particularly disabled veterans, in driving. Olds was a natural for this program because of its pioneering efforts with the HydraMatic transmission which made it much easier for handicapped people to drive.

A strike by the United Auto Workers kept Olds sales from really soaring in 1946. This is the body drop operation in Lansing on one of the first postwar Oldsmobiles built. The portion of the car being dropped onto the chassis was produced largely by Fisher Body Division. The bodies were received on an upstairs floor and various trim operations were performed by Olds before the actual "body drop" took place.

Convertible production was on the upswing in 1947 for the 60 (Special) series. Model number for the Special convertible was 473567. For 1947 60 series cars could be either six or eight cylinder powered. A total of 3,949 Series 66 convertibles were built, while 2,579 Series 68 convertibles were sold. The 66 sold for $1,627, while the 68 went for $1,680. Shipping weights were 3,520 pounds for the six cylinder and 3,595 pounds for the eight cylinder.

The strike in 1946 plus the staggering demand of the American public for new cars of almost any manufacture assured there would be few changes from Lansing in 1947. A total of 194,388 model year sales and 191,45 calendar year cars were good enough to hold onto seventh spot for Olds.

Changes between the 1946 and 1947 Oldsmobiles were almost non-existent. The most easily spotted difference is the front fender and door chrome strip, which was changed slightly between 1946 and 1947. Mechanically the 1946 and 1947 models were nearly identical.

An 8-cylinder engine popped back up in the Special Series, and again there were 66 and 68 model Oldsmobile available. Oldsmobile, while it was doing nothing new with this move, was checking ahead to see how well the relatively high powered 8-cylinder engine would sell in it lightest car. This is exactly the thinking that would lead to the 88 model a couple of years later.

Colors for 1947 were black, three greens, two reds, two beiges, two blues, two grays and six two-tone combinations. Special Series interiors were in tan mixture cloth standard Dynamic Cruisers were done in modern weave cloth and DeLuxe Dynamic Cruisers and Custom Cruiser were outfitted in gray custom broadcloth. Convertible offered either Bedford cord and leather combinations or all tan cloth with varying trim colors. The factory accessor list included Dual Flow heater and defroster, exhaust deflector, automatic underhood light and a Safety spotlight.

While the 1947's were nearly identical to offerings from the previous model year and closely resembled pre-war Oldsmobiles, stylists and engineers were busy working on things to change all that. Olds and GM stylists in 194 were putting final touches on what became Futuramic styling for the top of the line models in 1948.

A high compression, V-8 overhead valve engine had been a pet project of GM research director Charles Kettering for a number of years. On June 4, 1947 Boss Ket shoe horned his new V-8 into a stock looking 1947 Olds sedan for a demonstration at the Summer Meeting of the Society of Automotive Engineers. This demonstration powerplant was run on 99 octane gas and its compression ratio was 12:5 to 1.

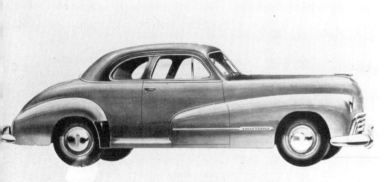

Sales on model number 473527, the 60 series club coupe, held up well in 1947. A total of 14,297 Olds buyers bought Special series club coupes. The 66 club coupe was the least expensive 1947 Olds at $1,308 and shipping weight was 3,315 pounds. All 60 series cars rode on a 119-inch wheelbase, and low pressure balloon 6.00 x 16-inch tires. Fifteen-inch tires and whitewalls were optional.

Station wagon production continued to be on a highly specialized basis in 1947. The 66 series wagon carried a price tag of $2,175. Station wagon colors included black, ambassador red, pawnee beige and ivy green. The standard station wagon interior was tan simulated leather. Production for the 66 station wagon was only 968 and very few of this model survive today.

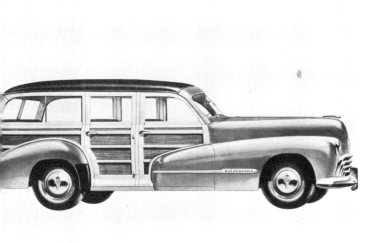

For the first time in several years a 68 station wagon was available, and this proved to be the rarest 1947 Olds built. Only 492 of the Special 68 series wagons were made. Price on this model was $2,228, making this the most expensive 1947 Olds. With both the center and rear seats installed, seating was available for eight adults. The tailgate on this model folded flat for easy loading.

Most popular among the Special models was number 473507, the club sedan. This fastback styled auto was available as a 66 priced at $1,334 and weighing 3,330 pounds and as a 68 priced at $1,387 and weighing 3,405 pounds. Production for the 60 series club sedan was 28,488. The standard interior fabric on Special series cars was tan mixture cloth with other interior options available.

Model number 473519 was the Special series four-door sedan. A total of 22,660 of this model were built. The 66 four-door sedan was priced at $1,369 and weighed 3,375 pounds, while the 68 cost $1,422 and tipped the scales at 3,450 pounds. Standard equipment on all 60 series cars included: safety glass, spare wheel, tire and tube, dual horns, dual windshield wipers, vacuum booster pump, two sun visors and a cigar lighter.

David Bond's 1947 club coupe is a 68 model from Huntington, West Virginia. The cowl vent, open in this photo, provided good ventilation for front seat passengers. The 68 club coupe sold for $1,361, and weighed 3,390 pounds. Chrome trim rings, like the wheels of this car are equipped with, sold for $10.60 as a dealer installed option. Optional equipment on Bond's car also includes either the $72.75 standard radio or the $82.75 deluxe radio.

The standard 70 (Dynamic) series club sedan carried model number 473607. This was the most popular Oldsmobile in 1947 and production totalled 38,152. Price on the 70 club sedan was $1,392 in 76 trim and $1,445 as a 78 model. Shipping weight was 3,460 pounds for the 76 and 3,535 pounds for the 78. The standard Dynamic series interior fabric was modern weave cloth.

The Dynamic series four-door sedan was model number 473609. Production of the standard model totalled 30,841. The 76 was priced at $1,459 and weighed 3,525 pounds. The 78 carried a price tag of $1,512 and weighed 3,600 pounds. Tire suppliers for the 1947 Oldsmobile assembly lines were Goodrich, U.S. Royal and Firestone. Four ply tires were standard with six ply tires available on special order.

The deluxe 70 series four-door sedan was model number 473609D and as with all Dynamic series offerings, it was available as either a 76 or 78. Price on the 76 was $1,565 and weight was 3,550 pounds, while the 78 deluxe sold for $1,618 and weighed 3,625 pounds. Total production for all Dynamic series four-doors with the deluxe package was 7,984. HydraMatic continued as a popular Olds option and it was priced at $135.

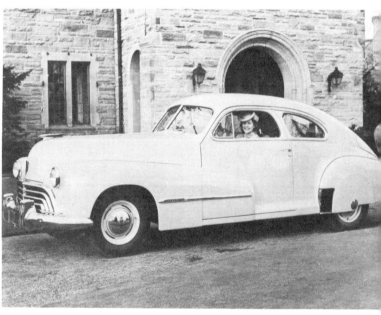

Model number 473607D was the deluxe 70 series club sedan. Production for this model totalled 6,697. Price on the 76 deluxe club sedan was $1,500 and shipping weight was 3,475 pounds. The 78 deluxe club sedan cost $1,554 and weighed 3,550 pounds. Deluxe equipment in the 70 series included a special instrument cluster, clock and steering wheel, gray custom broadcloth interior, foam rubber seat cushions, rear center armrests and 7.00 x 15-inch tires. This car also was equipped with fender skirts which sold for $17.35 and differed from those which were standard on all 98's.

Rarest among the top of the line 90 (Custom Cruiser) series was the convertible. It carried model number 473967. Price was $2,040 and shipping weight on this open car was 3,765 pounds. Production totalled only 3,940. All 98's rode on 7.00 x 15-inch tires and all came standard with their own distinctive fender skirts exclusive to the top of the line series.

Power on all Custom Cruiser models came from the tried and true 110 horsepower straight-eight engine. This car wore the standard convertible top done in black. Tan convertible tops were also available on special order. Whitewall tires were rather rare as 1947 factory equipment and this car sports the "plastic white sidewall disks." They carried part number 982392 and sold for $12.10 installed either as a factory option or by the dealer.

Charles "Boss" Kettering, head of GM's research operations for years, spent most of the World War II years working on various overhead valve engine designs. By 1947 these experimental engines had been stuffed into current year Oldsmobiles and were being tested at the proving grounds and on the highways. Even Kettering's early designs were based on high compression heads and the gradual raising of gasoline octane ratings.

The lone closed two-door in the 98 lineup continued to be the club sedan, model number 473907. Price on this model was $1,642 and shipping weight was 3,690 pounds. A total of 8,475 Custom Cruiser club sedans were produced. Standard interior fabric for closed 98 models was gray custom broadcloth. A rear window wiper could be added on this model for $14.60, an option that could be dealer installed.

By far the most popular 98 was the four-door sedan. It carried model number 473969. Price for this top of the line four-door was $1,690 and shipping weight was 3,775 pounds. Production for the Custom Cruiser was a surprisingly high 24,733. The factory mentioned in its dealer data book for 1947 that it would sell a 98 chassis including radiator, grille, hood, lamps, fenders and dash instruments for $1,263. These chassis were sold mainly to funeral coach and ambulance builders.

1948

The most expensive 1948 Oldsmobile six cylinder was the 66 series station wagon. It carried a price tag of $2,614 and had model number 483562. Production for the 1948 Sixty-Six wagon totalled 1,393. Standard wagon upholstery continued to be tan simulated leather. Regular wagon colors were black, ambassador red, tawnee buff and ivy green. This car was equipped with the rare cadet external sun visor which sold for $30.25 installed.

Olds continued to offer a 68 wagon in 1948. Production on this model totalled 1,314 and the price was $2,672, making this the most expensive 1948 Olds. This particular car is owned by Oldsmobile Club of America member Karl Foss of Middleton, Wisconsin. Foss found this car on an island in highly original condition with 78,000 miles on it. The wagon carries Wisconsin historical plate number 1, issued in recognition of the work Foss has done for historical vehicles in his state.

In 1948 Oldsmobile aggressively moved into a period (innovation that would carry it well into the 1950's as (automotive leader. The year marked the introduction (Futuramic styling in the 98 line and the completion (developmental work on the Rocket V-8 which wou. bow in 1949.

A total of 173,661 cars were built during the model ye; with a calendar year output of 194,755. With its ne styling and despite its later introduction, the 98 Seri(became the best selling Oldsmobile for the first time sinc the series was introduced in 1940. The division remained i its familiar 7th place niche despite increased 98 sale

Because of its new styling, the 98's were introduced i February, several months later than the 60 and 70 model But the wait was worthwhile as the new top of the lir Olds was quite a hit. This also began a tradition of offerir the next year's styling a year early on the 98 Series. Th new 98 looked longer and indeed was lower than the 194 offerings, but actually two inches were trimmed from th wheelbase from the previous year, dropping it to 12 inches. The new model was offered in three body style: the convertible, club sedan and 4-door sedan. The onl underhood change came when the horsepower of th Straight-8, in its last year of production, was upped fiv horsepower to 115.

Horsepower remained the same on both the 6 and 8 cylinder offerings of the 60 and 70 Series. Up front ther was a slightly different ornament treatment and a sligh re-style on the rearend around the tailite area. A con bination wood and metal Fisher Body was offered on th 60 Series station wagons replacing the Ionia bodies use on previous wagons. A slightly fancier interior trir package was also offered on 1948 models of the statio: wagon.

Standard upholstery on the 66 and 68 Series Old: mobiles was striped Bedford cord, while all other close(models (except wagons) were done in shadow strip broadcloth. Deluxe trim packages of either gray or brow.

1948

roadcloth could be ordered on any closed car. Open cars
ere available either in leather or Bedford cord in a variety
f colors.

Seventeen colors were available with 10 two-tone combi-
ations available. Station wagon owners were limited to
five-color choice and wagon interiors came standard in
rown simulated leather. Factory accessories for 1948
cluded two types of radios, heater, defroster, Cadet
ont visor, spotlight, exhaust deflector and windshield
asher.

News of the Kettering V-8 engine was widespread by
te 1948 and in September the press was called in for a
etailed briefing on the revolutionary powerplant. An
mbitious construction project was underway on the
outheast portion of Olds property to construct a plant
r Rocket V-8 protection. By September of 1948 the
ew plant was in full tilt operation. A total of 300 new
achines were in place and Oldsmobile was set to offer
s first V-8 since the ill-fated Viking departed the
utomotive scene in 1930.

The lone open car below the 98 series was the 60 series
convertible, model number 483567X. As with all 60 series
cars, the convertible was based on a 119-inch wheelbase.
Price on the 66 model was $1,725 and production totalled
1,801. The 68 model was priced at $1,780 and 2,091 were
built. Convertible interiors were done in either bedford cord
or a combination of leather and bedford cord.

The year 1948 continued to be a good one for club coupe
sales. Model number for the 60 series coupe was 483527 and
the suffix D indicated the deluxe package. The price on the
66 club coupe was $1,609, while the deluxe 66 went for
$1,749. The 68 club coupe went for $1,667 and the deluxe
68 sold for $1,808. A total of 8,226 Sixty series club coupes
were built with an additional 1,100 deluxes made. Standard
60 series interiors were done in striped bedford cord.

Model number 483519 was the 60 series four-door sedan
with deluxe models carrying the designation D as a suffix.
Production totalled 15,842 standard four-doors and an
additional 2,300 deluxes. A standard 66 series four-door was
priced at $1,677, while the deluxe 66 went for $1,815.
The 68 standard four-door was priced at $1,735 and the
deluxe sold for $1,876. This car was equipped with white-
wall tires which were a $15 option.

Most popular of the 60 series cars was the two-door club
sedan. It carried model number 483507 with deluxe models
carrying the suffix D. The 66 club sedan went for $1,634
and the deluxe 66 club sedan sold for $1,776. With the
bigger powerplant, the 68 club sedan sold for $1,693 and
the deluxe 68 club sedan brought $1,834. Deluxe equipment
in the 60 series included: special upholstery, deluxe steering
wheel and horn ring, foam rubber seat cushion, special
instrument cluster, deluxe rearview mirror, 7.10 x 15 tires
and electric clock. Production totalled 20,932 for all 60
series club sedans in standard trim. In addition, 2,800 more
deluxes were built.

The dash layout was changed very little in 1948 on 60 and
70 series models. Symmetry was obtained between the
instrument cluster and the glovebox clock which could be
ordered as part of the deluxe equipment package. The
standard radio was priced at $84.25 installed, and the
deluxe six tube radio went for $10 more. Instrumentation
included: a gas gauge, ammeter, oil pressure gauge and
temperature indicator.

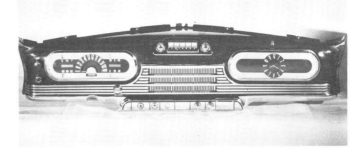

1948

Fastback styling continued to be eye appealing on 70 series four-doors. Model number for 70 four-doors was 483609 with the designation D used on deluxe models. Standard production totalled 12,444 and an additional 12,202 deluxes were built. Seventy series four-door prices were: standard 76 – $1,801; deluxe 76 – $1,947; standard 78 – $1,859; and deluxe 78 – $2,005. Two-tone paint schemes were popular options by 1948 and ten combinations were offered. The price was $12.45 and two-toning was not offered on the 98 club sedan.

This attractive fender skirt was offered in 1948 as part of the deluxe package on 70 series deluxe models. Skirts could also be ordered as an accessory on any standard 60 or 70 model for $17.35 installed. For 1948, all models had stainless steel rear fender gravel shields. The most distinctive rear styling change for 60 and 70 models was the new taillight design. The bottom round portion of the taillight served as a permanent warning reflector in case of taillight failure.

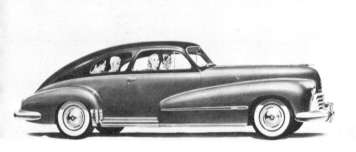

Seventy series Oldsmobiles, like the 60 series models, could be ordered with either the six cylinder or straight powerplant. The straight eight was in its final year of production in Lansing. Model number on the 70 club sedan was 483607 and the letter D appeared on deluxe models. Price on the standard 76 was $1,726, while the deluxe 76 went for $1,873. The standard 78 club sedan went for $1,785, while the deluxe was priced at $1,931. A total of 16,923 standards were built with an additional 8,249 deluxe 70 models made.

Oldsmobile waited until well into the 1948 model year before introducing its all new 98 series. This styling concept was tagged as Futuramic and it set the stage for the next generation of Oldsmobiles. For the final time all 98's were powered by the venerable 257 cubic inch, straight-eight. A slightly raised compression ratio gave it five more horsepower than the powerplant in 60 and 70 models. All 98's rode on a 125-inch wheelbase.

The new styling was particularly graceful on the 98 convertible. Model number 483867 X carried a price tag of $2,624, making it the most expensive of the 98 models. A total of 12,914 Ninety-Eight convertibles were built. Instrument panels on all 98's were two-tone with the center portion done in pearl beige and the rest of the panel color keyed to the upholstery. Convertible interiors were done in either two-tone bedford cord or bedford cord and leather in a variety of colors.

Despite its late introduction and totally new styling package, the deluxe 98 four-door sedan proved to be the most popular 1948 Olds. It carried model number 483869D and was priced at $2,256. Production totalled a whopping 32,456. Deluxe 98 models were upholstered in broadcloth. Other deluxe equipment in the top of the line series included: special front and rear floor mats, a clock, deluxe steering wheel, chrome wheel trim rings, 8.20 x 15 tires and rear center armrests.

The only closed two-door model in the 98 lineup for 1948 was the club sedan. It carried model number X-483807 and the deluxe model carried the suffix D. A total of 2,311 standard 98's were built. The base price for this car was $2,078. The deluxe 98 club sedan listed for $2,182 and production totalled 11,949. Standard model 98's were upholstered in shadow striped broadcloth.

Even with its top up, the 98 convertible was an attractive car. Convertible tops were done in either black or tan. All factory tops had the small rear window. All 98 convertibles rode on 8.20 x 15 tires. Factory tire suppliers in 1948 were U.S. Royal, Firestone and Goodrich. Four ply tires were standard with six ply tires available on special order.

The standard 98 four-door carried model number 483869. Base price on this model was $2,151. Production on the 98 four-door totalled only 5,605 as most buyers opted for the deluxe model. HydraMatic remained a strong selling point for Olds as its competitors were just beginning to offer automatic transmissions. The HydraMatic was listed as Olds option group H and by 1948 the price had risen to $185.

Model year 1948 provided an interesting assembly line model mix. Olds workers were familiar with the older style 60 and 70 series cars since they had been building them since before the war. But the all new Futuramic styled 98's were something altogether different. Very few parts — with the exception of the drive train — could be interchanged between 60 and 70 series cars and the all new 98.

1949

Not since the introduction of the curved dash model a half century before, did Oldsmobile make such an impact as with the Futuramic Rocket V-8 powered machines which were introduced from Lansing on September 15, 1948.

Despite the introduction of revolutionary changes, Olds retained seventh place in the sales race but put down the basis for its sales climb in years to come. A total of 288,310 cars were built in the model year, with a calendar year output of 282,885.

Biggest of the big 1949 news was under the hood of the 88 and 98 offerings. The Rocket V-8 had been under serious development since the war years, from both corporate and divisional levels. The Olds V-8, along with the introduction of a similar Cadillac engine, showed the way into a new type of mass-produced powerplant which would gradually attract all major car builders in the U.S.

The new Lansing-built V-8 offered some impressive statistics for the day: 7:25 to 1 compression ratio, 135 horsepower at 3,600 rpm and 263 pounds of torque 1,800 rpm. Advertising touted the five-bearing cranksha overhead valves and hydraulic valve lifters. Topping t new V-8 block was a new type of carburetor designed minimize vapor lock. As the Rocket powerplant w introduced, engineers were already saying that as gasoli Octane ratings could be upped, compression ratios wou rise to 12.5 to 1.

The new high powered V-8 was an even better mate the Hydra-Matic than the straight-eight offered previous In 1949, Olds talked about the special safety downsh device known as "Whirlaway." By 1949, Olds was proud mentioning the billions of miles of driving Hydra-Ma equipped cars had attained in nine years.

As if the new eight cylinder engine wasn't enough, a ne "Big Six" was offered as well. Both bore and stroke we upped for 1949 on the 6-cylinder, reaching 3-17/ inches by 4-3/8 inches. This new combination curious equalled the 257 cubic inches of the previous yea straight-eight cylinder engine.

The changeover to Futuramic styling began with t 1948 98's and was completed across the board in 194 Oldsmobiles were slated initially to be offered only two models, the 76 and the 98 — the popular 88 was last minute addition to the Olds lineup. The 76 and 8 models shared a 119½ inch wheelbase, while the 98 ro alone on a 125-inch wheelbase.

A total of six models were offered in both the 76 and 8 series. The 98's were restricted to only 4 models. An new station wagon, featuring a Fisher Body with spar use of real wood trim, was offered either as a 76 or 8 A luggage capacity of 80 square feet was realized with t second seat folded down. The wagon came equipped wi leather upholstery and mahogany veneer panels. Anoth attractive Olds offering new to the 1949 lineup, was t Holiday hardtop coupe. This car shared its unique Fish Body with the Buick Riviera and Cadillac DeVille and w offered initially only on 98 models.

For 1949 a total of 13 colors were offered singly, wi four special Holiday color schemes offered and fo 2-tones were available. Nine upholstery packages we available on 76's and 88's, and 10 upholstery choic were offered on the 98. Leather was available on any Ol model in 1949. Accessories for the year included: Sup Deluxe radio, traffic light viewer, fog lights, backup ligh and turn signals.

In addition to offering a unique line of cars, Oldsmobi also featured some different marketing tools for 1949. T show off its new Rocket V-8 engine, a plastic showroo display hood was made available to dealers. An amazing well-detailed plastic model of a four-door sedan was bui by Cruver Manufacturing Company. These tiny Olds were one of the first 1/25th scale models which ha since become popular with collectors.

For the first time in a long while, the attention of th auto racing world was focused on Oldsmobile. The pac car for the 1949 Indianapolis 500 was an 88 convertibl NASCAR stock car racers quickly got the idea that th new V-8 was a hot setup. Of the nine races staged by th NASCAR grand national division in 1949, Oldsmobi took the checkered cloth in six of them. The two to point standing drivers, Red Byron and Bob Flock, bot drove Oldsmobiles.

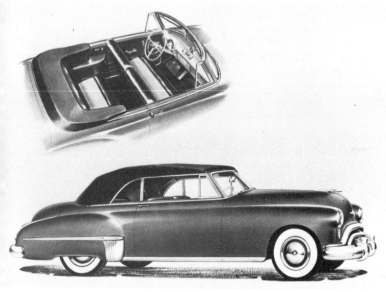

The 76 convertible, model number 493567X, was the second least popular model in the 1949 line. This model and the station wagon were offered in only the deluxe version rather than the standard and deluxe offerings in the rest of the 76 body styles. A price tag of $2,025 came on this car, with a shipping weight of 3,620 pounds. A total of 5,338 76 convertibles were produced in 1949.

The rather novel club coupe, model number 493527, was continued in 1949. This 76 model, as well as others, could be detected visually from the 88 by lack of the Futuramic chrome panel near the front of the chrome rocker panel moulding. A price tag of $1,630 made the 76 club coupe Oldsmobile's least expensive car in standard trim. The deluxe model was $135 more. Weight was 3,410 pounds. Production was 9,403 for the standard and 3,280 on the deluxe.

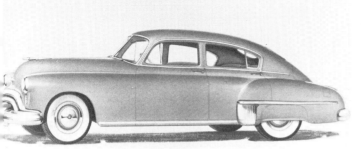

In a somewhat unusual production move, two types of four-door sedans were offered in the 1949 76 and 88 series. The town sedan offered a more attractive roofline. This 76 model carried the designation of 493508. The standard offering was priced at $1,715 and only 3,741 were built. A price tag of $1,850 on the deluxe town sedan cut sales volume to 2,725. As on 76 models, the deluxe equipment package consisted of two-tone upholstery, deluxe floor mats, special instrument cluster, aluminum sill plates, clock, deluxe steering wheel, 7.60 x 15 tires, turn signals and wheel trim rings. Shipping weight was 3,572 pounds.

Fastback styling came to the 76 lineup with the club sedan. Like all other models in Oldsmobile's lowest price series, it was powered by the improved 105 horsepower "Big Six" engine. Model number for the club sedan was 493507 and like all 1949 offerings deluxe equipped cars carried the D designation after the model number. A total of 23,059 standard 76 club sedans were built with a base price of $1,655. Production of this model in deluxe trim was 8,960 with a base price of $1,790.

By far the most popular 76 model was the four-door sedan. Carrying the model designation of 493569, this particular 76 four-door sported optional wide whitewall tires and a radio. The standard four-door sedan was priced at $1,725 — or $10 higher than the less popular 76 town sedan. A total of 23,631 standard models were produced. A price tag of $1,860 appeared on the deluxe model and 13,874 were made. Shipping weight was 3,580 pounds.

The rarest model in the total Oldsmobile line this year was the station wagon — and this is despite the fact that Olds actually had four different versions of its wagon available. Wagons were offered in both the 76 and 88 Series. The initial offerings were the wood-bodied variety shown here. Later in the year, the new all-steel wagon was introduced in both series. Thus, between the wood and steel bodies and the 76 and 88 series, a dealer could have four different 1949 Olds wagons on his floor at the same time. This particular car has the optional cadet sun visor. This is the wood version 76, as indicated by the rear quarter panel.

Although the all-steel version of the Olds wagon was very similar in style to the wood bodied cars, the rear end treatment was a dead giveaway as to what body was on the car. This is the wood bodied 76, which bore model number 493561-D. It was priced at $2,735, more than $700 higher than the next most expensive 76 series car. Only 1,545 of the 76 wagons were built, and these were divided between wood and steel bodied cars. No breakdown could be found as to how many had each type of body.

The new all-steel 76 Olds wagon came very close to the wood bodied car in styling, but a quick glance at the rear quarter quickly told the difference between the two vehicles. Besides the rear quarter styling, the tailgate also was a give-away, with the ribs on the all-steel model being far less defined than on the wood version. This body was almost identical to the all-steel wagon introduced by Chevrolet this year.

In addition to being a popular entry in Bill France's budding NASCAR circuit, the Olds 88 also served as 1949 pace car for the Indianapolis 500. A smiling Wilbur Shaw displays one of the two pace vehicles in front of the long-since-gone Pagoda on the Indy front stretch. Note the outsize chrome rocket on the front fender. Originally these were designed to give off a smokey vapor during the pace lap. This idea was quickly discarded for a variety of good reasons, but the garrish chromed rockets remained as ornamentation.

Workers who produced the 1949 Indianapolis pacing 88 convertible got a chance to see their handiwork during a shift change. This photo was snapped near the final assembly complex. Notice the 1949 Olds billboard and the neat 1948 Olds woodie wagon in the right corner of this photo.

The 88 club coupe carried the designation of 493527. A total of 6,562 were delivered in standard form, while 4,999 deluxe models came off the line. Prices on the standard models began at $2,025, making this model the cheapest 88 offered. A deluxe 88 club coupe was priced at $2,150. Both the club coupe and the fastbacked club sedan, powered by the Rocket V-8, enjoyed popularity with stock car racers of the day. As with all 88 and 98 models, the powerplant of this car was the new overhead valve V-8 turning out 135 horsepower. Shipping weight was 3,525 lbs.

An 88 Rocket engined convertible was one of the hottest cars on the road for 1949. This top-up shot shows the most popular black top that was offered on most 1949s. A price tag of $2,420 appeared on the convertible and production was 5,434. The model number was 493567 DX. Note the position of the 88 emblem on the rear fender of this car. Some cars also carried this trim on the lower front fender. A few 1949s also reportedly came out of the factory with no such trim. The 88 convertible shipping weight was 3,655 pounds.

1949

Fastback styling appealed to the 88 buyer and the 88 club sedan was a good seller. Carrying model number 493507, a total of 16,887 standard 88 club sedans were built with 11,820 of the deluxe models produced. Deluxe models of all 88s carried the designation D with their model numbers. The standard model was priced at $2,050 with the deluxe model going for $2,175. Deluxe equipment on the 88 series consisted of: two-tone upholstery, foam rubber seat cushions, deluxe floor mats front and rear, deluxe instrument cluster, aluminum sill plates, painted rearview mirror, electric clock, deluxe steering wheel and horn button, glove box light, wheel trim rings, turn signals and deluxe exterior chrome mouldings. These items could be ordered separately without ordering the deluxe package.

The most popular car in the 88 Olds line for 1949 was the four-door sedan, model number 493567. Production of standard models was 23,342 while deluxe production almost equalled it at 23,044. The standard four-door sedan was priced at $2,120, with the deluxe selling for $2,245.

The lowest production model in the entire 1949 line was the 88 station wagon, model number 493561-D. This was Oldsmobile's highest priced car, tagged at $3,120, which even placed it above the top of the line 98s. Only 1,355 total of this model were built, divided between the early production wood bodied versions and the mid-year introduced all-steel variety. Shown here is the wood bodied model — the last true "woodie" that Oldsmobile would produce.

While fastback styling appealed to the two-door buyer, it apparently didn't please the four-door purchaser, and sales on the 88 town sedan were relatively low. Despite a price tag $10 lower than the four-door sedan, Olds buyers still preferred the other four-door offering. Model number for the 88 four-door town sedan was 493508. A total of 2,859 standards were built with prices starting at $2,110. Deluxe models were slightly more popular with 2,974 sold and prices beginning at $2,235. The Futuramic styling seemed particularly appropriate on this model.

With its longer 98 wheelbase, the top of the line Olds convertible was a particularly graceful car. The convertible carried a model number of 493867X. Price of the 98 open top model was $2,810 and 12,602 were built. All 98 convertibles were deluxe equipped and only one version was offered, but there still was a healthy option list to choose from. Note the small rear window which was factory equipment on all 1949 convertibles. Shipping weight was 3,915 pounds.

Top seller in the 98 line was, of course, the four-door sedan. Unlike the bottom two series, only one four-door was offered. Model number of the four-door 98 sedan was 493869 and deluxe models carried the suffix D on this model number. A total of 8,820 standards were produced and a whopping 49,001 deluxes were made. Price on the standard model was $2,360 and the deluxe went for $2,450. Strangely enough, the most expensive four-door in the Olds line was also the top 1949 Olds seller. Weight on the 98 four-door sedan was 3,892 pounds.

A view from above accents the fastback styling of the 98 club sedan. This model was the lone closed two-door in the 98 series. Model number was 493807. The club sedan was the least expensive model in the top of the line Olds series. A standard model was priced at $2,290 with the deluxe going for $2,380. A total of 3,849 standards were built with 16,200 models turned out. The deluxe package on the 98s consisted of two-tone upholstery, rear seat armrest, deluxe instrument cluster, aluminum sill plates, deluxe floor covering front and rear, electric clock and deluxe steering wheel. The club sedan weighed 3,710 pounds.

The rarest and probably the most attractive of the 1949 98s was the Holiday coupe. This car had a late introduction date and its Fisher Body shell was shared with the Buick Riviera and the Cadillac Coupe DeVille. As the result of the February 1949 introduction, only 3,006 of this model were made. A model number of 493837X was used. The Holiday was the most expensive 98 at $2,973. The shipping weight on the hardtop was 3,750 pounds.

With its late introduction, the 1949 98 Holiday coupe caused quite a stir. This radio equipped hardtop was photographed near one of the Olds assembly buildings. This car sports the standard hubcaps with the accessory wheel trim rings.

At home on the range with a 98 was the apparent theme of this California scene. Two Rocket standards support the Olds slogan. The cowboy was obviously propelled by one horsepower, while the Olds passengers could count on 135 horsepower from 303 cubic inches. Notice the accessory passenger spotlight on this particular car.

To show off its new Rocket V-8 powerplant, the factory produced a limited number of hoods with plexiglass inserts. These units were made available to dealers and did turn a few heads in Olds dealerships across the country. No, they were not available to the hot rod contingent.

The big news in 1949 was under the hood. Olds cashed in on the name and fame of GM research chief "Boss" Kettering in promoting this all-new overhead valve V-8. Kettering envisioned this engine winding up with a compression ratio of 12 to 1. Had it not been for the federal government exhaust pipe sniffers he might have well been right.

Oldsmobile was not the only V-8 that caused a stir at the 1949 500. The crowd pleasing NOVI racers were V-8 powered also. Here car number 5 undergoes a sparkplug change. This car started in Row #1 of the 1949 event, but it was plagued by typical NOVI luck and fell out of the event with mechanical ills.

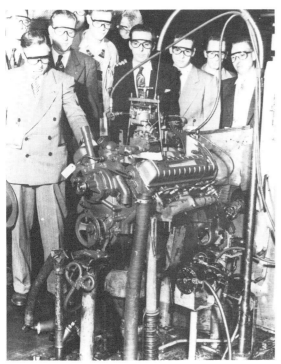

The Rocket V-8 was a new Oldsmobile product and it was built in the all-new Kettering Engine Plant. Naturally, the new plant was a stopping point on most tours. Here a group of V.I.P.s inspect a 1949 V-8 on a test stand.

The dash on all 1949 models was quite attractively laid out. Starter operation was via a push button. This particular car was equipped with the popular Hydra-Matic transmission and the center dash located clock and radio.

This front shot of a 1949 model shows the rather clean grille treatment and the unique styling surrounding the headlights. Notice also the driving lights which were a rare factory accessory.

Olds was big on posters, banners and other sales trinkets in 1949. Here posters featuring Wilbur Shaw and the Indy pace car are placed in a dealership display window. Other Olds gimmicks for 1949 included: Rocket 88 date books, scale model plastic Oldsmobiles, treasure hunt game, shoe-shine cloths and satin sales banners.

Plenty of trunk space was the message this little fellow was getting across from his perch in the rear of a 98 convertible. The Firestone spare tire is in stock position. This scene took place at the annual employee's showing of the new model Oldsmobiles.

Another one off the line. This four-door 1949 model bursts to life at the end of its long assembly line trip. Gathered is a group of plant visitors. Note the chalk writing on the passenger's windshield and also the high bank of lights for inspection purposes and to aid workers in doing fine detail work.

Olds rushed the 1949s into production as quickly as possible. This photo, taken in the fall of 1948, shows the 1949s sharing assembly line space with some late 1948s. The vast number of overhead lights, shown in this photo, helped with the final inspection process which is taking place here.

1950

In 1950 Oldsmobile drew heavily on the innovations of 1949 and moved up a notch in the sales standings to sixth position. A total model year production of 408,060— a new division record—was realized, with a calendar year total of 396,757 Oldsmobiles built.

Two long standing Oldsmobile offerings came to a temporary halt with the end of the 1950 model year. Station wagon production was stopped after the 1950 model, and also, the offering of a 6-cylinder engine was last seen for awhile in 1950. Station wagons came back to the Olds lineup in 1957, with the return of the 6-cylinder engine coming in 1963 in the F-85 lineup.

Olds pulled a styling page out of the 1948 book (that year the 1949 styling was previewed on the 1948 98's) by popping 1951 styling with the 1950 98 Series line of cars. In another styling move the Holiday hardtop coupe was expanded to all three Olds models for 1950.

The potent team of the Rocket V-8 engine and Whirlaway Hydra-Matic transmission remained virtually unchanged for 1950. The station wagon became an all-steel unit with imitation wood trim.

The newly restyled 98's came on a new wheelbase of 122 inches, down three inches from the 98 models of 1948 and 1949.

A total of 11 solid color options were offered with seven two-tone color schemes available. DeLuxe models were offered in all series and all models. All standard series closed models were upholstered in gray striped cloth. DeLuxe 76 closed models were done in dark grey broadcloth and light gray striped nylon cord. Other DeLuxe closed models had interiors of light gray nylon surrey weave and dark gray striped nylon cord. A variety of leathers were offered on convertibles, station wagons and Holiday coupes.

Accessories of 1950 included: two types of radios, traffic light viewer, Cadet sun visor, electric clock, spotlight and battery vitalizer.

By 1950 the main Oldsmobile plant covered 96 acres and included 50 buildings. The newly constructed forge plant complex covered 51 acres. The GM Division employed 9,242 hourly employees and 1,625 workers on salary. A dealer network of 3,908 were located throughout the 48 states.

Olds continued to make big news in the racing world. Joe Littleton established a new, two-way class speed record on Daytona Beach with a clocking of 100.28 mph in a stickshift 88 coupe. Hershel McGriff and Ray Elliott won the Carera Panamerica in an Olds. Oldsmobile continued to do well in the NASCAR grand national division. Rocket V-8's also began popping up under the hoods of modified short track race cars across the country, challenging the venerable Ford flathead V-8's. And even the hot rodders were casting a watchful eye on auto graveyards for wrecked 1949 and 1950 Oldsmobiles with good engines.

Oldsmobile offered two types of distinctly different styling in 1950. The 76 series is shown at the top, with the 88 in the middle and the top of the line 98 at the bottom.

Oldsmobile would not be in the station wagon business again until 1957 as high prices, combined with low volume sales, didn't justify continuation of the model. The 76 wagon was the most expensive model of the series at $2,360. It was also the lowest production 1950 Olds. Only 121 standards were built and 247 deluxe models were made. Model number for the 76 wagon was 503562.

An expanded 1950 lineup included Holiday two-doors across the board. This was the only year that the 76 line included a hardtop and it was also the last year of the 76 series for Oldsmobile. Model number for the Holiday was 503537 and, as with all 1950 models, a D was included on all deluxe model numbers. Price on the standard model was $1,885 with the deluxe selling for $1,995. Only 144 of the standard model were built with 394 of the deluxe model made.

1950

Convertibles are usually rare in the lowest priced series of any car maker, and the 76 Olds convertible was no exception. Only 973 of this model, number 503567X, were produced. The 76 convertible was priced at $2,010. As with all 76 models there were two external styling items which distinguished it from the other series. There were no front fender chrome strips on the 76 and the taillight housings were plain on the lowest priced series.

The new model in the Olds line for 1950 was the two-door sedan. With three two-door offerings, the Olds 76 series had the market completely covered. This particular model, number 503511, was the most expensive of the closed two-doors. The standard sold for $1,655 with the deluxe selling for $1,720. A total of 3,865 standards were built with deluxe production totalling 2,489.

Olds continued its fastback styling on the 76 club sedan. The model number for this offering was 503507. A total of 3,186 standard club sedans were built. Only 1,919 of the same model with deluxe equipment were made. The standard model came with a $1,640 price tag, while the deluxe sold for $1,705.

The 76 line had only one four-door in 1950, and it became the most popular model of the series. Model number for this car was 503569. Base price for the standard was $1,710 and 7,396 were built. The deluxe went for $1,775 and 9,159 of those were delivered. This side shot shows the Futuramic rear fender chrome, which was common to all 1950 Oldsmobiles — an easy way to tell them from 1949s.

Hanging on for another year, the 76 club coupe was the cheapest Oldsmobile built. Model number for this car was 503527. A total of 2,238 standards were built at a base price of $1,615. Production was even lower on the deluxe as only 1,126 were built. The deluxe price tag was $1,680.

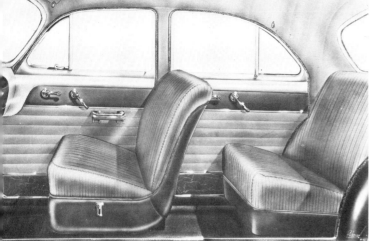

This was the interior on the 76 standard four-door. Interior fabrics for this model included either gray striped cloth or gray striped nylon cord. The only 1950 76 models featuring leather upholstery were the station wagon, deluxe Holiday coupe and convertibles. Coat hooks were fitted over the rear doors. The rear quarter windows did not open.

1950

Convertibles continued to be big business for Olds, as the 88 was among the hottest open cars on the road. The model number on the 88 convertible was 503767X. It was offered in deluxe form only. Base price for the 88 convertible was $2,160 and 9,127 were built. Notice the fender chrome strip which was common to all 88 and 98 offerings.

Carrying model designation 503707, the fastback styled 88 club sedan was a popular offering. A total of 14,705 club sedans were built with standard trim, while 16,388 deluxes were made. The standard model was priced at $1,790. Deluxe prices began at $1,865.

The Holiday coupe was most popular in the 88 series. Model number for the lone 88 hardtop was 503737. It's obvious that most buyers preferred the fancy edition of this model. Only 1,366 standard Holidays were built in the 88 series, while deluxe output was 11,316. The standards were priced at $2,035 and the deluxe model went for $2,135. This particular car is from the Oldsmobile factory collection, and is finished in Canto Cream with a black top. It was restored in 1971 for Olds general manager John Beltz who drove the car quite frequently on jaunts around Lansing.

An addition to the 88 lineup for 1950 was the two-door sedan. This model carried the designation of 503711. The two-door sedan proved to be the most popular of the three 88 two-door models offered. A total of 23,889 standards were built, while 26,672 deluxes were made. The standard sold for $1,805 and the deluxes brought $1,880. This model shows the special 88 taillight trim that marked the beginning of tail fins for Oldsmobile.

The least popular 88 continued to be the station wagon. This model carried the number 503762. For 1950 the station wagon was offered in both standard and deluxe fittings. A total of 1,830 wagons were built in standard trim, while only 552 deluxe wagons were made. Station wagons were the most expensive 88s with standards priced at $2,510 and the deluxe going for $2,585. After 1950, Olds went out of the station wagon business until 1957.

1950

The 1950 88 four-door sedan continued to be the bread and butter car for Oldsmobile. This model carried the designation of 503769. A total of 40,301 standards were built and price tags started at $1,860. The deluxe saw a production run of 100,816 and prices began at $1,925.

This is the deluxe interior package on the 88 four-door sedan. It was the most popular Oldsmobile for 1950. Deluxe 88 fabrics were light gray nylon surrey weave and dark gray striped nylon cord. This package was referred to as combination No. 3 on the serial number plate. On this model, the rear door vent windows were functional.

This closeup shows the 1950 76 and 88 instrument cluster and adjacent controls. The dash is little changed from 1949. Layout is attractive and functional and gauges inform the driver far better than the idiot lights that were down the road a few years. Olds this year used an internal hood latch.

Two more loads of 1950 Oldsmobiles receive final preparations. Note the tarps for protection of cars riding on the top layer. This shot also affords a good look at the rear 88 rocket emblems. In this era, the average transporter could carry only four cars at a time.

This is a fairly typical 1950 Olds dealership showroom floor. In the foreground is an 88 Holiday coupe with a 98 model in the background. Note the banners hanging from the dealership pillars. These were used quite extensively in 1949 and 1950. The 1950 banners were a red-like silk material with yellow lettering. Also note the Oldsmobile rug that the car is displayed on.

Oldsmobile again peaked its advanced styling on the top of the line models, as the 1950 98s tipped 1951 styling. The bulky new styling treatment made a particularly unique-looking car in the 98 convertible. The convertible came in deluxe trim only and carried Oldsmobile's top price tag, of $2,615. Only 3,925 of this model, number 503837X, were made.

1950

A longer and lower profile is particularly apparent on this 1950 98 Holiday coupe. This car carried the designation of 503837. Only 317 standard equipment cars were built with price tags of $2,245. The deluxe was far more popular with 7,946 produced. Deluxe prices began at $2,490. This particular car features the full wheel covers and two-tone paint scheme, both options.

Fastback styling carried over to the 98 line with the two-door club sedan. The model number was 503807. Standard production was 2,270 with a price of $2,095. Deluxes were more popular with 9,719 built and a base price of $2,185. The 1950 98 club sedan was the least expensive car in its series.

For some unexplained reason, Olds offered two four-doors in its top of the line series. Far and away the most popular 98 for 1950 was the four-door sedan. Note the bustle back design and the unique rear side window arrangement. A total of 7,499 standard-equipped four-door sedans were built with prices beginning at $2,165. The deluxe proved more appealing with 72,766 produced, all carrying a base price tag of $2,225. The model number for the four-door sedan was 503869.

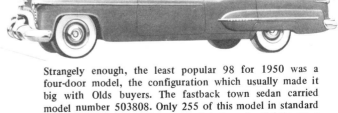

The engineer checking the frosty 98 four-door sedan didn't have the heater working for him as did the driver. Olds used this factory shot in various publications to point up General Motors' testing procedures under a variety of conditions, including quick starting and defroster and heater operation in sub-zero cold.

Strangely enough, the least popular 98 for 1950 was a four-door model, the configuration which usually made it big with Olds buyers. The fastback town sedan carried model number 503808. Only 255 of this model in standard trim were built. The deluxe proved to be only slightly more popular with 1,523 being sold. The standard priced out at $2,135 with deluxes selling for $2,225.

This seven car lineup shows the plastic hood used to give a bird's eye view of the mighty Rocket V-8. A few of these hoods can still be found tucked away in long-time Olds dealers' attics. They were available for both 88 and 98 models. The hoods didn't prove too practical for street use, but were great traffic builders in the showroom. They were sold to dealers strictly as promotional items, though no doubt some hot rodders eyed them with envy.

A touch of the bizarre was added with the oversize hood ornament on this 98. The car also features the plexiglass dealership hood. Note the factory Cadet sun visor and the driver's side spotlight on this car.

A specially built edition of the all-new 98 Holiday was called the Palm Beach. On the outside, this special auto show car was nearly stock, but it featured special paint and interior treatment. Door panels were done in green alligator hide, green leather and lacquered wicker. Floor mats and the seat base were in natural flax. The seats were covered in Irish linen weave nylon edged with alligator leather. The exterior was surf green with a crackle finished cabana sand colored top. Model Phyllis Nelson, pictured, was in several auto shows with the Palm Beach.

The very early 1950 models were handbuilt in the Olds engineering area. Here an engine is dropped into place, and two more prototype 98s can be seen in the background. While these cars were being built, probably in the late summer of 1949, the 1949 model Oldsmobiles continued to roll off the nearby assembly line.

In 1950 this is what a Body by Fisher consisted of. A Fisher Body, such as this 98 convertible, would arrive at the Olds assembly plant. Olds workers then joined this body to an assembled chassis and numerous other parts like front and rear fenders, steering column, spare tire, etc.

For 1951 Oldsmobile dropped back to its old familiar niche of Seventh place in the sales race. A total of 85,615 Oldsmobiles were built during the model year, with an early identical calendar year total of 285,634. The familiar Seventy series — which had been with the division since the early 1940s — was dropped in 1951, and with it went the 6-cylinder powerplant. For the first time since the company's founding in 1897, all Oldsmobiles were powered by 8-cylinder engines.

The all new Super 88 was a new model designation in 1951 and this model name would last a dozen years. Introduced two years previously as a middle of the line car, the 88 suddenly became Oldsmobile's "plain Jane" offering.

As was the Olds custom in the early 1950's, two distinctly different cars were offered. The 88 models were quite clearly holdovers as they drew heavily on the Futuramic concept first offered on the 1948 98 Series models. There were very few distinctions between 1950 and 1951 88's. Only two 88 models were available, 2-door and 4-door sedans. This was down from the seven-model lineup featured in 1950. Quite obviously the 88, Olds' largest selling model in both 1949 and 1950, was being de-emphasized in 1951. The result was that 88 sales were about one-fifth of Super 88 sales in 1951. Three different wheelbases were offered in the new Oldsmobiles. The 88 was based again on 119½ inches, while the Super 88 wheelbase was a half-inch more. The top of the line 98 was on a 122-inch wheelbase, the same as the 1950 98.

On the mechanical side of things, a new sealed-type starter was introduced across the line. A different carburetor, air cleaner and distributor topped off the 1951 version of the Rocket engine. The powerplant, however, remained basically unchanged from its introduction in 1949 as it still displaced 303 cubic inches and developed 135 horsepower. Slight suspension changes were built into the Super 88's and 98's with a new type shock absorber and angle mounted rear springs.

A total of 13 different solid color offerings were made in 1951, and 10 two-tone combinations could be ordered. Light and dark gray Chevron pattern striped cloth upholstery was used on standard 88's and standard 98 Holiday coupes. Dark and light gray nylon interior furnishings came on Deluxe 88's, closed models of the Super 88 and 98 Deluxe sedans. Leather was available in a variety of colors on open cars. Convertible tops came in either black or tan. Leather and nylon combination interiors could be ordered on any Holiday coupe.

Factory accessories of the day included: heater, radio, Hydra-Matic, backup lights, windshield washers, rear fender gravel shields, Cadet sun visors, driving lights and traffic light viewer.

Oldsmobile continued to fair well in the racing wars. Domination of NASCAR continued with grand national circuit victories for Olds in nearly half the races staged in 1951.

On the management side of the business, 1951 marked a change in the top position within the division. S. E. Skinner moved on to other corporate duties and Jack Wolfrom became Oldsmobile's 13th general manager. The smallish Wolfrom, nicknamed "Black Jack" by some of the employees he ruled over with an iron hand, had been with the division since 1928 and had been Olds chief engineer since 1944.

Four-year old styling, dating back to the 1948 Ninety-Eight models, was the basis for the 1951 Eighty-Eight series. This model was also called the 88-A series and was either left out entirely or mentioned very little in Olds sales literature for the year. Offered only in the two basic models, model number 513711 was the two-door sedan. This was Olds least expensive 1951 model at $1,815 and deluxe equipment added $77. Production was a surprisingly high 11,792. The 88's were phased out as the model year advanced.

Most popular of the abbreviated 1951 Eighty-Eight series was the four-door sedan, model number 513769. A total of 22,848 of this model were produced. Base price was $1,871, with the deluxe equipment package selling for $77 more. Wheelbase on all 88 models was 119.5 inches with an overall length of 202 inches. Delco two-way shock absorbers — with levers — were standard equipment on all 88 offerings.

Curtis Turner was one of the all-time great stock car drivers. Here "Pops" Turner stands with one of the many NASCAR Oldsmobile stock car rides he had in the 1950's. Of the 1951 Oldsmobiles, the 88-A two-door sedan was the lightest model offered, hence it became the racers' favorite. And it shared the same Rocket V-8 with the rest of the model lineup, making Olds a big winner in 1951. Notice the almost stock appearance of this Olds race car.

1951

Model number 513637DX was the Super 88 deluxe holiday coupe with hydraulic-electric window and seat controls. Externally this car was the same as the regular Super 88 deluxe holiday coupe. A total of 901 of this model – with power windows and seat – were built. Base price of the cars was $2,231. The power options added $130 and were not available separately. All Super 88 series cars came standard with either U.S. Royal, Firestone or Goodrich 7.60 x 15 tires.

The updated 1951 styling package was particularly attractive on the Super 88 deluxe holiday coupe. Model number 513637D came with standard seat and window controls. Base price was $2,231 and production totalled 13,279. In its third year of building two-door hardtops, this car continued a popular offering for Olds. As with all Super 88 models, the hardtop was on a 120-inch wheelbase.

Sales volume really didn't justify it, but Olds continued to offer a club coupe in its Super 88 series. It carried model number 513627D, and like all Super 88's it was designated as a deluxe model. Base price was $1,9 ? making it the least expensive offering in the series. Production totalled 7,328. HydraMatic continued to be a popular Olds offering and by 1951 the price of this option had risen to $150.

Most popular of all 1951 Olds two-door offerings was the Super 88 deluxe two-door sedan. It carried model number 513611 D and was base priced at $1,969. Production totalled 34,963. All Super 88 closed car interiors were done in either dark gray striped nylon cord or light and dark gray chevron pattern striped cloth. This particular car is equipped with some interesting accessories including fog and driving lights ($19.20 per pair), window ventshades ($14 per set) and full wheel covers ($17.60 per set).

The least expensive of the two 1951 Olds convertibles was the Super 88. It carried model number 513667 DX. Regular convertible production totalled 3,404, making it the rarest 1951 Olds built. This model convertible had a hydraulically operated top with manual seats and windows. Convertibles in the Super 88 series were base priced at $2,333. Tops were available in either black or tan, with black the standard color.

1951

The most popular 1951 Oldsmobile was the Super 88 deluxe four-door sedan, model number 513669D. Production totalled a surprisingly high 90,131. The base price on the lone 1951 Super 88 four-door offering was $2,025. A total of regular two-tone combinations were offered for $12.45, with special two-tone paint jobs available for $25. Whitewall tires were fairly common factory equipment and sold for $20.60 extra.

Oldsmobiles with special coachwork are relatively rare. Derham of Rosemont, Pa., built this 1951 Super 88 four-door into a formal limousine. The most attractive feature of this special automobile was a roof covering of weather-proofed black leather. Another distinctive touch was the functional continental kit. Derham added this feature to vastly increase the amount of luggage space available.

For the first time in several years external styling was quite similar between the Super 88 and 98 series. Main differences were in the taillight area and chrome side trim. All 98's came standard with fender skirts. Ninety-Eights rode on a 122-inch wheelbase, while the Super 88's were two inches shorter. All three Olds series got their power from a 303 cubic inch, 135 horsepower Rocket V-8 engine. Cars had an 18-gallon gas tank and premium gas was suggested.

Olds built an additional 450 Super 88 convertibles with model number 513667 DTX. These cars came equipped with hydraulically operated seats and windows as well as tops. This package cost $115 as a factory installed option and was of the troublesome hydra-electric design. Convertible interiors could be ordered in a variety of colors of full leather.

The 98 convertible was an attractive offering in 1951. It carried model number 513867X and was equipped with a hydraulic-electric system to operate the seat, top and windows. Base price was $2,644, making this the most expensive car in the 1951 lineup. Production totalled 4,468. Red, green, blue or black leather upholstery was available, along with two-color combinations of green or blue leather.

The standard Holiday coupe, model number 513837, was the rarest 1951 Ninety-Eight. It was base priced at $2,267. Production totalled only 3,917. The rear styling of this model was attractive with the split rear window treatment. The taillight-stoplight combination could also house the turn signal or backup light, if a car had these accessories. All 1951 Oldsmobiles carry their serial numbers on the left front door pillar.

1951

All other Oldsmobiles wearing the holiday designation were hardtops except the 98 deluxe holiday sedan. Olds was four years away from its first postless four-door model. This car carried model number 513869D. It was base priced at $2,277. This was by far the most popular car in the 98 series with a production run of 78,122. All 98 models were equipped with fender skirts. Rocket engine improvements for the year included a newly designed carburetor, slightly raised compression ratio and a more efficient exhaust system.

More popular than its standard equipped sister car was the 98 deluxe holiday coupe. It carried model number 513867X. Production totalled 4,468. Base price for this model was $2,517. The deluxe equipment package included: hydraulic-electric seats and windows, leather trimmed interior, exposed chrome-plated interior roof bars and a special deluxe clock and steering wheel.

A basically new chassis was offered to Super 88 and 98 buyers in 1951. The frame itself was considerably beefed up for the upper series cars. The frame was made a great deal stronger in the area of the X-member. Front and rear springs were revised. A new front stabilizer bar was also adopted. With the dropping of the "Big Six" engine in 1950, all Oldsmobile chassis were built to handle the bulk of the Rocket V-8 engine.

Interiors were revised on the 1951 Super 88 and 98 models. Instruments were tightly grouped in front of the driver and included: speedometer, odometer, temperature indicator, fuel gauge, oil pressure gauge and ammeter. This car carries the optional steering wheel with the center section consisting of a gold globe on a starry field of midnight blue. Radio and clock were once again mounted in the center of the dash.

General Motors' styling in the early 1950's seemed perfectly suited for the Cadet sun visor. This option could be had on any 1951 Olds, except for the convertibles. The installed price for the Cadet visor was $32.90, and this unit was pushed as a dealer installed item. A necessary accessory with the visor was a dash-mounted traffic light viewer. This device aided a driver in seeing a traffic light despite the visor overhang. Installed price was $5.00.

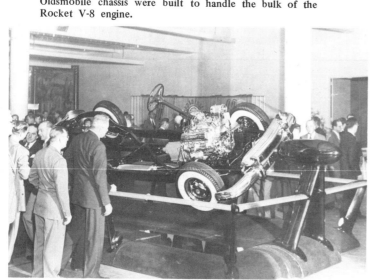

1952

A more streamlined and more powerful line of cars me from Lansing in 1952 and moved Oldsmobile back to Sixth position in the sales race. A total of 213,490 w cars were sold during the model year. Calendar year les totalled 228,452.

The plain 88 designation was dropped for 1952. Bottom the line models were called Deluxe 88's. Next up the le was the Super 88, and the 98 remained the top of e line from Lansing.

Soaring horsepower ratings were common in the auto dustry and Oldsmobile's Rocket engine was upgraded to main one of the most potent stock engines offered. enty of reserve capacity had been engineered into the ocket V-8 in the late 1940's. Some of that reserve was pped in 1952.

For the first time separate editions of the Rocket V-8 ere released. Both were based on a displacement of)3 cubic inches. The Deluxe 88 engine turned out 145 rsepower. The Super 88 and 98 models were powered a 160 horsepower engine. The main difference in the o engine packages was the Deluxe 88 motor had a al down-draft carburetor, while the more powerful gine was fueled by the all-new Quadri-Jet down-draft rb.

Oldsmobile's popular Hydra-Matic was also changed for ded performance in 1952. A super range was added to e transmission, and an "S" was placed as the fifth sition in the automatic shift pattern. The drive and low sitions were retained. The new super range was ggested for use in hill climbing and as a gentle brake on ep downgrades.

Again in 1952 the bottom of the line Oldsmobiles were tricted to two models, a 2-door and 4-door sedan. Both e 88 and Super 88 series were on a 120-inch wheelbase. e 98's ran on a wheelbase of 124 inches.

A total of 15 solid color options were available including: yal turquoise, regent maroon, canto cream and chariot d. Sixteen two-tone combinations were available in 1952. A gray basket weave cloth interior was provided on luxe 88 models. A combination of nylon sharkskin and lon bedford cord, in gray or green, was offered on all per 88's. Ninety-Eight models were done in a combi- tion of light and dark broadcloth in either gray or en. Various colored leather interiors were available in nvertibles with tops available in black or green. Holiday upe interiors were done in combinations of nylon and ther in assorted colors.

One rather revolutionary General Motor's accessory was fered for the first time in 1952: Saginaw Steering ar's power steering system. This unit — billed as GM ydraulic Steering — was offered on some late 1951 dillacs, but 1952 was the first year it was available Oldsmobiles. The increasing weight and length of the rs of the 1950's quickly made the new steering system popular option. List price of the system in its initial ar was $185.

Two other accessories for 1952 got plenty of ink in vision sales literature, but they fell more in the category gadgets than driving aids.

The Autronic Eye system automatically dimmed head- hts as an oncoming car approached and brightened lights en the road was again clear. A second oddball accessory as a steering wheel mounted automatic car watch which

Olds touted as an industry first. This unit wound itself as the steering wheel was used. Engineers allowed that five miles of city driving would keep the 15-jewel watch movement running for two days. The price on this option was $35.

Other factory options for 1952 included: a compass, oil filter, radio, turn signals, full wheel covers and a heavy duty air cleaner.

Oldsmobile began to fade on the racing circuits, but a Super 88 coupe did win the 1952 Southern 500 at Darlington, S. C.

The plain 88 designation disappeared with the mildly restyled 1952 model lineup. Bottom of the line series cars were now known as Deluxe 88's, and the series consisted again of just two models. Number 523611 was the two-door sedan. Production totalled 6,402. Base price on the Deluxe 88 two-door was $2,050, making this the least expensive 1952 Olds. All Deluxe 88's shared a 120-inch wheelbase with the Super 88's. Power came from a slightly detuned Rocket V-8 turning out 145 horsepower.

Rounding out the Deluxe 88 series for 1952 was the four-door sedan, model number 523669. Production was 12,215, making this the more popular car in the series. Base price on this model was $2,110. The Deluxe 88 series had its own distinctive side trim. Interiors on all of these bottom of the line cars were done in gray basket weave corded cloth.

1952

Olds continued to offer three different two-door models in the Super 88 series. By far the most popular was the two-door sedan, model number 523611D. Production totalled 24,963. Base price on this model was $2,172. Super 88 equipment included a 160 horsepower Rocket V-8 which was shared with the 98 series. This powerplant gained a good bit of its new horsepower via the new Quadri-Jet carburetor. Other engine modifications included a new air cleaner, new intake manifold and redesigned pistons and crankshaft.

The rarest Olds built in 1952 was the Super 88 club coupe. This was the final year for this model and it carried model number 523627D. Only 2,050 Super 88 club coupes were made. This was also the least expensive Super with a base price of $2,126. As with all Super 88's and 98's, power came from the improved 160 horsepower Rocket V-8. A full flow oil filter was an engine-saving option listing for $10.27 installed.

This Super 88 two-door sedan belongs to Melvin Melrose of Bay City, Mich. It sports one of sixteen two-tone paint combinations available in 1952. Retail price for these paint schemes was $14.22, except on the holiday coupes, where the cost of a two-tone job was included in the base price. All Deluxe and Super 88's rode on 7.60 x 15 tires. Whitewalls were $29.41 extra.

Model number 523637D was the Super 88 holiday coupe. Production totalled 15,777. Base price on this car was $2,430. The holiday coupe in the Super 88 could be ordered with a leather and bedford cord interior in four colors or a nylon sharkskin and bedford cord combination. By 1952 a number of Olds customers were sold on Hydra-Matic. During the year the price of the popular automatic transmission went to $165.

The largest Super 88 price tag belonged to the convertible. This car carried model number 523667TDX. Production totalled only 5,162. Base price was $2,595. Super 88 convertible interiors could be ordered in either red or black leather or combinations of light and dark green or light and dark blue leather. Convertible tops were available either in the old standby black or a new offering of green.

1952

The interiors on closed Super 88 models were done in nylon sharkskin and nylon bedford cord. Color selection included gray or green and headliner came in a matching shade. The use of chrome in the interiors became a bit more common in 1952. The overall width of the Super 88 backseat was slightly more than 63 inches, making it the widest backseat of any Olds four-door.

The most popular 1953 Oldsmobile was the Super 88 four-door sedan. It carried model number 523669D. Base price on this high volume model was $2,234. During this model year fender skirts remained a much ordered accessory on Super 88 and Deluxe 88 models. Price was $17.60 installed. This particular car is also equipped with the distinctive Cadet sunvisor. Price on this option, part number 982863M, was $32.75.

The flagship of the line for 1952 was the 98 four-door sedan. Carrying model number 523069D, a surprisingly high 58,550 of this model were sold. Base price on the 98 four-door sedan was $2,532. Closed 98 models could be upholstered in light and dark gray broadcloth or light and dark green broadcloth. All 98 models rode on a 124-inch wheelbase with overall length of slightly more than 213 inches.

One of the most attractive offerings in the 1952 lineup was the 98 holiday coupe. It carried model number 523037DX. Production totalled 14,150. A nice touch was the special holiday emblem located on the moulding between the back and rear side windows. Again for 1952 all 98 holidays were equipped with hydraulic seat controls and windows.

The most expensive 1952 Oldsmobile was the 98 convertible, model number 523067 DX. It was by far the rarest of the top of the line model as only 3,544 were built. Base price for this model was $2,940. All 98 convertibles rode on 8.00 x 15 tires supplied by either U.S. Royal, Firestone or Goodyear. This model had hydraulically operated top, seats and windows. By 1952 the convertible rear window had grown to nearly full size.

One of the top award winners in Oldsmobile Club of America judging has been Marlin Hoskins 1952 Ninety-Eight convertible. This car is from Mogadore, Ohio. It is finished in a deep green. It is also equipped with sparkling wire wheels. In 1952, Olds 98 convertible interiors could be ordered in red, green, blue or black leather or a dark and light green leather combination or a light and dark blue leather duo.

The 98 models offered the plushest interiors in the Olds lineup for 1952. Four-door 98 interiors were done in gray or green broadcloth with headliner and side panels to match. The rear seat of the 98 was more than 59 inches wide. All 1952 Ninety-Eight four-doors had a rear seat center armrest. The four-door was the only 98 on which there wasn't some type of leather trim available.

Saginaw Steering Gear's power steering system was introduced on 1952 Oldsmobiles, as well as other General Motors offerings. The hydraulic pump was the underhood heart of the power steering system. Olds claimed its power steering cut up to 77% of the driver effort. Power steering was available on any Olds as factory installed option Y. Price was $185.

The most unusual accessory in the 1952 catalog would probably be option M-2, the self-winding car watch. Its price was $32.21 and it could be dealer installed. In Deluxe and Super 88 models the deluxe steering wheel ($14.09) had to be ordered also. Olds claimed its unusual timepiece was a "precision-built Swiss watch." The clock was designed to be wound by the motion of the steering wheel and would run for eight days without winding.

The more powerful 1952 Olds Rocket powerplant could be distinguished from its forerunners by its larger carb and huge air cleaner. Horsepower output had risen to 160 on the Super 88 and 98 motor. The new fuel system was a complete downdraft unit. This improved winter starting. Electricity was supplied by a 45 amp generator and voltage regulator.

1953

Oldsmobile retained the industry's Sixth sales position in 1953 with a mildly restyled lineup. Model year totals were 334,462, with calendar year sales of 319,414. The biggest change for 1953 came with the conversion of the electrical system to 12 volts. Results were, of course, faster and easier starts in all weather and also more operating power for the additional electrical accessories the average buyer was loading on his new Olds.

A massive August fire at the Hydra-Matic plant in Livonia, Mich. quickly put a pinch on the supply of the popular automatic transmission. Olds shared Hydra-Matic with Pontiac and Cadillac, but Olds customers were particularly adjusted to the fully automatic unit since it had been available since 1939. General Motors moved with unaccustomed speed in reacting to the problem, and within a matter of several weeks after the devastating fire, new Oldsmobiles could be ordered with a Dynaflow Twin Turbine transmission. The sale of stickshift Oldsmobiles increased greatly for a few months. There is no record of how many Oldsmobiles came Dynaflow equipped, but estimates run as high as 7,000. General Motors estimated it lost 100,000 car sales — across all its car and truck divisions — as a result of the $30 million fire. A new Hydra-Matic plant, in the old Kaiser Motors plant in Willow Run, was in operation for the 1954 model run. Several other mechanical changes were offered on the new models. Output of the Rocket V-8 was upped five horsepower and compression ratio was raised to 8 to 1. The Quadri-Jet equipped V-8 was now turning out 165 horsepower, while the motor in the Deluxe 88 was rated at 150 horsepower. Other mechanical changes included: a new type of front wheel bearing, an improved differential design, wider front tread and new fender bracings and body mountings.

The interior was subject to revision for 1953, particularly the dashboard treatment. The new layout featured a large, round speedometer and instrument cluster balanced on the other side of the car by a round radio speaker-clock housing. The automatic transmission shift quadrant was moved to the instrument cluster, just below the speedometer. Previously this unit had been atop the steering column. Oldsmobile's new interior featured the liberal, yet attractive use of chrome throughout.

A total of seventeen solid colors were offered including: agate red, cove green, Acacia blue and royal marine. Sixteen two-tone color combinations were also available. Deluxe 88 models were upholstered in 2-tone weave gray pattern cloth. Super 88's came with the combination of light nylon striped cloth and dark nylon pattern cloth, in either gray, green or blue. Top of the line 98's were done in dark and light broadcloth, in blue or gray; or dark and light green gabardine. A variety of colored leathers could be ordered on convertibles. Convertible top selection was expanded to include the recommended black as well as green, tan or blue. Holiday coupe interiors were done in a combination of leather and striped cloth in the Super 88 series, and leather and waffle weave cloth on the 98 series. Tires available from the factory were U.S. Royal, Firestone and Goodrich.

Several popular accessories were offered for the first time on Oldsmobiles in 1953. As a companion to the 1952-introduced power steering, power brakes were now offered for $33. At the whopping price of $550 a Frigidaire air conditioning system could be ordered. G.M.'s first attempt at air conditioning offered a bewildering jungle of hardware both underhood and in the trunk. The cooled air was distributed by plastic tubes mounted in the headliner and running rear to front. Other accessories offered by the factory included: radio, deluxe steering wheel, electric clock, safety padded instrument panel and fender skirts.

Little emphasis was placed on the Deluxe 88 series again in 1953 and the model lineup was held at two. The two-door sedan carried model number 533611 and was Oldsmobile's least expensive and lightest 1953 model. Base price was $2,066 and shipping weight was 3,514 pounds. Production totalled 12,400. The Deluxe 88 models continued to be powered by a less powerful Rocket V-8 which generated 150 horsepower. Deluxe and Super 88 models shared the same 120-inch wheelbase.

The top volume machine in the Deluxe 88 lineup was the four-door sedan, model number 533669. This car was base priced at $2,126 and it weighed 3,622 pounds. Production totalled 20,405. Interiors on Deluxe 88 models were done in trim package number 61, gray basket pattern cloth. In 1953, Olds offered 17 basic colors and 16 recommended two-tone paint schemes.

1953

The Super 88 convertible could be ordered with hydraulic windows and seats. If so equipped, the model number was 533667DTX. A total of 803 of these cars were built. The special hydraulics added $131.29 to the Super 88 convertible base price of $2,615. The color selection for convertible tops was expanded in 1953 to include green, tan and blue. This was in addition to the long standard black.

Oldsmobile was forced out of the racing spotlight somewhat by the buzzing Hudson Hornet and the awesome Chrysler Hemi, but Oldsmobile won some big 1953 events including one at Daytona Beach. By the early 1950s General Motors was becoming increasingly involved in the dream car/auto show circuit. Oldsmobile was a natural to be involved in this activity. By 1953 two distinct Oldsmobiles were on the circuit: the Fiesta and the Starfire.

The Fiesta actually was shown in 1952 and by mid-1953 it had become a limited production car with only 458 built. It was offered only as a convertible, and Fiestas were not pictured in any Olds sales literature except an oversized greentone postcard devoted exclusively to that car. Unique features of the Fiesta were its lowness, almost three inches lower than a standard 98 convertible, and its special wraparound windshield. Powering the Fiesta was a warmed over Rocket V-8 turning out 170 horsepower and offering a slightly higher than normal production compression ratio.

The Starfire was a strictly one-off show car. Drawing its name from a Lockheed airplane, the car was built of fiberglass. The Starfire engine was rated at 200 horsepower. Several styling features from the Starfire were adopted in the next three years of Oldsmobiles, but the car was never considered seriously for production.

The hardtop holiday model continued to be a popular Super 88 body style. Model number 533637D carried a base price of $2,448 and was shipped weighing 3,585 pounds. Production was 34,500. Accessory U was hydraulic window and seat controls which could be ordered for $148.42. A total of 2,381 hydraulically equipped Super 88 holidays were built and they carried model number 533637DX.

The least expensive model in the Super 88 series was model number 533611D, the two-door sedan. Base price was $2,189. Shipping weight was 3,548 pounds. Production totalled 36,824, making this the highest volume two-door model for 1953. Interiors for Super 88 two-door and four-door sedans were done in dark and light nylon pin striped cloth in gray, green or blue. These were trim combinations 81, 82 and 83.

The biggest styling change for 1953 came with the adoption of a massive front end theme which Olds called power styling. Model number 533669D was the Super 88 four-door sedan, the most popular 1953 Oldsmobile. Base price was $2,252 and shipping weight was 3,657 pounds. Production totalled a whopping 119,317. All Deluxe and Super 88 models rode on 7.60 x 15 tires supplied by U.S. Royal, Firestone or Goodrich.

Super 88 buyers had to reach into their pockets the deepest if they wanted to own a convertible. Carrying model number 533667DX, it carried a base price of $2,615. Shipping weight was 3,642 pounds and production totalled 7,507. There were two one-color leather interiors – red and black – available on the Super 88 convertible along with a variety of mixed colored leather combinations.

Oldsmobile's good fortunes in automobile racing continued in 1953. Buck Baker, a long-time Olds stock car pilot, won the Southern 500 at Darlington, South Carolina in this Super 88 two-door sedan. Olds collected a total of 87 NASCAR grand national victories in 1953. This car carried the sponsorship of the Oldsmobile dealer in Florence, S.C., Griffin Motors, Airlift Corp., Champion Spark Plug and Pure Oil were other early stock car sponsors.

George Cale of West Jefferson, Ohio owns several Oldsmobiles including this sharp 1953 Super 88 two-door sedan. All 1953 Oldsmobiles had almost five inches of front seat travel. When the front door of any closed model Olds was opened a dome light came on. Also, locking an Oldsmobile door did not require a key. It could be accomplished by pushing the door sill lock button down and depressing the outside door handle release button until the door was closed.

One of the most attractive Olds offerings in 1953 was model number 533037DX, the 98 holiday coupe. Base price on this model was $2,771 and it weighed 3,680 pounds. Total production was 27,920. This 98 had hydraulic windows and seat as standard equipment. Interiors were quite attractive and included a variety of colored leathers blended with nylon waffle weave cloth. Two-tone paint was a no-cost option on either the Super 88 or 98 holiday.

The massive 98 four-door sedan again was the best seller in the top of the line series. It carried model number 533067D. Base price was $2,552 and shipping weight was 3,765 pounds. Production totalled 64,431. All four-door 98 interiors were done in dark and light blue or gray broadcloth, or dark and light green gabardine. All 98's rode on a 124-inch wheelbase.

The graceful 98 convertible was model number 533067DX. It was the highest priced 1953 Olds at $2,963. It weighed 3,741 pounds. In addition to a hydraulically operated top it also had hydraulic windows and seat. A total of only 7,521 Ninety-Eight convertibles were made in 1953. Standard tires on this model only were 8.00 x 15. Whitewalls cost $33.10 as an option.

Four color choices were offered in the 98 Fiesta. Solid colors were black and white with two-tone options being Noel and Nile green and surf and teal blue. Cars built late in the model year may have been painted other colors. Interiors were done in hand buffed leather of either light green, light blue or black and were trimmed in ivory leather. Some stainless steel was used as interior trim. Olds kept the Fiesta nameplate for its convertibles and later its station wagons long after this special model disappeared.

The Ninety-Eight four-door sedan offered the plushest non-leather interior in the Olds lineup. All Super 88 and 98 models came with foam rubber seat cushions front and rear. An extra comfortable seating package called custom lounge cushions was available on all Super 88 and 98 models. This package listed for $35 and included extra foam padding and reinforced cushion edges.

Big changes were made in the Rocket V-8 in 1952 and a few more modifications came in 1953. During the model year the millionth Rocket V-8 powerplant was built at Olds' Kettering Engine Plant in Lansing, Michigan. A 12-volt electrical system marked a giant step forward for Olds this model year. This change provided higher ignition voltage, increased generator output, faster starter turnover and greater battery capacity.

The Fiesta was a specially built auto show car that was popular enough that Oldsmobile put it into limited production. It had a number of differences from production 1953 models, the most radical being a wrap around windshield. Fiesta production totalled 458, shipping weight was more than 4,000 pounds. The price was a whopping $5,715. It was powered by a slightly hopped up version of the Rocket V-8 turning out 170 horsepower. HydraMatic was standard equipment on all Fiestas.

1953

The rear styling treatment was a bit different on the Fiesta, particularly the center chrome. Several cars appeared with continental kits in later years, but it is not believed the factory made these installations. Each Fiesta was loaded with accessories including: power steering, power brakes, super deluxe radio, heater defroster, Autronic Eye, white sidewall tires and backup lights. Tops were available in black or natural orlon (tan).

The Starfire was the second special model — the first being the limited production Fiesta — that appeared during the 1953 model year. The Starfire name was used at several points in later Oldsmobile history. For several years in the 1950's the Starfire nameplate appeared on all convertibles. In the 1960's a luxury Olds series carried the Starfire name, while in the 1970's an Olds small car was dubbed the Starfire.

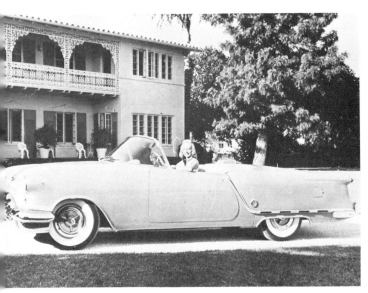

Starfire models were cleanly styled with a sparse use of chrome. Many Starfire features — most noticeably the large oval grille — found their way into the production 1956 models. The overall concept of the Starfire was the "sporty personal car." This theme was later used with success by Ford in the post 1957 Thunderbirds and by Oldmobile in its later Starfire series of production cars.

The Starfire drew its name from the Lockheed F-94B Starfire Fighter plane pictured here with the one-off dream car. The Starfire car had a fiberglass body — one of the early attempts at this type construction. A specially built Rocket V-8 topped the 200 horsepower mark. In its early stages the Starfire was finished in a striking turquoise finish with a turquoise and white leather interior.

1954

Oldsmobile sales were up slightly for 1954. This, coupled with a downturn in industry wide sales caused the Lansing based division to rise to an unexpected Fourth in the sales race. That milestone was the highest sales standing that Oldsmobile had enjoyed since it topped the sales race just after the turn of the century.

Despite its Fourth Place standing, the division fell well short of its 1950 model year mark. A total of 354,001 models were sold. Calendar year sales established a new Olds record with 433,810 deliveries.

The new models were completely redone. Across the line styling achieved a longer and lower look with a somewhat slab sided appearance. Coupled with several new two-tone packages, the new styling effort came off quite well.

The juggling of model names continued and for 1954 the designation of 88 was back on the bottom-of-the-line

Lightest and least expensive of the 1954 Oldsmobiles was the 88 Two-Door Sedan. It was designated model number 543611. Base price was $2,066 and weight was 3,584 pounds. Production on this model totalled 18,013. The 88 series for 1954 consisted of only three models, a pair of two-doors and a four-door. The 88 series shared an 122 inch wheelbase with the Super 88s. Overall length was slightly more than 205 inches.

This side view of an 88 Holiday Coupe shows one feature that was much talked about in 1954: the panoramic windshield. Literature of the era said it "opened a vast new range of unhampered driver vision." It provided 185 new square inches of glass area. Corner posts were moved back on 1954 models giving the driver a better view. Along with the new windshield design came newly designed front ventipanes. These were hand cranked and mounted in chrome frames.

Oldsmobile. Super 88 and 98 nameplates remained th same. The name Starfire was affixed to all 98 Seri convertibles. Eleven models were offered in the thr series. All featured the new panoramic windshield, whic was previewed by the 1953 Fiesta. All three series ha wheelbases extended two inches and each model wa lowered three inches without any decrease in groun clearance and interior dimensions. To achieve the low silhouette the frame and rear suspension were complete redesigned.

In its sales literature of the day, Olds claimed the ne models were really scheduled for 1955, but instea released as 1954's. This was probably just an advertisir claim as General Motors, with its inter-divisional sharir of body design, didn't operate that way.

The Rocket V-8 continued to creep up in horsepowe Ratings on the two engines increased to 170 horsepow and 185 horsepower. Displacement across the board wa upped to 324 cubic inches, with compression ratio goir to 8:25 to 1. In other mechanical areas improvements wer made. The basis for all models was a new and large X-member frame. Improved universal joints were adapte along with a new type coil front spring and a new re spring and shock absorber location.

A total of 18 solid colors were offered includin flare red, capri blue, maize cream and copper metalli Olds had 65 conventional 2-tone paint combinations, wit the top of a different color than the rest of the car. total of 11 special two-tone combinations were availab on the 98 Series 4-door and ten 2-tone schemes wer offered on the 98 Holiday, 98 Deluxe Holiday and th Starfire convertible.

Interiors on closed 88 Series models were done Elascofab bolster and pattern cloth, in gray, green or blu Super 88 closed car interiors were done in nylon bolst and orlon pin-striped cloth in gray, green or blue. Close models of the 98 Series were finished in gray, green or blu nylon bolster and nylon pillow tuft weave. Convertible continued to offer a variety of colored seat coverings leather, with tops of the recommended black, tan, gree blue, turquoise and natural orlon.

More and more power accessories were being ordered b Oldsmobile owners. Slight improvements for 1954 wer made in power steering, power brake and air conditionin systems. A hydraulic power window and power se system could be ordered on 98 Series 4-doors, while 4-wa electric seat and electric windows were available on mos other models. Other accessories available for 1954 Old mobiles were: signal seaking radio, cadet sun viso autronic eye, wire wheel covers, and padded dash pane

Two more of the popular Olds experimentals wer introduced in 1954. The Cutlass was a fastback mode built on a 110-inch wheelbase. The Cutlass' deep se grille would be put into production in 1956. Othe features included rear window louvers, extreme tail fin and copper tinted glass. The F-88 was a second one-of machine by Olds. It was a Corvette-sized, fiberglass tw seater. The F-88 was powered by a 250 horsepowe Rocket V-8 and sported a gold paint job.

Olds bought a new bumper production and plating plan on line in March of 1954. Assembly also began durin that year for Oldsmobiles at a 7th Buick-Oldsmobile Pontiac plant in Arlington, Texas.

1954

This 1954 88 Two-Door Sedan carried one of five types of wheel covers which were available from the factory. Standard on the 88 were the bottlecap hubcap which were on this car along with the optional trim rings (4 for $12.36). Stainless steel full wheel discs were an additional $14.67, while a spinner type deluxe stainless steel wheel disc cost $50 for a set. The ultimate wheel cover was "mimetic wire wheel" hubcaps. These retailed for $60 per set on 88s and Super 88 models and $46.23 on the Ninety-Eight models.

Model number 543637 was the sleak looking 88 Holiday Coupe. List price on this model was $2,230 and weight was 3,615 pounds. A total of 25,820 of this model were produced. A synchro-mesh transmission with an 11 inch single plate dry disc clutch was standard equipment on all models. Most buyers opted for HydraMatic which was a $165 factory installed option.

Most popular among the 88 series cars were the Four-Door Sedan. It was designated model number 543669. Price was $2,126 and weight was 3,692 pounds. Production totalled 29,028. A distinguishing feature of the 88 models were the 88 numerals near the back molding of the car. Power brakes were an option on all 1954 models equipped with HydraMatic. Price was $37.

The Super 88 Convertible was the least expensive open car that was available to Olds buyers. Super 88 open car interiors were available in red, green, dark blue, ivory, turquoise and light blue leather. Black tops were furnished on most Convertible Coupes but tan, green, blue and turquoise colored tops were offered. A natural orlon top was a $50 option on any Super 88 ragtop and a $45 option on the Ninety-Eight.

Least expensive of the four-model Super 88 series was the Two-Door Sedan. A total of 27,882 buyers went for model number 543611D. Its base price was $2,189 and weight was 3,618 pounds. Super 88 models carried an 88 logo, slightly different than 88 models, above the rear moldings. The Supers also sported a new decklid emblem of the rocket design.

By far the rarest Super 88 in 1954 was the Convertible Coupe. This open car carried model number 543667TDX. It was the most expensive Super 88 priced at $2,615. Weight on this machine was 3,712 pounds. For 1954 Oldsmobile had added a new parking light positioned below the headlight. These units were framed in chrome bezels designed to harmonize with the headlight contours. Production totalled 6,452.

1954

A popular offering in the Super 88 series was the Holiday Coupe, model number 543637D. It carried a base price of $2,448 and weighed 3,635 pounds. Production stood at 42,155 units. Super 88 interiors could be ordered in a combination of leather and waffle weave cloth. Colors included red, gray, green, blue and ivory. Interior color depended on the exterior color combination.

This Ohio based 1954 Olds Holiday Coupe from the Super 88 series was displayed at a national Oldsmobile Club of America meet. The Rocket V-8 engine displacement was up to 324 cubic inches in 1954. Compression ratio was 8.25 to 1. In the 88 models this engine developed 170 horsepower. Installed in the Super 88 and Ninety-Eight models the Rocket engine developed 185 horsepower. Olds claimed a 10% improvement in fuel economy with the 1954 powerplants.

Joseph Slagle of London, Ohio, displayed this nice Super 88 Four-Door Sedan at one of the national meets of the Oldsmobile Club of America. This car is radio equipped. Two radios were offered in 1954. A deluxe six tube unit with pushbuttons retailed for $100.82 installed. A super deluxe, eight tube signal seeking model sold for $129.36 installed. A rear speaker could be ordered in any 1954 Olds — except the convertible models — for $14.

More 1954 Oldsmobile buyers laid down their money for a Super 88 Four-Door Sedan than any other model. This car achieved sales totalling 111,326. Model number 543669D cost $2,251 and weighed 3,722 pounds. In Super 88 and Ninety-Eight four-doors "friction type" rear ventipanes were used. Olds claimed this helped air circulation with the Fisher body.

The highest production car in the Ninety-Eight series was the Four-Door Sedan. This car was designated model number 543069. Price was $2,552 and weight was 3,780 pounds. The roofline on the 1954 models was a full three inches lower than the 1953 models. New rear license plate lamps were mounted in the bumper guards. This location protected the lights from mud and stones. A total of 45,605 were built.

1954

A most handsome 1954 Ninety-Eight was the Starfire Convertible. Model number 543067DX was the most expensive car of the year with a price tag of $2,963. This car weighed 3,780 pounds. Production was only 6,800. Olds dubbed its top series convertible models Starfires after the 1953 dream car of the same name. Starfire interiors made generous use of deep hand buffed leathers.

Rarest among the 1954 models was the late introduced Deluxe Ninety-Eight Four-Door Sedan, model number 543069DX. Priced at $2,668 this car weighed 3,790 pounds. Production totalled only 2,367. Both models of the Ninety-Eight four-door had the rear center armrests. This model, the deluxe offering, also was equipped with all hydraulic controls. This particular car carried the $550 air conditioning system as indicated by the little scoops mounted on the rear fenders.

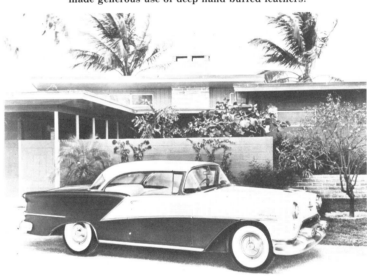

More popular among the two Ninety-Eight Holiday Coupes was the deluxe version. This car was designated model number 543037DX. Base price was $2,770 and weight was 3,760 pounds. A total of 29,688 of this model were built. Part of this deluxe model's equipment included all hydraulic controls. The interior fabrics in the Deluxe Holiday Coupes included a combination of leather and nylon weaves.

The standard Ninety-Eight Holiday Coupe was model number 543037. It weighed 3,750 pounds and was priced at $2,570. Production equalled only 8,865. This model had a somewhat less fancy interior than the deluxe models. All Ninety-Eight cars had special tailight assemblies which were larger than those units on the Super 88 and 88 models. All Olds tailights were clearly visable from the sides, which Olds touted as a safety feature.

Many people asked "Would You Buy a Used Car from This Man" when Richard Nixon took to the Presidential campaign trail. It wasn't a used car, but a new Ninety-Eight Four-Door that awaited Nixon on a visit to Lansing. Oldsmobile, like virtually all automobile manufacturers, was glad to loan some of its then new cars when VIP's made a local appearance.

Henry Parker of Palos Verdes, California had one of the most extensive collections of 1954 Oldsmobiles including this Ninety-Eight Holiday Coupe. This model included a full factory option list. It was equipped with: HydraMatic transmission ($165), Super Deluxe Radio ($129) electronically operated antenna ($20), power steering ($125), electric clock ($18.29), power brakes ($37), autronic eye ($45) and deluxe hubcaps ($36).

1954

The official Oldsmobile accessory catalog did not show a continental kit among the 1954 options available. Some after market outfitters made units like these available, however, and dealers did equip at least a few Oldsmobiles with rear mounted spare tires. This Hank Parker — owned 1954 Olds was found — continental kit and all — in a California junkyard and barely escaped the car crusher. This kit is also outfitted with one of the rare "mimetic wire wheel" hubcaps. The bumper sticker reads: "Saved From The Crusher By The Oldsmobile Club".

The Cutlass was one of two major "dream cars" on the auto show circuit in 1954. The Cutlass drew its name from the Chance-Vought Navy fighter plane of the same name. Body of the Cutlass was painted metallic silver with a white and copper leather interior. Wheelbase was 110 inches and it was more than 188 inches long. There was no outside decklid on this show model. Exhaust stacks were an integral part of the rear bumper.

This was the under hood compartment of the F-88 model. Both the Cutlass and the F-88 were powered by a 250-horsepower advanced version of the Rocket powerplant. Displacement was 324 cubic inches, the same as the 1954 models, while compression ratio was 9 to 1. Notice this special model used the odd sized General Motors battery. The F-88 was HydraMatic equipped with a tachometer and chronometer.

A Corvette-sized "dream car" was the second special show car for Oldsmobile in 1954. This was the F-88, a two-seater sports convertible. Both the F-88 and Cutlass bodies were made of reinforced plastic. The F-88 had a wheelbase of 102 inches and was just over 167 inches long. The car was painted metallic gold while the upholstery and steering wheel were finished in pigskin. Two 88s in six inch numerals were located on the front fenders ahead of the doors.

The F-88 was an interesting car both coming and going. High rear fenders terminated in two cone shaped taillights. Exhaust stacks were integral with the lower rear fenders in oval openings with decorative louvers just ahead of them on the fender panel. Seven vertical bumper guards were part of the rear bumper. This bumper unit dropped down to reveal a horizontal compartment for the spare tire.

Records tumbled for Oldsmobile in 1955 as the division completed its most successful year in nearly 60 years operation. Olds secured its hold on Fourth Place and established sales marks that would last for a decade. For the model year a whopping 583,179 cars were sold. Calendar year totals were 643,459.

This record shattering performance came with a model lineup mildly restyled from 1954. The most obvious and attractive style work was the deepset and chrome trimmed headlights. Other styling changes included new side mouldings, new emblems front and rear, and the extension of the sweep cut front fenders to 88 and Super 88 Series, matching 1954 98 Series styling.

The trend toward more powerful Rocket V-8's continued. Horsepower ratings climbed upward to 185 and 202. Compression ratio was bumped to 8.5 to 1. Internal engine modifications were newly designed combustion chambers and a redesigned camshaft. The carburetor on the smaller engine was also redone for 1955. In 1952, Oldsmobile began offering a lower horsepower engine for its lowest priced series. In 1955, for the first time, the higher rated engine was available on the 88 and for the modest sum of $35 any of the bottom of the line 88's could be equipped with the 202 horsepower Rocket V-8. The biggest mechanical change came as the result of a completely redesigned front suspension. Olds called its new independent-type front suspension Power Ride. It employed direct action shock absorbers, a new front stabilizer and newly calibrated front coil springs. Other changes for the new year included an improved manual steering gear and the adoption of tubeless tires for all series. Inside the new Oldsmobile both the standard and deluxe steering wheels were redone. The instrument cluster, radio dial, speaker grille and panel moulding on the 88 Series were now chrome, the same as all other series in 1954. Carpeting was made standard on Super 88's and optional on all 88's.

New 4-door Holiday hardtop models were added in each series for the first time in 1955.

A total of 10 solid colors were available for 1955 including: glen green, juneau gray, coral, bronze metallic, and burlingame red. A whopping total of 89 conventional 2-tone paint jobs were offered, and 20 special 2-tone combinations could be ordered on 88 and Super 88 2 and 4-door sedans and 98 4-door sedans. The 88 and Super 88 Holiday coupes and Super 88 convertibles could also be ordered in 10 special 2-tone combinations, and 19 additional special paint combinations were offered on 98 Holiday coupes and Starfire convertibles. Upholstery on 88 and Super 88 closed models was pattern bolster and pattern cloth in gray, green or blue. The 98 Series 4-doors could be ordered in the same color interiors of covert cloth bolster and pattern cloth. All series Holiday coupe interiors were done in pattern cloth with Super 88 and 98 models featuring leather bolster. Convertibles featured leather interiors and top colors of the recommended black, tan, green, blue, white Toptex and white orlon. Fifteen-inch tubeless tires were supplied by U.S. Royal, Firestone and Goodrich.

The newest power accessory to add to the 1955 option list was a power operated radio antenna listing for $20. An improved air conditioning system now saw all the hardware under the hood with three outlets featured in the dash. The price remained at $550, and few cars were so equipped because of the high cost. Other factory options included: electric clock, oil filter, rear radio speaker, electric windows and tinted glass.

The Delta was the new show car for 1955 and that model tipped some Olds' styling of the later 1950's. The Delta was a 4-passenger model on a 120-inch wheelbase. Special features included: dual fuel tanks, aluminum trim, a center console and dual headlights.

A multi-million dollar expansion effort was begun in June to double production capacity from the Lansing operation. The 5-millionth Olds was built in July.

Thirty-five years of Oldsmobile history are easily spanned in this side by side comparison of a 1920 Sedan — owned by Oldsmobile — and a 1955 convertible fresh off the assembly line. For 1955 Olds offered a massive new front bumper assembly which was contoured to blend with the hood and fender moldings. Olds also used a modern world emblem up front. This decoration was recessed into the hood. Headlights were recessed, hooded and rimmed with chrome.

Basic transportation in the Oldsmobile lineup for 1955 was an 88 Two Door Sedan. This model was designated number 553611. It was the least expensive 1955 Olds with a price tag of $2,297. Shipping weight was 3,690 pounds. Production for the 88 Two Door Sedan stood at 37,507. All 88 and Super 88 models rode on 122 inch wheelbases. Overall length was just over 203 inches, while width was more than 78 inches. Standard tire size was 7.10 x 15 inches.

This 1955 Oldsmobile Two Door Sedan showed the simplest two tone style available during the model year. Customers had a choice of 19 colors. This amounted to 89 conventional two tone options offered by the factory, plus other configurations available on other special models. Fourteen 1955 colors were new, while five colors were carryovers from 1954. Again the Oldsmobile lines were particularly well suited for two toning.

The open roofline styling wore well on the 88 Holiday Coupe. This was model number 553637. Base price on this auto was $2,474 and it weighed 3,705 pounds. The 88 Holiday Coupe was the most popular car in its series as production totalled 85,767. On 88 and Super 88 models the 1955's offered swept cut front fenders matching those on the Ninety-Eight series.

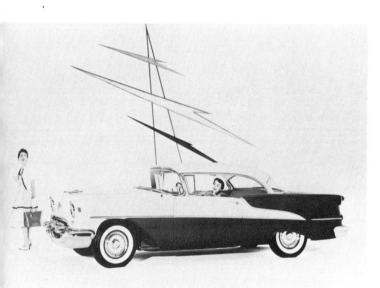

This 88 series Holiday Coupe typified the basic good looks of the 1955 Oldsmobiles. The base powerplant for all cars this year was the old standby 324 cubic inch unit. It had aluminum alloy pistons and hydraulic valve lifters. The 88 version of this engine was rated at only 185 horsepower by virtue of its dual downdraft two barrel carburetor. The more powerful Super 88/Ninety-Eight engine was an option on the 88 series.

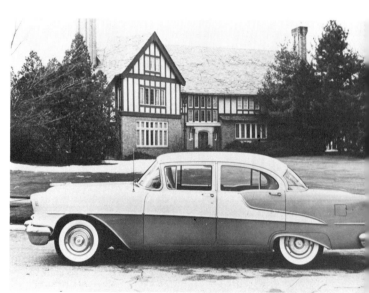

The 88 Four Door Sedan was a lot of car for its $2,362 base price. This car carried model number 553669 and weighed 3,710 pounds. Production for this model was 57,777. The syncro-mesh manual transmission was standard across the board for the last time in 1955. The HydraMatic - pioneered by Oldsmobile in its 1940 models - was option A and had a suggested list price of $165.

All literature put out very early did not include any of the Holiday Sedans and these models were introduced a bit later than the regular 1955 model introduction. The 88 Holiday Sedan was model number 553639. Base price on this model was $2,546 and weight was 3,695 pounds. Despite its later introduction this model sold 41,310. A feature on all 1955 models was a new fuel and vacuum pump with a one piece cover.

On-the-beach racing was still a factory proving ground in 1955 and Oldsmobiles could often be found frolicking on Daytona Beach. This posed NASCAR action shot saw two 88 Two Door Sedans ready to do battle on the sand. Drivers of the machines were Dick Rathman and Jim Pascal. Both cars came out of the well known Wood racing stable. Note the early NASCAR sponsors: Pure Oil, Air Lift, Grant Piston Rings and Wynn's Friction Proofing.

Front end allignment was critical even in the rough and tumble early days of NASCAR. Here Indianapolis 500 veteran Dick Rathman stands by his 1955 Olds racer while it receives a front end allignment. Oldsmobile had been active in NASCAR stock car racing since it introduced the Rocket V-8 in 1949. The Lansing factory officials and engineers would share their knowledge with racers and some special parts that helped racers could be found in the Olds parts catalog.

Rarest among all the 1955 Oldsmobiles was the Super 88 Convertible. It was designated model number 553667DTX. Base price was $2,894, making this the most expensive car in the series. Weight was 3,795 pounds. Production totalled only 9,007. One difference between the 88/Super 88 and Ninety-Eight models was the taillight design. Tire suppliers for 1955 were: U.S. Royal, Firestone or Goodrich.

One of only two open cars available in the 1955 lineup was the Super 88 Convertible. This particular car is equipped with the relatively rare rigid fiberglass top boot. It was an option and sold for $95. This car also has the deluxe hubcaps which listed for $50 installed on 88 and Super 88 models. The standard Super 88 tire size was 7.60 x 15. Oversize tires were 8.00 x 15 inches. Covertible top colors were black, tan, green, blue and white Toptex. The white orlon top was a $50 extra.

1955

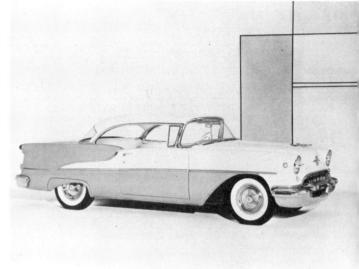

A relatively rare model was the Super 88 Two Door Sedan. This car carried model number 553611D. This was the least expensive car in the series with a price of $2,436. Weight of this model was 3,755 pounds. Production on the Super 88 Two Door Sedan totalled 11,950. The cooling system capacity on all 1955 Oldsmobiles was 21.5 quarts including the heater. The deluxe heater and defroster was a $74.50 option.

Enjoying popularity in the Super 88 series was the Holiday Coupe which achieved 62,534 sales. Model number 553637D sold for $2,714 and weighed 3,765 pounds. For 1955 Olds offered new standard and deluxe steering wheels. Each had a new recessed center design with the world emblem in the center. The 1955 dash had new, clean smooth surface with chrome control knobs.

This straight side shot of a Super 88 Holiday Coupe pointed out the clean styling of this model. This particular car is equipped with the electrically operated radio antenna which was available on any model for $20 installed. Two radio options were offered on 1955 Oldsmobiles. The deluxe radio - six tubes, pushbutton tuning - could be installed for $94.50. The super deluxe radio - 8 tubes, signal seeking and favorite station tuning - was $121 installed.

Oldsmobile's bread and butter car for 1955 was the Super 88 Four Door Sedan. The most popular Oldsmobile was model number 553669 D. It was priced at $2,503 and weighed 3,760 pounds. This car achieved a whopping sales total of 111,316. The easiest way to tell the difference between an 88 and Super 88 model was the difference in the front fender chrome emblem.

This was an early version of the Super 88 Holiday Sedan, model number 553639SD. Base price was $2,788 and shipping weight was 3,780 pounds. Despite an introduction later than the other four cars in the Super 88 series, the Holiday Sedan was responsible for 47,385 sales. One distinguishing feature of this early car was the Super 88 emblem on the front fender. Most of these cars had a holiday inscription on the front fender instead.

1955

Convertibles were seldom photographed with the top up but this 1955 Ninety-Eight Starfire Convertible was caught on a dealer backlot. A black top was supplied on all 1955 Oldsmobiles unless one of the five other colors of top materials available was specified. The top of the line series convertible standard equipment included: electric vertical seat adjustment, four way seat adjuster and electric window lifts.

The regal flagship of the Oldsmobile fleet was the Ninety-Eight Starfire Convertible. This graceful model was designated 553067 DX. It was Oldsmobile's most expensive 1955 model with a hefty $3,276 tab. Weight was 3,890 pounds. This also was the rarest car of the Ninety-Eight series with a production run of 9,149. Convertible upholstery included a variety of leather color combinations.

The side trim pattern was a bit different on Ninety-Eight models as demonstrated on this Holiday Coupe. Ninety-Eight series cars rode on their own exclusive 126 inch wheelbase with an overall length of more than 212 inches. Rear suspension of all 1955 Oldsmobiles consisted of two 2½ by 58 inch leaf springs. Angle mounted direct acting shock absorbers were used. A rear stabilizer bar was also used to aid handling.

A number of buyers opted for the Ninety-Eight Holiday Coupe, model number 553037 DX. This car was priced at $3,069 and it weighed 3,805 pounds. A total of 38,363 Olds buyers laid down their new car cash for this top series model. Special interior options were available on this model Ninety-Eight. All leather trim was available or an attractive combination of leather bolster cloth and pattern cloth in red, green, gray, blue, coral and turquiose could be ordered.

Top seller among the 1955 Ninety-Eight series cars was the Four-Door Sedan. This offering carried model number 553069D. It was priced at $2,833 and it tipped the scales at 3,865 pounds. Olds assembly plants across the country pumped out a total of 39,847 of this model. Olds supplied new design tubeless tires which were built to reduce the chances of blowouts and to give a smoother ride with less tire squeal. Oddly, this particular car was photographed at Ford Motor Company's test track at Dearborn, probably as part of a competition study that Ford was conducting at the time.

This Ninety-Eight Four Door Sedan was equipped with one unusual option. Part number 983103 was a factory left hand spot light. It could be ordered on any model and be either factory or dealer installed. Price was $23.95. Olds did offer some special equipment that police departments found useful in 1954. A package that included a heavy duty stick shift transmission and heavy duty seats and seat frames sold for $13.65.

1955

The last model in the top of the line Olds Ninety-Eight series was the Holiday Sedan. This car was model number 553039 SDX. Base price was $3,140 and weight was 3,875 pounds. Production for this model totalled 31,267. Standard equipment included windshield washers and front compartment courtesy lights. Backup lights were available on any model for $13.15.

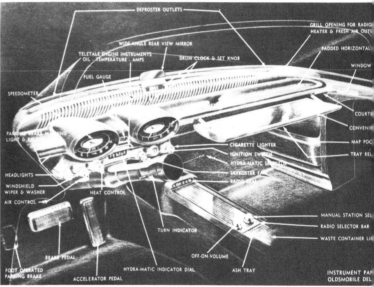

Oldsmobile continued with its strong involvement in the General Motors dream car scene in 1955. The representative was the 1955 Delta which pretold 1957 and 1958 Olds styling. The Delta was a four passenger coupe which had a height of 53 inches and a wheelbase of 120 inches. Its features included rear fender mounted fuel tanks, cast aluminum wheels and anodized aluminum trim.

It's probably a good thing Oldsmobile never went into production with dream cars like the Delta. Interior layouts seemed designed more to dazzle the auto show crowds than for actual use. It probably would have been tough to live with such an interior layout on a day to day basis. A center console was provided for radio controls and storage. Dual instrument pods housed a speedometer and tachometer.

Just entering the funeral car and ambulance field was the Comet Coach Co. of Memphis. This company, formed by Waldo J. Cotner and Robert Bevington, was to become one of the large firms in the future. Building on the Oldsmobile chassis, they offered a line of attractive and economical vehicles. This is the Comet limousine combination.

Comet's ambulance was this attractively styled Oldsmobile coach with finely etched rear quarter windows, tunnel type roof warning lights, and a centrally mounted roof siren warning light. Comet built on the Olds chassis mainly but did build a few cars on the Pontiac chassis.

1956

Sales slid slightly for 1956 and Olds found itself in Fifth Place in the sales standing with totals well below 1955's record level. For the model year, sales were 485,458. Calendar year totals were 432,903.

For the first time since its de-emphasis in 1951, the bottom of the line 88 became the division's top seller. By series, 1956 sales totals were 216,020 Eighty-Eights, 179,000 Super 88's and 118,626 Ninety-Eights. This was also the last year Oldsmobile used the plain designation 88 for any of its cars.

The biggest exterior styling change for 1956 was the deeply concave, heavily chromed grille. This styling idea came basically from the F-88 dream car of a couple of years earlier.

In the interior styling package the highly functional dashboard gauges for monitoring engine temperature, oil pressure and electrical system charging were replaced by "idiot lights." This change marred what otherwise had to be considered one of the best interior layouts in the business.

Drive train improvements were significant in 1956 as both the Hydra-Matic and Rocket V-8 were updated. Two Hydra-Matics were offered in 1956, for the first time since the automatic transmission was introduced in 1939. The initial automatic was the standard unit retailing for $175, and basically unchanged from 1955. For the first time an automatic transmission was made standard equipment on the 98 only. This unit was the new Jetaway Hydra-Matic, and its claimed improvement in smoothness came from a second fluid coupling in the transmission. The Jetaway unit was also available as an option on any Series 88 and Super 88 model for $15 more than the standard Hydra-Matic. Another change in the automatic transmission was the addition of a park position to the shifting quadrant for Jetaway equipped models.

The Rocket V-8 powerplant carried the additional designation of T-350 for the new model year. This referred to the engine's 350-foot-pound torque rating. Displacement remained at 324, but horsepower went up substantially from 202 to 240. The compression ratio was bumped to 9.25 to 1. A 10-horsepower less version of the Rocket V-8 was standard equipment on the 88, but the more powerful engine remained an option.

Nineteen colors were offered on the 1956 models including: festival red, ice green, nordic blue, citron cream and terra cotta. Regular 2-tone combinations — with the top and body of differing colors — were offered as well as several special 2-tones based on the chrome trim of the particular model. Interior trim packages came in a variety of fabrics in gray, green, blue and beige. Leather was still available in convertible interiors. Tops could be ordered in black, tan, dark green, dark blue and white.

Olds remained a leader in the power era with power steering (now standard on the 98), power brakes, air conditioning, 6-way seats, power radio antenna and power windows. Other factory accessories were: signal seaking radio, backup lights, deluxe steering wheel, electric clock and chrome exhaust extension.

In keeping with an Olds policy of introducing a dream car/show car per year, 1956 was no exception with the Golden Rocket. This model offered a 275-horse-power Rocket V-8. Other features included: plastic body construction, removable roof panels and swivel seats. The 1957 Oldsmobiles picked up their unique parking lights from the Golden Rocket.

Olds was gradually slipping from the racing spotlight as the highwinding overhead V-8 Ford and Chevrolets were taking over. Hot rodders still prowled the junk yards in hopes of finding a Rocket V-8 to do some engine swapping with. Lee Petty established a flying mile record at Daytona Beach with a run over 144 mph in an 88 Olds. Eighty-Eight and 98 sedans recorded class wins in the 1956 Mobil Gas Economy run. Olds finally completed canon and shell orders for the government in 1956, and this production area could be turned over to automotive uses. The division began its armament effort in 1941 and carried out the assignment through the Korean War.

The least expensive 1956 Oldsmobile was model number 563611, the 88 Two Door Sedan, with a base price of $2,166. Weight on this offering was 3,705 pounds — the lightest 1956 Olds. Production totalled 31,949, the lowest production car in the 88 series. All of the cars in this low priced series rode on a 122 inch wheelbase, the same as the Super 88 cars. Overall length was just over 203 inches.

As usual Oldsmobile dubbed its hardtop styled cars Holidays. The 88 Holiday Coupe was model number 563637. This was the largest selling 88 model with a production run of 74,739. Base price was $2,330 and weight was 3,715 pounds. Each 88 series car had a front tread width of 59 inches and a rear tread width of 58 inches.

A rare "Plain Jane" in the Olds lineup was this 88 Two Door Sedan. This car carried the standard blackwall tubeless 7.10 x 15 inch tires supplied by several manufacturers. Oversize tires were available on the 88 series and they were 7.60 x 15 inches. Whitewalls could be added on both the standard and oversize tires. If an Olds buyer didn't like the bottlecap hubcaps on the car pictured, a larger stainless steel wheel disc was offered.

1956

A bread and butter Oldsmobile was the 88 Four Door Sedan down through the years and 1956 provided no exception. Production on this model, number 563669, was 57,092. It weighed 3,761 pounds and base price was $2,226. The standard equipment on 88 models was a synchromesh three-speed transmission unit. The pedal operated clutch was 11 inches in diameter and of the semi-centrifugal type. The 88 standard shift rear end ratio was 3.64 to 1. This particular model was owned in 1958 by George Dammann, Crestline's general manager, and is shown in front of the Dammann home at that time, in Coldenham, N.Y.

Each of the three 1956 Oldsmobile series had a hardtop four door model. In the 88 series it was model number 563639, the Holiday Sedan. This car was base priced at $2,397 and weighed 3,776 pounds. Production equalled 52,239. The 88 series came with a 324 cubic inch engine rated at 230 horsepower. This engine had a dual downdraft two barrel carburetor which accounted for its lower horsepower output.

A very fine example of the Super 88 Convertible stayed right in the Lansing, Michigan area. This largely original car belongs to Max Hineman of DeWitt, Michigan. He is an employee in the service department of Story Oldsmobile, the world's largest Oldsmobile dealership. Max's car is equipped with the X-2 deluxe stainless steel wheel discs. They cost $38.95 for a set of four and appealed to hot rodders of a slightly later era.

The Super 88 Four Door Sedan like all other cars in its series was powered by the same Rocket engine that drove the 98 series cars. Again for 1956 no engine other than a V-8 was available from Olds. The Super 88 motor displaced 324 cubic inches and developed 240 horsepower and 350 pound feet of torque. Compression ratio was 9.25 to 1. Each of the Super series cars were fueled by a Quadri-Jet carburetor of four barrel design. For 1956 that unit featured larger primary venturi and larger throttle bores.

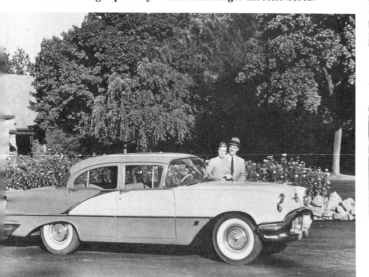

The largest series in terms of models for 1956 was the Super 88 group with five basic models. Among the rarest of all 1956 Oldsmobiles was the Super 88 Convertible. Only 9,561 were made. Base price was $2,726 making this the most expensive car in its series. Weight was 3,947 pounds and model number was 563667DTX. Standard Super 88 tire size was 7.60 x 15 inches with optional 8.00 x 15 tires recommended on air conditioned cars.

OLDS

A good seller in the Super 88 series was model number 563669 D, the Four Door Sedan. Production totalled a very sizable 59,728. Base price was $2,363 and weight was 3,897 pounds. A total of 17 all new colors were added in 1956 and this set up at least 129 conventional two tones that were offered by Olds. The Oldsmobile lines and styling provided one of the more attractive two toning schemes in the industry for 1956.

Rarest among all the 1956 Oldsmobiles was the Super 88 Two Door Sedan. This car was model number 563611D. Only 5,465 of this basic model were produced. Prices started at $2,301 making this the least expensive car in the series. It weighed 3,835 pounds. All Super 88 series cars shared a 122 inch wheelbase with 88 model cars, but were powered by the same 240 horsepower engine as the 98 models.

Model number 563637SD was the Super 88 Holiday Coupe. Base price was $2,520. It weighed 3,835 pounds. The production run on this car was 43,054. Super 88 and 88 models were nearly identical in appearance. The emblem on the lower front fender was slightly different on the two series cars. Windshield wipers were redesigned on 1956 models. Blades cleaned a ten percent larger area than before.

This Memphian limousine ambulance was mounted on an Oldsmobile chassis and featured a roof mounted gum ball type warning light and wrap around rear corner windows. This car was built on an extended Olds Super 88 chassis and was fitted out with all of the ambulance emergency equipment.

The largest selling 1956 Oldsmobile was the Super 88 Holiday Sedan. Production totalled a whopping 61,192. This car was designated model number 563639 SD. Base price on this selection was $2,586 and weight was 3,905 pounds. Olds harmonized the color treatment of the instrument panel and steering wheel to the interior and upholstery colors. Directional signals were standard on all 1956 Oldsmobiles.

The Super 88 Holiday Sedan was a graceful and handsome car. Holiday four door sedan models carried the holiday chrome lettering on the middle portion of the front fender. New for 1956 on the Super 88 and Ninety-Eight models was the Jetaway HydraMatic Drive. This unit virtually eliminated all sensations of the gear change. For the first time all upper series Oldsmobiles came with an automatic as standard equipment. Eight-Eight buyers could opt for a slightly different version of the HydraMatic.

Model number 563037 SDX was the Ninety-Eight Holiday Coupe. Production on this model was 19,433, base price was $3,138 and weight was 3,978 pounds. Oldmobile offered an improved air conditioning system in 1956. Cool air outlets were larger and dash mounted. Air compressor speed was increased to set up overall cooling capacity. Price on this option, part number 983415, was $425.

The longer wheelbased (126 inches) Ninety-Eights for 1956 were elegant and well equipped cars. Rarest of the top of the line series was the Starfire Convertible, model number 563067DX. This car was the most expensive 1956 Olds priced at $3,380. Weight was 4,107 pounds. Only 8,581 were produced. One easy way to distinguish the Ninety-Eight series cars from the 88's and Super 88's was the more rounded pattern of the side trim.

The Ninety-Eight Four Door Sedan was one of four models available in the top of the line Olds series. It was designated model number 563069D. This was a relatively popular car as it achieved 20,105 sales. Carrying a price tag of $2,969, it weighed 4,047 pounds. Standard on all Ninety-Eight models was the Saginaw Gear built Safety Power Steering system. For 1956 this unit was improved to take less effort in steering during highway driving.

Top seller in the Ninety-Eight series was the Holiday Sedan, model number 563039 SDX. It was base priced at $3,204 and weighed 4,061 pounds. A total of 42,320 were built. The Pedal-Ease power braking system was offered only on HydraMatic equipped cars. Olds claimed its power brakes offered easier and quicker stopping times due to the low-to-the-floor suspended brake pedal mounting.

The early General Motors air conditioning systems were bulky units, part of which was mounted in the trunk with outlets in the headliner. By 1956 all that had changed and the air outlets blended in very well with the overall dash layout. Olds had an attractive interior design for 1956. A large "racetrack" type speedometer was easy to read. Located below that was the fuel guage and still lower was a nicely layed out shaft quadrant.

Dream cars were big with all General Motors divisions in the 1950s and early 1960s and Oldsmobile had its share of these units. The Oldsmobile Golden Rocket was introduced in 1956 and revised several times to stay on the show circuit for several years. It was a two passenger model. Ahead of its time, the car was made of reinforced plastic and finished in a gold color.

Oldsmobile used the 1956 General Motors Motorama as a debut point for its Golden Rocket show piece. The car was used in numerous other auto shows across the land. Projectile shaped bumper guards were incorporated in the front and rear end of the car, giving an overall rocket effect. As either door was opened, the roof panel automatically raised and the seat came up three inches and swiveled outward for easy entry or exit.

Oldsmobile nomenclature sometimes ran toward aircraft themes with such items as: Rocket engine, B-42 models, Starfire, F-88 and Cutlass. It was no surprise then when an airport was used as a backdrop to photograph the Golden Rocket. This strictly experimental model had a 105 inch wheelbase and a length of 201 inches. It was powered by a "pepped-up" 275 horsepower Rocket V-8. Upholstery on this car was done in striking blue and gold leather.

1957

Sales were down again in 1957, but Oldsmobile managed to retain Fifth spot. For the model year 384,390 cars were sold, while calendar year deliveries were 390,091.

A major styling change was carried out with the 1957's, and this was the final chapter in the Futuramic styling book which began with the 1948 98's. The 1957's carried an updated version of the deep, chromed grille of the previous year. A completely redone rear styling treatment featured larger taillights than those of previous years. The divided back window was also a styling curiosity for the new models.

Oldsmobile continued to play the name change game. The bottom of the line models were now known as Golden Rocket 88's, a curious tag since the division 50th (golden) anniversary was 10 years before. No matter what nameplate Olds slapped on its lowest priced series it continued to pace sales with 172,657 Golden Rocket 88's delivered. The Super 88 name remained the same and 132,039 of that model were built. The prefix word Starfire was added to all 98's, not just the convertibles as in previous years. A total of 79,694 Starfire 98's were built in the 1957 model year.

For the 1957 lineup the station wagon made its reappearance, after being dropped in 1950. This model used another familiar Oldsmobile nameplate, Fiesta. The Fiesta sedan, a model offered with a post between the two side doors, was available only in the Golden Rocket 88 Series. The Fiesta, which had a hardtop effect between the two side doors, could be ordered in either the Golden Rocket or Super 88 Series. No Starfire 98 wagons were built in 1957.

The Rocket V-8 continued its climb toward even more powerful levels. Horsepower on the standard engine was upped to 277, interestingly enough more than double the original 1949 Rocket V-8 output of 135 horsepower. Displacement was upped to 371 cubic inches. Compression ratios continued to climb and the new Rocket was 9.5 to 1. Other improvements included: redesigned combustion chambers, improved carburetion, new air cleaner package and a more efficient exhaust system.

By January, the Rocket V-8 could be made even more powerful with the J-2 tri-carburetor option. This performance package included three 2-barrel carbs, a special manifold, a cylinder head gasket package to boost the compression ratio to 10 to 1, a new throttle linkage and unique air cleaner setup. Horsepower output of the J-2 was rated at an even 300. The J-2 could be ordered on any model of any series for $83. There was also a special unpublicized J-2 engine option with racing camshaft, pistons and other heavy duty internal engine parts. This option listed for $385 and was rarely offered to anyone but a serious racer.

The 88 Convertible was the lowest priced open car in the 1957 lineup. A total of 6,423 were made. Model number on this car was 573667TX and the base price was $2,895. As with all bottom of the line Oldsmobiles, this model bore the official designation Golden Rocket 88, even though it was the division's 60th year of car production. All 88 and Super 88 models were on a 122-inch wheelbase with an overall length of 208.2 inches. Shipping weight was 4,021 pounds.

The least expensive 1957 Olds was this plain Jane 88 two-door sedan, carrying a price tag of $2,478. Model number was 573611. Production on the 88 two-door sedan was 18,477. Overall width, as with all Golden Rocket 88s, was 76.38 inches. Shipping weight on this model was 3,952 pounds.

Other 1957 changes included 14-inch wheels and tires, slightly redesigned front and rear suspension and a recessed safety steering wheel.

A total of 22 standard Olds colors were offered for 1957 including: charcoal, cutlass bronze, royal glow and sapphire mist. Special 2-tone combinations were also available on all models. Interiors were done in a variety of black, green, blue and gray fabrics. Leather was still available on Super 88 and Starfire 98 convertibles. Convertible top colors included: white, black, green, blue and tan.

A special policy package consisting of special duty transmission parts, heavy duty shocks and springs and a special rugged front seat was available on Lansing-built cars. Other factory options included: seat belts, air conditioning, wonder bar radio, traffic light viewer and cadet exterior sun visor.

A few Oldsmobiles continued to run on the oval tracks including a 1957 Golden Rocket 88 on the old NASCAR convertible circuit piloted by a rookie driver named Richard Petty. The focal point of the 1957 Olds show circuit effort was a Holiday coupe dubbed the Mona Lisa and featuring interior and exterior appointments in pearlescent tangerine.

1957

This 88 Holiday coupe was photographed at the fountain located in the General Motors Technical Center in Warren, Michigan. Model number of the two-door Holiday was 573637 and base price was $2,591. This long-standing model was a popular offering in 1957 with production of 49,187. As with all 88 models, note the absence of front fender trim which was present on Super 88 and 98 offerings. Shipping weight on this model was 3,957 pounds.

Most popular of the entire 1957 Olds lineup was this four-door sedan. Model number for this offering was 573669 and base prices began at $2,538. Production for the 88 four-door sedan was 53,923. As with all 88 models, tire size was 8:50 x 14, with larger tires optional. Shipping weight was 4,013 pounds.

Hardtop styling continued to be offered in the bottom of the line four-door model. The 88 Holiday sedan carried model number 573636, with a base price of $2,663. Production was 33,830. Shipping weight for this model was 4,007 pounds.

The Fiesta Sedan was the other station wagon offered in the 88 series, and the 88 was the only series it was available in. Model number for the Golden Rocket 88 Fiesta Sedan was 573662F and base price was $2,914. Production was slightly less than its sister Fiesta wagon at 5,052. This particular Fiesta sedan was photographed at a 1957 auto show. Notice in the right side of the photo there is a Super 88 Fiesta featuring the hardtop styling of the pillarless Fiesta version.

Station wagons returned to the Olds model lineup in 1957 after being absent since the 1950 model year. Offered in both the 88 and Super 88 series, all wagons carried the Fiesta nameplate and were externally very similar. Pictured here is an 88 pillarless Fiesta, or just plain Fiesta model, which carried number 573665F. Base price was $3,017, making it the only 88 to top $3,000 in base price. Note the styligh lack of a doorpost in keeping with hardtop styling. Production of the pillarless Fiesta was 5,767. Shipping weight was 4,307 pounds.

Oldsmobiles were still seen on the NASCAR circuit despite the domination of high winding Ford and Chevrolet models. Here a trio of Petty Engineering cars await final race tuning in a NASCAR garage area. The 88 convertible was driven by ace pilot Lee Petty of Randleman, N. C. The late "Tiny" Lund drove 88 coupe number 188. And an unheralded rookie driver by the name of Richard Petty wheeled car number 43. Few people realized that the Pettys had an Olds "factory" racing deal in the late 1950s between lucrative factory deals with Chrysler.

Airlift Corporation, a Lansing-based firm, spent a number of years racing Oldsmobiles. This was their 1957 effort. This Golden Rocket 88 two-door sedan was clocked on the Daytona sands in excess of 144 MPH. The car was equipped with special wide wheels and tires, but note the otherwise stock appearance of the machine.

The Super 88 convertible carried model number 573667DTX. This model had a base price of $3,132. A total of 7,128 were built. The chrome designation – Super 88 – was carried on the front fender as with all cars in this series except the station wagon. Super 88s shared the 122-inch wheelbase with the 88 series. Convertibles came standard with 9:00 x 14 tires. Shipping weight was 4,073 pounds.

Hardtop styling appealed to Super 88 buyers as 31,155 Holiday coupes were sold in 1957. This model carried a base price of $2,884. Its model number was 573637SD. Deluxe wheel covers came on this particular car. As with all Super 88s, overall length was 208.2 inches. Shipping weight was 4,007 pounds.

Most popular offering in the Super 88 series was the four-door sedan. It carried a base price of $2,745 and its model number was 573669D. A total of 42,629 Super 88 four-door sedans were built. This car, as did all 88 and Super 88 offerings, came standard with the three-speed syncro-mesh transmission. But few cars were actually built that way, as most had Hydra-matic transmissions. Shipping weight was 4,049 pounds.

The Super 88 two-door sedan was the rarest of all 1957 Oldsmobiles as only 2,983 were produced. The two-door carried a model number of 573611D and a base price of $2,687, making it the least expensive Super 88. Standard size tires were 8:50 x 14s, and shipping weight was 4,002 pounds.

The Holiday Sedan in the Super 88 series was a particularly attractive car. This shot shows the unique pillared rear window design. Model number for the Super 88 Holiday Sedan was 573639SD and it carried a base price of $2,863. A total of 39,162 of this model were built. Shipping weight was 4,042 pounds. As with all 1957 Oldsmobiles, except J-2s, power came from a 371 cubic inch engine producing 277 horsepower.

1957

Only the pillarless Fiesta model was available in Super 88 trim, but it proved to be the single most popular 1957 Olds station wagon. It carried model number 573665SDF and was the most expensive Super 88 at $3,200. A total of 8,981 Super 88 Fiestas were made. This factory shot was aimed at the outdoorsman, with props that included outboard motor, tent, boat and camping lantern. Shipping weight was 4,357.

The most popular Starfire 98 offered was the Holiday sedan. It carried the second highest 1957 Olds base price at $3,649. A total of 32,099 were sold. Model number for this car was 573039SDX. Shipping weight was 4,343 pounds. As with all 1957 Olds, it was based on an I-beam frame with X-center member and five cross members.

Surprisingly, the 98 convertible was the most popular 1957 open car Olds offered, despite the fact that it was the most expensive 1957 Olds available. A total of 8,278 were produced. They carried model number 573067DX. Base price was $3,838. As with all 98s, a 126-inch wheelbase was used. Overall length was 216.7 inches and shipping weight was 4,364 pounds.

With its slightly longer wheelbase, the 98 Holiday coupe proved a graceful car. It carried the Starfire designation as did all 98s in 1957. Model number for this car was 573037SDX and it was priced at $3,578. A total of 17,791 were built. As with all Starfire 98s, standard equipment included power steering. Hydra-matic and power brakes, Shipping weight was 4,305 pounds.

A four-door sedan rounded out the four-model Starfire 98 line. Priced at $3,396, model number for this offering was 573069D. A total of 21,525 Starfire 98 four-door sedans were built. This view shows the bumper exited exhausts and the hidden gas tank filler below the left taillight that was General Motors vogue from 1956-58. This also gives a good view of the unique pillared rear window that was so popular that year.

1957

The test rolls are a treadmill type affair which allow driveline testing of new cars within the factory. Here a Super 88 sedan undergoes such testing. Cars were usually shipped like this — minus wheelcovers — and the dealer then added them during prep work.

The Comet Coach Company of Memphis continued to offer distinguished looking vehicles on the Oldsmobile chassis, as well as others, and this year offered this attractive limousine funeral coach, ambulance combination car. The standard Oldsmobile 98 chassis was lengthened and the smooth lined Comet body was dropped on. This car was finished in metallic gray with a white roof and white draperies.

Front sheet metal is added to a Fiesta model. The front fenders and hood are the only large pieces of sheet metal which Olds fabricates. The rest of the large pieces are built by Fisher Body. Note the worker in the pit underneath the car. Employees are stationed similarly throughout final assembly to handle build-up from the bottom up.

The J-2 option was what the Olds performance enthusiast went for in 1957. This engine was prepped for duty in auto shows across the country. It featured gold paint and liberal use of chrome. The cutaway air cleaner shows the tri-carb setup. The J-2 claimed 300 horsepower and a compression ratio of 10 to 1. Owners of this engine reported good performance, but not much gas mileage if the driver used all three carbs via a heavy foot. In normal operation, only the center carb fed the engine, but at full acceleration or fast running, all three units went to work.

Olds show car of 1957 was a nearly-stock on the outside Starfire 98 Holiday coupe called the Mona Lisa. It was painted an attention-grabbing pearlescent tangerine with a cream accent stripe. The interior was done in striped tangerine leather and fabric. Pictured here is Mona Lisa designer Peggy Sauer with a vanity case finished in cream leather to match the glove box interior.

rome was king in 1958. A completely redesigned line Oldsmobiles carried the division back into Fourth Place he sales race by virtue of 294,374 model year sales, 310,795 deliveries during the calendar year.

ther you loved or hated the 1958 Olds, as few people d on middle ground with regard to this model. For second straight year Oldsmobiles were completely led and like other offerings from General Motors tended to be chrome-laden and a bit bizarre. dsmobile continued to tinker with the name of its om line series. The Golden Rocket 88 of 1957 became Dynamic 88 of 1958. The lowest priced Olds continued be the big seller as 146,566 of this model were uced. A total of 88,992 Super 88's were constructed 60,816 top of the line 98's were sold.

heelbases on each series grew one-half inch, but 1958 ng was a complete break from what Olds had offered e past. For the first time the division, along with most he rest of the automotive world, offered quad head-s. As in 1957 the gas tank filler was cleverly hidden e tail light assembly.

emphasis on safety was begun by Olds in 1957, aps in response to the Ford effort of 1956. For 1958, continued to mention safety items including its so-d safety dash, its safety power steering system, the onal seat belts and its new "Safety Sentinel" which a speedometer gadget that could be preset to warn a er of excessive speeds.

teriors for 1958 were completely restyled to go along all new outside styling. The dashboard was completely ne and was styled in a stepdown fashion. A new type eadliner — called Starlite — was made from a sponge-vinyl more than a quarter inch thick. This headliner standard on Super 88 and 98 Holidays and optional all other non-convertible and station wagon models. e dramatic climb of horsepower ratings for the ket V-8 came to a temporary plateau in 1958. A ler output V-8, rated at 265 horsepower, was standard the Dynamic 88 and sales literature touted the fuel nomy of this powerplant. The upper two series were ered by a 305 horsepower engine which offered tly upped compression ratio, an improved generator a redesigned camshaft over 1957 offerings. A J-2 on, rated at 312 horsepower, was also available. More nomical rear-end ratios were also available on 1958's. dsmobile made much noise about its air bag suspen- system called New-Matic Ride. This system was lar to the other disastrous air suspensions offered by eral Motors. It featured variable ride and constant ht features. Parts included an underhood compressor, ame mounted storage tank and both oil filtering and eparation systems. It wasn't unusual to see one of these ems fail and the 1958 Olds assume the posture of a ered hot rod. Later, Olds quietly offered a dealer kit ndo the New-Matic ride system.

ds offered 17 basic exterior colors including: surf n, mountain haze and desert glow. Five additional rs — called custom salon high metallics — were also lable. A variety of 2-toning schemes were available. rior fabrics came in green, black, ivory, red, blue, beige silver.

he most publicized new accessory for 1958 was the l prupose Transportable radio. This transistorized unit

plugged into the dash and was operated as a standard car radio. It also could be removed from the car and operated with its own batteries as a portable. Other accessories included: air conditioning, remote control outside mirror, spotlight, autronic eye, deluxe wheel covers and the anti-spin differential.

On April 8, Olds achieved a production milestone as the 4-millionth Hydra-Matic equipped Oldsmobile rolled off the Lansing assembly line. The divisional dream car for 1958 was a mildly restyled station wagon with features aimed at truly stylish family travel.

One of two four door models offered in the Dynamic 88 series was the Holiday Sedan, model number 583639. This car achieved a production run of 28,241. Base price was $2,971 and weight was 3,980 pounds. Standard Dynamic 88 equipment included: anodized aluminum grille, oil filter, dual illuminated ash trays, printed circuit instrument cluster and Pivot-Poise front suspension with counter dive measures.

Dynamic 88 Holiday Coupes were designated model number 583637. This was the second most popular car in the series with a production run of 35,036. Base price was $2,893 and weight was 3,895 pounds. A 265-horsepower Rocket V-8 engine was standard in the Dynamic 88 series. This powerplant got 265 horses from 371 cubic inches. Equipped with a two-barrel carburetor called the Econ-O-Way, Olds touted the economy of this engine.

1958

The lone two door sedan in the 1958 lineup was the Dynamic 88 Two Door Sedan. This car was designated model number 583611. Base price was $2,772 and it weighed 3,900 pounds. Production totalled 11,833. All Dynamic and Super 88 models rode on 122.5 inch wheelbases. Overall length was just over 208 inches.

DYNAMIC 88

On display at a national meet of the Oldsmobile Club of America. This car was the Dynamic 88 Fiesta, which featured hardtop styling in a station wagon. It was one of two wagons offered in the series. Production on this heavy hauler was only 3,323. It was designated model number 583695. Base price was $3,395, making this the most expensive car of the series. Weight was a healthy 4,215 pounds.

The top 1958 seller under the Oldsmobile banner was the Dynamic 88 Four Door Sedan. It carried model number 583669. A whopping 60,429 of this model were produced. Price on this popular offering was $2,837 and weight was 3,985 pounds. In 1958 Olds introduced its New-Matic-Ride — a very short lived air suspension system. This system could be ordered on any 1958 Olds equipped with power steering. Also available on any 1958 Olds was the optional J-2, 312 horsepower engine. This plant included a three-carburetor manifold. Actually, the option had been introduced during the 1957 model year and was carried over into 1958.

Rarest among the 1958 Oldsmobiles was the Dynamic 88 Fiesta Sedan. This unit was similar to the other Fiestas but it had a centerpost between the doors. The Dynamic 88 Fiesta Sedan was model number 583693. Price on this unit was $3,284 and weight was 4,225 pounds. Production on this unusual offering was only 3,249.

As with all 1958 Oldsmobile station wagons, the 1958 Dynamic 88 Fiesta was a rare and useful automobile. With both seats in use the Fiesta models could seat six adults. With rear seats folded this car provided almost 65 feet of cargo space. A durable linoleum floor mat and vinyl plastic trim were used generously in the interior. One popular station wagon option was a roof mounted luggage carrier.

1958

AFTER — Now wearing Swedish license plates, George Dammann's 1958 Olds Dynamic 88 convertible is shown in Bodafors, Sweden, after it had undergone a total restoration in the shop of Clarence Engborg. The job must have been good — in 1978 the car took first prize overall in the national Swedish car show in Stockholm, and thus was featured on the cover and in the centerfolds of several Scandinavian auto magazines. Apparently this particular Olds likes Sweden better than America, because Clarence reports having had no trouble with the car whatsoever.

BEFORE — Wearing its Illinois Bi-Centennial license plates is this 1958 Olds Dynamic 88 Convertible once owned by George H. Dammann, Crestline's general manager. The relatively rare car had a production run of only 4,456. Designated model number 583667TX, it originally carried a base price tag of $3,221, thus qualifying as the least expensive of the three open Olds models offered this year. It weighed 3,995 pounds. The car, originally from Arizona, had an excellent body, but was far from trouble free — once converting a relatively simple 14 hour trip from Pennsylvania to Illinois into a 30 hour marathon, and another time backfiring through the carburetor while being worked on, thus giving George a rather painful and definitely unwanted shave and haircut. Finally the nasty car was shipped to Clarence Engborg, Crestline's Scandinavian distributor in Bodafors, Sweden.

Most popular among the Super 88 cars was the Four Door Sedan. Model number 583669 achieved a production run of 33,844. Base price on this unit was $3,112 and weight was 4,008 pounds. The standard equipment list was lengthy for Super 88 models and included: Safety Padded Instrument Panel, Safety-Vee Steering Wheel, deep twist carpeting, courtesy lights, chromed roof trim moldings, cowl vent trim and rocker panel moldings.

OLDSMOBILE

Rarest of the Super 88s was model number 583667DTX, the Convertible. Base priced at $3,529 with a weight of 4,010 pounds a production run of only 3,799 was made. Leather was an interior option on open Super 88 models. Steering on all 1958 models was the dual center control, recirculating ball nut gear type. Power steering was standard on the Ninety-Eight models and optional on other models.

Another very popular offering in the series was Super 88 Holiday Sedan. Model number 583639 SD achieved production totals of 27,521. Base price on this car was $3,339 and it weighed 4,005 pounds. As usual most Oldsmobiles of this model year came HydraMatic equipped. The popular automatic transmission was standard equipment on the Ninety-Eight and an option on the other two series.

Five models were offered in the Super 88 series for 1958 including the Super 88 Holiday Coupe. Designated model number 583637SD this car was base priced at $3,262. Weight was 3,925 pounds. The production run on this offering was 18,653. Super 88 and Ninety-Eight cars shared a 305-horsepower, 371 cubic inch Rocket V-8 fueled by a new Quadri-Jet carburetor. The J-2 remained an option for any car in any series.

Most expensive and among the rarest 1958 Super 88s was the Fiesta station wagon. Model number 583695SD achieved a production run of 5,175. Base price was $3,623 and weight was 4,257 pounds. Unlike the Dynamic 88 series, the Super 88 line offered only one station wagon model. In the late 1950s auto builders — particularly GM — played little tricks on hiding the gas filler. In 1958 Olds located it in the left rear fender just forward of the taillight assembly.

Flagship of the Oldsmobile fleet again in 1958 was the Ninety-Eight Convertible. Carrying the designation of number 583067 DX this car was base priced at an even $4,200. Weight was 4,340 pounds. Production totalled only 5,605. On any model 1958 Olds a buyer could order color coordinated wheel discs. These came in a choice of five colors to match or complement body colors.

Top seller in Oldsmobile's top series was the Ninety-Eight Holiday Sedan, model number 583039SDX. Production equalled 27,603 — a goodly run for this series. Base price for this model was $4,096 and weight was 4,310 pounds. Standard Ninety-Eight features included: HydraMatic, power steering, power brakes, dual exhausts, electric clock and lounge seats.

Another relatively popular top of the line Olds was the Ninety-Eight Four Door Sedan. Carrying model number 583069 D, this car was priced at $3,824 making it the least expensive car in the series. Weight was 4,316 pounds. All Ninety-Eight models rode on an exclusive 126.5 inch wheelbase. Overall length was almost 217 inches.

1958

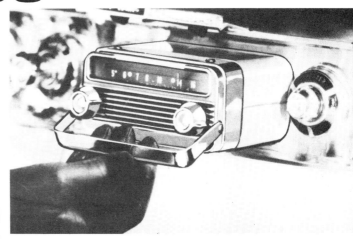

Three radios were offered to buyers of 1958 Oldsmobiles. Most unique of these units was the Transportable which slipped into the dash. It was designed to operate outside the car with its own speaker and battery supply pack. This radio was completely transistorized. The other Olds radios were the Super Deluxe-Wonderbar unit and the five tube Deluxe unit. Olds also had a dual speaker setup in 1958.

Perhaps the sharpest of the 1958 models offered by Olds was the Ninety-Eight Holiday Coupe. It was designated model number 583037SDX. Base priced at $4,020, weight was pegged at 4,270 pounds. Production on the Ninety-Eight Holiday Coupe was 11,012. Each Olds had a rear suspension consisting of 58 inch by 2½in leaf springs with outboard mounted, direct acting shock absorbers and a stabilizer bar.

Olds had the dubious distinction of sharing the air suspension package with several other divisions — and all these divisions soon regretted offering the package. Soon after midyear GM quietly introduced a kit to reconvert a car back to the standard suspension system. Olds claimed no metal to metal contact with this option. The car could be temporarily elevated up to four extra inches.

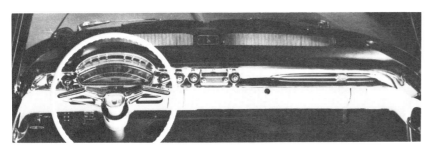

Oldsmobile called its 1958 interior layout "fashion flare." There was a generous use of chrome on the dash and for that matter in the styling of the entire car. This dash photo is of a non-air conditioned car — but air conditioning ducts were located in the lower corners of the dash and also flanking the electric clock. For 1958 Oldsmobile incorporated a new and larger compressor, condenser, blower and evaporator in its system. It was still a rare option in 1958.

Comet Coach Co. of Memphis, Tenn., (which later became the Cotter-Bevington Division of Miller-Meteor) continued to build their attractive professional cars on Oldsmobile chassis. This is the 1958 version which was available in either the limousine style shown here or in landau style. The cars were available set up as funeral vehicles, ambulances, or combination cars, which could be converted to either funeral or ambulance use in relatively short time. This particular unit utilizes the Olds 98 trim and chassis components.

1959

Sportiest of the six model Dynamic 88 series was the convertible which was also the rarest offering in the series. A total of 8,491 of model number 593267 were built. Base price of this car was $3,286 and shipping weight was 4,175 pounds. All Dynamic 88's carried their series designation in chrome script on the front fender. Olds called its 1959 styling the linear look.

The big seller from all three series continued to be the Dynamic 88 four-door sedan in 1959. A total of 70,995 of this model, number 593219, were delivered. Base price on the 88 four-door was $2,902 and shipping weight was 4,135 pounds. Standard equipment on the least expensive series continued to include: manual transmission and standard steering and brakes.

With 1959's complete restyling, the four-door hardtops proved to be extremely nice looking cars. Hardtops were renamed Holiday SportSedans. Note how the rear window blends in with the overall styling theme of the car. Model number for the Dynamic 88 Holiday SportSedan. was 593239 and base price was $3,036. Production stood at 48,707. Standard size tires were 8:50 x 14 inch with overall height on this model at 54.2 inches.

Oldsmobile sales were up slightly in 1959, but not enough to keep the division from sliding two spots back to Sixth in the sales race. A model year production of 382,865 was realized. Calendar year totals were 366,305.

For the third year running Oldsmobile went through a bumper to bumper styling change. The 1959's were offered for introduction on October 3, 1958. Two new body styles — the 4-door Holiday Sport Sedan and the 2-door Holiday SceniCoupe — were available in all series. For once Old's management decided to leave the series names as they were in the previous year.

The Dynamic 88 was the top selling series with a total of 194,103. Ninety-Eight sales were 81,102, while Super 88 totals were 107,660.

The exterior styling was dubbed as the "linear look" by company advertising writers. Wheelbase on the Dynamic and Super 88 series was stretched to 123 inches. The 98 wheelbase covered 126.3 inches. Styling differences between the cars included a separate taillight design on the 98. Oldsmobile offered up to 36% more glass on the 1959's over comparable 1958 offerings.

The interiors were also redone for 1959 with the most noticeable bit of gadgetry being the "Safety Spectrum" speedometer. Speed was indicated by a moving band of color — green from 0-35 mph, orange from 35 to 65 mph and red for speeds over 65 mph.

The frame on Dynamic and Super 88 models was nine inches wider and ten inches longer. This was the basis for the "Glide-Ride" tag hung on the new chassis. Other claimed improvements came from longer control arms, better shock absorbers, a heavier stabilizer bar and new ball joints.

For the first time since 1959, Oldsmobile offered engines with two different displacements. The standard Dynamic 88 motor stayed at 371 cubic inches. A 1/8-inch greater bore brought the Super 88 and 98 engine to 394 cubic inches. Both engines had compression ratios of 9.75 to 1. Horsepower ratings were 270 and 315. Internal engine improvements were redesigned pistons and connecting rods, camshaft machining changes, better air filtration, and larger intake valves.

A reduced total of 15 colors were offered in 1959 including: frost blue, cardinal red and burgundy mist. In addition to the solid color packages, two-tone combinations were available in three different layouts. Interior fabrics were available in gray, green, blue, beige, copper and red.

The only new power accessory for the model year was electrically operated vent windows. Other factory accessories included: electric clock, six-way seat, anti-spin differential, tri-tone horns, Roto-Matic power steering, padded dash, a redesigned Trans-portable radio and air conditioning.

Olds breathed its last gasp on the NASCAR circuit as Lee Petty drove a Dynamic 88 coupe to a photo finish victory in the Daytona 500 of that year. The division offered a 102-inch wheelbase F-88 III on the dream car/show car circuit in 1959.

Oldsmobile began construction of a huge new warehouse complex on a 100-acre site on the west edge of Lansing.

Again in 1959 the only two-door coupe with a roof post offered by Olds was in its least expensive series. The Dynamic 88 two-door sedan, model number 593211, was the least expensive 1959 Oldsmobile at a base price of $2,837. It tipped the scales at 4,095 pounds. A total of 16,123 of this model were produced. Wheelbase for the Dynamic 88 series was 123 inches with an overall length of 218.4 inches.

1959

A new name was tacked on the hardtop coupe, and the Dynamic 88 SceniCoupe became the division's top selling two-door offering in 1959. A total of 38,488 of model number 593237 were sold. Base prices began at $2,958 and shipping weight was 4,090 pounds. Standard engine on the Dynamic 88 was a 270 horsepower, 371 cubic inch V-8 with the Econ-o-Way carb. An optional 300 horsepower engine of the same displacement was also available on this series.

The most expensive of the Dynamic 88's was the Fiesta station wagon. Hardtop station wagon styling was dropped in 1959 by Olds and there was just one Fiesta model in the Dynamic 88 series. Model number was 593235, base price was $3,365 and shipping weight was 4,325 pounds. Production jumped to 11,298, making this the highest production Oldsmobile had ever achieved in the wagon market.

Rarest of the 1959 Oldsmobiles was the Super 88 convertible with a production of only 4,895. Base price on model number 593567 was $3,595. Shipping weight was 4,220 pounds. Options on this poolside car included special spinner hubcaps which were color coordinated with the body color of the car. All Super 88's shared wheelbase length with the Dynamic 88's, but a 394 cubic inch, 315 horsepower V-8 was the same powerplant as used in the heavier 98 model.

Olds added 13% to the cargo space of its 1959 station wagons over the 1958 models. A retractable rear window, as on this Dynamic 88 Fiesta, eliminated the two-piece rear gate. Station wagon options included a 1/3-2/3 divided rear seat and electric rear window lift. Station wagon floors and the inside of the tailgate were faced with a tough vinyl covering protected by a steel edging. Wheel housings were covered by molded grained rubber.

The Super 88 four-door sedan carried model number 593519. It had a base price of $3,178, making it the least expensive car in the Super 88 series. Shipping weight was 4,160 pounds. All Super 88's carried chrome spares front and rear. Special trim was also provided behind the headlights on the front fenders. Olds went to a new type of thick molded rubber body mounts in 1959 and these supposedly cut down on body drumming and vibration.

Hardtop styling looked good on the Super 88 Holiday SceniCoupe. Production for model number 593537 was 20,259. Base prices began at $3,328 and the scales were tipped at 4,140 pounds. Oldsmobile continued to expand its option list and available items included: power windows at $107.50, heater and defroster at $101.88, air conditioning at $430.40 and HydraMatic Drive at $231.34.

1959

Most popular of the five models of the Super 88 Olds series was the Holiday Sportsedan. Production totalled 38,467, base price was $3,405 and shipping weight was 4,154 pounds. In 1959, Olds went away from exiting the exhaust through the rear bumper, a practice it had used on several previous years' offerings. In 1959, the optional backup lights could be ordered to fill the area where the exhaust used to exit.

Super 88 buyers continued to be offered a Fiesta wagon in 1959. A total of 7,015 of model number 593535 were built. Base price was $3,669, making the Fiesta the most expensive Super 88. Shipping weight for this car was 4,350 pounds. All Super 88's carried the model designations on the front fender behind the wheel. 1959 station wagons enjoyed an eight-inch longer cargo area than 1958's.

The 98 SceniCoupe carried a base price of $4,086 and weighed 4,390 pounds. A total of 13,669 Ninety-Eight SceniCoupes were built in 1959. This car was model number 593837. All 98 models carried a chrome designation on the rear fender. With the redesigned 1959 styling, Oldsmobile trunk areas were up to 64% larger than previous years. A popular option for the year was the anti-spin rear axle available on any model.

The added grace of the top of the line Oldsmobiles came from the 126.3-inch wheelbase and the 223-inch overall length. Model number for the 98 convertible was 593867 and the base price was a whopping $4,366, making this the most expensive 1959 Oldsmobile by far. Shipping weight was 4,435 pounds and standard tire size on all 98's was 9.00 x 14 inches. Finishes for 1959 were an acrylic based lacquer which Olds claimed held its luster longer than paints from previous years.

Standard equipment on the 98 four-door sedan included: power steering, power brakes and HydraMatic transmission. Model number for this offering was 593819, base price was $3,890 and shipping weight was 4,420 pounds. A total of 23,106 Ninety-Eight four-door sedans were built. Olds also called its four-door post models celebrity sedans in 1959.

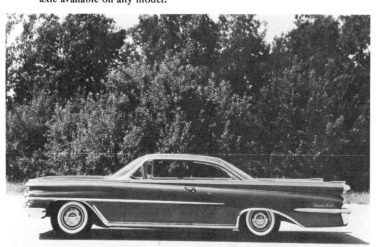

1959

This 98 SceniCoupe displays one of the two-tone paint combinations available in 1959. Olds offered three types of two-tone paint jobs, this being officially referred to as special two-tone, type I. With 15 base colors, hundreds of combinations could be dreamed up. Olds claimed it bonderized and then primed the car, followed by four coats of what it called Magic-Mirror-Finish paint. This gave bare metal a total of six coats.

The long and low styling reached a peak for Oldsmobile in 1959 as is obvious with this 98 Holiday SportSedan. Model number 593839 accounted for 36,813 sales. Base price was $4,162 and shipping weight was 4,418 pounds. Seat belts could be ordered in any 1959 Olds and colors included: beige, blue, green and grey. Another accessory Olds advertised as being safety related was the Safety Sentinel which buzzed when a driver exceeded a preset speed.

The Comet Coach Co. of Memphis continued to offer high quality funeral cars and ambulances on either the Oldsmobile or the Buick chassis. The Comet Oldsmobile was offered in both landau and limousine body styles, and as either a straight hearse or as an ambulance. This Comet Oldsmobile landau funeral car wears the modern landau panel styling sandwiched between vast expanses of glass.

The front end look for 1959 was rather unique and styling was streamlined. Lee Petty won the Daytona 500 NASCAR race with a 1959 Olds and then went back to racing Chrysler products for a long while. Front end Olds styling had a space age touch to it. Quad headlights were in their second year for General Motors, and parking lights were blended in rather nicely on Oldsmobiles.

COMET OLDSMOBILE

Comet also offered the high headroom emergency rescue type ambulance body that was becoming increasingly popular with the large coach makers. This car with a 48-inch head room roof over the patient's compartment is on an extended Oldsmobile chassis and wears a limousine type body style. The roof was made of fiberglass and adorned with chrome ornamentation.

Most basic among all the 1960 Oldsmobiles was the Dynamic 88 Two-Door Sedan. It was designated model number 60-3211, weighed 4,052 pounds and was priced at $2,835. Production totals were 13,545 with three additional cars exported. All 1960 Oldsmobiles were based on a Guard Beam frame with an X center member and a total of five cross members.

The plainest of the Dynamic 88 series four-doors carried the nametag of Celebrity Sedan. This car was the high production 1960 Olds as 76,377 were built with 16 more exported. This car was designated model number 60-3219. It was priced at an even $2,900 and weighed 4,109 pounds. All cars in the Super and Dynamic 88 series shared the same wheelbase of 123 inches and length of just over 217 inches.

This rear shot of a Dynamic 88 Celebrity Sedan shows the distinctive rear styling treatment for 1960. The Dynamic 88 series had five basic models with two choices in the station wagon area. A quick way to distinguish the Dynamic 88 from the Super 88 was the chrome model markings on the rear quarter panels. Rear suspension on all models was 58 inch by 2½ inch leaf springs with outboard mounted, direct acting shock absorbers.

Oldsmobile offered a clean styling package in 1960, and Sixth Place in the sales race was maintained. For the model year, 347,141 Oldsmobiles were delivered with an additional 224 for the export market. Calendar year totals were 402,612.

A steel strike early in the model year severely cut into the total Olds output. This labor dispute caused particular delivery problems for persons ordering a new car from the introductory showings. Production was actually halted in Lansing in the late fall of 1959 because there was no steel to feed the stamping presses.

The new Oldsmobiles were introduced October 1, with a total of seventeen models available. Few traces of the rather extreme styling of the 1959's remained, yet the updating process had not been too drastic on the new models. There were few internal or external innovations in the lineup, an unusual position for Oldsmobile at new model time.

The Dynamic 88 continued to be the division's bread and butter car as 189,864 were sold in 1960. Super 88 sales totalled 97,913, while 59,363 top of the line 98's were sold.

For years each successive Rocket V-8 carried a higher horsepower rating than its predecessor. Not so with the 1960 engines. A rating of 315 horsepower, exactly the same as in 1959, stayed on the Super 88 and 98 power plant. But 30 horsepower was dropped from the Dynamic 88 motor in 1960. This unit continued to displace 371 cubic inches, but was now rated at 240 horsepower.

A total of 15 solid colors were offered Olds buyers and these colors could also be arranged in two-tone schemes. Interiors came in cloth, vinyl or a combination of the two. Interior colors included grey, green, blue, brown, white, black and red. Convertible top color selections included white, black, green, blue, beige and turquoise.

Oldsmobile continued to offer a wide ranging list of optional equipment. These factory accessories included air conditioning, power steering, power brakes, Wonderbar radio, dual rear radio speakers, electric clock, dual exhausts and a roof-mounted luggage carrier for the Fiesta models.

Although no longer a winner on stock car racing circuits throughout the land, an Oldsmobile convertible did serve as the pace car for the 1960 Indianapolis 500. Work was also moving into high gear on an experimental series of front wheel drive cars that would eventually lead to the introduction of the revolutionary Toronado in 1966.

1960

One of the nicer looking 1960 models was the Dynamic 88 Holiday SceniCoupe. This was designated model number 60-3237. It was base priced at $2,456 and weighed 4,061 pounds. Production totalled 29,368 with 31 more cars exported. Standard tires were 8.50 by 14 inch with option 9.00 x 14s costing an extra $26.37. On the Dynamic 88 series cars whitewalls were $44.60 extra.

Rather graceful in its lines was the Dynamic 88 Holiday SportSedan, model number 60-3239. This unit was base priced at $3,034 and weighed 4,067 pounds. A production run of 43,761 made it the second most popular 1960 Oldsmobile. All Dynamic 88 cars were powered by a 371 cubic inch, 240 horsepower Rocket V-8. This engine had the Econ-O-Way two barrel carburetor.

The two-seat Fiesta station wagon gained its most popularity in the Dynamic 88 series. Model number 60-3235 was priced at $3,363 and weighed 4,278 pounds. Production of this model was 8,834 — the highest of any 1960 station wagon. Olds said the wagon tailgate could be opened with one hand. Every Fiesta was outfitted with a sound deading perforated headliner.

Sportiest of the Dynamic 88 series cars was the Convertible, model number 60-3267. This was the highest production 1960 Olds open car as 12,271 rolled off the assembly lines. Three more were built for export. Base price was $3,284 and weight was 4,184 pounds. Interiors in the Dynamic 88 Convertible were done in Moroceen. 1960 Olds buyers had a choice of 15 standard colors including: cordovan, citron and palmetto mist.

1960

Most expensive of the Dynamic 88 series cars was the three seat Fiesta station wagon with a base price of $3,471. It weighed 4,295 pounds and designated model number 60-3245. It was also the rarest car in the series as only 5,708 were built. Standard in all three-seat Fiestas was an electrically operated rear window. This was an option on two-seated models.

Most popular among the Super 88 series cars was the Celebrity Sedan, model number 60-3519. This was also the least expensive car in the series with a price tag of $3,176. It weighed 4,128 pounds. Production equalled 35,094 with 17 additional cars exported. Ninety-Eight and Super 88 models carried an Olds crest between each pair of headlamps, while the Dynamic 88s had block chrome numerals there.

As with all 1960 Oldsmobiles the Celebrity Sedans in the Super 88 series had air scoop brakes. These units had large flanges on the drums to direct air over the brakes. This reduced brake fade, increased safety margin and extended lining life. Olds used cast iron brake drums. Brake linings provided more than 191 square inches of stopping power. The Olds brakes were self energizing and used a step on parking brake with a foot operated release.

For a base price of $3,325 a Super 88 Holiday SceniCoupe was available. This model was designated number 60-3537. It weighed 4,080 pounds. Production was 16,464 with 21 more exported. Powerplant for the Ninety-Eight and Super 88 models was a 394 cubic inch unit. It was rated at 315 horsepower and 435 pound feet of torque. This larger displacement engine had a larger bore than the Dynamic 88 powerplant.

Rarest among the three open models offered in 1960 was the Super 88 Convertible. Only 5,830 of this model were produced. It was designated as model 60-3567. Base price was $3,592 and weight was 4,203 pounds. A Deluxe Radio — with transistors and push buttons — was availble installed in any model for $88.77. The Super Deluxe Radio — with automatic tuning bar and foot operated control — cost $124.82 installed.

The two-seat Fiesta station wagon was available in the Super 88 series for 1960. It was model number 60-3535. Production was only 3,765 with three additional cars exported. Base price on this model was $3,665 and weight was 4,298 pounds. Fuel tanks on 1960 models were of the 20 gallon capacity. A self-cleaning Saran filter helped keep the system free of water and dirt. Large ⅜ inch fuel lines promoted the smooth, easy flow of gas.

Most expensive, heaviest and rarest of the Super 88 series was the three-seat Fiesta station wagon. This rare car was model number 60-3545. Production was only 3,475 with 12 additional cars exported. Base price was $3,773 and weight was 4,306 pounds. The third seat was a rear facing unit which provided a good view for passenger and this often proved a favorite seating location for kids.

Another very popular 1960 Oldsmobile was the Super 88 Holiday SportsSedan. This car carried model number 60-3539. Base price was $3,402 and weight was 4,086 pounds. Production on this car was 33,285 with 19 more cars made for export. Power brakes were standard on all Ninety-Eight models and offered as an option on other series. The Pedal-Ease Power Brakes were option L and were factory installed for $43.

The most expensive 1960 Oldsmobile was the Ninety-Eight Convertible priced at a whopping $4,362. This was also the rarest car in the Ninety-Eight series as only 7,284 were built. Weight was 4,412 pounds. Model designation on the top line convertible was 60-3867. The interior on all Ninety-Eight Convertibles were done in a combination of moroceen and leather. Colors included gray, green, blue, fawn and red.

This nicely restored Ninety-Eight Convertible was on display at a national meet of the Oldsmobile Club of America. Four electric window lifts were standard on all Ninety-Eight models except Celebrity Sedans. A master switch located near the left front door allowed the driver to control all windows. Air conditioning was an option offered in 1960, but cars so equipped were rare. Price on option "N" (air conditioning) was $430.

1960

Another of the thin roof pillared hardtop Olds designs was found on model 60-3837, the Holiday SceniCoupe Ninety-Eight. This model carried a base price tag of $4,083 and it weighed 4,312 pounds. Production on this luxury hardtop coupe was 7,635 with 19 additional cars shipped for export. Standard equipment on all Ninety-Eights was Roto-Matic Power Steering by Saginaw Steering Gear. This was option C for any Dynamic or Super 88. It cost $107.50.

Least expensive offering in the top of the line Ninety-Eight series was the Celebrity Sedan. It carried model number 60-3837 and was base priced at $3,887. It weighed 4,353 pounds. This was a fairly popular model as production was 17,188 with three more cars exported. All Ninety-Eights had their own exclusive wheelbase of just over 126 inches. Overall length was just shy of 221 inches. The 315 horsepower Rocket V-8 was shared with the Super 88 models.

Front end styling was unique for 1960 as pointed out by this Ninety-Eight SportSedan, model number 60-3839. Base priced at $4,159, this car weighed 4,364 pounds. This was the most popular top of the line series car as 27,257 were made. For 1960 body mountings were live rubber and 50% thicker than those used in 1959. Olds called its overall chassis package: Quadri-Balanced Ride.

The Oldsmobile Ninety-Eight SportSedan shared its novel roof-line treatment only with the Super 88 and Dynamic 88 Holiday SportSedans. No other styles in this year's Olds line had this unique top, which featured both

the wrap-around windshield and very interesting wrap-around rear window of huge dimensions. Back-up lights on this year's Oldsmobiles were well protected by — and set into — the rear bumper.

Oldsmobile called its instrument panel a twin cove unit. Idiot lights were located below the Safety Spectrum speedometer which changed from green to orange to red depending on the miles per hour traveled. Flanking the speedometer was a new resistor type fuel gauge and a clock. The safety padded dash was standard on Super 88 and Ninety-Eight models.

The 1960 Oldsmobile was built on a rugged chassis. Several rear axle ratios were available on 1960 Olds models. these included: 2.87 to 1; 3.07 to 1 and 3.23 to 1. The HydraMatic transmission was standard equipment on all Ninety-Eight models. The Jetaway HydraMatic was a factory installed option that cost $231.34. Most of the Dynamic 88 and Super 88 models were equipped with the popular Olds automatic which had been around for 20 years.

National Coaches of Knightstown, Ind., offered a complete line of professional cars on almost any General Motors chassis. This Oldsmobile is an excellent representative of their Minute Man ambulance. This body was also mounted on Chevrolet and Pontiac chassis and offered a headroom of 42 inches.

The newly named Cotner Bevington Corp. offered a complete selection of professional cars on the Oldsmobile chassis. These cars were offered in both limousine and landau styling and as funeral cars, combinations, and ambulances. This attractive Cotner Bevington limousine funeral coach features smooth flowing styling with a large amount of glass area and formal draperies. Note the new Cotner Bevington star emblem on the lower part of the rear fender. With the new name, the company moved to new quarters in Blytheville, Ark.

The Comet Coach Company of Memphis sold the rights to the name Comet to the Ford Motor Company in 1959 for use on a new compact car that Ford wanted to market under the Comet name. The 1960 vehicles from the old Comet firm were renamed to honor the company's founders, Waldo Cotner and Robert Bevington. The new Cotner Bevington Corp. produced a line of medium priced funeral cars based on the Oldsmobile chassis. These cars were built in both the landau and limousine styles with consistent quality and built-in prestige. This is the 1960 Cotner Bevington landau funeral car that was competing directly with the Flxible Premier landau.

OLDSMOBILE

More models still spelled declining sales for Oldsmobile in 1961. For the first time since 1949 the division offered more than three series. The new model lineup included the familiar Dynamic 88, Super 88 and 98 coupled with the small F-85 — which bowed late in the model year — and the limited production Starfire model.

Olds remained in Sixth spot, as industry-wide sales were in an even bigger slump than Oldsmobile's. The model year total was 318,550 and calendar year output was pegged at 321,550. A total of 219 Oldsmobiles were built

The bread and butter car for the newly introduced F-85 series was the four-door sedan. Four doors were available in both standard and deluxe trim. The standard F-85 four-door was the least expensive 1961 Olds at $2,384. Price tag on the deluxe four-door was $2,681. A total of 19,765 standards were built with 26,311 deluxes produced. Shipping weight on this model was 2,566 pounds.

Oddly enough Oldsmobile chose to debut its 1961 F-85 line with the four-doors and station wagons. The station wagon was a particularly nicely sized little Oldsmobile. Two-seat wagons came in both standard and deluxe models. As on all F-85's, the deluxe package consisted of: deluxe steering wheel, carpets front and rear, padded dash and special interior appointments. Weight for the two-seat wagon was 2,742 pounds. Price on the two-seat standard station wagon was $2,519 with 6,667 built. The deluxe sold for $2,816 with only 526 made.

for export. By series, the breakdown was 29,304 F-85, 47,090 F-85 Deluxe's, 138,380 Dynamic 88's, 53,1.. Super 88's, 43,012 98's, and 7,600 Starfires.

General Motor's new look in this model year was to t. smaller cars, as the automotive giant was casting a co.. cerned glance at growing import sales in the U. S. Olds w. right in the middle of this automotive happening with. all-new F-85. The new series was a full two feet short. than the full-sized Oldsmobile. Developmental work f. GM's small cars (F-85, Pontiac Tempest and Buick Speci. began in 1957. The new little Olds was based on a 11. inch wheelbase and utilized a 215 cubic inch, 155 hor. power V-8 engine. Because of the aluminum used in t. motor, a lot of warranty problems with heater co. developed as there was an apparent chemical reacti.. between engine metals and those used in the heater co. This situation cost Oldsmobile a bundle of money. warranty repairs and customer good will.

The F-85 came in coupe, 4-door sedan and station wag.. models. Deluxe editions were available in each line wi. the 2-door Deluxe F-85 carrying the Cutlass namet.. marking the first time that nameplate had been used on. regular line of Oldsmobiles.

The other new series for 1961 was the Starfire. This w. not a new nameplate for Olds as it previously had be. variously applied to a show car, 98 convertibles and. 98 models. The Starfire series wasn't introduced un. January of 1961, and it was only offered in a convertib. model. Wheelbase was shared with the Dynamic and Sup. 88 series and the division was unclear — in 1961 — as. whether the Starfire was a separate series or a part of t. Super 88 series. Starfires came loaded with a standa. equipment list that included: brushed aluminum si. panels, console, tachometer, 3:42 to 1 rear axle, leath. interior, power seats, special mufflers and dual exhaus. and a special 330 horsepower engine.

Four engines were available on the 1961 models. T. Rockette V-8 aluminum powerplant was the only engi. offered on F-85's. The standard Rocket V-8 turned o. 250 horsepower from 394 cubic inches and was standa. on Dynamic 88 models. The Skyrocket engine w. standard on the Super 88 and 98 models and an option. Dynamic 88's. It developed 325 horsepower from 39. cubic inches. The fourth engine was the Starfire powe. plant, which was rated at 330. It had a slightly high. compression ratio than the Skyrocket's 10 to 1.

Mechanical improvements for the big 1961 mode. included a redesigned guardbeam frame, nylon sleeve. shock absorbers, coil springs moved to a location on t. rear axle housing and a vertically mounted fuel tank. Ne. models also offered more passenger space and a larg. trunk compartment. The Hydra-Matic offered on the fu. sized cars was improved with a 22-vane rotor which l. Olds to claim improved reliability and performanc. coupled with simpler construction.

A total of 15 standard paint selections were offere. including: saddle mist, antique rose, pacific mist a. holiday red. Interior fabrics came in grey, green, blu. fawn, red and turquoise. Convertible tops were availab. in white, black, green, blue, fawn and red.

Accessories included: air conditioning, electric antenn. power brakes, station wagon roof rack, radio, pow. steering, wheel covers and clock.

The advantages of the three-seat F-85 wagon are rather evident. As with all F-85 models, power came from a rather interesting aluminum V-8 turning out 155 horsepower from only 215 cubic inches. Weight on the three-seat wagons was up to 2,798 pounds. Price tag on the standard F-85 three-seater was $2,694 and 10,087 were built. The deluxe F-85 three seated wagon sold for $3,091 and production amounted to 757.

1961

The two-door coupe was the third basic body style to be added to the F-85 series. It is not listed in any of the early product literature and was not offered until midyear. The coupe weighed in at 2,712 pounds. It was available as a standard coupe priced at $2,502 and as a fancier Cutlass model offered for $2,753. Only 2,336 of the coupes were made in standard trim, while a total of 9,935 Cutlass models were built. The Cutlass nameplate came from a mid-1950's Olds dream car.

While the F-85 was by far the least expensive Oldsmobile series, interiors on these small cars were well turned out. This deluxe F-85 sedan interior shot shows the plain dash treatment with all instrumentation housed in a pod in front of the driver. Trim on all models was in a material Olds literature identified as "Morocceen." Seat coverings could be ordered in either vinyl or cloth. Exterior color options on F-85 numbered 15.

A high volume model was the Dynamic 88 Celebrity Sedan which carried a price tag of $2,900. Production on this car was 42,584 with an additional 13 cars built for export. Shipping weight was 4,024 pounds. Whitewalls from the factory remained fairly wide in 1961. Standard whitewalls (8:00 x 14) cost an additional $40.78 on any Dynamic 88 model with oversize whitewalls (8:50 x 14) going for $62.89.

With the 1961 styling any of the Holiday two-doors were graceful looking cars. This two-door Holiday coupe carried a base price of $2,956. The two tone paint added $15.82 to the sticker price. Shipping weight on this model was 3,969 pounds. A total of 19,872 Holiday Coupes were produced with an additional 28 made for export. All Dynamic 88's were built on a 123 inch wheelbase with an overall length of 212 inches.

The "Plain Jane" of the full sized Oldsmobiles was the Dynamic 88 two-door sedan. As with all Dynamic 88 models it was offered with the 250 horsepower, 394 cubic inch Rocket V-8 engine. The higher horsepower Sky Rocket engine was an option in this series for 1961. This model carried a price tag of $2,835. Only 4,920 were built. Shipping weight for the Dynamic 88 two-door sedan was 4,152 pounds.

The top selling 1961 Oldsmobile was the four-door Holiday Sedan in the Dynamic 88 series. It carried a price tag of $3,034. Shipping weight was 4,037 pounds. Production for this car was 51,562 with 26 more built for export. Oldsmobile called its suspension package for 1961 "Vibra-Tuned." They also boasted that the standard-equipment Rocket V-8 would perform well on regular gas.

1961

Pride of the Dynamic 88 fleet again in 1961 was the convertible. Carrying a price tag of $3,592, only 2,624 of these cars were produced. Shipping weight was 4,244 pounds. Although not particularly popular on open cars, Oldsmobile's most expensive option continued to be its air conditioning system. Priced at a stiff $430 Olds claimed this unit delivered cooled, purified and dehumidified air. This option also included oversize tires.

Oldsmobile continued to be in the station wagon business for 1961, offering two choices in both the Dynamic 88 and Super 88 series. The basic model in the Dynamic 88 series was the two-seat wagon, also tabbed the Fiesta. Price tag on the two-seat Fiesta was $3,665. Production totalled 5,374. Shipping weight on this Fiesta was 4,317 pounds. An optional roof-mounted luggage carrier was listed for $98.35.

The Celebrity Sedan was one of the more popular cars offered in the 1961 Super 88 series. Super 88 and Dynamic 88 models shared the same wheelbase, but Super 88's came standard with the high compression, 325 horsepower Sky Rocket engine. Shipping weight on this model was 4,063 pounds. Price tag on the Super 88 Celebrity Sedan was $3,176 making it the lowest priced car in the series. Production totalled 15,328.

The three-seat Fiesta was a rather comfortable nine-passenger vehicle in the Dynamic 88 series. This was the rarest car among the Dynamic 88's as only 4,013 of this three-seat Fiesta rolled off the assembly lines. Price tag on this model was $3,773 making it the most expensive car in the series. With seats folded in the down position, the cargo area of any Fiesta model exceeded 85 cubic feet. Shipping weight was 4,334 pounds. The deep pile carpeting was complimented by matching vinyl cargo floor covering.

The lone closed two-door in the 1961 Super 88 series was the Holiday Coupe. This model carried a price tag of $3,325. Proudction was a relatively low 7,009 with 26 additional cars exported. Shipping weight was 4,003 pounds. Oldsmobile offered two basic radio packages in 1961: the Deluxe radio for $88.77 and the signal seeking Super Deluxe for $124.82.

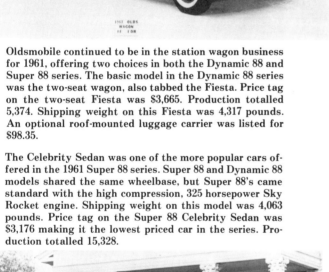

Like the Dynamic 88 series, the more expensive Super 88 classification offered two station wagon models. The two-seat Super 88 station wagon, or Fiesta as all 1961 wagons were called, cost $3,665. Production totalled only 2,761. Shipping weight on the two-seat wagon was 4,357 pounds. An exclusive two-seat station wagon option was the "luggage locker." This option consisted of a locking compartment beneath the rear floor. It cost $21.52.

Most popular among the Super 88 series cars was the Holiday Sedan. Production for this model was 23,272. List price was $3,402 and shipping weight was 4,092 pounds. With a new trunk design for 1961, luggage space was increased in all big cars. This new design included moving the fuel tank forward and relocating the spare tire horizontally. Trunk compartments were lined on all Super 88's for protection to trunk contents.

The most expensive Super 88 model in 1961 was the three-seat station wagon. This Fiesta sold for $3,773. It also proved to be the rarest of all 1961 Oldsmobiles as only 2,170 were produced. Shipping weight on this model was 4,378 pounds. An electric rear window package was standard on any three-seat Fiesta model, and it was a $26.47 option on two-seat station wagons.

The Super 88 convertible was a relatively rare 1961 Oldsmobile which saw a production run of 2,624. Price on the convertible was $3,592 and shipping weight amounted to 4,275 pounds. Convertible interiors on the Super 88 series were tri-toned and available in five color combinations. Six different convertible top colors were available: white, black, green, blue, fawn and red.

There was little actual difference between Oldsmobile's two 1961 Ninety-Eight hardtop four-doors. The Holiday sedan had six side windows and a relatively flat rear glass treatment. List price on the Holiday Sedan was $4,021 and shipping weight was 4,179 pounds. Production on this model totalled 13,331 with eight more cars outfitted for export. As in all Ninety-Eight models, the engine was the 325 horsepower SkyRocket V-8.

The least expensive 1961 Ninety-Eight model was the Town Sedan. It was the lone model in the top of the line series priced under $4,000 with a list price of $3,887. A total of 9,087 of this model were built. Shipping weight was 4,208 pounds. Standard 98 tires were 8:50 x 14 with an option of oversize tires (9.00 x 14) available. Price on this oversize tire option was $23.67, with it being offered at no additional charge on all air conditioned cars.

1961

With a wraparound rear window treatment was the 1961 Ninety-Eight Sport Sedan. This was a relatively low production Olds as only 4,445 were built. Shipping weight was 4,187 pounds and the sticker price was $4,083. All the Ninety-Eight series cars rode on their own exclusive 126 inch wheelbased chassis. Overall length was 218 inches.

Only one closed two-door model was offered in the 1961 Ninety-Eight grouping. The Holiday Coupe saw a limited production run of 4,445. Price was $4,083 and shipping weight was 4,156 pounds. Ninety-Eights came standard with Oldsmobile's redesigned HydraMatic drive featuring Accel-A-Roter action. Other standard equipment on the top series included: Rota-Matic power steering and Pedal-Ease power brakes.

Rarest among the Ninety-Eight models was the convertible. Production on this open car totaled only 3,804. In addition to being a rare car, the Ninety-Eight convertible was also the most expensive car in the series with a base price of $4,362. Leather interior packages were available on Ninety-Eight ragtops and the high grade seat coverings came in a variety of attractive colors.

Mounted on one of the most attractive Oldsmobile chassis ever built, the 1961 Cotner-Bevington professional cars were very attractive. All of the large Cotner-Bevington models were now built on an extended Oldsmobile Ninety Eight chassis and were called Cotingtons. 1961 saw a totally new styling approach by Cotner-Bevington and the cars were very tastefully appointed and styled. The Cotington landau in funeral car form sold for $8,088, while the landau combination went for $8,221. The Cotington ambulance sold for $8,354 in landau form.

To bring Oldsmobile some ammo in the sales war against the Thunderbird type cars, 1961 saw the introduction of the Starfire. Olds again turned to its fleet of mid-1950 dream cars to come up with a nameplate. Starfire shared its wheelbase of 123 inches with the Super 88 series, but it was powered by a special engine exclusive to the Starfire. Starfires were convertibles only in 1961. Price was $4,647, making it the most expensive 1961 Olds. Production totalled 7,800.

1962

Oldsmobile made a strong sales showing in 1962 by snatching fourth place in the sales race with 447,594 cars sold. This marked a dramatic improvement over previous years and gave Olds the best sales totals since the boom year of 1956.

The bottom of the line big car series - the Dynamic 88 - was again the bread and butter series with 188,537 sales spread across six models. Super 88 buyers accounted for 58,147 sales with 64,154 Ninety-Eights sold. The top of the line, two-model Starfire series appealed to 41,988 buyers and the second year F-85 offerings went to 93,968 buyers.

New front and rear styling was imparted to the big cars and although wheelbases stayed the same overall lengths increased by a couple of inches. The most obvious styling change was the new roofline on some hardtop models.

Introduction day came on Friday September 22, 1961. A number of unseen mechanical improvements were offered on the big cars. The popular HydraMatic transmission was improved by the incorporation of a pressure compensated shift pattern to make smoother shifts. Olds was touting improvement on its Rocket and Skyrocket engines including a new combustion chamber shape and a higher compression (10:25 to 1) ratio on the standard engine. Four horsepower ratings were offered in big car engines for 1962 including an optional, low compression (8:75 to 1) ratio, 260-horsepower Rocket; the standard 280 horsepower Rocket V-8 powerplant and the Skyrocket, a four-barrel carburetor engine which was standard equipment on Super 88 and 98 series cars and developed 330 horsepower. Most powerful among the 1962 Olds engines was the ultra high compression (10.5 to 1) ratio engine rated at 345 horsepower that was found under the hood of the exclusive Starfire series.

The Starfire series was expanded in 1962 to include a coupe as well as the convertible introduced in 1961. Standard Starfire equipment included automatic transmission, power steering, self adjusting power brakes, dual exhaust and leather upholstered bucket seats.

Other unseen big car changes for 1962 included: replacement of open end lubrication fittings with factory sealed units, longer main camshaft bearings and improved air conditioning systems on those cars so equipped.

Much of Oldsmobile's sales success could be traced to the second year F-85 series which introduced a sports convertible and Cutlass convertible in 1962. The Cutlass package included special interior trim and a 185 horsepower aluminum V-8 engine. The Cutlass package came only on the new convertible and a coupe, but the Cutlass engine option was offered on any F-85 model. Standard powerplant for the F-85 was the aluminum Rockette V-8 engine which produced 155 horsepower.

Styling changes for the F-85 series included a revised front end with new hood, grille and headlamp housings coupled with a restyled rear section with twin tail lamps on each side. The F-85's came in the full range of 15 Mirror-Magic exterior colors. Interior trims on the small series came in five basic colors:

gray, green, blue, fawn and red. A new, extra-cost 1962 F-85 option was the anti-spin differential unit.

In April of 1962 Olds introduced its Jetfire at the New York Automobile Show. The Jetfire was an F-85 coupe which was equipped with a startling fluid-injection, turbo-charged V-8 engine. The package featured hardtop styling and a sporty center console.

Oldsmobile continued its strong emphasis on divisional engineering pride with a new engineering center which was opened in August of 1962. The building more than doubled the previous amount of space allotted to Olds engineering.

Two very similar F-85 four doors were offered in 1962. The F-85 four sedan, model number 62-3019, saw a production total of 8,074 and weight of 2,719 pounds. The deluxe F-85 four door sedan, model number 62-3119, weighed 2,725 pounds and 18,736 were made. The standard four door was priced at $2,457 while the deluxe model went for $2,492. Deluxe features included: a special steering wheel, front and rear carpets, exterior body molding package and padded instrument panel.

A total of three station wagon models were available in the F-85 Series: the two-seat station wagon (62-3035), the deluxe two-seat station wagon (62-3135) and the three-seat station wagon (62-3045). The two-seat wagon cost $2,754, weighed 2,805 pounds and had a production run of 3,204. In the deluxe package, the two-seat wagon's list price was $2,889, weight was 2,815 and production totalled 4,974. Least popular of the wagons was the three-seat model which sold for $2,835, weighed 2,820 pounds and had production of only 1,887.

F-85 CLUB COUPE

The Jetfire Sports Coupe was a late 1962 introduction by Oldsmobile and it was the most expensive F-85 listing for $3,042. Standard Jetfire equipment included: dual exhausts, 3:36 to 1 rear axle, bucket seats, special console and a fluid injected turbo-charged 215 cubic inch aluminum V-8 that delivered one horsepower for every cubic inch of displacement. Only 3,765 of this model were built and shipping weight was 2,744 pounds. Model number was 62-3147. Of course, this dealer's display model has been fitted with a definitely non-standard transparent hood.

The least expensive 1962 Oldsmobile was model number 62-3027, the F-85 Club Coupe. Priced at only $2,403, a production total of 7,909 was achieved. Car weight was 2,691 pounds. The standard F-85 powerplant was a two-barrel version of the aluminum Rockette V-8, developing 155 horsepower. Bore was 3.5 inches, stroke was 2.8 inches.

The 1962 Cutlass Coupe was the overwhelming sales leader in the F-85 series and gave an indication of things to come in years ahead. It carried model number 62-3117 and was priced at $2,694. Weight totalled 2,698 pounds. Cutlass models gained extra performance from a higher horsepower engine and a standard 3.36 to 1 rear axle ratio. Stopping power on the F-85 series came from cast iron drum brakes of 130 square inches of lining area.

The fancier of the F-85 convertibles was the Cutlass Convertible, model 62-3167. Carrying a rather hefty small car price tag of $2,971, the Cutlass convertible weighed 2,785 pounds. This was a popular F-85 offering as 9,898 were sold. The Cutlass V-8 was a high performance version of the 215 cubic inch Rockette. It produced 185 horsepower with the help of a four-barrel carb, special heads and a fiberglass packed muffler.

Olds added two convertibles to the 1962 F-85 lineup with the base model being this sports convertible, 62-3067. Shipping weight on the sports convertible was 2,780 pounds with a price tag of $2,760 and production totalling only 3,660. All F-85-s were on a 112-inch wheelbase. The aluminum V-8 engine was found on each of the Olds small cars and gave the series a nearly ideal 50/50 weight distribution.

The new "convertible look" hardtop styling was evident in the Dynamic 88 Holiday Coupe, model number 62-3247. This model was priced at $3,054 and was the most popular 1962 Olds two door with a production run of 39,676. Shipping weight totalled 4,165 pounds. Olds was ahead of the times by touting gas mileage in its 1962's. The standard Dynamic 88 rear-end ratio was 2.56 to 1 and this helped stretch a gallon.

1962

Model number 62-3269 was the Dynamic 88 Celebrity Sedan. This was the least expensive full size Olds carrying a price tag of $2,997. Shipping wieght was 4,179 pounds and production was 68,467. The Dynamic 88 had a number of hidden features including: 94 rubber body to frame contacts, hood insulation, aluminized muffler and a two-stage automatic choke.

Among the more popular big cars was the Dynamic 88 Holiday Sedan, model number 62-3239. This basic model carried a price tag of $3,131 and weighed 4,173 pounds. Production totalled 53,438. Olds offered generous trunk capacity in its big cars of 38.5 cubic feet on four door models. Spare tire location was to the rear of the trunk compartment making the trunk an easy one to load.

The most popular 1962 Olds convertible was model number 62-3267, the Dynamic 88 Convertible. Priced at $3,381, it weighed 4,255 pounds and 12,212 were produced. Standard 1962 Dynamic 88 features included: a Rocket V-8 rated at 280 horsepower, front compartment courtesy lamps, safety padded instrument panel and full floor carpeting.

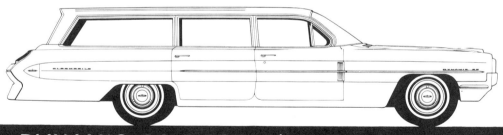

DYNAMIC 88 FIESTA (2- and 3-Seat)

A pair of station wagons were offered in the 1962 Dynamic 88 series: the two-seat Fiesta (62-3235) and the three-seat Fiesta (62-3245). A total of 8,527 of the two-seat model, weighing 4,305 pounds were made. The price was $3,460. In the three-seat Fiesta only 6,417 were produced with a weight of 4,325 pounds. Price tag on the three-seater was $3,568.

Just the one station wagon was offered in the Super 88 series for 1962, the two seat Fiesta — model number 62-3535. This was the most expensive Super 88 priced at $3,762. Weight was 4,312 pounds and only 3,837 of this model were built. With its second seat folded down, 1962 big Olds wagons had 85 cubic feet of cargo space. There was also an optional, below-deck luggage locker which held an additional 8 cubic feet.

Most popular among the Super 88 series cars was the Celebrity Sedan, 62-3569. Production totalled 24,125 with a price tag of $3,273 and a weight of 4,199 pounds. All Super 88's shared the 123-inch Olds wheelbase with the Dynamic 88's and Starfires. Power for all series cars came from a 394 cubic inch, 330 horsepower powerplant which was dubbed the Skyrocket. This engine was shared with the 98 Series.

1962

The lone closed two-door model in the 1962 Super 88 series was the Holiday Coupe, 62-3547. This model was priced at $3,422, weighed 4,182 pounds and 9,010 were sold. Standard tire size on the Super 88 series was 8.00 x 14. Optional 8.50 x 14 inch tires were available on any Super 88 and the larger size tires came automatically on air conditioned cars.

Hardtop styling looked good on the Super 88 Holiday Sedan, model number 62-3539. The price tag on this model was $3,499. It weighed 4,197 pounds and a total of 21,175 were sold. Olds went after silence in its big car models. There was a fiberglass lining on the hood and cowl. Sound deadening was sprayed in doors, rear quarter panels and around the transmission. The passenger compartment floor was covered by layers of jute and felt.

The flagship of the Ninety-Eight series was the convertible, model number 62-3867. This was the most expensive Ninety-Eight at $4,459. It weighed 4,494 pounds and was the rarest of the Olds big cars as only 3,693 were made. The list of Ninety-Eight standard convertible equipment was impressive and it included: 4-S HydraMatic, power steering, power windows and power seat.

One of the new additions to the 1962 Olds fleet was the handsome Starfire coupe. Carrying model number 62-3647, the Starfire Coupe weighed 4,335 pounds and was priced at $4,131. Production was a significant 34,839, helping Olds sales over the previous year when there was no Starfire Coupe. All Starfires sported leather upholstered bucket seats, a console-controlled HydraMatic and a console-mounted tachometer.

The Starfire convertible, model number 62-3667, was in its second year as the basis for a separate Olds series. This was the most expensive 1962 Olds, listing for a whopping $4,744. Weight was 4,488 pounds and production totalled 7,149. All Starfires came standard with a special V-8 developing 345 horsepower. This was teamed with the Olds 4-S HydraMatic Drive and other standard equipment which usually was reserved for the option list.

The Ninety-Eight Holiday coupe carried model number 62-3847. It was priced at $4,180 with a weight of 4,375 pounds. Production totalled 7,546. Each Ninety-Eight model rode on an exclusive 126 inch wheelbase with an overall length of 220 inches. Standard tire size was 8.50 x 14, while 9.00 x 14's were available as an option. Power brakes came standard on all Ninety-Eights.

By far the most popular of the three Ninety-Eight four doors offered in 1962 was the Sports Sedan, model number 62-3839. Price tag on this offering was $4,256, it weighed 4,384 pounds and it was the most popular of the series with a production run of 33,095. Olds said that under normal driving conditions its 1962 chassis would never need lubrication or brake adjustment.

The only non-hardtop four-door in the 1962 Ninety-Eight lineup was the Ninety-Eight Town Sedan, 62-3819. Production on this 4,392-pound model totalled 12,167 with a base price of $3,984 — making it the least expensive Ninety-Eight. Among standard series features were: power steering, electric clock, two-speed electric windshield wipers, windshield washers and full floor carpeting.

Olds called its vinyl interior material Morocceen. Pictured is the 1962 Cutlass Coupe interior. This was the second year for the Cutlass Coupe package. Special Cutlass interior appointments included: extra seat padding, carpeted lower door panels, full floor carpeting, vinyl headlining and chrome window frames.

The Ninety-Eight Holiday Sedan, model number 62-3829, offered a slightly different rear roof line than other Ninety-Eight four-doors. It carried a base price of $4,118, weighed 4,399 pounds and had a production run of 7,653. Like all Ninety-Eights, the Holiday Sedan offered a long line of standard features: parking brake, signal lamp, Safety-Vee steering wheel, heavy duty air cleaner, hood insulation and aluminized muffler.

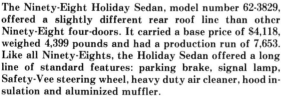

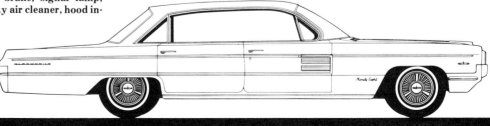

NINETY-EIGHT HOLIDAY SEDAN

Oldsmobile continued to exhibit dream cars in 1962. The new F-85 chassis was the basis for the X-215 show/dream car. This was a custom convertible with a fiberglass tonneau, rollbar and airfoil combination. The X-215 was finished in a bright silver gray with a black racing stripe. Other features of this one-off model were: functional air scoops for brake cooling, a full width concave grille and long range driving lights.

Exact records were not available on chassis production in 1962, but some Oldsmobiles wound up outside the passenger car field like this Cotner-Bevington hearse. The Ninety-Eight chassis was a natural for this line of work with its 394 cubic inch engine which developed 440 foot pounds of torque. A total of 192 square inches of brake lining gave the big Oldsmobiles plenty of stopping power too.

To help the funeral director to match his fleet, many coach builders began to offer limousines with styling that matched their coaches. Cotner-Bevington offered this interesting Oldsmobile limousine that would seat 8 passengers in luxurious comfort. Powered by the large Olds 330 horsepower engine, these cars rode on the same 150-inch wheelbase that the Cotington professional coaches used.

COTNER

BEVINGTON CORPORATION
BLYTHEVILLE, ARK.

The distinguished craftsmanship of the Cotner-Bevington line was displayed with the 1962 Cotington Oldsmobile line of long wheelbase professional cars. The Cotington was offered in both landau and limousine body styles again this year. The landau funeral car went for $8,524 while the limousine version went for $8,391. The landau combination cost $8,657 and the limousine combination sold for $8,524. A service car version of the Cotington cost $8,391 and featured the same clean lines as the limousine funeral car with the notable exception of having blanked off upper rear side panels.

The Cotington ambulance was offered in both landau and limousine body styles in this year. The Cotington limousine ambulance carried a price tag of $8,221, while the landau ambulance commanded a full $8,354. A special 44-inch headroom version of the limousine ambulance was offered for $8,688.

Even though total sales were up over the previous year, in 1963 Oldsmobile dropped back a notch into fifth sales position with total car sales of 476,753.

The F-85 series grew even more popular, however, in 1963 and this series accounted for a solid 118,811 Oldsmobile sales. The solid Dynamic 88 series continued to be the bread and butter line for Olds and it accounted for 199,315 sales. Super 88 sales were up modestly to 62,770, while Starfire sales totals slipped dramatically to 25,549. Ninety-eight production was up also in 1963 with 70,308 sales recorded.

Revised Oldsmobile styling greeted lookers and buyers on new model introduction day of October 4, 1962. The biggest styling change came on the third-year F-85 series which was growing more each year into what Oldsmobile buyers had come to expect from Lansing. Biggest news in the accessory area was the introduction of the Saginaw Steering Gear tilt steering wheel. The first shot in the automotive war against air pollution was fired with Olds introduction of the positive crankcase ventilation system across the line.

As with all auto manufacturers in the 1960's Olds followed the trend toward bigger and more luxury filled products. New Olds models for 1963 included the Ninety-Eight Luxury Sedan and Ninety-Eight Customer Sports Coupe. All big cars were now equipped with a new door interlock system which increased resistance to door openings in crash situations.

In the full size models the heating, ventilating and air conditioning systems were operated by a single control unit to maintain constant temperatures. There was a nearly 50 percent reduction in the size of the front floor tunnel, while the rear tunnel area was four inches narrower than on 1962 models. All 1963 Olds radios were transistorized for instant response. In addition to the deluxe and super deluxe radio models, Olds picked 1963 to introduce its new line of AM-FM radios.

Other major mechanical changes for 1963 on full size models included: a revised rear suspension system, newly designed body mountings and an improved Delcotron generator which was said to prolong battery life. The speedometer was now driven off the left front wheel instead of through the transmission.

All full size Olds offering were powered by 394 cubic inch engines in various stages of horsepower output. The Rocket engine, rated at 280 horsepower with a two barrel carburetor was standard on the Dynamic 88 models. The Super 88 and most 98 models were equipped with the 330 horsepower SkyRocket engine. The high performance engine - the 345 horsepower Starfire powerplant - was standard on both Starfire and the new Ninety-Eight Custom Sports Coupe. The only engine option was a lower compression ratio, 260 horsepower Rocket engine offered on any Dynamic 88 model.

The HydraMatic transmission, standard on Starfire and Ninety-Eight models, was an option on all F-85's, Dynamic 88's and Super 88's. A three-speed synchromesh transmission was standard on these series cars.

Despite its major restyling treatment, F-85 models were just four inches longer in 1963. One area of significant improvement in the smaller Olds series was in the HydraMatic transmission offered on these cars. New shifting controls made shifts a great deal smoother throughout the F-85 lineup.

On all F-85's the instrument panel was restyled for improved appearance and readability with recessed control knobs for greater safety. Standard on all deluxe models for 1963 and available at extra cost on all other F-85's was a padded instrument panel. Steering wheel diameters were reduced on all F-85 models for easier entrance and exit.

Standard F-85's came with the Rockette aluminum V-8, 155 horsepower engine. The Cutlass engine, delivering 195 horsepower, was optional on any F-85. A 215 horsepower, 215 cubic inch aluminium V-8 was offered exclusively on the second-year Jetfire model. To lessen maintenance costs self adjusting brakes were made standard on the small cars in 1963. Brake operations was improved through the use of a new lining material which gave a more positive pedal feel.

In February of 1963 Oldsmobile built its 5 millionth V-8 engine. In the spring of that same year Olds also announced a major expansion and rearrangement program that affected more than 70 percent of the division's manufacturing operations.

The F-85 Club Coupe was the least expensive 1963 Oldsmobile priced at $2,403. Model number 63-3027 weighed 2,684 pounds and saw a production run of 11,276. The F-85 series continued to be based on the popular General Motors 112 inch wheelbase. Overall length on the smallest series Oldsmobile was just over 192 inches — up slightly for 1963 — while width was 73.7 inches.

Two slightly different versions of the F-85 Four-Door Sedan continued to be offered in 1963. Model number 63-3019, the F-85 Four-Door Sedan was priced at $2,457, weighed 2,747 pounds and had a production run of 8,937. Model number 63-3119 was the F-85 Deluxe Four-Door Sedan. This model was priced at $2,592, weighed 2,767 pounds and was the second most popular 1963 F-85 with a production run of 29,269.

Coming in two slightly different trim packages for 1963 were the two F-85 station wagons. Both were two-seat models. The F-85 Station Wagon, model number 63-3035, was priced at $2,754, weighed 2,792 pounds and had sales of only 3,348. The Deluxe F-85 Station Wagon, model number 63-3135, sold for $2,889 and weighed 2,814 pounds. A total of 6,647 of the deluxe version were built.

The most popular F-85 again in 1963 was the stylish Cutlass Coupe, model 63-3117. This was the overwhelming sales leader in the small Olds series with a total of 41,343 sales. List price for the base Cutlass Coupe was $2,964 and it weighed 2,704 pounds. This model came standard with a three-speed synchromesh standard transmission and an optional 4-speed stick shift or HydraMatic were available. Standard rear end ratio was 3.36 to 1.

The Cutlass Convertible, model 63-3167, continued to be a handsome Oldsmobile offering. A total of 12,149 of this model were built. The price tag on the Cutlass open model was $2,971 and weight was 2,784 pounds. The Cutlass engine, available as an option on any F-85, had a compression ratio of 10.75 to 1, four barrel carburetion and torque rating of 235 pound feet. The horsepower rating was 195 with HydraMatic shift and 185 with the standard transmission.

The Jetfire Coupe, model 63-3147, continued to be the most exotic Olds available in 1963. It carried a base price of $3,048-making it the most expensive car in the F-85 series. Curb weight was 2,884 pounds. The production run of only 5,842 hardly justified such a special offering. This car was displayed at a national Olds meet in Bowling Green, Ohio and is owned by Alvin Lindgren of Northbrook Illinois.

As in 1962 the main claim to fame for the Jetfire F-85 was its one horsepower per cubic inch rating achieved from an aluminum, 215 cubic-inch, turbo-charged V-8. This engine was rated as having 300 pound feet of torque. Aside from goodies under the hood the Jetfire package for 1963 included: bucket seats, a center console and special aluminum side trim exclusive to the Jetfire.

The lowest priced Olds in the 1963 Super 88 series was the Celebrity Sedan priced at $3,246. Model number 63-3569 weighed 4,196 pounds and its production run equalled 24,575. Standard equipment for the Super 88 series included: the deluxe steering wheel, padded dash, parking brake signal lamp, front compartment courtesy lamps and two-speed electric windshield wipers. Standard tires were 8.00 x 14 inches.

The only two door offered in the Super 88 series was the Holiday Coupe, 63-3547. It weighed 4,184 pounds and was priced at $3,408. Production totalled 8,930. The standard Super 88 powerplant was the SkyRocket V-8 developing 330 horsepower from 394 cubic inches. This engine used premium fuel through a four-barrel carburetor and developed 440 pound feet of torque.

Hardtop four-door styling came to the Super 88 series via the Super 88 Holiday Sedan. It was designated model number 63-3539 and proved to be the most popular car of the series with production totalling 25,387. Base prices started at $3,473 and curb weight was 4,202 pounds. Olds dubbed its 1963 power steering system as Roto-Matic Power Steering. It was an option on all Super 88, Dynamic 88 and F-85 models.

Nope, not room enough for a horse to ride in there. Just a single station wagon model was offered in the Super 88 series for 1963. The two-seat Super 88 Fiesta was model number 63-3535. It was the most expensive car it its series priced at $3,748. Curb weight on this model was 4,314 pounds and it was the rarest of all full sized Oldsmobiles as only 3,878 were made. Special station wagon options for 1963 included: electric roll down tailgate window and a hidden rear luggage locker.

One of the best looking and cleanest 1963 Oldsmobiles was the Dynamic 88 Holiday Coupe. It carried model number 63-3247 and was priced at $3,052. Curb weight was 4,165 pounds and production totalled 39,071. This particular car was equipped with the optional wire-wheel hubcaps. Non air conditioned Dynamic 88 models — except convertibles and station wagons — came with 8.00 x 14 tires. An option of 8.50 x 14's were available.

1963

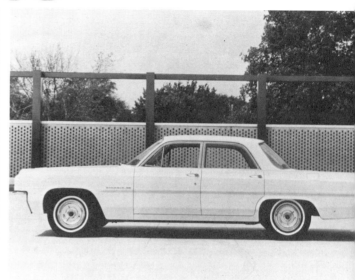

The Dynamic 88 Convertible, model number 63-3267, was the most popular 1963 open Olds built. A total of 12,551 of this convertible were sold. It was priced at $3,379 and weighed 4,240 pounds. All Dynamic 88 models carried full floor nylon fabric carpeting. The rear axle ratio for Dynamic 88's equipped with standard shift was 3.23 to 1, while it was 2.56 to 1 on HydraMatic optioned cars.

The most popular 1963 Oldsmobile was model number 63-3269 the Dynamic 88 Celebrity Sedan. This was also the lowest priced full sized Oldsmobile in 1963 with a price tag of $2,995. Production totalled 68,611 and it weighed 4,184 pounds. All Dynamic and Super 88 models rode on an 123 inch wheelbase. The overall length for cars in both series was 214.4 inches.

Two slightly different versions of the Dynamic 88 station wagon were available in 1963. Model number 63-3235 was a two-seat version of the Fiesta. It was priced at $3,459, weighed 4,280 pounds and saw production totals of 9,615. Model number 63-3245 was the three-seat Fiesta. It weighed 4,292 pounds and cost $3,566, making it the most expensive Dynamic 88. This model sold 7,116.

This Ninety-Eight Holiday Sport Coupe, model number 63-3847, found a limited number of buyers in 1963. Only 4,984 sales were made. The price tag was $4,178, while curb weight was 4,390 pounds. Most of the Ninety-Eight models came standard with a 330 horsepower, 394 cubic inch powerplant. This engine was shared with the Super 88 series and because of its 10.25 to 1 compression ratio it required premium fuel.

Hardtop styling was evident in model number 63-3239 the Dynamic 88 Holiday Sedan. Carrying a price tag of $3,130 this model weighed 4,172 pounds. Production totalled a whopping 62,351. All big cars were equipped with 394 cubic inch engines with various horsepower outputs. A special 260 horsepower version of this engine — turned for regular gas usage — was optionally available on any Dynamic 88.

Carrying model number 63-3819 in the Ninety-Eight series was the Town Sedan. With a base price of $3,982, it weighed 4,395 pounds. Production totalled 11,053. Each Ninety-Eight series car rode on an exclusive 126 inch wheelbase and was over 221 inches long. The overall width was 77.9 inches, the same as Dynamic 88 and Super 88 models.

The Holiday Sports Sedan, model number 63-3839, was one of six 1963 Ninety-Eight models offered. Priced at $4,254, this model weighed 4,396 pounds. Production totalled 23,330 making this the most popular Ninety-Eight built in 1963. The HydraMatic transmission came standard in all Ninety-Eight models. The standard rear end ratio was 3.08 to one.

The 1963 Oldsmobile Ninety-Eight Luxury Sedan, model number 63,3947, was one of two new models added to the top of the line series. Price on this car was $4,332 and weight was 4,411 pounds. A total of 19,252 Ninety-Eight Luxury Sedans were sold. In this model built-in door armrests housed the controls for electric windows. Both front and rear seats contained center arm rests and assist grips were built into the back of the front seats to aid entry and exit.

The most expensive and lowest production 1963 Ninety-Eight was the convertible, model number 63-3867. This awesome Oldsmobile carried a beefy price tag of $4,457 and weighed 4,465 pounds. The production run of 1963 Olds Ninety-Eight Convertibles was only 4,267. Each full size 1963 Olds could carry 21 gallons of gasoline, five quarts of oil (with filter) and slightly more than 20 gallons of radiator coolant.

Posed against a Grant Park, Chicago, background is another new model offered in the 1963 lineup. It is the Ninety-Eight Custom Sport Coupe, model number 63-3847. Priced at $4,381, a total of 7,422 of this car were built. Curb weight was 4,384 pounds. This was the lone model in the Ninety-Eight series to be powered by the Starfire engine. The interior featured a center console and bucket seats. It carried other Ninety-Eight standard equipment of automatic transmission, power steering, power brakes and power windows.

1963

The Olds Starfire series was the only one to drop in popularity between 1962 and 1963. One feature of the 1963 Starfire Coupe, model number 63-3657, was the novel hardtop roofline treatment. The Starfire Coupe, now in its second year, carried a hefty price tag of $4,129. Shipping weight was 4,349 pounds. Production dropped to a rather disappointing 21,148 for this model in 1963.

The most expensive 1963 Oldsmobile was again the Starfire Convertible, model number 63-3667. It sold for the sizable sum of $4,742 and that was a big reason only 4,401 were sold. Shipping weight was 4,492 pounds. Both Starfires were powered by an ultra-high compression, 345 horsepower V-8 which carried a maximum torque rating of 440 foot pounds. This was absolutely a premium fuel engine.

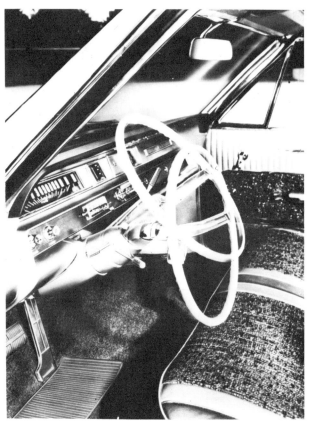

Finding its way on to the rather extensive Oldsmobile option list in 1963 was the Tilt-Away steering wheel. This popular factory installed accessory was built by the innovative GM Saginaw Steering Gear Division. The unit was available on all full sized Oldsmobiles equipped with power steering. By operating a small lever near the turn signal lever, the steering wheel could be tilted to any one of seven angles.

As in previous years, the Cotner-Bevington Co. of Blytheville, Ark., continued to offer a strong line of professional coaches mounted on Oldsmobile chassis. The long wheelbase Cotington models were offered in landau and limousine style, and were also converted into 8-passenger luxury limousines. The landau model sold for $8,636 as a funeral car, or as shown here, for $8,937 as combination which could be switched from ambulance to hearse form. It was also available as a standard headroom ambulance for $9,036, or as a 46-inch headroom ambulance for $10,501. On the other end of the scale, a funeral director's service car version, which really was a luxury panel truck, sold for $8,551. The short wheelbase Seville models on the standard Oldsmobile 98 chassis ranged in price from $6,180 for the economy funeral car and/or service car to $6,393 for the ambulance. Obviously, all medical equipment carried in the ambulance was at additional cost. The roofs on these cars continued to be covered in leather-like vinyl in colors compatible to the paint, and were set off by large chromed decorative landau irons.

1964

For 1964 Oldsmobile added several series of cars to its model mix, yet the division slipped to sixth position in the sales race. Model year sales totals increased to 546,112 for 1964 and calendar year sales stood at 510,931.

From relatively low sales totals in its infant years of 1961-62, the F-85/Cutlass group had developed into a significant part of the Oldsmobile lineup by 1964. This was the largest selling series of cars for the year and it accounted for roughly one-third of the division's sales in 1964.

Olds introduced its new cars on Friday October 4, 1963 and a number of the new features was used on the F-85 line. A new design — using a 115-inch wheelbase version of the new features was used on the new models. Brakes on the F-85s were bigger and a foot operated parking brake was used. Gasoline tank capacity was 20 gallons and an oil filter was standard in all models. As the smallest Olds grew in popularity, some of the more popular Olds options were made available in the F-85 series. These included for the first time Tilt-Away steering wheels. ($44.03) and the electric 4-way bench seat adjuster ($66.71). A sports console was offered in Cutlass models and the V-6 Sports Coupe. This unit featured a tachometer, storage compartment and shift controls.

The 1964 F-85s came in standard and deluxe versions with the top of the series being the Cutlass models. Three powerplants were offered in addition to the midyear offering of the 4-4-2 engine. The economy engine was a 155 horsepower V-6 with 230 horsepower and 290 horsepower versions of the 330 cubic inch V-8 powerplant available. Transmission choices included as standard equipment a column-mounted three-speed stick, and an optional floor-mounted four-speed manual unit or a Jetaway HydraMatic.

Since the mid-1950's the Olds high performance image had been slipping badly and in mid model year the 4-4-2 package was made available to dealers and customers without much fanfare. Most of the items contained in the package had been offered on police cars, so little new equipment was made necessary. The unique option (#B-09) was available on any F-85 and stood for 4-barrel carburetion, 4 on the floor and 2 (dual) exhausts. Features of the package boosted the horsepower rating to 310 and other items included heavy duty shocks and springs, red-line tires, special air cleaner, and special fender emblems.

While things were happening in its smaller car camp, Olds didn't forget about its bread and butter full sized car lineup. New for 1964 was the Jetstar 88 series and also the Jetstar I. The Jetstar I was designed as a lower priced companion car to the Starfire, a personal luxury car that Olds had introduced in 1961. Jetstar I equipment included: bucket seats, console, Starfire roof styling and a 345 horsepower, high compression, 394 cubic inch V-8. The Jetstar 88 series was the budget priced offering of the full sized lineup. Models included: a four-door sedan, hardtop sedan, convertible, and a coupe. This series was based on a 123-inch wheelbase and this was the lone big car series to use the 330 cubic inch V-8.

Continuing to be produced under the Olds banner were the Dynamic 88, Super 88 and Starfire models sharing the 123-inch wheelbase chassis. Workhorse powerplant of the 1964 full sized cars was a redesigned 394 cubic inch engine which ranged in horsepower output from 280 to 345. Improvements were made in the Jetaway automatic transmission for the new model year. New styling treatments were found in each series. Interior fabrics were upgraded on the full sized cars and included heavy duty vinyls and satin weave nylons.

Corner lamps ($34.43) were a new Olds accessory offering for 1964 and other popular full sized car options included: Tilt Away Steering Wheel ($44.03), AM-FM radio ($150.64), Reverbatone rear speaker ($53.80) and cruise control ($91.46). Ten interior colors were offered on the big Oldsmobiles in 1964 with 15 exterior colors available on full sized models.

Another chief engineer found his way to the general manager's spot as Harold Metzel succeeded Jack Wolfram as top man at Oldsmobile. By 1964 Olds could build 2,400 cars daily at its plants across the country with 1,400 of this daily production capability in Lansing. Olds employed 14,184 in its Lansing operations and payroll exceeded $100 million in 1964.

The price leader for the 1964 Olds lineup was the F-85 Club Coupe, model number 64-3027. With the 155 horsepower V -6 engine this little car cost $2,332 and weighed 2,875 pounds. A total of 8,314 were made. With the standard V-8 the price for the Club Coupe rose to $2,404, weight was 3,025 pounds. and production totaled 7,984. The V-6 powerplant displaced 225 cubic inches, had a one-barrel carb and used regular gasoline.

The F-85 four door was available several different ways in 1964. Model number 64-3069 was the standard four door sedan which sold for $2,386, weighed 2,920 pounds and saw a production run of 6,531 with the V-6 engine. With a V-8 the standard F-84 four door cost $2,458, weighed 3,107 pounds and a total of 5,575 were built. With the deluxe package 7,428 with the V-8 engine were made. Price was $2,494 and weight was 3,066 pounds. Big seller of the F-85 line was the V-8 equipped deluxe four door. It cost $2,566, weighed 3,158 pounds and 42,237 were built.

1964

The Deluxe Sports Coupe came exclusively powered with the V-6 engine — which produced 155 horsepower — equalled the horsepower output of the 1963 F-85 V-6 engine — which produced 155 horsepower — equalled the horsepower output of the 1963 F-85 V-8 engine. A major change for the F-85's in 1964 was in the engine compartment with more horsepower being added across the board.

Least expensive among the Cutlass series cars was the Sports Coupe, model number 64-3227. This car was priced at $2,663 and weighed 3,140 pounds. Production was 15,440. The Cutlass package included bucket seats. A mainstay of the Cutlass option was a 290 horsepower Rocket V-8 engine displacing 330 cubic inches. Olds called this powerplant a Jetfire, but it was not turbo-charged like previous Jetfire offerings.

Most popular among the Cutlass offerings was the Holiday Coupe, model number 64-3237. This popular car saw a production run of 36,153. Base price was $2,773 and weight was 3,155 pounds. For 1964 all F-85 models rode on wheelbases of 115 inches with an overall length of 203 inches. The standard tire size on Cutlas models was 7.00 x 14 inches.

The Vista Cruiser was introduced by Oldsmobile at the 1964 Chicago Auto Show and this model grew into one of the industry's best selling and best looking station wagons. The body style was shared for a number of years with Buick. As a Cutlass 3,320 Vista Cruiser two-seat models were sold. These were priced at $3,055 and weighed 3,365 pounds. Designation for this model was 64-3255. As a three-seater — model number 64-3265 — 7,286 Cutlass models were built. Base price was $3,122 and weight was 3,405 pounds.

The station wagon was a market that would open up tremendously over the next few years to intermediate car makers. Model number 64-3035 was the F-85 station wagon. It was priced at $2,678, and weighed 3,254 pounds and saw a production of 4,047. In deluxe trim this model was designated 64-3135. Price was $2,876, weight was 3,290 pounds and only 909 were made.

1964

For those Olds buyers who wanted a somewhat sporty car, the lone open car in the F-85 series was model number 64-3267 the Cutlass Convertible. This car sold for $2,973, weighed 3,307 pounds and 12,822 were built. A total of four top color choices were offered to convertible buyers in 1964. These included: white, black, blue and saddle.

A late addition to the 1964 Olds lineup was the Vista Cruiser Station Wagon. In the F-85 series it carried model number 64-3055 as a two seater. It was priced at $2,942, weighed 3,350 pounds and only 1,305 were made. As a three-seater in the F-85 series, 2,089 Vista Cruisers were made. Base price was $3,112 and weight was 3,377 pounds. Model number was 64-3065.

Oldsmobile took a look at the newly introduced Pontiac GTO and by mid-year the division had a tiger-like machine of its own. The 4-4-2 was a combination of extra horsepower (310 total) and a special handling package. Also part of the option were redline tires with the wire wheel covers shown on this car as an option. Genuine 4-4-2 equipped cars for 1964 are rare, but the exact production of this option package is unknown. The 4-4-2 stood for four barrel carburetor, four on the floor transmission, and dual exhaust.

Almost as an after thought the 4-4-2 package was offered in the mid-model year. The package caught on reasonably well and the car became a street terror — real competition for the Pontiac GTO's, Mopars and fast Mustangs of the era. Over the years Oldsmobile engineers developed the 4-4-2 into a separate model and off the showroom floor it was equal to just about any production car. This rare 1964 Cutlass from Tennessee with the 4-4-2 option was photographed at a national Oldsmobile meet in Ohio.

The price tag was quite high on the Starfire models for 1964 and it was reflected in slumping sales for that series. Added to the Olds lineup in 1964 was the Jetstar I, a less costly personal luxury car powered by a 345-horsepower Starfire engine. The Jetstar I sold reasonably well with 16,084 sales in its first year. Base price was $3,592, weight was 4,028 pounds and the model number 64-3457.

1964

One of the rarest cars in the 1964 lineup was the Jetstar 88 Convertible. Only 3,903 of model number 64-3367 were produced. This was the rarest car of the new series and also the most expensive with a price tag of $3,308. This model weighed 3,817 pounds. The powerplant for this new series of Oldsmobiles was a 245 horsepower, 330 cubic inch engine.

The least expensive full sized Oldsmobile was the Jetstar 88 Celebrity Sedan, model number 64-3369. Base price on this model was $2,924 and weight was 3,739 pounds. Production totalled 24,614 making this the best seller in the Jetstar 88 group. Transmission choices included the Jetaway HydraMatic, three-speed column mounted stick shift or a floor mounted four speed manual unit.

A handsome Olds offering for 1964 was the Jetstar 88 Holiday Coupe, model number 64-3347. List price was $2,981 and weight was 3,720 pounds. A total of 14,663 of this model came off the assembly lines. Standard Jetstar 88 equipment included: foam padded front seat, safety padded instrument panel, wheel opening and rocker panel moldings and an automatic dome light.

Another four door offering in the new Jetstar 88 series was the Holiday Sedan, model number 64-3339. Base price on this car was $3,058 and shipping weight was 3,758 pounds. Production totalled 19,325. This series offered all moroccen upholstery as standard equipment along with harmonizing deep pile carpeting.

A series that had been coming out of Lansing for a number of years was the Dynamic 88 series. For 1964 model number 64-3447 was the Holiday Coupe. Base price on this offering was $3,051 and weight was 3,912 pounds. Production totalled a substantial 32,369. Engines of the V-8 design and putting out 260, 280 and 330 horsepower were available in this series cars. All were 394 cubic inch units.

Model number 64-3467 was the Dynamic 88 Convertible, one of five open models built by Olds this model year. Production of this model totalled 10,042. Base price was $3,378 and weight was 4,005 pounds. Standard Dynamic 88 series equipment included: chrome side moldings, courtesy and map lights and carpeting.

Olds offered two versions of its Fiesta in the Dynamic 88 series. The two-seat model number 64-3435 sold for $3,458 and weighed 4,155 pounds. Production on this version was 10,747. The three-seat Fiesta was model number 64-3445. It carried a price of $3,565 and weighed 4,180 pounds. Production was 6,599. An electric rear window was standard on three-seat models.

Once again the best selling Oldsmobile was found in the popular Dynamic 88 series. Model number 64-3469 was the Celebrity Sedan and it was the big volume car in 1964. A total of 57,590 of this model went to new car buyers. This was the least expensive car in the series at $2,924. Weight was 3,952 pounds.

The Super 88 series for 1964 had dwindled to just two models and both were four doors. The Super 88 Celebrity Sedan carried model number 64-3569. Base price was $3,250 and weight was 4,021 pounds. This was the better seller of the series with a production run of 19,736. Standard equipment included: chrome window frames, deluxe steering wheel and parking brake signal lamp.

Another high volume Oldsmobile in 1964 was the Dynamic 88 Holiday Sedan, model number 64-3447. Production on this model was a sizable 50,327. This car cost $3,129 and weighed 3,980 pounds. The standard tire size for this series was 8.00 by 14 inches. Fuel tank capacity on all full sized models was 21 gallons.

Model number 64-3539 was the Super 88 Holiday Sedan. Base price was $3,472 and weight was 4,054 pounds. Production totals were 17,778. Super 88 models came with the standard three speed transmission, although few were actually equipped that way. Most buyers opted for the popular HydraMatic which listed for $231.34.

1964

Most popular among all the top of the line Oldsmobiles in 1964 was the Holiday Sports Sedan, model number 64-3839. This offering was base priced at $4,254 and weighed in at 4,231 pounds. A total of 24,791 Ninety-Eight Holiday Sports Sedans were sold. This particular car from Ohio was displayed at one of the national meets of the Oldsmobile Club of America in Lansing, Michigan.

Model Number 64-3947 was the Ninety-Eight Custom Sports Coupe. This car was priced at $3,831 and weighed 4,207 pounds. Production for this version two door was only 4,954. Standard Ninety-Eight equipment included a variety of things that were options on other models like: window washers, power windows, power seat and a deluxe steering wheel.

The Ninety-Eight lineup was well populated in 1964 and sales held up well across the board. One of three Ninety-Eight four doors was the Town Sedan, model number 64-3819. Base price on this model was $3,982 and weight was 4,189 pounds. Production on the Nienty-Eight Town Sedan was 11,380. All top series Oldsmobiles rode on an exclusive 126 inch wheelbase.

Another four door in the Ninety-Eight series was the Luxury Sedan, model number 64-3829. Base price on this model was $4,331 and weight was 4,238 pounds. The production run on this car was 17,346. All Ninety-Eight models were powered by a 330 horsepower, 394 cubic inch engine which required premium quality fuel.

Oldsmobile offered a pair of two door models in the Ninety-Eight series and the more popular of the two was the Holiday Sports Coupe. This car carried model number 64-3847. Base price was $4,177 and weight was 4,175 pounds. Production totalled 6,139. Standard 98 equipment included: power steering, power brakes and automatic transmission.

Rarest among the top of the line Oldsmobiles was the Ninety-Eight Convertible, model number 64-3947. This was the most expensive car in the series at $4,457 — but it fell several hundreds of dollars short of Starfire convertible of 1964. Weight on this model was 4,315 pounds. Production was only 4,004. Tire size on all Ninety-Eight models was 8.50 x 14 inches.

The rarest full sized automobile in the Olds lineup and also the most expensive Olds was the Starfire Convertible. Its price tag of $4,742 made it hundreds of dollars more than other models. Weight was 4,275 and its model number was 64-3667. Production on this model was only 2,410. Both Starfires came standard with a floor mounted automatic shifter.

Because of high prices the Starfire continued to drop in popularity in 1964 with the coupe remaining the more popular of the two models. It carried model number 64-3657. Base price was $4,128. Weight was 4,153 pounds and production totalled only 13,753. Starfire models were powered by the most powerful Olds engine, a 394 cubic inch unit putting out 345 horsepower.

Continuing with anticipated success was the Cotner-Bevington line of long wheelbase professional cars built on modified Olds 98 chassis. Marketed under the name Cotington, the long wheelbase series offered this limousine style car both as a hearse and as a combination hearse/ambulance. The funeral version went for $8,220, while the combination cost $8,335. Both versions were also offered in landau styling, which was the same basic car only with a vinyl top, blind quarter panels, and decorative landau irons. This version sold for $8,410 as a funeral car or $8,525 as a combination. The Cottington line also featured two ambulances, one with 41 inches of headroom that sold for $8,585, and one with a headroom of 46 inches which cost $9,160. Cotner-Bevington cars competed directly with Pontiac based cars being built by Superior, and Bucik based cars being turned out by Flxible.

The Cotner-Bevington Co. of Blytheville, Ark., offered both long and short wheelbase professional cars, all built on Oldsmobile's modified 98 chassis. The short wheelbase models, such as this ambulance, were marketed under the name Seville. This unit sold for $6,800, while a combination version, which allowed the vehicle to be converted from ambulance to hearse, sold for $6,685. The straight funeral car version cost $6,575 with limousine styling similar to this ambulance, or $6,715 with landau styling, which featured blind quarter panels and decorative landau irons and a leatherette-vinyl top. The combination car was also available in landau styling and sold for $6,945.

Oldsmobile held on to sixth position in the 1965 sales race, with totals for both model year and calendar year going up substantially over the previous year. A total of 591,701 model year sales were made with calendar year production jumping to 650,801.

The F-85 series continued to soar in sales. In its introduction year of 1961 less than 80,000 of the little Olds model were sold, but by 1965 the F-85 sales total had grown to 212,870.

After substantial changes in 1964, the 1965 F-85 series offered mild changes. These included a redesigned grille and front bumper, redone tail lights and redesigned side trim. A brushed aluminum strip in the instrument panel and some new interior fabrics were the big changes inside the small Oldsmobiles.

The 330 cubic inch Jetfire Rocket V-8 engine remained the mainstay for the F-85's and all cars in the Jetstar 88 series. Horsepower ratings ranged from 250 to 315 on these small block Olds engines. The closest thing to an economy car in the Olds lineup was an F-85 equipped with the Econ-O-Way engine. That powerplant remained unchanged from the previous year, developing 155 horsepewer from 225 cubic inches. Smoother ride and better handling characteristics were claimed by Olds due to revised body mounts, springs and rear suspensions.

Two packages introduced in 1964 within the small Olds series made it even bigger in 1965. The Vista Cruiser station wagon, with its uniquely styled Vista Roof, was offered in four basic packages this year:

Again in 1965 the least expensive and lightest Olds was the Club Coupe in the F-85 series. As a V-6 this model was number 65-3327. It was priced at $2,344 and weighed 2,655 pounds. A total of 5,289 were built. With a V-8 the Model designation became 65-3427. This car weighed 2,789 pounds, base price was $2,415 and production was 7,720. This marked the final year Olds used the Econ-O-Way V-6.

For those desiring a little bit fancier V-6, the F-85 Deluxe Sports Coupe was still available. Carrying model number 65-3527 this car weighed 2,704 pounds and was base priced at $2,538. Only 6,141 were made. The F-85 grille was die cast and the factory claimed this method of construction was stronger and allowed more styling detail to be built into the finished product.

two-seat and custom two-seat; three-seat and custom three-seat. Sales were up nearly double on this model over 1964 introduction levels and this was the th most attractive General Motors station wago package since Chevrolet dropped the true Nomad i 1957. With the surface barely scratched on the 4-4-: market with its mid-1964 introduction, Olds polishee its performance package in 1965. The new 4-4-2 wa powered by an exclusive 400 cubic inch powerplan which was conservatively rated at 345 horsepower Other goodies in the package included: four barre carb, twin exhausts, 10.25 to 1 compression ratic heavy duty suspension and red line tires. Either standard three speed, optional four speed, o automatic transmission could be coupled with a '3.5 to one rear axle. External emblems were displayee front, rear and side on the hottest 1965 and th automotive press began to acknowledge this as one o the best performance packages for the money. Th 4-4-2 package was available on any F-85 coupe or con vertible.

Introduction day, which was Thursday Septembe 24, 1964, found the big Oldsmobile lineup shufflee around slightly. Missing was the long standing Supe 88 nameplate which dated back to 1951 and in it: place appeared the Delta 88 series, which the factory billed as "glamorous companion to the popula Dynamic 88."

Restyling was done on the big cars and new feature: included more interior room, curved side glass in mos models and new rooflines on all models. Big change: could also be found in the full size car power trains a: the 1965 Olds big block grew to 425 cubic inches Horsepower ratings on the new engine ranged fron 310 to 370. Coupled with the new powerplant was new Turbo HydraMatic transmission which wa: equipped with a variable vane feature to giv smoother shifts and better performance at driving speed. For the first time in all 88, Jetstar and Starfir models a floor-mounted four-speed manual transmis sion was offered. This unit was fully synchronized i all gears.

Other full-sized model changes included increasing fuel tank capacity to 25 gallons and the addition of u to 4 cubic feet of trunk space in some models. A feature offering added style and comfort in the nev models was a split back front seat with a large cente: arm rest. This new front seat was standard on Delt: 88 Holiday Sedans and Coupes and on the Ninety Eight Sports Sedan, Coupe and Convertible.

Throughout the industry Oldsmobile had carried tag of being a major innovator, and in 1965 the fina touches were being put on an innovation that woule rank with the Rocket V-8 of 1949 and the HydraMati transmission of 1940. As early as 1959 Oldsmobile er gineers had begun working with experimental fron wheel drive cars. By 1963, the "Toronado concept" ha been locked in by designers and work was under way t build a car the likes of which the American auto indus try hadn't seen for 30 years. In 1965 final testing of th Toronado was being done and facilities were alread being renovated for the production of an all new mode the following year.

The V-6 engine never was a real popular seller on the Four Door F-85 Sedan. As pictured in deluxe trim this model carried model number 65-3569. It was priced at $2,505 and weighed 3,012 pounds. Only 4,989 were built. As a standard model the V-6 F-85 Four Door sold only 3,089. It was priced at $2,398 and weighed 2,991 pounds. Model number was 65-3369.

As a V-8 the F-85 Four Door Sedan was a big seller. The largest selling model — for the first time ever — came from the smallest Olds series. A total of 47,767 buyers opted for model number 65-3669, the F-85 V-8 Deluxe Four Door Sedan. Base price was $2,576 and weight was 3,188 pounds. In standard V-8 form the F-85 Four Door Sedan — model number 65-3469 — sold for $2,465 and weighed 3,167 pounds. Production was 5,661.

Several combinations were available on the F-85 two-seat Station Wagon. Model number 65-335 was V-6 equipped, with a base price of $2,689 and weight of 3,236 pounds. Only 714 were made. The deluxe V-6 model was designated 65-3535, priced at $2,797 and weighed 3,258 pounds. Production was 659. The standard equipped V-8 carried model number 65-3435, weighed 3,408 pounds and cost $2,760. A total of 2,496 were built. Model number 65-3635 was the deluxe V-8. It was priced at $2,868, weighed 3,445 pounds and had a production run of 10,365.

The Vista Cruiser continued to offer something sporty to those needing practical transportation. For 1965 the Vista Cruiser had its own wheelbase of 120 inches. All Vista Cruisers were V-8 powered. In standard two-seat equipment the model number was 65-3455, price was $2,937 and weight was 3,685 pounds. Production was 2,110. In the custom offering, the model number was 65-3855 for the two-seater. Base price was $3,146 and weight was 3,747 pounds. Production equalled 9,355.

The Vista Cruiser was the lone three-seat wagon offered since the Dynamic 88 Fiesta wagon was dropped after the 1964 model run. In standard equipment a three-seated Vista Cruiser was designated model number 65-3465. It weighed 3,762 pounds and cost $3,072. Production was 3,335. In custom equipment the same Vista Cruiser cost $3,270 and weighed 3,814 pounds. Production totals for model number 65-3865 were 17,205.

1965

Another extremely popular Cutlass model was the Sports Coupe, model number 65-3827. This was the least expensive Cutlass at $2,643. Weight was 2,784 pounds. Production for the Cutlass Sports Coupe totalled 26,441. Five transmission combinations were offered in the Cutlass series: three speed column shift, three speed floor shift, Jetaway automatic with column shift, the automatic with a floorshift or a floor mounted four speed manual transmission.

A total of three Cutlass models were offered in 1965 and each was a balanced good looking and good performing car. Model number 65-3837 was the Holiday Coupe, the lone hardtop in the F-85 series. It was priced at $2,784 and weighed 2,799 pounds. A whopping 46,138 of this model rolled off the assembly lines. Cutlass models came standard with the 315 horsepower, 330 cubic inch V-8. Premium fuel was suggested for this motor.

The lone open car in the popular F-85 series was model number 65-3867, the Cutlass Convertible. Priced at $2,983, this was the most expensive Cutlass. This model tipped the scales at 2,901 pounds. Production totals were 12,628, making this by far the most popular open Olds model in 1965. All divisional engines for this model year featured V-design, hydraulic valve lifters, full flow oil filter, dual fuel filters, positive crankcase ventilation and Delcotron generator.

The 4-4-2 package — introduced halfway through the previous model year — was tremendously improved for 1965. Pictured here on a Cutlass Convertible the popular high performance option could also be ordered on the two other Cutlass models or the F-85 V-8 Club Coupe. In the

F-85 series the package cost $190.45 and on Cutlass cars it cost $156.02. Power for the 4-4-2 came from an exclusive 345 horsepower, 440 pound-foot torque, 400 cubic inch, 10.25 to 1 compression ratio engine.

The Jetstar 88 series continued to be offered to budget minded Olds buyers in 1965. Again this series shared the 123-inch wheelbase with all full sized models except the Ninety-Eights. The Jetstar 88 Holiday Coupe was designated model number 65-5237. It weighed 3,701 pounds and was priced at $2,995. Production on this, the lone closed two-door in the series, was 13,911.

The 4-4-2 package was rather complete and it competed with just about anything else off the showroom floor. The package included: heavy duty frame, engine mountings, shock absorbers and suspension with front and rear stabilizer bars; heavy duty wheels with 7.75 x 14 nylon Red-line tires, special propeller shaft and performance axle; dual exhausts; heavy duty radiator and distinctive identification including grille, headlamp housing and medallions.

Rarest among the four models offered in the Jetstar 88 series was the convertible, in its final year of production. Model number 65-5267 was the highest priced Jetstar 88 with a tab of $3,337. Weight was 3,853. Only 2,980 of this model were sold in 1965. Oldsmobile convertible tops were available in white, black, blue and fawn. Interiors were done in a variety of colors of Morocceen.

The best seller in the Jetstar 88 lineup was the Celebrity Sedan. This was the least expensive full sized Olds, priced at $2,938. It weighed 3,734 pounds and carried model number 65-5267. For the first time a choice of three transmissions could be ordered in the Jetstar. Standard was a column mounted three speed stickshift. Optional units were the Jetaway automatic and a new floor shift four speed.

Model number 65-5239 was the Jetstar 88 Holiday Sedan. Base price on this model was $3,072 and it weighed 3,755 pounds. Production totalled 15,922. Three engines were available on this series and all were based on the 330 cubic inch V-8. A 250 horsepower regular fuel engine was offered. Also available was a 260 horsepower unit and a 315 horsepower V-8.

It was a short life for the Jetstar I, as Oldsmobile's attempt at a lower priced personal luxury car found its second year also was also its last. A number of styling gimmicks produced only 6,552 sales in a market that was probably hurt by the growing poupularity of the 4-4-2 option. Model number 65-5457 was priced at $3,602 and weighed 3,936 pounds. Power for this model came from a 425 cubic inch, 370 horsepower Starfire V-8.

The Super 88 series nameplate, with Olds since the 1951 model year, was dropped in favor of the Delta 88 tag in 1965. In that new series model number 65-5837 was the Holiday Coupe. It was priced at $3,253 and weighed 3,907 pounds. Production was low on all three Delta 88 models at 23,194. This was one of the cars equipped with the new split back front seat with the large center armrest.

Two four doors were offered in the Delta 88 series and model number 65-5869 was the Celebrity Sedan. Base priced at $3,158 this was the least expensive Delta 88. Weight was 3,948 pounds and production totalled 29,915. This series of cars came standard with a 310 horsepower Super Rocket engine. Horsepower ratings of 300, 360 and 370 were also available. All were versions of the new 425 cubic inch, big block powerplant.

The Dynamic 88 series continued to be a solid basis for Olds full sized car sales and three of its four models topped the 24,000 sales mark. Second best seller in the series was the Holiday Sedan, one of the two four doors offered. Model number 65-5639 was priced at $3,143 and weighed 3,942 pounds. Sales totals were an impressive 38,889. The new 425 cubic inch engine had a bore and stroke of 4.125 and 3.975 inches.

Rounding out the new Delta 88 series was its most popular model, the Holiday Sedan. Model number 65-3839 weighed 3,959 pounds and was priced at $3,330. Production was 37,358 making this one of the more popular full sized Oldsmobiles. Transmission selections included three and four speed manuals and the new Turbo-HydraMatic. Most full size car buyers opted for the automatic which cost $242.

1965

The largest selling 1965 full sized Olds was the Dynamic 88 Celebrity Sedan, which was also the price leader in the series. A whopping 47,030 of this model were built. Model number 65-5669 sold for $3,008 and weighed 3,914 pounds. One of the design improvements in 1965 was more interior space on the larger cars. Rear passengers were given extra foot room by a ¾ inch reduction in rear tunnel height in new models.

Rooflines were sporty on most 1965 coupe models as shown on the Dynamic 88 Holiday Coupe. Model number 65-5637 was priced at $3,065 and weighed 3,847 pounds. Production totalled 24,756. Olds touted a new self-tightening hood latch on full sized models as well as a full fiberglass under the hood insulation blanket to deaden noise.

Convertibles were starting to wind down in popularity in the big Olds lineup which was one factor which ultimately lead to their demise. Model number 65-5667 was the rarest of the Dynamic 88's, the Convertible. With a base price of $3,408, weight was 4,036 pounds. The production run was 8,832. All Dynamic and Delta 88 models rode on 8.25 by 14 inch tires. Oversize fourteen inch tires and also fifteen inch rubber were options offered on most 1965 Oldsmobiles.

The Starfire, never as successful in the personal luxury class as Oldsmobile would have liked, was in its final years as an offering. In 1966 the Toronado was scheduled for introduction and this sealed the Starfire's fate. For 1965 the Starfire Coupe was model 65-6657 and it weighed 4,132 pounds. The price was a hefty $4,148. Production stood at 13,024. The Starfire as usual had no engine of its own. It was powered by a top of the line 370 horsepower, premium fuel burner.

In its final year was the extremely low production Starfire Convertible. The 1965 model run was only 2,236 making this the rarest full sized Olds. Model number 65-6667 weighed 4,347 pounds. This was the highest priced Olds again, this year selling for $4,778 — which at least in part accounted for the low sales totals. The Starfire models could be ordered either with a floor shifted Turbo HydraMatic or a floor shifted four speed manual unit.

1965

Lowest production among the three Olds Ninety-Eight four doors was the Town Sedan. It was designated model number 65-8469. This was the least expensive car in the series at $4,001. Weight was 4,201 pounds. Production equalled 13,266. Standard rear end ratio on Ninety-Eights was 3.08 to 1. Optional ratios were 2.73 to 1 or 3.42 to 1.

The Ninety-Eight Holiday Sports Coupe was designated model number 65-8437. Base price was $4,197. Weight was 4,164 pounds. A total of 12,166 buyers purchased this model in 1965. Standard on all top series Oldsmobiles was a 360-horsepower Rocket V-8. Optional was the 370 horsepower Starfire powerplant. Both were premium fuel engines.

Rarest among all Ninety-Eights was the Convertible. Production on this top line open car was limited to 4,903. Model number 65-8467 was the highest priced car in the series at $4,493. Weight was 4,335 pounds. All Ninety-Eights required premium fuel regardless of engine choice. The only transmission offered in the series was the standard equipment Turbo HydraMatic.

Model number 65-8439 was the Ninety-Eight Holiday Sedan. Weight on this model was 4,232 pounds and base price was $4,273. Production run on this top line car was 28,480. Standard equipment included: two-way power seat, chrome body moldings, deluxe steering wheel, full wheel discs, windshield washers and 8.55 x 14 tires.

A total of three four door models were offered in the Ninety-Eight series. Most popular among these was model number 65-8669, the Luxury Sedan. Base priced at $4,351, weight was 4,249 pounds. Production was a series high 33,591. Standard equipment included: Pedal-Ease Power Brakes, Roto-Matic Power Steering, clock, padded instrument panel and deluxe armrests.

Oldsmobile did not have a Limousine style available, but that didn't mean that Olds dealers could not offer such a style to their customers. The Cotner-Bevington Co. of Blytheville, Ark., was quite happy to produce this rather interesting high-headroom Limousine on a semi-custom, special order basis. The car could be fitted with a wide variety of interiors, ranging from super-plush 4-passenger style to 9-passenger livery form. The car was based on a stretched version of the 98 Sedan, and prices depended upon equipment ordered, starting at about $7,800.

Cotner-Bevington again offered its short wheelbase professional cars under the name Sevilles. These cars used the 98's standard 126-inch wheelbase chassis with a 62.5-inch front tread. This is the combination version, which could be converted from ambulance to funeral car, allowing livery companies and rural funeral homes to do double duty with one vehicle. As shown, the car sold for $7,065, but with landau styling with a vinyl top, blind rear quarter, and decorative landau irons, the car cost $7,237. The same body was available as a limousine ambulance for $7,165 or a landau ambulance for $7,337, or as a straight limousine hearse for $6,921 and the landau hearse for $7,093. Also available was a funeral service car, which really was a glorified panel truck. This sold for $7,093, the same as the landau hearse.

The stretched versions of the Cotner-Bevington line were marketed under the Cotington name. The ambulance this year offered increased headroom for attendants. It was available in 42-inch headroom for $8,910, or as the 48-inch headroom model shown here for $8,447. The roof of the high-headroom version was made of fiberglass to lessen the total weight of the vehicle and to improve handling characteristics. Olds provided plenty of stopping power for heavy bodies such as this, with its power brakes and 229 square inches of brake lining.

The top line Cotner-Bevington furneral car this year was the Cotington landau coach, which sold for $8,702. It featured a large blind panel set off by decorative landau irons, and covered in vinyl. The standard limousine funeral coach sold for $8,472. The style was also available as a combination ambulance/hearse, and in that form sold for $8,824 in landau style and $8,587 as a limousine. A service car, which had completely enclosed side panels similar to a panel truck, but much more luxurious, was marketed for $8,702, which was the same price as the top of the line hearse. In constructing these cars, C-B stretched the Olds 98 chassis to a 150-inch wheelbase length. Power was by the 360-horsepower Super Rocket. This year Cotner-Bevington of Blytheville, Ark., became part of the Wayne Co., but this did not effect its building of professional cars on Olds chassis.

On the strength of a new look lineup, Oldsmobile jumped two spots into fourth place in the sales race for 1966. Model year sales totals were 586,381 with calendar year sales standing at 594.069.

The big news in the Olds camp was the long awaited front wheel drive Toronado. Olds officials probably never introduced a car with more fanfare and results included Motor Trend Car of the Year award and the Car Life Engineering Excellance selection.

Research on the Toronado dated back to the 1950's and even included looking at some of the classic front wheel drive products built by E.L. Cord. The Toronado was billed as a six-passenger hardtop coupe. It was 211 inches long, only 52.8 inches high and utilized a wheelbase of 119 inches. Innovations on this Lansing-built car included: complete elimination of the transmission hump, torsion bar suspension and some unique placement of power train components.

A look under the hood found the engine offset slightly right of center. The torque converter for the transmission was attached to the rear of the engine. The remaining section of the Turbo HydraMatic was turned around and mounted along the left side of the engine facing forward. A link chain assembly transfered power from the converter across and through the transmission gear to a differential. Transmission power flow had to be reversed so driving torque could be applied to the front wheels. This was accomplished by dividing the Turbo HydraMatic into two units.

A differential unit had to be specially designed for the new car. It used planetary gears rather than traditional ring and pinion set-up. Differential torque was split between two front drive axles, one connected to the planetary gears the other to an internal sun gear. While turning, the planetary gears revolved with differential action, allowing the drive axles to rotate at different speeds.

Front suspension was based on two specially hardened steel torsion rods which worked from each lower control arm to special anchors. A rugged stabilizer bar was used up front and 17.8 to 1 ratio power steering was standard on all Toronados. The

rear suspension was a U-channel axle cushioned b two single leaf springs and four shock absorber Another unique Toro feature was a retractab headlight system which was completely automatic. large vacuum reserve tank was the basis of th system.

Were there any weak points in the new Olds? A co ple to be sure. The author's family owned a brand ne 1966 and two problems — common to the early mode and cured in later versions — surfaced. The doors wer bulky and hard to manage, particularly for smaller i dividuals. Secondly, the early Toros had a real tende cy to chew up front tires — even the expensive 8.85 15 tires they came equipped with.

New car introduction day for Olds was Thursda October 14, 1965 and although over shadowed by th new Toronado the rest of the Olds lineup drew atter tion as well. The F-85 series continued to grow in sale popularity and some changes were made in that serie for 1966. For the first time a pair of four-door hardtop were available in the Olds intermediate offerings. Th top of the line four-door hardtop was the Cutlas Supreme, a name that would grace many Oldsmobile — in many body styles — in years to come.

Performance continued to be popular with buyers i the F-85/Cutlass series. The 4-4-2 option was in it third year and continuing to grow in popularity. Par of the Olds performance package for 1966 included specific grille and tail lamps, recessed front fende scoop and special ornamentation. The 4-4-2 model continued to be powered by a 400 cubic inch V-8 with 1966 horsepower rating of 350 with a single ca buretor. Another 10 horsepower could be gained in th 4-4-2 with the first factory tri-carb set-up since the J option package of 1957-58. Another speciality smalle Olds that continued to sell well was the Vista Cruise which was in its second year built on an exclusiv 120-inch wheelbase.

The biggest change under the hood of the F-85s, a least for economy minded buyers, was the switch fron the V-6 motor to the Action — Line L-head 6-cylinde engine displacing 250 cubic inches and developing 15 horsepower. The bread and butter powerplant of th F-85 series remained the 330 cubic inch V-8 whic could be ordered in several different forms betwee 250 and 320 horsepower.

The stylists attempted to give the full size models longer and lower look in 1966. Rectangular headlam housings and new grilled designs were to add to th impression of additional width in the big cars. Th Starfire coupe was done at the end of model year 1966 as some of this car's potential buyers certainly moved into the Toronado camp. A convertible model was add ed to the Delta 88 series, but open cars were eliminated from the Jetstar and Starfire series in 1966.

The basic big car powerplant — with the exception

The biggest news in years from Oldsmobile was the exciting new Toronado. Model number 66-9487 was the standard Toronado Coupe. It was priced at $4,585, weighed 4,366 pounds and a production run of 6,333 was made on the standard model. The only engine selection on the Toro was a 385 horsepower Rocket V-8.

f the Jetstar 88 series — remained the 425 cubic inch ig block. Most of the improvements under the hood temmed from a redesigned Quadrajet carburetor hich the factory claimed would give better performance, up fuel economy and idle better.

Some new big car accessories were manually adustable reclining Strato bucket and bench seats. ruise control — an option for several years on the full ized cars — was expanded to the F-85 lineup in 1966. afety, both government mandated and voluntary, as becoming more a part of the auto industry. eatures for this model year included: front and rear eat belts, back-up lights, outside rear-view mirror, indshield washers, padded sun visors and glare educing surfaces on wiper arms and instrument anels.

Olds added more than 400,000 square feet of anufacturing space to its main complex in Lansing. new administration building was also added in 1966 nd a large addition was made to the growing parts arehouse complex.

By far the more popular of the Toronados was the deluxe model. Deluxe equipment included front center armrest, chrome windshield and window interior moldings, strato bench seat and wheel trim rings. The deluxe Toronado was model number 66-9687. Base price was $4,779 and weight was 4,410 pounds. An impressive first year production total of 34,630 was achieved.

The new Toronado was a handsome car from any angle. All Toronado models came standard with dual exhuasts and chrome exhaust extension sticking through the bumper. The standard Toronado tires were 8.55 x 14 blackwalls. The early models sometimes chewed up front tires at alarming rates. Optional 8.85 x 14 tires were available for $23 in blackwall and $71 in the thin whitewalls.

A special version of the 425 cubic inch V-8 engine was offered on all Toronados as the only engine selection. This unit turned out 385 horsepower, the highest rating of any Olds engine. This Rocket V-8 powerplant produced 475 pound feet of torque. It carried a compression ratio of 10.5 to 1 and used a four barrel carburetor. Only premium fuel could be used.

The early Toronados were real sleepers in the handling department. They handled as well as just about anything on the road once a driver got used to the front wheel drive. A beefy suspension system was built around torsion bars. Despite its heft some Toronados found their way into racing. Here Indy 500 winner Bobby Unser boldly charges up Pike's Peak in a specially modified Olds Toronado.

An impressive part of the Toronado was the vast expanse of flat floor. This was made possible by the elimination of the driveshaft and transmission hump. One of the problems with the early Toros was the heavy doors which smaller people had trouble opening or closing. The tilt and telescope steering column was option N-37 and cost $78.

A heavier styling approach was used on 1966 F-85 models. Apparently buyers liked the treatment as sales continued to rise in this grouping. The Olds price leader again was model number 66-3307, the six cylinder Club Coupe. Base price was $2,332, weight was 2,855 pounds and production was 6,341. The F-85 V-8 Club Coupe was model number 66-3407. Base price was $2,401, weight was 3,145 pounds and production was 6,353.

The least expensive of all the four doors offered in the F-85 series were the two standard four door sedans. Model number 66-3369 was the six cylinder unit base priced at $2,384 and weighing 3,023 pounds. Only 2,862 were built. With the larger V-8 engine the model number became 66-3469. Base price was $2,453 and weight was 3,210 pounds. Production was 3,754.

The Deluxe Holiday Coupe was model number 66-3517 in the F-85 series when powered by the 155 horsepower six cylinder engine. Base price was $2,495 and weight was 2,955 pounds. A total of 2,974 were built. With the 330 cubic inch V-8 this car was model number 66-3617. Base price was upped to 2,564 and weight was 3,245 pounds. A total of 16,968 of this stylish hardtop model were produced.

New to the intermediate Olds series was the F-85 Deluxe Holiday Sedan. Model number 66-3539 was the six cylinder version. Base price was $2,610 and weight was 3,043 pounds. Only 1,002 were made. With the V-8 the model number for this car became 66-3639. Base price was $2,680 and weight was 3,251 pounds. Production equalled 6,911.

Buyers continued to take a long look at the Deluxe F-84 four door sedans. Model number 66-3569 was powered by the in-line six cylinder. Base price was $2,479 and weight was 3,058 pounds. Production was 3,568. A total of 27,452 buyers opted for the V-8 version which carried model number 66-3669. It was base priced at $2,549 and weighed 3,245 pounds.

The lowest priced group of Olds station wagons was the two standard F-85 models. With a six cylinder model number 66-3335 was base priced at $2,605. Weight was 3,350 pounds and the production was only 508. With the 330 cubic inch V-8 the F-85 station wagon model number became 66-3435. Base price was $2,744 and weight was 3,520 pounds. Only 1,652 of this cargo hauler were built.

The deluxe package on the 1966 F-85 station wagons meant a bit more chrome on the outside and better interior trim on the inside. Powered by the new L-six cylinder, the F-85 Deluxe Station Wagon was model number 66-3535. Only 434 were built. This car was base priced at $2,773 and weighed 3,386 pounds. With a V-8 under the hood the little wagon became 66-3635. Base price was $2,842 and weight was 3,555 pounds. Production totals were 8,058.

All the models in the Cutlass series were popular and the Sports Coupe was no exception. Model number 66-3807 was base priced at $2,614 and weighed 3,185 pounds. Production totals were 17,455. Cutlass models came standard with a premium fuel 320 horsepower engine. Options included a regular fuel 310 horsepower V-8 and a buyer could also order one of the two 4-4-2 powerplants.

This Cutlass Holiday Coupe was equipped with the popular 4-4-2 package. Model number for this unit was 66-3817 (this didn't change due to designation).The Cutlass Holiday Coupe was Oldsmobile's big seller in 1966 with a total of 44,633 built. Base price was $2,750 and weight was 3,197 pounds. The 4-4-2 option was available on F-85 and Cutlass coupes and convertibles. It was number L-78 and cost $185 on F-85s and $151 on Cutlass models.

Actually two 4-4-2 packages were offered in 1966. Option L-69 was the tricarb set up and L-78 utilized a single four barrel unit. The tri-carb cost about $100 more and delivered 10 more horsepower. Both packages included a beefed up suspension, external styling gimmicks and Redline tires. Transmission choices included heavy duty clutched three or four speeds or a special duty Jetaway automatic.

Almost tripling the popularity of the other open Oldsmobile models was model number 66-3867 the Cutlass Convertible. Production on this model was 12,154. It was base priced at $2,944 and weighed 3,352 pounds. Two standard shift packages — a three speed and four speed, both with Hurst shifters — were offered by Olds in 1966. The Jetstar automatic was also available on the Cutlass.

New on the Cutlass scene was the Supreme four door hardtop. In an impressive first year sales total 30,871 buyers opted for model number 66-3839. This car was base priced at $2,825 and its weight was 3,255 pounds. Vinyl tops were in vogue in the mid-60's and such equipment on the Cutlass Supreme cost $73. It was option CO8.

This was the first year Cutlass buyers had a shot at four door models. A second addition to the top of the line F-85 group was model number 66-3869, the Cutlass Celebrity Sedan. Base price was $2,654 and weight was 3,243 pounds. Production totals were 9,017. Each Cutlass took five quarts of oil with a filter change, held 17 quarts of coolant and could hold up to 20 gallons of gasoline.

Again this model year the Vista Cruiser stood between the F-85 series and full sized models. It rode on its own 120 inch wheelbase. In standard trim a two-seat Vista Cruiser was model number 66-3455. It was priced at $2,914, weighed 3,753 pounds and only 1,660 were made. A standard three-seater was model number 66-3465. Base price was $3,065 and weight was 3,787 pounds. Production equalled 1,869.

The Jetstar 88 was an experiment to offer a lower priced full sized Olds and 1966 was the end of the line for that experiment. Model number 66-5237 was the Jetstar 88 Holiday Coupe. This was the lowest priced Olds at $2,962. Weight was 3,752 pounds. Production was only 8,575. All Jetstar models shared the 330 cubic inch with Cutlass models.

More popular in the Vista Cruiser series were the custom equipped models. The two seat custom was designated 66-3855. It cost $3,114, weighed 3,769 pounds. A total of 8,910 came off the assembly lines. Model number 66-3865 was the three-seat custom. It weighed 3,804 pounds and was priced at $3,270. A total of 14,167 were produced.

Most popular of the three model Jetstar 88 series was the Celebrity Sedan, model number 66-5239. Production on this four door was 13,734. Base price was $2,907 and weight was 3,776 pounds. One weak point of the Jetstar was the brakes which tended to be much smaller than other full sized Oldsmobiles. Self adjusting brakes were standard on this model.

Model number 66-5239 was the Jetstar 88 Holiday Sedan. This was the most expensive car in the series carrying a price of $3,038. Weight was 3,752 pounds. Only 7,938 of this model were built. Jetstar 88s came standard with a three speed manual transmission. A four speed manual or Jetaway automatic were the options in the transmission department.

The biggest seller in the big car lineup was the Dynamic 88 Celebrity Sedan, model number 66-5669. A total of 38,742 buyers went for this model. It was also the least expensive car in the series with a price tag of $2,992. Weight was 3,930 pounds. The standard engine in this series was a 310 horsepower, 425 cubic inch unit. Also available were 300 horsepower and 365 horsepower versions of the same motor.

Another popular model was the Dynamic 88 Holiday Sedan. Model number 66-5639 was base priced at 3,123 and weighed 3,945 pounds. A total of 30,784 were built. Standard equipment on this model was a three speed manual column shift. Optional were the fully synchromesh four speed floor shift or the popular Turbo HydraMatic.

1966

The lone closed two door in the Dynamic 88 group was the Holiday Coupe which was designated model number 66-5637. A total of 20,768 of this model were produced. The cost was $3,048 and weight was 3,913 pounds. With the Turbo HydraMatic unit the standard Dynamic 88 rear end ratio was 2.93 to 1. Optional ratios were 2.73 to 1 or 3.42 to 1.

Full sized convertibles were getting to be rare in the Olds lineup by 1966. Model number 66-5667 was the Dynamic 88 open car. It was the most expensive car in the series with a price tag of $3,381. Weight was 4,017 pounds and production was limited to 5,540. Trunk capacity on this series of cars exceeded 19 cubic feet.

Newest of the Oldsmobile series was the Delta 88 group which drew its name from past Oldsmobile dream cars of the 1950's. By far the rarest of this series was the convertible, which was designated model number 66-5867. Base price on this car was $3,564 which made the convertible the most expensive car in the series. Weight was 4,055 pounds. Production totalled only 4,303, including this California based beauty.

Olds stylists had made even the big cars look graceful from the rear. Model number 66-5837 was the Delta 88 Holiday Coupe. It was base priced at $3230 and weighed 3,917 pounds. A total of 20,857 were built. This series came standard with a 310 horsepower big block engine as standard equipment. Optional horsepowered engines included: 300, 365 and 375.

Best seller among the four Delta 88 models was model number 66-5839, the Holiday Sedan. This car carried a base price of $3,306 and weighed 3,984 pounds. Production totalled 33,326. Standard series equipment included: full carpeting, heater and defroster, backup lights, seat belts, deluxe steering wheel and two speed windshield wipers and washers.

1966

Model number 66-5869 was the Delta 88 Celebrity Sedan. A total of 30,140 customers purchased this new Oldsmobile. Base price was $3,138 and weight was 3,963 pounds. The four season air conditioning system cost $418 on Delta 88 models and the new Comfortron air conditioning system listed for $480.

Alone as a closed two-door in the Ninety-Eight series was model number 66-8437, the Holiday Coupe. Base priced at $4,129 this car weighed 4,140 pounds. Production run for this sharp two-door was 11,488. All top of the line Oldsmobiles came standard with a 365 horsepower Super Rocket V-8 or with the optional 375 horsepower Starfire V-8. Both engines were 425 cubic inches.

Waiting for the Hyde St. cable car to go past on its way to San Francisco's Fisherman's Wharf is this Starfire, which in 1966 had been cut to a one-car series. This was the Starfire's final year as a personal luxury car, and as a result, production was only 13,019. Carrying model number 66-5457, this car was priced at $3,540 and weighed 4,013 pounds in basic form. Known officially as the Starfire

One of the best selling Oldsmobiles this model year — and the most popular Ninety-Eight model — was the Luxury Sedan. Model number 66-8669 was base priced at $4,279 with a weight of 4,197 pounds. Production totalled a whopping 38,123. All Ninety-Eight models came standard with Turbo HydraMatic and no transmission options were even offered.

Coupe, this particular model was equipped with extra cost option N95, which was the simulated wire wheels with spinner hubs. These cost $53 a set. That's the San Francisco Maritime Museum in the background, which consists of several historically important ships at permanent mooring.

Model number 66-8469 was the Ninety-Eight Town Sedan. This was the rarest of the top series four doors with a production run of only 10,892. This was also the least expensive car in the series with a price tag of $3,939. Weight was 4,197. All Ninety-Eights came standard with 8.55 x 14 inch tires. Optional 8.45 x 15 inch tires were also offered.

One of three four doors offered in the Ninety-Eight series was the Holiday Sedan, model number 66-8439. Base priced at $4,204 and weighing 4,184 pounds, a total of 23,048 of this car came off the assembly lines. All Ninety-Eights came standard with a 3.08 to 1 standard rearend ratio when equipped with the standard motor. Optional ratios were 2.73 to 1 and 3.42 to 1.

The flagship of the Ninety-Eight fleet again in 1966 was the top of the line convertible. Model number 66-8467 weighed 4,245 pounds and was the most expensive car in the series with a price tag of $4,413. Only 4,568 of this model were built. Standard Ninety-Eight equipment included: Pedal-Ease power brakes, Turbo HydraMatic, Roto Matic power steering and self adjusting air scoop brakes. This particular car, missing its rear skirts and part of its side chrome, was owned in 1976 by Eric Dammann, son of Crestline's general manager. At that time, it was part of a fleet of about a dozen convertibles owned by the Dammanns, which included the Buick in the background, the Pontiac in the foreground, and seven Cadillacs.

Again Cotner-Bevington Co. of Blytheville, Ark., introduced its line of fine medium priced ambulances and hearses (professional cars) on either stock or extended Olds 98 chassis. The line was divided into two series, the Seville, which was built on the standard 126 inch wheelbase chassis, and the Cotington, which used a stretched version of this chassis, having a wheelbase of 150 inches. These cars ran an overall length of 247 inches, were 79 inches wide, and except for the high headroom ambulance, averaged 69 inches in height and 5,250 pounds in weight. The Seville line included the limousine style combination ambulance/hearse shown here, which sold for $7,363, and included both straight ambulances and funeral cars in either limousine or landau style. The same choices held true for the long wheelbase models. Prices on the smaller cars ranged from $7,200 through $7,500, while the Cotington line had prices ranging from $8,500 through $9,500 for the ambulance with 48 inches of headroom. Illustrations of these body styles, which were not changed all that much from the previous year, can be found in the 1965 section. C-B also continued to offer its rather ungainly Limousine, based on the Olds 98 Sedan. This car, in basic 7-passenger form, now sold for $7,934.

1967

Oldsmobile dropped a couple of notches in the sales race for 1967 as they wound up in sixth place with 558,762 calendar year sales and 548,390 model year sales.

Olds was still searching for the right model mix in 1967 with a reallignment and elimination of several big car series taking place. Introduction on the new models came on September 29, 1966 and the full size lineup appeared without the Jetstar 88 and Starfire nameplates which were eliminated. The new Toronado cut deeply into the Starfire sales and the Jetstar 88 was a budget full size Olds that never really caught on. The series which for several years had been tagged the Dynamic 88 in 1967 in effect became the Delmont 88s. Models in the Delmont 88 category could be ordered as either: a pillared sedan, hardtop sedan, hardtop coupe or convertible. Power came from either a 330 cubic inch or 425 cubic inch powerplant. Delmont's with the big block motor were identified with a 425 logo on the front fender.

The 425 cubic inch Super Rocket V-8 was the standard powerplant for the Delta 88 series. For those desiring a bit fancier trim package, a Delta 88 Custom was offered in the hardtop coupe or hardtop sedan. A new styling treatment was employed for the five-model Ninety-Eight series. Olds was touting an optional black custom Royale trim package — with white leather inserts — for the 1967 Luxury Sedan.

No radical changes were made in the Toronado for 1967, but some key improvements made this an easier car to live with, in some respects, than its 1966 counterpart. Front tire wear problems were greatly reduced thanks to a combination of suspension system improvements and better tire industry technology. A smoother and quieter ride was developed for the 1967 front wheel drive car. Spring-operated door opening assistors made doors open much easier. Styling changes for the Toro included a new egg-crate type grille, flush-with-the-hood headlight covers and newly styled tail lamps. Horizontal paint striping was a Toronado option as were bucket seats in the deluxe offering. Despite all these changes for the better, Toronado sales dropped almost in half in 1967 over the previous introduction year.

Olds continued to concentrate on its intermediate offerings and more buyers than ever seemed interested in the luxury equipped small Oldsmobiles. For 1967 the F-85 line had shrunk to three basic body styles, while five offerings were made in the Cutlass series. Because of its success in 1966, the Cutlass Supreme series also had five offerings in 1967. A new option in the Supreme coupe models was the turnpike cruising package which combined excellent economy with equally good performance. This package was especially put together for the driver who racked up a lot of super-highway driving. The 4-4-2 package continued to be offered to the muscle car buyers and functional hood louvers were added this model year. The division continued to offer a 3-seat Vista Cruiser, and both a 2 and 3-seater in the Custom Vista Cruiser line. Wood grain exterior panels on the sides and tailgate further set off the custom offering.

There was a long list of mechanical advances in 1967, with a great number of them relating to safety. These included: dual master cylinder, four-way emergency flasher system, a padded glareproof rearview mirror and shoulder harness anchors. Steering columns were of the General Motors energy absorbing design and the steering wheel itself was padded. Braking power was boosted in 1967 models with capacity and effectiveness increased by using a larger vacuum cylinder on the power brake equipped cars. Optional for the first time in 1967 were front wheel disc brakes. Other new options included a climate controlled air inlet system, a more effective limited slip differential unit and a transistor ignition system.

On the corporate side of things a total of 91,000 square feet of floor space was added to the main plant in 1967. In additon to that, construction was started on a 57,000 square foot building in the main plant complex to house paint inspection and repair facilities. Work was also started on the expansion of the Olds parts warehouse and work was progressing to add more space to the press plant complex.

The number of cars offered in the basic F-85 series was shrinking, but the divisional price leader remained the F-85 Club Coupe. As model number 3307 it was a six-cylinder powered machine priced at $2,410 and weighing 2,965 pounds. Production was 5,349. As a V-8 the F-85 Club Coupe was designated number 3407. Price was $2,480, weight was 3,150 pounds. Production was 6,700.

The smaller wheelbased of the two basic Olds station wagons offered in 1967 was the F-85 Station Wagon which rode on an 120-inch wheelbase. Model number 3335 was the six cylinder version which cost $2,749, weighed 3,200 pounds and had a production run of 2,751. The V-8 edition of this car was priced at $2,818, weighed 3,406 pounds and had sales of 1,625. It was designated model number 3435.

Rounding out the three-model F-85 series was the four door Town Sedan. With six cylinder power this car was designated model number 3369. Price was $2,457, weight was 3,015 pounds and production was 2,458. With the old standby 330 cubic inch V-8 the car became model number 3469. Base price was $2,527, weight was 3,206 pounds and production was 5,126.

The 4-4-2 package was available on the three Cutlass Supreme two doors offered in 1967. Here is the Holiday Coupe with the 4-4-2 set-up. New treatments for the model year included functionally louvered hood and paint striping. Either bucket or bench type seats could be ordered. The heart of this muscle car option was the 400 cubic inch, 350-horsepower Rocket V-8. It was fed through a four barrel carb.

Certainly the most sporty looking of the 4-4-2 optioned cars were the convertibles. This front shot shows the clean front hood look and the 4-4-2 emblem inset in the grille. There were some special options which interested the 4-4-2 buyers. These included: the UHV transistorized ignition, several special axle ratios and a tachometer and engine gauge package.

For 1967 any of the five Cutlass models could be ordered with either a six or an eight cylinder engine. Model number 3517 was the six cylinder Holiday Coupe. Base price was $2,574, weight was 2,998 pounds and 2,564 of this model were built. Model number 3617 was the V-8 cutlass Holiday Coupe. It was the most popular car in the series with 29,799 produced. Base price was $2,644 and weight was 3,190 pounds.

Another model made popular by the 4-4-2 option was the Sports Coupe. The 4-4-2 package was listed as option L-78 and it sold for $184.31. It included: a special engine, dual exhaust, F-70 x 14 wide tread redline tires and various heavy duty components. The package also included a variety of external trims displaying the 4-4-2 logo.

1967

The more popular of the two Cutlass four doors built in 1967 was the pillared Town Sedan. Model number 3569 was the six cylinder model which saw a production run of 2,219. Price on this model was $2,552 and weight was 3,054 pounds. Powered by a V-8 the model number became 3669. Production totalled a whopping 29,062. Base price was $2,662 and weight was 3,228 pounds.

The Cutlass series offered a station wagon in 1967. Model number 3535 was the six cylinder powered wagon of which only 365 were produced. Base price was $2,848 and weight was 3,245 pounds. Carrying model number 3635 was the V-8 Cutlass wagon. Production totalled 8,130. List price on this model was $2,917 and weight was 3,462.

Hardtop styling wore well on the Cutlass Holiday Sedan. Model number 3539 drew its power from the 155 horsepower Action Line Six. Base price was $2,683, weight was 3,074 and only 644 were made. With the V-8 engine the model designation for the Cutlass Holiday Sedan became 3639. Base price was $2,753, weight was 3,251 pounds and 7,344 rolled off the assembly lines.

Rarest among the Cutlass series cars was the convertible. With the 250 cubic inch six cylinder engine a scant 567 were produced. Model number 3567 base price was $2,770 and weight was 3,145 pounds. When the 330 cubic inch V-8 was underhood the model number became 3667. Base price was $2,839, weight was 3,315 pounds and 3,770 of this attractive open car were made.

All models in the Cutlass Supreme series enjoyed extreme popularity. A number of those sales were with the 4-4-2 option (not pictured here). Model number 3807 was the Cutlass Supreme Sports Coupe. Base price was $2,694 and weight was 3,140 pounds. Production was 18,256. All cutlass Supremes came base equipped with a 320 horsepower Jetfire V-8 engine.

A surprisingly popular car — certainly the most popular open Olds built this model year — was the Cutlass Supreme Convertible. It carried model number 3867. A total of 10,897 were produced. Base price was $3,026, making this the most expensive F-85 small model. Weight was 3,385 pounds. All Cutlass Supreme models came standard with a three-speed manual transmission.

The most popular offering in the 1967 Oldsmobile lineup was the Cutlass Supreme Holiday Coupe, model number 3817. A whopping 57,858 of this hardtop model rolled off the Olds assembly lines. Base price was $2,831 and weight was 3,152 pounds. Option C08 was on this car was the vinyl roof covering. It was available on sedans and coupes and cost $84.26.

Least popular in the Cutlass Supreme series was strangely enough the Town Sedan, model 3869. Only 8,346 of this four door were built. Base price was $2,726 and weight was 3,262 pounds. The standard tires on this series were two-ply, 7.75 x 14 inch blackwalls unless the 4-4-2 or turnpike cruising package was ordered from the factory.

A handsome car from any angle was the Cutlass Supreme Holiday Sedan, model number 3839. Base priced at an even $2,900 the weight on this unit was 3,284 pounds. A total of 22,571 buyers laid down their money for this 1967 Olds. All Cutlass Supremes came standard with: full floor interior carpets, courtesy lamps, deluxe steering wheel and chrome inside rearview mirror.

Across the country freeway driving had become a way of life and Cutlass Supreme buyers could be at home on the road with option L-66 "the Turnpike Cruising package." The heart of this option was a 300 horsepower, two barrel version of the 400 cubic inch V-8. Other items in the $142.18 package included: a new air induction system, a special Turbo HydraMatic, 7.75 x 14 inch white line nylon cord tires and several special chassis items. The Turnpike Cruising "TC" emblem appeared along with the Cutlass emblems.

The Vista Cruiser rode again in 1967 and it was offered in three versions. Without the woodgrain treatment was model 3465, the three-seat standard. It was priced at $3,136 and weighed 3,815 pounds. Only 2,748 were built. All Vista Cruisers rode on an exclusive wheelbase of 120 inches.

Stylish from almost any angle was the hardtopped Delmont 88 Holiday Sedan. Powered by the faithful 330 cubic inch motor it was designated model number 5239. Base price was $3,139 and weight was 3,894 pounds. The production run was 10,600. With the 425 under the hood the model number became 5639. Base price was $3,202 and weight was 3,987 pounds. Production was a series high 21,909.

Two versions of the custom Vista Cruiser were offered in 1967. The two-seat cruiser was designated model 3855. A total of 9,513 were made with a base price of $3,228 and weight of 3,789 pounds. By far the most popular Vista Cruiser was the three-seat custom, model number 3865. Production reached 15,293. It was the most expensive car in the series, priced at $3,369 and weighing 3,897 pounds.

A bread and butter car in the Delmont 88 series in 1967 was the Holiday Coupe. Model number 5287 was that car with the 330 cubic inch V-8 engine. Base price was $3,063, weight was 3,876 pounds and 10,786 were made. With the big block 425 cubic inch motor the model designation was 5687. Base price was $3,126, weight was 3,781 pounds and production amounted to 16,699.

1967

Most popular among the Delmont 88 offerings was the Town Sedan. As model number 5269 the car was powered by the 330 cubic inch engine. It was base priced at $3,008 and weighed 3,850 pounds. The production run was 15,076. The 425 cubic inch model of this car was model number 5669. It carried a base price of $3,071 and weighed 3,955 pounds. Production was 21,909.

Relatively rare in the 1967 Olds lineup was the Delmont 88 Convertible. Only 3,525 of this model were built and all were powered by the big 425 cubic inch motor. this car carried model number 5667 and weighed 4,058 pounds. It was the most expensive car in the series priced at $3,462. This particular car is equipped with wire wheel hubcaps — option N-95 — priced at $52.66.

One of the distinctively trimmed Delta 88 Customs was the Holiday Sedan, model number 5439. Carrying a base price of $3,582 this model tipped the scales at 4,027 pounds. Production was 14,306. Standard powerplant for the Delta 88 Customs was a 399 horsepower Super Rocket V-8 regular fuel engine. The standard transmission was a column mounted three speed manual unit.

A large side chrome strip was one identifying factor of the Delta 88 Custom model. The Delta 88 Custom Holiday Coupe carried model number 5487. Base price on this car was $3,522. Weight was 3,975 pounds. A total of 12,192 of the Delta 88 Custom Holiday Coupes rolled off the Oldsmobile assembly lines in 1967.

Olds claimed it was using its Toronado as the styling trend setter across the board in 1967. The Delta 88 Holiday Coupe was model number 5887. It was priced at $3,310 and tipped the scales at 3,915 pounds. Only 2,447 of this model were built. The 8.45 x 15 two-ply whitewall tires were option P04 and listed for $42.54.

A "meat and potatoes" car in the 1967 Olds lineup was the Delta 88 Town Sedan. Carrying model number 5869, production totalled 21,909. Base price was $3,218 and weight was 3,993 pounds. All Delta 88 models came standard with a stick shift transmission and a 300 horsepower, 425 cubic inch Super Rocket V-8 engine that used regular gasoline.

Another high sales volume Oldsmobile was the Delta 88 Holiday Sedan, model number 5839. This car was base priced at $3,386 and weighed 3,951 pounds. The production total was 22,270. Delta 88 standard equipment included: deluxe steering wheel, deluxe armrests, full-floor carpeting, courtesy lamps and chrome roof drip moldings.

The lone open car the Delta 88 series was the Delta 88 Convertible. Priced at $3,646 this was the most expensive car of its series. Model number was 5867 and weight was 4,178 pounds. Production was surprisingly high total of 14,471. A deluxe convertible interior package was option Y67 and cost $17.85. Most Delta 88 ragtops were so equipped.

The lone closed two-door in the Oldsmobile Ninety-Eight lineup was the Holiday Coupe. Carrying model number 8457, base price on this model was $4,214. Weight was 4,184 pounds. A total of 10,476 of this model were built. This particular car is equipped with option CO-8, a vinyl roof covering. On top series cars this factory installed option sold for $110.59.

Flagship of the stylish Ninety-Eight series was the Convertible, model number 8467. In addition to being the highest priced car in the series it was also the rarest. Base price on the Ninety-Eight Convertible was $4,498 and the weight was 4,405 pounds. Only 3,769 of these open cars hit the road in 1967.

Surprisingly the best selling single full sized model in 1967 was in the Ninety-Eight series. It was the Luxury Sedan, which carried the designation of 8669. Base price was $4,351 and weight was 4,247 pounds. Production equalled a whopping 35,511, making it by far the most popular offering in the top of the line Olds series.

Another relatively popular top of the line Olds was the Ninety-Eight Holiday Sedan. Carrying model number 9439 this car was base priced at $4,276 and weighed 4,285 pounds. Production totalled 17,533. The standard engine for the Ninety-Eights was a 365 horsepower Super Rocket V-8 displacing 425 cubic inches. It was a premium fuel engine.

One of three four doors offered in the Ninety-Eight series was the Town Sedan. Carrying model number 8469 this car achieved a production run of 8900. Base price was $4,009 and weight was 4,222 pounds. Among the items on the standard equipment list for this series were: power windows, Roto-matic power steering, 8.85 x 14 inch tires, electric clock and Turbo HydraMatic transmission.

Far more popular in the second-year Toronado models was the deluxe version, which carried model number 9687. Production was 20,020 on this front drive model. Base price on the Deluxe Toronodo Coupe was $4,869 and weight was 4,357 pounds. Again this year all Toronados were equipped with a specially built automatic transmission system.

The more rare of the two Toronados offered in 1967 was the standard which was model number 9487. Only 1,770 of this model were produced. Base price was $4,674 and weight was 4,330 pounds. Only one Toronado engine package was available in 1967. It featured a 385 horsepower big block with dual exuasts.

The Toronado proved to be an attractive car from whatever angle it was viewed. Options for 1967 included horizontal paint stripes and bucket seats. Standard equipment included: armrests, Pedal-Ease power brakes, Roto-Matic power steering, deluxe steering wheel, automatic transmission, 8.85 x 14 inch special 2-ply tires, wheel trim rings, lamp package, electric clock and full carpeting.

In 1967 and several years after this strange looking — but awesomely powerful Oldsmobile Cutlass was making exhibition runs at dragstrips across the country. The car featured two complete supercharged Toronado engines — one to power each pair of wheels. The car carried 4-4-2 trim and featured a complete rollcage inside. Exhibition cars like these were the forerunners of drag racing's colorful funny cars. This scene took place at the Niagara Dragstrip in Upstate New York.

Oldsmobile did not have a limousine model, but the Cotner-Bevington Co. was happy to fill in that gap. The 7-passenger vehicle utilized a streched chassis with a 150-inch wheelbase and was 247 inches long overall. The car offered everything but pleasing style. Priced at $9,487 f.o.b. Blytheville, Ark., the car was fitted with three folding auxiliary seats for extra passengers, and came complete with air conditioning, AM-FM radio with signal seeker tuner and rear speakers, power steering and brakes, heavy-duty shock absorbers and drive shaft with center bearing, power operated front seat, and deluxe steering wheel.

The Divco-Wayne Corp., the parent company of Cotner-Bevington, continued to offer its ambulance line based on Oldsmobile chassis. This is not the 48-inch headroom unit, which utilized a specially-designed fiberglass roof unit to give additional inside space. It sold for $9,923. The standard 42-inch headroom unit sold for $9,324. These and the hearse units rode on a stretched chassis of 150-inches wheelbase. A smaller ambulance and hearse line, called the Seville Series, used a chassis of 126-inch wheelbase and was 223 inches long overall. These smaller cars cost about $2,000 less than the big models, even though both series used the Olds 98 as its base.

Oldsmobile continued to supply some chassis to selected hearse and ambulance companies in 1967. One of their best customers continued to be Cotner-Bevington. The Olds Ninety-Eight chassis was a good one for commercial use. Chassis features for this model year included: Guard-beam frame, front suspension stabilizer bar, coil springs all around, foot-operated parking brakes, low profile tubeless tires and self adjusting brakes. The landau model shown here with its large blind quarters, sold for $9,277 as a long-wheelbase model, or $7,882 as the 126-inch Seville version. Cotner-Bevington, a direct descendant of the old Comet Coach Co. of Memphis, Tenn., was now located in Blytheville, Ark. It now was a division of the Divco-Wayne Corp. of Richmond, Ind.

1968

Sales went up substantially in 1968, but the Lansing based G.M. Division stayed in sixth place in the sales race this year. A total of 562,459 Oldsmobiles were sold this model year. Model lineups wre juggled slightly in 1968 with a total of 31 models now coming in from ten series.

Biggest news in the Olds camp came from the growing performance muscle car front. For the first time since its introduction in 1964 the 4-4-2 became a full fledged series of its own rather than an option package on F-85 and Cutlass models. Although not completely produced within the Olds factory walls, the famed Hurst/Olds models were originated this model year.

The 4-4-2 series was offered this year with three basic models: holiday coupe, sports coupe and convertible. Standard powerplant for the 4-4-2's was a 400 cubic inch, 350 horsepower (325 horsepower with automatic transmission) Rocket V-8. Standard equipment included a Hurst shifted, floor-mounted three speed manual heavy duty transmission; dual exhausts; wide rims, and wide oval redline tires. Options on this new series included a four speed manual or Turbo Hydramatic transmission, forced air induction system, power front disc brakes, transistorized ignition, rally stripes, anti-spin differential, and special instrumentation package.

If the 4-4-2 model was noted for its brutish performance, the new Hurst/Olds quickly became acknowledged for its combination of high performance and luxury motoring. Designed initially as a one-off customized car for high performance component manufacturer George Hurst, the Hurst/Olds quickly caught the eye of supercar fans across the country. The initial Hurst/Olds was designed by Hurst performance master Jack (Doc) Watson. When the demand for a car of this type surfaced George Hurst and Watson quickly huddled with Olds officials and Lansing industrialist John Demmer. Demmer, a long time Oldsmobile supplier through his Demmer Engineering firm, set up a limited production area within his Lansing complex to produce Hurst/Oldsmobiles. The basic car was supplied off the Olds assembly line and even carried a warranty by the General Motors division. Demmer added the many finishing touches to the package and the cars were then marketed by selected Olds dealerships.

The H/O car equipment included a 390 horsepower 455 cubic inch engine, high performance heads,

The least expensive, lightest and cheapest 1968 Olds was the F-85 Club coupe. As a six cylinder this model was number 3177, was priced at $2,512 and weighed 3,065 pounds. With a V-8 this car was tagged model number 3277, weighed 3,150 pounds and sold for $2,617. A total of 4,052 of the six cylinders were built, while 5,426 of the V-8 powered F-85's were made. Available only in the bottom two of the F-85/Cutlass series was the 155-horsepower Action Line six.

crankshaft and camshaft, a specially modified Turbo Hydramatic with Hurst shifter, forced air induction system, oversized G-70 x 14 Goodyear polyglass tires special interior and exterior emblems and a heavy duty rear end assembly.

The regular 1968 Olds line was introduced September 11, 1967. Officials said power train changes across the board would give additional mid-range performance, better fuel economy, new quietness of operation and more durability. This year Olds tagged its two door intermediates Cutlass S cars. Wheelbase on the F-85, Cutlass and Cutlass Supreme four door was lengthened to 116 inches. Vent windows were no crank operated on the smaller Oldsmobiles replacing the friction type openers of earlier years. The Vista Cruiser rolled on a wheelbase of 121 inches. Legroom headroom and luggage capacity was upped for 1968 on this series. For the first time Olds offered its 400 cubic inch engine as an option on the Vista Cruiser.

New styling was found on the larger Oldsmobiles the Delmont and Delta 88's, the Delta Custom, the Ninety-Eights and the Toronado. Headlamps were concealed behind twin grilles which retracted upward when the Toronado's lights were turned on. Suspension changes resulted in a softer ride for the top of the line front wheel drive Olds. Oldsmobile had expected more of a share of the personal luxury car market from the Toronado and this car would be changed several times over the next few years looking for the right combination. An optional Toro high performance package for 1968 included a cold air induction system and a high speed camshaft. All Toronados had a new and simplified ring and pinion drive axle in place of the more complicated 1966-planetary unit.

Displacement for the F-85, Cutlass and Delmont 88 cars with V-8's was increased from 330 to 350 cubic inches. Engines on the larger Oldsmobiles climbed from 425 to 455 cubic inches. Maximum torque ratings on all Olds V-8's were up substantially over last year's cars. In addition to the larger displacement engines, transmissions were re-calibrated and rear axle ratios were lowered slightly. Olds met 1968 federal emission laws with a simpler combustion control system. This new system, for the time being eliminated an extra belt drive, air pump and a jungle of pipes and valves from the former Air Injection Reaction system.

There were a host of other minor improvements across the board for 1968. Larger wheel cylinders were found within the braking system of most models. A larger windshield wiper coverage area was outfitted along with a convoluted fuel tank filler that would contain fuel in case of a crash. Other safety related improvements, in an era of vast Ralph Nader influence, included redesigned armrests, control knobs and door handles, wider vision outside rearview mirror and the elimination of metal in the seatbacks.

Physical plant additions in 1968 included a new medium press plant, a new shipping preparation building and another addition to the parts warehouse. Cars Magazine named the 4-4-2 the top performance car of 1968. Toronados finished in the first three spots in the Pike's Peak Hill Climb.

1968

One of the Olds plain-Jane offerings was the F-85 town sedan. This car was designated model number 3169 as a six cylinder. Priced at $2,560, weight was 3,115 pounds. Production was 1,847. As a V-8 the town sedan carried model number 3269. It sold for $2,665 and weighed 3,206 pounds. Production was 3,984. Although lowest on the Olds model ladder, the two-car F-85 series had the following standard equipment: dual master cylinder; backup lamps; chrome windshield and rear window moldings; heater, and 12-volt Delco-Eye Energizer battery.

Although not as popular as its cousin the Vista Cruiser, the Cutlass station wagon was a decent seller in 1968. Carrying model number 3535 as a six cylinder, this model was priced at $2,969 and weighed 3,345 pounds. Production was only 354. A total of 9,291 of the V-8 powered Cutlass station wagons were made. Base price was $3,074 and weight was 3,562 pounds. Model number was 3635. The Cutlass wagon was based on a 116-inch wheelbase and came only as a two-seater.

Hardtop styling wore well on this Cutlass holiday sedan which was far more popular with a V-8 sitting under the hood. With that equipment it was model number 3639. Base price was $2,909 and weight was 3,351 pounds. Production totalled 7,839. As a six cylinder the holiday sedan was model number 3539. It was priced at $2,804 and weighed 3,174 pounds. Only 265 were built. Standard tire size on Cutlass models was 7.75 by 14 inches.

Open cars remained popular in 1968, and the Cutlass convertible was no exception. The V-8 model shown here had a total run of 13,667. Designated Model number 3667, it was priced at $3,054 and weighed 3,415 pounds. In the six cylinder division, however, the production was a different story. A total production of only 410 proved that the buyers of convertibles were not the type of people who wanted low-powered economical engines. The six cost $2,949, weighed 3,245 pounds, and bore Model designation 3567. All of the Cutlass convertibles were outfitted with Strato bucket seats covered in Morocceen, and trimmed out with matching interior panels and top boot. This particular example, well covered with Illinois mud, was owned in the early 1970s by George H. Dammann, general manager of Crestline Publishing Co.

The more popular of the two Cutlass four doors was the town sedan. As a six cylinder this car was model number 3569. Base price was $2,674 and weight was 3,154 pounds. Production was 1,305. A total of 25,994 of the V-8 Cutlass town sedan, model number 3669, were made. Price was $2,779 and weight was 3,328 pounds. Some standard Cutlass items were full fiberglass hood insulation; deluxe steering wheel; four-way hazard blinkers; energy absorbing steering column; padded instrument panel, and side marker lights.

1968

Revised Cutlass styling was quite pleasing in 1968. The sports coupe tag was hung on the two-door post sedan in this series. As a six cylinder model it was designated model number 3577. Base price was $2,632 and weight was 3,216 pounds. Production was 1,181. Once again V-8 production was much higher as 14,586 of model 3677 were built. Base price was $2,737 and weight was 3,412 pounds. Cutlass models were outfitted with the V-8 were equipped with a 61-amp hour Delco battery with a 37 amp Delcotron alternator.

Adding a bit of confusion to the 1968 model lineup within the Cutlass series was the fact that all two-doors within that series were also known as Cutlass S models. This subgrouping included two coupes and the convertible. This is the holiday coupe, the single most popular 1968 Olds with a whopping V-8 production total of 59,577 with another 1,492 six cylinders made. As a V-8 the model number was 3687, while six cylinders were tagged 3587. Price on the six was $2,696 and the V-8 was $2,801. Weight on the six was 3,099 pounds and 3,294 on the eight.

If an Olds owner wanted to move up the line a bit and still stay within the intermediate bracket, the Cutlass Supreme series filled the bill. The Cutlass Supreme holiday sedan was designated model number 4239. Cars in this series came only with V-8 power. Base price was $3,057 and weight was 3,240 pounds. Production here totalled 15,067. Cars in this series rode on 7.75 by 14 inch, two-ply blackwall tires. The vinyl top on this car was option CO-8 and came in gold, brown, blue or green. A chrome roof molding package was included with this option.

Cutlass Supreme Holiday Coupe

Cutlass Supreme Town Sedan

Shown here was a pair of Cutlass Supremes, the holiday coupe and town sedan. The coupe — the lone two-door in the series — was model number 4287. Price was $2,982 and weight was 3,335 pounds. This was the most popular Supreme as 33,518 were built. Model number 4269 was the town sedan. Only 5,524 rolled off the Olds assembly lines. Base price was $2,884 and weight was 3,334 pounds. This model had a trunk capacity of 17.5 cubic feet.

Taking a page from the Greyhound Bus styling book, Olds continued to offer a Vista Cruiser in 1968. The Vista Cruiser was a bit larger than the Cutlass wagon and buyers developed a loyalty to this model. Model number 4855 was the two-seater. Production was 13,375. Price was $3,367 and weight was 3,842 pounds. Wheelbase was 121 inches. Tire size on the Vista Cruiser was 8.25 x 14 inches. Cars in this series were all V-8 powered.

More popular in the Vista Cruiser group was the three-seater which carried model number 4865. Production here was 22,768. Base price was $3,508 and weight was 3,957 pounds. The Vista Cruiser had more than 100 cubic feet of storage space including a bit of under floor storage. Some popular 1968 station wagon options included nylon blend cargo area carpeting (B-39); rear radio speaker (V-80); chrome roof rack (V-55); tinted Vista roof windows (AA-3), and a tailgate air deflector (C-51).

4-4-2 Sports Coupe

For the first time the 4-4-2 models were sold as a series rather than an option package for Cutlass/F-85 buyers. A trio of 112-inch wheelbased two-doors were offered in this performance oriented series. Model number 4477 was the sports coupe. Production was 4,282. Base price was $3,087 and weight was 3,450 pounds. All cars in this series were powered by an exclusive 350 horsepower, 400 cubic inch V-8. Premium fuel was suggested and a 20-gallon tank was outfitted.

A pair of fairly popular options were shown on this 4-4-2 holiday coupe. The superstock wheels were option PO-5. A vertical rally stripe, exclusive to this year, was option W-36. This car, model 4487, was the most popular 4-4-2 with a produciton run of 24,183. Base price was $3,150 and weight was 3,470 pounds. Cars in this series rode on F-70x14 inch, two-ply, wide oval redline nylon cord tires. Stick shift cars, three or four speed, were all Hurst shifted.

Performance buffs who liked open cars were drawn to model number 4467, the 4-4-2 convertible. This was the highest priced car in the series, tagged at $3,341 and weight was 3,540 pounds. Production totalled 5,142. The 4-4-2 featured a heavy duty suspension package consisting of special front and rear springs; heavy duty shock absorbers; stabilizer bars, and wide wheels. Two special engine packages were available in this series, a 290 horsepower highway cruising option and a fire breathing 360 horsepower force air induction powerplant.

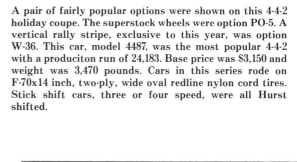

One of the rarest cars in the entire 1968 model lineup was the Delmont 88 convertible, model number 5467. This was the last year for the Delmont 88 grouping. Only 2,812 of this model were built. Price was $3,515 and weight was 3,964 pounds. This convertible was covered by a vinyl coated fabric top with a glass rear window. A hydro-electric mechanism raised the top. All cars in this series had trunk capacities of 19 cubic feet.

The lone closed two-door in the Delmont 88 series was the holiday coupe. Designated model 5487, this car weighed 3,874 pounds and sold for $3,202. Production was 18,391. Standard equipment on this full size Olds series included dual master cylinder; four-way flashers; backup lights; side markers; heater and defroster combination; fiberglass hood insulation; rubber trunk mat, and chrome wheel discs.

Carrying model designation 5439 was the Delmont 88 holiday sedan. Production on this car was 21,056. Price was $3,278 and weight was 3,977 pounds. Last year two engines were available on Delmont 88 cars, and this year the same thing existed with both big and small blocks offered. Standard powerplant was a 250-horsepower, 350 cubic inch V-8. A second 310 horsepower 350 cubic inch unit was offered along with three 455 cubic inch V-8's ranging between 310 and 365 horsepower. Standard equipment included a three-speed manual transmission, but few cars were so built.

Most popular among the four models in the Delmont 88 series was model number 5469, the town sedan. A price tag of $3,146 and weight of 3,922 pounds were found on this car. Production totalled 24,365. Two automatic transmissions were available on Delmont 88's. The first was option M-31, the Jetaway transmission. Option M-40 was the Turbo-Hydramatic. Air conditioning was a popular option in 1968 and well over half the cars in this series were outfitted with the $421 system.

A three model series was the Delta 88 grouping. All cars rode on a wheelbase of 123 inches. Standard tire size was 8.55 by 14 inches. The holiday sedan was model number 6439. Weight was 4,090 pounds and price was $3,525. A sizeable production run of 30,048 was achieved. Standard Delta 88 engine was a 310 horsepower, 455 cubic inch V-8. Optional was a 320 horsepower version of the same big block V-8.

Most popular among the Delta 88's was model number 6469, the town sedan. A total of 33,689 were made. This car weighed 4,030 pounds and was priced at $3,357. Interiors on Delta 88 models featured full floor carpeting, walnut grained applique on the instrument panel and a deluxe steering wheel. The Delco battery on this series was a 73 amp hour, 78-plate unit. Regular fuel was suggested on the lower horsepower V-8, while the larger engine was to run on premium.

A single two-door was offered in 1968 in the Delta 88 series. Model number 6487 was the Delta 88 holiday coupe. This machine tipped the scales at 3,990 pounds and cost $3,661. Production was 18,501 — making this the lowest production Delta 88. Folks buying a car this year could get a price break by ordering accessory packages rather than buying options singly. A popular grouping was accessory group Number 2 which included a power trunk opener; chrome door edge moldings; electric clock; radio, and convenience lights.

Olds had a seeming desire to offer as many series as possible during this era and one rather unnecessary group seemed to be the two-model Delta 88 custom series. Shown is model 6687, the Delta 88 custom coupe. Base price was $3,661 and weight was 4,055 pounds. Production was 9,540. Rounding out the series was holiday sedan, model 6639. Production on this four door was 10,727. Price was $3,721 and weight was 4,115 pounds. There were few changes between the Delta 88 and custom series.

Luxury continued to abound on the Ninety-Eight series from Olds. Model number 8439 was the popular holiday sedan. Base price was $4,422 and weight was 4,347 pounds. Production totalled 21,147. Electrical things on this top of the line series were powered by a 75 amp hour, 90-plate Delco-Eye Energizer battery. Pedal-Ease power brakes were standard on this series in 1968.

Model 8457 was the lone closed two door in the Ninety Eight series, the holiday coupe. With a base price of $4,360 a total of 15,319 of this car were made. Weight was 4,247 pounds. Standard equipment here included interior courtesy lamps; foam padded seat cushions; Roto-matic power steering; backup lights, and two-speed windshield wipers and washers. Trunk carpeting was also standard equipment as were 8.85 x 14 inch, two-ply tires.

By far the rarest Ninety-Eight was the convertible, model number 8467. This was also the most expensive car in the series priced at $4,618. Weight was 4,295 pounds and production totalled only 3,942. Standard on the top line Olds convertible was a vinyl coated fabric top with glass rear window; Morocceen top boot; all nylon cut pile floor carpeting; two-way power seat adjuster; power side windows, and dual exhausts. All Ninety-Eights were Turbo Hydramatic equipped.

1968

The Ninety-Eight town sedan was model number 8469. This Olds series presented really luxurious interiors. Deep foam seat cushions were topped with color keyed deluxe lap belts and front seat shoulder belts. Full carpeting was fitted and the instrument board was covered by a walnut grained vinyl applique. Shipping weight was 4,258 pounds and price was $4,155. A production run of 10,584 was achieved. All Ninety-Eights rode on a wheelbase of 126 inches.

Surprising numbers of Olds buyers were willing to plop down $4,497 for the Ninety-Eight luxury sedan. This car was model number 8669 and weighed 4,318 pounds. Production was 40,755. There were no engine options on this series as all Ninety-Eights were powered by a 365 horsepower, 455 cubic inch Rocket V-8. The factory cautioned that only premium fuel be used. Power brakes were standard on all cars in this series with power front discs optional.

The 1966-7 Toronado was one of the cleanest styling packages ever offered by General Motors. By 1968 the Toronado got a rather heavy dosage of chrome upfront in the form of a new grille and massive wrap around bumper. The Toronado was model number 9487. Weight was 4,280 pounds and base price was $4,750. Production totalled 26,454. The Toro rode on a wheelbase of 119 inches. Standard tire size was 8.85 inches.

From the rear the Toronado offered more resemblance to the 1966-7 models. Standard Toronado powerplant was a 375 horsepower Rocket 455 cubic inch V-8. Optional was a big-block 400 horsepower unit with forced air induction and dual exhausts. All of these front wheel drive cars came with a special Turbo Hydramatic transmission, modified for smoother operation in 1968.

All new for Olds in 1968 was the Hurst/Olds. This luxury-performance package began as a one-off car built for performance accessory manufacturer George Hurst. All these machines were finished in a special silver and black paint scheme, while later year Hurst/Olds were done in white and gold. This photo was taken in front of Hurst Performance, Inc. headquarters. This car is probably the most collectable Olds built in the decade of the 1960's.

1968

Two of the 515 Hurst/Olds paused long enough on an Ohio backroad to be photographed. Being trailered is a C/Stock Automatic H/O carrying the sponsorship of Columbus, Ohio, Oldsmobile dealership Chesrown Oldsmobile. The tow car is also a Hurst/Olds. Note the superstock factory wheels on the tow car and also the air induction ducts peeking out from under the front bumper.

Although the basic Hurst/Olds was built by Oldsmobile, the finishing touches and some of the unique options were done at Demmer Engineering. The Lansing, Michigan-based corporation devoted some floor space in 1968 to turning out the new Olds offering. A total of 515 Hurst/Olds were built this year. Of that total 451 were based on 4-4-2 holiday coupes and just 64 were 4-4-2 sport coupes. Air conditioning was found on 153 of the H/O cars.

A few specialty manufacturers continued to use the Olds chassis and front sheet metal this year. One such manufacturer was Cotner-Bevington which produced this hearse based on a Ninety-Eight chassis. All Ninety-Eights were fueled from a 25-gallon tank and the factory suggested that it be filled only with premium fuel. Most Olds V-8's this year were outfitted with a UHV transistorized ignition system.

Another Cotner-Bevington offering in 1968 was this ambulance. The center grille piece was slightly altered but this was a Ninety-Eight based vehicle. Olds made braking improvements on its big chassis in 1968. A dual master cylinder worked through corrosion resistant brake lines. Pedal-ease power brakes — with a larger vacuum booster — were standard on all Ninety-Eights. A new type of shock absorber was also fitted on top line cars.

In 1968 Olds returned to the show car circuit with the Toronado Granturisimo. A total of nine inches was removed from the standard Toro wheelbase. Overall height was also reduced by modifying the springs. The engine was a bored big block of 475 cubic inches and three two barrel Rochester carbs fueled this job. Olds outfitted several innovations inside this special front driver, including digital-read instruments; safety warning system; special ventilation package, and a four-overhead-speaker stereo system. The car was finished in an electric blue.

Sales were up for Oldsmobile in 1969 as 655,241 units moved Olds ahead of Plymouth into fifth place in the industry sales race. The larger Oldsmobiles got even bigger along with a restyling job in 1969. Olds offered just mild restyling on the intermediate F-85/ Cutlass cars.

Model introductions came on September 12, 1968. Ralph Nader continued to hound the auto makers in general and G.M. in particular. As a result all General Motors divisions were making some safety inroads and publicizing them. On the 88 and 98 models, new side impact bars were installed inside the doors. These units were positioned horizontally within each door to protect passengers in the case of a side impact. Also in the safety area was an improved energy absorbing steering column, head restraints outfitted behind seats and larger rear view mirrors. A newly designed windshield header was fitted to give greater front seat passenger protection in case of a crash.

Directly opposed to the Nader influence — stressing safety — was the potent high performance equipment offered by Olds this year. The 4-4-2 was in its second year as a full series, rather than as the optional basis package that it was introduced under in late 1964. Exclusive 4-4-2 equipment included a four-hundred cubic inch V-8 (rated at 325 or 350 horsepower depending upon transmission selection); distinctive outside and inside emblems; special suspension; heavy duty wheels, and F-70x14 red stripe wide oval tires.

The most awesome 1969 Olds was a 4-4-2 which could be ordered with the 360-horsepower, air inducted W-30 package. This could be ordered with up to a 4.66 to 1 rear end. The W-31 package was a 325 horse-

Introduced as an the entire intermediate series just a few years back, just a single model was left in the F-85 grouping for 1969. Available as either a six cylinder, model 3177, or a V-8, model number 3277, the F-85's were all sports coupes. Base price on the six was $2,561, weight was 3,221 pounds and production was 2,899. On the V-8 the base price was $2,672, weight was 3,421 pounds and production was 5,541. Regular fuel was permitted in either F-85 engine choice.

power, 350 cubic inch Cutlass. The limited production specially built Hurst/Olds was again available in 1969. The color scheme was switched to the familiar gold and white this year. Production for this 4-4-2 base model rose to 906.

For 1969 a total of 30 models were spread across ten series. Gone was the Delmont 88, which for several years had attempted to be a "budget" big Olds. Replacing it as a series was the single model Delta Royale which fit atop the three different 88 series lineup. In the Olds intermediate group the F-85 had dwindled to a single car — the sports coupe. In the intermediate line were Cutlass, Cutlass Supreme and 4-4-2 models. Two-door Cutlass models continued to be tagged Cutlass "S" models this year. The Vista Cruiser remained a popular car slightly up the ladder from the intermediates with several inches more wheelbase than Cutlass models. The 88 lineup went like this: four models of Delta 88; three Delta 88 customs, and a lone Delta Royale. Six Ninety-Eight models were offered and a lone Toronado topped the field.

The wheelbase on 88 series cars was up to 124 inches. The Ninety-Eights went to a 127-inch wheelbase and two luxury four doors were now offered. The Toronado also grew longer in 1969 with 3 inches added to its overall length. On F-85 Cutlass models a new three-speed Turbo HydraMatic transmission was offered. Front vent windows were eliminated on most models. The ignition lock was now found on the steering column. The Ninety-Eights and Toronado were now outfitted with a new variable ratio power steering system which was standard equipment. Fiberglass belted tires were now available on any Olds as optional equipment. On all two-barrel carbed engines there were choke improvements. Olds offered a six cylinder in F-85 and Cutlass models. A trio of V-8's, displacing 350, 400 and 455 cubic inches were offered in many different horsepower ratings. Any Olds model could be ordered with V-8 power in 1969.

Olds continued to do a good business in station wagons and again this year two wagons were offered: the Cutlass and the slightly larger and more stylish Vista Cruiser. A swing tailgate, hinged to open either as a door or as a loading platform, was optional on both the Cutlass and Vista Cruiser. A deep well luggage compartment was standard on all 1969 wagons. Fuel tank capacity in all wagons was upped to 23 gallons for greater cruising range.

During 1969 Harold Metzel stepped down from a five-year tenure as Olds general manager. Replacing Metzel was the young and extremely talented Olds chief engineer John Beltz, who had so much to do with the development of cars like the 4-4-2 and Toronado.

Construction was begun on a 144,000-square foot addition to the Rocket V-8 engine plant. Inside that engine plant in 1969 Olds introduced an energy saving program using compressed air instead of natural gas to test run newly built engines. In November of this year the 12,000,000th Olds ever built, a red Cutlass Supreme coupe, rolled off the main assembly line in Lansing.

Wagon buyers who were budget minded elected to purchase a Cutlass station wagon. As a six cylinder this was an exceedingly rare car as only 180 were made. Model number 3535 had a base price of $3,055. Weight was 3,701 pounds. As a V-8 the weight went up to an even 3,900 pounds. Model number was 3635 and production was a respectable 8,559. Popular wagon options for this year included: A-33 power tailgate window at $34; B-39 cargo area carpeting for $15, and C-51 rear wind deflector for $20.

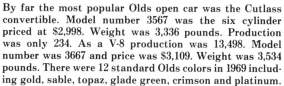

By far the most popular Olds open car was the Cutlass convertible. Model number 3567 was the six cylinder priced at $2,998. Weight was 3,336 pounds. Production was only 234. As a V-8 production was 13,498. Model number was 3667 and price was $3,109. Weight was 3,534 pounds. There were 12 standard Olds colors in 1969 including gold, sable, topaz, glade green, crimson and platinum.

For some reason the hardtopped version of the Cutlass four door sedan wasn't as popular as the post version. Model number 3539 was the six cylinder Cutlass holiday sedan and only 236 were sold. Price was $2,853 and weight was 3,353 pounds. As a V-8 the model designation became 3639 and 7,046 were made. Price was $2,964 and weight was $3,548 pounds. Olds continued to call its six cylinder the Action-Line Six. It developed 155 horsepower from 250 cubic inches.

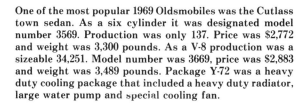

One of the most popular 1969 Oldsmobiles was the Cutlass town sedan. As a six cylinder it was designated model number 3569. Production was only 137. Price was $2,772 and weight was 3,300 pounds. As a V-8 production was a sizeable 34,251. Model number was 3669, price was $2,883 and weight was 3,489 pounds. Package Y-72 was a heavy duty cooling package that included a heavy duty radiator, large water pump and special cooling fan.

Cutlass two doors continued to also be known as Cutlass S models. The six cylinder sports coupe, model number 3577, was a low production car as only 483 were made. The scales were tipped at 3,237 pounds and the price was $2,681. The V-8 was designated model number 3677. Production totalled 10,682. Price was $2,792 and weight was $3,437 pounds. The basic Cutlass V-8 was 350 cubic inches of V-8 developing 250 horsepower.

Cutlass Supreme buyers had three models to select from in 1969. Model number 4239 was the holiday sedan. It was priced at $3,111 and weighed 3,586 pounds. The production run was 8,714. Exclusive power in this series was the 350 cubic inch V-8. This car was vinyl roof equipped. It was option CO8 and the price was just over $100.

The most popular 1969 Olds was the Cutlass holiday coupe. With the V-8 production was a sizeable 66,495. Model number 3687 was priced at $2,855 and weight was 3,465 pounds. As a six cylinder the model number as 3587, weight was 3,277 pounds and the price was $2,742. Only 566 were made. The attractive wheels on this coupe were option N-66, superstock II wheels and they sold for $73.

Most popular car in the series was the model number 4287, the Cutlass Supreme holiday coupe. Base price was $3,036 and weight was 3,496 pounds. Production was a respectable 29,193. Cars in this series had a three-speed column shifted, fully synchronized standard transmission. Transmission options included a floor mounted three speed manual, M-14 for $84; a four-speed manual unit, M-21 for $143 and the turbo hydramatic, M-38 for $205.

A dandy tow rig was this three-seat Vista Cruiser, model 4865. This car was priced at an even $3,600 and weight was 4,237 pounds. This was the best selling Olds wagon with a production run of 21,508. The factory listed several options that would benefit trailer haulers: Y-72 heavy duty cooling package - $57; G-66 super iift rear shocks - $42; G-51 heavy duty rear springs - $3; M-55 transmission oil cooler - $15, and V-89 trailer wiring harness - $10.

Rarest of the Cutlass Supreme series was the town sedan, model number 4269. Production was only 4,522. Price was $2,938 and weight was 3,509 pounds. As a standard equipped car the Cutlass Supreme models were outfitted with single exhaust. Option N-10 was a dual exhaust system. List price for the dual pipes was just $30. The standard tire on this series was the 7.75 x 14 inch, 2-ply blackwall.

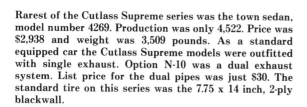

A pair of Vista Cruisers continued to rack up sales in the Olds column. Model 4855 was the two-seater model. A total of 11,879 were made. Base price was $3,457 and weight was 4,101 pounds. The standard powerplant for these Olds wagons was a 250 horsepower, 350 cubic inch Rocket V-8 outfitted for regular fuel. A fully synchronized three speed standard tranny was standard equipment—but few cars left the factory so equipped.

Olds buyers who wanted to go a bit faster continued to buy the 4-4-2 series cars. For 1969 this series included the following equipment as standard: a 70 amp hour/66 plate battery; 400 cubic inches motor rated at 325 or 350 horsepower depending upon transmission selection; dual exhausts; heavy duty engine mounts; special hood paint; strato bucket seats; heavy duty springs and shocks, and stabilizer bars both front and rear.

Overwhelming Olds 4-4-2 buyers preferred the holiday coupe over the other cars in the series. Model number 4487 saw production totals of 19,587. Base price was $3,204 and weight was 3,675 pounds. A popular 4-4-2 option was D-55 the sports console. It included a lockable map case, courtesy and map lights. Price on this factory installed accessory was $61 and it could be ordered with either standard or automatic transmission.

4-4-2 Sports Coupe

Carrying the biggest price tag in the 4-4-2 series was model number 4467, the convertible. Price was $3,395 and weight was 3,743 pounds. Only 4,295 of this open model were built. The air conditioning package offered on the 4-4-2's was option C-60, the four season unit. It was priced at $375 and could not be ordered with the close ratio four-speed transmission, heavy duty radiator or performance rear axles.

Rarest of the 4-4-2 models was the sports coupe, model 4477. Only 2,475 of this machine were built. Price was $3,141 and weight was 3,665 pounds. The W-30 package was an exclusive to the 4-4-2 series. It included air induction scoops, special air cleaner, exclusive heads and high performance camshaft. All standard shift 4-4-2's were Hurst shifter equipped in 1969.

For 1969 the Delta 88 series became the bottom line cars in the big car Olds lineup with the demise of the budget Delmont 88's of previous years. Model number 5437 was the Delta 88 holiday coupe. A total of 46,947 of this model were built. Base price was $3,277 and weight was 4,070 pounds. The standard Delta 88 powerplant was a 250-horsepower, regular fueled 350 cubic inch Rocket V-8. Engine options for this series 455 cubic inch motors ranging from 310 to 390 horsepower.

Another very popular 1969 Delta 88 was model number 5439, the holiday sedan. A production run of 42,690 was achieved. Base price was $3,353 and weight was 4,148 pounds. Standard equipment in this series included a three-speed manual transmission. Most buyers opted for either M-31 the much maligned Jetaway automatic for $184, the turbo hydramatic 400 option M-40 for $227, or M-41 the heavy duty turbo hydramatic 400 for $242.

Model number 5469 was the most popular car in the series, the Delta 88 town sedan. Production here was 49,995. It was priced at $3,222 and thus was the least expensive full sized Olds. Weight was 4,098 pounds. A popular method of buying options in 1969 was the factory grouping. Accessory group number two included power trunk latch, chrome door moldings, deluxe steering wheel, courtesy lamps, electric clock, and radio. Price was $166.

By far the rarest car in the Delta 88 series was the convertible. Designated model 5467, this car was priced at $3,590 and weighed 4,129 pounds. Production on this open car totalled only 5,294. The standard tire on the 88 as an 8.55 x 15 inch, 2-ply blackwall. Tire options included: P-26 8.55 x 15 2-ply whitewalls at $43; P-83 H-78 x 15 inch fiberglass belted wide oval whitewalls or PQ-9 8.55 x 15 inch 4-ply polyester custom whitewalls for $64.

The Delta custom series was upped to a three-model lineup this year. The holiday sedan was model number 6439. This was the biggest seller in the series with a production run of 36,502. Price was $3,600 and weight was 4,254 pounds. In the Delta custom series, engine selection was limited to three big block 455 cubic inch motors. Standard was the 310-horsepower Rocket built to run on regular fuel.

Second among the Delta 88 custom series four doors was model number 6469, the town sedan. A model run of 31,012 was realized. Price was $3,432 and weight was 4,189 pounds. Interiors on the Delta customs had nylon blend loop pile carpeting. A front seat fold down armrest was fitted. Foam padded seat cushions were used and front and rear seat belts—along with front shoulder belts—were utilized.

1969

Production on the Delta 88 custom holiday coupe was 22,083. Model number 6437 was priced at $3,525 and weight was 4,169 pounds. Olds called its big car frame the Torque-Beam Frame. Coil springs supported all wheels. The chassis was on a 124-inch wheelbase. Self adjusting brakes were fitted and all cars in the series rolled on 15-inch welded steel wheels with low profile tires.

Several Oldsmobile series contained just one car and an example was the new Delta 88 Royale grouping. Olds borrowed a nameplate from early crosstown rival Reo, as more than three decades before Reo introduced a true classic car called the Royale. The Delta 88 Royale, model number 6647, came just as a holiday coupe. A total of 22,564 were built. Price was $3,836 and weight was 4,197 pounds.

Again the Olds Ninety-Eight series did well in the upper crust auto market this year. A very popular car was the Ninety-Eight holiday coupe, the lone closed two-door in the series. Model number 8457 was priced at $4,462 and weighed 4,359 pounds. A total of 27,041 were made. Olds continued to offer Fisher bodies. Fifteen colors were available in 1969 accented by body side paint stripes.

New to the Ninety-Eight lineup was the luxury hardtop sedan. This model was designated model number 8639. Production was 25,973. It weighed 4,447 pounds and cost $4,599. All cars in the series rolled on a wheelbase of 127 inches. Front tread was 62.5 inches and rear tread was 63 inches.

The least expensive offering in the Ninety-Eight series was the town sedan. Designated model number 8469, a total of 11,169 were made. Price was $4,256 and weight was 4,372 pounds. Again in 1969 a single engine selection was offered. All cars in this series were powered by a 365-horsepower, 455 cubic inch Rocket V-8. Fuel came from a 25-gallon tank with a rear filler. Standard equipment included a 400 turbo hydramatic.

1969

Again the rarest offering in the Ninety-Eight series was the convertible, model number 8467. This was one of four convertibles offered by Olds in 1969. It was the highest priced cars in the series at $4,720. Weight was 4,457 pounds. Production here was only 4,288. Upholstery on this model was a combination of Morocceen and leather. Power side windows were standard equipment as was a two-way power seat adjuster.

A basic Ninety-Eight model was the holiday sedan, model 8439. A total of 17,294 of this car were built. Price was $4,524 and weight was 4,456 pounds. The Ninety-Eight models were well outfitted cars and standard equipment included Pedal-ease power brakes, electric clock, Vari-ratio power steering, and full chrome wheel discs.

Most popular car in the exclusive Ninety-Eight series was model 8669, the luxury sedan. A sizeable production run of 30,643 was made. Price here was $4,693 and weight was 4,515 pounds, making this the heaviest 1969 Oldsmobile. In this series Olds offered two optional air conditioning systems—the four season unit at $421 and the Comfortron at $500.

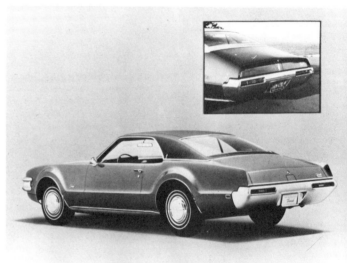

Highest priced of any Oldsmobile this year was the Toronado coupe, model 9487. Base price was $4,836 with a weight of 4,478 pounds. A total of 28,494 of this unique model were built. The Toro came standard with a bench front seat and a special bench seat or Strato bucket seats were available optionally. The flat floor—allowed because there was no driveshaft hump—was responsible for a more spacious interior.

Biggest styling change in the Toronado line came in the rear end for 1969. Inset on this photo is a shot of the rear end treatment for 1968. This top of the line Olds model was 3½ inches longer for 1969. It came only as a two-door and was the country's leading front drive car. Standard powerplant was a 375-horsepower, 455 cubic inch V-8. Premium fuel was demanded.

For years Olds had a tendency to name its cars after things that flew: Starfire, Delta and Cutlass were all airplane names. The Rocket engines and B-44 models also represented flying things. This special 1969 showcar 4-4-2 was named the Apollo after the space project of the same name. This one-of-a-kind car was finished in a bright red with shiny leather seats in the same striking hue.

For 1969 all Hurst/Olds cars were based on model 4487, the 4-4-2 holiday coupe. The H/O package was listed as option W-46. Never a very high production machine, in 1969 a total of only 906 Hurst/Oldsmobiles hit the streets. And, this nearly doubled the output of the previous year. Some new items appeared on the 1969 H/O's including a new type hood scoop and nifty rear deck spoiler.

For awesome straight line performance, an all out W-30 equipped 4-4-2 could probably outdo a Hurst/Olds. But for a combination of luxury and high performance motoring the Hurst/Olds had no equal within the Olds lineup. Items like the rear deck spoiler and striking gold and white color scheme really set these cars off on the street. Power for all Hurst/Olds came from a special 455 cubic inch, 380 horsepower V-8. It could be coupled with a heavy duty turbo hydramatic, or close or wide ratio four speed manual transmissions. All were Hurst shifted.

Although produced in limited numbers and then only in certain years, the Hurst Olds was extremely popular with collectors. This nice example of a 1969 Hurst/Olds was displayed at the 1980 national meet of the Oldsmobile Club of America in Bowling Green, Ohio. This machine was owned by Tom Bechtold of Northbrook, Illinois. Paint scheme for this year was changed to white and gold from the previous year's silver and black.

1969

Oldsmobile was relatively quiet on the racing circuits in the late 1960's—but an old combination fielded this car in 1969. Once again Oldsmobile and Air Lift Corporation of Lansing, Michigan were together with a stocker. Bob and Jody Pemberton of Air Lift owned this 1969 Cutlass which ran on the USAC stock car circuit. This pair had in the earlier years of NASCAR owned several potent racers. This particular Olds was driven by a pair of Indiana chauffeurs, Bruce Jacobi and Eldon Rassmussen.

In late 1968, comedian Dick Smothers became involved in drag racing Oldsmobiles and in 1969 a trio of drag cars were fielded under the Smothers Brothers banner. This G/Stock machine, a Cutlass convertible with the W-31 package, was maintained and driven by Jim Waibel. Helping with these racers was performance clutch manufacturer Carl Schiefer. Also very active with any racing of the era was "General Dale" Smith from Olds engineering. Dale for years was the Olds man behind the scenes at the races and he became one of the best liked and most widely respected factory men involved in racing.

In 1969 Oldsmobile continued to offer a limited number of chassis for commercial car production. This was Cotner-Bevington model 42 ambulance. This machine was built on a Ninety-Eight chassis. Power was from a 455 cubic inch, 365 horsepower Rocket V-8 workhorse engine—the same powerplant found in all Ninety-Eight models.

Another Cotner-Bevington offering was this all-steel funeral car. Again the Ninety-Eight chassis was used. In addition to offering chassis to funeral car and ambulance manufacturers, Olds built a limited number of police cars. It offered packages for both city cruiser and highway patrol models. An Olds police car could be ordered as a Delta 88, Delta 88 custom or Delta 88 Royale. A limited option list included things like special seats, air conditioning, several engine choices and a certified police speedometer.

The new Cotner-Bevington Oldsmobile series of Cotington professional cars rode on a wheelbase of 150 inches with an overall length of 248½ inches. The Cotington was offered in this year, as in past years, in both landau and limousine body styles. The landau funeral car sold for $10,079, while the combination with landau styling cost $10,108. As a limousine the funeral car version cost $9,836, while the combination went for $9,871.

1970

Another good year, with sales of 633,981, allowed Oldsmobile to retain fifth place in the industry sales race of 1970. The F-85/Cutlass cars became even more prominent in the model mix. High performance cars were also important to Olds in 1970.

Headlining the Olds performance team in 1970 were the 4-4-2 series cars. The standard powerplant was upped to a 365-horsepower, 455 cubic inch V-8. Other series equipment included: special interior and exterior markings, dual exhausts with straight through mufflers, heavy duty suspension, heavy duty steel wheels and G-70 wide oval fiberglass belted tires. The biggest firebreather in the entire Olds lineup again was the W-30 equipped 4-4-2. This package included a slightly underrated 370-horsepower, force air inducted 455 cubic inch V-8. In addition to higher horsepower, engineers went after weight reduction in the areas of a fiberglass hood, aluminum intake manifold and reduced sound deadener. The W-31 continued to be offered on Cutlass or F-85 two-doors. It featured an air inducted, 325-horsepower, 350 cubic inch V-8. A Hurst shifter was outfitted along with a 3.91 to 1 anti-spin rear end and dual exhausts. The W-33 was a rare first year performance package for Delta 88 models, while the W-34 was a Toronado appearance and performance option.

Available only on V-8 Cutlass S models the sports coupe and holiday coupe—was option W-45, the Rallye 350 appearance package. It was difficult for one of these cars to sneak up on anybody as they were finished in a bright color Olds called Sebring Yellow. The package included black and orange decaling, urethane-coated yellow front and rear bumpers, blacked-out grille, yellow Super Stock II wheels and G-70 x 14 wide oval tires. Production was 3,547.

It had been a decade since Oldsmobile had appeared at the Indianapolis Motor Speedway as the official pace car. In 1970 a 4-4-2 convertible—pearl white with a white top, black interior and special red striping—paced the Indy 500. Some replicas of this pace car were sold at Olds dealerships and a fleet of specially trimmed Oldsmobiles were loaned to 500 track and festival officials in the month of May. One of the original two pace cars was awarded to 1970 race winner Al Unser.

For this model year Olds offered 29 models spread across 10 series. In introducing the new models Olds general manager John Beltz played up the better durability and easier servicing of the new cars. For this year a hardtop coupe and convertible were added to the Cutlass Supreme lineup. All intermediate models received a styling update. A Cutlass SX package was added to the Cutlass Supreme line option list. It was option Y-79 and featured a 320 horsepower, 455 cubic inch engine, two barrel carb, dual exhaust, special fender ornaments and special rear bumper with exhaust pipe cutouts. Price on the package was $139. The Toronado was again restyled with new wheel openings, a new front end treatment and the elimination of the troublesome but attractive disappearing headlights.

On the mechanical side of things Olds introduced positive valve rotators on the V-8 engines. These units allowed better valve seating and increased compression. A new connecting rod design, in the Rocket V-8's, increased engine durability. The choke was redesigned as well. The 455 cubic inch big block engine was made standard equipment on the 4-4-2 series cars and it became optional on some Cutlass Supremes. Front wheel power disc brakes were standard on Toronado and Ninety-Eight models. On other models front power disc brakes were optional. For this year all automatic transmissions were three speed turbo hydramatics and the troublesome Jetaway unit was gone. An inside hood release was now outfitted on most Oldsmobiles. The electric rear defogger, introduced in 1969 on Toro models, became an option this year on all full sized cars. Fiberglass belted tires were standard equipment this year.

In 1970 construction was begun on a giant water clarification system at the main plant. This unit was designed to work on storm water runoff and industrial waste to protect the nearby Grand River. A ten-week United Auto Worker strike in the fall of 1970 caused the potential production loss of up to $180,000 Oldsmobiles.

Once again the F-85 series was confined to a single model, a sports coupe. Carrying model number 3,177 as a six cylinder and 3277 as a V-8, weight on the six was 3,294 pounds and the eight was 3,505 pounds. The price tag on the six was $2,676 and $2,787 on the eight. Production totals were 2,836 for the six and 8,274 on the V-8. Olds continued to rate its Chevy built six cylinder at 155 horsepower. This engine was fitted with a single barrel carb.

Cutlass series buyers again in 1970 had a station wagon to consider. Model number 3535 was a six cylinder wagon that saw a production run of only 85. Price was $3,234 and weight was 3,749 pounds. As a V-8 the model designation was 3635 and production totaled 7,680. Price was $3,334 and weight was 3,956 pounds. The standard Cutlass V-8 was a 250 horsepower, 350 cubic inch Rocket.

The most popular car this model year was the Cutlass holiday coupe. With a V-8 powerplant, model number 3687 had a production run of 88,578. Price was $2,970 and weight was 3,556 pounds. It was a different story for model 3587, the six cylinder coupe. Production was only 729. Price was $2,859 and weight was 3,342 pounds. Optional V-8's in this series were a 310-horsepower, 350 cubic inch V-8 and a 320-horsepower, 455 cubic incher.

From the back the Cutlass was a sharp car. This is the sports coupe which was model number 3577 as a six cylinder. Only 484 were made. Price was $2,796 and weight was 3,305 pounds. As a V-8 production jumped to 10,677. Price was $2,907 and weight was 3,520 pounds. Model number was 3677. Cutlass models came standard with a column shifted manual transmission. Options included either a 350 or 400 turbo hydramatic (depending upon engine selection), floor shifted three speed manual, or a wide close ratio four speed.

Hardtop styling was found on the Cutlass holiday sedan. As model number 3539 it was a six cylinder. Only 238 were built. Price was $2,968 and weight was 3,430 pounds. As model 3639 production was a more sizeable 9,427. Price on the V-8 was $3,079 and weight was 3,641 pounds. On its mufflers, Olds aluminum coated its inner walls, baffles, tubing, outside mufflers, resonators and tailpipes.

Another big seller in the Cutlass lineup was the town sedan. As a V-8 a total of 35,239 were sold. Base price was $2,948 and weight was 3,572 pounds. Model number was 3669. As model number 3569, the six cylinder, production was only 1,171. Price was $2,837 and weight was 3,361 pounds. In the Olds cooling systems of 1970, Daycron fan belts were outfitted with special radiator hose material that resisted ozone deterioration.

Model number 4239 was the Cutlass Supreme holiday sedan. Production here totaled 10,762—making this the rarest car in the three-model series. Base price was $3,226 and weight was 3,662 pounds. The standard powerplant for the Cutlass Supreme series was the 250 horsepower, 350 cubic inch, regular fueled Rocket V-8. Three other V-8's were available on an optional basis. In this year Olds eliminated the heat riser valve in the exhaust manifold of all V-8's.

1970

Seen front and rear is the most popular car in the series and second most popular in the entire 1970 Olds lineup, the Cutlass Supreme holiday coupe, model number 4257. Production was a sizeable 68,309. Price was $3,151 and weight was 3,575 pounds. Rear end ratios on this series ranged from 2.56 to 1 to 3.91 to 1. Option G-80 was the anti-spin rear axle priced at $42. Option W-27 was an aluminum axle carrier and cover. Price was $157.

Dozing under the spreading limbs of a live oak tree in the backyard of George Dammann, Crestline's general manager, is an example of the most popular open Oldsmobile of 1970. It is this Cutlass Supreme, Model 4267, owned by Eric Dammann of Sarasota, Fla. Its base price of $3,335 and weight of 3,614 pounds did not reflect the options found on this car, such as 4-speed transmission with factory installed Hurst shifter; dual exhaust; bucket seats; center console; "Tic-Toc" tachometer; heavy-duty suspension package, and matching-color Rallye wheels. Power is by the 350 cubic inch block with 4-barrel carb.

Cutlass owners this year were treated to a very pleasing and sensible dash panel, set off with wood-grain trim and vinyl. Door panels were also trimmed in the wood-grain material. This is the Cutless Supreme Convertible set up with optional bucket seats, factory-installed Hurst shifter, and the very handy console with its own lockable storage compartment. In addition, Olds offered several sound system selections in Cutlass models for 1970. Option U-63 was the standard AM radio for $69; U-58 was an AM-FM stereo for $238; U-57 was a stereo tape player for $133; and U-80 was a biphonic rear speaker for $16.

New to the Olds option list in 1970 was the SX package, offered only on Cutlass Supreme models as option Y-79. Depending on engine choice this package ranged from $107 to $172. The package included a two barrel carb, dual exhausts, special ornaments and special bumpers. All cars in the option package were 455 powered. This option gave boosted power, decent mileage and stopped short of the W-option all out performance packages.

For those not wanting the overpowering wallop of the wall to wall cubic inches of the 455 Olds, the W-31 package was desirable option on Cutlass two-doors. The package cost a sizeable $585 and included a 325-horsepower, 350 cubic-inch motor; air induction; aluminum intake manifold; heavy duty clutch; manual front disc brakes; light weight clutch; light body insulation, dual air scoop fiberglass hood, special stripes, and external emblems. This car also included option W-35, rear deck lid spoiler which sold alone for $73.

1970

Probably the most performance for the money in the Olds lineup came from the 4-4-2 series cars. This was the high-point as far as performance cars went. Next year's pollution control laws and no lead engines would make such cars much harder to build. Again three models, all two-doors, were offered in this series. Standard equipment was 455 cubic-inch V-8; heavy duty suspension with front and rear stabilizer bars; G-70x 14-inch glass belted tires; heavy duty 7-inch wheels; strato bucket seats; custom stripes, and external and internal 4-4-2 emblems.

By far the most popular car in the three-model 4-4-2 series was the hardtop coupe, model 4487. Production was 14,709. The base price was $3,376 and weight was 3,817. This version, owned by Ken Stephens of Sarasota, Fla., sports the W-30 package, which included an air inducted 455 cubic inch engine; fiberglass hood with functional scoops; chrome tie-downs; front disc brakes; clutch fan; aluminum intake manifold; sports mirrors; G-70 glass belted white letter tires, and special stripes. This version was also finished in Rallye Red paint with matching Super Stock II wheels, and fitted with the heavy duty FE-2 suspension package; anti-spin performance rear end, and the W-400 Turbo-hydramatic transmission. Being a Florida car, it also has factory air.

One of the most collectable cars in the 1970 Olds lineup was the 4-4-2 convertible, model 4467. Only 2,933 of this open model were made. Base price was $3,567 making it the most expensive car in the series. Weight was 3,844 pounds. A sports coupe was also offered in this series. It was model number 4477, was priced at $3,312 and weighed 3,771 pounds. Only 1,688 were built. This was the seventh year for the 4-4-2 package at Olds.

Introduced as an option rather than standing as a full fledged model, the Rallye 350 was available only on two-door Cutlass and F-85 models. Called Option W-45, the package included a bold Sebring yellow paint scheme with black and orange decaling. Urethane-coated yellow bumpers front and rear and yellow super stock of Rallye wheels made this a very striking package. The rear deck lid spoiler was also included in the package, which was ordered by only 3,547 customers in 1970. This model, owned by Eric Dammann of Sarasota, Fla., is missing the rear quarter decal proclaiming it Ralley 350. Otherwise, it is just as it left the factory, complete with power steering, power brakes, air conditioning, bucket seats, automatic transmission with dual gate shifter, heavy duty suspension package, and disc brakes. The engine is the 350 cubic inch block developing 325 horsepower. The chrome beauty rings on the wheels are not standard, but were added to enhance the car's appearance.

Several times Olds provided special cars for the Indianapolis Motor Speedway. Indy involvement dated back to 1933 and in 1949 and 1960 Olds provided convertible pace cars. Again in 1970 Olds was designated the official pace car. A limited number of replica pace cars—some with lettering, some without—were available through selected dealers. A pace car like this one was awarded to 1970 race winner Al Unser.

An interesting page was turned in the Olds performance book with the single year Rallye 350. Just 3,547 intermediate models were released with this colorful package outfitted. In introducing the car Olds General Manager John Beltz said, "It is designed to communicate its sporting spirit, and while we expect people to be impressed with the young look of this Oldsmobile, we believe they will be even more impressed when they drive it."

This is the end of the Rallye 350 that most motorists saw. The rather rapid car was hard to mistake in its Sebring Yellow paint, decked out with rear deck spoiler, and often rumbling a heavy exhaust note from non-stock mufflers running through the stock dual exhaust system. These big canaries still draw a healthy interest today, from both the collector car and muscle car contingents.

Wagon buyers continued to like the pair of Vista Cruisers offered in 1970. Model 4855 was a two-seater that saw a production run of 10,758. Price was $3,636 and weight was 4,183 pounds. The standard Vista Cruiser engine was the much used 250-horsepower, 350 cubic inch Rocket V-8. Wheelbase on this model was an exclusive 121 inches. A three speed manual transmission was standard equipment here.

The ultimate Olds station wagon was model 4865, the three-seat Vista Cruiser. A total of 23,336 of this stylish hauler were built. Price was $3,778 and weight was 4,284 pounds. Some special station wagon options were C-51, rear air deflector—$20; B-39 cargo area pile carpeting—$15; G-66 superlift rear shocks—$42; V-55 chrome rooftop luggage carrier—$63, and M-55 special transmission cooler—$15.

A popular full sized offering was the Delta 88 hardtop coupe, model number 5437. Production was 33,017. Price was $3,590 and weight was 4,034 pounds. The Delta 88 series had the familiar 250-horsepower, 350 cubic inch V-8 as standard equipment. Several big block 455 cubic inch V-8's could be ordered optionally in this series. All the Deltas rolled on a wheelbase of 124 inches.

Rarest car in the series was the Delta 88 convertible, model 5467. Only 3,095 of this open machine were made. It was the most expensive Delta 88 priced at $3,903. Weight was 4,119 pounds. Convertibles were upholstered in full Morocceen. A bench front seat came standard in this car. Lamps included: instrument panel, ashtray, courtesy, map, and rear armrest courtesy.

A lot of automotive value was contained in a car like the Olds model 5439, the Delta 88 holiday sedan. This car attracted 37,695 buyers in 1970. Base price was $3,666 and weight was 4,120 pounds. Standard equipment on this series included a three-speed, column-shifted manual transmission. Few cars were built that way as most buyers selected one of the pair of turbo hydramatics offered this year.

Three cars appeared in the Delta 88 custom series and the lone two-door was model 6437, the holiday coupe. A total of 16,149 were made. Base price was $3,848 and weight was 4,133 pounds. The standard wheels were six-inch wide, 15 inch welded steel units. Standard tires were H-78 x 15 inch blackwall fiberglass belted units supplied by several manufacturers.

Big seller in the Delta 88 group was the least expensive car in the series—the $3,534 town sedan. Model number 5469 saw a production run of 47,067. Weight was 4,078 pounds. The standard rear end on this series was a 3.23 to 1 ratio. Olds built it in its own plant. The driveshaft was a precision balanced unit with two universal joints. A 25-gallon fuel tank gave a good cruising range.

The only car in the Delta 88 custom series not to utilize hardtop styling was model 6469, the town sedan. Base price was $3,755 and weight $4,174 pounds. Production was 24,727. There were a number of appealing options available on this series: A-31 power windows—$110; K-30 cruise control—$62; M-40 turbo hydramatic—$227; N-33 tilt steering wheel—$46; P-26 whitewall tires—$33, and U-35 electric clock—$16.

All models in the Delta 88 custom series sold relatively well, but sales leader for the series was the holiday sedan—model 6439. Base priced at $3,924, this car weighed 4,221 pounds. The production run was 28,432. A pair of air conditioning systems were optional in 1970 on this series. Option C-60 was the four season system which sold for $421. Option C-61 was the Comfortron which sold for $500.

Remaining as a single car series in 1970 was the Delta Royal holiday coupe, model 6647. Base priced at $4,159, production here totaled 13,249. Weight on this car was 4,136 pounds. This car was outfitted with a vinyl top as part of its standard equipment package. Other standard items included full floor carpeting; vari-ratio power steering; power brakes with front discs, and a 310 horsepower-455 cubic inch V-8.

Part of the six-car 1970 Ninety-Eight series lineup was model 8457, the holiday coupe. Production was 21,111. Base price was $4,656 and weight was 4,391 pounds. The Ninety-Eight series cars rode well partially because of a combination of a 127-inch wheelbase and J-78x 15 inch fiberglass belted tires. A total of 17 standard colors and an additional pair of special order colors were available on 1970 Ninety-Eights.

As per usual the rarest car in the Ninety-Eight series was the convertible. This machine saw a production run of just 3,161. Base price was $4,914 making this the most expensive car in the series. Weight was 4,423 pounds and the model number was 8467. Upholstery on this ragtop was a combination of Morocceen and leather. A two-way seat adjuster was standard equipment as was an automatic transmission, power steering and power brakes with front discs. This was the last year for the Ninety-Eight convertible.

One of the four, four-door sedans offered in the 1970 Ninety-Eight series was the luxury sedan, model 8669. A total of 29,005 of this model were produced, making it the most popular car in the series. Base price was $4,793 and weight was 4,490 pounds. There was just a single engine available on this series—a 365-horsepower, 455 cubic inch Rocket V-8. It drank premium fuel from a rear filler, 25-gallon gas tank.

Model 8639 was the Ninety-Eight luxury sedan hardtop. Base priced at $4,888, weight on this well equipped model was 4,534 pounds, making it the heaviest 1970 Oldsmobile. A total of 19,377 were built. Cars in this series had a 2.56 to 1 ratio rear end. This car was outfitted with option C-08, the vinyl roof covering. This popular option went for $139.

Coming or going the Ninety-Eight Olds was a graceful auto. A lot of competition existed between General Motors divisions for the big buck car market. The Ninety-Eight competed for buyers with bottom of the line Cadillacs, top of the line Chevrolets and Pontiacs and the Buick Electras. This was model 8439, the holiday sedan. A total of 14,098 were built. Base price was $4,582 and weight was 4,463 pounds. All cars in this series had slightly more than 20 cubic feet of trunk space.

Rounding out the Ninety-Eight series was model 8469, the town sedan. Production here totaled only 9,092 and the base price was $4,451. Weight was 4,397 pounds. Some models in this series could be ordered with full custom leather interior. This was option WJ-3 and it was priced at $368. Option Y-70 was side body and trunk lid paint stripes. Price on this option was $15.

In its fifth year was the Olds Toronado, still the most popular front wheel drive car produced in this country. A big change this year was fixed headlights up front. Model number 9487 was base priced at $5,023 making it the most expensive Olds for this year. Weight was 4,459 pounds. Production totaled 25,433. Standard powerplant was a 375-horsepower, 455 cubic inch unit.

A very popular Toro option was the Y-79 custom interior. About 90% of the Toros built this year had this package. It could be ordered with either bench or bucket seats. Color selections included black, blue, brown, gold or green. A rare 1970 Toronado option was an F-41 heavy duty suspension package that included special torsion bars, rear springs and shock absorbers. The package sold for just $21.

Cotner-Bevington continued to offer a line of funeral cars, professional cars and ambulances on Ninety-Eight chassis. Several heavy duty Ninety-Eight options were utilized on cars like these. Option J-55 was a heavy duty power braking system with special rough service front discs. This option sold for $15. Option K-81 was a heavy duty, 60 amp/hour alternator with a solid state transistorized regulator.

The Cotner-Bevington Division of the Wayne Corp., an Indian Head Company, offered their Cotington Oldsmobile professional car line in both landau and limousine body styles. The Cotner-Bevington models were all sprayed with Ziebart rust-proofing to preserve the life of the coach and to make it look like new longer. The Cotington series rode on a wheelbase of 150 inches inches with an overall length of 248½ inches. These cars were powered by the famous Oldsmobile 365 horsepower 455-cubic-inch engine with a Quadrajet carburetor and a Turbo-Hydramatic 400 transmission. The limousine funeral carried a price tag of $10,397, while the limousine combination went for $10,432. The landau funeral car cost $10,641 and the landau combination went for $10,669.

1971

Production totals of 558,899 grabbed sixth place for Oldsmobile in the 1971 auto industry sales race. A completely restyled Toronado was added to updated Cutlass, 88 and 98 models. For the first time since 1964 a full-sized station wagon—the Custom Cruiser—was available from Olds.

On September 10, 1970 the new Oldsmobiles were first shown. A drastic styling change was well received in the front drive Toronado. That car had not lived up to Oldsmobile expectations in the personal luxury auto market. Through 1971 this model failed to top the 40,000 sales mark achieved during its introductory year of 1966. For 1971 the Toro grew three inches in wheelbase to 122 inches. Room was added in front and rear seat and shoulder room. Exclusive to the Toronado were high level brake lamps and turn signals located near the rear window line. Toronado interiors could be had in either fabric or vinyl. Option Y-69 was a new brougham interior package. It cost $157 and featured full foam divided front seats with dual controls. The Toro instrument panel was now similar to the Ninety-Eight. All Toronados were front wheel drive and powered by a 455-cubic-inch, 275 horsepower engine. Chassis changes on this model included a new frame; new nodular iron steering knuckles; coil springs at the rear, and a newly refined power steering system. The Toronado continued to be built on its own exclusive assembly line within the Olds complex in Lansing.

Olds, like auto manufacturers across the board, went to building engines that could run on unleaded fuel in 1971. Horsepower ratings dropped dramatically this year as all premium fueled engines bit the dust. Compression ratios dipped to 8.5 to 1. Olds engineers did their best to maintain driveability by doing things like installing higher axle ratios, improving air intake flows and making the exhaust system freer breathing.

If the above items were a bit annoying to the regular motorists, they were downright discouraging for Olds performance car buffs. Gone were the potent small block W-31 option packages. The last avenue of performance for Olds was the 4-4-2 series and sales fell there dramatically as 1971 models were not able to keep up with screamers from the past. The W-30 package—in rather limited numbers—was again available, but it was as shadow of its past fire breathing performance level.

If going fast was a bit tougher in a 1971 Olds, it was a bit easier to haul things in selected models for this year. Oldsmobile dug way back into its name bin of the 1940's and came up with the Custom Cruiser tag to hang on a new big wagon. This new car rode on a wheelbase of 127 inches and it had the largest cargo area ever offered in an Olds wagon. Featured was a power operated back glass that receded into the lower body. Two and three seat versions of both the Custom Cruiser and Vista Cruiser were offered this year along with a single Cutlass wagon.

The Olds model total in 1971 slipped just one from 29 to 28, spread across eleven series. The convertible began its fade out of the Olds lineup as the Ninety-Eight open car, first offered in 1940, was gone.

A few other items of note appeared on 1971's. Instrument panels were now designed with better service accessibility built in. Snap-in switches were used. The main wiring harness was now encased in plastic conduit. Suspension changes were made across the board including more efficient stabilizer bars and springs along with shocks that had teflon-coated pistons. All 1971 Oldsmobiles were outfitted with the evaporative emission control system developed by Olds and introduced on 1970 California cars. Bumpers on the new full sized cars were of heavier stock which offered increased protection.

In 1971 Olds developed an exclusive re-inspection program called Sentinel, which examined a major portion of Lansing-built cars. The 13 millionth Olds was built in Lansing in 1971. As an industry trend setter, Olds expanded its home plant capability of production of plastic parts to six dozen of these weight saving units.

Despite sagging sales, Oldsmobile kept the F-85 series and it remained the price leader for the firm. It continued as a single model series, and this year that model was designated a town sedan. Model 3169 was the $2,884 priced six cylinder. Weight was 3,358 pounds and only 769 were made. The V-8 was designated 3269. Production here was a more sizeable 3,650. Price was $3,005 and weight was 3,569 pounds.

This year Olds concentrated on its lineup of station wagons. This was the bottom rung on the wagon ladder. As a six cylinder the Cutlass station wagon was model 3536. Only 47 of this combination were made. Price was $3,453 and weight was 3,680 pounds. The heaviest and most expensive car in the Cutlass series was the V-8 wagon. It was model number 3636, with a base price of $3,574 and weight of 4,054 pounds. It was a relatively low production car with 6,742 made.

Again very popular with Cutlass buyers was the four door town sedan. As a V-8, model number 3669, production was 31,904. Price was $3,119 and weight was 3,598 pounds. It was a different story with the six cylinder, model 3569. Only 618 were made. Base price was $2,998 and weight was 3,358 pounds. As with all engines this year horsepower ratings dropped dramatically on the 110 horsepower Action-line six. This was the last year for the inline six from Chevy.

Pictured in the background are the two remaining Cutlass Supremes, the convertible on the left and the hardtop sedan. Model 4267 was the convertible which was base priced at $3,506 and weighed 3,631 pounds. Production run was 10,255. The lone four door in the Supreme lineup was model 4239, the hardtop sedan. It sold for $3,397 and weighed 3,690 pounds. Production was 10,458. This series of Oldsmobiles came standard with a fully synchronized three speed column shifted manual transmission. In the foreground is the second most popular among the 28 Olds models offered this year. It is the Cutlass Supreme holiday coupe, model 4257, which had a production run of 60,599. Base price was $3,332 and weight was 3,562 pounds. The Supreme was a three-car series now and the standard engine was a 180-horsepower, 350 cubic inch V-8. Also optionally available was a 160 horsepower, small block and a 250-horsepower, 455 cubic inch motor.

Another popular Cutlass offering was the hardtop coupe —model 3287—as a V-8. A total of 32,278 were made. Base price was $3,021 and weight was 3,552 pounds. As a six cylinder only 1,345 were made. Model number 3187 was priced at $2,900 and weight was 3,339 pounds. Standard V-8 powerplant for the Cutlass was a derated 160 horsepower, 350 cubic inch Rocket V-8.

In a somewhat confusing move, Olds offered two Cutlass two-door hardtops in 1971. For several years Olds called its two-door Cutlass models Cutlass S's. This year there were slight differences between a Cutlass S and Cutlass hardtop coupe. Despite this, the Cutlass S hardtop coupe V-8 model 3687 was the most popular 1971 Olds. A total of 63,145 were built. Base price was $3,141 and weight was 3,561 pounds. As a six cylinder the model number was 3587, price was $3,020 and weight was 3,346.

The Cutlass S was essentially a series within a series for 1971. Two hardtop coupes were produced, but just a single pillared sports coupe was built. The Cutlass S sports coupe, shown here in the background, was model 3577 as a six cylinder. Only 113 were made. Base price was $2,957 and weight was 3,334 pounds. As a V-8 production rose to 4,339. Base price was $3,078 and weight was 3,550 pounds.

1971

As far as a series of performance cars, the 4-4-2 was just about dead. This was the final year for these cars as series and the next model year this group of cars was relegated to option status as in earlier days. With drastic pollution controls placed on engines this year these cars—even the W-30's—were far behind previous 4-4-2's in straight line performance. This showed up heavily in sales figures and the series this year was reduced to just a pair of cars.

A very rare car this year was this sharp looking 4-4-2 convertible. Carrying model number 4467, only 1,304 of this car were built. Base price was $3,742 and weight was 3,792 pounds. This car was outfitted with one of the three super stock wheel options offered by the factory in 1971. They were either option N-66, N-67 or P-05. Prices ranged from $73 to $90. These special wheels could be finished in either gray or the lower body color of the car.

Remaining alone as the closed car in the 4-4-2 series was model 4487, the hardtop coupe. It weighed 3,835 pounds and cost $3,551. A total of 6,285 of this car were made. Some items that came standard on this series included special suspension; three-speed heavy duty manual floor shifted transmission; special stripes; a special 455-cubic inch motor, and G-70 whitewall oval tires.

An old standard in the Olds wagon offerings was the Vista Cruiser, model 4856 as a two-seater. This version was priced at $3,865 and weighed 4,293 pounds. The three-seater was tagged model 4866 and saw production of 20,566. It was priced at $4,007 and weighed 4,414 pounds. Option F-41 was a special suspension system which offered heavy duty springs and shocks front and rear, special sway bars and it was a good buy at $21.

With things like performance on the decline in 1971, an area of increased emphasis for Olds was the station wagon. Now three distinctly different Olds wagons were available. Olds listed a station wagon among its regular products from 1940 through 1950. Wagon production picked up again in 1957. Never a large volume seller, the Vista Cruisers began to change that in the 1960's. Oldsmobile hoped to capitalize on the market more with the addition of the Custom Cruiser in 1971.

1971

New to Olds this year was the two model Custom Cruiser series. The two-seat car was model 6835. It sold for $4,539 and weighed 4,888 pounds. A total of 4,049 were built. Option V-55 was a chrome rooftop luggage carrier which sold for $84. Other popular options for this large wagon included: C-49, rear window defogger-$63; B-39, cargo area deep-pile carpeting-$52; V-56, special locking rear storage compartment-$15, and AV-3, power door locks-$70.

More popular of the two Custom Cruisers was model 6845, the three-seater. A total of 9,932 of this car were built. Price was $4,680 and this was by far the heaviest Olds built at 5,008 pounds. The standard powerplant in this series was a 455 cubic inch V-8 rated at 185 horsepower. A 225 horsepower version of that same engine was option L-31 and cost an additional $47.

Most popular in the Delta 88 series this year was model 5469, the town sedan. It saw production of 38,298. Base priced at $3,770, this car weighed 4,198 pounds. Cars in this series had a wheelbase of 124 inches. Powering this machine was a 455 cubic incher which had an output of 185 horsepower. In May of 1971 a turbo hydramatic transmission replaced a column shifted three-speed manual unit as standard equipment. A 25-gallon gas tank was fitted on this hauler.

A few different pieces of external trim and a bit fancier interior trim spelled the difference between the Delta 88 and Delta 88 customs. Model 6439 was the Delta 88 custom hardtop coupe. It was priced at $4,134 and weighed 4,360 pounds. Production was 24,251—making it the sales leader in the series. Standard equipment on the customs included vari-ratio power steering and power brakes outfitted with front discs.

Balanced sales were achieved across the three model Delta 88 series. The lowest sales totals came from model 5457, the Delta 88 hardtop coupe. Production was 27,031 on the car pictured in the far background of this grouping. Base price was $3,826 and weight was 4,165 pounds. Shown in front of this group was model 5439, the Delta 88 hardtop sedan. Production here was 31,420. Base price was $3,888 and weight was 4,221 pounds.

A pair of four doors were offered as Delta 88 customs this year. Shown is model 6439, the hardtop sedan. It was priced at $4,134 and weighed 4,360 pounds. A total of 24,251 were made. The other four door was model 6469, the town sedan. A total of 22,209 of this car were made. Base price was $3,966—the lowest in the series. Weight was 4,308 pounds.

Again this year the top of the line 88's were the Delta Royales. In 1971 there were two cars in the series. The hardtop coupe was designated model 6647. A total of 8,397 were made. Base price was $4,317 and weight was 4,254 pounds. A two-barrel carburetor, 455 cubic inch Rocket V-8 was standard in this series. Other standard equipment included power brakes, power steering, turbo hydramatic transmission, and full carpeting front and rear.

Down to just a single full size open car, Oldsmobile offered convertible model 6667 in the Delta 88 Royale series this year. Only 2,883 were made. This was the most expensive car in the series priced at $4,325. Weight was 4,223 pounds. The convertible came standard with a full foam front bent seat. Interior colors included black, jade green, blue, maize, briar, white sandalwood, and sienna. Convertible top colors were black, white, green, or sandalwood.

An obvious problem in prior years for the Ninety-Eight series was too many models and too much overlap. In 1971 a giant step was taken to eliminate this, as two body styles were offered in two types of trim. Two coupes were available. Shown is the Ninety-Eight hardtop coupe, model 8437. Production was 8,335. Base price was $4,828 and weight was 4,482 pounds. As a luxury coupe, model 8637, production totalled 14,876. Base price was $5,197 and weight was 4,582 pounds.

In the streamlined Ninety-Eight series, a pair of hard-topped sedans were built. Sales leader in the series was model 8639, the luxury hardtop sedan. It achieved a surprising sales total of 45,055. Base priced at $5,197, weight was 4,582 pounds. The companion four door hardtop in the top of the line series was the sedan, model 8439. The production run here was 15,025. Base price was $4,890 and weight was 4,548 pounds.

New styling and larger dimensions were obvious on model 9657, the Toronado. It cost $5,499 for a new Toro, making this the most expensive 1971 Oldsmobile. It weighed 4,532. Production run on this model was 28,980—far short of introduction year 1966 Toro sales totals of more than 40,000. This year the Toro wheelbase was upped three inches to 122 inches. The new size also added space in the area of front and rear shoulder room.

General Motors and Olds stylists had done a good job with the Toronado this year. From the rear this was a particularly stylish auto. A single engine—a 275 horsepower, 455 cubic inch Rocket V-8—was the only motor available in this series. A popular Toro option was Y-69 the brougham interior which featured a divided front seat with dual controls. Price was $157. Another popular option was Y-60, a convenience group that included trunk and underhood lamps, visor vanity mirror and several interior courtesy lamps. Price was $21.

Olds performance took a real step backwards this year— but it hit other manufacturers equally hard. Things were relatively quiet on the circle track in 1971, but some good running Oldsmobiles could still be found on the drag strip. This Vista Cruiser, nicknamed the "Vista Bruiser," was still a strong stock class performer. The heavy station wagon body allowed the car to run in a lower class with the 455 cubic inch motor.

If lack of performance in 1971 bothered high performance buyers, it probably didn't thrill ambulance operators either. This Cotner-Bevington ambulance was quite a hulk to push down the road. A 455 cubic inch motor could be coupled with either a 2.73 to 1 or 2.93 to 1 rear end ratio. On cars like these, Olds continued to build the front sheet metal to the windshield. Fisher Body had no part in the remaining production, and firms like C/B did the coachwork.

Oldsmobile and the Cotner-Bevington Co. of Blythesville, Ark., again combined this year to offer several specialty cars on Ninety-Eight chassis. Pictured here is a hearse with an extremely long rear quarter sporting large landau irons. Most of these cars automatically were outfitted with option Y-72, the heavy duty cooling system. It offered a larger capacity radiator, special water pump, special fan and transmission oil cooler.

1972

This was an action filled year for Oldsmobile. An all time sales mark was set and Olds moved ahead of rivals to the industry's coveted third sales spot in 1972. Oldsmobile also paused to celebrate its seventy-fifth year in the auto business.

Sales totaling 758,711 were good enough to knock GM rival Pontiac out of third place in the auto industry. In an automotive homecoming Olds products from across the country gathered in Lansing, Michigan in August to mark seven and one-half decades of Olds in the car business. A giant parade, several large banquets, a special mailing to employees and retirees, a flyover by the Goodyear blimp and a national meet of the Oldsmobile Club of America were the highlights of this community wide celebration.

This year also brought a couple of special production cars as Olds offered a Regency version of Ninety-Eight four door sedan and the Hurst/Olds was re-introduced to pace the field at Indianapolis.

Once again Olds performance admirers had to take their lumps, with the only good news coming with the re-appearance of the Hurst/Olds. Just over 600 of the H/O cars were divided between Cutlass Supreme hardtop coupes and convertibles. For the second time in three years an Olds would pace the Indy 500. The H/O package this year included the familiar gold and white paint scheme. Standard equipment included a pepped up 455 cubic inch motor, rallye suspension, dual exhausts and a Hurst dual gate shifter. Options for this already loaded Cutlass were the W-30 performance package, a special electric sunroof, a security alarm system and a digital readout performance computer. A decal set, identical to the one on the actual pace cars, was optionally available on the H/O ragtop.

Banished from the status of a full fledged series was the 4-4-2. It became simply an optional appearance and handling package in 1972. The 4-4-2 option this year included: special hood and body stripes, a distinctive grille, hood louvers and some suspension modifications. If a buyer wanted any kind of performance boost the W-30 package could be ordered. It included: a high performance 455, dual exhausts, dual intake fiberglass hood and an anti-spin rear end. The 4-4-2 option could be added on Cutlass or Cutlass S coupes or Cutlass Supreme convertible. Also dropped this model year was the SX performance package previously offered on the Cutlass Supreme series.

By the mid 1960's Oldsmobile's model lineup was a jumble of models that heavily overlapped. In the 1970's an effort was made to correct this and in 1972 that trend continued. For this year 25 models were spread across ten series. Gone were the 4-4-2 series and the Delta 88 custom grouping.

F-85/Cutlass sales were to become even more important to Olds in the future and these intermediates were in the final year with the old body design. Again this year a new grille was fitted. Gone from the intermediate series was the Chevrolet Action-Line six cylinder and for this year Olds was again all V-8 powered. In all Cutlass models 350 cubic inch power was offered with the 455 cubic inch V-8 optional. Some chassis modifications were made and the side terminal battery was now offered on the smaller cars.

For this year there were just two Delta 88 series cars, the Delta 88 and the Delta 88 Royale. Grilles and rear end styling were revised. Fifteen colors were offered on these models, while interiors were done in either vinyl or fabric. Both 350 and 455 cubic inch motors were offered. A midyear change in 1971 saw the turbo hydramatic become standard 88 equipment. Again the Ninety-Eight series offered a pair of coupes and a pair of hardtop sedans. A new styling treatment was made on the rear of Ninety-Eight models.

In late February of 1972 Olds announced a special Ninety-Eight for the 64th annual Chicago Auto Show. The Regency began appearing in Olds dealerships in March. Interiors were done either in black or gold velour fabric. Exterior color was gold. The Regency instrument panel had an electric clock from Tiffany and Co. Each original owner was sent a sterling silver key ring and a special jeweled ignition key. Again a mild restyle was added to the top of the line Toronado. Chassis refinements made for a smoother ride. The standard Toro axle ratio was lowered slightly and carb adjustments and timing changes allowed slightly better fuel economy.

In keeping with federal safety standards, big Oldsmobiles were fitted with a new spring steel bumper support system. Front and rear bumpers on the 88 and Ninety-Eight models and the front Toronado bumper were fitted with protective rubber strips. Bumper guards were optional on any 1972 Olds.

On the corporate side of things Olds general manager since 1969—John Beltz—died an untimely death and he was replaced by Olds chief engineer Howard Kehrl. Beltz was one of the most talented men ever to guide Oldsmobile and he led some really good automotive thinking and engineering to bring out cars like the Toronado, Cutlass and 4-4-2.

After a five year stint as automotive editor of the Saginaw, Michigan News the author joined the Oldsmobile public relations staff as chief writer and photographer. He took a number of the original factory photos used in this book and was an active participant in the factory's 75th anniversary program and also several Indianapolis pace car programs.

Sales probably didn't justify it, but Olds continued to offer three lines of station wagons this year. Model 3636 was the Cutlass Cruiser. Base price was $3,497 making it the most expensive car in the series. It was also the heaviest Cutlass, weighing 4,049 pounds. Production totalled only 7,979. Any car in this series could be outfitted with option Y-72, the heavy duty cooling package which included special radiator; double capacity transmission oil cooler; heavy duty water pump, and a Thermo Cool fan.

1972

Again, and for the last time, the F-85 was offered as a single car series with just a town sedan. Carrying model number 3269 only 3,792 of this car were built. This was the least expensive 1972 Oldsmobile, carrying a base price of $2,957. Weight was 3,536 pounds. The only engines offered in the F-85, Cutlass and Cutlass S group were V-8's. Two 350 cubic inch units were available with two optional 455 cubic inch motors offered.

A bread and butter combination offered by Olds this year was the Cutlass hardtop coupe—model 3287—and the Cutlass town sedan—model 3669. The coupe, shown in the foreground, sold for $2,972 and weighed 3,509 pounds. A total of 37,790 were made. The town sedan sold for $3,065 and weighed 3,549 pounds. Production was 38,893. Standard Cutlass transmission was a three-speed, column shifted manual unit.

Performance was not a byword with Oldsmobile in 1972 and for this model year the once potent 4-4-2 was reduced to an option rather than a full fledged series. Actually the 4-4-2 package this year was an appearance and handling package (option W-29) offered on Cutlass, Cutlass S and Cutlass Supreme models. This option included side and deck stripes; black hood louvers; 4-4-2 emblems; Hurst shifter, and heavy duty suspension components.

If an Olds buyer wanted any performance at all from his 4-4-2 he would have had to order option W-30, the $599 factory performance package. It included a special 455 cubic inch four barrel V-8 with dual exhausts; forced air fiberglass hood; heavy duty radiator; front disc brakes; 3.42 to 1 rear axle, and a special paint scheme. Even with this package the 1972 performance models were just a shadow of some of the Olds screamers offered between 1964 and 1970.

A very popular Olds was model 3687, the Cutlass S hardtop coupe. Sales here were 78,461. Base price was $3,068 and weight was 3,509 pounds. Rounding out the Cutlass S series was model 3677, the sports coupe. It sold for $3,026 and weighed 3,503 pounds. Production was only 4,141. A number of Cutlass models were outfitted with option C-60, the four seasons air conditioning system. This popular accessory sold for $397.

Rarest among the Cutlass Supreme models was 4267, the convertible. This would mark the final year for the Olds intermediate ragtop. In 1972 Olds produced just two open models. Production here was 11,571. It was the most expensive car in the series tagged at $3,432. Weight was 3,614 pounds. Convertibles came with a choice of either a bench or bucket seats. Upholstery could be done in either black, white, or saddle vinyl.

This strikingly handsome Olds model—the Cutlass Supreme hardtop coupe—was by far the most popular 1972 Oldsmobile. Model 4257 saw a whopping production run of 105,087. Base price was $3,257 and weight was 3,520 pounds. Cars in this series were outfitted with full floor carpeting in a variety of colors. Lower door panels and seat backs were also carpet covered in Cutlass Supreme models.

Pictured in the foreground is the popular Vista Cruiser, which was in its final year with the Greyhound Bus style roof. Again this year the Vista Cruiser came in two slightly different versions. Model 4856 was the two-seat model. A total of 10,573 were made. Base price was $3,773 and weight was 4,285 pounds. Model 4866 was the even more popular three-seat model. Production totals were 21,340. Price was $3,907 and weight was 4,373 pounds.

Rounding out the Cutlass Supreme series was the hardtop sedan, model 4239. Production totalled 14,955. Weight was 3,582 pounds and base price was $3,328. The standard tire in this series was the F-78 x 14 belted bias ply blackwall. Cars with air conditioning, heavy duty suspension, or the 455 cubic inch motor came with G-78 x 14 inch tires. Whitewalls cost an additional $32 and option PK-5 was raised letter wide ovals which cost $86 more.

1972

Station wagon buyers had a variety of choices in 1972 and the top of the line was the Custom Cruiser models. Model 6835 was the two-seat Custom Cruiser. A total of 6,907 were made. Base price was $4,700 and weight was a whopping 5,109 pounds. Designated model 6845 was the three-seat version. It sold for $4,834 and weighed 5,204 pounds. Production totalled 18,087. The rooftop luggage carrier shown on this car was option V-55 and listed for $82.

Offering solid sales across its three models was the Delta 88 series. The model 5457 was the hardtop coupe. This was the first model Oldsmobile purchased new by the author and he enjoyed several years of good service from it. Production on this model was 32,036. It was the least expensive car in the series tagged at $4,001. Weight was 4,296 pounds. Buyers in the Delta 88 class looked at a standard 350 cubic inch V-8 with an optional extra horsepower 350 available as well as a 455 cubic inch unit.

A total of 35,538 customers bought Delta 88 hardtop sedans this year. Base price on model 5439 was $4,060. Weight was 4,375 pounds. For many years Olds offered a manual transmission on this series, but few cars actually were so equipped. By 1972 the column shifted turbo hydramatic was on the standard equipment list. The vinyl roof shown on this Olds was option C-08 and cost $123.

Biggest seller in the Delta 88 grouping was the town sedan, model 5469. Production was 46,092. Base price was $3,948 and weight was 4,324 pounds. A popular Delta 88 option was the Y-60 convenience group priced at $19. It included underhood and trunk lamps; glove compartment and map lamps, and a visitor vanity mirror. An unusual option was Y-71 an outside thermometer mounted near the rearview mirror.

If an Olds buyer desired to move up just a bit in class on the full size ladder, then he or she probably chose one of the Delta 88 Royales. The lone two-door closed car in this series was the two-door hardtop, model 6457. Production here was a respectable 34,345. Base price was $4,179, while it weighed 4,316 pounds. Although Olds built few police cars, it did offer several items in this area including special suspension, heavy service brakes and certified speedometer.

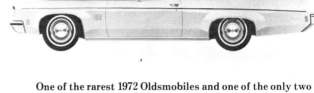

One of the rarest 1972 Oldsmobiles and one of the only two open cars offered this year was model 6467, the Delta 88 Royale convertible. It was both the heaviest at 4,442 pounds and the most expensive—$4,387—car in the series. Just 3,900 were made. All cars in the Royale grouping had side moldings which were color coordinated with the body color selection.

Most popular in the Delta 88 Royale grouping was the hardtop sedan. It was designated model 6439. A total of 42,606 were made. Base price was $4,238 and the car tipped the scales at 4,404 pounds. All Royale interiors used bench seats. Interiors could be ordered in either vinyl or cloth. Colors available in this series included black, green, blue, gold, white, or saddle.

Model 6469 was the Delta 88 Royale town sedan. This model was base priced at $4,101 and 34,150 buyers made a purchase. Weight was 4,369 pounds. Olds gained some popularity during this era as a trailer towing car. Options which helped were: F-41—a special suspension package for $21; F-G-2—special shock absorbers at $5; G-66 superlift shock at $41; N-99—heavy duty wheels for $10, and V-89 a special trailer wiring harness at $10.

A pair of body styles in the Ninety-Eight series worked out to four models for 1972. A coupe and sedan could be found in standard and luxury versions. Model 8437 was the Ninety-Eight coupe. Price was $4899 and weight was 4,537 pounds. Just one engine was found in the series, the L-74 four barreled 455 cubic inch Rocket V-8. All cars in the series were outfitted with a column shifted turbo hydramatic.

The second Olds two-door in the Ninety-Eight series was the luxury coupe, model 8637. Production on this model was 24,452. Price was $5,008 and weight was 4,549 pounds. Equipment level was high on these models and included power front disc brakes; variable ratio power steering; seven interior lamps, and a remote controlled outside rear-view mirror.

A pair of four doors were offered in the Ninety-Eight series for this model year. Shown is the most popular car in the series, the luxury sedan, model 8639. A total of 69,920 were made. Base price was $5,907 and weight was 4,658 pounds. The other four door was the Ninety-Eight sedan, model number 8439. A total of 17,572 were made. Base price was $4,806 and weight was 4,608 pounds.

As a recognition of Oldsmobile's seventy-fifth anniversary a special midyear Ninety-Eight Regency model was offered in 1972. A special pillowed velour interior was offered in either black or gold. A Tiffany clock was fitted and each owner was presented with a special key and a sterling silver key ring. Paint on each car was anniversary gold. In later years Olds would add the Regency to its regular Ninety-Eight lineup.

Olds absolute top of the line offering continued to be the Toronado, model 9657. A total of 48,900 of this front wheel drive vehicle were built. This was the most expensive 1972 Olds with a price tag of $5,340. Weight was 4,660 pounds. One change in the Toro this year was a heavy vinyl strip insert on the front bumper. Because of its limited production, yearly changes in the Toronados were held to a minimum compared to other better selling Oldsmobiles.

Under the massive hood of the Toronado was a 455 cubic inch Rocket V-8 outfitted with dual exhausts for better breathing. Although far from a mileage champion, factory literature of the day touted improved fuel economy due to a different axle ratio, new carburetion calibration, different valve timing, and ignition timing. Standard Toro equipment this year included full time power ventilation; power steering; power front disc brakes; automatic transmission, and a remote controlled outside mirror.

From any angle the 1972 Toronado was a handsome and graceful machine. Cloth interiors were offered in this series in pewter, black, dark green, gold, or dark blue. Vinyl could be ordered in black, gold, or saddle tan. An interior benefit of the Toro front wheel drive layout was a flat floor. Some popular Toro options were power windows, power seats, power door locks, and rear window defogger.

1972

Coming all the way from Illinois was this Hurst/Olds Pace Car convertible belonging to Steve Hemmingas. This shot came from the National Meet of the Oldsmobile Club of America in Bowling Green, Ohio. Standard equipment on the H/O models included cameo white body color; gold body stripes; twin sports mirrors; Goodyear Polysteel tires; Super Stock wheels in Hurst Gold; 3.23 to 1 rear axle, and power front disc brakes.

Again in 1972 Oldsmobile supplied the pace car for the Indianapolis 500. This convertible was a Hurst/Olds. It was based on a Cutlass Supreme. Powerplant was the proven 455 cubic inch Rocket V-8. Other goodies supplied on the H/O pace car replicas included power disc brakes; Rallye suspension; dual exhausts with trumpet outlets; forced air hood, and a Hurst Dual Gate shifter housed in a center console.

With a backdrop of Hurst/Olds machinery, this 1972 Hurst offering was displayed at a national Oldsmobile Club of America meet. The coupe is owned by Texan Jim Ghedi. The H/O models were options W-45 or W-46. A total of 499 of the Hurst/Olds coupes were built. An additional 130 H/O convertibles were made. Hurst produced these cars from its Southfield, Michigan headquarters.

In 1972 Olds continued to offer some commercial cars. A major user of the Olds chassis continued to be Cotner-Bevington of Blytheville, Ark. Again the bulk of these machines were based on the sturdy Ninety-Eight chassis. The Ninety-Eight continued to roll on a wheelbase of 127 inches, the longest vehicles in the Olds lineup. Power came from a 455 cubic inch V-8 which was fueled by a four-barrel carburetor.

Another commercial car offered by Cotner-Bevington in 1972 was this Seville Limousine. This car also was based on a Ninety-Eight chassis. One popular option ordered on most of these commercial chassis was Y-72, a supplemental cooling package which included a heavy duty radiator; double capacity transmission oil cooler; larger capacity water pump; Thermo-Cool engine fan, and a 63-ampere alternator. Price for this package was just $57.

Landau

1973

In 1973—based largely on a redesigned Cutlass lineup that was enthusiastically received by the buying public—Oldsmobile grabbed a solid hold on third place in the industry sales standings. A total of 938,970 sales was an all-time model year high.

The totally new Cutlass series cars were based on extremely clean styling, good engineering and Oldsmobile's traditional reliability. Gone from the Cutlass grouping was the convertible, town sedan and the Cutlass Cruiser wagon. For 1973 the redesigned Vista Cruisers were for the first time recognized as Cutlasses. Also in the model lineup for this year were a Cutlass "S" hardtop, a Cutlass hardtop and hardtop sedan, Cutlass Supreme hardtop and hardtop sedan. A new front styling treatment featured seven-inch single side headlamps, new energy absorbing bumpers and bottom hinged grilles which retracted with mild front impact. The rear Cutlass design featured large vertical taillamps. Front disc and rear drum brakes were standard on all Cutlasses.

The 1973 Vista Cruisers rolled on a 116-inch wheelbase with an overall length of slightly less than 220 inches. Gone was the Greyhound Bus glass roof section and replacing it was what Olds called a Vista Vent, a section of movable hinged tinted glass over the front seat. This roof treatment was also available as an option on hardtop coupes. The Vista Cruiser was offered in two and three seat models and featured a lift open tailgate with a fixed window. Power brakes were standard equipment on all wagons.

A pair of special packages were offered in the Cutlass group: the 4-4-2 and Salon. The 4-4-2 by this time had been reduced to an appearance and handling option. It came optionally on Cutlass and Cutlass "S" coupes. This package consisted of special grille, hood louvers, and stripes the hood and deck lid. Special suspension items included front and rear stabilizer bars, higher rate springs and heavy duty shock absorbers. Performance was just abut dead in the Oldsmobile camp for 1973 with hot car options like the forced air fiberglass hood, sports console, the fabled W-30 engine

package and the heavy duty clutch all gone from th factory order book. For four-door fanciers an all ne salon option attempted to give a European touch t selected Cutlass Supreme hardtop sedans. The $36 option included: contoured reclining front seats, ste belted radial tires, front and rear stabilizer bars, a fro compartment console and a headlight dimmer switc which was actuated by the turn signal lever.

In a move a long time in coming Olds eliminated th slow selling, one-car F-85 series. This added to deal pleas for lower priced models to build showroom traff and for the 1973 model year a thinly disguised Chev Nova was added to the Olds model list. Called th Omega, the new Olds rode on an 111-inch wheelbase. came in three body styles: a two-door coupe, four-do sedan and a hatchback coupe. Standard powerplan was the Chevy-built in line 250 cubic inch six cylind which just a couple of years earlier had been droppe from the Cutlass engine list. An Olds Rocket 350 cub inch Rocket V-8 was optional Omega equipment. Oth Omega options included: power brakes (drum or disc variable ratio power steering and Turbo Hydramat transmission.

While the redesigned and smaller Oldsmobile grabbed a lot of attention, the full sized Oldsmobile continued to be good sellers. The Ninety-Eight grou was beefed up with the addition of a Regency sedan, a offering which was a limited production anniversar special the previous model year. Regency features fo 1973 included a special plush interior trim with 60/4 split seats and a special clock. On the big cars ther were mild styling revisions which changed hood fenders, front panels and parking lamps. A hydrauli front bumper system helped cars meet more rig federal safety standards. Also revised were decklid rear quarter panels and taillamps. Standard full size car equipment included power front disc brakes, powe steering and Turbo Hydramatic. Eighty-Eight model used a 350 cubic-inch V-8 as standard equipment, wit the 98 and Custom Cruisers using a 455 cubic inc motor as standard. The Custom Cruiser wagon continued to be by far the most ponderous Oldsmobile offered. Two or three-seat versions were offered eithe with or without the traditional woodgrain side trim.

Again topping the Olds lineup was the Toronad outfitted with a new bumper, modified rear quarte panels and decklid, and redone vertical taillamps. popular option on the lone front wheel drive Olds wa Y-69, the Brougham interior package which include full foam 60/40 front seat with dual controls. Price o this option was $154.

Buyers were not the only ones who recognized th outstanding nature of the all new Cutlass models a Car and Driver Magazine named the Cutlass as th best domestic family sedan in 1973. On the corporat side of things both Olds and Fisher Body announced major 3-year expansion program in Lansing, Michiga to add more than one and one-half million square feet o floor space. In November of 1973 John Baker wa named Olds general manager replacing Howard Keh who moved up the corporate ladder. Just a month late Baker, who came to Oldsmobile from GM operations i Canada, died.

New to Oldsmobile in 1973 was the Omega compact series, a slightly warmed over version of the popular Chevy Nova. Most popular of the three models offered was the two-door coupe, model B-27. Production was 26,126. This was the least expensive 1973 Olds base priced at $2,612. It was also the lightest Olds built this year weighing just 3,094 pounds. Standard transmission on this series was a fully synchronized three-speed manual.

The first Oldsmobile ever offered with the popular hatchback configuration was model B-17, the Omega hatchback coupe. A total of 21,433 of this model were produced. Base price was $2,761 and weight was 3,283 pounds. The Omegas were built at several General Motors plants, with major production coming from Willow Run, Mich. Omegas came down the same assembly line as Chevrolet Novas, Buick Apollos and Pontiac Venturas.

Not since 1941, when Olds offered a Nash-style fold down interior package, had the division encouraged sleeping in an Oldsmobile. This novel tent package was available as a factory option rather late in the model year. Although a little push was made to promote the accessory, it is believed that relatively few of these units were sold.

Rounding out the Omega series was the four door sedan, model B-69. A total run of 12,804 of this model were built. Base price was $2,640 and weight was 3,117 pounds. Omega sedans had bench front seats done in black or white cloth or green, blue or saddle vinyl. Standard powerplant was the Chevrolet-built L-six cylinder. It had a single barrel carb and single exhaust. Seven main bearings were fitted and 100 horsepower were developed.

Carrying model number F-37 was the Cutlass series coupe. Production totalled 22,022. Base price on this model was $3,048 and weight was 3,905 pounds. All Cutlass models were Rocket V-8 powered. A pair of 350 cubic inch V-8's were available, developing 160 or 180 horsepower depending upon carburetion choice. The top of the line performance came from option L-75, a 455 cubic inch motor which turned out 250 horsepower.

More popular than the coupe was the four-door Cutlass sedan, model G-29. A total of 35,578 of this model were built. The base price on this model was $3,136. Weight was 3,905 pounds. Cutlass models were fitted with a fully synchronized three-speed column shifted standard transmission. Option M-20 was a Hurst shifted manual four speed for $190. A pair of Turbo Hydramatics, costing $215 and $236, were offered depending upon engine selection.

1973

General Motors called this roof styling treatment colonnade in its 1973 models, including this Cutlass "S" offering. Attractive from any angle the new design allowed good visibility from a variety of motoring conditions. This car is outfitted with option PX-6, the F-78 x 14 inch whitewall, belted, bias ply tires. Cost was just $30. Also outfitted were option N-67, the Super Stock wheels with stainless steel trim rings. Price on this stylish option was $98.

A very popular car for this model year was G-37, the Cutlass "S" coupe. Production totals were 77,558. Base price was $3,158 and weight was 3,840 pounds. This car was the lone model carrying the Cutlass "S" nameplate. The Olds intermediates could be ordered in 16 different exterior colors. Additionally seven vinyl top and body stripe colors were available.

Star of the Olds show in 1973 was the sharply styled Cutlass Supreme coupe, model J-57. An incredible 219,857 of this model were sold. Base price was $3,394 and weight was 3,920 pounds. Setting this particular car off rather nicely was option N-95, the simulated wire wheel discs. They sold for $98 per set. Another popular Olds option this year was U-M-2, the AM/FM stereo tape player combination. It listed for $363.

Sharing the Cutlass Supreme series with the coupe was this four-door sedan, model J-29. A total of 26,099 of the Cutlass Supreme sedans were made. Base price was $3,323 and weight was 3,824 pounds. If a buyer didn't care for dash mounted idiot lights, option V-21 consisted of panel gauges for temperature and oil pressure. Price was $31. Option V-31 was the $18 electric clock.

A pair of special packages were offered on Cutlass models this year. One was the 4-4-2 package. This was option W-29 and it included special stripes, special emblems, special hood and grille. There were also heavy duty suspension components included in this option. Cost of the 4-4-2 package was $121. This factory photo was one of many taken by the author while he was the official photographer for Oldsmobile.

The second of the special Cutlasses was the four-door based Cutlass Salon. This package was put together to duplicate some of the features of expensive European touring cars. The salon was option Y-78 and it featured reclining seats, special interior trim, steel belted radial whitewall tires, a specially tuned ride and handling package and a headlight dimmer built into the turn signal lever.

A three-seater Vista Cruiser was also available and it was designated model J-45. Production here was 13,531. Base price was $3,901 and weight was 4,392. Gone was the Greyhound Bus like roof styling that had been found on previous cars in this series. In its place was a new fliptop roof unit called the Vista Vent. It could be ordered as an option on several Cutlass models.

All cars in the Cutlass group underwent drastic changes this year, but none more than the Vista Cruisers. Just two wagon groups were offered in 1973: the Vista Cruisers and Custom Cruisers. Gone for this year were the bottom of the line Cutlass Cruisers. The two-seater Vista Cruiser was model J-35. Base price was $3,788 and weight was a sizeable 4,357 pounds. Production was 10,894. Note the new, fixed window, flip-up rear gate.

Although a bit overshadowed by the all-new Cutlass models, the full-sized Oldsmobiles continued to attract customers. A total of 27,096 buyers selected model L-57, the Delta 88 hardtop coupe. Base price was $4,047, the least expensive 1973 full sized Oldsmobile. Weight was 4,313 pounds. A seldom seen option in this series was BT-1, the police apprehender package. It features heavy duty suspension, high output alternator and certified speedometer. Price was $42.

Model L-39 was the hardtop sedan from the Delta 88 series. Production equalled 27,986. Base price was $4,108 and weight was 4,420 pounds. A total of four radios were offered in this series. V-63 was the $85 AM pushbutton model. V-69 was the $144 AM/FM pushbutton unit. V-58 was the $233 AM/FM stereo radio. Top of the line was VM-2, the $363 AM/FM stereo tape unit. A rear speaker was offered for $18 and a power antenna was $32.

1973

Most popular offering in the Delta 88 group was the town sedan, model L-69. This full sized Olds carried a base window sticker of $3,991. Weight was 4,379 pounds. A total of 42,476 of the Delta 88 town sedans were built. A popular 88 option was Y-60, the lamp and mirror group. It included underhood and trunk lamps, courtesy and glove box lights and a visor vanity mirror.

A notch above the Delta 88 series was the four model Delta 88 Royale group. Model N-57 was the two-door hardtop coupe. It cost $4,221 and weighed 4,341 pounds. A total of 27,096 were manufactured. Standard power in the series was a 350 cubic inch Rocket V-8 with the 455 cubic inch V-8 a popular option.

Two sedans were offered in the Delta Royal series for 1973. Pictured is N-39, the hardtop sedan. Priced at $4,293, weight was 4,448 pounds. Production totalled 49,145—making this the most popular Royale offering. Also available was the town sedan, model N-69. It was priced at $4,156, and carried a weight of 4,379 pounds. A total of 42,672 were made. All cars in the series were Turbo Hydra Matic fitted.

A very rare 1973 Olds was the lone open car in the divisional lineup, the Delta 88 Royale convertible. It was designated model N-67. Only 7,088 were made and soon after they came off the assembly line they achieved a status of collectibility. It was the most expensive car in the series, priced at $4,442. Weight was 4,430 pounds. All convertibles were bench seated with black, red, white or saddle upholstery.

Although not achieving overwhelming popularity in 1973, the Custom Cruiser could actually be ordered four ways this model year. Q-35 was a two-seat model priced at $4,630 and weighing 4,942 pounds with 5,275 built. Q-45 was the three-seat Cruiser with a price of $4,769, weight of 5,035 pounds with 7,341 built. The R-35 was a woodgrained two-seater. Base price was $4,785, weight was 4,944 pounds and 7,142 were manufactured. Most popular of these big wagons was the three-seat woodgrained Cruiser with a model run of 19,163. Model R-45 was priced at $4,924 and weighed 5,039 pounds.

The second closed Ninety-Eight two-door was the luxury coupe, model V-37. A total of 26,925 of this model were made. It was base priced at $5,070 and weighed 4,601 pounds. Interior designers this year worked with six interior colors for the Ninety-Eight. Colors were black, green, blue, chamois, red and beige. A new type of vinyl grain pattern was used this year. Fabric upholstery was also offered.

Climbing back up to a five car series in 1973 was the Ninety-Eight group. Model T-37 was the hardtop coupe. Base price was $4,798 and weight was 4,545 pounds. Production on this model was 7,850, making it the rarest car in the series. A Ninety-Eight buyer got a well equipped car with standard power steering, power front disc brakes and the proven Turbo Hydramatic transmission.

Model T-39 was the Ninety-Eight hardtop sedan. A total of 13,989 were built in 1973. Base price was $4,859 and weight was 4,611 pounds. As usual only a single engine was available in the Ninety-Eight group. It was a 250-horsepower, 455 cubic inch Rocket V-8 fitted with a four barrel carburetor. A larger 26-gallon fuel tank was new for this year in Ninety-Eight models.

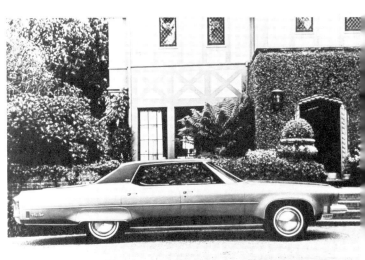

Most popular among Ninety-Eight series cars was the luxury sedan, model number V-39. It achieved a very respectable production run of 55,695. Base price on this upper crust auto was $5,163. Weight was 4,686 pounds. An unseen and fortunately seldom used new feature on Ninety-Eight models was a new jacking system. Slots were now built into the bumpers. These slots assured the correct positioning every time and also gave better contact between the bumper surface and the jack head.

In 1972 Oldsmobile marked its seventy-fifth year in the auto business by offering a limited edition of its Ninety-Eight four-door called the Regency. Acceptance was so good that in 1973 the Regency sedan became a regular part of the Ninety-Eight group. It was designated model X-39 and a total of 34,009 were built. Base price was $5,417 —the highest in the series. Weight was 4,695 pounds. Interiors in this model were the plushest Olds offered.

1973

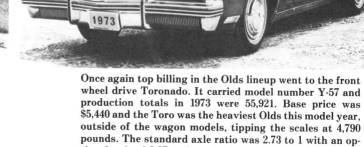

Once again top billing in the Olds lineup went to the front wheel drive Toronado. It carried model number Y-57 and production totals in 1973 were 55,921. Base price was $5,440 and the Toro was the heaviest Olds this model year, outside of the wagon models, tipping the scales at 4,790 pounds. The standard axle ratio was 2.73 to 1 with an optional unit of 3.07 to 1 available.

The Regency was a concept that Olds buyers appreciated and any edge Olds could get was welcomed in the tough luxury car market. Olds called its big car suspension "G-Ride." It was additionally refined this year by the use of new body mounts, revised spring rates and new shock absorber valving. A new visual wear indicator was also built into lower suspension ball joints to simplify service inspection.

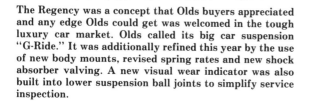

Although no radical changes were found on the Toronado series in 1973, there were refinements none the less. Suspension adjustments allowed a smoother ride this year. Engine noise was cut back with exhaust system tuning and improved motor compartment sound deadener. A brake wear indicator was built into front disc brakes. A new steel belted tire option was offered this year. It was option PS-3 and it sold for $70.

The Cotner-Bevington Co. of Blytheville, Ark., continued to offer a full range of professional cars on modified Oldsmobile chassis. These ranged from the expensive Cotington series of ambulances and hearses on a 151-inch wheelbase chassis to the lowest priced Seville series, of which this was the limousine style hearse. This vehicle could also be ordered as an ambulance or in combination car form, which meant that it could be converted from a hearse to a basic-equipment ambulance with little trouble. The Seville series had a wheelbase of 127 inches. All of these vehicles used the 455 cubic inch Oldsmobile engine.

Again in 1973 there was a Hurst/Olds. The new Cutlass styling treatment seemed to agree with the H/O concept. In 1973 this option was W-45 and it came only on the Cutlass S coupe. The color scheme was changed in 1973 to an attractive—but hard to keep clean—black with gold trim. A total of 1,097 of the Hurst/Oldsmobiles were built this model year.

For 1974 Oldsmobile retained its third place sales standing by virtue of a production run of 619,168. Cutlass models continued to highlight Olds sales with a solid backup from big car offerings.

Introduction date for the 1974 model year was September 20, 1973. New to the Olds lineup this year was a new Cutlass Salon series, a new Ninety-Eight Regency coupe, addition of the Toronado Brougham and the resumption of Cutlass series station wagons. The federal government continued to poke its massive nose into the auto business with even more onerous pollution and safety regulations.

It was a year of evolution rather than revolution as the highly successful Cutlass series of the previous year was just mildly updated this year. The Salon, introduced as an option on the Cutlass Supreme sedan last year, was expanded in 1974 to include a hardtop coupe and sedan. The exterior of this Cutlass featured a distinctive flag plaque and Cutlass Salon script. Interior features on the Salon included velour or perforated vinyl contour seats with center console and floor shift. The salon handling package was built around 15-inch GM spec radial tires on special seven-inch rims. The reactivated Cutlass Supreme Cruiser wagons were in two or three-seat versions and rode on a 116-inch wheelbase. They shared body design with the higher priced Vista Cruisers that had woodgrain vinyl body inserts and Vista Vent roof ventilator as standard equipment. The Cutlass S coupe, Cutlass Supremes, Cutlass Salons and Vista Cruisers shared the same front styling treatment with vertical-bar grilles and parking lamps mounted in the fiberglass front end panels. Standard Cutlass models had a horizontal-bar design with the parking and turn signals in the bumper. The 4-4-2 remained an option on Cutlass or Cutlass S coupes. Standard engine for the entire Cutlass group became a four-barreled 350 V-8 with a 455 cubic inch unit optional. Other standard equipment this year included: Turbo hydramatic transmission, power steering and front disc brakes.

Oldsmobile again provided the pace car at the Indianapolis 500 this year. This year's pace setter was a distinctive Hurst/Olds that featured removable top panels. The author served as public relations coordinator for the 1974 pace car project for Oldsmobile. It proved to be one of the most interesting assignments in his automotive and public relations career. A selected number of pace car replicas were offered through Olds dealers. An optional W-30 package on the Hurst/Olds included: Rallye suspension, dual snorkel air cleaner, sport steering wheel, heavy duty cooling system, special automatic transmission and high energy ignition. The H/O package was available either in white with black and gold trim or black with white and gold trim.

Although it didn't make as large a splash as Cutlass model introduction the previous year, Olds big car styling was completely redone for 1974. Cars in the Eighty-Eight group received a dramatic revision with the hardtop coupes showing increased upper glass area. In the Delta 88 group the standard engine was the 350 cubic inch four barrel Rocket V-8. The Custom Cruiser continued to be offered in four slightly different versions. The 455 cubic inch four barrel engine was standard on the haulers. Added to the Ninety-Eight group was the Regency coupe. Discontinued was the standard Ninety-Eight coupe. A deflectable stand-up hood ornament was used on Ninety-Eight series cars. Options on this luxury series included high energy ignition, pulse wipers and Tempmatic air conditioning. Minimum design changes were added to the Toronado line in 1974. A new grille was used and a deflectable T-emblem hood ornament was fitted. A special landau padded roof option — including opera window — was available. A Toronado Brougham model was officially added this year and five interior fabric colors were offered on the 60/40 seat.

During the 1974 model year Olds delivered a Toronado Brougham with the first production air cushion restraint system. The car — after a press conference within the manufacturing complex — went to GM president Ed Cole. The system, though never very popular, was pushed heavily by Federal officials. It was offered on selected Delta 88, Delta 88 Royale, Ninety-Eight and Toronado models.

In early 1974 Robert J. Cook, a 33-year Olds veteran with a strong Olds manufacturing background, replaced the late John Baker as Olds general manager. Cook became the eighteenth man to hold the chief executive's position in Olds history.

The Omega was just mildly restyled in 1974 and it continued as a bit fancier version of Chevy's Nova. Model B-27 was the Omega two-door, the least expensive 1974 Olds priced at $2,762. It weighed 3,334 pounds—the lightest Olds this year. With a production run of 27,075 this was by far the most popular car in the series. This car is shown with option Y-70, the paint stripe decal package which cost $21.

Many automotive enthusiasts concluded Oldsmobile missed the boat by not offering a Cutlass hatchback. The lone Olds hatchback this year, however, was the Omega. Model B-17 saw a production run of 12,449 and weighed 3,438 pounds. Base price was $2,911—the highest priced car in the series. Standard engine in the Omega group was the 250 cubic inch L-head six cylinder.

1974

Rounding out the Omega series was the four-door town sedan, model B-69. Base priced at $2,790, weight was 3,382 pounds. This was the rarest car in the series with a model run of 10,756. Standard transmission on the Omega was a fully synchronized manual three-speed. Option M-11 was a floor shifted three-speed manual for $26 and option M-32 was the $190 Turbo Hydramatic.

An attractive model was the Cutlass hardtop coupe, model F-37. Base price was $3,453, weight was 3,984 pounds. Production on this intermediate was only 16,063. The standard Cutlass engine was a four barrel version of the long popular 350 cubic inch V-8. Available optionally was a 455 cubic inch Rocket V-8. All Cutlass models were fitted with a Turbo HydraMatic transmission.

Easy to pick out of this metropolitan airport parking lot was the Cutlass sedan. It carried model number G-69 and was priced at $3,528. Weight was 4,040 pounds. The production run was 25,718. Standard equipment on this popular series included: front disc brakes, rocker panel moldings, vari-ration power steering, automatic transmission and wall to wall carpeting.

Moving up to the Cutlass Supreme series, the sedan was model J-29. Base price was $3,816 and weight was 4,085 pounds. Production was 12,525. Standard tires were F-78 x 14 inch of bias ply construction. Seven tire options were offered, ranging from white walled steel belted radials to raised lettered wide oval blackwalls. Option VJ-9 was California emission equipment and a special testing procedure. It cost an extra $20, and obviously was included on this California-based model.

Pictured in the background is the single-car series Cutlass S coupe, model G-37. This was a popular offering as 50,860 were made. Base price was $3,550 and weight was 3,993 pounds. Cutlass coupes could be ordered as 4-4-2's by ordering option W-29 for $58. It was basically deck lid, hood and body-side stripping. Option F-E-2 was a rallye suspension package that sold for $17 and included special springs, shocks and stabilizer bars.

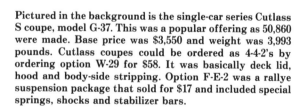

1974

Not actually full fledged models, but rather an option package offered on the Cutlass Supreme series, were the two Salons offered in 1974. Pictured is the coupe with the Salon option Y-78. A total of 31,207 of the two-door with the Salon treatment were built. This option cost $361. The Salons were Oldsmobile's answer to the growing sales of European touring cars in this country.

The overwhelming sales favorite in the 1974 Cutlass lineup this year again was the Cutlass Supreme coupe. It was tagged model J-57. Base price was $3,745 and weight was 3,998 pounds. Production was 172,360. A number of sporty options were available on this car including N-67 Super Stock wheels—$72; D-55 sports console—$59; N-34 sports steering wheel—$31, and D-35 sport mirrors—$22.

Introduced as a four-door model the previous year, the Salon was in its second year. Only 6,766 of this model were made in 1974. The Salon package consisted of contoured reclining front seats, special interior trim, special wheels surrounded by steel belted radial tires, painted wheel discs, ride and handling package, console, and a European styled headlight dimmer switch mounted in the turn signal lever.

Back again in 1974 was another edition of the highly collectible Hurst/Olds. This model was based on the Indianapolis 500 pace car and a good many of the cars saw actual duty as part of the Olds Indy 500 fleet. All H/O cars this year were based on the Cutlass S hardtop coupe. Only 380 of this model were built—making this the rarest year of Hurst/Olds production. The Indy lettering package was an option on these cars, but such decal lettering did not hold up well over the years.

Olds had several special versions of its popular Cutlass models in 1974. One of these was the GMO. Believe it or not, this nametag stood for "Gallant Men of Oldsmobile." This Cutlass carried a number of special options and an external decal on the lower front fender and decklid. The package was initially put together for the Chicago Auto Show and dealers within that Olds zone sales office.

Olds offered both a two and three-seat version of the Cutlass Supreme Cruiser this year. Model H-35 was the two-seater. It sold for $3,970 and weighed 4,485 pounds. A total of 3,437 were made. The three-seat version was model H-45. Base price was $4,083 and weight was 4,521 pounds. Production was only 3,101. The luggage rack was option V-55 and it was priced at $63.

Again in 1974 the long standing Vista Cruiser series was offered by Olds. Two versions of this Olds hauler were built. The two-seater was model J-35. It was priced at $4,180 and weighed 4,496 pounds. Production here was 4,191. The three seater was designated model J-45. Base price was $4,293 and weight was 4,532 pounds. Production was 7,013. If a Vista Cruiser buyer elected to have the Vista Vent not fitted he could knock off $95.

Oldsmobile continued to offer a variety of cars that appealed to buyers looking in the full sized market. Model L-39 was the hardtop sedan, one of a trio of models offered in the Delta 88 group. Base price was $4,181 and weight was 4,568 pounds. Production totaled 11,941. Standard equipment on this series included: power front disc brakes, full carpeting, Turbo Hydramatic transmission, variable ratio power steering, and a concealed windshield radio antenna.

Rounding out the Delta 88 series was model L-69, the town sedan. This was the most popular car in the series with a production run of 17,939. Base price was $4,064 and weight was 4,536 pounds. This car was equipped with a vinyl roof, option CO-9 priced at $123. Other popular options included K-30 Cruise Control—$67; N-33 Tilt-Away Steering Wheel —$44; VE-8 Electric Digital Clock—$38, and A-90 Power Trunk Release—$14.

The lone two-door Eight-Eight was the hardtop coupe, model L-57. Base price was $4,120, weight was 4,515 pounds and production equaled 11,615. A 350 cubic inch four barrel V-8 was standard on Delta 88 and Royale models. Optional on these two series cars was the 455 cubic inch V-8. The 455 was the lone powerplant offered in California where more stringent emission standards were in force.

New styling was evident on this rear shot of the Delta 88 Royale coupe, model N-57. Base price was $4,275 and weight was 4,537 pounds. This was the most popular car in the series with a production run of 27,515. A police package was offered as option BT-1 and it cost just $42. The Lansing, Michigan police force has been a long time Olds police car user.

One of the author's assignments while serving as Oldsmobile's photographer was shooting new car pictures as soon as the cars became available. In very early 1973 this photo was taken within the studios of General Motors Photographic. What looks like a mountain scene in the west with a functional Olds is not what it seems. This photo was set against a special projected background. The car? It's actually a fiberglass model with no running gear. The girl behind the car? She was very real.

A pair of four-doors were offered in the Delta 88 Royale series. Model N-69 was the town sedan pictured. It cost $4,204. Weight was 4,554 pounds. Production totaled 22,504. Slightly more popular was the hardtop sedan, model N-39. Production was 26,363. Base price was $4,341. Weight was 4,602 pounds. Standard tires on this series were H-78 x 15 blackwalls of bias ply construction.

Moving down the line to extinction was the Olds convertible. After years of offering several series of open cars, the 1974 Delta 88 Royale convertible was the lone ragtop for this year. Model N-67 was priced at $4,490—the highest priced car in the series. Weight was 4,594 pounds. This was the rarest 88 offering as only 3,716 were made. Convertible top colors included: white, black, cranberry and saddle.

Model T-39 was the Ninety-Eight hardtop sedan. It was priced at $4,930 and weighed 4,870 pounds. This was by far the rarest car in the series with a production run of 4,395. The powerplant offered in the 98 group was the Rocket 455 cubic inch four-barrel V-8. The lone transmission was a column shifted Turbo Hydramatic. Option G-80 was the $48 anti-spin rear axle.

A total of four versions of the Custom Cruiser were built in 1974, none of which were very popular. Model Q-35—the two seater without woodgrain—was priced at $4,665, weight was 5,239 pounds and production was 1,481. Model Q-45—the three-seater without woodgrain—cost $4,804, weighed 5,300 pounds and 2,528 were built. Model R-35, shown here, was the woodgrained two-seater. It cost $4,820, weighed 5,239 pounds and 2,960 were built. Model R-45 was the three-seated woodgrained wagon. Price was $4,959, weight was 5,300 pounds and 8,947 were produced.

Comfortable on any city street, including downtown San Francisco, was model V-39, the Ninety-Eight luxury sedan. Base price was $5,234 and weight was 4,892 pounds. A total of 21,896 were made. A special cooling package— $56 option Y-72 — was offered on this series. It included a heavy duty radiator, larger transmission oil cooler, special water pump, and Delcotron.

One of a pair of coupes offered in the Ninety-Eight series
was the luxury coupe, model V-37. Base price was $5,141
and weight was 4,778 pounds. A total of 9,236 of this
model were made. Option UM-2 was the AM-FM stereo
pushbutton radio with a stereo tape player. This package
included two rear speakers. Price was a sizable $362. Op-
tion U-75 was the power antenna. It listed for $32.

A pair of Regency models were the highlight of the
Ninety-Eight series. Shown is model X-37, the Regency
coupe. It was priced at $5,403 and weighed 4,789 pounds.
A total of 10,719 were made. The Regency sedan was even
more popular, with 24,310 produced. Model number X-39
was base priced at $5,496, making it the most costly in the
series. Weight was 4,802 pounds. For cold climates option
KO-5, an engine block heater, was offered for $10.

Not particularly attractive, but none the less offered in
the Ninety-Eight lineup late in the model year was this
special coupe model. Olds called this treatment the
Elegance. It could be ordered on either the Luxury or
Regency coupe. A factory press release said, "the opera
roof treatment provides more privacy and adds to the
car's distinctiveness." The special padded roof was made
of leather grained vinyl and could be ordered in any one of
seven colors.

Olds stayed with its high level lights in its 1974
Toronados. Several improvements were made in the braking system this year. Semi-metallic disc brake pads
became standard equipment. Option JL-9 was the optional
True Track Braking System. It cost $190 and monitored
braking action and prevented lockup. Brake wear indicators introduced in 1973, were standard equipment and
provided an audible warning when front disc pads needed
replacement.

The standard Toronado carried the designation of
Custom, as model Y-57. Price was $5,559, the most expen-
sive Olds for this year. Weight was 4,838 pounds. Total
Toro production for 1974 was 27,582. A popular Toronado
option was Y-60, the convenience light/mirror group. It included a visor vanity mirror, trunk and underhood lamps,
door courtesy lights and open-door warning lights.
Another option was Y-67, a low washer fluid/fuel level and
headlamp-on indicator. Price was $22.

There were several options that made the 1974 Toronado an even more attractive car. This was one, the landau roof with the opera window treatment. It was option CB-4 and sold for $363. A special Brougham interior package was V1-J, and it sold for $154. The Brougham interior was based on a full foam 60/40 divided front seat. Power windows were another popular Toro feature. They were option A-31 and sold for $129.

A very rare option in the top of the line Olds model was CA-1, the sliding electric sunroof. One reason this was so rarely ordered was the price, a sizable $589. To order this option, power windows had to be fitted as well. In the special use section of the option list was F-41, the heavy duty suspension system. It was suggested for strenuous use, trailer towing, and heavy trunk loading. It included heavy duty torsion bars, larger shock absorbers and heavier rear springs and stabilizer bars.

A pair of specially built Hurst/Oldsmobiles paced the Indianapolis 500 in 1974. The unique T-top treatment was stylish and allowed race officials to use a partially open car, but engineers had to beef the chassis up to make up for structural loss from the roof cutting. Cars like this were not offered for sale, but a limited number of H/O coupes were built this year. Driver of this car was Indy 500 veteran Jim Rathman. The author had the chance to drive this car around the Indy oval in a private session in 1974.

It is far more complicated than imagined to provide pace cars for the Indy 500. More than a handful of cars are needed, as this photo shows only a portion of the special cars Olds brought to Indianapolis for the month of May. Some were Hurst/Oldsmobiles. Others were full sized 88 convertibles. The author, who had to do a great deal of photo work at the racetrack, had a specially built and trimmed Custom Cruiser with a roof mounted photo platform.

A very special handbuilt Olds was provided for late Indy 500 track owner Tony Hulman. This was a Cutlass Salon that was modified to Hulman's specs by the Olds engineering garage. One special feature of this car was swivel bucket seats which were not normally offered on four doors. Since all the other Cutlasses used at Indy were two doors, this car had special stripes as well.

Government continued to intrude on the auto business and one thing long pushed by the Feds was an air bag system. A specially built Toronado, outfitted with an air cusion system, was presented to GM president Ed Cole by Olds officials. The air cushion system was offered for several years by Olds on a variety of models and it proved to be one of the least popular options ever listed in the factory accessory books.

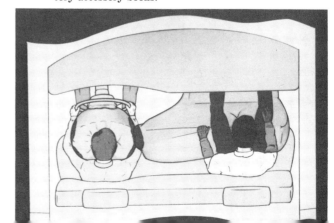

1975

Third place in the industry sales race again belonged to Oldsmobile by virtue of 628,720 sales. Big mover in the Olds lineup continued to be Cutlass cars, with the Supreme series again topping the popular intermediate group. Full sized autos gave Olds a sales backup for the year.

Big news in this model year came with the introduction of the new Starfire, which was a re-designed version of the Chevy Monza. Rolling on a wheelbase of 97 inches, the Starfire was the smallest car built by the division since the Curved Dash was dropped in 1908. The nameplate was a familiar one for Olds followers as it was used for a 1950's dreamcar, mid-1950's convertibles, and also used on 1957 Ninety-Eight models.

Oldsmobile's newest car was powered by a 231 cubic inch V-6 motor hooked to either a four-speed manual transmission or a three-speed Turbo Hydramatic. Dual rectangular headlamps were set in a soft plastic front end. Functional louvers were found in the rear quarter area to exit air from the passenger compartment. An energy absorbing rear bumper was also surrounded by a special resilient plastic. All Starfires were hatchback coupes outfitted with high backed bucket seats covered with either vinyl, velour or leather. A space-saver tire and inflator bottle were stored in the right rear quarter well. Front disc and rear drums were fitted with 13-inch steel belted radial tires as standard equipment.

Moving up the Olds model lineup by size, the Omega group offered three body styles — coupe, hatchback and sedan — in either standard or Salon trim. A major restyle job was done on this series. This was a 111-inch wheelbased auto powered with a standard 250 cubic inch inline six cylinder. Optional were 260 or 350 cubic inch Olds V-8's. Transmission selection included a three-speed manual unit either floor or column shifted with the Turbo Hydramatic optional. Salon offerings featured reclining front contour bucket seats, head-lamp dimmer switch built into the turn signal lever, a center console, special steering wheel and special suspension package. Variable speed pulse windshield wipers, power door locks, power windows, power trunk

New to the Oldsmobile lineup this year was the Starfire, the smallest car built by Olds since the days of the Curved Dash. To start with, Starfire power came from a 231 cubic inch V-6 powerplant, later a four cylinder would be offered. Brakes were power assisted and self adjusting, discs in front and drums at the rear. A dual master cylinder was fitted with a dash warning light. Rear axle ratio was 2.56 to 1.

lid release and a "headlamp-on" reminder system were all available on Omega models for the first time in 1975

Oldsmobile officials continued to realize the Cutlass lineup was its bread and butter and 11 Cutlass models were available from four basic body styles. Series offerings included: the Cutlass, Cutlass S, Cutlass Supreme, Cutlass Salon and Vista Cruiser. Back in the intermediate lineup for this year was a 250 cubic inch L-six cylinder and the three-speed manual transmission was again standard equipment except on the Salon and Vista Cruisers. Optionally available on various Cutlass models were the 260, 350 and 455 cubic inch Olds built motors. Slight grille variations were made within the Cutlass group to distinguish the various series. Swivel bucket seats were available on coupes. Tempmatic air conditioning, introduced on full sized cars in 1974, was available on Cutlass models in 1975.

Olds stayed with the same basic full sized lineup in this year, again offering the Delta 88, Delta 88 Royale, Custom Cruiser and Ninety-Eight series. Sedans this year featured a new upper body styling treatment with more side glass. All 88 cars came standard with the 350 cubic inch V-8, while Custom Cruiser and Ninety-Eights were built with the 455 cubic inch engine. Two-way electric power seats, power windows, power steering and power brakes were all standard equipment on the Ninety-Eight models.

Rounding out the product lineup was the luxury Toronado and two models were officially listed the Custom Coupe and Brougham Coupe. Both were fitted with opera windows. The Brougham came with a 60/40 dual controlled seat. Horizontal taillamps were used and vertical chrome bumper bars with body colored inserts were added. The 455 cubic inch engine and Turbo Hydramatic transmission were standard equipment. A new option was a theft deterrent system that featured flashing exterior car lamps and rapid horn blowing in the event of an attempted forced entry. The system was armed by locking the door with the key. It also monitored improper opening of the trunk or hood.

Several milestones were passed in 1975 by Oldsmobile. With sales totals mounting each year, Olds built its 16 millionth car during this year. The first Olds built in 1897 was an open air model and the first closed cars were very rare and didn't appear at all until 1908. The end of open Oldsmobiles came this model year as the last Olds convertible—a red Delta 88 Royale—rolled off the Lansing assembly line July 11, 1975. A combination of improved factory air conditioning and increased safety regulation had sent convertible sales on a slide for the past decade and at Olds another era had officially ended.

Some specially built Oldsmobiles came from Lansing, as 32 Toronado chassis were packaged for motor homes and 150 Ninety-Eight chassis were sold to Cotner-Bevington for ambulance and hearse construction. A 1975 Hurst/Olds—marking the last time for several years this model would be offered—saw a sizable production run of 2,535. The cost of the Hurst package was $1,095 over the base price of the J-57 Cutlass Supreme hardtop coupe it was built on.

The Starfire was designated model DO-7. It weighed 2,937 pounds and cost $4,156. The new car was fairly well received as 31,081 were sold. Olds dealers wanted a small car as a showroom traffic builder and often used the Starfire to move customers up to Cutlass models where profit margins were better. With some option loading, this model could approach $7,000, and most Cutlass models could be had for that.

A complete restyle job was added to the Omega this model year and Salon packages were offered in each of the three body styles. The standard sedan was designated B-69. It was priced at $3,463 and tipped the scales at 3,471 pounds. A total of 13,971 were made, making it the most popular car in the series. Standard powerplant on this model continued to be the Chevrolet-built in-line 250 cubic inch six cylinder.

Olds figured that if Cutlass buyers went for the Salon package during the past two years, perhaps Omega people would order a bit fancier version as well. The Salon Omega sedan was model C-69 and sales amounted to a disappointing 1,758. Base price was $4,205 and weight was 3,561 pounds. The Salon models came standard with a Turbo Hydramatic transmission and a lot fancier interior trim. There was also a special suspension system in place.

One of the most utilitarian cars in the entire 1975 Olds lineup was the little Omega hatchback coupe. It was designated model B-17 in standard form. Price was $3,435 and weight was 3,426 pounds. Production was 6,287. As a Salon the Omega hatchback was C-17. Weight was 3,601 pounds and cost was $4,310. An AM radio was option U69 in this series and cost $69. A rear speaker cost an additional $19.

Another relatively popular Omega was the coupe. The standard version was designated model B-27. It weighed 3,518 pounds and sold for $3,558. A total of 15,979 were built. As a Salon Coupe, the model number was C-27. Weight was 3,512 pounds and price was $4,194. Production amounted to only 2,176. This particular car is fitted with the padded vinyl roof, option CO-8 which sold for $82.

The bottom of the line Olds intermediate now was the Cutlass series. Model F-37 was the Colonnade hardtop coupe. It sold for $3,755 and weighed 3,773 pounds. Production was 12,797. At least partially because of the fuel crunch Olds went back to the 250 cubic inch six cylinder and manual transmission as standard Cutlass equipment in 1975. Power steering remained part of the standard equipment package this year.

A fairly good sales mark of 30,144 was set by the Cutlass series sedan, model G-29. Base price here was $3,820 and weight was 3,845 pounds. If the buyer did not want the Chevy-built six cylinder powerplant, a trio of Olds Rocket V-8's could be optionally ordered. These included 260, 350 and 455 engines. Prices on these engine choices ranged from $78 to $298.

Carrying designation G-37 was the Cutlass S coupe. It was priced at $3,852 and weighed 3,779 pounds. Production was 42,921. This was one of the models that could be ordered with the 4-4-2 appearance package. This was option W-29 and cost the buyer $128. It was available with any engine selection in 1975 so there may even be some six cylinder 4-4-2's running around somewhere!

While not nearly as popular as its sister car the coupe, the Cutlass Supreme sedan was back for another year. Model J-29 sold for $4,104 and weighed 3,891 pounds. Production totaled 15,517. In this series Olds offered a number of special use options. They included two special suspension systems, special shock absorbers, wider and heavier wheels, a special trailer wiring harness and a heavy duty cooling system.

For the third consecutive year Cutlass buyers went absolutely wild for the Cutlass Supreme coupe. This year's sales totals were 150,874—a larger output than the entire Olds lineup in years not so distantly past. This was model J-57 and it was priced at $4,047. Weight was 3,793. This particular car rides on the popular Super Stock Wheels, option N-72 which sold for $69 a set.

Offering a bit more than the standard Cutlass Supreme were the Salon models for 1975. Model K-57 was the coupe. It cost $4,654 and weighed 4,033 pounds. A total of 39,050 were made. A popular option shown on this car was CB-1 the landau vinyl roof. It cost $110 and included a special body paint stripe. Option NO-5 was a locking fuel cap which cost $6.

Rounding out the Cutlass Supreme Salon offerings was the hardtop sedan, model K-29. This was the most expensive car in the series tagged at $4,726. It weighed 4,133 pounds and 5,810 were built. The driver that wanted to be informed of underhood conditions on his Olds ordered option U-21, instrument group gauges. It cost $33 and replaced dashboard idiot lights.

Most popular Hurst/Olds offering to date was this sharp 1975 model. Production run was 2,535. Each H/O of this year was built on a J-57 Cutlass Supreme hardtop coupe. Not every year produced a Hurst/Olds, but when they were offered, they usually did not last very long on the showroom floor. The Hurst conversation cost $1,095 over the list price of the standard Cutlass Supreme in 1975.

Olds was in its last year of convertible production, but this T-top was another way of building an open air Oldsmobile. This concept was taken from the previous year's Indy 500 pace car. The unit was called the "Hurst Hatch" roof. It had two removable tinted safety glass panels backed by a heavily padded vinyl top. The panels were stored in a special case located in the trunk. The H/O came in either black or white with gold stripes.

Slightly more popular than the Cutlass Cruiser models were the Vista Cruisers. Model designation was J-35. Production on this Olds hauler was 14,189. Base price was $4,790 and weight was 4,496. The optional roof rack on this car was option V-55 in the Olds accessory book. It could be installed on any Cutlass series wagon and cost $68.

A pair of Cutlass Cruiser wagons were again offered in 1975, a two-seater and a three-seater. Model number was H-35, weight was 4,492 pounds and base price was $4,678. A total of 8,329 were built. Option B-36 was a special luggage compartment made for station wagons. It cost $9. A locking rear storage compartment was available only on two seat models as option V-56. It listed for $13.

Bread and butter Olds sales continued to come from the full sized Oldsmobiles this year. Sales leader in the Delta 88 series was its least expensive offering, the town sedan. Base priced at $4,787 this car was designated model L-69. It weighed 4,496 pounds. A total of 16,112 were built. Standard tire for this series was the HR-78x15 GM spec steel belted radial blackwall. Several tire options could be ordered.

1975

The Delta 88 hardtop coupe was model L-57. It was base priced at $4,843 and had a production run of 8,522. Weight on this model was 4,483. The Delta came standard with the tried and true 350 cubic inch Rocket V-8. For 1975 standard equipment also included the electronic, high energy ignition system that had been a successful Olds option in past years.

Sales leader in the four-model Delta 88 Royale group was the hardtop sedan. It carried model number N-39 and was responsible for 32,481 sales. Base price was $5,064 and weight was 4,946. Wheelbase on the 88 series cars was 124 inches with overall length of just over 226 inches. Regular rear axle ratio was 2.73 to one.

The Delta 88 Royale coupe was model N-57. A total of 23,465 of this model were built in 1975. Base price was $4,998 and weight was 4,526 pounds. A hardtop sedan was also offered in this series and was model N-67. It was the least popular car in the series priced at $4,927 and weighing 4,525 pounds. Production totaled 7,181.

Rounding out the Delta 88 series was the hardtop sedan, model L-39. A total of 9,283 of this rather routine Olds were produced. Base price was $4,904 and weight was 4,544. A pair of option wheel disc could be had on this series. PA-3 were the optional deluxe hubcaps which sold for $35. The fancier N-95 simulated wire wheel discs sold for $89 and were a favorite target for hubcap thieves.

An era came to an end for Oldsmobile in 1975 as in July the final convertible rolled off the Lansing main plant assembly line. The convertible sold for $5,213, making it the most expensive Delta 88 Royale offered. Weight was 4,595 pounds and production was just 21,038. The Royales were decently outfitted cars with standard equipment including power steering, power front disc brakes, deluxe steering wheel, steel belted radial tires and a 350 cubic inch V-8.

The largest Olds built this year was the Custom Cruiser station wagon. Carrying model number Q-35, a total of 16,068 were made. Base price was $5,426 and weight was 5,223 pounds. The cruiser could be ordered with or without woodgrain side decals and in either a two or three seat version. Options included a power operated tailgate, rooftop luggage carrier and rear window defogger.

Model X-37 was the Regency Coupe, part of the Ninety-Eight series. Base price was $6,225 and this was one of two coupes offered in this group for 1975. Weight was 4,761 pounds and production was 16,697. All Ninety-Eights rode on their own exclusive 127-inch wheelbase and extended over 232 inches long. The lone engine offered in the series was again a four barrel version of the 455 cubic inch motor.

Initially the Regency was introduced 1972 as a special anniversary model. It proved to be such a welcome addition to the top end of the Olds lineup that it stayed on. Model X-39 was the Regency sedan, the top seller in the Ninety-Eight group. It had sales of 35,264. A base price of $6,366 made it the most costly car in the series. Weight was 4,895 pounds.

Model V-39 was the Ninety-Eight luxury sedan. It sold for $6,104 and weighed 4,883 pounds. Production was 18,091. These were well equipped cars with standard items like power steering and brakes, remote control rear mirror, power driver's seat, courtesy and map lights, steel belted radial tires, and inside hood release.

Rarest among the four Ninety-Eight offerings was the Luxury Coupe. Model V-37 had a production total of just 8,798. Base price was $5,963 and weight was 4,731 pounds. A good number of cars in this series were outfitted with either option C-60, Four Season air conditioning for $487 or option C-65 Tempmatic air conditioning for $524. Option C-49 was the $73 rear defogger.

This year the Toronado series offered a pair of slightly different models. The custom was tagged model Y-57. It sold for $6,536 and weighed 4,787 pounds. A total of 4,419 were made. The Toro continued to be one of the few cars built in America with front wheel drive. A popular Toro option was radio UM-2—the AM-FM stereo radio and tape player. It was a costly unit priced at $363.

From the rear the Ninety-Eight series cars received a restyle for 1975. Upon minor impact, the taillights moved with the new bumper system into flexible soft plastic rear quarter end caps. Rear end ratios available on this series included either 2.56 to one or 2.73 to one. All cars in this series had deflectable stand up hood ornaments.

Top of the line for the 1975 Olds lineup was the Toronado Brougham. It was model Z-57 and saw a production run of 18,882. Base price was $6,766—the most expensive Olds ever built. Weight was 4,792 pounds. A new theft deterrent system was offered this year on Oldsmobiles. It flashed car lights and blew the horn if someone tampered with the doors, hood or trunk. This was option UA-6 and cost just over $100.

Since introduction of the Rocket V-8 in 1949, Oldsmobile had been a solid leader in V-8 engine technology. For 1975 the emphasis was more and more on economy, so Olds brought out a gas stingy version of the V-8. This powerplant was fitted with a two-barrel carb and was the standard motor in Salon models, while optional on other series.

The swivel bucket seats had been offered for several years in Cutlass models, but in 1975 removable and reversible seat cushions were now an option. This option could be had on either the Cutlass S coupe or Cutlass Supreme coupe. Vinyl or cloth upholstery was offered in this package. Four color selections were offered.

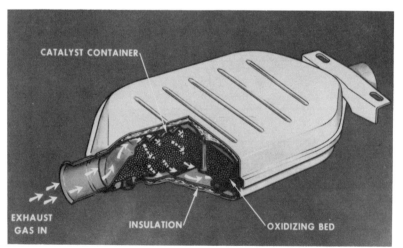

The long arm of the federal government continued to reach into the auto business and in 1975 the only way car builders could economically meet tightened pollution standards was with the underfloor catalytic converter. This unit contained one-eighth inch diameter beads coated with platinum/paladium catalyst. The life of the unit was predicted at 50,000 miles and the American public soon found ways to overcome the system—primarily by cutting the dumb things off and replacing them with standard pipes.

Although a bit on the expensive side, the all new Starfire was a well appointed car on the inside. High backed bucket seats were fitted and could be covered with either vinyl, cloth or leather. A center console was standard equipment with a floor shifter and a sport steering wheel. The instrument panel included a tachometer.

Oldsmobile again grabbed third place in the industry sales race in 1976 with total sales of 874,618. Cutlass models again proved the strongest seller in the Olds lineup with a solid backup performance from the Delta 88 Royale, Omega and Ninety-Eight models.

In its second year the Starfire was offered as a sport coupe and as the more popular SX coupe. Again this year the lone powerplant was the 231 cubic inch V-6. Transmission choices were a floor shifted four or five speed manual unit or the long standing Turbo HydraMatic. Little body or chassis changes were recorded this year on this model, which was basically shared with several other GM division. Fourteen color choices were offered on the smallest Oldsmobile. White, black or gold body stripes were also offered. Interior colors were blue and red in cloth and black, blue, white and buckskin vinyl with cloth upholstery.

The Omega lineup again offered two different packages along with the divisional price leader — the 3,389 F-85 coupe. This year the Brougham package replaced the Salons of the previous year. A new front styling treatment was adopted on the Omega and this remained a thinly disguised version of the Chevy Nova. Like the Starfire, it too was shared with several other GM divisions. Both the Omega and Starfire models were set up as basic showroom traffic builders and many buyers elected to move up into the lower priced Cutlass offerings. Neither the Omega nor Starfire were built in Oldsmobile's main Lansing plant, and only a few parts were built in that complex. The Omega in 1976 featured bumpers mounted on hydraulic shock absorbers. Fourteen exterior colors were offered along with seven vinyl top choices and nine stripe decal packages. A new Omega SX package included special stripes and a heavy duty suspension system. Engine choices started with the 250 cubic inch inline six cylinder with optional 260 cubic inch or 350 cubic inch V-8 powerplant. A new stronger and lighter rear axle was fitted in this series. The option list here was expanded to include simulated wire wheel discs, air conditioning, and AM/FM stereo radio and tape player.

Looming large again on the Oldsmobile horizon was the Cutlass intermediate group. Sales totals for just the Cutlass Supreme coupe surpassed some annual sales for the entire Olds lineup for years not so far passed. A new top of the line Cutlass, the Supreme Brougham, was added in 1976. All Cutlass models now used rectangular headlamps set in new front end styling. The 4-4-2 appearance and handling package was offered this year — but no Hurst/Olds was available this year. Velour or vinyl interior trims were offered and by the time a buyer moved through the Supreme to a Brougham, model interiors were quite plush. Cutlass models, except the Salon and station wagons, used the in-line six cylinder as standard equipment. Engine options included three Olds-built V-8's; the 260, 350, and 455 cubic inch units. Transmission choices included three and five speed manually shifted devices and the long popular Turbo Hydramatic. Among mechanical upgrades offered this year were heavier rear drum brakes on all cars within the series.

On the full sized front, the Royale convertible — the last fully open car offered by the division — was gone. A new crown landau hardtop option was added to the Royale group. Full sized models used a new, federally prodded bumper design. Front end styling was also updated with dual rectangular headlamps and front panel changes. The Delta 88 models offered the 350 cubic inch motor as standard equipment. Other standard items included: Turbo Hydramatic transmission, power steering, and power brakes. An upfront styling change was also carried out on the Ninety-Eight. Three different vinyl roof styles were offered on the Ninety-Eight. Power on this series again came from the 455 cubic inch motor hooked to a Turbo Hydramatic.

Again in 1976 the very top of the Olds lineup was the Toronado, this year offered as a custom and brougham. Rectangular headlamps were fitted here too. A sturdy, standing hood ornament was used upfront. The custom model was fitted with a normal bench seat, while the brougham again offered the popular 60/40 divided front seat. Standard driveline features again included a 455 cubic inch motor coupled to a special Turbo Hydramatic. New drive axle seals were among the minor mechanical changes for the year. Also new this year was the Stowaway spare tire.

Despite record sales level performances for Oldsmobile, the division suffered a number of cutbacks, in personnel and projects, like all other GM divisions in this era. In late 1974 Olds began work on an all new Cutlass assembly plant that would ultimately have impact on the Olds final assembly effort. By 1976 the shell on this building was completed and work inside that vast building was resumed.

Despite their recent successes in holding third place in the auto sales race, Oldsmobile officials kept fine tuning their automotive lineup. Shown here are three new models offered for the 1976 model year. In the foreground was the Cutlass Brougham coupe, which was well received in the market place. Behind that is one of the new Omega Brougham offerings that replaced Salon offerings from the previous year. In the rear is the crown landau option which could be obtained on the Delta 88 Royale coupe.

1976

The smallest Oldsmobile again in 1976 was the Starfire. Shown is the sport coupe, model TO-7 which achieved a production run of just 8,305. Very few Lansing built parts were found on this car. Base price was $3,936. This was the lightest 1976 Oldsmobile, tipping the scales at just 2,985 pounds. The lone powerplant for this model this year was the V-6 motor which had 231 cubic inches.

Next notch up the Starfire model lineup was the SX sport coupe. It was designated DO-7 and was top seller in the series with 20,854 produced. Base price was $4,116 and weight was 3,014 pounds. New this year in the Starfire was the five-speed transmission which was option M-75 and sold for $144. A four speed manual trans was standard equipment with a Turbo HydraMatic optional.

Available as an option was the GT package. It was designated Y-64 and its price was $391. The package consisted of body and hood stripes, special chrome wheels, raised letter wide oval tires, a rear stabilizer bar, tachometer and gauge package, and an electric clock. With the 4-4-2 just an appearance package in 1976 this was the closest Olds has to a sports car.

Three versions of the Omega coupe were offered this year. Shown is the Brougham coupe, model E-27. It was priced at $3,674 and weighed 3,391 pounds. Only 5,363 were made. Model B-27 was the standard coupe which had a production run of 15,347. Price was $3,484 and weight was 3,341 pounds. Least expensive 1976 Olds was the F-85 version of the Omega coupe. It cost $3,389, weighed 3,305 pounds and 3,918 were sold.

Sedans proved to be the most popular Omegas this year. Model E-69 was the Brougham sedan. It was base priced at $3,703 and weighed 3,432 pounds. A total of 7,578 were made. Also available was the standard Omega sedan, model B-69. A total of 20,221 were made. Base price was $3,513 and weight was 3,382 pounds. All Omegas came standard with the long standing 250 cubic inch inline six cylinder motor.

Several versions of each Omega body style were offered. The SX package was option Y-66 and was offered for $171. It included special decals and stripes, rocker panel moldings, wheel opening moldings, sports mirrors, heavy duty suspension components, and a custom sport steering wheel. Option Y-70 offered just decals and cost $23.

Rounding out the Omega group in 1976 was the hatchback coupe. For this year Olds dropped the Salon models and added the Broughams. The Brougham hatchback was model E-17. Only 1,235 were made. Base price was $3,816 and weight was 3,464 pounds. As a standard, hatchback production was 4,497. Base price on model B-17 was $3,389 and weight was 3,305 pounds.

Olds added a nice touch with its front styling treatment on the S cars. Model G-29 was the sedan. It was priced at $4,032 and weighed 3,870 pounds. Production was 34,994. Due mainly to economy considerations, Olds went back to the Chevrolet built in-line six cylinder for its base Cutlass engine. Most buyers bypassed the 250 cubic inch six in favor of a Rocket V-8.

The 4-4-2 option hung on another year and for 1976 it was a handling and appearance package only. Factory high performance was a long dead issue at Olds and all other General Motors divisions by this year. Option W-29 was priced at $134. Included were special body stripes, heavy duty springs, firm ride shocks, larger sway bars, and seven-inch wheels.

Olds kept slicing models off the bottom end of the Cutlass series and adding them on the top. Several years ago the Cutlass S offerings were in the middle of the group, but for 1976 they were the bottom of the ladder. Model G-37 was the Cutlass S coupe. It saw a production run of 59,179. Base price of $3,998 made it the least expensive Cutlass. Weight was 3,825 pounds. Officially, it was still called the Colonnade Hardtop Coupe.

Olds was doing more things right than wrong in the 1970's and one thing its was doing very well was the building and marketing of the Cutlass Supreme coupe. This car achieved an incredible sales mark of 186,647 in 1976. Model number was J-57. Base price was $4,290 and this Cutlass held one of the highest resale values in the entire market. Weight was 3,758. Outfitted on this car was option N-72, the $120 Superstock wheels.

1976

Added on the top end of the Cutlass group was the Brougham hardtop coupe, model M-57. It was also a fantastic seller with totals of 91,312. Weight here was 3,792 pounds and price was $4,579. Olds offered a number of special use options for its Cutlass model, including two special suspension systems, a leveling system, heavy duty wheels, trailer wiring harness and two cooling system options.

Also offered in the Supreme group was a four-door sedan. It did not begin to approach record setting sales of the coupe. Model number J-29 was responsible for 37,112 sales. Base price was $4,414 and weight was 3757 pounds. A three-speed manual transmission was standard on this series but most buyers shelled out $262 for a Turbo Hydramatic unit.

Achieving a good degree of popularity was the Cutlass Salon coupe, model K-57. It saw sales of 48,440. Base price was $4,889 and weight was 3,968 pounds. In the Salon group the downsized 260 cubic inch V-8 was standard equipment. Both the 350 and 455 V-8 engines were optional on this series. The Turbo HydraMatic transmission was standard equipment on this series.

Following trends set in other Cutlass series, the four doors were far less popular than their coupe counterparts. Model K-29 was the Salon four-door and it saw a model run of just 7,921. Base price was $4,964 and weight of 4,084 pounds. A popular option of this model was UM-2, the $337 stereo tape player and AM/FM stereo radio. Olds insisted on officially calling this model the Colonnade Hardtop sedan, even though it was a true sedan, not a hardtop.

A pair of Cutlass sized wagons were again available this year. Carrying model number H-35 was the Cutlass Supreme Cruiser. Production was 13,964. Base price was $4,878 and weight was 4,449 pounds. Coil springs were used on the Cutlass Cruiser and a 116-inch wheelbase was employed. Two seats were standard equipment with a fold down third seat optional.

Offered on a continuous basis since 1964, the Vista Cruiser this year was designated model J-35. Production totaled 20,560. Base price was $4,991 and weight was 4,459 pounds. A power equipment lover could get his fill on Cutlass models as options included; power windows, power seats, cruise control, tilt-away steering wheel, and anti-spin rear axle.

1976

Rarest of the three model Delta 88 series was the lone two door, model L-57 the coupe. Only 7,204 were built. Base price was $5,104 and weight was 4,383 pounds. Option Y-72 was a special cooling package that consisted of increased capacity radiator, special transmission oil cooler, heavy duty water pump and Thermo-cool fan. This option was strongly recommended for trailer towing.

The Delta 88 series cars offered clean front end styling in 1976. Model L-39 was one of two four-doors offered, the hardtop sedan. A total of 9,759 of this model was made. Base price was $5,188. Weight was 4,481 pounds. The base engine in this series was the 350 cubic inch V-8 with the 455 cubic inch Olds motor optional. A column shifted HydraMatic was also standard equipment.

Most popular in the Delta 88 series was the least expensive model also, the town sedan. This car was designated model L-69. A total of 17,115 were made. Base price was $4,917 and weight was 4,441 pounds. Standard tire size on the 88 series was HR-78-15 inch GM spec steel belted radial tires. Whitewalls were were available as an option.

Offered as an option on the Delta 88 Royale coupe was the crown landau package. This was option Y-61. It included a padded vinyl roof with wide brushed metal top band, special wheel covers and a standup hood ornament. The coupe carried model number N-57. Production totaled 33,364. Base price was $5,145 and weight was 4,515 pounds. As usual the Royale series was far more popular than similar Delta 88 models.

Model N-39, the hardtop sedan, proved to be the most popular car in the Delta 88 Royale series. Production was 52,103. Base price was $5,260 and weight was 4,515 pounds. Wheelbase for the 88 models was 124 inches. Springs were computer selected according to the exact car weight including options. Velour interiors were available on this series.

Rounding out the Royale group was model N-69, the town sedan. Production equaled 33,268. Base price was $5,127—the least expensive car in the series. Weight was 4,420 pounds. Olds said its 88 models, using unleaded fuel, could go 22,500 miles on a set of spark plugs, 15,00 miles between oil filter changes, 7,500 miles between oil changes, and 17 miles on a gallon of no lead fuel.

Full sized buyers had a station wagon model to look at again this model year. Model Q-35 was the Custom Cruiser. Base price was $5,620. This was the heaviest 1976 Oldsmobile, tipping the scale at 5,118 pounds. Production was 23,216. Special wagon options include B-39—full cargo area carpeting, C-49—electric rear window defogger, and A-96—locking storage compartment.

Model V-39 was the Ninety-Eight series luxury sedan. Production on this model was 16,802. Base price was $6,301 and weight was 4,820. Standard engine on the Ninety-Eight group was the 455 cubic inch V-8, in its last year as an Olds powerplant. Other standard equipment here included Turbo Hydramatic, power steering, power brakes, power seats and high energy electronic ignition.

A pair of coupes were offered in the Ninety-Eight series this year. Model S-37 was the Regency coupe. It cost $6,410 and weighed 4,697 pounds. A total production run of 26,282 was made. A second coupe, model V-37—the luxury coupe, also was offered. It was the rarest car in the series with only 6,056 made. Base price as $6,160. Weight on this version was 4,683 pounds.

Available again in two basic forms this year was the Toronado. Model Y-57 was the Toronado Custom. It listed for $6,728 and weighed 4,760 pounds. Only 2,555 were made. A pair of air conditioning units were offered on the Toro. Option C-60 was the Four Season system. Option C-65 was the more expensive Tempmatic air conditioning system.

Topping the Ninety-Eight series was the Regency sedan, model X-39. Base price was $6,550—the highest priced car in the series. It was also the best selling 1976 Ninety-Eight with total sales of 55,339. Weight on this model was 4,833 pounds. A seldom seen Ninety-Eight option was W-J7, leather interior trim. It was available only in black and then only on the Regency offerings.

More popular of the two Toronado offerings was the Brougham coupe, model Z-57. This was the most expensive 1976 Olds tagged at $6,815. Weight was 4,781 pounds. Production here was 21,746. The Toronados rolled on their own exclusive wheelbase of 122 inches. Options included the air cushion restraint system, the anti-theft system, rear window defogger, electric lamp monitor, and six-way power seat.

Olds stayed with front drive on this model, a feature it reintroduced to the domestic car market in 1966 with the first Toros. Advantages included placing engine weight over the drive wheels. This gave better winter and wet weather traction. Another advantage of the front wheel drive system was the flat floor area permitted because of the lack of a drive shaft hump.

Last year's Hurst/Olds offered a feature called the Hurst Hatch roof and this year such a feature was offered on certain Cutlass coupes. Called the Olds hatch roof it was based on two removable tinted glass panels. It was option AE-1 and listed for a hefty $550. It also required the space saver spare tire to allow more trunk storage for the top panels when in storage.

With the downplaying of the 4-4-2 package in recent years, perhaps the closest thing Oldsmobile had to a sports car off the showroom floor was the Starfire sports coupe. This specially modified Starfire saw action in sports car events in California. Although not thought of as a really gutty motor, the 231 cubic inch V-6 did have decent racing performance.

Olds had been off the racing scene for several years and its most recent successes had probably been on the drag strip in the earlier 1970's. Veteran racer Bob Silvers selected an Olds Cutlass S coupe for his 1976 race at Pike's Peak Hillclimb. Silvers was a veteran of that demanding event and he did receive a bit of help and encouragement from Lansing.

Oldsmobile continued to offer its swivel bucket seats on certain Cutlass coupes. Shown here is the special bucket seat interior on a Cutlass S coupe. This was option AN-7 and was priced at just $79. Also pictured here is option D-55, the sports console which cost $71. A five-speed manual transmission was available this year on certain Cutlass models.

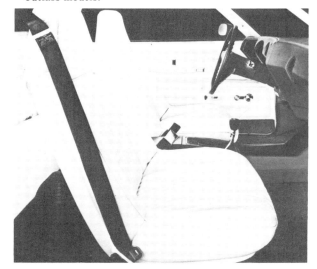

1977

Third place again belonged to Oldsmobile in 1977 with sales totaling 1,135,909. This was the first time Olds had topped the million car mark for a single year.

The Cutlass sales totals continued to swell, paced by an awesome 242,874 sales mark set by the Cutlass Supreme coupe. The downsized full size models also sold well this year. The divisional lineup had been slimmed to 28 models this year. Added was a four door in the Cutlass Brougham series and relined 88 and Royale offerings. Gone were the Cutlass Cruiser wagon, Cutlass Salon sedan, the Delta 88 and Royale hardtop sedan and the Toronado custom.

For the third year the Starfire series was found on Olds dealership showrooms and sales dwindled slightly for the two-model series this year. A new grille design was used. This year the standard powerplant became a 140 cubic inch four cylinder with the previously standard 231 V-6 now optional. Transmission selection continued to be between four and five speed manual units and a Turbo HydraMatic. The Starfire SX was a bit fancier than the sport coupe. A GT package was available on either model and included the V-6 motor, special hood and side stripes and a handling package. Special rallye wheels were offered this year as an option.

A move up the line in size found the Omega with three basic body styles in either standard or Brougham trim. The Olds price leader continued to be the Omega F-85 coupe priced at $3,653. A redesign was made upfront and also a mild rear end restyle was carried out. A newly designed instrument panel and new steering wheel were fitted.

Standard Omega offerings had interiors in cloth or vinyl while the Brougham interiors were done in brushed knit cloth. Standard powerplant for all cars in the series was the 231 cubic V-6 for the first time. The 260 cubic inch V-8 was optional. Transmission choice spanned a column shifted three-speed manual, floor shifted five-speed manual and a Turbo HydraMatic. A new front system design permitted a softer ride. All cars in the series rode on a wheelbase of 111 inches. The SX option could be ordered for $187 on any coupe model. Other options included air conditioning, electric windows, power door locks, power brakes, power steering, cruise control and vinyl roof.

Prime money makers in the 1977 lineup continued to be the Cutlass cars. Eight different models were available. Changes included front end modifications, a new instrument panel and wider selection of engines. The 4-4-2 was again offered as a $169 option, this year just on the Cutlass S coupe. It featured a special front end panel, stripes and a handling package. No Hurst Olds models were produced.

The 231 V-6 was standard on all Cutlass S and Supreme offerings. The Olds built 260 cubic inch V-8 was the standard powerplant on Salon and Brougham offerings. The 350 cubic inch was the standard motor on the Vista Cruiser and optional on all other Cutlasses. A 403 cubic inch V-8 was also an option. The three speed manual trans was standard on all models except the Salon, Brougham and station wagon. The Turbo HydraMatic was standard on these models and optional on the others. Standard Cutlass equipment included power steering and power brakes and steer

An option rather than a model was the GT package in 1977. This was option Y-64 and it cost $567. It was available on either the sport coupe or SX model. The package consisted of the V-6 engine, body and hood decals and stripes, special chrome wheels, raised letter white oval radial tires, stabilizer bar, tachometer and gauge instrumentation and bright wheel opening moldings.

Just about every Olds series showed increased sales this model year, except the Starfire group. Few changes had been made over the three-year run of this car. Model TO-7 was the sport coupe. Base price was $3,802 and this was the lightest 1977 Olds tipping the scales at 2,793 pounds. Production was 4,910. Standard transmission was a four speed, floor shifted unit with a five-speed and an automatic optional.

Far more popular in the Starfire series was model DO-7, the SX coupe. A production run of 14,181 was made. Base price was $3,999. Weight was 2,800 pounds. The Starfire continued to ride on a wheelbase of 97 inches with an overall length of 179 inches. Fuel capacity for lead free gasoline was 18½ gallons.

belted radial tires. Coupes rode on a wheelbase of 112 inches, while sedans and wagons rolled on 116-inch wheelbase.

The full sized Delta 88's, Royales and Ninety-Eights were redesigned and downsized substantially this year. Both the Delta 88 and Royale became two-car series. The V-6 was the standard powerplant on 88 and Royale models with standard Turbo HydraMatic trans. Optional were the 260, 350 and 403 cubic inch offerings. Options included an all electric sunroof, CB radio combinations and air conditioning. The Ninety-Eight remained a four car series and it too was redesigned bumper to bumper. The 88's used a wheelbase of 116 inches, the 98's used 119 inches. The 350 cubic inch motor became standard equipment on both the 98 and Custom Cruiser. All full sized models used a new four-link rear suspension system. The top of the line Olds remained the Toronado which this year was powered by a 403 cubic inch motor. Two models were offered, the Brougham and the new XSR. The latter had a large wrap around rear window and a sunroof provision.

Oldsmobile had long cast its divisional lot with production of the V-8 motor. The last Lansing built non-V-8 motor was dropped in 1950 with the Big Six engine. A great deal of research was done by Olds to offer more economical powerplants and final work was carried out this year for a diesel powerplant.

Oldsmobiles again this year appeared on bigtime NASCAR racing tracks as several astute racers took advantage of the slippery design of Cutlass bodies. Chevy motors remained underhood, however.

For its first two years the exclusive Starfire engine was the 231 cubic inch V-6. That motor was available optionally this year, but the new standard Starfire engine was this inline four cylinder from Chevrolet's New York engine plant. This unit developed 84 horsepower and had a compression ratio of 8 to 1. This was the first four cylinder offered by Olds since it dropped the model 43 A in 1923.

Some businesses develop loss leader items to attract customers to their stores and this is probably what Olds did with its Omega F-85. Few people bought this Olds, the lowest priced 1977 with a price of $3,653. Weight was 3,205 pounds. Only 2,241 of this model were sold. For the first time this year the 231 cubic inch V-6 was standard on the Omega. This engine was built by Buick in Flint.

Model B-27 was the standard Omega coupe. Production was 18,611. Base price was $3,740 and weight was just 3,281 pounds. Again this year the Omega rolled on a wheelbase of 111 inches. Overall length was 199 inches. The standard transmission was a three speed manual. Optionally available was a Turbo Hydramatic. The optional automatic was M-38 and price was $283.

Model B-17 was the standard Omega hatchback, base priced at $3,904. Only 4,739 of this car were made. Weight was 3,361 pounds. Interior choices on this series included either soft knit cloth or vinyl upholstery. The dash was done in a walnut grain plastic. Styling changes on the Omega were highlighted by a new grille treatment.

Available again this year was a standard Omega sedan and it proved to be the most popular car in the series with production of 21,623. Most of the cars in this series were produced in Willow Run, Michigan. Base price here was $3,797 and weight was 3,309 pounds. Standard Omega tires were E-78x14 blackwalls of bias ply construction. Radials and whitewalls were optional.

A total of 6,478 of the Omega Brougham coupes were built by Olds in 1977. Model number on this little car was E-27. Base price was $3,934 and weight was 3,290 pounds. This series could be air conditioned by ordering option C-60, the Four Season air conditioning. It cost $488. Power steering and power brakes were suggested options with the air conditioning order.

Moving into the Omega Brougham series, model E-17 was the hatchback coupe. Base price was $4,104 and weight was 3,381 pounds. Production was only $1,189 making this the rarest car in the series. This car was fitted with the $187 SX option Y-66. It consisted of special moldings, decals and stripes, heavy duty suspension, and deluxe interior appointments.

For not a whole lot more than an Omega or Starfire cost, an Olds buyer could move up to a Cutlass S model. The least expensive 1977 Cutlass was model G-57, the Cutlass S coupe. It cost $4,350 and weighed 3,678 pounds. Production was 70,923. Cutlass coupes this year rode on wheelbases of 112 inches, while the sedans used 116 inches.

Again this year there was a 4-4-2, although in 1977 there were no Hurst/Oldsmobiles built. This was option W-29 and it sold for $169. The package consisted of a special front end styling package, decals and stripes, heavy duty suspension components, and rocker panel and wheel opening moldings. This option could be ordered only on coupes.

Most popular in the Omega Brougham group was the four door sedan. It carried model number E-69 and production totaled 9.003. Base price was $3,997 and weight was 3,349 pounds. Olds mentioned by name the Audi 100LS, Volvo 244, and Saab 99GL, as direct competition for this series car. The Olds catalog said, "European luxury sedans had a good idea. Brougham just made it more practical."

The Cutlass S sedan—model G-29—base price was $4,923 and weight was 3,740. Production here was a respectable 42,923. The Flint built V-6 powerplant was the standard Cutlass S/Supreme powerplant—but most buyers opted for a Lansing built V-8 with its additional pep and power.

1977

Model J-29 was the Cutlass Supreme sedan. It was priced at $4,733 and weighed 3,800 pounds. Production on this series four door was 37,929. Olds stressed its safety features for this year including seat belts, energy absorbing steering column, safety door latches and hinges, thick safety glass windows, safety steering wheel and pressure lock radiator cap.

The 4-4-2 was far from the screamer it was from 1964 through 1971. This photo was found in the Olds 1977 catalog and it kind of traded on the early performance image of Oldsmobiles. Notice the Futuramic Rocket parked in the garage behind the 4-4-2. In addition to the 4-4-2 option this Cutlass is also fitted with the Super Stock III wheels which sold for $89 a set.

An absolutely incredible sales total of 242,874 was achieved by the Cutlass Supreme coupe. Model number J-57 had a base price of $4,669. Weight was 3,707 pounds. In this series the V-6 engine was standard with 260, 350 and 403 cubic inch V-8's available on an optional basis. A three-speed manual transmission was standard but few cars were so equipped.

Only one Salon model was offered in the Cutlass group in 1977. Model K-57 was base priced at $5,268 and weight was 3,904 pounds. Production was 56,757. This car is fitted with the hatch roof option. It was AE-1 and was offered on selected coupes. Price was a hefty $587. The space saver spare tire had to be ordered to give enough trunk storage space for the roof panels.

Model M-29 was the Cutlass Supreme Brougham sedan. A total of 16,738 were built. Base price was $5,032 and weight was 4,000 pounds even. The top of the line Cutlass had a 60/40 divided front seat which could be upholstered in rich velours of the loose cushion design. The luxury level on the Cutlass models had come a long way in a few years.

Another awesomely powerful seller in the Cutlass group was the Supreme Brougham coupe. Model M-57 had production totals of 124,712. Base price was $4,968 and weight was 3,907 pounds. The standard powerplant on this series was the 260 cubic inch V-8 which was built by Olds in Lansing. It developed 110 horsepower. Compression ratio on this V-8 was 7.5 to 1.

Model L-37 was the totally redesigned Delta 88 coupe. Although the Cutlass models carried the bulk of the 1977 sales loads, the larger Oldsmobiles were the really new product. Base price on this coupe was $5,144 and weight was 3,536 pounds. Production was just 8,788. Standard powerplant on this series was the 231 V-6 engine. This is the first time an 88 model was not powered by a V-8.

This year there was just one Cutlass type station wagon, model number H-35, the Vista Cruiser. Gone was the Cutlass Cruiser of the past few years. Base price was $5,242 and weight was 4,393. Production was 25,816. Olds stressed the 350 cubic inch powerplant in this model and the computer selected springs as helping to carry whatever cargo that could be shoved in the rear hatch.

A sedan was also found in the Delta 88 group this year. Model L-69 had a production total of 26,084. Base price was $5,204. Weight was 3,576 pounds. Another first took place with these smaller 88's as it was the first time these machines weighed less than cars from the Cutlass group. The Turbo HydraMatic was standard equipment on this

Big wagon fans had to put up with a bit smaller Custom Cruiser this year. Model Q-35 was the big Olds wagon. Production was 32,827. Base price was $5,922 and weight was 4,145, the lightest Custom Cruiser ever. Standard powerplant was the 350 cubic inch V-8. It was the four barrel version which continued to be built in the Lansing, Michigan Rocket engine plant.

Far more popular than the 88 models were cars from the Delta 88 Royale group. Model N-37 was the coupe. Just two models were offered in each of the two 88 series. Base price was $5,362 and weight was 3,545 pounds. Production here was 61,138. This car was fitted with option CA-1, the electric sliding sunroof. This was an expensive option at $734.

More popular than the coupe was the Delta 88 Royale sedan, model number N-69. Production here was 117,571. Base price was $5,432 with weight at 3,602 pounds. Option Y-67 was the reminder package. For $44 it included indicators for low washer fluid, low fuel, low coolant, voltage problems, and headlamps left on.

The Ninety-Eight models had always been known for their luxury and the new dowsized models were no exception. Model V-69 was the luxury sedan. Base priced at $6,785, weight was 3,940 pounds. Production was 14,323. The luxury coupe, model V-37, was also offered in 1977. Only 5,058 were made. Base price was $6,085 and weight was 3,880 pounds.

One of the plushest machines offered by Olds continued to be in the Ninety-Eight Regency. Model X-37 was the coupe. It was priced at $6,948 and weighed 3,935 pounds. Production was 32,072. Standard Ninety-Eight equipment included the 350 cubic inch engine, Turbo HydraMatic transmission, power steering, power brakes, steel belted radial tires and power windows.

Model X-69 was the Regency sedan. It was by far the most popular car in the series with sales of 87,970. It was the most expensive car in the series with a price tag of $7,132. Weight on this model was 3,964 pounds. Option UP-6 was an AM/FM radio, and 4-channel Citizen's Band combination. It listed for $547.

The top of the line Oldsmobile was the rare Toronado XSR. This was the most expensive regular production Olds ever built with a base sticker of $10,683. Only 2,714 of this front wheel machine were made. Weight on model W-57 was 4,781 pounds. This would be the last year for Toronados built in Lansing. Since their introduction in 1966 the Toro had its own exclusive assembly line in Lansing. This model marked the first time ever that an Oldsmobile had a base price in excess of $10,000.

Again the top of the line Oldsmobile was the Toronado. This was model Z-57, the Brougham. It had model run of 31,371, base price of $8,133 and weight was 4,744 pounds. Gone was the 455 cubic inch big block motor and in its place as the standard Toro powerplant was an Oldsmobile built 403 cubic inch V-8. This engine developed 185 horsepower and a compression ratio of 8 to 1.

The XSR had a number of striking features. These included the so called panoramic rear window along with an electrically operated astro roof. There was also special striping on the package. In addition to regular production Toros a total of 179 Toro chassis were built for special use. Several major motorhome manufacturers used Toronado components in the construction of their products.

Oldsmobile was beginning to get quite attached to third place in the industry sales race as in 1978 sales totals of 1,015,805 grabbed those honors again.

Big news this year came from underhood on the full sized models. Locked in heavily on continued production of V-8 engines, Olds engineers came up with a 5.7 litre diesel V-8 introduced on Eighty-Eight, Ninety-Eight and Custom Cruisers in 1978. The engine shared dimensions and some features with the long running 350 cubic inch gas engine. Some major components — block, heads, crankshaft, pistons and rods — were substantially modified for the diesel application. Olds engineers did their homework to come up with just a few second "wait to start" period. Cold starts could be made at 10 degrees below zero without the use of a block heater. Fuel economy tests showed a 25% improvement over similar gasoline fueled cars. The diesels carried a hefty price tag, however. With a 27 gallon fuel tank, range on some diesels was well over 600 miles. Added body insulation on the front of the dash kept engine noise down and a muffler on the engine's air intake also kept noise levels down.

The smallest Olds series, the Starfire, continued to be marginal in the sales department. Again two models, the sport coupe and SX coupe, were available. Standard motor was the 151 cubic inch four cylinder. The option list was expanded to include the new 305 cubic inch V-8 and the old standby 231 cubic inch V-6. GT stripes in black, white or gold were available. Other options included Rallye wheels, raised white letter tires and an instrument package wtih a tachometer and gauges.

Next up the line was the Omega, which was another group Olds had little to do with the actual production of. Five models were offered in 1978, three standard models and a pair of Broughams. Front appearance was again modified. Standard powerplant was the 231 cubic inch V-6 with optional 305 or 350 cubic inch V-8's. An SX option package included special moldings, a stripe/decal package, sports mirrors, special suspension and custom sport steering wheel. A bit fancier LS package was offered on the Omega Brougham sedan. This group included automatic transmission, air conditioning, AM/FM stereo, painted wheel discs, special lower accent paint and LS emblems.

The star of the Oldsmobile show continued to be the Cutlass model group. An all new Cutlass line bowed this year and yet sales, particularly in the Supreme series, continued to soar. The average weight reduction was 657 pounds and fuel mileage was boosted accordingly. Eight models were offered in 1978. Singular rectangular headlamps and vertical park and turn lamps were found upfront. A new Calais version was introduced and the 4-4-2 was still around, this time as an option on the Salon and Salon Brougham coupes. A single station wagon, the Cutlass Cruiser, was found this year. Standard engine across the board was the 231 cubic inch V-6 with optional 260 and 305 cubic inch V-8's.

On the full size front the Delta 88 and Royale models came in coupe and sedan models. Standard engine was the 231 cubic inch V-6 coupled with the Turbo Hydra-Matic. Optional engines included the diesel and gas fired 260, 350 and 403 cubic inch V-8's. The Custom Cruiser continued to be Oldsmobile's full sized station wagon. The station wagon shared the 116-inch wheelbase of the 88 models. The Ninety-Eight group continued to offer a pair of luxury and a pair of Regency models. The 350 gas fired V-8 was standard with the diesel and the 403 cubic inch gas V-8 optional. Leather upholstery was offered on the Regency models. The Toronado was available just as a two door. A new grille was found on the Toro. Standard engine on the Toro was the 403 cubic inch V-8.

Sizes on Oldsmobiles had been reduced dramatically on all Oldsmobiles by this year. Starfires continued to ride on a 97-inch wheelbase, while the Omegas used 111 inches. Cutlass models were cut to 108 inches, while 88 models used 116 inches. The Ninety-Eight group rolled on a wheelbase of 119 inches and the Toronado was now the largest Olds on its 122 inch wheelbase.

In the fall of 1978 Olds formally opened its all new Cutlass assembly plant in Lansing. This was the largest single car assembly complex in this country. Production of 88 and 98 models continued at a separate complex in Lansing. Assembly of the all new 1979 Toronado would be moved to Linden, New Jersey's GMAD plant. The new assembly lineup would give Oldsmobile a 1979 model production capability of 120 cars hourly.

Oldsmobile continued to offer Starfire models in 1978, mainly as traffic builders in dealer showrooms. Model DO-7 was the sport coupe. It was priced at $3,925 and weighed just 2,806 pounds—the lightest Oldsmobile of this year. Production was 9,265. Standard engine on this model was the 151 cubic inch, four cylinder. Front disc brakes and rear drum brakes were fitted.

The other model in the Starfire group was the SX coupe, model TO-7. Production here was 8,056. Base price was $4,130 and weight was 2,811 pounds. Standard transmission was the four-speed manual with an option five-speed manual and a Turbo HydraMatic. This car is fitted with the GT package, option Y-64.

1978

A three model Omega series was found this year. The standard coupe was B-27. Base price was $3,974 and weight was 3,118 pounds. Production was 15,632. The two-model Brougham series also offered a coupe, model E-27. It was priced at $4,179 and weighed 3,276 pounds. Production on the Brougham was just 3,798. Standard Omega powerplant was the V-6.

The fancier four door in the Omega lineup was this Brougham sedan, model E-69. Production was 7,125. Weight was 3,305 pounds and base price was $4,254. A standard sedan, model B-69, was the most popular car in the series with 19,478 built. The price was $4,048 and weight was 3,287. A three-speed manual transmission was standard Omega equipment.

The hatchback was again the least popular standard Omega and it was only offered in standard form this year. Just 4,084 of model B-17 were built in 1978. Base price was $4,137 and weight was 3,251 pounds. The Omegas all sported a 21 gallon fuel tank. Computer selected front springs were matched to each car's option list and total weight.

On the bottom end of the Cutlass scale this year was the downsized Salon. Model G-87 was the coupe. A total of 21,198 were built. Base price was $4,408—the least expensive Cutlass offered. Weight was 3,159 pounds which put the Cutlass models down with Omega offerings, and with their 108-inch wheelbase they were actually smaller. Computer selected coil springs were used all around on this model.

The Salon series was a rare case where a Cutlass four door outsold its companion two door. Model GO-9 saw a model run of 29,509. Base price was $4,508 and weight was 3,205 pounds. Base motor was the Buick built V-6 which used 231 cubic inches. A high energy ignition—which Olds claimed gave fast starts and improved highway economy—was fitted.

It had been a long time since the 4-4-2 represented any really breathtaking performance level factory stock, and yet the option continued to be fairly popular. For this year the package was option W-29 and included a special grille, special side stripes, rear deck numbers, and a special suspension with heavy duty springs, shocks and sway bars.

Model J-87 was the four door Cutlass Salon Brougham. It had a production run of 21,902. Base price was $4,795 and weight was 3,255 pounds. Two special Cutlass cooling packages were offered this year. Option VO-2 was the high capacity system recommended for normal driving in hot temperatures. Y-72 was the heavy duty system suggested for severe usage and trailer towing.

Shown at Riverside Raceway in California, this model was added to the Cutlass Salon group this year. It was the Brougham edition, Model JO-9. The coupe had a production run of 10,741. Base price was $4,695 and weight was 3,210 pounds. Depsite the fact that size and weight had been trimmed substantially on Cutlass models, the 1978's actually had more headroom and legroom than comparable 1977's.

The magic was continued with the Cutlass Supreme coupe, as 240,917 of this popular Oldsmobile were built this year. Model number was R-47. Base price was $4,844 and weight was 3,197 pounds. Olds claimed its new Cutlass suspension system was patterned after the 98 models, long known for their good riding qualities. Olds continued to stay with full frame construction for its Cutlass models.

Moving up the Cutlass Supreme ladder another notch brought the buyer to the new Calais. The nameplate was a new one for Olds, but for years Cadillac used it for their least expensive offering. Model number was K-47 and a total of 40,842 were built. Weight was 3,234 pounds and base price was $5,195. It was quite unusual for any manufacturer to offer a series of cars with three coupe models, but Olds did it successfully with the Supremes.

A buyer looking for a slightly fancier version of the Supreme would probably have moved up to a Cutlass Supreme Brougham. Model M-47 saw a sizable production run of 117,880. Base price was $5,240 and weight was 3,225 pounds. Standard engine here was the Lansing built 260 cubic inch V-8. Standard transmission was the manual, floor shifted three-speed. Few cars left the factory so equipped.

1978

This is what a well optioned Calais would look like. Special painted wheel discs were standard on this model. Option N-94 was the simulated wire wheels shown on this car. Also available was option N-66, the Super Stock wheels, popular over so many past years. Also available was option N-76, the die cast aluminum wheels with special ornaments.

For 1978 the Vista Cruiser nameplate was officially dead and Olds went back to calling its smaller wagon the Cutlass Cruiser again. This was model H-35 and 44,617 were built. Base price was $5,241 and weight was 3,306 pounds. The V-6 was the standard powerplant on this Olds hauler. Optional motors included 260, 350 and 305 cubic inch V-8's.

The Delta 88 series consisted of just two cars this year. Model L-37 was the coupe. A total of 17,469 were built. Base price was $5,706 and weight was 3,585 pounds. As usual this series had disc brakes up front and drums on the rear. They were power assisted. The parking brake used just a single cable to improve efficiency and eliminate brake drag.

This year brought a two piece tailgate operation on the Cutlass Cruiser. The counterweighted upper glass portion swung up. The solid lower tailgate swung down. This section was all welded construction with sturdy hinges. An optional rear window air deflector was painted to match the body color. It was built of aluminum and directed air flow to keep the rear window clean.

More popular than the coupe was the Delta 88 four door sedan. This car was designated model L-69. It was priced at $5,806 and weighed 3,611 pounds. Production totals were 25,322. Standard engine on this series was the 231 cubic inch V-6. Engine options included the diesel and 260, 350 and 403 cubic inch V-8's fueled by gasoline. Yes, the car is parked in front of Magic Mountain, a major theme park in the greater Los Angeles area.

Model N-37 was the Delta 88 Royale coupe. Base priced at $5,4358, this car weighed 3,613 pounds. A total of 68,469 were built. A four-link design was engineered into the Royale suspension. It saved weight and also increased ride travel. Cars in the Royale group continued to use computer selected springs matched to the car's option load.

Offerings from the Delta 88 Royale group were far more popular than the plain 88 group. The Royale sedan was model N-69. Production was 131,430. Base price was $5,482 and weight was 3,654 pounds. An improvement in the area of serviceability found major components in the instrument panel removable from the front on this model.

The big wagon this year continued to be the Custom Cruiser. Model Q-35 was this Olds hauler. It cost $6,323 and weighed 4,160 pounds. Production totaled 34,491. The Cruiser had a three-way tailgate that allowed a variety of loading options. A lockable third seat was offered as an option on any Cutlass or Custom Cruiser.

This was the Delta 88 Royale with the all new diesel V-8 powerplant. Diesel cars could be told by the standup hood ornament, rear script, and usually by the slightly "dirty" exhaust plume not normally associated with a late model car. The diesel shared some components with the long running 350 cubic inch gas engine. Olds called its diesel "light duty" and did not encourage trailer towing with the package.

A bit more popular than the coupe was model V-69, the luxury sedan from the Ninety-Eight series. A total of 9,136 were built. Base price was $7,240 and weight was 3,973 pounds. All cars in this series came standard with the long standing 350 cubic inch gasoline V-8. The Turbo Hydramatic was the standard transmission on this top of the line Olds series.

Again two different pairs of Ninety-Eight models were available. The luxury coupe was model V-37. It cost $7,063 and weighed 3,980 pounds. Just 2,956 were produced. Ninety-Eights this year took a page from Cutlass Salon models as the dimmer switch was built into the turn signal indicator. This was common practice on many import models.

1978

The largest production Ninety-Eight model was the Regency Sedan. This model originated as a special anniversary option in 1972 and evolved into the most popular 98 over the years. Model number was X-69 and production was 78,100. Base price was $7,610—the most expensive car in the series. Weight was 3,998 pounds. Olds cars in this series came standard with GM spec steel belted radial tires.

The next step up the Olds ladder was the Ninety-Eight Regency models. The coupe was designated model X-37 and cost $7,426. This model tipped the scales at 3,919 pounds. Production was 28,573. There were several special options for Ninety-Eights including firm ride shock absorbers, heavy duty suspension package, superlift shock absorbers and the automatic load leveling.

The Ninety-Eight was one of three series cars that could be obtained with the new diesel engine in 1978. This was really a test marketing year for the diesel and demand was substantial. Over the next few years Olds would expand the diesel engine to other lines of its cars and other General Motors began offering Olds diesel power in some of their cars.

This would mark the final year of Toronado production from the Lansing plant. These front wheel drive models had been built, since their introduction, on a slower moving assembly line that had better quality than other faster moving assembly lines. For next year an all new Toro model would be built in an east coast General Motors Assembly Division plant at Linden, New Jersey.

The Toronado once again just came in the coupe configuration. Model number was Z-57 and the Toros were by now the largest Oldsmobiles offered. Production was 24,715. This was again the most expensive Olds offered at $8,899 and also was the heaviest car offered as it weighed in at 4,769 pounds. The 403 cubic inch V-8 was the standard motor offered.

1978

The compression ratio in the Olds diesel engine was nearly three times that in its gasoline engines. That required most major components in the diesel to be strengthened. Beefed up were the block, crank, camshaft, rods and lifters. The Olds diesel used a rotary fuel injection pump which performed the functions of both the distributor and carburetor in the gas engine.

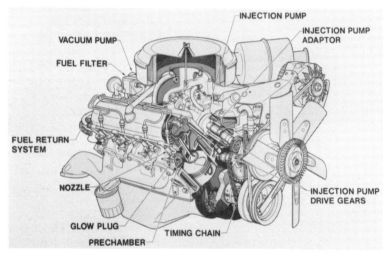

VACUUM PUMP • FUEL FILTER • INJECTION PUMP • INJECTION PUMP ADAPTOR • FUEL RETURN SYSTEM • NOZZLE • GLOW PLUG • PRECHAMBER • TIMING CHAIN • INJECTION PUMP DRIVE GEARS

Olds was popping back up in the racing scene by this model year. Here a Cutlass Salon coupe has been prepped for sports car racing. The Salon could be ordered from the factory with a five-speed standard transmission which could be modified into a pretty good unit for road racing. The GM five-speed manual oddly enough was lubricated by automatic transmission fluid.

Pretty girls and new model cars were usually a combination that made newspaper editors and readers sit up and take notice. The Oldsmobile public relations department sent this photo out to hundreds of newspapers across the country seeking a bit of extra ink for the new Olds diesels. The women in the photos worked the auto show circuit across the country. Oldsmobile continued to have factory exhibits at major auto shows and the new diesels attracted a lot of attention.

The Olds diesel "wait to start" system ranged from a few seconds on a warm day to 60 seconds or more on subzero mornings. Number two diesel fuel was to be used above 20 degrees and number one diesel was to be used in colder temperatures. Oil and filter changes were required every 3,000 miles and these were critical intervals. Very little other routine maintenance was required on diesels.

This Cutlass Supreme found itself in a rather unusual position for an Olds, on the tough rally circuit. Most popular cars in this activity were small nimble foreign cars and Jeeps. This was the particularly tough "Press On Regardless" event staged on logging roads in northern Michigan. Note the car has been fitted with Olds Super Stock wheels, grille mounted driving lights and a CB or two-way radio.

Third place again belonged to Oldsmobile in 1979, with sales totals of 1,068,155. The diesel introduction of the previous year was a big hit and a new diesel powerplant was added this year. Diesel availability was expanded to include Toronado and Cutlass models this year. The Toronado was also downsized this year and production of that front drive car was moved from Lansing to a GMAD plant in Linden, New Jersey.

Olds offered 26 models in 1979 and none was newer than the Toronado. The Toronado was the third Olds series to be drastically downsized and it was also General Motors' way of moving into the smaller car front wheel drive arena. The new Toros rode on a wheelbase of 114 inches. Available as a four-passenger hardtop coupe, the 1979 vehicle was approximately 900 pounds lighter than the previous year's offering. Standard was the 350 cubic inch gasoline engine. The optional 350 cubic inch diesel V-8 was offered and it would deliver 21 miles per gallon in the new model. New front end styling featured rectangular grille openings, dual headlamps and long horizontal parking and turn signal lamps. The Toro had what Olds called a "formal" roof design with stationary quarter windows that were covered when the landau or full vinyl top was ordered. Standard equipment on this series included air conditioning, a divided power seat, power windows, remote control mirror, automatic transmission, AM/FM stereo radio, steel belted radial tires, power steering, and power brakes.

The Starfire continued to be offered in two models, the coupe and SX. Both were two doors with hatchback and fold down rear seat. Standard powerplant remained the 151 cubic inch four cylinder. The GT package was available as an option and it included body and hood stripes in black, white or gold, the 231 cubic inch V-6 motor, special wheels, raised white letter tires and an instrument panel that included a tach and gauges. A Firenza option, introduced late in the 1978 model year, was again available. It included a special front air dam, rear spoiler, flared wheel openings, sport mirrors, wide oval tires, and heavy duty suspension.

This would be the final year for existing Omega styling as an all new Omega was in the wings for 1980. Three body styles were offered in standard Omega trim and two of these body styles were repeated in the Omega Brougham group. Standard powerplant here was the 231 cubic inch V-6. An optional SX package was available on the regular Omega coupe and hatchback coupe. This option was Y-66 and cost $231. The Omega LS package, option Y-61, cost a whopping $2,078 but it included automatic transmission, Four Season air conditioning, special emblems, painted wheel discs and special paint scheme.

Big news in the hot selling Cutlass group was the addition of a 260 cubic inch diesel on all models except the Cutlass Cruisers which had the 350 cubic inch diesel. Both diesels were optional, at costs ranging from $735 to $895 extra. A total of 38,672 buyers went for the diesel options in the Cutlass series. A new model in the Cutlass group was the Brougham station wagon which was added to eight existing models transferred from 1978. The 4-4-2 appearance and handling package, option W-29, was available for $122 on either the Salon or Salon Brougham coupe. This option consisted of paint striping and lettering on the lower body sides and deck lid, bucket seats, sports console, Rallye suspension and a special grille treatment. Standard engine on all Cutlasses was the 231 cubic inch V-6.

After an absence of several years, a Hurst/Olds again popped up this model year. It was option W-30 and was available only on the Calais model. Included in the package was the 350 cubic inch gas engine, aluminum sports wheels, sports mirrors, raised white letter tires, sports console with Hurst shifter, power steering and brakes, contour reclining bucket seats, ride and handling package, and full instrumentation. A total of 2,499 of this desirable Olds were built and 536 of these came fitted with the T-top option.

The full sized lineup remained essentially unchanged this year. A pair of Delta 88 and Delta 88 Royales again were offered. A new grille design was used and a new wrap around sidemarker design was employed. The V-6 engine was again standard and diesels were popular in the 88 group as 48,879 buyers opted for the 350 cubic inch diesel. A special holiday package, $288 option Y-78. was available on Delta 88 coupes. The Custom Cruiser continued essentially unchanged from 1978. Ninety-Eight models were offered in four models for this year, a pair of luxury models and a pair of Regency offerings. A newly designed grille was fitted up front. Standard powerplant here was the 350 cubic inch gasoline engine and 21,231 buyers went for the similar cubic inch diesel V-8.

The Starfire model was to become less important in the Olds lineup as the division continued to downsize its cars and make them lighter. Pictured, from the top, are the standard Starfire coupe, the Starfire with the GT package and the Starfire with the Firenza option. This series continued to ride on a wheelbase of 97 inches with an overall length of 179 inches. Height was just over 50 inches.

A pair of Starfire models were offered in 1979. The coupe was model TO-7 and had a production run of 13,144. Base price was $4,095 and weight was 2,754 pounds. As the SX model coupe model designation was DO-7. Production was 7,155. Base price was $4,295 and weight was 2,760 pounds. Standard powerplant continued to be a Pontiac built 4 cylinder displacing 151 cubic inch.

A popular option on the Starfire group was Y-65, the Firenza Sport Package. It cost $375 extra and was actually introduced late in the previous model year. It included a front air dam, rear spoiler, fender flares, special lettered blackwall radial tires, sport wheels, a special paint scheme, and special instrumentation. Styling on this series Olds had changed little over the years.

The Omega coupe again came in two versions for 1979. The standard ccoupe was model B-27. It sold for $4,180 and weighed 3,190 pounds. Production was 4,806. In the Brougham series the Omega coupe was model E-27. Base price was $4,386 and weight was 3,228 pounds. Production was just 1,078. The car pictured was fitted with option C-04, the $190 landau roof covering offered only on coupes.

Rarest among all Oldsmobile models in 1979 was model B-17, the Omega hatchback coupe. Only 956 of that little car were produced. Base price was $4,345. Weight was 3,267 pounds. This car was fitted with option Y-66, the SX package. It cost $231 extra and included special moldings, body side decals, sports styled mirrors, sports steering wheel, heavy duty springs, firm ride shocks and larger stabilizer bars.

Big news this year in the Cutlass group was the availability of the 260 cubic inch V-8 diesel engine. For the second year in a row Olds engineers succeeded in converting a gas powerplant to a diesel. This motor cost over $700 and it took a lot of fuel savings for a buyer to recover the initial cost of the engine option. Diesels carried special hood ornaments and also rear identification.

A pair of sedans was also available in the Omega group this year. Pictured was E-69, the Omega Brougham sedan. It was priced at $4,486 and weight was 3,243 pounds. A total of 2,145 were made. As model B-69, the standard sedan, price was $4,280. This car tipped the scales at 3,228 pounds. Production was 5,826—the largest total of the Omegas.

The Cutlass Salon looked good with its fastback styling. It was model GO-9 and a total of 20,266 were made. Base price was $4,722 and weight was 3,172 pounds. Standard equipment here was the three-speed manual transmission, but very few cars came that way. A floor shifted three speed, four speed, or five speed manual transmission was offered as was the $355 Turbo Hydramatic.

Model G8-7 was the Cutlass Salon coupe. Only 8,399 were made. Base price was $4,622—the least expensive Cutlass offered for 1979. This car tipped the scales at 3,53 pounds, lighter than any Olds except the Starfire. Base engine was the Buick built V-6 with options being the 260 cubic inch diesel V-8, the Olds built 260 cubic inch gas motor, or the Chevy built 305 cubic inch gas V-8.

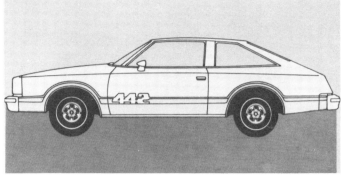

High performance was just a memory around the car factories by 1979 and yet the 4-4-2 package did enough business to justify continuing it. This year the 4-4-2 was $276 option W-29. The package included a specific grille, a special paint scheme, deck decals, special moldings, heavy duty springs, firm ride shock absorbers, special steering box, and larger stabilizer bars.

A step up the Cutlass ladder brought a prospective buyer to the Cutlass Salon Broughams. Model JO-9 was the sedan from that series. Production totaled 18,714. Base price was $5,032 and weight was 3,218 pounds. This car was fitted with one of four wheel discs available this year from the factory. The wires were option N-94 and they cost $140.

The sales leader continued to be the extremely popular Cutlass Supreme coupe. It achieved the output of some entire makes of cars with a total of 277,944 sales. Base price was $5,062 and weight was 3,183 pounds. Olds designated this popular model the R-47. The Supreme came standard with a manual, floor shifted three-speed, but most left the factory with automatics.

A car that was surprisingly rare was the Cutlass Salon Brougham coupe, model J8-7. A production run of only 3,617 was made. Base price was $4,907 and weight was 3,153 pounds. In addition to a good selection of hubcaps, the factory also offered several wheel options. This car is fitted with the long standing Super Stock wheels, option N-67. The cost was $88.

Model M-47 was the Cutlass Supreme Brougham coupe. A total of 137,323 of this model were produced. Base price was $5,491 and weight was 3,207 pounds. A leather interior was available on this series. It was option WJ-7 and cost $264. Leather was available in either carmine red or camel tan. A popular option on all Oldsmobiles was N-33, tilt away steering wheel for $75.

1979

For more than a decade the Hurst/Olds had been around. An H/O model was not offered every year, but when they were offered they were eagerly received by the buying public. Two different color schemes were offered this year. The white model saw production of 1,165. Both white and black versions featured gold stripes. All Hurst/Oldsmobiles this year were based on Cutlass Calais coupes and the cost was $2,054 over the car's base price plus other options.

The Hurst/Olds could also be ordered in basic black with gold stripes. This actually was the more popular of the color choices as 1,334 were made. The Hurst package was option W-30, an old number for a popular performance option in past years. The Hurst models came standard with a 350 cubic inch gasoline engine. A number of these cars are already on their way to becoming collector items, and several were displayed at the most recent Oldsmobile national meet.

The Cutlass Supreme Calais was another top of the line model that had been around for awhile. It was model K-47. Production totals were 43,780. Base price was $5,490 and weight was 3,214 pounds. A heavy duty coolings system, option Y-72, was available for $29. It featured a high capacity radiator, larger transmission oil cooler, heavy duty water pump and larger fan unit.

There were a number of ways the tailgate on the Cutlass Cruiser could be operated. With both the top and bottom opened cargo loading was quite easy. Special station wagon options this year included C-49—the $99 rear window defogger, V-55—the rooftop luggage carrier for $99, and C-51—the $30 rear window air deflector.

A pair of Cutlass Cruiser wagons were available in 1979. The Brougham was a new offering that carried model H-35, cost $5,517 and weighed 3,337 pounds. A total of 42,953 were built. The regular Cutlass Cruiser was model G-35. It had a production run of just 10,755. Base price was $4,980 and weight was 3,293 pounds. Standard engine here was the V-6 powerplant.

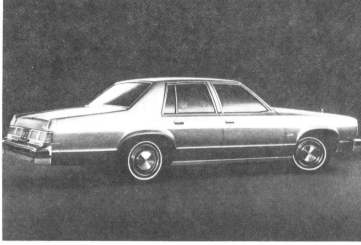

Carrying designation L-37 was the Delta 88 coupe. It was base priced at $5,782 and weighed 3,598 pounds. Total production was 16,202. This car was fitted with option N-65, the custom sport wheels. They were quite attractive and probably worth the optional $133 price tag. Also offered were the old standby Super Stock wheels.

Offered as an Olds model since 1949, the 88 series was still a bread and butter model for Oldsmobile. Model L-69 was the Delta 88 sedan. A total of 25,532 were made. Price was $5,882 and weight was 3,624 pounds. The most expensive factory radio package was option UP-6, the AM/FM stereo radio and 40-channel CB unit. Price was $574 and this included a power antenna.

Moving up the Olds ladder a bit, a buyer would next look at the Delta 88 Royale group. Two models were offered here. The sedan was N-69 and it was by far the most popular 88 with sales totals of 152,626. Base price was $6,154 and weight was 3,649 pounds. As a coupe, the Royale was designated model N-37. It was priced at $6,029 and weighed 3,607 pounds. The production run was 60,687.

Full sized wagon buyers agian found the Custom Cruiser models waiting for them. Model Q-35 was base priced at $6,742. Production was 36,648 and weight was 4,136 pounds. Although the factory suggested that the diesel engine not be used for heavy trailer hauling, a number of wagons were fitted with the optional 350 cubic inch diesel V-8.

A pair of coupes awaited the Ninety-Eight buyer once again in 1979. The luxury coupe had a production run of just 2,104. Model number V-37 was priced at $7,492 and weight was 3,942. The Regency coupe, model X-36, was a lot more popular with sales of 26,965. Price was $7,815 and weight was 3,946 pounds. The 98 models came standard with the 350 cubic inch gasoline engine.

Most popular among the four Ninety-Eights built in 1979
was the Regency sedan, model X-69. It had a sales total of
91,862. Base price was $8,063 and weight was 4,021
pounds. Also available this year was model V-69, the
Ninety-Eight luxury sedan. Only 6,720 were built. Base
price was $7,637 and weight was 3,986 pounds. A leather
interior was offered on this series for an extra $264.

Oldsmobile owners continued to use their vehicles to tow
trailers like this 98 sedan hooked up with a medium Air-
stream trailer. Olds cautioned trailer towers to fit their
cars with a hitch that permitted normal operation of the
energy absorbing bumper system. The $68 G-80 limited
slip differential was a suggested option for trailer towing.
This option was not available on the all new Toronado.

All new for 1979 was the Toronado. For the first time since
that model was introduced in 1966, the Toro was not built
in Lansing. It carried model X-57 and had a production
run of 50,056. This was by far the highest priced Olds with
a price tag of $10,684. Weight was reduced substantially
here, down to 3,851 pounds. The Toro came standard with
a 350 cubic inch gas V-8 and the only engine option was the
350 cubic inch diesel.

Sports car racing seemed particularly well suited to this
Cutlass Salon coupe. This car was fitted with the optional
305 cubic inch V-8, which was a Chevrolet built engine and
a cousin to the long standing small black Chevrolet
powerplant. A number of the special heavy duty suspension parts offered by Oldsmobile optionally were ideal for
road racing and sports car racing. These included special
shocks, springs and sway bars.

General Motors used the all new Toronado and other
similar GM division cars to work with smaller front drive
cars. The Toro wheelbase dropped from 122 inches in 1978
to 114 inches in 1979. The new Toro Fisher body had a
flush fitted rear window glass. The deck lid was counterbalanced with gas cylinders. The trunk was carpeted and
fitted with a space saver tire.

Despite a slight slippage in sales totals for 1980, Oldsmobile retained its third position in the industry sales race with a production run of 910,306. Diesels continued to grow in popularity as Olds built 278,851 diesel V-8's this year. All of this output did not go in Oldsmobiles, however, as other GM divisions offered th Olds diesel powerplants.

A total of 27 models were offered this year and diesel power could be ordered in 21 of these models. Fuel economy had become the name of the game and by 1980 Olds was in relatively good shape here. Engineering tests showed a fleet fuel economy average of over 21 miles per gallon, a 35% improvement in just five years. The top mileage miser was a 1980 Omega with the four cylinder motor and manual transmission. It rolled to 38 mpg on the highway. Several diesel models rolled to 34 mpg on a highway driving course.

The final Oldsmobile to be downsized was the Omega, which was introduced a bit earlier than other 1980 models. The all new Omega featured front wheel drive and a different looking transverse mounted engine. General Motors engineers achieved a weight reduction of 750 pounds over 1979 Omegas. The new Omegas racked up at least six miles per gallon better fuel economy than similar 1979 models. Four models were offered, a coupe and sedan in the standard and Brougham series. A sunroof, $250 option AD-4, was now available on the Omega. A total of 14 exterior colors were now available. Standard powerplant here was the gas-stingy, Pontiac-built four cylinder. Available optionally was a V-6. The wheelbase on the all-new models was 105 inches. Special packages on the Omega included the sporty SX group, option Y-66 for $303.

In its last year was the Starfire group. Dwindling sales levels and the fact that all other Oldsmobiles were getting smaller made this car expendable. Two models were offered—the two-door sports coupe and SX sports coupe. Both were hatchbacks with fold-down rear seating. The Firenza package again included items like air dam, rear spoiler, wheel flares, special wheels and tires, and special paint was again offered to buyers. A

GT option was also available. Standard powerplant was the Pontiac four cylinder with a Buick built V-6 optional.

Over the past few years the sales of Cutlass coupes had been fantastic and this year the division added several models in hopes of beefing up sedan sales. A total of 10 Cutlass models was offered this year. A 4-4-2 was available this year as option W-30. This year the package came only on the Calais coupe with either black or white exterior colors. It appeared the division was trying to offer a combination of past 4-4-2 and Hurst/Olds models. The package sold for $1,255 and included special grilles and stripes, W-30 and 4-4-2 emblems, a special 350 cubic inch V-8 gas engine, Rallye suspension, special radial tires, and special interior trim. Standard Cutlass engine was the V-6 with a pair of gas V-8's offered along with the diesel V-8.

Newly added at the 88 level was a Royale Brougham series. Now a coupe and sedan could be ordered as either a Delta 88, Delta 88 Royale or Delta 88 Brougham. Fronts on the 88 models had been lengthened and rears had shortened. Other aerodynamic improvements included flatter wheel discs, rounded front corners, and the addition of a small spoiler at the deck lid. A special holiday option was again available on the Delta 88 coupe. This package was option Y-78 and price was $295. It included special emblems, contour bucket seats, sports console with shifter, sport mirrors, custom sport steering wheel and special color-keyed wheel discs.

The Ninety-Eight series was cut to just three models as the low selling Luxury Coupe was no longer offered. Left were the Regency coupe and sedans in both the Regency and luxury trim. Slight styling changes were made in the Ninety-Eight group to clean up the aerodynamics. A 307 cubic inch V-8 was the standard powerplant with an optional gas V-8 and the optional V-8 diesel available.

The Toronado received a slight restyle and 111 pounds was shed from the all new model introduced a year ago. New light weight components—including aluminum bumper reinforcements, hoods, and intake manifolds—helped take weight levels down. A new option—called the XSC—was offered for $331. It offered a special ride and handling package, bucket seats, console, gauge package, and leather-wrapped steering wheel.

The Firenza was one of several special option packages offered on the 1980 Starfire. The package included special stripes and side markings, a front air dam, rear spoiler, fender flares, several heavy duty suspension components, styled wheels, and raised letter steel belted radial tires. This was a nimble handling Olds and was basically a remake of the Chevy Monza.

It was no secret that the Starfire was being phased out and by midyear this model didn't even appear in some factory literature. Built were the DO-7 SX coupe and the TO-7 sports coupe. Production totals were 8,237. Base prices began at $4,195. Weight was 2,751 pounds. The interior on this model again featured contour bucket seats in either vinyl or velour.

This angle gives another idea of the devices used on this special Starfire to better direct airflow. Changes to accomplish this same thing were made in 88 and 98 models this year. Oldsmobile was concerned about every bit of fuel mileage it could squeeze out of its cars. The Starfire was one of two Oldsmobiles that the diesel was not offered in.

The biggest changes in the Olds lineup this year came with the all new Omega models. Riding on a wheelbase of just under 105 inches, weight levels came down drastically on this series. Mileage ratings went up dramatically as well. Gone this year was the relatively unpopular hatchback coupe. There were two standard Omegas offered as well as two Broughams.

A driver who wanted the sportiest version of the Omega selected the SX option. It came only on standard coupes and sedans. This was option Y-66 and it cost $303. The package included gloss black lower finish, special hubcaps, special decals, sport mirrors, special tires, and rear spoiler. Standard Omega transmission was a floor shifted four speed.

Even more popular were the Omega sedans. The standard sedan was model B-69. Base price was $5,447 and weight was just 2,497 pounds. This was the second best selling Omega, with a production run of 42,172. Standard powerplant was the 2.5 litre, 151 cubic inch Pontiac-built four cylinder. Omegas with this engine and a standard transmission got up to 38 mpg on the highway.

Model E-37 was the Omega Brougham coupe. Production was 21,595—way up for all models from 1979 levels. Base price was $5,561 and weight was 2,511 pounds. The standard Omega coupe was model B-37. Production was 28,267 and weight was 2,470 pounds—the lightest Oldsmobile produced this year thanks to some nifty weight trimming by Olds engineers. Base price was $5,281.

This was the fancier Omega Brougham sedan, model number E-69. Production here was the most ever for an Omega model, 42,289. This was the most costly Omega, tagged at $5,711 and weight was 2,542 pounds. An optional 173 cubic inch V-6 powerplant, bulit by Chevrolet, was optional on this model for $225. This was the only engine option as no diesel Omegas were built this year.

After fantastic success in the coupe market the last few years, Olds added several "notchback" sedans to its Cutlass group this year. Model G-69 was the Cutlass sedan. Production was 36,923. Base price was $5,750 and weight was 3,161 pounds. Olds emphasized that one out of every two Oldsmobiles sold was a Cutlass. Standard Cutlass power cam from a 231 cubic inch V-6.

The fastback styling continued to be applied to the Cutlass Salon, model G-87. Production here was just 3,429. Base price was $5,590 and weight was 3,157 pounds. The Salon rolled on a wheelbase of just over 108 inches. A pair of special suspension packages was offered. The Rallye suspension was FE-2 for $40 and the F-41 was the heavy duty suspension.

Rarest offering in the Cutlass lineup was the Cutlass Salon Brougham. Just 965 of this coupe were made. Base price was $5,879 and it tipped the scales at 3,157 pounds. This car carried option N-78, the aluminum die cast wheels. Price tag was $315. The long running Super Stock wheels were also an option on this series. They cost $95.

Continuing as the biggest selling Cutlass was the Supreme coupe, model R-47. It racked up 169,597 sales—the leader once again in the Olds lineup. Base price was $6,455 and weight was 3,283 pounds. Option U-89 was a $25 optional wiring harness for those using their cars to pull trailers. Heavy duty wheels, for $12, were suggested for trailer pullers.

Moving up the Cutlass ladder another notch brought the buyer to the Cutlass Supreme Broughams. Model M-49 was the sedan. A total of 52,462 were built. Base price was $6,993 and weight was 3,298 pounds. A trio of optional hubcaps were available on this series. The most expensive were fitted on this model. Option N-91 was the simulated wires which sold for $186 including locks.

Added to the Olds lineup was the LS Cutlass sedan, model R-69. A total of 86,868 were built. Base price was $6,570 and weight was 3,271 pounds. Base engine was the 3.8 litre V-6 and the Turbo Hydramatic was again the standard transmission in this series. Power steering and power front disc brakes were also standard.

The Cutlass Supreme Brougham continued to be a good seller as a coupe. It was model M-47 and was responsible for 77,875 sales this year. Base price was $6,894 and weight was 3,293 pounds. The diesel was offered optionally in this model and it was popular. In 1980 a total of 46,990 Cutlass buyers opted for the 260 cubic inch diesel motor.

Model K-47 was the Calais coupe. It was offered only as a two-door and had total sales of 26,269. Base price was $6,919, Weight was 3,293 pounds. A 4-4-2 package was offered this year, but it was actually a combination of prior 4-4-2's and Hurst/Oldsmobiles. This option cost over $1,200 and among other things it offered a special 350 cubic inch gas fueled V-8. It probably was the best performer in the Olds lineup.

A pair of Cutlass Cruiser wagons were available this year. Pictured was the H-35, the Brougham edition. A total of 22,791 were sold. Base price was $6,594 and weight was 3,392 pounds. Also available was the standard Cutlass Cruiser, model G-35. Only 7,815 were made. Base price was $6,195 and weight was 3,335 pounds. A new one-piece bumper was adopted this model year.

Not an overwhelmingly popular model was the Delta 88 coupe. It was designated model L-37. Only 6,845 were made. Base price was $6,627 and weight was 3,459. More than half the Delta 88 coupes built this year utilized option Y-78, pictured here. It was the $295 holiday coupe option. It included special emblems, bucket seats, console, sports steering wheels, and sports mirrors.

The other car in the Delta 88 series was model L-69, the Delta 88 sedan. It was priced at $6,722 and weighed 3,492 pounds. Production was 15,285. Olds did some styling alterations on the 88 cars including making the front end lower and slightly longer to reduce aerodynamic drag. Standard engine was the 231 cubic inch V-6.

Model N-69 was again the most popular 88 offered, the Delta 88 Royale sedan. It saw a production run of 71,052. Base price was $7,034 and weight was 3,470 pounds. Interiors could be ordered in black, green, blue, brown or tan velour. A light tan leather interior package was also offered as special trim 85.

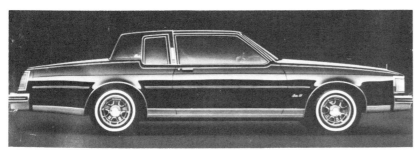

The lone two-door in the Delta 88 Royale series was model N-37, the coupe. Production here was 34,203. Base price was $6,627 and weight was 3,459 pounds. Diesel production was highest of any series on the 88 group with a total of 49,087 cars fitted with the second year 350 cubic inch V-8 diesel. This was engine option LF-9 and it cost $790.

Several years ago Olds cut the 88 down to two body styles: a coupe and a sedan. In 1980, however, they decided to add a Delta 88 Royale Brougham as another series. The coupe was model Y-37. Just 2,100 of this first year model were made. Base price was $7,249 and weight was 3,496 pounds. This particular car is shown with option N-91, the simulated wire wheel discs. They sold for $175 and included locks.

Rounding out the new Brougham 88 group was the sedan, model Y-69. It cost $7,330—making it the most expensive 88 ever offered by Olds. Weight was 3,505 pounds. Production was 16,026. All Eighty-Eight models came standard with a Turbo Hydramatic transmission. Engine selection determined which version of the long-popular Olds automatic transmission would be fitted.

The full-sized Oldsmobile station wagon continued to be the Custom Cruiser. Model Q-35 saw a production run of 17,067. Base price was $7,614 and weight was 4,024 pounds. Olds literature claimed that station wagon ride had been improved for 1980. Olds had an on-again off-again record in the station wagon business. The first Olds wagons were listed in factory literature in 1940 and up through postwar years the wagons were woodies.

Oldsmobiles continued to be used to pull a variety of trailers. Several special options were fitted just for trailer pulling customers. A 6,000-pound trailer was the heaviest unit that Olds suggested one of its cars pull. Officials suggested that the diesels not be used as trailer pullers. Options suggested included limited slip differential, heavy duty wheels, heavy duty suspension, superlift rear shocks, and special cooling package.

Just one lone coupe model was left in the Ninety-Eight series by 1980. The Regency coupe was designated model X-37. Production was 12,391. Base price was $9,817 and weight was 3,946 pounds. Standard engine in the series was the 307 cubic inch gas V-8. A total of 18,446 buyers opted for diesel power when they purchased their Ninety-Eights this year.

A pair of sedans were built for Ninety-Eight series buyers this year. Sales leader by far was this Regency sedan, model X-69. A total of 58,603 were made. It was the highest priced car in the series tagged at $9,939. Weight was 3,966 pounds. One of the most expensive options offered on 98 models was CF-5, the electric sliding Astroroof. Few cars were so fitted, mostly due to the $1,058 cost. Also offered this year was the Luxury sedan, model V-69. It cost $9,310, weighed 3,924 pounds, and 2,640 were built.

The Olds Toronado was a handsome car from any angle. Also, the luxury car buying public had accepted the new Toronado concept. The Toronado buyer was very aware of option LF-9, the 350 cubic inch diesel engine. It cost $860 and an original buyer had to do a lot of driving to recover that cost. A total of 12,362 diesel Toronados were built in 1980.

Its' $11,638 price tag made the 1980 Toronado the most expensive Oldsmobile ever made. Model Z-57 saw a production run of 43,440. Weight was 3,730 pounds. The Toro models offered a dramatic increase in fuel economy over the past few years. The 1980 front drive Olds was more than 54% more efficient than its 1975 counterpart.

Oldsmobile was running its diesel engine plant just as hard as it could to keep up with fitting the popular powerplant just to Cutlass, 88, 98, and Toronado models. So the Omega had to come up with its way of achieving good fuel economy. One way was to trim weight from the newly designed cars. Another was to stuff a small V-6 powerplant sideways into the front wheel driven chassis. This sure is a far cry from the engines that used to grace American cars just a decade before.

By the 1981 model year it seemed Oldsmobile had swung full circle in the products it offered and the sales pitch it was using. In the early 1900's the Curved Dash models were touted for their economic nature and were among the best selling cars built. In later years Oldsmobiles became known for their reliability, luxury and finally their high performance levels. For 1981 Oldsmobile was again touting the economy of its models and again Oldsmobiles were among the most popular cars built.

In this model year Olds offered 23 models, ranging from the compact Omega through the Toronado. The division's fleet fuel economy average went to more than 22 miles per gallon. But, several long running Oldsmobile models were dropped this year. Gone were the Salon models and the Starfires were actually discontinued midway through the previous year.

The Omega group was now the smallest Oldsmobile offered. A pair of standard Omegas and a pair of Omega Broughams were available in 1981. A new grille treatment was used this year and a new tail lamp design was employed. A new Omega option was a floor mounted automatic transmission shifter and console. Again several Omega options were offered. The Sport Omega was highlighted by a blacked out grille and a wraparound front bumper. Flexible light-weight fenders were also fitted. The ES package used a soft front end treatment with a bumper done in a body matching color. A ride and handling package was also fitted. The option was available only in silver metallic exterior with maple red or dark blue interior. The SX option could be ordered on any standard Omega coupe or sedan. Special blacked out parts were fitted along with sport mirrors, special wheel trim and body stripes.

Eight Cutlass models were found in 1981. Aerodynamics were improved on the sales-leading Cutlass Supreme. A soft front end extended to the bumper. All Cutlass models were now rolling on lower resistance tires designed to be inflated to 35 pounds per square inch. This improved fuel economy. Suspension and structural changes were made to offset the effects of higher tire pressure. A new windshield washer system was now standard on Cutlass and Toronado models.

Aerodynamic improvements continued to be made on 88 and 98 models this year. These cars were now fitted with 25-gallon fuel tanks which made for extended mileage range. Full sized models were also fitted with the new increased pressure tires. Low drag front disc brakes with quick take-up master cylinders were standard. The 88, Royale and Royale Brougham series were each available in a choice of coupe or sedan models. The Custom Cruiser wagon received a new front styling treatment. The 98 group continued to be a Luxury Sedan and Regency coupe and sedan. A new grille was fitted on the 98 cars.

The Toronado continued to be offered as a Brougham coupe. A plush XSC option was available this year. Fuel economy improvements were offered on this front wheel drive group. The higher pressure tires were used. Additional structure was added in the window pillars, underbody and rear wheelhouses. Front wheelhouses were now reinforced with fiberglass.

This year just seven engines were offered in the Olds family. They included: a 151 cubic inch four cylinder, 173, 231 and 252 cubic inch V-6 motors, 260 and 307 cubic inch V-8 gas fed motors and a 350 cubic inch diesel powerplant. The diesel was offered on 19 of the 23 Olds models and it continued to be a hot seller despite a heavy price tag. Diesel improvements included a roller hydraulic valve lifter system and increased intervals on oil changes. A better emmission system was fitted this year on both gas and diesel powered cars. Diesels also were fitted with an improved water separation system. A diesel fuel heater option was also available. Heavy duty suspension packages were available this year also. Puncture sealing tires were also on the 1981 Olds option list.

Despite some relatively gloomy times in the auto industry, Olds moved ahead with another expansion program in Lansing. Thanks to some good engineering by Olds personnel, the diesel kept the Olds V-8 competitive for a few more years—but new and smaller engines would be needed in the near future. Olds launched a new plant—Plant 5—several years ago. Located near Lansing, in Delta Township, this large manufacturing complex was built to turn out new Olds engines of the future. The plant was in partial operation by late 1981 and would be fully operational for the 1982 models. This entirely new plant location allowed Oldsmobile plenty of expansion room near Lansing in the future. Plans were also announced to totally re-fit and re-tool the Rocket Engine Plant within the main plant complex. A good deal of this plant and tooling dated back to the Rocket V-8 introduction in the late 1940's and early 1950's.

In the foreground of this photo was the least expensive 1981 Oldsmobile, the Omega coupe. It carried model designation B-37 and was priced at $6,343. This was also the lightest car offered by Olds this year as it tipped the scales at just 2,71 pounds. For this year the standard Omega was offered in just two body styles: the coupe and the sedan. This series and the Toronado were the only front drive cars built by Olds.

A pair of sedans were available in the Omega series this year. Pictured is the Brougham sedan, model E-69. It was priced at $6,855 and weighed 2,537 pounds. A standard Omega sedan, model B-69, was also offered. It sold for $6,514 and weighed 2,501 pounds. All cars in this series came standard with the 151 cubic inch four-cylinder motor. The standard transmission was a manual, floor shifted four speed. P 185 x 13 inch glass belted radial tires were standard equipment here.

Model E-37 was the Omega Brougham coupe. It sold for an even $6,700. Weight on this model was 2,515 pounds. Extra Brougham equipment included cloth upholstered custom sport bench seat, carpeted lower doors, standup hood ornament, deluxe steering wheel and extra modlings. Some popular Omega options included six way power seats, vinyl roof, remote control mirror, cruise control, luggage roof rack and power steering.

Omega offered almost as many special packages as it did models. Shown is the Sport Omega. This treatment was offered only on the coupe. It included a soft frontend, flex fenders, blackened bezels and grille work, sport mirrors, heavy duty suspension components, custom steering wheel, deluxe color keyed wheel discs, instrument/gage package, and special orange and red body stripes. This package was normally offered only on white cars.

Oldsmobile long seemed fascinated by the European touring cars and the latest offering to try to copy that concept was the Omega ES. This package was available only on silver Omega Brougham sedans with dark blue or red interiors. Either the four cylinder or V-6 powerplant could be ordered. Equipment included a soft front end with scoop, wide body side mouldings, special tires, power front disc brakes, custom sport steering wheel, power steering and special swirled instrument panel.

A long standing Omega package was the SX, which again was offered for 1981. This treatment included low gloss paint on the lower body, special rub strip bumpers, rallye trimmed wheels, special decal striping and sport mirrors. This car was built only as a coupe. This particular car was fitted with the sunroof. Since the factory built convertible disappeared a number of buyers were turning to sunroofs of one design or another. Some opted for factory installed units, while others went to aftermarket installers.

The least expensive car in the Cutlass group, in fact the only one base priced under $7,000, was model G-69 the Cutlass sedan. It cost $6,955. Weight was an even 3,400 pounds. The standard Cutlass engine was the 231 V-6 engine. Optional powerplants included the 260 cubic inch V-8 and the 350 cubic inch diesel V-8. Standard transmission for this car was the fully synchronized three speed manual unit. Wheelbase on all Cutlass models was just over 108 inches.

The long standing Oldsmobile sales favorite was the Cutless Supreme coupe, model R-47. It was priced at $7,715 and weighed 3,320 pounds. Once the top of the line Cutlass, by this year the Supreme had slipped a few notches in the Cutlass pecking order. Olds engineers were able to salvage a great deal of the interior room in the smaller Cutlass models, but one area that suffered was the trunk. All cars in this series carried a compact spare tire for better trunk space usage.

1981

Olds was throwing more emphasis on its four door sedan models this year in hopes that the sedans would catch up with coupes in the sales department. The Cutlass LS was model R-69. It was base priced at $7,552 and weighed 3,414 pounds. A long option list kept any buyer busy for some time outfitting his car just right. Accessories included six way power seat, power door locks, tinted windows, bucket seats (on coupes), power trunk release, pulse wiper system, and limited slip differential.

Another part of the beefed up Olds four-door Cutlass lineup was the Brougham sedan. It was model M-69 and was priced at $8,100. Weight for this offering was 3,427 pounds. In addition to a long option list for Cutlass models, Olds made several special use items available in 1981. These included heavy duty suspension package, high capacity electrical system, heavy duty wheels, trailer wiring harnesses, and high capacity cooling system. Olds recommended that diesel engined cars not pull trailers.

The most expensive Cutlass offered in 1981 was the Calais coupe. It was base priced at $8,285. This car was designated model K-47 and it weighed 3,372 pounds. It is obvious from this photo that this model was designed with air flow in mind. Olds literature said this styling treatment reduced aerodynamic drag by at least 15 percent when compared to the same 1980 models.

Model M-47 was the Cutlass Supreme Brougham coupe. It was priced at $8,250 and weight was 3,360 pounds. A variety of radio packages were available on this year's Cutlass models. They started with the AM pushbutton, AM-FM stereo with tape player and digital display, AM-FM stereo with tape player, AM-FM stereo with cassette player, AM-FM stereo with 40-channel CB, AM-FM stereo and AM-FM mono system.

Luxury liner of the Cutlass wagons this year was the Cutlass Cruiser Brougham. The dolled-up "utility" vehicle was designated Model H-35 and wore a base price of $7,726. It weighed 3,427 pounds. In addition to sporting wood-grained side trim, the brougham version had a front center armrest and a fully carpeted cargo floor. Upholstery could be ordered in all-vinyl; all-fabric, or fabric front seat and vinyl rear. The roof rack and air deflector shown here were accessories, as were the spoked wheel covers. An under-floor compartment held the spare tire and provided some space for safe storage of valuables.

CUTLASS CRUISER

Station wagon buyers had two choices in the Cutlass group. Model G-35 was the Cutlass Cruiser. It cost $7,417 and weighed 3,418 pounds. Model H-35 was the Cutlass Cruiser Brougham. Base price was $7,726 and weight was 3,427 pounds. Wagon models came standard with the 231 cubic inch V-6 powerplant. An automatic transmission-column shifted-was also standard equipment.

Model L-37 was the Delta 88 coupe. It was base priced at $7,655 and weighed 3,459 pounds. Available only on this two-door model was the holiday package which had been offered for several years. This model got about as sporty as an 88 could get, with bucket seats, a T-bar shifter, and a beefed up suspension. This was a relatively rare option package.

In the foreground of this photo was model L-69, the Delta 88 sedan. Base price was $7,751 and weight was 3,492 pounds. Standard Delta 88 powerplant was the long standing 231 cubic inch V-6 engine. A column shifted Turbo HydraMatic was also on the standard equipment list along with electronic ignition, front disc brakes, power steering and full wheel discs.

Moving up a bit in the 88 group brought a buyer to the Delta 88 Royale models. Again a coupe and sedan were offered. The coupe was model N-37. Base price was $7,689 and weight was 3,491 pounds. All 88 models rolled on a wheelbase of 116 inches. Length was over 218 inches. Gas cars were fitted with a 25 gallon fuel tank, the diesel models held 27 gallons of fuel.

The top of the line in the 88 group was the pair of Broughams. Model Y-37 was the Delta 88 Royale Brougham coupe. It cost $8,284 and weighed 3,501 pounds. Model Y-69 was the sedan in the same series. It was base priced at $8,367 and weighed 3,528 pounds. Cars in the 88 group had more than 20 cubic feet of usable trunk space. A compact spare helped increase that space.

Model N-69 was the Delta 88 Royale sedan. It was base priced at $8,019 and weighed 3,512 pounds. A variety of special use equipment was available in 1981 on this series. Included were suspension packages, automatic leveling equipment, a high capacity alternator, heavy duty wheels, special trailer wiring harness, high capacity cooling system and oversize tires. Some of these options were for trailer towers, but Oldsmobile did not suggest towing with its diesels.

1981

Model P-35 was the big Olds station wagon, the Custom Cruiser. Base price was $8,678 and weight was 4,024 pounds. This car has a pair of the sharp optional wire wheel discs which did not last long around hubcap thieves. A 307 cubic inch, gas-fed V-8 was the standard big wagon engine. It was hooked to a four-speed overdrive automatic transmission. The wagons shared the 116-inch wheelbase of the 88 models.

Oldsmobile retained a single model in its long standing luxury Ninety-Eight offerings. Model V-69 was the Luxury Sedan. It was base priced at $10,289 and weighed 3,966 pounds. Standard engine was the 252 cubic inch gas fueled V-6. Standard tires were P215 steel-belted radial whitewalls. An AM-FM stereo radio was standard equipment on this Olds series as was an electric digital clock.

The lone coupe in the Ninety-Eight series was the Regency coupe, model X-37. It sold for $10,778 and weighed 3,946 pounds. Wheelbase on this series was 119 inches and length was just over 221 inches. Cars in this series had an energy absorbing bumper system. Included were bumper guards and special impact strips.

Rounding out the Ninety-Eight series was model X-69, the Regency sedan. This model dated back to Olds' 75th anniversary year of 1972 when it came in just one color and was a midyear introduction. Base price was $10,896 — the most expensive Ninety-Eight built this year. Weight was 3,978 pounds — the heaviest car in the series. Long travel springs and a new type of shock absorber this year accounted for a good 98 ride.

The real top of the line car in the 1981 lineup was the Toronado XSC, a special option on the single-car Toro series. Offered in this exclusive package was contour front bucket seats, sports console, leather wrapped custom steering wheel, instrument panel gauges, larger front and rear stabilizer bars, over-size tires, special painted wheel discs, special paint stripes, and XSC emblems.

Around since 1966, the Toronado had seen a lot of changes over the years. For awhile this front wheel drive car was built in a special Lansing plant. By 1981 production had been shifted to a General Motors Assembly Division plant on the east coast. The Toro was designated model Z-57 and price was $12,526. Weight was 3,730 pounds. Grille changes were made on cars built in this model year, but mechanics remained about the same as on the 1980 models.

About the author

Prior to joining the utility company seven years ago, Casteele worked from 1972 to 1975 directly for Oldsmobile. This was valuable experience used in writing this volume. He served as chief photographer and writer for the Olds public relations department. Before his Oldsmobile work experience, Casteele was in the newspaper business, briefly as a sports writer for the Athens Ohio Messenger and later as automotive editor for the Saginaw Michigan News.

Casteele lives with his wife Diane, son Scott, a cow, two dogs and a cat in the small, historic village of Vermontville, Michigan.

He is a prolific free-lance writer and has authored many magazine and newspaper articles. Casteele is generally recognized as one of the nation's leading authorities on vintage Oldsmobiles. He edits the monthly publication for the 3,800-member Oldsmobile Club of America and is a member of the Board of Directors for the R.E. Olds Museum in Lansing, Michigan. His collection of auto related items includes: a 1951 Cadillac Fleetwood 60, 1954 Mercury coupe, 1957 Corvette and 1962 Thunderbird. In addition to his cars, he also maintains an extensive collection of automobile literature with a specialization on Oldsmobile. This book would have been impossible to research and write about without that collection.

A nearly life-long love of sports is still carried on and has found a logical automotive link. After a high school career as a multiple letter winner in both football and basketball on championship teams at Troy (Ohio) High School, Casteele entered the University of North Carolina on a full football scholarship. A series of injuries cut short a promising career as a college defensive lineman, and Casteele was forced to give up football. He transferred to Ohio University where he earned a journalism degree. Admidst several part time jobs—including driving giant Euclid earth moving equipment—Casteele developed an interest in auto racing. Not content to watch from the grandstands, he soon found himself behind the wheel of a variety of racing equipment including the deadly quick, fuel injected, open wheeled sprint cars. Since that time Casteele has blended a career of driving race cars with officiating at race tracks as a racing director, starter and pit steward. Today he is recognized as one of the midwest's top race track announcers and serves as the voice of several weekly racing programs including Michigan's NASCAR racing activities. He still will slip behind the controls of a race car from time to time in between announcing chores.

Over his career Casteele has received numerous awards for his reporting, writing, public relations and announcing efforts. Although finding the time to research and write is difficult, Casteele has found his work with Crestline Publishing among the most satisfying aspects of a nearly 20-year writing career. Casteele is currently working with publisher George Dammann on a complete history of GMC trucks in the Crestline format and adding some later chapters to several Crestline books produced nearly a decade ago.

Dennis Casteele is an automotive writer whose experience goes far beyond simply writing about cars. He is an automotive collector, restorer, merchant, mechanic and racer.

Automobiles have always enjoyed a position of special interest in Dennis' family. His maternal grandfather, Roy Knoop, had one of the first motorized vehicles in the Ohio community of Troy. Mr. Knoop was a well known tinkerer and could usually work some type of mechanical magic to coax a balky motorcycle or car back to life. His father, Frank Casteele, has spent most of his working career on wheels either pushing 18-wheelers around cross-country highways or running some type of garage or auto/truck repair facility. Some of Dennis' earliest memories are playing with a batch of discarded Cummings diesel parts from one of his father's Mack LTL log trucks while in a truck garage in northern California. At age eight he got his first vehicle as a birthday present, a 1934 vintage Mopar pickup he wishes he had back today. His eight-year old son Scott shows a strong interest in carrying on a family tradition as he spends time penning drawings of jet assisted race cars and enjoys helping his Dad at auto flea markets.

Currently Casteele is employed as public relations director for Michigan's largest municipal utility operation, the Lansing Board of Water and Light. His technical background serves him well in directing communications for this $200 million a year business. The BWL's largest customer is Oldsmobile's Lansing operation.